SCHAUM'S OUTLINE OF

THEORY AND PROBLEMS OF

ELEMENTS OF STATISTICS II

INFERENTIAL STATISTICS

STEPHEN BERNSTEIN, Ph.D.

Research Associate
University of Colorado

RUTH BERNSTEIN, Ph.D

Associate Professor
University of Colorado

SCHAUM'S OUTLINE SERIES

McGRAW-HILL

New York San Francisco Washington D.C. Auckland Bogotá Caracas Lisbon
London Madrid Mexico City Milan Montreal New Delhi
San Juan Singapore Sydney Tokyo Toronto

Stephen Bernstein, Ph.D., *Research Associate, Department of Environmental, Population, and Organismic Biology, University of Colorado at Boulder*

Dr. Stephen Bernstein has taught biostatistics, quantitative reasoning, and general biology in his current position. Previously as an Assistant Professor in the Department of Psychiatry at UCLA he taught animal behavior, and at the University of Wisconsin he taught statistics for psychologists. He received his B.A. from Princeton University and his Ph.D. in psychology from the University of Wisconsin. A recipient of various NIMH fellowships and awards, he attended the University of Zürich and the University of Paris for postdoctoral studies. His published research is in animal behavior, neurophysiology, and brain-body allometry. He is co-author with Ruth Bernstein of three general biology textbooks.

Ruth Bernstein, Ph.D., *Associate Professor, Department of Environmental, Population, and Organismic Biology, University of Colorado at Boulder*

Dr. Ruth Bernstein currently teaches ecology and population dynamics, and has taught general biology. Previously, she taught general biology at the University of California, Los Angeles. She received her B.S. from the University of Wisconsin and her Ph.D. in biology from UCLA. Her published research is in evolutionary ecology, with emphasis on ants and beetles. She is the co-author with Stephen Bernstein of three general biology textbooks.

This book is printed on recycled paper containing 10% postconsumer waste.

Schaum's Outline of Theory and Problems of
ELEMENTS OF STATISTICS II: INFERENTIAL STATISTICS

1 2 3 4 5 6 7 8 9 10 11 12 13 14 15 16 17 PRS PRS 9 0 9 8 7 6 5 4 3 2 1 0 9

ISBN 0-07-005023-6

Sponsoring Editor: Barbara Gilson
Production Supervisor: Tina Cameron
Editing Supervisor: Maureen B. Walker

Library of Congress Cataloging-in-Publication Data

McGraw-Hill
A Division of The McGraw-Hill Companies

PREFACE

Statistics is the science that deals with the collection, analysis, and interpretation of numerical information. Having a basic understanding of this science is of importance not only to every research scientist, but also to anyone in modern society who must deal with such information: the doctor evaluating conflicting medical research reports, the lawyer trying to convince a jury of the validity of quantitative evidence, the manufacturer working to improve quality-control procedures, the economist interpreting market trends, and so on.

The theoretical base of the science of statistics is a field within mathematics called *mathematical statistics*. Here, statistics is presented as an abstract, tightly integrated structure of axioms, theorems, and rigorous proofs. To make this theoretical structure available to the nonmathematician, an interpretative discipline has been developed called *general statistics* in which the presentation is greatly simplified and often nonmathematical. From this simplified version, each specialized field (e.g., agriculture, anthropology, biology, economics, engineering, psychology, sociology) takes material that is appropriate for its own numerical data. Thus, for example, there is a version of general statistics called *biostatistics* that is specifically tailored to the numerical data of biology.

All introductory courses in general statistics or one of its specialized offshoots share the same core of material: the *elements of statistics*. The authors of this book have learned these elements in courses, used them in research projects, and taught them, for many years, in general statistics and biostatistics courses. This book, developed from our experience, is a self-help guide to these elements that can be read on its own, used as a supplement to a course textbook, or, as it is sufficiently complete, actually used as the course textbook.

The science of statistics can be divided into two areas: *descriptive statistics* and *inferential statistics*. In descriptive statistics, techniques are provided for processing raw numerical data into usable forms. These techniques include methods for collecting, organizing, summarizing, describing, and presenting numerical information. If entire groups (*populations*) were always available for study, then descriptive statistics would be all that is required. However, typically only a small segment of the group (a *sample*) is available, and thus techniques are required for making generalizations and decisions about the entire population from limited and uncertain sample information. This is the domain of inferential statistics.

All courses in introductory general statistics present both areas of statistics in a standard sequence. This book follows this sequence, but separates these areas into two volumes. *Volume I* (Chapters 1–10) reviews the mathematics required for understanding this book (aspects of high-school algebra), deals with the fundamental principles and techniques of descriptive statistics, and also presents the main theoretical base of inferential statistics: *probability theory. Volume II* (Chapters 11–20), this volume, deals with the concepts and techniques of inferential statistics. Each chapter of the book has the same format: first a section of *text* with fully solved problem-examples for every new concept and procedure; next a section of *solved problems* that both reviews the same material and also makes you look at the material from a different perspective; and finally a section of *supplementary problems* that tests your mastery of the material by providing answers without the step-by-step solutions. Because this is a book on general statistics, an attempt has been made throughout to have a diverse selection of problems representing many specialized fields. Also, we have tried in these problems to show how decisions are made from numerical information in actual problem-solving situations.

To master statistics you must both read the text and do the problems. We suggest that you first read the text and follow the examples, and then go back to re-read the text before going on to the solved and supplementary problems. Also, the book is cross-referenced throughout, so that you can quickly review earlier material that is required to understand later material.

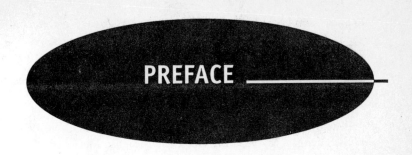

If you go on to work with statistics, you will likely use a computer and one of the many available packages of statistical programs. This book does not deal with how to use such computer programs, but instead gives you the mastery required to understand which aspects of the programs to use and, as importantly, to interpret the output-results that the computer provides. A computer is not required for doing the problems in this book; all problems are solvable with an electronic calculator.

We would like to thank the following people at the McGraw-Hill Companies who have contributed significantly to the development of this book: Barbara Gilson, Elizabeth Zayatz, John Aliano, Fred Perkins, Arthur Biderman, Mary Loebig Giles, and Meaghan McGovern. I am grateful to Roger E. Kirk for permission to reprint Table D.10 from *Elementary Statistics*, 2nd Ed., and to all the other individuals and organizations that gave us permission to use their published materials (specific credit is given where the material is presented). We would also like to thank the anonymous reviewers of the chapters.

CONTENTS

CHAPTER 11

Discrete Probability Distributions

11.1 DISCRETE PROBABILITY DISTRIBUTIONS AND PROBABILITY MASS FUNCTIONS

In Chapter 10 of Volume 1 we examined the general characteristics of discrete probability distributions. We indicated there (see Volume 1, Section 10.3) that such distributions are probability functions that assign probabilities to events in a sample space that have been defined by a discrete random variable. These probability functions have as their domain all values that the discrete random variable can assume ($X = x$), and as their range, the probabilities assigned to these values [$P(X = x) = f(x)$]. The probability function for a discrete probability distribution is called a probability mass function because probability is massed at discrete values of the random variable.

While all discrete probability distributions are defined by a unique and specific formula for a probability mass function, they each can be presented in four ways: as the function itself, or as a list, table, or graph of the probabilities calculated with the function (see Volume 1, Table 10.1 and Fig. 10-1). While to a mathematician the terms "discrete probability distribution" and "probability mass function" are synonymous, we will distinguish between the defining function of a discrete probability distribution and a theoretical distribution of probability values calculated with the function.

In this chapter we will examine the specific characteristics and uses of four of the most important discrete probability distributions: the *binomial distribution*, the *multinomial distribution*, the *hypergeometric distribution*, and the *Poisson distribution*. We will begin with the binomial distribution.

11.2 BERNOULLI EXPERIMENTS AND TRIALS

To understand the binomial distribution, it is necessary to first understand two basic concepts: the *Bernoulli experiment* and *Bernoulli trials*; which are named after *James Bernoulli* (also known as *Jakob Bernoulli*) (1645–1705), the Swiss mathematician who first investigated their properties. [Among his other contributions to probability theory, he developed Bernoulli's theorem (see Volume 1, Section 8.2).] The Bernoulli experiment and Bernoulli trials have the following properties:

(1) A Bernoulli experiment has only two possible outcomes, which we refer to as "success" and "failure." The two outcomes are randomly determined and mutually exclusive.

(2) Bernoulli trials are a fixed sequence of n identical repetitions of the same Bernoulli experiment.

(3) For each trial, the probability of a success is p and the probability of a failure is $q = 1 - p$.

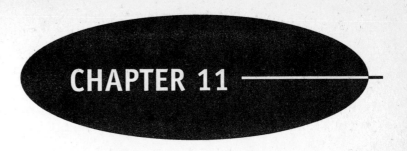

(4) The Bernoulli trials are *independent* (see Volume 1, Section 9.4): no outcome or sequence of outcomes affects any subsequent outcome.

(5) The probability of success p is the same (remains *constant*) for every Bernoulli trial (which means that the probability of failure, q, also remains constant).

EXAMPLE 11.1 You have a bowl of 20 marbles that are identical except for color: 10 are red and 10 are green. Which of the following are Bernoulli trials: (*a*) you blindly pick 10 marbles out in succession, determine for each pick whether the marble is red, and then replace the marble in the bowl after each pick, (*b*) the same experiment as in (*a*) except you do not replace the marble after each pick?

Solution

(*a*) These are Bernoulli trials, where on each trial: success = red, failure = green, $p = 10/20 = \frac{1}{2}$, $q = 1 - \frac{1}{2} = \frac{1}{2}$, and the trials are independent.

(*b*) These are not Bernoulli trials. Because the marble is not replaced after each pick, p does not remain constant over trials and the trials are not independent (the outcome of one trial has an effect on the outcomes of subsequent trials).

In the trials described in Example 11.1(*b*), suppose the bowl contained 150 red marbles and 150 green marbles, rather than 10 red and 10 green, and again the experiment is to blindly pick 10 marbles in succession, determining for each pick whether the marble is red, and not replacing the marble after the pick. The trials seem the same as the ones described in Example 11.1(*b*), but to a statistician they are very different because of the change in sample size. With 300 marbles, the ratio of sample size n to population size N is $10/300 = 0.033$, whereas with 20 marbles the ratio is $10/20 = 0.50$. It is generally agreed among statisticians that if in these sampling conditions the ratio of sample size to population size is no more than 0.05 (i.e., the sample is no more than 5% of the population, or $n \leq 0.05N$), with less conservative statisticians saying no more than 0.10 ($n \leq 0.10N$), then we can assume p is "essentially" constant, the trials are "essentially" independent, and that these are Bernoulli trials if all other assumed properties of the Bernoulli trials are met.

The problem we are dealing with here we have dealt with before and will deal with many times again: the conflict between the requirements of the pure, abstract models of statistics and the demands of real-world problem solving. Statistical techniques are based on theoretical, mathematical models of idealized situations that rarely exist in the real world, and therefore it is often the case that the strict assumptions and requirements of a statistical model cannot be exactly met. However, in many cases it has been determined, as here, that if the assumptions and requirements are "essentially" met, then a given statistical technique can give reasonably accurate results.

The assumptions of Bernoulli trials are only perfectly met under two conditions: (1) *random sampling with replacement* (see Volume 1, Section 3.16) *from a finite or infinite population*, and (2) *random sampling without replacement from an infinite population*. In the first condition, the population may be small or large relative to the sample but with replacement of the sampled item each time, p remains constant and the trials are independent. In the second case, the population is so large that for all practical purposes it is unaffected by removal of a sample item. Here again, p remains constant and the trials are independent.

11.3 BINOMIAL RANDOM VARIABLES, EXPERIMENTS, AND PROBABILITY FUNCTIONS

If a discrete random variable X (see Volume 1, Section 10.2) is used to count the number of successes ($X = x$) that occur in n Bernoulli trials, then this random variable is called a *binomial random variable* and the sequence of n Bernoulli trials is considered to be a *binomial experiment* (*bi*, two; *nomial*, terms, or outcomes). Finally, if a probability function is used to assign a probability value to every sample point in the sample space defined by such a binomial random variable, then this function is called a *binomial probability mass function*, or a *binomial probability function*, or a *binomial probability distribution*, or a *binomial distribution.*

EXAMPLE 11.2 Using the definitions above and in Section 11.2, show that the discrete probability distribution for number of heads in three flips of a coin (see Fig. 10-2 and Table 10.2 in Volume 1) is a binomial distribution.

Solution

To be a binomial distribution there must be these basic components: a Bernoulli experiment, Bernoulli trials, a binomial random variable, a binomial experiment, and a probability function that assigns a probability value to every sample point in the sample space defined by the binomial variable.

In this problem, the Bernoulli experiment is the flip of the coin. It has only two possible outcomes, head or tail, which are randomly determined and mutually exclusive. Either of these outcomes could be classified the success-outcome; this choice is determined by the probability question being investigated. Here we classify observing a head as a success, with the goal of determining the probability distribution for the variable number of heads. It should be noted that classifying one of the outcomes as a success does not mean it is the preferred outcome; it only indicates it is the outcome being investigated. In any event, having classified a head as success and thus a tail as failure, we can now complete the definition of a Bernoulli experiment by stating that the probability of a success (a head) is $p = \frac{1}{2}$, and thus the probability of a failure (a tail) is $q = 1 - \frac{1}{2} = \frac{1}{2}$.

The fixed sequence of n repetitions of the Bernoulli experiment are the three flips of the coin. Each flip is a Bernoulli trial. It is true for each trial in this sequence that: (1) only the same two mutually exclusive, randomly determined outcomes are possible, success (head) or failure (tail), (2) the probability of success remains constant over trials $p = \frac{1}{2}$, and (3) the trials are independent [assuming it is an idealized game (see Volume 1, Section 8.1), no outcome of a coin affects the outcome of any subsequent flip].

The binomial random variable, the discrete random variable X that counts the number of successes $(X = x)$ that occur in the $n = 3$ Bernoulli trials, is the variable number of heads. This makes the sequence of Bernoulli trials a binomial experiment. Finally, a probability function is used (see Volume 1, Example 10.5) to assign probability values to every sample point in the sample space defined by the binomial random variable $S = \{0, 1, 2, 3\}$, and thus the resulting probability distribution (see Volume 1, Table 10.2) is a binomial distribution.

11.4 THE BINOMIAL COEFFICIENT

Three counting rules were introduced in Chapter 9 of Volume 1: multiplication principle (see Section 9.12), permutations (see Section 9.13), and combinations (see Section 9.14). The *binomial coefficient*, a component of the binomial probability function (see Section 11.5 below), is another counting rule. It determines the number of possible permutations that can be made of n objects when the n consists of only two types of objects, x of one type and $n - x$ of the other. It turns out this number of permutations is given by the formula for the number of combinations of n different objects taken x at a time [equation (9.20), Volume 1]

$$\text{Binomial coefficient } = {}_nC_x = \binom{n}{x} = \frac{n!}{x!(n-x)!} \tag{11.1}$$

To understand what this means we will use four marbles, two reds R and two greens G, and ask: How many ways can these $n = 4$ objects be arranged *in order* in a line? As we are concerned with order of the objects, this is clearly a permutations problem, and if the four objects were all different then the answer would be (see Problem 9.30, Volume 1)

$${}_nP_n = n! = 4! = 24$$

If the four objects were all different and we were not concerned about order, only about the number of possible combinations of n objects taken four at a time, then the answer would be (see Problem 9.41, Volume 1)

$${}_nC_n = 1$$

Neither of these answers is correct when $n = 4$ and there are $(x = 2)$ reds and $(n - x = 2)$ greens, as can be seen by actually putting the marbles in all of the unique four-marble lines that are possible

$$RRGG \quad RGRG \quad RGGR \quad GGRR \quad GRGR \quad GRRG$$

There are only six possible permutations of $(n = 4)$ objects where $x = 2$ are of one type and $n - x = 2$ are of another, and we can see that the binomial coefficient gives this answer:

$$\binom{n}{x} = \frac{n!}{x!(n-x)!} = \frac{4!}{2!2!} = 6$$

EXAMPLE 11.3 A bowl contains 20 marbles that are identical except for color: 12 are red and 8 are green. You blindly pick 6 marbles from the bowl, returning each marble after its color has been observed. How many ways can you pick 4 red marbles in 6 trials?

Solution

In this binomial experiment, $n = 6$ and $x = 4$. Using the binomial coefficient

$$\binom{n}{x} = \frac{n!}{x!(n-x)!} = \frac{6!}{4!2!} = 15$$

11.5 THE BINOMIAL PROBABILITY FUNCTION

The probability function used in Example 10.5 of Volume 1 to calculate the probability values for the binomial distribution: number of heads in three flips of a coin, is based on both the generalization of the special multiplication rule for k independent events [equation (9.9), Volume 1] and the generalization of the special addition rule for k mutually exclusive events (Property 4, Section 8.6, Volume 1). Now we present a formula, called the *binomial probability function*, that condenses these multiplications and additions into one calculation formula

$$f(x) = \binom{n}{x} p^x q^{n-x}, \qquad \text{for } x = 0, 1, 2, \ldots, n \tag{11.2}$$

This states that the probability of x successes in the n Bernoulli trials of a binomial experiment $[f(x)]$ is equal to the product of the binomial coefficient [equation (11.1)] times the probability of success p raised to the xth power (p^x) (see Section 1.9, Volume 1) times the probability of failure q raised to the $(n - x)$th power (q^{n-x}).

EXAMPLE 11.4 From the bowl containing 12 red marbles and 8 green marbles in Example 11.3, 6 marbles are again picked, one after the other, and each is returned to the bowl after its color has been observed. What is the probability of picking 4 red marbles in the 6 picks?

Solution

We know from Example 11.3 that the binomial coefficient $\binom{n}{x}$ is 15; that there are 15 ways of picking 4 red marbles in the sample of 6. Thus, to find the probability of getting 4 red marbles $[P(X = 4) = f(4)]$, we need only to multiply this coefficient times the probabilities of getting 4 red marbles and 2 green marbles. For each trial, the probability of getting a red marble (p) is $\frac{12}{20} = 0.6$ and the probability of getting a green marble (q) is $1 - p = 0.4$. The probability of picking a red marble on each of four trials is (0.6)(0.6)(0.6)(0.6), or 0.6^4, and the probability of picking a green marble on each of two trials is $(0.4)(0.4) = 0.4^2$. Using equation (11.2), the probability of picking 4 red marbles in the sample of 6 is

$$f(x) = \binom{n}{x} p^x q^{n-x}$$

$$f(4) = (15)(0.6)^4(0.4)^2 = 0.311$$

11.6 MEAN, VARIANCE, AND STANDARD DEVIATION OF THE BINOMIAL PROBABILITY DISTRIBUTION

Every discrete probability distribution has a mean, a variance, and a standard deviation. The general equation for the expected value (or mean) of the probability distribution of a discrete random variable is given by equation (10.10), Volume 1,

$$E(X) = \mu = \sum_x xf(x)$$

To get the equation for the *mean of a binomial probability distribution*, we simply substitute equation (11.2) for $f(x)$:

$$E(X) = \mu = \sum_x x\left[\binom{n}{x}p^x q^{n-x}\right] \tag{11.3}$$

It can be proven mathematically that this equation simplifies to

$$E(X) = \mu = np \tag{11.4}$$

The computational version of the general equation for the variance of a discrete probability distribution is given by equation (10.22), Volume 1,

$$\sigma^2 = \sum_x x^2 f(x) - \mu^2$$

Substituting equation (11.2) for $f(x)$ and equation (11.4) for μ, we get the equation for the *variance of the binomial probability distribution*:

$$\sigma^2 = \sum_x x^2\left[\binom{n}{x}p^x q^{n-x}\right] - (np)^2 \tag{11.5}$$

It can be proven mathematically that this equation simplifies to

$$\sigma^2 = npq \tag{11.6}$$

The standard deviation of a discrete probability distribution is

$$\sigma = \sqrt{\sigma^2}$$

and so the *standard deviation of a binomial probability distribution* is

$$\sigma = \sqrt{npq} \tag{11.7}$$

EXAMPLE 11.5 Find the mean, variance, and standard deviation of the binomial probability distribution: number of heads in three flips of a coin.

Solution

For this experiment, p = probability of getting a head on a single flip of a coin $= \frac{1}{2}$, q = probability of getting a tail $= \frac{1}{2}$, $n = 3$. Inserting the values of n and p into equation (11.4),

$$E(X) = \mu = np = 3\left(\frac{1}{2}\right) = 1.5$$

Inserting the values of n, p, and q into equation (11.6),

$$\sigma^2 = npq = (3)\left(\frac{1}{2}\right)\left(\frac{1}{2}\right) = 0.75$$

The standard deviation is calculated by taking the square root of the variance,

$$\sigma = \sqrt{npq} = \sqrt{0.75} = 0.87$$

11.7 THE BINOMIAL EXPANSION AND THE BINOMIAL THEOREM

The binomial probability function and binomial distribution take their names from their relation to the *binomial expansion.* A *binomial algebraic expression* has two (*bi*, two) terms (see Section 1.11, Volume 1). Whenever such an expression takes the form of $(a+b)$ raised to the nth power and the product is multiplied out to produce a *sum of terms*, then this sum of terms is called a binomial expansion. The following are examples of binomial expansions:

$$(a+b)^2 = a^2 + 2ab + b^2 \qquad (a+b)^3 = a^3 + 3a^2b + 3ab^2 + b^3$$

The *binomial theorem* is the following general formula for expanding $(a+b)^n$, in which a and b are real numbers and n and x are positive integers

$$(a+b)^n = \sum_{x=0}^{n} \binom{n}{x} a^{n-x} b^x \tag{11.8}$$

It is the sum for $x = 0$ to $x = n$ of the product of: (1) the binomial coefficient [equation (11.1)], (2) a raised to the $(n-x)$th power (a^{n-x}), and (3) b raised to the xth power (b^x). For example, the binomial expansion of the binomial expression $(a+b)^2$ is

$$\begin{aligned}(a+b)^2 &= \sum_{x=0}^{2} \binom{2}{x} a^{2-x} b^x \\ &= \binom{2}{0} a^{2-0} b^0 + \binom{2}{1} a^{2-1} b^1 + \binom{2}{2} a^{2-2} b^2 \\ &= \frac{2!}{0!2!} a^2 + \frac{2!}{1!1!} ab + \frac{2!}{2!0!} b^2 \\ &= a^2 + 2ab + b^2\end{aligned}$$

If we let $a = q$ and $b = p$, where q and p are the probabilities of failure and success on a single Bernoulli trial, n = number of Bernoulli trials, x = number of successes, then

$$\begin{aligned}(q+p)^n &= \sum_{x=0}^{n} \binom{n}{x} q^{n-x} p^x \qquad (11.9) \\ &= \binom{n}{0} q^{n-0} p^0 + \binom{n}{1} q^{n-1} p^1 + \cdots + \binom{n}{n-1} q^{n-(n-1)} p^{n-1} + \binom{n}{n} q^{n-n} p^n \\ &= q^n + nq^{n-1}p + \cdots + nqp^{n-1} + p^n\end{aligned}$$

(Note that the order of p and q have been reversed, to conform with the order in which the two parameters appear in the binomial theorem, where a^{n-x} precedes b^x.) From this expansion, you can see the relationship between the binomial probability function and the binomial expansion $(q+p)^n$: For each integer value of x successes, the probability of x corresponds to a term in this binomial expansion.

EXAMPLE 11.6 Use the binomial theorem to find the probability distribution for the binomial variable: number of 5s in five rolls of a die.

Solution

Using equation (11.9) with $n = 5$,

$$
\begin{aligned}
(q+p)^5 &= \sum_{x=0}^{5} \binom{5}{x} q^{5-x} p^x \\
&= \binom{5}{0} q^{5-0} p^0 + \binom{5}{1} q^{5-1} p^1 + \binom{5}{2} q^{5-2} p^2 + \binom{5}{3} q^{5-3} p^3 + \binom{5}{4} q^{5-4} p^4 + \binom{5}{5} q^{5-5} p^5 \\
&= \frac{5!}{0!5!} q^5 + \frac{5!}{1!4!} q^4 p + \frac{5!}{2!3!} q^3 p^2 + \frac{5!}{3!2!} q^2 p^3 + \frac{5!}{4!1!} q p^4 + \frac{5!}{5!0!} p^5 \\
&= q^5 + 5q^4 p + 10q^3 p^2 + 10q^2 p^3 + 5qp^4 + p^5
\end{aligned}
$$

If you compare this expansion with the probability distribution for this variable in Table 11.1, you will see that for each value of x successes, the probability of x corresponds to a term in the expansion.

Table 11.1

Number of 5s x	Probability $f(x) = \binom{n}{x} p^x q^{n-x}$
0	$f(0) = \binom{5}{0}(1/6)^0(5/6)^{5-0} = 0.40187$
1	$f(1) = \binom{5}{1}(1/6)^1(5/6)^{5-1} = 0.40188$
2	$f(2) = \binom{5}{2}(1/6)^2(5/6)^{5-2} = 0.16076$
3	$f(3) = \binom{5}{3}(1/6)^3(5/6)^{5-3} = 0.03215$
4	$f(4) = \binom{5}{4}(1/6)^4(5/6)^{5-4} = 0.00322$
5	$f(5) = \binom{5}{6}(1/6)^5(5/6)^{5-5} = 0.00013$
Σ	1.00001

As success and failure are the only possible outcomes for each Bernoulli trial and the outcomes are mutually exclusive

$$q + p = 1$$

and therefore

$$(q+p)^n = \sum_{x=0}^{n} \binom{n}{x} q^{n-x} p^x = 1$$

This relationship between the binomial probability function and the binomial theorem confirms what is demonstrated empirically in Table 11.1: that, as should be true for a discrete probability distribution (see

Property 7, Fig. 10-3 in Volume 1),

$$\sum_x f(x) = \sum_x \binom{n}{x} p^x q^{n-x} = 1$$

11.8 PASCAL'S TRIANGLE AND THE BINOMIAL COEFFICIENT

Pascal's triangle is an arrangement of the binomial coefficients for the expansion of $(a+b)^n$. The triangle, extended to $n = 5$, is shown in Fig. 11-1. You can see that the first and last number in each row is a 1 and that any number within a row can be calculated by taking the sum of the two numbers that are immediately above it and to its left and right. Thus, for example, both 5s in row $n = 5$ are the sums of the numbers 1 and 4 that are above them to their left and right. In row $n = 5$ are the coefficients for $(a+b)^5$ [or $(q+p)^5$]: 1, 5, 10, 10, 5, 1. You can see these are the same as the coefficients we found for $(q+p)^5$ in Example 11.6.

n											
0						1					
1					1		1				
2				1		2		1			
3			1		3		3		1		
4		1		4		6		4		1	
5	1		5		10		10		5		1

Fig. 11-1

EXAMPLE 11.7 Use Pascal's triangle to find the binomial coefficients for the expansion of $(q+p)^6$.

Solution

Using the above calculation procedures, the coefficients are: 1, 6, 15, 20, 15, 6, 1.

11.9 THE FAMILY OF BINOMIAL DISTRIBUTIONS

There is only one binomial probability function [equation (11.2)]

$$f(x) = \binom{n}{x} p^x q^{n-x}$$

but it defines an infinite number of specific binomial probability distributions, one for each unique combination of numbers assigned to the constants n and p. It is not necessary to also specify q, since $q = 1 - p$. Because specifying n and p completely determines which specific binomial distribution we are considering, n and p are said to be the *parameters of the binomial distribution*. Note that this use of the term parameter is different from the descriptive population parameters we introduced in Section 3.4 of Volume 1: descriptive measures calculated from measurement populations. While a parameter of a theoretical equation is a defining constant in the equation, the parameter of a measurement population is a descriptive measure of that population.

When a theoretical equation can take many different forms as a function of which numbers are assigned to its parameters, then it is said that there are a *family of equations*. Therefore, we can say that the binomial probability function defines an infinitely large *family of binomial probability distributions*. Six of these are shown in Fig. 11-2 to illustrate how changes in n and p affect the distribution. Thus, in

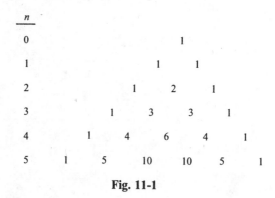

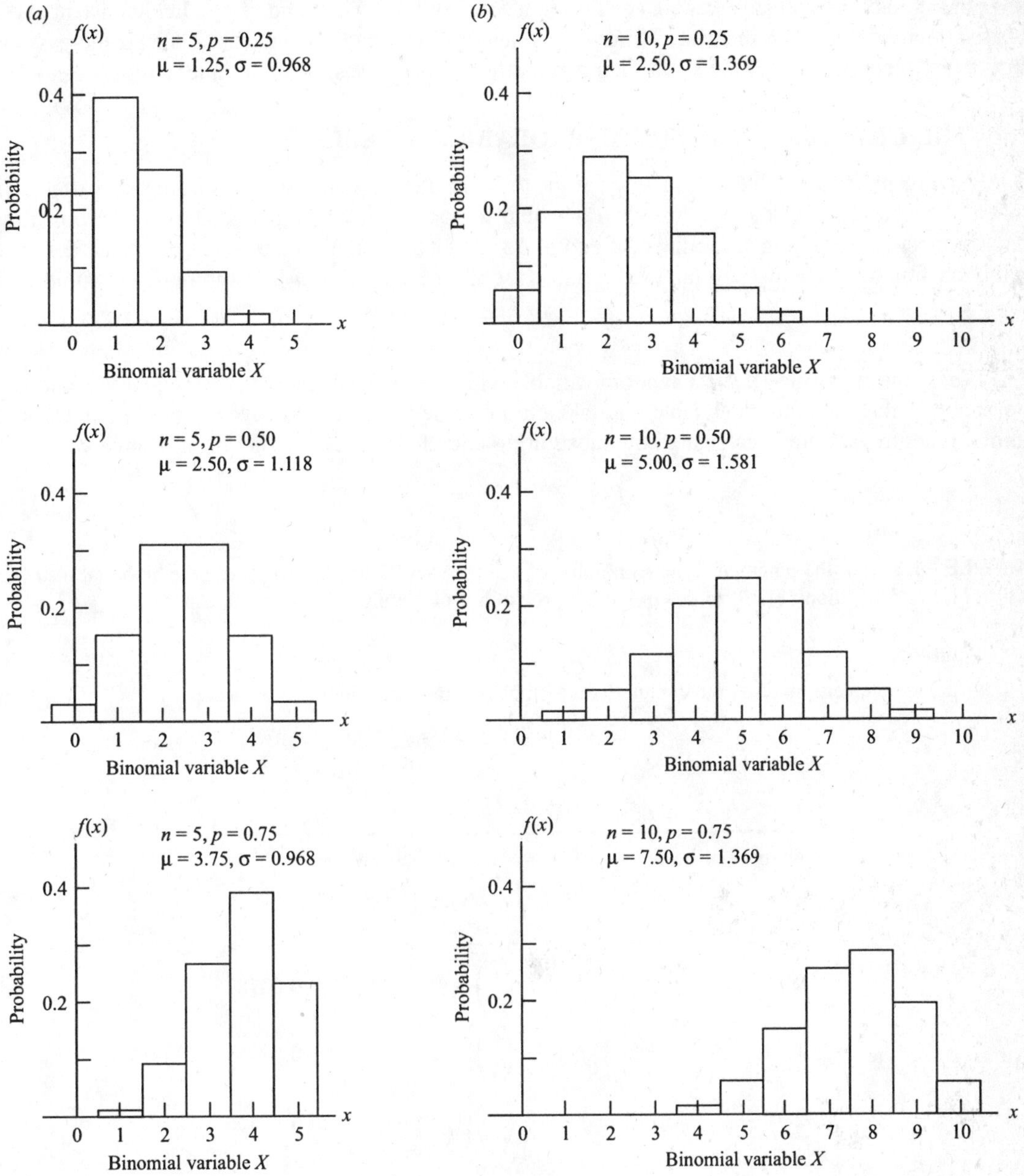

Fig. 11-2

Fig. 11-2(*a*), n is held constant at 5 as p is changed (top to bottom) from 0.25 to 0.50 to 0.75, and in Fig. 11-2(*b*), n remains at 10 as p is changed (top to bottom) from 0.25 to 0.50 to 0.75. The distribution values for Fig. 11-2(*a*) were calculated using the expansion of $(q+p)^5$ (see Example 11.6) and the distribution values for Fig. 11-2(*b*) were calculated using

$$(q+p)^{10} = q^{10} + 10pq^9 + 45p^2q^8 + 120p^3q^7 + 210p^4q^6 + 252p^5q^5 + 210p^6q^4 + 120p^7q^3 + 45p^8q^2 + 10p^9q + p^{10}$$

Several characteristics of the binomial distribution can be seen in Fig. 11-2. First, the distribution is symmetrical at $p = 0.50$, and asymmetrical when $p < 0.50$ (positively skewed, see Problem 5.6, Volume 1) and when $p > 0.50$ (negatively skewed, see Problem 5.5, Volume 1). Second, if p is held constant and n is increased, then both μ and σ increase. Third, if n is held constant and p is increased, then μ increases with p, but σ first increases to $p = 0.50$ and then symmetrically decreases as p continues to increase.

11.10 THE CUMULATIVE BINOMIAL PROBABILITY TABLE

In solving practical problems, we often want to know the probability that a binomial variable (i.e., number of successes in n trials) is less than or equal to some whole number, such as the probability of getting at most two heads in seven flips of a coin. To compute such a probability, we use the cumulative distribution function of a discrete random variable for any real number a [equation (10.3), Volume 1]

$$F(a) = \sum_{x \leq a} f(x)$$

where $F(a)$ is the probability that the random variable will take on a value less than or equal to a and $f(x)$ is the probability that the random variable will take on the value x. The cumulative distributive function of a binomial random variable is calculated by substituting equation (11.2) for $f(x)$ in the above equation:

$$F(a) = \sum_{x \leq a} \left[f(x) = \binom{n}{x} p^x q^{n-x} \right] \tag{11.10}$$

EXAMPLE 11.8 For the binomial variable: number of heads in seven flips of a coin, use the binomial distribution in Table 11.2 and equation (11.10) to determine the probability of getting at most two heads.

Solution

This problem involves the cumulative distribution function, where

$$F(2) = P(X \leq 2) = \sum_{x \leq 2} f(x)$$

Table 11.2

Number of heads x	Probability $f(x) = \binom{n}{x} p^x q^{n-x}$
0	$f(0) = \binom{7}{0}(1/2)^0(1/2)^{7-0} = 0.00781$
1	$f(1) = \binom{7}{1}(1/2)^1(1/2)^{7-1} = 0.05469$
2	$f(2) = \binom{7}{2}(1/2)^2(1/2)^{7-2} = 0.16406$
3	$f(3) = \binom{7}{3}(1/2)^3(1/2)^{7-3} = 0.27344$
4	$f(4) = \binom{7}{4}(1/2)^4(1/2)^{7-4} = 0.27344$
5	$f(5) = \binom{7}{5}(1/2)^5(1/2)^{7-5} = 0.16406$
6	$f(6) = \binom{7}{6}(1/2)^6(1/2)^{7-6} = 0.05469$
7	$f(7) = \binom{7}{7}(1/2)^7(1/2)^{7-7} = 0.00781$
$\sum$	1.00000

Therefore, using the values from Table 11.2 (rounded to four decimal places),

$$F(2) = f(0) + f(1) + f(2)$$
$$= 0.0078 + 0.0547 + 0.1641 = 0.2266$$

Table A.3 in the Appendix (*Cumulative Binomial Probabilities*) gives cumulative probability values $F(a)$ calculated with equation (11.10) for binomial distributions that have these values of the parameters n (left column) and p (top row): $n = 2, 3, \ldots, 10$; $p = 0.01, 0.05, \ldots, 0.50$.

EXAMPLE 11.9 For the binomial variable number of heads in seven flips of a coin, use Table A.3 in the Appendix to determine the probability of getting at most 2 heads.

Solution

The part of the table that we need for this problem is reproduced in Table 11.3, which shows the cumulative probabilities for $n = 7$ and $p = 0.01, 0.05, \ldots, 0.50$ for $a = 0, 1, \ldots, 7$. From Example 11.8 we know for this question that

$$F(2) = P(X \leq 2) = 0.2266$$

Using Table 11.3, we can see from the intersection (right circled number) of row ($a = 2$) and column ($p = 0.50$) that again $F(2) = 0.2266$.

Table 11.3

		p											
n	a	0.01	0.05	0.10	0.15	0.20	0.25	0.30	1/3	0.35	0.40	0.45	0.50
7	0	0.9321	0.6983	0.4783	0.3206	0.2097	0.1335	0.0824	0.0585	0.0490	0.0280	0.0152	0.0078
	1	0.9980	0.9556	0.8503	0.7166	0.5767	0.4449	0.3294	0.2634	0.2338	0.1586	0.1024	0.0625
	2	1.0000	0.9962	0.9743	0.9262	0.8520	0.7564	0.6471	0.5706	0.5323	0.4199	0.3164	0.2266
	3	1.0000	0.9998	0.9973	0.9879	0.9667	0.9294	0.8740	0.8267	0.8002	0.7102	0.6083	0.5000
	4	1.0000	1.0000	0.9998	0.9988	0.9953	0.9871	0.9712	0.9547	0.9444	0.9037	0.8471	0.7734
	5	1.0000	1.0000	1.0000	0.9999	0.9996	0.9987	0.9962	0.9931	0.9910	0.9812	0.9643	0.9375
	6	1.0000	1.0000	1.0000	1.0000	1.0000	0.9999	0.9998	0.9995	0.9994	0.9984	0.9963	0.9922
	7	1.0000	1.0000	1.0000	1.0000	1.0000	1.0000	1.0000	1.0000	1.0000	1.0000	1.0000	1.0000

To save space in a statistical table, it is often the case that only the essential values are given, from which other needed values can be calculated. Thus, in Table A.3 there are no cumulative probabilities for $p > 0.50$ because for the given n values these probabilities can be calculated from the probabilities provided. To find $F(a)$ for $p > 0.50$: enter Table A.3 at the appropriate n, but then use $n - (x + 1)$ for the a value and $1 - p$ for the p value. The cumulative probability found at the intersection of row $n - (x + 1)$ and column $1 - p$ is then subtracted from 1.

EXAMPLE 11.10 Use the section of Table A.3 shown in Table 11.3 to find $F(a = 3)$ for $n = 7$ and $p = 0.7$.

Solution

For this problem, the intersection (left circled number) of row $[7 - (3 + 1) = 3]$ and column $(1 - 0.7 = 0.3)$ is 0.8740, and therefore

$$F(3) = 1 - 0.8740 = 0.1260$$

To check this use of Table A.3, we calculated $F(3)$ directly using equation (11.10) for $n = 7$ and $p = 0.7$.

$$\begin{aligned} F(3) &= P(X \leq 3) = f(0) + f(1) + f(2) + f(3) \\ &= (0.3)^7 + 7(0.7)(0.3)^6 + 21(0.7)^2(0.3)^5 + 35(0.7)^3(0.3)^4 \\ &= 0.00022 + 0.00357 + 0.02500 + 0.09724 \\ &= 0.12603, \text{ or, rounded to four decimals, } 0.1260 \end{aligned}$$

11.11 LOT-ACCEPTANCE SAMPLING

Lot-acceptance sampling (or simply *acceptance sampling*) is a quality-control procedure used in industry. It uses binomial-distribution techniques to develop *statistical decision rules* for the acceptance or rejection of raw materials and manufactured products. A standard of quality is set, and if the materials or products meet this standard, then they are accepted; if not, they are rejected.

Raw materials and products move through an industrial process in units called *lots*. A lot is a large number of the same items, such as 1,000 steel rods, 10,000 screws, or 5,000 electric drills. To ensure the quality of the final product, it would be optimal to have all components of each lot tested for defects, but this is rarely possible. The lots are typically so large that such testing would be prohibitively expensive and time consuming, and often the testing of an item destroys it (e.g., test-firing bullets). Therefore, a much smaller random sample is taken from each lot, and every item in the sample is tested for defects. In advance of taking the sample, a *sampling plan* is devised that specifies a sample size (n) and an *acceptance number* (a). If the sample has a or less defective items in it, then the entire lot it came from is accepted, but if the sample has more than a defective items then its entire lot is rejected.

To determine which sampling plan is appropriate for a given stage of an industrial process, binomial-distribution techniques are used to develop *operating characteristic curves* for a variety of sampling plans. These curves show, for a given sampling plan with parameters n and a, the probability that a lot will be accepted (P_a) given different possible proportions of defective items in the lot (p). Four such operating characteristic curves are shown in Fig. 11-3, with P_a on the vertical axis and p on the horizontal axis, for the following plans: $n = 10$, $a = 0$; $n = 10$, $a = 1$; $n = 50$, $a = 0$; and $n = 50$, $a = 1$.

To understand these curves we will go through the reasoning and calculations for the sampling plan where $n = 10$ and $a = 1$, which means that a random sample of 10 will be taken from the lot and if the sample contains one or fewer (0) defective items, then the lot will be accepted (more than one and the lot will be rejected). We do not know the actual proportion of defective items in the lot (p), but if the sampling plan meets the assumptions of Bernoulli trials (see Section 11.2), then we can use binomial-distribution techniques to determine the probability of accepting the lot (P_a) for any hypothetical p. While this type of sampling is typically without replacement, whenever the sample size n is no more than 5% of the lot (the population) ($n \leq 0.05N$, see Section 11.2), we can assume that p remains essentially constant over independent trials and that therefore this is a binomial experiment. If so, then for any given hypothetical p value

$$P_a = P(X \leq a) = F(a) = \sum_{x \leq a} \left[f(x) = \frac{n!}{x!(n-x)!} p^x q^{n-x} \right] \tag{11.11}$$

Thus, for example, for $n = 10$, $a = 1$, and $p = 0.01$,

$$\begin{aligned} P_a &= \frac{10!}{0!(10-0)!}(0.01)^0(0.99)^{10} + \frac{10!}{1!(10-1)!}(0.01)^1(0.99)^9 \\ &= (0.99)^{10} + 10(0.01)(0.99)^9 = 0.9957 \end{aligned}$$

If you now look at Fig. 11-3, you will see that this is the P_a value plotted for sampling plan ($n = 10$, $a = 1$) for $p = 0.01$. Also, you can verify this number by finding $F(1)$ in Table A.3 for $n = 10$, $p = 0.01$.

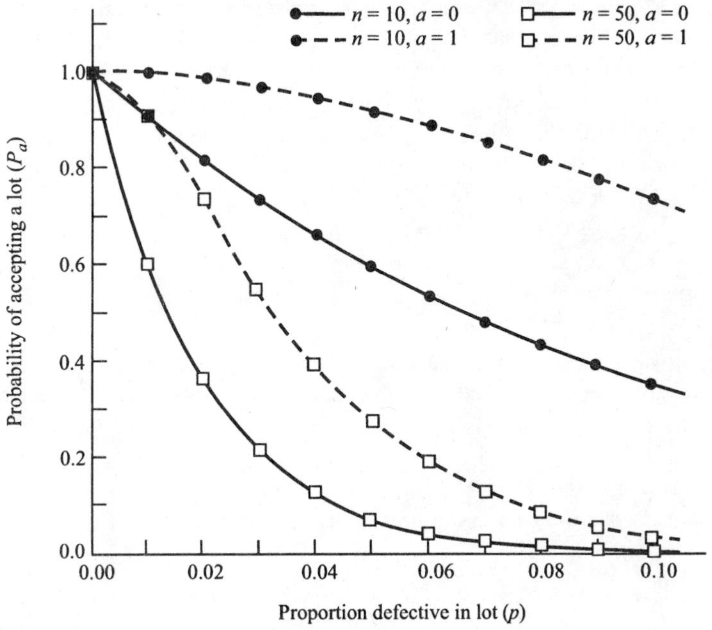

Fig. 11-3

This same technique was used to find all the plotted values in Fig. 11-3. For another example, consider the sampling plan ($n = 50$, $a = 1$) for $p = 0.06$:

$$P_a = \frac{50!}{0!(50-0)!}(0.06)^0(0.94)^{50} + \frac{50!}{1!(50-1)!}(0.06)^1(0.94)^{49}$$
$$= (0.94)^{50} + 50(0.06)(0.94)^{49} = 0.1900$$

From the curves in Fig. 11-3 you can see two important general characteristics of lot-acceptance sampling. First, the larger the acceptance number (a) for a given sample size (n), the higher the P_a value for a given p. For example, for $p = 0.04$ for sample size $n = 50$, P_a increases from 0.1299 for $a = 0$ to 0.4005 for $a = 1$. The second important general characteristic is that the larger the sample size (n) for a given acceptance number (a) the smaller the P_a value for a given p. For example, for $p = 0.04$ for acceptance number $a = 1$, P_a decreases from 0.9418 for $n = 10$ to 0.4005 for $n = 50$.

11.12 CONSUMER'S RISK AND PRODUCER'S RISK

Quality-control engineers, in determining the appropriate sampling plan (see Section 11.11) for a given stage of an industrial process, must take into account many factors: the cost, effort, and time required to test each sample item; the maximum proportion of defectives in a lot that the company can tolerate; the minimum proportion of defectives the supplier of the lot can economically and consistently achieve; and so on. If we call the receiver of the lot the consumer, then *consumer's risk* is the probability of accepting a lot that has a higher p than the consumer can tolerate. If we call the supplier of the lot the producer, then *producer's risk* is the probability of a lot being rejected that is actually in conformity with the consumer's requirements.

To understand consumer's risk, let us assume that a consumer will tolerate no more defective items in a lot than $p = 0.01$. Then the probability of accepting a lot with a larger p value is the consumer's risk. Thus, for example, if the lot actually has 2% defective items, these are the consumer's risks for the four sampling plans illustrated in Fig. 11-3: for $n = 10$, $a = 0$, the consumer's risk $= P_a = 0.8171$; for $n = 10$, $a = 1$, the consumer's risk $= P_a = 0.9838$; for $n = 50$, $a = 0$, the consumer's risk $= P_a = 0.3642$; and for $n = 50$,

$a = 1$, the consumer's risk $= P_a = 0.7358$. You can see from the curves in Fig. 11-3 that the consumer's risk declines for each plan as p increases.

To understand producer's risk, let us assume that the producer is actually meeting the $p = 0.01$ requirement. Then the producer's risk is the probability that a lot that has 1% defectives will be rejected, which is 1 minus (the probability that the lot will be accepted). Therefore, for the examples in Fig. 11-3 for a lot with $p = 0.01$: for $n = 10$, $a = 0$, the producer's risk $= 1 - P_a = 1 - 0.9044 = 0.0956$; for $n = 10$, $a = 1$, the producer's risk $= 1 - P_a = 1 - 0.9958 = 0.0042$; for $n = 50$, $a = 0$, the producer's risk $= 1 - P_a = 1 - 0.6050 = 0.3950$; and for $n = 50$, $a = 1$, the producer's risk $= 1 - P_a = 1 - 0.9106 = 0.0894$. You can see from these examples that for a given p value required by a consumer, the producer's risk increases as n is increased or a is decreased.

EXAMPLE 11.11 You are a consumer who tolerates no more than $p = 0.05$ as the proportion of defectives in a lot. If you use a sampling plan where $n = 100$ and $a = 3$, what is the consumer's risk if the actual proportion in the lot is $p = 0.06$?

Solution

The solution to this problem is the probability of accepting a lot (P_a) that has 6% defectives, given $n = 100$ and $a = 3$.

$$P_a = \sum_{x\leq 3}\left[f(x) = \frac{n!}{x!(n-x)!}p^x q^{n-x}\right]$$

$$= \frac{100!}{0!(100-0)!}(0.06)^0(0.94)^{100} + \frac{100!}{1!(100-1)!}(0.06)^1(0.94)^{99}$$

$$+ \frac{100!}{2!(100-2)!}(0.06)^2(0.94)^{98} + \frac{100!}{3!(100-3)!}(0.06)^3(0.94)^{97}$$

$$= 0.1430$$

11.13 MULTIVARIATE PROBABILITY DISTRIBUTIONS AND JOINT PROBABILITY DISTRIBUTIONS

Statistical techniques can be classified by the number of variables being analyzed. When just one variable is analyzed, the techniques are called *univariate statistics*; when relationships between two variables are analyzed, the techniques are called *bivariate statistics*; and when relationships between more than two variables are analyzed, the techniques are called *multivariate statistics*. These distinctions are relevant here because, while to this point in our consideration of discrete probability distributions we have dealt entirely with univariate techniques, now, with the next discrete probability distribution we will consider—the *multinomial distribution* (see Sections 11.14 through 11.19)—we will deal with multivariate techniques.

Discrete probability distributions are classified as univariate, bivariate, or multivariate depending on the number of discrete random variables being considered. Thus, binomial probability distributions are *discrete univariate probability distributions* because they give the probabilities for all possible values of a single discrete random variable X (number of successes) [equation (11.2)]

$$f(x) = P(X = x) = \binom{n}{x}p^x q^{n-x}$$

Such a univariate probability distribution is appropriate when an experiment has only one outcome of interest or there are several outcome categories and you want to consider each separately. Quite often, however, you are interested in relationships between several outcomes from an experiment, and if it is possible to measure each outcome with a separate discrete random variable, then *discrete bivariate* or *multivariate probability distributions* can be calculated that give the probabilities of all possible mixtures of outcomes on these variables. Thus, if two outcomes are being measured by discrete random variables X

and Y that can take on specific values $X = x$ and $Y = y$, then the discrete probability distribution of these variables can be defined as

$$f(x, y) = P(X = x, Y = y)$$

which has the properties

$$(1)\quad f(x, y) \geq 0$$
$$(2)\quad \sum_{f(x,y)>0} f(x, y) = 1$$

These properties indicate that all $f(x, y)$ values are greater than or equal to zero, and that the sum of all $f(x, y)$ values that are greater than zero is 1.

Similarly if k different outcomes per trial are measured by the discrete random variables $X_1, X_2, \ldots, X_k$ that can take on specific values $X_1 = x_1, X_2 = x_2, \ldots, X_k = x_k$, then the discrete multivariate probability distribution for these variables can be defined as

$$f(x_1, x_2, \ldots, x_k) = P(X_1 = x_1, X_2 = x_2, \ldots, X_k = x_k)$$

which has the properties

$$(1)\quad f(x_1, x_2, \ldots, x_k) \geq 0$$
$$(2)\quad \sum_{f(x_1, x_2, \ldots, x_k)>0} f(x_1, x_2, \ldots, x_k) = 1$$

These properties indicate that all $f(x_1, x_2, \ldots, x_k)$ values are greater than or equal to zero, and that the sum of all $f(x_1, x_2, \ldots, x_k)$ values that are greater than zero is 1.

In both the bivariate and multivariate cases, we are simultaneously considering the related or *joint outcomes* of two or more random variables. Because of this, if a bivariate or multivariate probability distribution is determined for these discrete random variables, then it is said that they are *jointly distributed discrete random variables*, and that the distribution is a *discrete joint probability distribution* or a *joint probability mass function*. If it is clear from the context of the discussion that we are dealing with discrete random variables, then these distributions will be referred to simply as *joint probability distributions* or *joint probability functions*.

To understand these concepts, let us consider a specific example. There are 10 marbles in a bowl, identical except for color: 4 are red R, 3 are green G, and 3 are blue B. The experiment is to blindly pick 5 marbles from the bowl, identifying the color and replacing the marble after each pick. Now, if we only consider the discrete random variable X = number of reds, that can take on the specific values $x = 0, 1, \ldots, 5$, we can calculate the discrete univariate binomial probability distribution. If instead we consider the three discrete random variables X_1 = number of reds, X_2 = number of greens, and X_3 = number of blues, which on each trial can take on the specific values $x_1 = 0, 1, \ldots, 5$, $x_2 = 0, 1, \ldots, 5$, and $x_3 = 0, 1, \ldots, 5$, then we can determine the multivariate probability distribution

$$f(x_1, x_2, x_3) = P(X_1 = x_1, X_2 = x_2, X_3 = x_3)$$

If, say, we are interested in the probability of the joint outcomes—two Rs, two Gs, and one B—we would determine

$$f(2, 2, 1) = P(X_1 = 2, X_2 = 2, X_3 = 1)$$

This distribution/function is called a joint probability distribution or joint probability function, and the specific joint probability function for this marble problem, which is the *multinomial probability function* will be given in Section 11.16.

11.14 THE MULTINOMIAL EXPERIMENT

As the binomial probability distribution is based on the binomial experiment (see Section 11.3), so also is our next discrete probability distribution, the *multinomial distribution*, based on an experiment: the *multinomial experiment*. This experiment has these properties:

(1) It consists of n identical trials.

(2) For each trial, there are k possible mutually exclusive and exhaustive events $A_1, A_2, \ldots, A_k$.

(3) For each trial, the probability of A_i is p_i (where $i = 1, 2, \ldots, k$) and p_i remains constant over trials.

(4) For each trial

$$\sum_i p_i = p_1 + p_2 + \cdots + p_k = 1$$

(5) The trials are independent; no event or sequence of events affects any subsequent event.

(6) The discrete random variables $X_1, X_2, \ldots, X_k$ are used to count the number of times $A_1, A_2, \ldots, A_k$ occur in the n trials, with the actual count values denoted by $X_1 = x_1$, $X_2 = x_2, \ldots, X_k = x_k$. The variables are called *multinomial random variables*.

If you now compare these multinomial properties with the properties of a binomial experiment (see Sections 11.2 and 11.3), you will see why it is said that the *multinomial experiment is a generalization of the binomial experiment*. Another way to state the relationship between the two kinds of experiments is: *The binomial experiment is a special case of the multinomial experiment where* $k = 2$. For this special binomial case, the multinomial properties read:

(1) The experiment consists of n identical trials.

(2) For each trial, there are $k = 2$ possible mutually exclusive and exhaustive events $A_1 = \{\text{success}\}$ and $A_2 = \{\text{failure}\}$.

(3) For each trial, the probability of A_i is p_i ($p_1 = p$ = probability of success; $p_2 = q$ = probability of failure) and p_i remains constant over trials.

(4) For each trial

$$\sum_{i=1}^{2} p_i = p + q = 1$$

(5) The trials are independent.

(6) The single discrete random variable X is used to count the number of times $A_1 = \{\text{success}\}$ occurs in the n trials, with the actual count values denoted by $X = x$.

11.15 THE MULTINOMIAL COEFFICIENT

As the multinomial experiment is a generalization of the binomial experiment (see Section 11.14), so also is the *multinomial coefficient* a generalization of the binomial coefficient [equation (11.1)]. The multinomial coefficient counts the number of possible permutations of n objects where the n consists of k different types of objects, x_1 of type $1, x_2$ of type $2, \ldots, x_k$ of type k. If x_i is a nonnegative integer and $x_1 + x_2 + \cdots + x_k = n$, then the multinomial coefficient can be defined as

$$\text{Multinomial coefficient} = \binom{n}{x_1, x_2, \ldots, x_k} = \frac{n!}{x_1!x_2!\ldots x_k!} \tag{11.12}$$

EXAMPLE 11.12 For the bowl of 10 marbles in Section 11.13 (four R, three G, three B), how many ways can the 10 marbles be picked, in sequence, from the bowl (i.e., how many ways can the three kinds of 10 marbles be arranged *in order* in a line)?

Solution

The question is, how many permutations can be made from four R, three G, and three B marbles? If we define X_1 = number of Rs $= x_1 = 4$, X_2 = number of Gs $= x_2 = 3$, and X_3 = number of Bs $= x_3 = 3$, then the number of permutations is given by the multinomial coefficient

$$\binom{n}{x_1, x_2, x_3} = \frac{n!}{x_1!x_2!x_3!}$$

$$\binom{10}{4, 3, 3} = \frac{10!}{4!3!3!} = \frac{3{,}628{,}800}{864} = 4{,}200$$

11.16 THE MULTINOMIAL PROBABILITY FUNCTION

As the multinomial experiment is a generalization of the binomial experiment (see Section 11.14) and the multinomial coefficient is a generalization of the binomial coefficient (see Section 11.15), it is also true that the *multinomial probability function* is a generalization of the binomial probability function [equation (11.2)]. While the binomial probability function

$$f(x) = \binom{n}{x} p^x q^{n-x}, \qquad \text{for } x = 0, 1, 2, \ldots, n$$

gives the probability of x successes in the n trials of a binomial experiment, the multinomial probability function gives the probability in the n trials of a multinomial experiment of observing x_1 occurrences of event A_1, x_2 of A_2, ..., x_k of A_k. This joint probability function (see Section 11.13) is

$$f(x_1, x_2, \ldots, x_k) = \binom{n}{x_1, x_2, \ldots, x_k} p_x^{x_1} p_2^{x_2} \cdots p_k^{x_k} = \frac{n!}{x_1!x_2!\cdots x_k!} p_1^{x_1} p_2^{x_2} \cdots p_k^{x_k} \tag{11.13}$$

where x_i is the number of times event A_i occurred in the n trials, p_i is the probability of A_i on each trial, $x_1 + x_2 + \cdots + x_k = n$, and $p_1 + p_2 + \cdots + p_k = 1$.

EXAMPLE 11.13 For the bowl of 10 marbles in Example 11.12 (four R, three G, three B), the experiment is to pick 5 marbles from the bowl, identifying the color and replacing the marble after each pick. This experiment satisfies the multinomial properties: (1) it has $n = 5$ identical trials; (2) for each trial, there are three possible, mutually exclusive, and exhaustive events: $A_1 = \{R\}$, $A_2 = \{G\}$, $A_3 = \{B\}$; (3) for each trial, $P(A_1) = p_1 = 4/10$, $P(A_2) = p_2 = 3/10$, and $P(A_3) = p_3 = 3/10$; (4) for each trial, $\sum p_i = 4/10 + 3/10 + 3/10 = 1$; (5) the trials are independent; and (6) discrete random variables X_1 = number of Rs, X_2 = number of Gs, and X_3 = number of Bs are used to count the number of times A_1, A_2, and A_3 occur in the n trials. For the five picks, what is the probability of getting $X_1 = x_1 = 2$, $X_2 = x_2 = 2$, and $X_3 = x_3 = 1$? Calculate this probability by using: (*a*) the rules of probability, and (*b*) the multinomial probability function [equation (11.13)].

Solution

(*a*) One sequence of five events that would give this is $RRGGB$. Knowing p_i for each trial and that the trials are independent, we can say from the generalization of the special multiplication rule [equation (9.9), Volume 1] that

$$P(R \cap R \cap G \cap G \cap B) = P(R)P(R)P(G)P(G)P(B)$$

$$= \left(\frac{4}{10}\right)\left(\frac{4}{10}\right)\left(\frac{3}{10}\right)\left(\frac{3}{10}\right)\left(\frac{3}{10}\right) = 0.00432$$

which we can write in the multinomial form as

$$P(A_1 \cap A_1 \cap A_2 \cap A_2 \cap A_3) = p_1^2 p_2^2 p_3^1 = \left(\frac{4}{10}\right)^2 \left(\frac{3}{10}\right)^2 \left(\frac{3}{10}\right) = 0.00432$$

But this is just one of the many possible sequences of five events that would yield $X_1 = 2$, $X_2 = 2$, $X_3 = 1$. The actual number is given by the multinomial coefficient [equation (11.12)]. Thus

$$\binom{n}{x_1, x_2, x_3} = \frac{n!}{x_1!x_2!x_3!} = \frac{5!}{2!2!1!} = 30$$

Combining these results, we can see that

$$P(X_1 = 2, X_2 = 2, X_3 = 1) = (30)(0.00432) = 0.12960$$

(*b*) Using equation (11.13) directly, we get the same result:

$$f(x_1, x_2, x_3) = \binom{n}{x_1, x_2, x_3} p_1^{x_1} p_2^{x_2} p_3^{x_3} = \frac{n!}{x_1!x_2!x_3!} p_1^{x_1} p_2^{x_2} p_3^{x_3}$$

$$f(2, 2, 1) = \binom{5}{2, 2, 1}\left(\frac{4}{10}\right)^2\left(\frac{3}{10}\right)^2\left(\frac{3}{10}\right)^1 = \frac{5!}{2!2!1!}\left(\frac{4}{10}\right)^2\left(\frac{3}{10}\right)^2\left(\frac{3}{10}\right)^1$$

$$= (30)(0.00432) = 0.12960$$

11.17 THE FAMILY OF MULTINOMIAL PROBABILITY DISTRIBUTIONS

Recall from Section 11.9, that n and p are parameters, defining constants, in the binomial probability function [equation (11.2)], and that each unique combination of n and p values defines one member of an infinitely large family of binomial distributions. Similarly, we now say that $n, p_1, p_2, \ldots, p_k$ are parameters in the multinomial probability function [equation (11.13)], and that each unique set of $n, p_1, p_2, \ldots, p_k$ values defines one member of an infinitely large *family of multinomial distributions*. Each such multinomial distribution can be presented as the defining function with the parameters specified, or as a complete list or table of probabilities.

Table 11.4

Number of Rs, Gs, Bs x_1, x_2, x_3	Probability $f(x_1, x_2, x_3) = \binom{n}{x_1, x_2, x_3} p_1^{x_1} p_2^{x_2} p_3^{x_3}$
1, 1, 0	$f(1, 1, 0) = \binom{2}{1, 1, 0}(0.4)^1(0.3)^1(0.3)^0 = (2)(0.4)(0.3)(1) = 0.24$
1, 0, 1	$f(1, 0, 1) = \binom{2}{1, 0, 1}(0.4)^1(0.3)^0(0.3)^1 = (2)(0.4)(1)(0.3) = 0.24$
0, 1, 1	$f(0, 1, 1) = \binom{2}{0, 1, 1}(0.4)^0(0.3)^1(0.3)^1 = (2)(1)(0.3)(0.3) = 0.18$
2, 0, 0	$f(2, 0, 0) = \binom{2}{2, 0, 0}(0.4)^2(0.3)^0(0.3)^0 = (1)(0.16)(1)(1) = 0.16$
0, 2, 0	$f(0, 2, 0) = \binom{2}{0, 2, 0}(0.4)^0(0.3)^2(0.3)^0 = (1)(1)(0.09)(1) = 0.09$
0, 0, 2	$f(0, 0, 2) = \binom{2}{0, 0, 2}(0.4)^0(0.3)^0(0.3)^2 = (1)(1)(1)(0.09) = 0.09$
$\sum > 0$	1.00

EXAMPLE 11.14 For the bowl of 10 marbles in Example 11.13 (four R, three G, three B), the experiment is now to pick two marbles from the bowl, identifying the color and replacing the marble after each pick. Thus, $n = 2$; $A_1 = \{R\}, A_2 = \{G\}$, and $A_3 = \{B\}$; $X_1 =$ number of Rs $= x_1, X_2 =$ number of Gs $= x_2$, and $X_3 =$ number of Bs $= x_3$; $p_1 = 0.4, p_2 = 0.3$, and $p_3 = 0.3$. Present, in a table of probabilities, the multinomial distribution for this experiment.

Solution

The requested multinomial distribution is shown in Table 11.4.

11.18 THE MEANS OF THE MULTINOMIAL PROBABILITY DISTRIBUTION

The multinomial probability distribution has a mean (expected value) for each of its discrete random variables, which is the expected number of times that each random variable will occur in n trials. When the random variables of the distribution are $X_1, X_2, \ldots, X_k$, then the *means of the multinomial probability distribution* are

$$E(X_1) = \mu_1 = np_1, \qquad E(X_2) = \mu_2 = np_2, \ldots, \qquad E(X_k) = \mu_k = np_k \tag{11.14}$$

EXAMPLE 11.15 For the multinomial distribution in Table 11.4, what are the means of X_1, X_2, and X_3?

Solution

The means are

$$E(X_1) = \mu_1 = np_1 = 2(0.4) = 0.8$$
$$E(X_2) = \mu_2 = np_2 = 2(0.3) = 0.6$$
$$E(X_3) = \mu_3 = np_3 = 2(0.3) = 0.6$$

11.19 THE MULTINOMIAL EXPANSION AND THE MULTINOMIAL THEOREM

The multinomial probability distribution is related to the *multinomial expansion* and the *multinomial theorem*, just as the binomial probability distribution is related to the binomial expansion and the binomial theorem (see Section 11.7).

If a *multinomial algebraic expression* (see Section 1.11, Volume 1) of the form $a_1 + a_2 + \cdots + a_k$ is raised to the nth power, and if this product is multiplied out to produce a sum of terms, then this sum of terms is called a multinomial expansion. Furthermore, if $a_1, a_2, \ldots, a_k$ are real numbers and n is a positive integer, then the following is a general formula for expanding $(a_1 + a_2 + \cdots + a_k)^n$ that is called the multinomial theorem,

$$(a_1 + a_2 + \cdots + a_k)^n = \sum_{x_1+x_2+\cdots+x_k=n} \binom{n}{x_1, x_2, \ldots, x_k} a_1^{x_1} a_2^{x_2} \cdots a_k^{x_k} \tag{11.15}$$

where the symbol $\sum\limits_{x_1+x_2+\cdots+x_k=n}$ means take the sum over all possible combinations of nonnegative integers that add up to n.

EXAMPLE 11.16 For the multinomial distribution in Table 11.4, use $n = 2$, $a_1 = p_1$, $a_2 = p_2$, and $a_3 = p_3$, to demonstrate the relationship between the multinomial probability distribution and the multinomial expansion and theorem.

Solution

Using these parameters in equation (11.15), the multinomial expansion for all possible sets of nonnegative integers x_1, x_2, and x_3 that satisfy $x_1 + x_2 + x_3 = 2$ is

$$\begin{aligned}(p_1 + p_2 + p_3)^2 &= \sum_{x_1+x_2+x_3=2} \binom{2}{x_1, x_2, x_3} p_1^{x_1} p_2^{x_2} p_3^{x_3} \\ &= \binom{2}{1,1,0} p_1^1 p_2^1 p_3^0 + \binom{2}{1,0,1} p_1^1 p_2^0 p_3^1 + \binom{2}{0,1,1} p_1^0 p_2^1 p_3^1 + \binom{2}{2,0,0} p_1^2 p_2^0 p_3^0 \\ &\quad + \binom{2}{0,2,0} p_1^0 p_2^2 p_3^0 + \binom{2}{0,0,2} p_1^0 p_2^0 p_3^2 \\ &= 2p_1p_2 + 2p_1p_3 + 2p_2p_3 + p_1^2 + p_2^2 + p_3^2\end{aligned}$$

From this you can see that for every probability value in the multinomial distribution in Table 11.4 there is a corresponding term in the multinomial expansion. Indeed, it is this relationship to the expansion that gives the multinomial probability distribution its name.

11.20 THE HYPERGEOMETRIC EXPERIMENT

As with the previous discrete probability distributions in this chapter (see Sections 11.3 and 11.14), the next distribution we will consider, the *hypergeometric probability distribution*, is also based on an experiment: the *hypergeometric experiment*. This experiment resembles the binomial experiment except that the hypergeometric experiment involves sampling from a finite population *without replacement*, and so the trials are not independent and the probability of "success" changes as the sample is removed from the population. The characteristics of the hypergeometric experiments are:

(1) A random sample of n objects is taken one at a time (n trials) from a finite population of N_T objects by sampling without replacement.

(2) Of the N_T objects in the population, N_S are of one type, called "successes," and N_F are of another type, called "failures" ($N_S + N_F = N_T$).

(3) The discrete random variable X, here called a *hypergeometric random variable*, is used to count the number of successes ($X = x$) in the sample.

11.21 THE HYPERGEOMETRIC PROBABILITY FUNCTION

The *hypergeometric probability function* determines the probability of x successes in the n trials of a hypergeometric experiment. It is different from the binomial probability function [equation (11.2)] because, in sampling without replacement, the probability of success changes after each trial. The hypergeometric probability function, therefore, utilizes a different calculation method based on three aspects of probability: the classical probability ratio [equation (8.1), Volume 1], the counting rule: multiplication principle (see Section 9.12, Volume 1), and the counting rule:combinations (see Section 9.14, Volume 1).

In the classical interpretation of probability (see Section 8.1, Volume 1), the probability of an event A [denoted by $P(A)$] is the ratio of the number of possible outcomes favorable to A (denoted by N_A) to the total number of possible outcomes for the experiment (denoted by N), with the assumption that all outcomes are equally likely. Thus

$$P(A) = \frac{N_A}{N}$$

This ratio is the basic structure of the hypergeometric probability function, with N_A representing the total number of ways x successes can occur in the n trials of a hypergeometric experiment, and N representing the total number of n-trial outcomes that can occur in the experiment. To determine N_A and N we use the two counting rules.

To understand how this works, consider again the experiment in Example 11.4: picking 6 marbles from the bowl of 20 ($12R, 8G$), and determining the probability of picking 4 Rs in the six picks. In

Example 11.4, the sampling was with replacement, the probability remained constant over trials, and so the binomial probability function was used to determine that $f(4) = 0.311$. Now, let us consider the probability of picking 4 Rs in the six picks, if the sampling is without replacement. These are the conditions of the hypergeometric experiment (see Section 11.20), where: $n =$ number of picks $= 6$, $N_T =$ total number of marbles $= 20$, $N_S =$ number of Rs $= 12$, $N_F =$ number of Gs $= 8$, $x =$ number of successes $= 4$. From this we will calculate the ratio

$$P(\text{picking 4 } Rs) = P(X = 4) = \frac{N_A}{N}$$

where N_A is the total number of ways 4 Rs can be picked in the six picks and N is the total number of possible six-pick outcomes for the experiment. To determine N_A we use both types of counting rules. First, we use the counting rule: combinations to determine the number of ways in six picks that 4 Rs can be picked from the 12 Rs,

$${}_{N_S}C_x = {}_{12}C_4 = \frac{N_S!}{x!(N_S - x)!} = \frac{12!}{4!(12-4)!} = \frac{11{,}880}{24} = 495$$

and the number of ways in six picks that 2 Gs can be picked from the 8 Gs,

$${}_{N_F}C_{n-x} = {}_8C_2 = \frac{N_F!}{(n-x)![N_F - (n-x)]!} = \frac{8!}{2!(8-2)!} = \frac{56}{2} = 28$$

Now we use the counting rule: multiplication principle to determine N_A:

$$N_A = {}_{N_S}C_x \times {}_{N_F}C_{n-x} = 495 \times 28 = 13{,}860$$

To determine N, the number of possible six-pick outcomes, we again use the counting rule: combinations. Thus,

$$N = {}_{N_T}C_n = {}_{20}C_6 = \frac{N_T!}{n!(N_T - n)!} = \frac{20!}{6!(20-6)!} = \frac{27{,}907{,}200}{720} = 38{,}760$$

Therefore,

$$P(X = 4) = \frac{13{,}860}{38{,}760} = 0.3576$$

To generalize from this example, if the conditions of a hypergeometric experiment are met and a probability function is used to assign probability values to every sample point in the sample space defined by a hypergeometric variable, then this function is called a *hypergeometric probability distribution*, or a *hypergeometric distribution*, or a *hypergeometric probability mass function*, or simply a *hypergeometric probability function*. It is defined as follows:

$$f(x) = P(X = x) = \frac{{}_{N_S}C_x \times {}_{N_F}C_{n-x}}{{}_{N_T}C_n} = \frac{\binom{N_S}{x}\binom{N_F}{n-x}}{\binom{N_T}{n}} \tag{11.16}$$

and, substituting equation (9.20) of Volume 1, we get

$$f(x) = P(X = x) = \frac{\left[\dfrac{N_S!}{x!(N_S - x)!}\right]\left[\dfrac{N_F!}{(n-x)!(N_F - (n-x))!}\right]}{\left[\dfrac{N_T!}{n!(N_T - n)!}\right]}, \qquad \text{for } x = 0, 1, 2, \ldots, n \tag{11.17}$$

where: $x \le N_S$ (number of successes in sample must be less than or equal to number of successes in population); $n - x \le N_F$ (number of failures in sample must be less than or equal to number of failures in population); and N_T, n, and N_S are positive integers such that $N_S \le N_T$ and $n \le N_T$.

EXAMPLE 11.17 A manager must select a committee of three from his staff of six men M and four women W. He writes their names on separate identical pieces of paper, puts the papers in a bowl, and then blindly picks a sequence of three papers from the bowl. Find the probability that he picks two women by using: (*a*) the conditional-probability techniques from Chapter 9 of Volume 1, and (*b*) the hypergeometric probability function.

Solution

(*a*) There are three sequences of picks that include two women: $W \cap W \cap M$, $W \cap M \cap W$, and $M \cap W \cap W$. Using equation (9.5), Volume 1,

$$P(W \cap W \cap M) = \frac{4}{10} \times \frac{3}{9} \times \frac{6}{8} = 0.10$$

$$P(W \cap M \cap W) = \frac{4}{10} \times \frac{6}{9} \times \frac{3}{8} = 0.10$$

$$P(M \cap W \cap W) = \frac{6}{10} \times \frac{4}{9} \times \frac{3}{8} = 0.10$$

Then, using the generaliztion of the special addition rule [Property 4, Section 8.6, Volume 1]

$$\begin{aligned} P(2 \text{ women}) &= P[(W \cap W \cap M) \cup (W \cap M \cap W) \cup (M \cap W \cap W)] \\ &= P(W \cap W \cap M) + P(W \cap M \cap W) + P(M \cap W \cap W) \\ &= 0.10 + 0.10 + 0.10 = 0.30 \end{aligned}$$

(*b*) These are the conditions of a hypergeometric experiment and so we can use equation (11.16). For this,

$$_{N_T}C_n = {}_{10}C_3 = \frac{10!}{3!(10-3)!} = 120$$

$$_{N_S}C_x \times {}_{N_F}C_{n-x} = {}_4C_2 \times {}_6C_1 = \left(\frac{4!}{2!2!}\right)\left(\frac{6!}{1!5!}\right) = (6)(6) = 36$$

Therefore,

$$P(\text{selecting 2 } W\text{s}) = \frac{36}{120} = 0.30$$

11.22 THE FAMILY OF HYPERGEOMETRIC PROBABILITY DISTRIBUTIONS

As is true for the binomial (see Section 11.9) and multinomial (see Section 11.17) distributions, the hypergeometric distribution is also a family of probability distributions. It has the parameters N_T, N_S, and n.

EXAMPLE 11.18 For the experiment in Example 11.17, determine the entire hypergeometric probability distribution by placing the values given for the parameters in equation (11.17).

Solution

The requested hypergeometric distribution is shown in Table 11.5.

Table 11.5

Number of Ws x	Probability $f(x) = \dfrac{\binom{N_S}{x}\binom{N_F}{n-x}}{\binom{N_T}{n}}$
0	$f(0) = \dfrac{\binom{4}{0}\binom{6}{3}}{\binom{10}{3}} = \dfrac{(1)(20)}{(120)} = 0.16667$
1	$f(1) = \dfrac{\binom{4}{1}\binom{6}{2}}{\binom{10}{3}} = \dfrac{(4)(15)}{(120)} = 0.50000$
2	$f(2) = \dfrac{\binom{4}{2}\binom{6}{1}}{\binom{10}{3}} = \dfrac{(6)(6)}{(120)} = 0.30000$
3	$f(3) = \dfrac{\binom{4}{3}\binom{6}{0}}{\binom{10}{3}} = \dfrac{(4)(1)}{(120)} = 0.03333$
Σ	1.00000

11.23 THE MEAN, VARIANCE, AND STANDARD DEVIATION OF THE HYPERGEOMETRIC PROBABILITY DISTRIBUTION

Without deriving them, we will state that for a hypergeometric distribution the mean (expected value) is

$$E(X) = \mu = \frac{nN_S}{N_T} \tag{11.18}$$

the variance is

$$\sigma^2 = \frac{nN_S N_F (N_T - n)}{N_T^2 (N_T - 1)} \tag{11.19}$$

and the standard deviation is

$$\sigma = \sqrt{\sigma^2} = \sqrt{\frac{nN_S N_F (N_T - n)}{N_T^2 (N_T - 1)}} \tag{11.20}$$

EXAMPLE 11.19 Find the mean and variance of the hypergeometric distribution shown in Table 11.5.

Solution

Using equation (11.18),

$$\mu = \frac{nN_S}{N_T} = \frac{3 \times 4}{10} = 1.2$$

Using equation (11.19),

$$\sigma^2 = \frac{nN_S N_F(N_T - n)}{N_T^2(N_T - 1)} = \frac{3 \times 4 \times 6 \times (10 - 3)}{10^2(10 - 1)} = 0.56$$

11.24 THE GENERALIZATION OF THE HYPERGEOMETRIC PROBABILITY DISTRIBUTION

As the multinomial probability function is a generalization of the binomial probability function (see Section 11.16), there is also a joint probability function (see Section 11.13) that is a *generalization of the hypergeometric probability function*. This function is appropriate for hypergeometric experiments with the following properties:

(1) A random sample of n objects is taken from a finite population of N_T objects by sampling without replacement.

(2) Of the N_T objects in the population, N_1 are of type one, N_2 are of type two, ..., N_k are of type k, and $N_1 + N_2 + \cdots + N_k = N_T$.

(3) The discrete random variable $X_1, X_2, \ldots, X_k$ are used to count the number of times types one, two, ..., k appear in the sample, with the actual count values denoted by $X_1 = x_1, X_2 = x_2, \ldots, X_k = x_k$.

The joint probability function that gives the probability of obtaining x_1 of type one, x_2 of type $2, \ldots, x_k$ of type k, also simply called the hypergeometric probability function, is

$$\begin{aligned} f(x_1, x_2, \ldots, x_k) &= P(X_1 = x_1, X_2 = x_2, \ldots, X_k = x_k) \\ &= \frac{\binom{N_1}{x_1}\binom{N_2}{x_2}\cdots\binom{N_k}{x_k}}{\binom{N_T}{n}} \end{aligned} \tag{11.21}$$

where $x_1 + x_2 + \cdots + x_k = n$.

EXAMPLE 11.20 You randomly draw 10 cards from a deck of 52 playing cards without replacing the card between draws. What is the probability that you draw 2 clubs, 2 hearts, 2 diamonds, and 4 spades?

Solution

In this problem we are dealing with a hypergeometric experiment where: X_1 = clubs in sample $= x_1 = 2$, X_2 = hearts in sample $= x_2 = 2$, X_3 = diamonds in sample $= x_3 = 2$, X_4 = spades in sample $= x_4 = 4$, $N_T = 52$, $N_1 = N_2 = N_3 = N_4$ = number of cards in each suit = 13, and $n = 10$. Using these values in equation (11.21), we get

$$f(2, 2, 2, 4) = \frac{\binom{13}{2}\binom{13}{2}\binom{13}{2}\binom{13}{4}}{\binom{52}{10}} = \frac{(78)(78)(78)(715)}{(15{,}820{,}024{,}220)} = 0.0214$$

11.25 THE BINOMIAL AND MULTINOMIAL APPROXIMATIONS TO THE HYPERGEOMETRIC DISTRIBUTION

The hypergeometric distribution is the appropriate discrete probability distribution to use for probability questions involving *sampling without replacement from finite populations*, either two-outcome questions or multiple-outcome questions. However, in large populations there is essentially no difference between sampling with replacement and sampling without replacement. Thus, if $n \leq 0.05N$, then the binomial distribution can be used to solve two-outcome sampling-without-replacement problems and the multinomial distribution can be used to solve multiple-outcome sampling-without-replacement problems. In the binomial case this approximation is called the *binomial approximation to the hypergeometric distribution* and in the multinomial case it is called the *multinomial approximation to the hypergeometric distribution*.

11.26 POISSON PROCESSES, RANDOM VARIABLES, AND EXPERIMENTS

In the three previous discrete probability distributions in this chapter, we determined the probability of random events occurring in a fixed number of trials, n. Now, with the fourth and last probability distribution to be discussed in the chapter, the *Poisson probability distribution*, we will determine probabilities for *random events occurring in continuous fixed units* (see Section 2.6, Volume 1) *of time and space*. The Poisson is similar to the binomial in that it deals with the number of occurrences of one of two possible outcomes (again called the "*success*" outcome), but while the number for the binomial is a finite number of trials when success occurs, the number for the Poisson can be an infinitely large number of occurrences in a continuous unit of time or space. Some examples of discrete random variables in the real world whose outcome-probabilities might appropriately be calculated with Poisson techniques are: number of phone calls arriving at a switchboard during the interval 10 AM to 11:30 AM, number of emitted particles recorded during a ten-second interval by a Geiger counter placed near a radioactive substance, number of defects in four meters of electrical cable, number of white blood cells in one cubic centimeter of blood, number of defects in the surface of a new car, and number of bacterial colonies growing on an agar plate.

To use Poisson techniques to determine outcome-probabilities for such random variables, it is necessary that the *process* generating the random outcomes be a *Poisson process*. This is true if the following assumptions are met:

(1) For a given continuous unit of time or space, there is a known, empirically determined positive constant, denoted by λ (Greek lowercase *lambda*), that is the *average rate of occurrence of successes* in the given unit. This rate λ characterizes the success-generating process being observed and is the same for all similarly defined units.

(2) For any size of subunit of the given unit, the number of successes occurring in the subunit is *independent* of the number of successes in any other nonoverlapping subunit.

(3) If the specified unit is divided into very small subunits denoted by h, then the probability of exactly one success occurring in an h is very small and it is the same (is constant) for all hs in the unit no matter when (or where) they appear. This very small probability of one success in h gets closer and closer to the value λh as h is made smaller and smaller.

(4) The probability of more than one success occurring in any very small subunit h is essentially zero. As h is made smaller and smaller, this probability gets closer and closer to zero.

If the process that generates random events in a given unit of time or space is a Poisson process, then if a discrete random variable X is used to count the number of successes ($X = x$) occurring in the given unit (or in one of its subunits), this variable is called a *Poisson random variable*, and the experiment of counting the number of successes is a *Poisson experiment*. These concepts and the *Poisson probability function* (see Section 11.27) are named after their discoverer, the French mathematician *Siméon D. Poisson* (1781–1840).

To understand these concepts, consider this Poisson experiment. A manufacturer of electrical cable, knowing that defects appear "randomly" in the cable as it is produced, wants to use Poisson techniques to determine the probabilities for different numbers of defects (successes) in a fixed length (unit) of cable. He decides to use 4 meters as the fixed unit and, after counting defects in many 4-meter lengths, he finds that the average (arithmetic mean) of these counts is 4.0 defects per 4 meters. This satisfies assumption (1): for the 4-meter unit, there is an empirically determined positive constant ($\lambda = 4.0$ defects per 4 meters) that is the average rate of random occurrences of the defects (successes) in the unit, and it is reasonable to believe that λ will be the same for all 4-meter lengths. If we now consider a 10 cm section (subunit) from the 4 meters, then assumption (2) is met if the number of defects occurring in this subunit is independent of the number occurring in any other nonoverlapping subunit. If we now consider a very small subunit h of the 4 meters, then assumption (3) is met if there is a very small but constant probability that exactly one defect will occur in any h $[P(X = 1) \approx \lambda h = (4.0)h]$ regardless of where the h is located in the 4-meter unit. Finally, assumption (4) is met if the probability of more than one defect in any subunit h is essentially zero $[P(X > 1) \approx 0]$.

EXAMPLE 11.21 At the end of each week, the receptionist at a big-city clinic counts the number of new cases that have come to the clinic that week with the same highly contagious disease. These counts, increasing over the past three weeks, were 2, 10, and 30. Explain why this is probably *not* a Poisson experiment.

Solution

For this experiment to be a Poisson experiment, the process that generates the successes (new cases at the clinic) in the given unit of time (one week) must be a Poisson process. For this to be true, none of the four Poisson assumptions can be seriously violated, and in this example it would appear that at least three of them may be badly violated.

The essence of assumption (1) is that for the given unit (one week) there is a characteristic empirically determined average rate of occurrence of successes (new cases), λ, that is the same for all similarly defined units. Clearly this is not the case here, as it is apparent that the generating process is not stable but is instead a rapidly changing epidemic. Under these conditions, a λ calculated from these three weeks ($\lambda = 42/3 = 14$ cases per week) cannot be assumed to be valid for subsequent weeks.

The essence of assumption (2) is that the number of new cases appearing in any subunit of the week (say, on a Friday) will be independent of the number occurring in any other nonoverlapping subunit (say, on a Monday). But, under epidemic conditions in a crowded city neighborhood it is very likely that this assumption will be violated. As patients early in the week become infected and learn of the disease at the clinic, they will return to the neighborhood, infecting and informing their neighbors, sending new cases to the clinic later in the week.

The essence of assumption (3) is that there is a small but constant probability of the occurrence of exactly one success in all equal, very small subunits (i.e., seconds) within the unit (week), but under these epidemic conditions it is not reasonable to expect this moment-by-moment probability to remain constant.

Finally, for assumption (4), the case numbers are as yet small enough that the probability of more than one new case in a very small subunit would be close to zero, but if the numbers greatly increase this could also be violated.

11.27 THE POISSON PROBABILITY FUNCTION

In Section 11.26, we indicated that one assumption of a Poisson process is that for any given unit of time or space there is a known, empirically determined average rate of occurrence of successes λ that is the same for all similarly defined units. It follows from this and the other three assumptions, though we will not attempt to prove it, that the average (expected) rate of occurrence of successes in any multiple of the defining unit, denoted by t, is λt. Thus, for the cable-defect experiment in Section 11.26, where $\lambda = 4.0$ defects per 4 meters, the average rate of occurrence of defects in 24 meters ($t = 6$ units) would be

$$\begin{aligned}\lambda_t &= (4.0 \text{ defects per 4 meters}) \times (6 \text{ units})\\ &= 24.0 \text{ defects per 24 meters}\end{aligned}$$

and for 1 meter ($t = \frac{1}{4}$ unit)

$$\begin{aligned}\lambda t &= (4.0 \text{ defects per 4 meters}) \times (\tfrac{1}{4} \text{ unit})\\ &= 1.0 \text{ defect per meter}\end{aligned}$$

The *Poisson probability function* utilizes this constant λt to determine the probability of occurrence of $(X = x)$ successes in some multiple t of the defining unit for a Poisson experiment. Without attempting to derive the function, it is

$$f(x) = P(X = x) = \frac{(\lambda t)^x e^{-\lambda t}}{x!}, \qquad \text{for } x = 0, 1, 2, \ldots \tag{11.22}$$

where e is the base of the natural logarithm and is equal to $2.71828\ldots$ [see Problem 1.23(*b*), Volume 1], and $x = 0, 1, 2, \ldots$ means that the domain of this function (see Section 1.17, Volume 1) consists of all the nonnegative integers.

EXAMPLE 11.22 Assuming that the cable-defect experiment described in Section 11.26 is a Poisson experiment, what is the probability of two defects occurring in one meter of a cable?

Solution

Using equation (11.22) to determine the probability of two defects in one meter of cable ($t = \frac{1}{4}$ units)

$$f(2) = P(X = 2) = \frac{(4.0 \times \frac{1}{4})^2 e^{-(4.0\times 1/4)}}{2!} = \frac{(1)^2 e^{-1}}{2} = \frac{e^{-1}}{2}$$

If your calculator has an e^x key, you can get the solution directly:

$$f(2) = 0.1839$$

If your calculator does not have an e^x key, then knowing that $e = 2.71828\ldots$ and that $e^{-x} = 1/e^x$ [see Example 1.16(*a*), Volume 1], you can use the following solution:

$$f(2) = \frac{e^{-1}}{2} = \frac{1}{2e} = \frac{1}{2(2.71828)} = 0.1839$$

11.28 THE FAMILY OF POISSON PROBABILITY DISTRIBUTIONS

As was true for the previous distributions in this chapter, the Poisson distribution is also a family of probability distributions. It has the single parameter λt.

EXAMPLE 11.23 Use equation (11.22) to determine the Poisson probability distribution for the cable-defect experiment in Section 11.26, where $\lambda = 4.0$ defects per 4 meters, $t = \frac{1}{4}$ units, and thus $\lambda t = 1.0$ defect per meter.

Solution

Because the domain of equation (11.22) consists of all nonnegative integers, a countably infinite number of values (see Section 10.2, Volume 1), it is never possible to determine an entire Poisson probability distribution. What we do present in Table 11.6 are the distribution values for $x = 0, 1, \ldots, 6$ to show how rapidly $P(X = x)$ goes toward zero as $(X = x)$ increases, and thus how much of the total probability of 1.0 in the distribution is taken by $x = 0, 1, \ldots, 6$

$$\sum_{x=0}^{6} f(x) = 0.99992$$

Table 11.6

Number of defects x	Probability $f(x) = \frac{(\lambda t)^x e^{-\lambda t}}{x!}$
0	$f(0) = \frac{(1.0)^0 e^{-1.0}}{0!} = 0.36788$
1	$f(1) = \frac{(1.0)^1 e^{-1.0}}{1!} = 0.36788$
2	$f(2) = \frac{(1.0)^2 e^{-1.0}}{2!} = 0.18394$
3	$f(3) = \frac{(1.0)^3 e^{-1.0}}{3!} = 0.06131$
4	$f(4) = \frac{(1.0)^4 e^{-1.0}}{4!} = 0.01533$
5	$f(5) = \frac{(1.0)^5 e^{-1.0}}{5!} = 0.00307$
6	$f(6) = \frac{(1.0)^6 e^{-1.0}}{6!} = 0.00051$
Σ	0.99992

11.29 THE MEAN, VARIANCE, AND STANDARD DEVIATION OF THE POISSON PROBABILITY DISTRIBUTION

For a Poisson distribution where λ is the average rate of occurrence of successes in the given defining unit and λt is the average rate of occurrence of successes in an interval of t units, then, without deriving them, we will state that

Mean of distribution = expected number of successes in an interval of t units

$$\mu = E(X) = \lambda t \tag{11.23}$$

$$\text{Variance of distribution} = \sigma^2 = \mu = \lambda t \tag{11.24}$$

$$\text{Standard deviation of distribution} = \sigma = \sqrt{\sigma^2} = \sqrt{\lambda t} \tag{11.25}$$

As indicated in Section 11.28, the Poisson distribution has a single parameter λt, which we now see is both the mean and the variance of the distribution. Because of this, equation (11.22) is often written

$$f(x) = \frac{\mu^x e^{-\mu}}{x!}, \qquad \text{for } x = 0, 1, 2, \ldots \tag{11.26}$$

EXAMPLE 11.24 For the Poisson distribution shown in Table 11.6, what are its mean, variance, standard deviation, and parameter?

Solution

For this Poisson distribution, in which λ is equal to 4.0 and t is equal to $\frac{1}{4}$, the mean is

$$\mu = \lambda t = 4.0 \times \frac{1}{4} = 1.0$$

the variance is

$$\sigma^2 = \mu = \lambda t = 1.0$$

the standard deviation is

$$\sigma = \sqrt{\sigma^2} = \sqrt{1.0} = 1.0$$

and the parameter is

$$\lambda t = 1.0$$

11.30 THE CUMULATIVE POISSON PROBABILITY TABLE

In Section 11.10, we introduced Table A.3 in the Appendix (*Cumulative Binomial Probabilities*) that gives cumulative probability values calculated with equation (11.10)

$$F(a) = \sum_{x \leq a} \left[f(x) = \binom{n}{x} p^x q^{n-x} \right]$$

for selected binomial distributions. Similarly, Table A.4 in the Appendix (*Cumulative Poisson Probabilities*) gives cumulative Poisson probability values calculated with this equation

$$F(a) = \sum_{x \leq a} \left[f(x) = \frac{\mu^x e^{-\mu}}{x!} \right] \tag{11.27}$$

for $\mu = 0.001, \ldots, 1.00$; and $\mu = 1.1, \ldots, 8.0$. To find the required $F(a)$ in Table A.4, go to the intersection of the appropriate μ column and a row.

EXAMPLE 11.25 A physicist places a Geiger counter near a radioactive substance and then notes the number of emitted particles recorded by the counter every 10 seconds for a 2-hour period. From this set of data, he calculates the average rate of recording particles (successes) in a 10-second interval (unit) to be $\lambda = 5.5$ particles per 10 seconds. Assuming this is a Poisson experiment, find the probability of recording more than three emitted particles in a 10-second interval. First, calculate the probability by cumulating the probabilities, and then find it by using Table A.4 in the Appendix.

Solution

The first step is to find the Poisson probability distribution for $x = 0, 1, 2, 3$ particles in a 10-second interval. Using equation (11.26),

$$f(x) = \frac{\mu^x e^{-\mu}}{x!}$$

with the values $\mu = \lambda t = 5.5 \times 1 = 5.5$,

$$f(0) = \frac{5.5^0 e^{-5.5}}{0!} = \frac{e^{-5.5}}{1} = 0.00409$$

$$f(1) = \frac{5.5^1 e^{-5.5}}{1!} = \frac{5.5 \times e^{-5.5}}{1} = 0.02248$$

$$f(2) = \frac{5.5^2 e^{-5.5}}{2!} = \frac{30.25 \times e^{-5.5}}{2} = 0.06181$$

$$f(3) = \frac{5.5^3 e^{-5.5}}{3!} = \frac{166.375 \times e^{-5.5}}{6} = 0.11332$$

The calculation of the probability by cumulation is

$$P(X > 3) = 1 - P(X \leq 3) = 1 - F(3)$$

where

$$F(3) = \sum_{x \leq 3} \left[f(x) = \frac{\mu^x e^{-\mu}}{x!} \right]$$

$$\begin{aligned} F(3) &= f(0) + f(1) + f(2) + f(3) \\ &= 0.00409 + 0.02248 + 0.06181 + 0.11332 \\ &= 0.20170 \end{aligned}$$

And thus

$$P(X > 3) = 1 - 0.20170 = 0.79830, \quad \text{or } 0.798$$

Now, finding the same probability by using Table A.4 of the Appendix, we need to find $F(3)$, which is the intersection of column ($\mu = 5.5$) and row ($a = 3$). The value at this intersection is 0.202. This solution is the same as the one above,

$$P(X > 3) = 1 - 0.202 = 0.798$$

11.31 THE POISSON DISTRIBUTION AS AN APPROXIMATION TO THE BINOMIAL DISTRIBUTION

The Poisson probability distribution can be used to approximate the binomial probability distribution under the following conditions: the random occurrence of success in the binomial experiment is a *rare event*, where n is "large" and p is "small." Without attempting to show this relationship between the two distributions, we simply state that the following is true:

> A binomial distribution $f(x) = \binom{n}{x} p^x q^{n-x}$ has two parameters, n and p, and a mean $\mu = np$. If np remains fixed while n is increased and p is decreased, then as n approaches infinity and p approaches zero, the binomial distribution approaches the Poisson distribution $f(x) = \dfrac{\mu^x e^{-\mu}}{x!}$ with a mean of $\mu = np$.

There is no unanimous agreement among statisticians about what is "large" and "small" in this context, but one common rule of thumb is that *Poisson approximations are good if* $n \geq 20$ *and* $p \leq 0.05$ *and very good if* $n \geq 100$ *and* $p \leq 0.01$.

EXAMPLE 11.26 A large factory has accepted 100 new people into a training program. The manager of the program knows from thousands of previous trainees that 4% of the trainees will not finish the program. Use both binomial and Poisson techniques to calculate the probability that exactly six will not finish.

Solution

If we accept that p is constant over independent trials, then this is a binomial experiment where: success = trainee not finishing, $n = 100$, $p = 0.04$, and $q = 1 - 0.04 = 0.96$. Thus, using the binomial probability function [equation (11.2)]

$$\begin{aligned} f(x) &= \binom{n}{x} p^x q^{n-x} \\ f(6) &= \binom{100}{6} (0.04)^6 (0.96)^{94} \\ &= (1{,}192{,}052{,}400)(0.0000000041)(0.021552) \\ &= 0.1053 \end{aligned}$$

As $n \geq 100$ and $p \leq 0.05$, we can use the Poisson approximation to the binomial. Thus, using equation

(11.26) with $\mu = n \times p = 100 \times 0.04 = 4$

$$f(x) = \frac{\mu^x e^{-\mu}}{x!}$$

$$f(6) \approx \frac{4^6 e^{-4}}{6!} = \frac{(4{,}096)(0.018316)}{720} = 0.1042$$

Solved Problems

THE BINOMIAL PROBABILITY DISTRIBUTION

11.1 Which of the following are binomial experiments?

(*a*) From many previous studies it has been established that drug A successfully cures a specific skin condition 64% of the time. You are a dermatologist, and you give this drug to the first 10 patients who come to you with this condition, counting how many of them it cures.

(*b*) Out of the population of 150,000 families, you call a random sample of 150 and ask the person who answers what the family income is.

Solution

(*a*) For this to be a binomial experiment, the following must be true: (1) the cure rate of 64% must remain constant over the 10 patients, (2) the drug treatments are independent, (3) the population N with this condition must be large. If we can assume these to be true, then this is a binomial experiment, where: success = cure, $p = 0.64$, $q = 1 - 0.64 = 0.36$, the binomial trials are the 10 patients, and the binomial variable is the number cured.

(*b*) This is not a binomial experiment because you do not have outcomes that can be classified as success or failure.

11.2 Which of the following are binomial experiments?

(*a*) Your factory has a machine that produces a part for an electric drill. You test the machine by taking 30 parts consecutively produced by the machine and counting how many of them are defective.

(*b*) You survey 100 randomly selected people out of the 50,000 registered to vote in an election, counting how many of them prefer candidate A over candidate B.

Solution

(*a*) This is not a binomial experiment because the trials are not independent. If the machine begins to produce defective parts, then in all likelihood each subsequent part will be defective.

(*b*) Here $n \leq 0.05N$ [$n = (100/50{,}000)N = 0.002N$], so we accept that p is constant over independent trials. Therefore, this is a binomial experiment, where: success = prefer A, p = unknown % of 50,000 who prefer A, $q = 1 - p$, the Bernoulli trials are the 100 voters surveyed, and the binomial variable is the number who favored A.

11.3 Which of the following are binomial experiments?

(*a*) From past experience, a tire dealer expects a 2% defective rate for each 1,000-tire shipment of one type of tire. He takes a random 20-tire sample from such a shipment and counts the number of defective tires in the sample.

(*b*) For the same 1,000-tire shipment in (*a*), instead of taking a 20-tire sample and counting the number of defectives, the dealer randomly removes tires from the shipment, counting how many he must remove until he finds the first defective tire.

Solution

(*a*) As $n \leq 0.05N$, we can assume p is constant over independent trials, and that therefore this is a binomial experiment.

(*b*) Not a binomial experiment because there is not a fixed number of trials n.

11.4 The tire dealer in Problem 11.3 receives a 1,000-tire shipment with the 2% defective rate. This time he takes a random sample of 5 and counts the number of defective tires in the sample. Using equation (11.2), find the probability distribution for the binomial variable: number of defectives. What is the mean, variance, and standard deviation of this variable?

Solution

The requested distribution is shown in Table 11.7, and the calculations of the mean, variance, and standard deviation are shown below the distribution.

Table 11.7

Number of defectives x	Probability $f(x) = \binom{n}{x} p^x q^{n-x}$
0	$f(0) = \binom{5}{0}(0.02)^0(0.98)^{5-0} = 0.9039208$
1	$f(1) = \binom{5}{1}(0.02)^1(0.98)^{5-1} = 0.0922368$
2	$f(2) = \binom{5}{2}(0.02)^2(0.98)^{5-2} = 0.0037648$
3	$f(3) = \binom{5}{3}(0.02)^3(0.98)^{5-3} = 0.0000768$
4	$f(4) = \binom{5}{4}(0.02)^4(0.98)^{5-4} = 0.0000008$
5	$f(5) = \binom{5}{5}(0.02)^5(0.98)^{5-5} = 0.0000000$
Σ	1.0000000

$$\mu = np = (5)(0.02) = 0.10$$
$$\sigma^2 = npq = (5)(0.02)(0.98) = 0.098$$
$$\sigma = \sqrt{\sigma^2} = \sqrt{0.098} = 0.313$$

11.5 In Example 10.5 in Volume 1, for the binomial experiment of flipping a coin three times with the random variable number of heads, it was found that the probability of getting two heads in the three flips is

$$f(2) = P(H_1 \cap H_2 \cap T_3) + P(H_1 \cap T_2 \cap H_3) + P(T_1 \cap H_2 \cap H_3) = 3(0.125) = 0.375$$

Redo this calculation using the binomial probability function [equation (11.2)], and then show why the two results are the same.

Solution

Using equation (11.2) with: success = getting a head, failure = getting a tail, $p = \frac{1}{2}$, $q = \frac{1}{2}$, and $n = 3$

$$f(x) = \binom{n}{x} p^x q^{n-x}$$

$$f(2) = \binom{3}{2}\left(\frac{1}{2}\right)^2\left(\frac{1}{2}\right)^{3-2} = \frac{3!}{2!(3-2)!}\left(\frac{1}{2}\right)^2\left(\frac{1}{2}\right)^1 = 3\left(\frac{1}{2}\right)^3 = 3(0.125) = 0.375$$

To see why the binomial probability function gives the same result as the original calculation, we will convert the original to the binomial form. Thus

$$\begin{aligned} f(2) &= P(H_1 \cap H_2 \cap T_3) + P(H_1 \cap T_2 \cap H_3) + P(T_1 \cap H_2 \cap H_3) \\ &= (p \times p \times q) + (p \times q \times p) + (q \times p \times p) \end{aligned}$$

which can be rearranged to be

$$f(2) = (p^2q) + (p^2q) + (p^2q) = 3(p^2q)$$

Here we see the two components of the binomial probability function; the 3 is the binomial coefficient, and the p^2q is the p^xq^{n-x} component.

11.6 Use equations (11.4), (11.6), and (11.7) to find the mean, variance, and standard deviation of the binomial distribution in Table 11.2.

Solution

$$\mu = np = (7)\left(\frac{1}{2}\right) = 3.5$$

$$\sigma^2 = npq = (7)\left(\frac{1}{2}\right)\left(\frac{1}{2}\right) = 1.75$$

$$\sigma = \sqrt{\sigma^2} = \sqrt{1.75} = 1.3229, \text{ or } 1.32$$

11.7 For the binomial distribution in Table 11.1, use equations (11.4), (11.6), and (11.7) to find the mean, variance, and standard deviation.

Solution

$$\mu = np = (5)\left(\frac{1}{6}\right) = 0.8333, \text{ or } 0.83$$

$$\sigma^2 = npq = (5)\left(\frac{1}{6}\right)\left(\frac{5}{6}\right) = 0.69444, \text{ or } 0.694$$

$$\sigma = \sqrt{npq} = \sqrt{0.69444} = 0.83333, \text{ or } 0.833$$

11.8 Use Pascal's triangle to find the binomial coefficients for the expansion of $(q+p)^7$ and $(q+p)^8$.

Solution

These coefficients are found by first adding the row for $n = 6$ (Example 11.7) to the triangle in Fig. 11-1, and then using the calculation procedures from Section 11.8. The coefficients for $n = 6$, $n = 7$, and $n = 8$ are shown in Fig. 11-4.

n									
6	1	6	15	20	15	6	1		
7	1	7	21	35	35	21	7	1	
8	1	8	28	56	70	56	28	8	1

Fig. 11-4

11.9 For the binomial variable: number of heads in seven flips of a coin, use the binomial distribution in Table 11.2 to determine the probability of getting: (*a*) at most 5 heads, (*b*) more than 2 heads but at most 5 heads, (*c*) 2, 3, 4, or 5 heads.

Solution

(*a*) $F(5) = P(X \leq 5) = f(0) + f(1) + f(2) + f(3) + f(4) + f(5)$

$$= 0.0078 + 0.0547 + 0.1641 + 0.2734 + 0.2734 + 0.1641 = 0.9375$$

(*b*) For a discrete random variable, equation (10.4) in Volume 1 states that

$$P(a < X \leq b) = F(b) - F(a)$$

We know from Example 11.8 that $F(2) = 0.2266$, and from part (*a*) that $F(5) = 0.9375$. Therefore,

$$P(2 < X \leq 5) = F(5) - F(2) = 0.9375 - 0.2266 = 0.7109$$

(*c*) For a discrete random variable, equation (10.5) in Volume 1 states that

$$P(a \leq X \leq b) = F(b) - F(a) + f(a)$$

Therefore,

$$P(2 \leq X \leq 5) = F(5) - F(2) + f(2) = 0.9375 - 0.2266 + 0.1641 = 0.8750$$

11.10 For the binomial variable: number of heads in seven flips of a coin, use the results from Problem 11.9 and the binomial distribution in Table 11.2 to determine the probability of getting: (*a*) more than 2 heads but fewer than 5 heads, (*b*) at least 2 heads but fewer than 5 heads.

Solution

(*a*) For a discrete random variable, equation (10.6) in Volume 1 states that

$$P(a < X < b) = F(b) - F(a) - f(b)$$

Therefore,

$$P(2 < X < 5) = F(5) - F(2) - f(5) = 0.9375 - 0.2266 - 0.1641 = 0.5468$$

(*b*) For a discrete random variable, equation (10.7) in Volume 1 states that

$$P(a \leq X < b) = F(b) - F(a) + f(a) - f(b)$$

Therefore,

$$P(2 \leq X < 5) = F(5) - F(2) + f(2) - f(5) = 0.9375 - 0.2266 + 0.1641 - 0.1641 = 0.7109$$

11.11 For the binomial variable: number of heads in seven flips of a coin, use the cumulative binomial probabilities in Table A.3 of the Appendix to determine the probability of getting: (*a*) at most 2 heads, (*b*) at most 3 heads, (*c*) 3 heads.

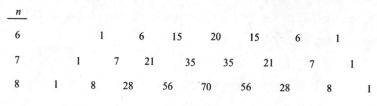

Solution

(*a*) From the intersection in Table A.3 of row ($n = 7$, $a = 2$) and column ($p = 0.50$),

$$F(2) = P(X \leq 2) = 0.2266$$

This agrees with the result in Example 11.8.

(*b*) From the intersection in Table A.3 of row ($n = 7$, $a = 3$) and column ($p = 0.50$)

$$F(3) = P(X \leq 3) = 0.5000$$

(*c*) $f(3) = P(2 < X \leq 3)$

Using equation (10.4) of Volume 1,

$$P(2 < X \leq 3) = F(3) - F(2)$$

Therefore, using the values from parts (*a*) and (*b*),

$$f(3) = 0.5000 - 0.2266 = 0.2734$$

This result is the same as the $f(3)$ value given in Table 11.2 (rounded to four decimals).

11.12 For the binomial variable: number of heads in seven flips of a coin, use Table A.3 in the Appendix and results from Problem 11.11 to determine the probability of getting: (*a*) at least 3 heads, (*b*) more than 3 heads, (*c*) more than 2 heads but fewer than 5 heads.

Solution

(*a*) $P(X \geq 3) = 1 - P(X \leq 2) = 1 - F(2)$

From Problem 11.11(*a*), we know that $F(2) = 0.2266$, so

$$P(X \geq 3) = 1 - 0.2266 = 0.7734$$

(*b*) $P(X > 3) = 1 - P(X \leq 3) = 1 - F(3)$

From Problem 11.11(*b*), we know that $F(3) = 0.5000$, so

$$P(X > 3) = 1 - 0.5000 = 0.5000$$

(*c*) Equation (10.6) in Volume 1 states that

$$P(a < X < b) = F(b) - F(a) - f(b)$$

Therefore, here we want to determine

$$P(2 < X < 5) = F(5) - F(2) - f(5)$$

We know from Problem 11.11(*a*) that $F(2) = 0.2266$. From Table A.3 we find that the intersection of row ($n = 7$, $a = 4$) and column ($p = 0.50$) is $F(4) = 0.7734$, and the intersection of row ($n = 7$, $a = 5$) with column ($p = 0.50$) is $F(5) = 0.9375$. Therefore,

$$f(5) = F(5) - F(4) = 0.9375 - 0.7734 = 0.1641$$

and thus, $$P(2 < X < 5) = 0.9375 - 0.2266 - 0.1641 = 0.5468$$

This agrees with the result in Problem 11.10(*a*).

11.13 Everyone applying for a laboratory job at a large drug company is given an eight-question multiple-choice exam in basic chemistry. Each question has four choices. If the applicants have no knowledge of chemistry and are answering randomly, then: (*a*) On the average how many questions do they answer correctly? (*b*) What is the probability that an applicant randomly answering will get correct at most one more than the average number in (*a*)?

Solution

(*a*) If the applicant is answering randomly, then this is a binomial experiment where: success = correct answer, $n = 8$, and $p = 0.25$. Therefore, using equation (11.4), the average number correct is

$$\mu = np = (8)(0.25) = 2.0$$

(*b*) From Table A.3 in the Appendix, for $n = 8$, $a = 3$, and $p = 0.25$

$$P(X \leq 3) = F(3) = 0.8862$$

11.14 Using Table A.3 in the Appendix, determine for the multiple-choice exam in Problem 11.13: (*a*) If applicants are required to get six or more correct to be considered for employment, what is the probability that a randomly answering applicant will be so considered? (*b*) What is the probability that a randomly answering applicant will get two, three, or four correct?

Solution

(*a*) $P(X \geq 6) = 1 - F(5)$
From Table A.3 for $n = 8$, $a = 5$, and $p = 0.25$,

$$F(5) = 0.9958$$

Therefore,

$$P(X \geq 6) = 1 - 0.9958 = 0.0042$$

(*b*) Using equation (10.5) of Volume 1, we must determine

$$P(2 \leq X \leq 4) = F(4) - F(2) + f(2)$$

From Table A.3 for ($n = 8$, $a = 1$, $p = 0.25$), ($n = 8$, $a = 2$, $p = 0.25$), and ($n = 8$, $a = 4$, $p = 0.25$),

$$F(1) = 0.3671, F(2) = 0.6785, F(4) = 0.9727$$

Thus,

$$f(2) = F(2) - (1) = 0.6785 - 0.3671 = 0.3114$$

And therefore,

$$P(2 \leq X \leq 4) - 0.9727 - 0.6785 + 0.3114 = 0.6056$$

THE MULTINOMIAL PROBABILITY DISTRIBUTION

11.15 Of the registered voters in a city, 40% are Democrats, 35% are Republicans, and the other 25% are not affiliated with either party. If you take a random survey of 10 registered voters, what is the probability that all 10 are Republicans?

Solution

The 10 voters are only a small fraction of the city's registered voters ($n \leq 0.05N$), so the survey is a multinomial experiment where: $n = 10$, $A_1 = \{\text{Democrat}\}$, $A_2 = \{\text{Republican}\}$, $A_3 = \{\text{not with either}\}$, $X_1 = \text{number of Democrats} = x_1, X_2 = \text{number of Republicans} = x_2, X_3 = \text{number not with either} = x_3$, $p_1 = 0.40$, $p_2 = 0.35$, $p_3 = 0.25$. Using equation (11.13),

$$f(x_1, x_2, x_3) = \frac{n!}{x_1!x_2!x_3!} p_1^{x_1} p_2^{x_2} p_3^{x_3}$$

$$f(0, 10, 0) = \frac{10!}{0!10!0!}(0.40)^0(0.35)^{10}(0.25)^0 = (1)(1)(0.0000276)(1) = 0.000028$$

11.16 For the random survey of 10 registered voters in Problem 11.15, use equation (11.13) to determine the probability that: (*a*) two are Democrats, two are Republicans, and six are not affiliated with either party, (*b*) five are Democrats and five are Republicans.

Solution

(*a*) $f(2, 2, 6) = \frac{10!}{2!2!6!}(0.40)^2(0.35)^2(0.25)^6 = \left(\frac{3{,}628{,}800}{2{,}880}\right)(0.16)(0.1225)(0.0002441) = 0.006028$

(*b*) $f(5, 5, 0) = \frac{10!}{5!5!0!}(0.40)^5(0.35)^5(0.25)^0 = \left(\frac{3{,}628{,}800}{14{,}400}\right)(0.01024)(0.005252)(1)$

$= 0.013553$

11.17 After cross-breeding two types of plants, a geneticist predicts from Mendelian theory that the resulting offspring-population will have a 9:3:3:1 ratio of (tall purple-flowered plants *TP*) to (short purple-flowered plants *SP*) to (tall white-flowered plants *TW*) to (short white-flowered plants *SW*). Assuming she is correct, if 16 seeds from the offspring-population are randomly selected and planted, then what is the probability of exactly 4 plants of each type?

Solution

If it can be assumed that the 16 seeds are only a small fraction of the present and future offspring-population ($n \leq 0.05N$), then this is a multinomial experiment where: $n = 16$, $A_1 = \{TP\}$, $A_2 = \{SP\}$, $A_3 = \{TW\}$, $A_4 = \{SW\}$, $X_1 =$ number of TPs $= x_1$, $X_2 =$ number of SPs $= x_2$, $X_3 =$ number of TWs $= x_3$, $X_4 =$ number of SWs $= x_4$, $p_1 = 9/16$, $p_2 = 3/16$, $p_3 = 3/16$, $p_4 = 1/16$. Using equation (11.13),

$$f(x_1, x_2, x_3, x_4) = \frac{n!}{x_1!x_2!x_3!x_4!}p_1^{x_1}p_2^{x_2}p_3^{x_3}p_4^{x_4}$$

$$f(4, 4, 4, 4) = \frac{16!}{4!4!4!4!}\left(\frac{9}{16}\right)^4\left(\frac{3}{16}\right)^4\left(\frac{3}{16}\right)^4\left(\frac{1}{16}\right)^4$$

$$= (63{,}063{,}000)(0.100113), (0.001236)(0.001236)(0.000015)$$

$$= 0.000145$$

11.18 For the 16 seeds planted in Problem 11.17: (*a*) What is the probability of 9 *TP*s, 3 *SP*s, 3 *TW*s, and 1 *SW*? (*b*) What are the expected values and parameters of this distribution?

Solution

(*a*) Using equation (11.13),

$$f(9, 3, 3, 1) = \frac{16!}{9!3!3!1!}\left(\frac{9}{16}\right)^9\left(\frac{3}{16}\right)^3\left(\frac{3}{16}\right)^3\left(\frac{1}{16}\right)^1$$

$$= (1{,}601{,}600)(0.005638)(0.006592)(0.006592)(0.0625)$$

$$= 0.02452$$

(*b*) Using equation (11.14), the expected values are

$$E(X_1) = \mu_1 = np_1 = 16\left(\frac{9}{16}\right) = 9 \qquad E(X_2) = \mu_2 = np_2 = 16\left(\frac{3}{16}\right) = 3$$

$$E(X_3) = \mu_3 = np_3 = 16\left(\frac{3}{16}\right) = 3 \qquad E(X_4) = \mu_4 = np_4 = 16\left(\frac{1}{16}\right) = 1$$

The parameters are (see Section 11.17)

$$n = 16, \qquad p_1 = \frac{9}{16}, \qquad p_2 = \frac{3}{16}, \qquad p_3 = \frac{3}{16}, \qquad p_4 = \frac{1}{16}$$

THE HYPERGEOMETRIC PROBABILITY DISTRIBUTION

11.19 For the committee-selection experiment in Example 11.17, determine the probability that the manager picked three men.

Solution

For this experiment: X is a hypergeometric random variable that counts the Ms in the three picks $(x = 0, 1, 2, 3)$, $N_T =$ staff members $= 10$, $n =$ sample size $= 3$, $N_S = M$s on staff $= 6$, $N_F = W$s on staff $= 4$, $x = M$s in sample, and $n - x = W$s in sample. Placing these values in equation (11.17),

$$f(x) = P(X = x) = \frac{\left[\dfrac{N_S!}{x!(N_S - x)!}\right]\left[\dfrac{N_F!}{(n-x)!(N_F - (n-x))!}\right]}{\left[\dfrac{N_T!}{n!(N_T - n)!}\right]}$$

$$f(3) = \frac{\left[\dfrac{6!}{3!(6-3)!}\right]\left[\dfrac{4!}{(3-3)!(4-0)!}\right]}{\left[\dfrac{10!}{3!(10-3)!}\right]} = \frac{20}{120} = 0.1667$$

11.20 A bowl contains 20 marbles that are identical except for color: 10 are red R and 10 are green G. You blindly pick 10 marbles, without returning the marbles after they have been picked. Find the probability of picking 4 red marbles in the 10 picks.

Solution

As this is sampling without replacement, the trials are not Bernoulli trials, and thus this problem must be solved using hypergeometric techniques. For this experiment: X is a hypergeometric random variable that counts the Rs in the 10 picks $(x = 0, 1, 2, \ldots, 9, 10)$, $N_T = 20$, $n = 10$, $N_S = 10$, $N_F = 10$, $x = R$s in sample, $(n - x) = G$s in sample. Therefore, using equation (11.16),

$$f(x) = \frac{\dbinom{N_S}{x}\dbinom{N_F}{n-x}}{\dbinom{N_T}{n}}$$

$$f(4) = \frac{\dbinom{10}{4}\dbinom{10}{6}}{\dbinom{20}{10}} = \frac{(210)(210)}{(184{,}756)} = 0.2387$$

11.21 A factory receives electrical fuses in lots of 40. The receiving department randomly tests four fuses from each lot, and if any are defective it rejects the remainder of the lot. If 10% of a lot is actually defective, then what is the probability that one of the four tested fuses is defective?

Solution

This is a hypergeometric experiment where: X = number of defectives, $N_T = 40$, $n = 4$, $N_S = 4$, $N_F = 36$, $x = 1$, $n - x = 3$. Therefore, using equation (11.16),

$$f(x) = \frac{\binom{N_S}{x}\binom{N_F}{n-x}}{\binom{N_T}{n}}$$

$$f(1) = \frac{\binom{4}{1}\binom{36}{3}}{\binom{40}{4}} = \frac{(4)(7{,}140)}{(91{,}390)} = 0.3125$$

11.22 For the four-fuse test in Problem 11.21, what is the probability that the lot will be accepted?

Solution

In Section 11.11, binomial techniques were used to solve lot-acceptance-sampling problems. If, however, as here, binomial techniques are inappropriate [sampling without replacement and $(n/N = 0.10) > 0.05$], then hypergeometric techniques can be used to find the probability of accepting the lot P_a for a given acceptance number a. Therefore, using equation (11.16) for $a = 0$,

$$P_a = P(X = 0) = \frac{\binom{4}{0}\binom{36}{4}}{\binom{40}{4}} = \frac{(1)(58{,}905)}{(91{,}390)} = 0.6445$$

Thus, there is a 64% probability of accepting the lot even though 10% of the lot is defective.

11.23 The factory in Problems 11.21 and 11.22 now receives its fuses in lots of 50. A decision is made to randomly test six fuses from each lot, and to reject the lot if more than one is defective. If 12% of the lot is actually defective, then what is P_a?

Solution

This is a hypergeometric experiment where: X = number of defectives, $N_T = 50$, $n = 6$, $N_S = 6$, $N_F = 44$, $x = 0$ or 1, $n - x = 6$ or 5. The problem can be solved by placing equation (11.16) in equation (10.2) of Volume 1 to get

$$P_a = P(X \leq a) = F(a) = \sum_{x \leq a} \left[f(x) = \frac{\binom{N_S}{x}\binom{N_F}{n-x}}{\binom{N_T}{n}} \right]$$

For this problem

$$P_a = P(X \leq 1) = F(1) = \frac{\binom{6}{0}\binom{44}{6}}{\binom{50}{6}} + \frac{\binom{6}{1}\binom{44}{5}}{\binom{50}{6}}$$

$$= \frac{(1)(7{,}059{,}052)}{(15{,}890{,}700)} + \frac{(6)(1{,}086{,}008)}{(15{,}890{,}700)}$$

$$= 0.442 + 0.4101 = 0.8543$$

Thus, there is an 85% probability of accepting the lot even though 12% of the lot is defective.

11.24 What are the mean, variance, and parameters of the hypergeometric distribution from the fuse-testing experiment in Problem 11.23?

Solution

Using equations (11.18) and (11.19),

$$\mu = \frac{nN_S}{N_T} = \frac{6 \times 6}{50} = 0.72, \qquad \sigma^2 = \frac{nN_S N_F(N_T - n)}{N_T^2(N_T - 1)} = \frac{6 \times 6 \times 44(50 - 6)}{50^2(50 - 1)} = 0.569$$

and the parameters are (see Section 11.22) $N_T = 50$, $N_S = 6$, and $n = 6$.

11.25 A group of painters has painted 38 houses. Of these paint jobs: 14 of the homeowners are very satisfied V, 16 are moderately satisfied M, and 8 are dissatisfied D. The owner of the painting company decides to take a random survey of 12 of these homowners. What is the probability the survey will include $4V$s, $2M$s, and $6D$s?

Solution

This is a hypergeometric experiment for which the generalized version of the hypergeometric probability function [equation (11.21)] is appropriate. In this experiment: $X_1 = V$s in sample $= x_1 = 4$, $X_2 = M$s in sample $= x_2 = 2$, $X_3 = D$s in sample $= x_3 = 6$, $N_T = 38$, $N_1 = V$s in population $= 14$, $N_2 = M$s in population $= 16$, $N_3 = D$s in population $= 8$, $n = 12$. Therefore,

$$f(x_1, x_2, x_3) = \frac{\binom{N_1}{x_1}\binom{N_2}{x_2}\binom{N_3}{x_3}}{\binom{N_T}{n}}$$

$$f(4, 2, 6) = \frac{\binom{14}{4}\binom{16}{2}\binom{8}{6}}{\binom{38}{12}} = \frac{(1{,}001)(120)(28)}{(2{,}707{,}475{,}148)} = 0.00124$$

THE POISSON DISTRIBUTION

11.26 For the Geiger-counter Poisson experiment in Example 11.25, the average rate of recording particles was calculated to be $\lambda = 5.5$ particles per 10 seconds. Use Table A.4 in the Appendix and the rules from Section 10.7 in Volume 1 to determine the probability in a 10-second interval of recording 6 particles.

Solution

Using equation (10.4) of Volume 1,

$$P(5 < X \leq 6) = F(6) - F(5) = f(6)$$

and from Table A.4 for $\mu = 5.5$, $F(5) = 0.529$ and $F(6) = 0.686$. Therefore,

$$f(6) = 0.686 - 0.529 = 0.157$$

11.27 For the Geiger-counter Poisson experiment in Problem 11.26, use the results from Problem 11.26 and the rules from Section 10.7 of Volume 1 to determine the probability in a 10-second interval of recording: (*a*) at least 6 particles, (*b*) 6, 7, or 8 particles.

Solution

(*a*) $P(X \geq 6) = 1 - P(X \leq 5) = 1 - F(5)$
From Problem 11.26, we know that $F(5) = 0.529$. Therefore,

$$P(X \geq 6) = 1 - 0.529 = 0.471$$

(*b*) Using equation (10.5) of Volume 1,

$$P(6 \leq X \leq 8) = F(8) - F(6) + f(6)$$

From Problem 11.26, we know that $F(6) = 0.686$ and $f(6) = 0.157$, and from Table A.4 for $\mu = 5.5$, $F(8) = 0.894$. Therefore,

$$P(6 \leq X \leq 8) = 0.894 - 0.686 + 0.157 = 0.365$$

11.28 Poisson techniques are commonly used in business in *inventory control systems*. Thus, in this problem the manager of a seafood restaurant wants to use such techniques to determine how many live lobsters he should have available each day, given that on the average seven lobsters are ordered by customers each day. Assuming this is a Poisson experiment, then: (*a*) If on a given day he has nine lobsters on hand, what is the probability that more than nine will be ordered? (*b*) If on a given day he wants to be more than 95% certain of having enough lobsters, how many does he need?

Solution

(*a*) The question is: Given that $\mu = \lambda t = 7 \times 1 = 7$, what is $P(X > 9)$? We know that

$$P(X > 9) = 1 - P(X \leq 9) = 1 - F(9)$$

and from Table A.4 for $\mu = 7$, $F(9) = 0.830$. Therefore, the probability of not having enough lobsters on hand is

$$P(X > 9) = 1 - 0.830 = 0.170$$

(*b*) The question is: Given that $\mu = 7$, what is a in the following?

$$P(X \leq a) = F(a) > 0.950$$

As from Table A.4 for $\mu = 7$, $F(11) = 0.947$ and $F(12) = 0.973$, if he wants to be more than 95% certain he should have 12.

11.29 A large factory has accepted 100 people into a training program. The manager of the program knows from thousands of previous trainees that 4% of the trainees will not finish the program. Determine the probability of 5 or more of the $n = 100$ trainees not finishing the program.

Solution

This problem can not be solved with Table A.3 because, as is true with most binomial tables, it does not include values for large n. We can, however, solve the problem with Table A.4, as n appears only in $\mu = n \times p = 100 \times 0.04 = 4$. To do this we must solve this equation

$$P(X \geq 5) = 1 - P(X \leq 4) = 1 - F(4)$$

and from Table A.4 for $\mu = 4$, $F(4) = 0.629$. Thus,

$$P(X \geq 5) \approx 1 - 0.629 = 0.371$$

11.30 A vaccine has been effective in immunizing against a disease 98.4% of the many times it has been tried. Use Table A.4 in the Appendix and the rules from Section 10.7 in Volume 1 to answer the following. Of the next 125 people vaccinated, what is the probability that the vaccine will not be effective for: (*a*) three of them, and (*b*) more than three of them?

Solution

(*a*) If we accept that this is a binomial experiment, then it can be approximated with Poisson techniques $[(n = 125) > 100;\ (p = 0.016) < 0.05]$. Thus, using equation (10.4) of Volume 1,

$$P(2 < X \leq 3) = F(3) - F(2) = f(3)$$

and from Table A.4 for $\mu = n \times p = 125 \times 0.016 = 2$, $F(3) = 0.857$ and $F(2) = 0.677$. Therefore,

$$f(3) \approx 0.857 - 0.677 = 0.180$$

(*b*) $P(X > 3) = 1 - P(X \leq 3) = 1 - F(3) \approx 1 - 0.857 = 0.143$

11.31 The restaurant in Problem 11.28 has an average of 280 customers each day. If the manager decides to do his inventory control for numbers of customers rather than units of time, for the next 200 customers rather than for daily demand, then what is the probability that $x = 8, 9, 10, 11$ of the next 200 customers will order lobster?

Solution

If we accept that this is a binomial experiment, then it can be approximated with Poisson techniques $[(n = 200) > 100;\ (p = 7/280 = 0.025) < 0.05]$. Therefore, using equation (11.26) with $\mu = n \times p = 200 \times 0.025 = 5$,

$$f(x) = \frac{\mu^x e^{-\mu}}{x!}$$

$$f(8) \approx \frac{5^8 e^{-5}}{8!} = \frac{(390{,}625)(0.006738)}{40{,}320} = 0.06528$$

$$f(9) \approx \frac{5^9 e^{-5}}{9!} = \frac{(1{,}953{,}125)(0.006738)}{362{,}880} = 0.03627$$

$$f(10) \approx \frac{5^{10} e^{-5}}{10!} = \frac{(9{,}765{,}625)(0.006738)}{3{,}628{,}800} = 0.01813$$

$$f(11) \approx \frac{5^{11} e^{-5}}{11!} = \frac{(48{,}828{,}125)(0.006738)}{39{,}916{,}800} = 0.00824$$

Supplementary Problems

THE BINOMIAL PROBABILITY DISTRIBUTION

11.32 Which of the following are binomial experiments?

(*a*) You randomly pick 10 cards in succession from a deck of 52 playing cards, following this same procedure after each pick: determining whether the card is a red card, replacing the card in the deck, and shuffling the deck. You count the number of red cards in the 10 picks.

(*b*) The same experiment as in (*a*) except that you do not replace the card after each pick.

Ans. (*a*) binomial experiment, (*b*) not a binomial experiment

11.33 The following is a binomial experiment: rolling a die five times and counting the number of 4s that occur in the five rolls. For this binomial experiment, what are: success, failure, p, q, and the binomial random variable?

Ans. Success = observing a 4 on a roll, failure = observing any other outcome (1, 2, 3, 5, or 6), $p = 1/6$, $q = 1 - 1/6 = 5/6$, the binomial random variable is the number of 4s on the five rolls

11.34 A professional basketball player has shot thousands of free throws and has been successful 80% of the time. In a series of nine attempts, what is the probability of his making: (*a*) at least five, (*b*) at most five, and (*c*) fewer than five?

Ans. (*a*) 0.9804, (*b*) 0.0856, (*c*) 0.0196

11.35 Fifty salespeople for a magazine are each required to make 10 telephone calls each evening to people randomly selected from names in directories. The salesperson's task with each call is to sell a subscription to the magazine. From thousands of such calls, the magazine knows that only 15% are successful; i.e., result in a new subscription. For every 10 calls: (*a*) What is the mean and standard deviation of the number of subscriptions the company expects? (*b*) What is the probability of two or fewer subscriptions?

Ans. (a) $\mu = 1.50$, $\sigma = 1.129$; (*b*) 0.8202

11.36 For the 50 salespeople in Problem 11.35, what is the probability, every 10 calls, of getting more than one new subscription?

Ans. 0.4557

THE MULTINOMIAL PROBABILITY DISTRIBUTION

11.37 The multinomial experiment is to pick 6 cards from a standard 52-card deck of playing cards, replacing the card and reshuffling the deck after each pick. If for each trial the mutually exclusive and exhaustive possible events are $A_1 = \{\text{ace}, 2, 3, 4, 5\}$, $A_2 = \{6, 7, 8\}$, $A_3 = \{9, 10\}$, $A_4 = \{\text{jack, queen, king}\}$, then what are: (*a*) $f(0, 0, 0, 6)$, (*b*) $f(2, 1, 3, 0)$?

Ans. (*a*) 0.000151, (*b*) 0.007458

11.38 For the probability distribution for the card-picking experiment in Problem 11.37, what are: (*a*) the expected values, (*b*) the parameters?

Ans. (*a*) $E(X_1) = 2.31$, $E(X_2) = 1.38$, $E(X_3) = 0.92$, $E(X_4) = 1.38$; (*b*) $n = 6$, $p_1 = \frac{5}{13}$, $p_2 = \frac{3}{13}$, $p_3 = \frac{2}{13}$, $p_4 = \frac{3}{13}$

11.39 The administrators of a college want to send 8 students to a national meeting. The college consists of 350 freshmen, 250 sophomores, 200 juniors, and 200 seniors. Their names are placed in a barrel and thoroughly mixed. The dean draws, without looking, 8 names. As the eight are only a small fraction of the student population ($n < 0.05N$), this is a multinomial experiment. What is the probability that two students from each class have been selected?

Ans. 0.0309

11.40 A wildlife biologist traps and releases (i.e., samples with replacement) a sequence of 15 mice from a small island community that consists of 25 mice of species A, 20 mice of species B, and 15 mice of species C. Assuming that the mice enter the trap at random with regard to species, what is the probability that the sample of 15 will include 5 mice from each species?

Ans. 0.0382

THE HYPERGEOMETRIC PROBABILITY DISTRIBUTION

11.41 The administrators of a college want to send eight upperclassmen to a national meeting. Twelve juniors and eight seniors volunteer. Their names are placed in a hat and thoroughly mixed. The dean draws, without looking, eight names. What is the probability that four juniors were selected?

Ans. 0.275

11.42 A wildlife biologist traps 10 mice, one after the other, from a population of 60 mice (36 males and 24 females). He does not return the trapped mice to the population, but instead takes them to his laboratory for behavioral studies. Assumming that the mice enter the trap at random with regard to gender, what is the probability that there are 5 males in the sample of 10?

Ans. 0.213

11.43 An algebra class consists of 16 men and 14 women. Assuming that all students attend class and that they enter the class at random with regard to gender, what is the probability that the first 5 students to enter will be females?

Ans. 0.0140

11.44 An acre of forest contains 100 mature pine trees that show no signs of a fungal infection. However, previous studies have shown that 30% of such trees are in the very early stages of the infection, and that this can only be detected by examining inner tissues. Assuming the 30% figure is true, if a forester cuts 10 trees and examines these tissues, what is the probability that he will find 5 infected trees?

Ans. 0.0996

THE POISSON PROBABILITY DISTRIBUTION

11.45 For the Geiger-counter Poisson experiment in Problem 11.26, use Table A.4 in the Appendix and the rules from Section 10.7 in Volume 1 to determine the probability in a 10-second interval of recording: (*a*) more than 2 particles but fewer than 6, (*b*) more than 6 particles but at most 9?

Ans. (*a*) 0.441, (*b*) 0.260

11.46 For the vaccine in Problem 11.30, which has been effective in immunizing against a disease 98.4% of the many times it has been tried, use Table A.4 in the Appendix and the rules from Section 10.7 in Volume 1 to answer the following. Of the next 125 people vaccinated, what is the probability that the vaccine will not be effective for: (*a*) more than zero of them but less than three, and (*b*) zero, one, two, or three of them?

Ans. If we accept that this is a binomial experiment, then it can be approximated with Poisson techniques. (*a*) ≈ 0.542, (*b*) ≈ 0.857

11.47 On a difficult rock climb, 10 climbers fall each week during the summer months. If these falls are distributed according to a Poisson distribution, what is the probability that there will be 12 falls during a particular two-week period in July?

Ans. 0.0176

11.48 An ornithologist studying the nests of juncos walks along a fence line, in junco habitat, and counts the number of nests that he can see from the fence. He counts 30 nests within a one-kilometer (1,000 meters) segment of the fence. What is the probability that he finds two nests within a particular 200-meter segment of the fence?

Ans. 0.0446

11.49 Thirty cars pass a crosswalk every hour. What is the probability that, for a particular 5-minute period, no cars will pass the crosswalk?

Ans. 0.0821

11.50 For the cars described in Problem 11.49, what is the probability that, for a particular 5-minute period, the number of cars that pass the crosswalk is 4 or less?

Ans. 0.891

CHAPTER 12

The Normal Distribution and Other Continuous Probability Distributions

12.1 CONTINUOUS PROBABILITY DISTRIBUTIONS

In Chapter 11 we examined the specific characteristics and uses of four discrete probability distributions: the binomial distribution, the multinomial distribution, the hypergeometric distribution, and the Poisson distribution. Now in this chapter we examine three continuous probability distributions: the *normal distribution*, the *uniform distribution*, and the *exponential distribution*. Before we discuss these distributions, however, we will first review, in Example 12.1, the general properties of continuous distributions that were presented in Chapter 10 of Volume 1.

EXAMPLE 12.1 For the continuous probability distribution shown in Fig. 12-1, what are: (*a*) $f(a)$, (*b*) $P(X = a)$, (*c*) $F(a)$, (*d*) $P(a \leq X \leq b)$, (*e*) $P(a < X < b)$, (*f*) $P(-\infty < X < \infty)$, (*g*) $P(b < X < \infty)$, (*h*) μ, (*i*) σ^2 and σ?

Solution

(*a*) The continuous curve shown in Fig. 12-1 represents a probability density function (also called a continuous probability distribution), denoted by $f(x)$, that is based on a continuous random variable X that can take on an infinite and not countable number of specific values x (see Section 10.4, Volume 1). If $X = a$ is substituted into $f(x)$, the resulting value is $f(a)$.

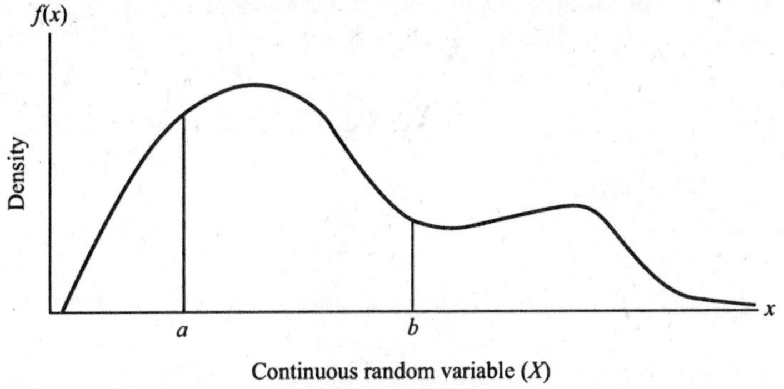

Fig. 12-1

(*b*) From Property (4) in Fig. 10-3(*b*) of Volume 1, we know that $P(X = x) = 0$. This means that the probability of X assuming any specific value a is zero: $P(X = a) = 0$.

(*c*) From Section 10.8 of Volume 1, we know that for $X = a$ the cumulative distribution function of a continuous random variable is [equation (10.8), Volume 1]

$$F(a) = P(X \leq a) = \int_{-\infty}^{a} f(x)\,dx$$

This means that the probability that X will assume a value that is less than or equal to a is the area under the curve in Fig. 12-1 that is to the left of the vertical line above a.

(*d*) From Property (6) in Fig. 10-3(*b*) of Volume 1, we know that

$$P(a \leq X \leq b) = \int_{a}^{b} f(x)\,dx$$

This means that the probability that X will assume a value in the interval from a to b is the area under the curve in Fig. 12-1 that is bounded by the curve, the X axis, and the vertical lines above a and b. From equation (10.9) of Volume 1, we also know that

$$P(a \leq X \leq b) = F(b) - F(a)$$

(*e*) From equation (10.9) of Volume 1, we know that

$$P(a < X \leq b) = P(a \leq X \leq b) = P(a < X < b) = P(a \leq X < b) = F(b) - F(a)$$

(*f*) From Property (7) in Fig. 10-3(*b*) of Volume 1, we know for continuous probability distributions that

$$P(-\infty < X < \infty) = \int_{-\infty}^{\infty} f(x)\,dx = P(S) = 1.00$$

This means that as the probability distribution contains the probabilities for all possible outcomes of the continuous random variable X, the total area under the curve is 1.00.

(*g*) From parts (*c*) and (*f*),

$$P(b < X < \infty) = 1 - F(b)$$

(*h*) From Section 10.10 of Volume 1, we know that the mean or expected value of a continuous random variable X [also the continuous probability distribution $f(x)$] is equation (10.14):

$$E(X) = \mu_x = \mu = \int_{-\infty}^{\infty} Xf(x)\,dx$$

(*i*) From Section 10.13 of Volume 1, we know that the variance of a continuous random variable X [also continuous probability distribution $f(x)$] is equation (10.24):

$$\text{Var}(X) = \sigma_x^2 = \sigma^2 = E[(X - \mu)^2] = \int_{-\infty}^{\infty} (x - \mu)^2 f(x)\, dx$$

and the standard deviation is

$$\sigma = \sqrt{\sigma^2}$$

12.2 THE NORMAL PROBABILITY DISTRIBUTION AND THE NORMAL PROBABILITY DENSITY FUNCTION

The *normal probability distribution* (or *normal distribution*) is the most important theoretical continuous distribution used in statistics because: (1) it has played a central role in the development of inferential statistics, (2) many real-world random variables exhibit frequency (or relative frequency) distributions that closely resemble normal distributions, and (3) it can conveniently be used to approximate many other probability distributions, such as the binomial and the Poisson (see Sections 12.12 and 12.13). The normal distribution has already appeared in several contexts in Volume 1 and will appear regularly throughout the remainder of this volume.

As was true for discrete probability distributions (see Chapter 11), all continuous probability distributions are defined by a specific and unique probability function. The normal probability distribution is defined by this function called the *normal probability density function* (or *normal probability function*) (see Section 10.4, Volume 1), which for the continuous random variable X can take on specific values $X = x$.

$$f(x) = \frac{1}{\sigma\sqrt{2\pi}} e^{-(x-\mu)^2/2\sigma^2}, \qquad \text{for } -\infty < x < \infty \tag{12.1}$$

where $e = 2.71828\ldots$ [see Problem 1.23(*b*), Volume 1]

$\pi = 3.14159\ldots$ (see Section 1.12, Volume 1)

$\mu = E(X) =$ mean of the normal distribution

$\sigma^2 = E[(X - \mu)^2] =$ variance of the normal distribution

$\sigma = \sqrt{\sigma^2} =$ standard deviation of the normal distribution

$-\infty < x < \infty$ means this function is defined for all real numbers

The graph of a typical normal distribution is shown in Fig. 12-2. The horizontal axis represents specific x values of the continuous random variable X and the vertical axis represents specific values of the normal probability density function $f(x)$. The smooth curve, called the *normal curve*, was constructed by calculating $f(x)$ values (ordinates, see Section 1.20, Volume 1) for a sufficient number of $X = x$ values (abscissas, see Section 1.20, Volume 1). You can see that the resulting curve has a bell-like shape that is completely symmetrical about the vertical line above the mean μ. Thus, 50% of the area under the curve is to the left of this vertical line, and 50% is to its right. It cannot be shown in a graph, but the curve extends continuously outward to both minus and plus infinity, getting closer and closer to the horizontal axis in both directions but never reaching it. As with any continuous probability distribution, the total area under the curve is 1.0, and the graph also shows the percentage of the area lying above the intervals $\mu \pm \sigma$ (68.3%), $\mu \pm 2\sigma$ (95.4%), and $\mu \pm 3\sigma$ (99.7%). We gave these percentages in Section 7.16 in Volume 1 as the *empirical rule*, and we will show that they are correct for normal distributions in Problem 12.5.

The equation for the normal distribution was first published in 1733 by the French mathematician *Abraham de Moivre* (1667–1754), who used it to approximate the binomial distribution. While the French mathematician-astronomer *Pierre Simon de Laplace* (1749–1827) extended de Moivre's work, it is the

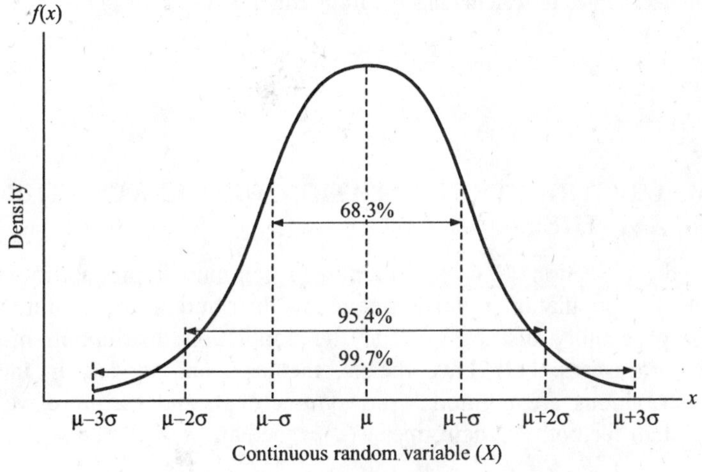

Fig. 12-2

German mathematician-astronomer-physicist *Karl Friedrich Gauss* (1777–1855) who is credited with being the first to really explore its properties and uses. Because of this, the normal distribution is also called the *Gaussian distribution.*

If the frequency (or relative frequency) distribution of a set of data can be reasonably fit by a normal curve, then the data is said to be normally distributed. As we indicated earlier (see Section 7.16, Volume 1), this statement is often made even when the empirical distribution only approximates a normal distribution by being unimodal, roughly mound-shaped, and essentially symmetrical. Many real-world continuous random variables generate such distributions: the heights in a population of men, the aptitude test scores of job applicants, the weights in a population of melons, the diastolic blood pressures in a population of women, and so on. While the normal curve is common for real-world variables, it is not called "normal" because anything other than this curve is "abnormal." The term normal was used early in the historic development of this distribution because it resembles another curve called the *normal curve of errors.*

12.3 THE FAMILY OF NORMAL PROBABILITY DISTRIBUTIONS

As was true for the discrete probability distributions in Chapter 11, continuous probability distributions are also families of distributions, with the specific distribution being considered determined by its parameters (or parameter). For the normal distribution you can see from equation (12.1) that there are two parameters: the mean μ and the variance σ^2 (some statistical books say μ and σ).

EXAMPLE 12.2 Use equation (12.1) to calculate $f(x)$ for $X = 1$ for a normal distribution with the parameters $\mu = 0$ and $\sigma^2 = 1$.

Solution

Inserting $\mu = 0$ and $\sigma^2 = 1$ into equation (12.1),

$$f(x) = \frac{1}{\sigma\sqrt{2\pi}} e^{-(x-\mu)^2/2\sigma^2}$$

$$f(1) = \frac{1}{\sqrt{1} \times \sqrt{2\pi}} e^{-(1-0)^2/2\times 1}$$

$$= \frac{1}{\sqrt{2 \times 3.14159}} e^{-1/2} = \frac{1}{2.50663} e^{-1/2} = 0.39894e^{-1/2}$$

Then, using the techniques for calculating e^{-x} from Example 11.22,

$$f(1) = (0.39894)(0.60653) = 0.24197$$

12.4 THE NORMAL DISTRIBUTION: RELATIONSHIP BETWEEN THE MEAN (μ), THE MEDIAN ($\tilde{\mu}$), AND THE MODE

As was indicated in Section 10.6 of Volume 1, continuous probability distributions serve as mathematical models for population relative frequency distributions of continuous random variables. For this reason, the probability distribution and the population distribution must be describable by comparable statistical measures: both have means, medians, and modes. In the case of the normal distribution, both distributions are unimodal and symmetrical, and therefore we know from Problem 6.29(*a*) of Volume 1 that, for both of them, mean (μ) = median ($\tilde{\mu}$) = mode.

EXAMPLE 12.3 For the two normal distributions (A and B) shown in Fig. 12-3, which has the larger: (*a*) μ, (*b*) σ, (*c*) σ^2?

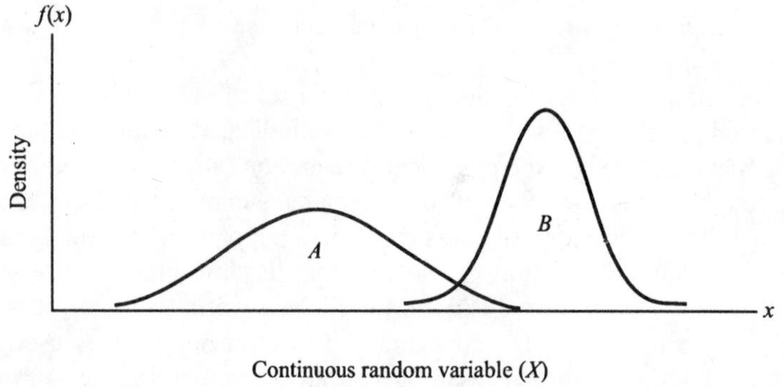

Fig. 12-3

Solution

(*a*) Because in any normal distribution the mean μ indicates the location on the horizontal axis (continuous random variable) of the median of the distribution, we know that a vertical line erected above μ to $f(x)$ will divide the distribution into two mirror-image halves (see Fig. 12-2). From this you can see in Fig. 12-3 that the mean of B (μ_B) is to the right of the mean of A (μ_A). Therefore, as it is true for any rectangular Cartesian coordinate system that the numbers along the horizontal axis are positive and increasing to the right of the origin (see Section 1.20, Volume 1), we know that $\mu_A < \mu_B$.

(*b*) From Section 7.9 of Volume 1 we know that the standard deviation is a measure of the dispersion (or spread) of the values around the mean. We also know from the empirical rule (see Section 12.2) that 68.3% of the area in a normal distribution will always lie within one standard deviation from the mean ($\mu \pm \sigma$). Therefore, the smaller the standard deviation the more values will be packed close to the mean, and consequently the distribution will have a more distinct peak, or greater *peakedness*. From this we can see in Fig. 12-3 that $\sigma_B < \sigma_A$.

(*c*) Therefore, $\sigma_B^2 < \sigma_A^2$.

12.5 KURTOSIS

Not all unimodal, symmetrical distributions are normal distributions. They may differ from a normal in terms of *kurtosis*, which is the degree of peakedness [see Example 12.3(*b*)]. Three distributions that differ in kurtosis are shown in Fig. 12-4. The middle distribution is a normal distribution, which is called *mesokurtic* (*meso*, middle). The distribution on the left, which is flatter and less peaked than the normal with a relatively even distribution of values and with shorter tails, is called *platykurtic* (*platy*, flat). The distribution on the right, which is more peaked than the normal with values concentrated in the middle and with long tails, is called *leptokurtic* (*lepto*, slender).

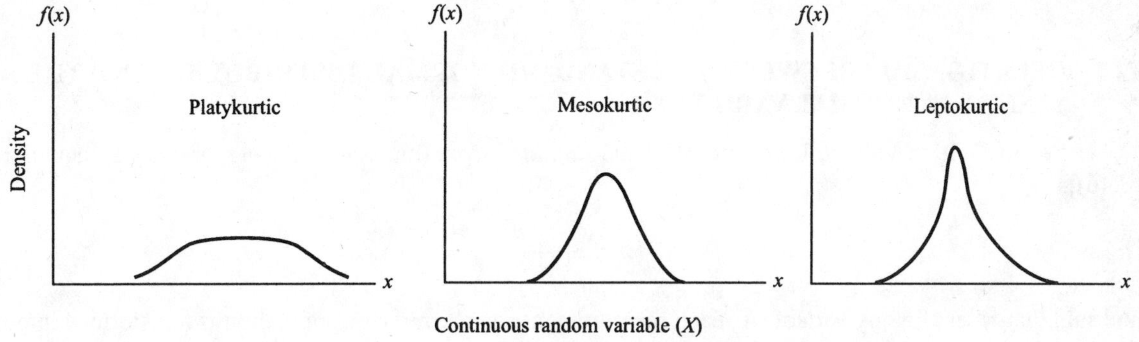

Fig. 12-4

12.6 THE STANDARD NORMAL DISTRIBUTION

The *standard normal distribution* (or *standard normal probability distribution*, or *standardized normal distribution*, or *unit normal distribution*) is a normal distribution with the specific parameters: $\mu = 0$ and $\sigma^2 = 1$. Placing these parameters in equation (12.1) produces the *standard normal probability density function* (or *standard normal density function*):

$$f(x) = \frac{1}{1\sqrt{2\pi}} e^{-(x-0)^2/2(1)^2} = \frac{1}{\sqrt{2\pi}} e^{-x^2/2} \tag{12.2}$$

The graph of the standard normal distribution is shown in Fig. 12-5. As with any other normal distribution, the smooth curve, here called the *standard normal curve*, was constructed by calculating density values $[f(x)]$ for a sufficient number of $X = x$ values. Note that because $\mu = 0$ and $\sigma^2 = \sigma = 1$, this distribution is always symmetrical about the vertical (density) axis, and the scale along the horizontal

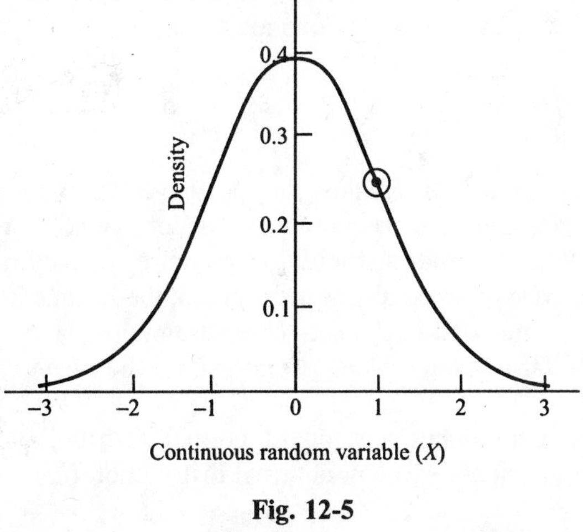

Fig. 12-5

axis is always shown for the range -3 to 3. This is done because 99.7% of the $f(x)$ values are known to lie between $\mu - 3\sigma$ and $\mu + 3\sigma$ (see Section 12.2), and thus for the standard normal distribution this range is 0 ± 3.

In Example 12.2 we calculated that $f(1) = 0.24197$ for a normal distribution with $\mu = 0$ and $\sigma^2 = \sigma = 1$, which we now know is the standard normal distribution. This value is shown as the circled dot on the standard normal curve in Fig. 12-5.

12.7 RELATIONSHIP BETWEEN THE STANDARD NORMAL DISTRIBUTION AND THE STANDARD NORMAL VARIABLE

In Section 7.19 in Volume 1 we introduced the *standard score* (or *normal deviate*, or *z score*) [equation (7.46)]:

$$z_i = \frac{x_i - \mu}{\sigma}$$

and said that when, for any variable X, each measurement x in a sample or population is transformed into a z value, the process is known as *standardizing* (or *normalizing*) the variable. The resulting variable Z is called a *standardized variable*. We then showed in Problem 7.37 in Volume 1 that, for any sample or population from a standardized variable, it is always true that the mean is zero ($\bar{z} = 0$, or $\mu_z = 0$) and the standard deviation (and thus the variance) is one ($s_z^2 = s_z = 1$, or $\sigma_z^2 = \sigma_z = 1$).

These concepts can be applied to continuous random variables and their probability distributions. Thus, if a continuous random variable X has a normal distribution with mean μ and variance σ^2, and every $X = x$ value is transformed into a standard score (or in this context a *standard normal deviate*), then the transformation generates a new continuous random variable Z. This variable, called a *standard normal variable*, is

$$Z = \frac{X - \mu}{\sigma} \tag{12.3}$$

which can take on any specific value

$$z_i = \frac{x_i - \mu}{\sigma} \tag{12.4}$$

in the range $-\infty < z < \infty$.

By the same reasoning that was used in Problem 7.37 in Volume 1, we could show that the mean of the standard normal variable will always be zero ($\mu = 0$) and its variance and standard deviation will always be one ($\sigma^2 = \sigma = 1$). Thus, the probability distribution for the standard normal variable is the standard normal distribution as defined by this version of equation (12.2):

$$f(z) = \frac{1}{\sqrt{2\pi}} e^{-z^2/2}, \qquad \text{for } -\infty < z < \infty \tag{12.5}$$

What this means is that any normal distribution can be converted to the standard normal distribution simply by applying the Z transformation to its continuous random variable X. This is true for any of the infinitely large family of theoretical normal distributions, and also for empirical distributions that can be fitted by a normal curve. In the case of an empirical distribution, the Z transformation converts the original measurement units (e.g., grams) into *standard units*. These are multiples of the standard deviation of the distribution; they indicate how far a given x value deviates from the mean of its distribution in terms of standard deviations.

The Z transformation of X produces a standard normal distribution only when X is normally distributed to begin with. It does not convert a nonnormal distribution (e.g., a skewed distribution) into a standard normal distribution.

12.8 TABLE OF AREAS IN THE STANDARD NORMAL DISTRIBUTION

We know from the general properties of continuous probability distributions (see Example 12.1) that: (1) the total area in the distribution is 1.0, (2) the probability that the continuous random variable X will assume a value in the interval a to b is the area in the distribution bounded by the curve, the X axis, and the vertical lines above a and b, and (3) such areas can be determined by applying the techniques of integral calculus to the specific probability function being considered.

While integral calculus could thus be used to solve area/probability problems for any of the infinitely large family of normal distributions, this is fortunately not necessary. Because any normal distribution can be transformed into a standard normal distribution, all normal distribution area/probability problems can be solved by applying integral calculus to equation (12.5), the density function for this one distribution.

Table A.5 in the Appendix (*Areas of the Standard Normal Distribution*) provides a summary of this integration of equation (12.5):

$$P(0 \le Z \le z) = \int_0^z \left[f(z) = \frac{1}{\sqrt{2\pi}} e^{-z^2/2} \right] dz \tag{12.6}$$

for positive z values ranging from 0.00 to 3.99. The results of this integration are areas bounded by the standard normal curve, the Z axis, the vertical axis at $z = 0$, and a vertical line erected above the z value of interest.

EXAMPLE 12.4 Use Table A.5 to answer these questions: (*a*) What area of the standard normal distribution lies under the curve over $0 \le z \le 0.45$? (*b*) What proportion of the standard normal distribution lies under the curve over $0 \le z \le 0.45$? (*c*) What is the probability that the standard normal variable Z will take on some value in the interval $0 \le z \le 0.45$?

Solution

(*a*) The area under the curve above $0 \le z \le 0.45$ is the shaded area in the standard normal distribution shown in Fig. 12-6. It is bounded by the curve, the Z axis, the vertical density axis at $z = 0$, and a vertical line above $z = 0.45$. This area can be found in Table A.5 by first locating z to one decimal place in the left column (0.4) and then finding z's second decimal place in the column headings (0.05). The part of Table A.5 needed to find this area is shown in Table 12.1, where you can see that at the intersection of row $z = 0.4$ and column 0.05, the area (circled) is 0.1736.

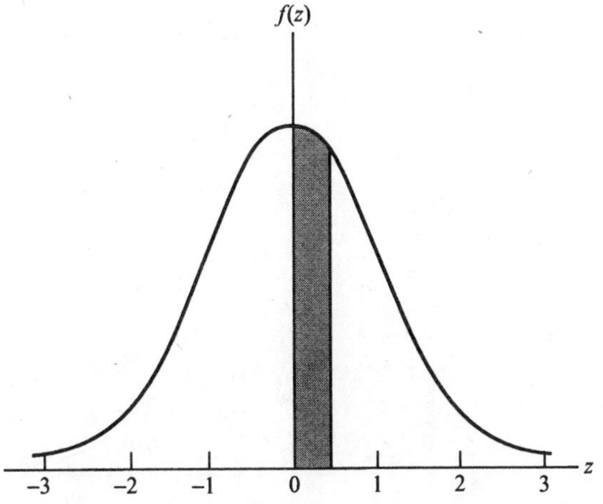

Fig. 12-6

Table 12.1

z	0.00	0.01	0.02	0.03	0.04	0.05	0.06	0.07	0.08	0.09
0.0	0.0000	0.0040	0.0080	0.0120	0.0160	0.0199	0.0239	0.0279	0.0319	0.0359
0.1	0.0398	0.0438	0.0478	0.0517	0.0557	0.0596	0.0636	0.0675	0.0714	0.0754
0.2	0.0793	0.0832	0.0871	0.0910	0.0948	0.0987	0.1026	0.1064	0.1103	0.1141
0.3	0.1179	0.1217	0.1255	0.1293	0.1331	0.1368	0.1406	0.1443	0.1480	0.1517
0.4	0.1554	0.1591	0.1628	0.1664	0.1700	0.1736	0.1772	0.1808	0.1844	0.1879

(*b*) Because the total area in the standard normal distribution is 1.0, Table A.5 gives areas as a proportion of 1.0. Thus, the proportion of the standard normal distribution that lies under the curve above $0 \leq z \leq 0.45$ is also 0.1736.

(*c*) Because area = probability in a continuous probability distribution,

$$P(0 \leq Z \leq 0.45) = \int_0^{0.45} \left[f(z) = \frac{1}{\sqrt{2\pi}} e^{-z^2/2} \right] dz = 0.1736$$

EXAMPLE 12.5 Use Table A.5 to find the area of the standard normal distribution that lies under the curve above $-1.69 \leq z \leq 0$.

Solution

The density axis $[f(z)]$ at $z = 0$ (see Fig. 12-6) divides the standard normal distribution into mirror-image halves. This means that if $+a$ and $-a$ are points on the Z axis that are to the right and left of $z = 0$, respectively, and equidistant from $z = 0$, then the areas under the curve above $0 \leq z \leq a$ and $-a \leq z \leq 0$ are equal and mirror-images of each other. Because of this, the area given in Table A.5 for $0 \leq z \leq a$ is also the area for $-a \leq z \leq 0$. Thus, for this problem as Table A.5 gives 0.4545 as the area under the curve above $0 \leq z \leq 1.69$, this then is also the area above $-1.69 \leq z \leq 0$. This area between -1.69 and 0 is the shaded area in the standard normal distribution shown in Fig. 12-7.

EXAMPLE 12.6 From what was determined in Examples 12.4 and 12.5, what is $P(-1.69 \leq Z \leq 0.45)$?

Solution

$P(-1.69 \leq Z \leq 0.45)$ is the shaded area under the curve above $-1.69 \leq z \leq 0.45$ in the standard normal

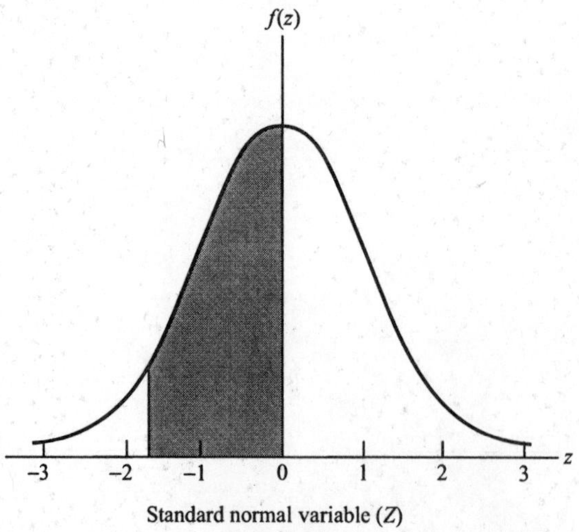

Fig. 12-7

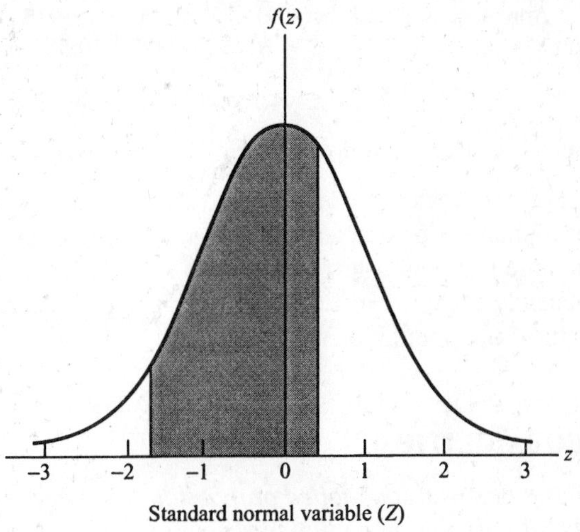

Fig. 12-8

distribution shown in Fig. 12-8. It is the sum of the areas found in Examples 12.4 and 12.5:

$$P(-1.69 \le Z \le 0.45) = 0.4545 + 0.1736 = 0.6281$$

12.9 FINDING PROBABILITIES WITHIN ANY NORMAL DISTRIBUTION BY APPLYING THE *Z* TRANSFORMATION

It can be proven mathematically that

$$P(a \le X \le b) = P\left(\frac{a-\mu}{\sigma} \le Z \le \frac{b-\mu}{\sigma}\right) = P(z_a \le Z \le z_b) \qquad (12.7)$$

This states that for any normal distribution with mean μ and standard deviation σ, the probability that its random variable X will take on a value in the interval $a \le x \le b$ is the same as the probability in the standard normal distribution that Z will take on some value in the interval

$$\left(\frac{a-\mu}{\sigma} \le z \le \frac{b-\mu}{\sigma}\right) = (z_a \le z \le z_b)$$

EXAMPLE 12.7 A physiologist wants to know the effect of winter hibernation on the weight of ground squirrels. He designs an experiment in which 1,000 adult male ground squirrels are weighed in late summer and in early spring. For the late-summer measurements, he finds that the weights are normally distributed with an average of 400 grams and a standard deviation of 100 grams. What is the probability that a particular ground squirrel will weigh between 350 grams and 450 grams in late summer?

Solution

To answer this question, we need to transform $P(350\text{ g} \le X \le 450\text{ g})$ into $P(z_a \le Z \le z_b)$. First, 350 g and 450 g are transformed into z scores using equation (12.4):

$$z_a = \frac{350\text{ g} - 400\text{ g}}{100\text{ g}} = -0.5 \qquad z_b = \frac{450\text{ g} - 400\text{ g}}{100\text{ g}} = 0.5$$

Next, the z scores are substituted into equation (12.7)

$$P(a \le X \le b) = P(z_a \le Z \le z_b)$$

$$P(350\text{ g} \le X \le 450\text{ g}) = P(-0.5 \le Z \le 0.5)$$

From Table A.5 in the Appendix, we find that $P(0 \leq Z \leq 0.5) = 0.1915$. Because of the symmetry of the normal curve (see Example 12.5), $P(-0.5 \leq Z \leq 0) = P(0 \leq Z \leq 0.5)$, and so

$$P(-0.5 \leq Z \leq 0.5) = 2(0.1915) = 0.3830$$

The probability that a ground squirrel will weigh between 350 grams and 450 grams is 0.3830.

Note that in Example 12.7 we treated a sample of 1,000 squirrels as if it were a population, using formulas that include the population parameters μ and σ. We did this because the standard-normal techniques in this chapter require population-level information, either directly from the population itself or from samples that are sufficiently large, as in Example 12.7, to give accurate information on the shape, mean, and standard deviation of the population's distribution.

12.10 ONE-TAILED PROBABILITIES

Many statistical procedures deal with *one-tailed probabilities*, in which only the area in the *upper tail* (*right tail*) or the *lower tail* (*left tail*) of a probability distribution is of interest. If we denote the area in the upper tail by α (the lowercase Greek letter *alpha*), then for the variable X the specific value x_α is the number such that

$$P(X > x_\alpha) = \alpha \tag{12.8}$$

In words, this states that the area (probability) under the distribution curve to the right of x_α is α. If X is a continuous normally distributed variable, then it can be proven mathematically that

$$P(X > x_\alpha) = P\left(Z > \frac{x_\alpha - \mu}{\sigma}\right) = P(Z > z_\alpha) = \alpha \tag{12.9}$$

This probability is the shaded area in the standard normal distribution shown in Fig. 12-9.

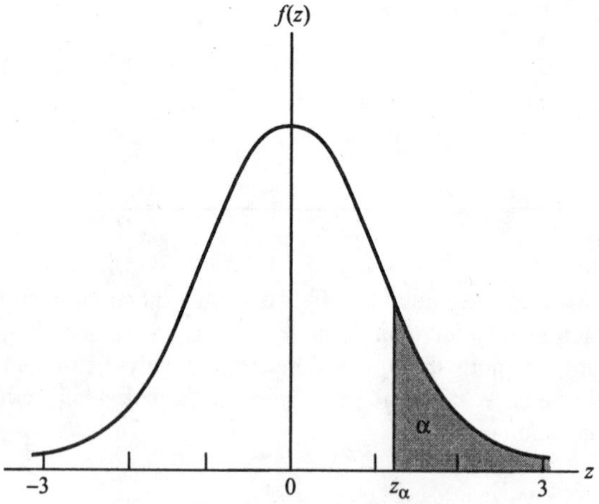

Fig. 12-9

Similarly, if we now denote the area in the lower tail by α, then for the variable X the specific value $x_{1-\alpha}$ is a number such that

$$P(X < x_{1-\alpha}) = \alpha \tag{12.10}$$

In words, this states that the area (probability) under the distribution curve to the left of $x_{1-\alpha}$ is α. (The subscript $1-\alpha$ indicates that the area to the right of $x_{1-\alpha}$ is $1-\alpha$.) If X is a continuous normally distributed variable, then it can be mathematically proven that

$$P(X < x_{1-\alpha}) = P\left(Z < \frac{x_{1-\alpha} - \mu}{\sigma}\right) = P(Z < -z_\alpha) = \alpha \tag{12.11}$$

This probability is the shaded area in the standard normal distribution shown in Fig. 12-10.

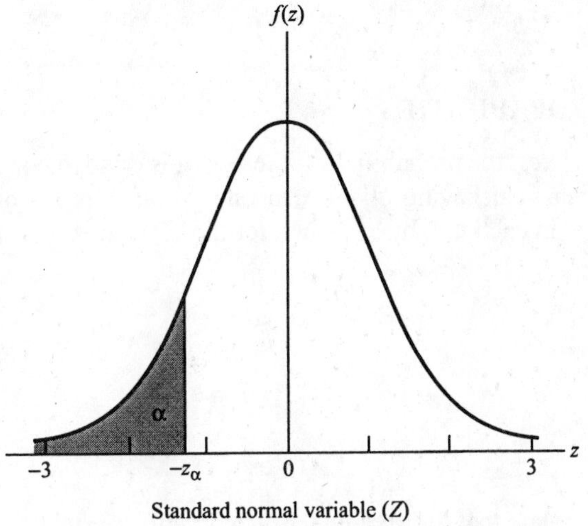

Fig. 12-10

EXAMPLE 12.8 If the normally distributed variable X has the parameters $\mu = 14.5$ and $\sigma = 2.1$, then for $\alpha = 0.05$, what are: (*a*) z_α and x_α, (*b*) $-z_\alpha$ and $x_{1-\alpha}$?

Solution

(*a*) From equation (12.9), we know that

$$P(Z > z_\alpha) = \alpha = 0.05$$

Thus, to find z_α we must find the z value associated with the area in Table A.5 in the Appendix that is closest to $0.5 - 0.05 = 0.45$

$$P(0 \le Z \le z_\alpha) = 0.45$$

We find that instead of just one "closest area," there are two areas that are exactly 0.0005 different from 0.45:0.4495 with $z = 1.64$ and 0.4505 with $z = 1.65$. Therefore, we use the average of these z values as z_α

$$z_\alpha = z_{0.05} = \frac{1.64 + 1.65}{2} = 1.645$$

Now, to find $x_\alpha = x_{0.05}$ we rearrange the terms in equation (12.4) to form

$$x_i = \mu + z_i\sigma \tag{12.12}$$

Substituting x_α and z_α for x_i and z_i,

$$x_\alpha = \mu + z_\alpha\sigma$$
$$x_{0.05} = \mu + z_{0.05}\sigma$$
$$= 14.5 + (1.645 \times 2.1) = 14.5 + 3.4545 = 17.9545, \qquad \text{or } 18.0$$

(*b*) From equation (12.11) we know that

$$P(Z < -z_\alpha) = \alpha = 0.05$$

and thus, because of the symmetry of the standard normal distribution, we know from (*a*) that

$$-z_\alpha = -z_{0.05} = -1.645$$

To find $x_{1-\alpha}$ we substitute $x_{1-\alpha}$ and $-z_\alpha$ for x_i and z_i in equation (12.12):

$$x_{1-\alpha} = \mu + (-z_\alpha \sigma)$$

$$x_{1-0.05} = \mu + (-z_{0.05}\sigma)$$

$$= 14.5 + (-1.645 \times 2.1) = 14.5 - 3.4545 = 11.0455, \qquad \text{or } 11.0$$

12.11 TWO-TAILED PROBABILITIES

With *two-tailed probabilities*, the probability of interest, α, is divided equally between the two tails of a probability distribution rather than having all of α in one tail as it is for one-tailed probabilities. If we denote these equal areas, one in each tail, by $\alpha/2$, then for the variable X the specific values $x_{\alpha/2}$ and $x_{1-\alpha/2}$ are numbers such that

$$P(X > x_{\alpha/2}) = \alpha/2 \tag{12.13}$$

$$P(X < x_{1-\alpha/2}) = \alpha/2 \tag{12.14}$$

$$P(x_{1-\alpha/2} \le X \le x_{\alpha/2}) = 1 - \alpha \tag{12.15}$$

In words, these formulas state that the area under the curve to the right of $x_{\alpha/2}$ is $\alpha/2$, that to the left of $x_{1-\alpha/2}$ is also $\alpha/2$, and therefore, the area between $x_{1-\alpha/2}$ and $x_{\alpha/2}$ is $1 - \alpha/2 - \alpha/2 = 1 - \alpha$. If X is a continuous normally distributed variable, then it is also true that

$$P(X > x_{\alpha/2}) = P\left(Z > \frac{x_{\alpha/2} - \mu}{\sigma}\right) = P(Z > z_{\alpha/2}) = \alpha/2 \tag{12.16}$$

$$P(X < x_{1-\alpha/2}) = P\left(Z < \frac{x_{1-\alpha/2} - \mu}{\sigma}\right) = P(Z < -z_{\alpha/2}) = \alpha/2 \tag{12.17}$$

$$P(x_{1-\alpha/2} \le X \le x_{\alpha/2}) = P(-z_{\alpha/2} \le Z \le z_{\alpha/2}) = 1 - \alpha \tag{12.18}$$

These areas are shown for the standard normal distribution in Fig. 12-11.

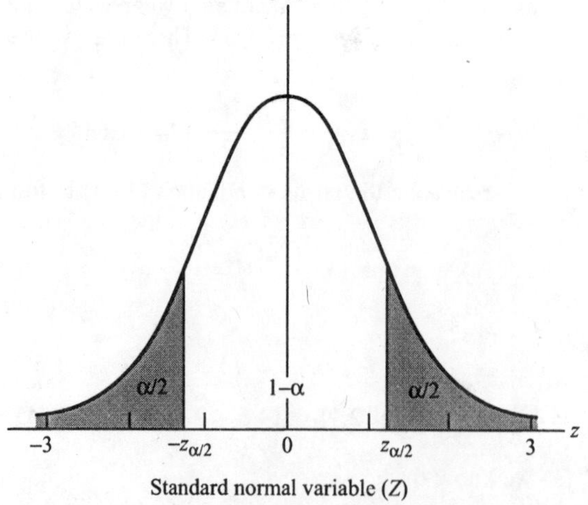

Fig. 12-11

EXAMPLE 12.9 For a normally distributed variable X that has $\mu = 14.5$ and $\sigma = 2.1$, if $\alpha = 0.05$, then what are $z_{\alpha/2}$, $-z_{\alpha/2}$, $x_{\alpha/2}$, and $x_{1-\alpha/2}$?

Solution

From equation (12.16), we know that

$$P(Z > z_{\alpha/2}) = \alpha/2 = 0.05/2 = 0.025$$

Therefore, to find $z_{\alpha/2} = z_{0.05/2}$ we must find the z value associated with the area in Table A.5 in the Appendix that is closest to $0.5 - 0.025 = 0.475$

$$P(0 \leq Z \leq z_{\alpha/2}) = 0.475$$

This "closest area" is exactly 0.4750 and thus $z_{\alpha/2} = z_{0.05/2} = 1.96$. Because of the symmetry of the standard normal distribution, we know that $-z_{\alpha/2} = -z_{0.05/2} = -1.96$. Next, to find $x_{\alpha/2}$ we substitute $x_{\alpha/2}$ and $z_{\alpha/2}$ in equation (12.12),

$$x_{\alpha/2} = \mu + z_{\alpha/2}\sigma$$

$$x_{0.05/2} = \mu + z_{0.05/2}\sigma$$

$$= 14.5 + (1.96 \times 2.1) = 14.5 + 4.116 = 18.616, \qquad \text{or } 18.6$$

and then to find $x_{1-\alpha/2}$ we substitute $x_{1-\alpha/2}$ and $-z_{\alpha/2}$ in equation (12.12),

$$x_{1-\alpha/2} = \mu + (-z_{\alpha/2}\sigma)$$

$$x_{1-0.05/2} = \mu + (-z_{0.05/2}\sigma)$$

$$= 14.5 + (-1.96 \times 2.1) = 14.5 - 4.116 = 10.384, \qquad \text{or } 10.4$$

12.12 THE NORMAL APPROXIMATION TO THE BINOMIAL DISTRIBUTION

To determine a probability for a binomial distribution, one must sum the relevant terms for the binomial expansion $(q + p)^n$ (see Section 11.7), a tedious process that may require a computer when n is large. In Section 11.31, however, we saw that under certain conditions (i.e., when $n \geq 20$ and $p \leq 0.05$), approximate binomial probabilities can be found using the Poisson distribution. Similarly, the normal distribution gives a good approximation to the binomial distribution under certain conditions, and so it also can be used to calculate the probabilities of a binomial experiment. Since these probabilities only approximate the true binomial probability values, this use of the normal distribution is called the *normal approximation to the binomial distribution*.

This normal-approximation method is appropriate only when the given binomial distribution resembles (i.e., approximates) a normal distribution in being both symmetrical and bell-shaped, and this will be true under two conditions:

(1) The binomial distribution becomes increasingly symmetrical the closer p (the probability of success) is to 0.5 (see Fig. 11-2).

(2) For any value p, however far it is from 0.5, if n (the number of trials, or the sample size) is increased as p is held constant, then the resultintg binomial distributions with $\mu = np$ and $\sigma^2 = npq$ become more and more similar in shape to a normal distribution with $\mu = np$ and $\sigma^2 = npq$.

Because of condition (2), when n is "sufficiently large" we can treat the binomial distribution as if it were a normal distribution with $\mu = np$ and $\sigma^2 = npq$, and then use standard-normal techniques to approximate the true binomial probability values.

There is no absolute rule for when p is "close enough" to 0.5 or for when n is "sufficiently large," but there are many rules of thumb for when it is appropriate to use the normal approximation. One such rule, found in many statistics books, is that

> The normal approximation to the binomial distribution can be used when both np and nq are greater than or equal to 5 ($np \geq 5$ and $nq \geq 5$).

A more stringent version of this rule specifies that both np and nq be greater than 5 ($np > 5$ and $nq > 5$).

EXAMPLE 12.10 For the binomial variable, number of heads in 14 flips of a coin, determine the probability of getitng 8, 9, or 10 heads in the 14 flips by using: (*a*) binomial-distribution techniques, (*b*) normal-approximation techniques.

Solution

(*a*) To solve this problem using binomial-distribution techniques, one must determine the binomial probability distribution for the variable. First, the binomial theorem is used to find the terms of the binomial expansion $(p+q)^{14}$ (see Section 11.7)

$$\begin{aligned}(q+p)^{14} &= q^{14} + 14q^{13}p + 91q^{12}p^2 + 364q^{11}p^3 + 1001q^{10}p^4 + 2002q^9p^5 \\ &\quad + 3003q^8p^6 + 3432q^7p^7 + 3003q^6p^8 + 2002q^5p^9 + 1001q^4p^{10} \\ &\quad + 364q^3p^{11} + 91q^2p^{12} + 14qp^{13} + p^{14}\end{aligned}$$

Then, the probability of getting a head ($p = \frac{1}{2}$) and of getting a tail ($q = \frac{1}{2}$) are inserted into the expansion to give the distribution shown in the histogram in Fig. 12-12. In this histogram, the discrete binomial variable is treated "as if it were continuous" (see Problem 5.9 in Volume 1), with probability values for each number-of-heads represented by both the height and area (height $\times$ 1.0) of the bar above the number. Thus, for example, the probability of 8 heads is both the height of the bar above it (0.1833) and the area of the bar ($0.1833 \times 1.0 = 0.1833$). As this is a probability distribution, the total area represented by the histogram is 1.0, and for this binomial probability distribution the mean is $\mu = np = (14)(\frac{1}{2}) = 7$, the variance is $\sigma^2 = npq = (14)(\frac{1}{2})(\frac{1}{2}) = 3.5$, and the standard deviation is $\sigma = \sqrt{npq} = \sqrt{3.5} = 1.8708$.

From Property 4 in Section 8.6 of Volume 1, we know that

$$P(A_1 \cup A_2 \cup \cdots \cup A_k) = P(A_1) + P(A_2) + \cdots + P(A_k)$$

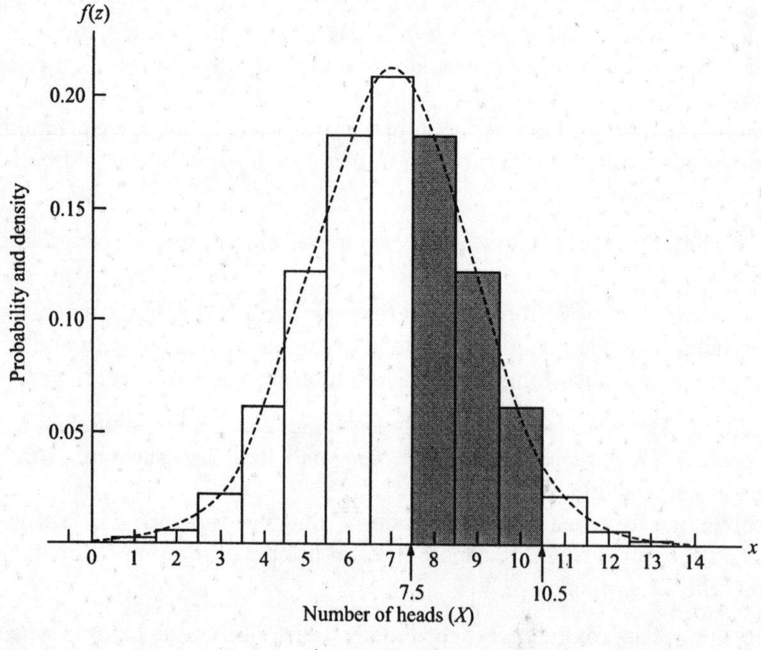

Fig. 12-12

Therefore, because the binomial is a discrete variable, the requested probability for this problem is

$$P(8 \leq X \leq 10) = P[(X = 8) \cup (X = 9) \cup (X = 10)] = P(X = 8) + P(X = 9) + P(X = 10)$$

From the binomial expansion $(q + p)^{14}$ we know that

$$P(X = 8) = 3003q^6p^8 = 3003(\tfrac{1}{2})^6(\tfrac{1}{2})^8 = 0.1833$$

$$P(X = 9) = 2002q^5p^9 = 2002(\tfrac{1}{2})^5(\tfrac{1}{2})^9 = 0.1222$$

$$P(X = 10) = 1001q^4p^{10} = 1001(\tfrac{1}{2})^4(\tfrac{1}{2})^{10} = 0.0611$$

Therefore,

$$P(8 \leq X \leq 10) = 0.1833 + 0.1222 + 0.0611 = 0.3666$$

This probability is the shaded area in the histogram in Fig. 12-12.

(*b*) As $np = nq = 7$, it is appropriate by either version of the rule of thumb to use the normal approximation. To show this, a normal distribution with parameters $\mu = np = 7$ and $\sigma^2 = npq = 3.5$ has been superimposed (as a dashed line) on the binomial distribution in Fig. 12-12.

It would seem that the normal approximation to the binomial value $P(8 \leq X \leq 10) = 0.3666$ would be the area under this normal curve over the interval $8 \leq x \leq 10$, but this would be ignoring the fact that the area for this probability in the binomial histogram actually extends over the interval $7.5 \leq x \leq 10.5$ (see Fig. 12-12). In order to use this continuous distribution to approximate the discrete distribution, each discrete value must be treated as an interval—as if the discrete value is the midpoint of the implied range of a measurement category (see Section 2.10, Volume 1), which extends 0.5 above and below the value. Then, in this problem, we are finding the area under the normal curve that is above the interval $7.5 \leq x \leq 10.5$, which extends from the implied lower boundary of measurement category 8 to the implied upper boundary of measurement category 10. This addition and subtraction of 0.5 from the discrete values is called the *continuity correction* (or *correction for continuity*, or *half-unit correction for continuity*).

To find $P(7.5 \leq X \leq 10.5)$ in a normal distribution where $\mu = np = 7$ and $\sigma = \sqrt{npq} = \sqrt{3.5} = 1.8708$, we use equation (12.7) to convert normal probability values into standard-normal values.

$$P(a \leq X \leq b) = P\left(\frac{a - \mu}{\sigma} \leq Z \leq \frac{b - \mu}{\sigma}\right) = P(z_a \leq Z \leq z_b)$$

$$P(7.5 \leq X \leq 10.5) = P\left(\frac{7.5 - np}{\sqrt{npq}} \leq Z \leq \frac{10.5 - np}{\sqrt{npq}}\right)$$

$$= P\left(\frac{7.5 - 7}{1.8708} \leq Z \leq \frac{10.5 - 7}{1.8708}\right) = P(0.27 \leq Z \leq 1.87)$$

Now, we know from Table A.5 in the Appendix that

$$P(0 \leq Z \leq 0.27) = 0.1064 \qquad P(0 \leq Z \leq 1.87) = 0.4693$$

Therefore

$$P(0.27 \leq Z \leq 1.87) = 0.4693 - 0.1064 = 0.3629$$

Comparing the true binomial result in (*a*) with the normal approximation, we can see that they are identical through the second decimal place:

$$P(8 \leq X \leq 10) = 0.3666 \approx P(0.27 \leq Z \leq 1.87) = 0.3629$$

12.13 THE NORMAL APPROXIMATION TO THE POISSON DISTRIBUTION

The normal distribution can be used to approximate the Poisson distribution. Recall that the parameter of the Poisson distribution is $\mu = \lambda t$ (see Section 11.28). It turns out that as $\mu = \lambda t$ increases, the Poisson distribution approaches a normal distribution with $\mu = \sigma^2 = \lambda t$. Thus, whenever λt is "large enough" we can treat the Poisson distribution as if it were a normal distribution with $\mu = \sigma^2 = \lambda t$, and $\sigma = \sqrt{\lambda t}$. We can then use standard-normal techniques to find the area (probability) values. Because these values only approximate the true Poisson probability values, this use of the normal distribution is called the *normal approximation to the Poisson distribution.*

There is no absolute rule for when λt is "large enough" but there are, again, as with the binomial distribution, many rules of thumb for when it is appropriate to use the normal approximation. One such rule, found in many statistics books, is that

> The normal approximation to the Poisson distribution can be used when λt is greater than or equal to $5 (\lambda t \geq 5)$.

A more stringent version of the rule specifies that λt must be greater than or equal to $10 (\lambda t \geq 10)$.

EXAMPLE 12.11 The cable manufacturer in Section 11.26 has determined that for a 4-meter unit of cable there are $\lambda = 4.0$ defects per 4 meters. Determine the probability of getting 6, 7, or 8 defects in $t = 1.5$ units of cable, using: (*a*) Poisson-distribution techniques, (*b*) normal-approximation techniques.

Solution

(*a*) Assuming this is a Poisson experiment (see Section 11.26), then what is requested is $P(6 \leq X \leq 8)$ in a Poisson distribution where $\mu = \sigma^2 = \lambda t = (4.0 \text{ defects per 4 meters}) \times (1.5 \text{ units}) = 6.0$ defects per 6 meters. We will determine this probability using equation (10.5) of Volume 1:

$$P(a \leq X \leq b) = F(b) - F(a) + f(a)$$
$$P(6 \leq X \leq 8) = F(8) - F(6) + f(6)$$

and equation (10.4):

$$P(5 < X \leq 6) = F(6) - F(5) = f(6)$$

From Table A.4 in the Appendix, we find for $\mu = 6.0$: $F(5) = 0.446$, $F(6) = 0.606$, and $F(8) = 0.847$. Thus: $f(6) = 0.606 - 0.446 = 0.160$, and $P(6 \leq X \leq 8) = 0.847 - 0.606 + 0.160 = 0.401$.

(*b*) Because we are using a continuous distribution to approximate a discrete distribution, we must correct for continuity [see Example 12.10(*b*)]. Thus, to find $P(6 \leq X \leq 8)$ we must find $P(5.5 \leq X \leq 8.5)$ in a normal distribution where $\mu = \sigma^2 = \lambda t = 6.0$ and $\sigma = \sqrt{6.0} = 2.4495$:

$$\begin{aligned}
P(5.5 \leq X \leq 8.5) &= P\left(\frac{5.5 - \lambda t}{\sqrt{\lambda t}} \leq Z \leq \frac{8.5 - \lambda t}{\sqrt{\lambda t}}\right) \\
&= P\left(\frac{5.5 - 6.0}{2.4495} \leq Z \leq \frac{8.5 - 6.0}{2.4495}\right) \\
&= P(-0.20 \leq Z \leq 1.02)
\end{aligned}$$

We know from Table A.5 in the Appendix that

$$P(0 \leq Z \leq 0.20) = P(-0.20 \leq Z \leq 0) = 0.0793$$
$$P(0 \leq Z \leq 1.02) = 0.3461$$

Therefore,

$$P(-0.20 \leq Z \leq 1.02) = 0.0793 + 0.3461 = 0.4254$$

Comparing the true Poisson result with the normal approximation, we can see that they differ by 0.024:

$$P(6 \leq X \leq 8) = 0.401 \approx P(-0.20 \leq Z \leq 1.02) = 0.425$$

12.14 THE DISCRETE UNIFORM PROBABILITY DISTRIBUTION

A uniform probability distribution is characterized by an equal probability for all the values of its random variable X. While this chapter is devoted to continuous distributions, we describe here the discrete version of a uniform probability distribution as an introduction to the continuous version.

In a *discrete uniform probability distribution* (or *discrete uniform distribution*, or *discrete rectangular distribution*), the random variable X can assume any integer value from 1 to k, and all k values have the same probability. The probability function that assigns this same probability value to each of the k possible outcomes, the probability function that defines the distribution, is this function, called the *discrete uniform probability function*

$$f(x) = \frac{1}{k}, \qquad \text{for } x = 0, 1, \ldots, k \tag{12.19}$$

As this is a discrete probability distribution, it must be true that: $f(x) \geq 0$ for any x and $\sum_x f(x) = 1.00$ [see Fig. 10-3(a) in Volume 1]. The mean of the discrete uniform distribution is

$$\mu = \frac{k+1}{2} \tag{12.20}$$

the variance is

$$\sigma^2 = \frac{k^2 - 1}{12} \tag{12.21}$$

and the standard deviation is

$$\sigma = \sqrt{\sigma^2} = \sqrt{\frac{k^2 - 1}{12}} \tag{12.22}$$

The discrete uniform probability distribution is, again, a family of distributions, with the single parameter, k.

EXAMPLE 12.12 For the experiment of rolling a die once, the probability distribution for the random variable, number of dots on the final upward face, is a discrete uniform probability distribution. For this distribution, determine: (a) the probability function $f(x)$, (b) the mean μ, (c) the variance σ^2, (d) the standard deviation σ, (e) the parameter, (f) $P(3 \leq X < 5)$.

Solution

(a) $f(x) = \frac{1}{k} = \frac{1}{6}$, for $x = 1, 2, \ldots, 6$

(b) $\mu = \frac{k+1}{2} = \frac{6+1}{2} = 3.5$

(c) $\sigma^2 = \frac{k^2 - 1}{12} = \frac{6^2 - 1}{12} = \frac{35}{12} = 2.92$

(d) $\sigma = \sqrt{\sigma^2} = \sqrt{2.92} = 1.71$

(e) $k = 6$

(f) $P(3 \leq X < 5) = P(X = 3) + P(X = 4) = f(3) + f(4) = \frac{1}{6} + \frac{1}{6} = \frac{2}{6} = 0.3333$. This probability is the shaded area in the probability histogram for this distribution shown in Fig. 12-13.

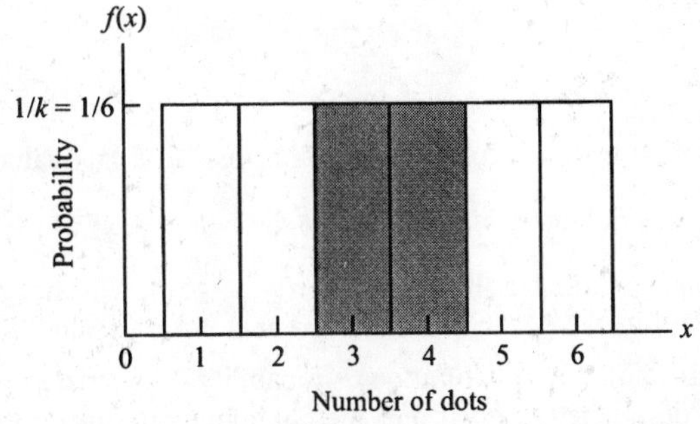

Fig. 12-13

12.15 THE CONTINUOUS UNIFORM PROBABILITY DISTRIBUTION

If a continuous random variable X can assume any value in the interval $a \le x \le b$ and only these values, and if its probability density function $f(x)$ is constant (uniform) over that interval and equal to zero elsewhere, then X is said to be *uniformly distributed*, and its distribution is called a *continuous uniform probability distribution* (or *continuous uniform distribution*, or *continuous rectangular distribution*). The probability density function that defines this distribution, called the *uniform probability density function*, is the following

$$f(x) = \frac{1}{b-a}, \quad \text{for } a \le x \le b, \quad \text{and} \quad f(x) = 0 \quad \text{elsewhere} \tag{12.23}$$

As this function defines a continuous probability distribution, it must be true that $f(x) \ge 0$ for any x and $\int_{-\infty}^{\infty} f(x)\,dx = 1.00$ [see Fig. 10-3(*b*), Volume 1]. The mean of the continuous uniform distribution is

$$\mu = \frac{b+a}{2} \tag{12.24}$$

the variance is

$$\sigma^2 = \frac{(b-a)^2}{12} \tag{12.25}$$

and the standard deviation is

$$\sigma = \sqrt{\sigma^2} = \sqrt{\frac{(b-a)^2}{12}} \tag{12.26}$$

The continuous uniform probability distribution is a family of distributions with the parameters a and b.

EXAMPLE 12.13 A continuous random variable X can assume values only in the interval $1 \le x \le 6$. If X has a continuous uniform probability distribution, then for this distribution determine: (*a*) the probability density function $f(x)$, (*b*) the mean μ, (*c*) the variance σ^2, (*d*) the standard deviation σ, (*e*) the parameters, (*f*) $P(3 \le X < 5)$.

Solution

(*a*) $f(x) = \frac{1}{b-a} = \frac{1}{6-1} = \frac{1}{5} = 0.2$, for $1 \le x \le 6$, and $f(x) = 0$ elsewhere

(*b*) $\mu = \frac{b+a}{2} = \frac{6+1}{2} = 3.5$

(*c*) $\sigma^2 = \frac{(b-a)^2}{12} = \frac{(6-1)^2}{12} = \frac{25}{12} = 2.08$

(*d*) $\sigma = \sqrt{\sigma^2} = \sqrt{2.08} = 1.44$

(*e*) $a = 1$ and $b = 6$

(*f*) The graph of a continuous probability distribution that only has values in the interval $a \le x \le b$ is a continuous horizontal line above that interval at the height $f(x) = \frac{1}{b-a}$. Because this is a probability distribution, the total area under the line over $a \le x \le b$ is 1. The graph for the distribution in this problem is shown in Fig. 12-14, with the shaded area representing $P(3 \le X \le 5)$.

As always with continuous distributions, probability is calculated for an interval; it is the area under the curve over the designated interval. For the continuous uniform distribution, as you can see in Fig. 12-14, the area is a rectangle with its base the length of the designated interval ($5 - 3 = 2$) and its height

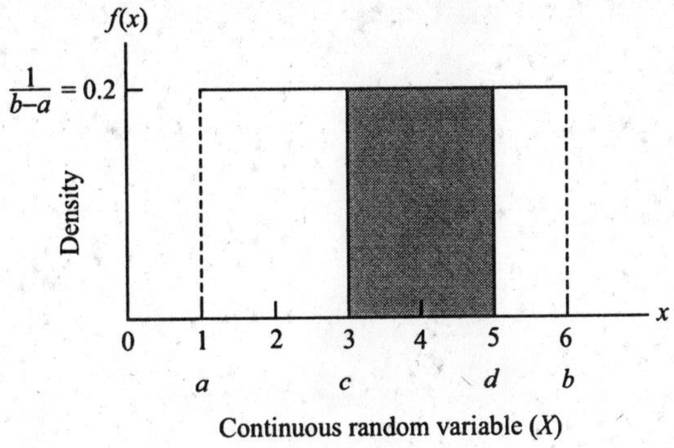

Fig. 12-14

the density function [$f(x) = 0.2$]. In general then, if $c \leq x \leq d$ is an interval equal to or within the defining interval $a \leq x \leq b$, then

$$P(c \leq X \leq d) = (\text{base})(\text{height}) = (d - c)\left(f(x) = \frac{1}{b-a}\right) = \frac{d-c}{b-a}$$

As this is a continuous variable it does not matter whether the endpoints of an interval are included. Therefore,

$$P(c \leq X \leq d) = P(c \leq X < d)$$

and thus

$$P(3 \leq X < 5) = \frac{d-c}{b-a} = \frac{5-3}{6-1} = \frac{2}{5} = 0.4$$

12.16 THE EXPONENTIAL PROBABILITY DISTRIBUTION

A continuous random variable X is said to be *exponentially distributed* if, for any $\lambda > 0$, its probability density function is given by the *exponential probability density function*

$$f(x) = \lambda e^{-\lambda x} \quad \text{for } x \geq 0, \quad \text{and} \quad f(x) = 0 \quad \text{for } x < 0 \tag{12.27}$$

where $e = 2.71828\ldots$ [see Problem 1.23(*b*) in Volume 1]. The *exponential probability distribution* (or *exponential distribution*) is a family of distributions with the single parameter λ. Versions of the exponential distributions for $\lambda = \frac{1}{2}$ and $\lambda = 2$ are shown in Fig. 12-15. For such exponential distributions,

$$\mu = \frac{1}{\lambda} \tag{12.28}$$

$$\sigma^2 = \frac{1}{\lambda^2} \tag{12.29}$$

$$\sigma = \frac{1}{\lambda} \tag{12.30}$$

Without deriving it, we simply state that the *cumulative distribution function* $F(x) = P(X \leq x)$ *of an exponential random variable* X is

$$F(x) = 1 - e^{-\lambda x}, \quad \text{for } x \geq 0, \quad \text{and} \quad F(x) = 0 \quad \text{for } x < 0 \tag{12.31}$$

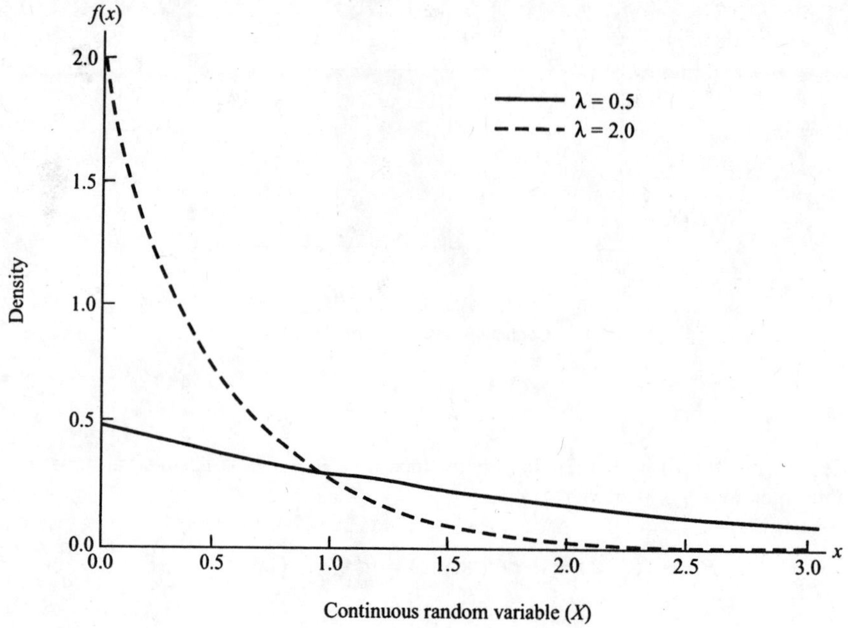

Fig. 12-15

EXAMPLE 12.14 For both exponential distributions shown in Fig. 12-15, determine the mean, variance, standard deviation, parameter, and cumulative distribution function.

Solution

For the distribution with $\lambda = \frac{1}{2}$,

$$\mu = \frac{1}{\lambda} = \frac{1}{1/2} = 2$$

$$\sigma^2 = \frac{1}{\lambda^2} = \frac{1}{(1/2)^2} = 4$$

$$\sigma = \frac{1}{\lambda} = \frac{1}{1/2} = 2$$

The parameter is $\lambda = \frac{1}{2}$, and the cumulative distribution function is

$$F(x) = 1 - e^{-\lambda x} = 1 - e^{-(1/2)x}$$

For the distribution with $\lambda = 2$,

$$\mu = \frac{1}{\lambda} = \frac{1}{2}$$

$$\sigma^2 = \frac{1}{\lambda^2} = \frac{1}{2^2} = \frac{1}{4}$$

$$\sigma = \frac{1}{\lambda} = \frac{1}{2}$$

The parameter is $\lambda = 2$, and the cumulative distribution function is

$$F(x) = 1 - e^{-\lambda x} = 1 - e^{-2x}$$

12.17 RELATIONSHIP BETWEEN THE EXPONENTIAL DISTRIBUTION AND THE POISSON DISTRIBUTION

You have probably noted that the positive constant λ (the lower-case Greek letter *lambda*) appears in both the exponential probability density function [equation (12.27)] and the Poisson probability function [equation (11.22)]. Both functions have the same parameter, λ, because the two distributions have the following relationship:

> If a certain event (success) is being generated randomly over a given unit of time (or space) by a Poisson process (see Section 11.26), then the continuous random variable—amount of time (or space) between successive occurrences of the event—is exponentially distributed. Furthermore, if λ is the average rate of occurrence of the event in the given unit, then the reciprocal of λ, or $\frac{1}{\lambda}$, is the average time (or distance) between successive events.

EXAMPLE 12.15 It is known that on Sundays between 6 PM and 10 PM an average of 5 emergency cases arrive per hour at the emergency room of a hospital. If the discrete random variable, number of arrivals, has a Poisson distribution, then during this time period what is: (*a*) the expected time between arrivals, (*b*) the probability that the next arrival will be within 15 minutes of the previous arrival, (*c*) the standard deivation of the exponential distribution for the continuous variable time between arrivals?

Solution

(*a*) We know that the number of arrivals has a Poisson distribution with $\lambda = 5$ arrivals per hour. Thus, the continuous random variable, time between arrivals, has an exponential distribution with $\mu = 1/\lambda = 1/5 = 0.2$ hours. This is the expected time between arrivals.

(*b*) The exponential probability density function [equation (12.27)] for the continuous random variable, time between arrivals, with $\lambda = 5$ is

$$f(x) = 5e^{-5x}, \quad \text{for } x \geq 0, \quad \text{and} \quad f(x) = 0 \quad \text{for } x < 0$$

This exponential distribution is presented in Fig. 12-16, with the requested probability shown as the shaded area under the curve above the interval $0 \leq x \leq$ (15 minutes or 0.25 hours). The value of this probability can be determined by using equation (12.31):

$$F(x) = P(X \leq x) = 1 - e^{-\lambda x}, \quad \text{for } x \geq 0, \quad \text{and} \quad F(x) = 0 \quad \text{for } x < 0$$

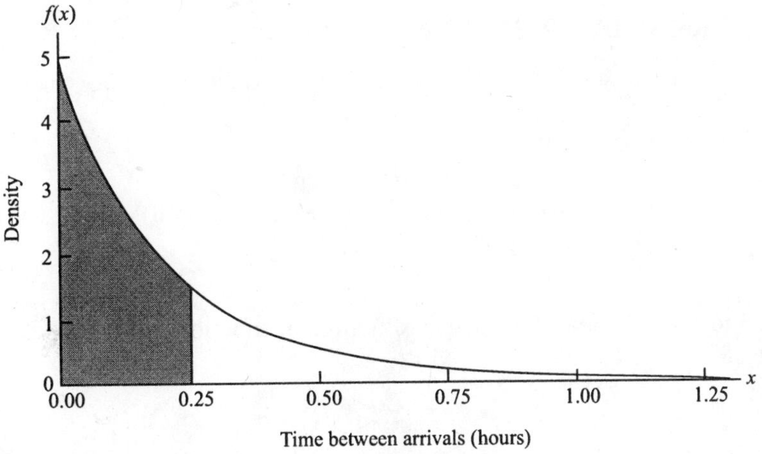

Fig. 12-16

Therefore, for $\lambda = 5$ and $x = 0.25$ hours,

$$F(0.25) = P(X \leq 0.25) = 1 - e^{-(5\times 0.25)} = 1 - e^{-1.25}$$

Using the techniques for finding e^{-x} from Example 11.22,

$$F(0.25) = 1 - 0.2865 = 0.7135$$

Therefore, the probability is 0.7135 that the next arrival will occur within 15 minutes of the previous arrival.

(*c*) Using equation (12.30),

$$\sigma = 1/\lambda = 1/5 = 0.2 \text{ hours}$$

Solved Problems

THE NORMAL DISTRIBUTION

12.1 Calculate $f(x)$ for $X = 1$ for a normal distribution with parameters $\mu = 0$ and $\sigma^2 = 4$.

Solution

Using equation (12.1),

$$f(x) = \frac{1}{\sigma\sqrt{2\pi}} e^{-(x-\mu)^2/2\sigma^2}$$

$$f(1) = \frac{1}{\sqrt{4} \times \sqrt{2\pi}} e^{-(1-0)^2/2\times 4}$$

$$= \frac{1}{(2)(2.50663)} e^{-1/8}$$

$$= (0.19947)(0.88250) = 0.17603$$

THE STANDARD NORMAL DISTRIBUTION

12.2 Use Table A.5 to find the area of the standard normal distribution that lies under the curve above $-1.21 \leq z \leq -1.05$.

Solution

The area above $-1.21 \leq z \leq 0$ is 0.3869, the area above $-1.05 \leq z \leq 0$ is 0.3531, and therefore, the area above $-1.21 \leq z \leq -1.05$ is $0.3869 - 0.3531 = 0.0338$.

12.3 Use Table A.5 to find the area of the standard normal distribution that lies under the curve above $0.32 \leq z \leq 1.85$.

Solution

The area above $0 \leq z \leq 0.32$ is 0.1255, the area above $0 \leq z \leq 1.85$ is 0.4678, and therefore, the area above $0.32 \leq z \leq 1.85$ is $0.4678 - 0.1255 = 0.3423$.

12.4 In Example 12.6, we found that for the standard normal distribution, $P(-1.69 \leq Z \leq 0.45) = 0.6281$. What is $P(-1.69 < Z < 0.45)$?

Solution

Equation (10.1) of Volume 1 states for a continuous probability distribution that

$$P(a < X \leq b) = P(a \leq X \leq b) = P(a < X < b) = P(a \leq X < b)$$

Therefore,

$$P(-1.69 < Z < 0.45) = P(-1.69 \leq Z \leq 0.45) = 0.6281$$

12.5 In Section 7.16 of Volume 1 we said that the *empirical rule* can be stated for populations roughly as follows:

> For a population that is approximately normally distributed, $\approx 68\%$ of the data lies in the interval $\mu \pm \sigma$, $\approx 95\%$ of the data lies in the interval $\mu \pm 2\sigma$, and $\approx 100\%$ of the data lies in the interval $\mu \pm 3\sigma$.

Then, in Section 12.2 we indicated that the exact percentages for the empirical rule are 68.3%, 95.4%, and 99.7%. Use Table A.5 to show that these values are correct.

Solution

The mean of the standard normal distribution is $\mu = 0$ and its standard deviation is $\sigma = 1$. Therefore, the area under the curve above $-1 \leq z \leq 1$ is the proportion (or percentage) of the distribution lying between $\mu - \sigma$ and $\mu + \sigma$. This area, the shaded area in the standard normal distribution shown in Fig. 12-17(*a*), is the sum of the equal areas over the intervals $-1 \leq z \leq 0$ and $0 \leq z \leq 1$. From Table A.5 the area above $0 \leq z \leq 1$ is 0.3413, and therefore the proportion (or percentage) of the distribution within $\mu \pm \sigma$ is

$$2(0.3413) = 0.6826, \text{ or } 68.3\%$$

By the same reasoning, the area above $-2 \leq z \leq 2$ [shaded area in Fig. 12-17(*b*)] is the proportion (or percentage) of the distribution lying within $\mu \pm 2\sigma$. From Table A.5 the area above $0 \leq z \leq 2$ is 0.4772, and therefore the proportion (or percentage) of the distribution within $\mu \pm 2\sigma$ is

$$2(0.4772) = 0.9544, \qquad \text{or } 95.4\%$$

Finally, the area above $-3 \leq z \leq 3$ [shaded area in Fig. 12-17(*c*)] is the proportion (or percentage) of the distribution lying within $\mu \pm 3\sigma$. From Table A.5, the area above $0 \leq z \leq 3$ is 0.4987, and therefore the proportion (or percentage) of the distribution within $\mu \pm 3\sigma$ is

$$2(0.4987) = 0.9974, \qquad \text{or } 99.7\%$$

As the intervals $-1 \leq z \leq 1$, $-2 \leq z \leq 2$, and $-3 \leq z \leq 3$ in the standard normal distribution represent, respectively, $\mu \pm \sigma$, $\mu \pm 2\sigma$, and $\mu \pm 3\sigma$ in any normal distribution, it is clear that the empirical rule holds true for all theoretical and empirical normal distributions.

12.6 For the continuous variable X that is normally distributed with $\mu = 4.0$ sec and $\sigma = 0.4$ sec, transform the following $X = x$ values into $Z = z$ values: (*a*) $x = 4.0$ sec, (*b*) $x = 3.6$ sec.

Solution

(*a*) Using equation (12.4), $z = \dfrac{4.0 \text{ sec} - 4.0 \text{ sec}}{0.4 \text{ sec}} = 0.00$

(*b*) $z = \dfrac{3.6 \text{ sec} - 4.0 \text{ sec}}{0.4 \text{ sec}} = -1.00$

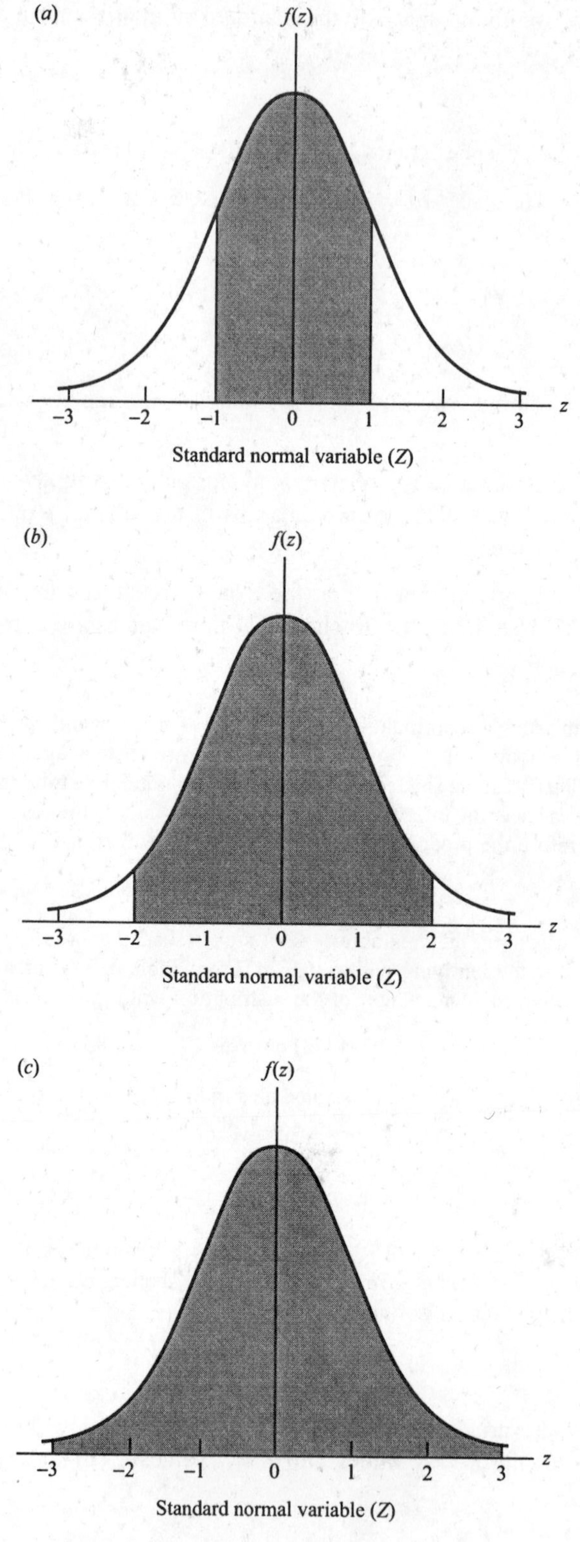
(a)
f(z)
−3
−2
−1
0
1
2
3
z
Standard normal variable (Z)
(b)
f(z)
−3
−2
−1
0
1
2
3
z
Standard normal variable (Z)
(c)
f(z)
−3
−2
−1
0
1
2
3
z
Standard normal variable (Z)

Fig. 12-17

12.7 For the continuous random variable X in Problem 12.6, transform the following $Z = z$ values back into $X = x$ values: (*a*) $z = -2.32$, (*b*) $z = 1.97$.

Solution

(*a*) Using equation (12.12), $x = 4.0 \text{ sec} + (-2.32 \times 0.4 \text{ sec}) = 4.0 \text{ sec} - 0.928 \text{ sec} = 3.1 \text{ sec}$

(*b*) $x = 4.0 \text{ sec} + (1.97 \times 0.4 \text{ sec}) = 4.0 \text{ sec} + 0.788 \text{ sec} = 4.8 \text{ sec}$

12.8 A geneticist working for a seed company develops a new carrot for growing in heavy clay soil. After measuring 5,000 of these carrots, it can be said that carrot length, X, is normally distributed with $\mu = 11.5$ cm and $\sigma = 1.15$ cm. What is the probability that X will take on a value in the interval $10.0 \text{ cm} \le x \le 13.0 \text{ cm}$?

Solution

Using equation (12.7),

$$P(10.0 \text{ cm} \le X \le 13.0 \text{ cm}) = P\left(\frac{10.0 \text{ cm} - 11.5 \text{ cm}}{1.15 \text{ cm}} \le Z \le \frac{13.0 \text{ cm} - 11.5 \text{ cm}}{1.15 \text{ cm}}\right)$$
$$= P(-1.30 \le Z \le 1.30)$$

From Table A.5 the area above $0 \le z \le 1.30$ is 0.4032, and this is also the area above $-1.30 \le z \le 0$. Therefore

$$P(10.0 \text{ cm} \le X \le 13.0 \text{ cm}) = P(-1.30 \le Z \le 1.30) = 2(0.4032) = 0.8064$$

12.9 The seed company in Problem 12.8 wants to state in its catalog that these new carrots "grow to between 10 cm and 13 cm." To do this, however, the company requires that at least 80% of the carrots are between 10 cm and 13 cm and that at least 90% of the carrots are 10 cm or more. Can the company use this phrase?

Solution

We know from Problem 12.8 that

$$P(10.0 \text{ cm} \le X \le 13.0 \text{ cm}) = 0.8064$$

and, therefore, that the first requirement is met: 80.6% of the carrots are in the interval $10.0 \text{ cm} \le x \le 13.0 \text{ cm}$.

To determine whether the second requirement is met, we must find

$$P(X \ge 10.0 \text{ cm}) = P\left(Z \ge \frac{10.0 \text{ cm} - 11.5 \text{ cm}}{1.15 \text{ cm}}\right) = P(Z \ge -1.30)$$

This probability is represented by the shaded area in Fig. 12-18.

We know that

$$P(Z \ge -1.30) = P(-1.30 \le Z < \infty) = P(-1.30 \le Z \le 0) + P(0 \le Z < \infty)$$

and that

$$P(0 \le Z < \infty) = 0.5$$

From Problem 12.8 we know that

$$P(-1.30 \le Z \le 0) = 0.4032$$

and so

$$P(-1.30 \le Z < \infty) = 0.4032 + 0.5 = 0.9032$$

Therefore,

$$P(X \ge 10.0 \text{ cm}) = P(Z \ge -1.30) = 0.9032$$

and the second requirement is met: 90.3% of the carrots are 10 cm or longer.

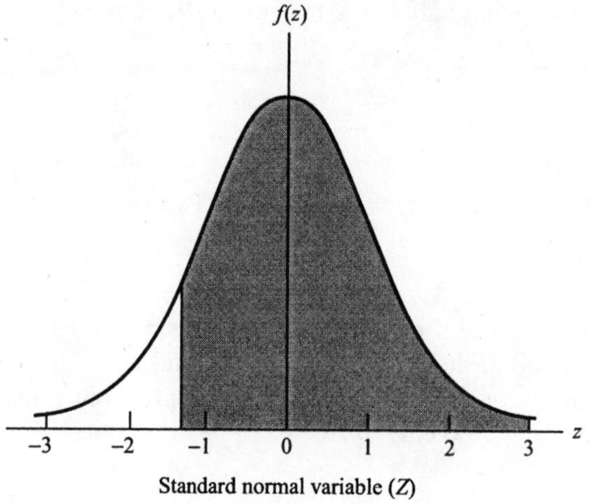

Fig. 12-18

12.10 Of the 5,000 carrots measured in Problem 12.8, how many are: (*a*) between 10 cm and 13 cm, (*b*) 10 cm or longer, (*c*) 13 cm or shorter?

Solution

(*a*) From Problem 12.8 we know that

$$P(10 \text{ cm} \leq X \leq 13.0 \text{ cm}) = 0.8064$$

Therefore, the number of carrots that are between 10 and 13 cm is

$$0.8064 \times 5{,}000 = 4{,}032$$

(*b*) From Problem 12.9 we know that

$$P(X \geq 10.0 \text{ cm}) = 0.9032$$

Therefore, the number of carrots that are 10 cm or longer is

$$0.9032 \times 5{,}000 = 4{,}516$$

(*c*) Because of the symmetry of the normal distribution, the number of carrots that are 13 cm or shorter is also 4,516.

12.11 For the carrots in Problems 12.8 to 12.10, what length is greater than or equal to 96% of the other lengths?

Solution

We know that

$$P(X \leq x_?) = P(Z \leq z_?) = 0.96$$

To solve for $x_?$ we first need to use Table A.5 to find $z_?$ and then transform this value back to $x_?$. To find $z_?$ we use these known relationships

$$\begin{aligned} P(Z \leq z_?) = 0.96 &= P(-\infty < Z \leq z_?) \\ &= P(-\infty < Z \leq 0) + P(0 \leq Z \leq z_?) \\ &= 0.5 + P(0 \leq Z \leq z_?) \end{aligned}$$

Therefore,

$$P(0 \le Z \le z_?) = 0.96 - 0.5 = 0.46$$

The area in Table A.5 that is closest to 0.46 is 0.4599, with a z value of 1.75. Therefore, using equation (12.12)

$$x_? = 11.5\text{ cm} + (1.75 \times 1.15\text{ cm}) = 11.5\text{ cm} + 2.0125\text{ cm} = 13.5\text{ cm}$$

Thus, a length of 13.5 cm is greater than or equal to 96% of the other lengths.

12.12 For the carrots in Problems 12.8 to 12.11, if two new carrots are harvested, what is the probability that both of them will be longer than 13.5 cm?

Solution

First, we know from Problem 12.11 that

$$P(X \le 13.5\text{ cm}) = 0.96$$

Therefore,

$$P(X > 13.5\text{ cm}) = 1 - 0.96 = 0.04$$

There is a 0.04 probability that a harvested carrot will be longer than 13.5 cm. Therefore, as carrot harvests are presumably independent events, we know from the special multiplication rule (see Section 9.5 in Volume 1) that

$$P(A \cap B) = P(A)P(B)$$

and so here, if we let X_1 and X_2 denote the lengths of the first and the second carrot, then

$$P[(X_1 > 13.5\text{ cm}) \cap (X_2 > 13.5\text{ cm})] = (0.04) \times (0.04) = 0.0016$$

12.13 A sociologist has been studying the criminal justice system in a large city. Among other things, she has found that over the last 5 years the length of time an arrested person must wait between their arrest and their trial is a normally distributed variable X with $\mu = 210$ days and $\sigma = 20$ days. What percent of these people had their trial between 160 days and 190 days after their arrest?

Solution

Using equation (12.7),

$$P(160\text{ days} \le X \le 190\text{ days}) = P\left(\frac{160\text{ days} - 210\text{ days}}{20\text{ days}} \le Z \le \frac{190\text{ days} - 210\text{ days}}{20\text{ days}}\right)$$
$$= P(-2.50 \le Z \le -1.00)$$

As

$$P(-2.50 \le Z \le -1.00) = P(-2.50 \le Z \le 0) - P(-1.00 \le Z \le 0)$$

and, from Table A.5,

$$P(-2.50 \le Z \le 0) - P(-1.00 \le Z \le 0) = 0.4938 - 0.3413 = 0.1525$$

Therefore, 15.25% came to trial between 160 days and 190 days after they were arrested.

12.14 For a given large population (e.g., all 12-year-old children in the United States), *intelligence quotient scores* (*IQ scores*) that are acquired by using the *Stanford–Binet Intelligence Scale* tend to be normally distributed with $\mu = 100.0$ and $\sigma = 16.0$. For such an *IQ* distribution, what *IQ* score ($X = x$) is the 67th percentile?

Solution

Normal-distribution techniques are routinely used to solve such *IQ*-distribution problems even though modern *IQ* scores are always integers and thus the *IQ* variable X is always a discrete variable. It is an example of treating a discrete measurement variable "as if it were continuous" because it is assumed that there is an underlying hypothetical variable (i.e., intelligence) that is continuous (see Problem 5.9 in Volume 1).

To use the normal distribution to find the 67th percentile ($Q_{67/100} = P_{67}$), we must determine the $x_?$ value below which are 67% of the data (see Section 6.13 in Volume 1). We find this value by using the techniques from Problem 12.11 to solve this equation for $x_?$

$$P(X < x_?) = P(X \leq x_?) = P\left(Z \leq \frac{x_? - 100.0}{16.0}\right) = P(Z \leq z_?) = 0.67$$

where

$$P(Z \leq z_?) = 0.67 = P(-\infty < Z \leq z_?) = 0.5 + P(0 \leq Z \leq z_?)$$

Thus,

$$P(0 \leq Z \leq z_?) = 0.67 - 0.5 = 0.17$$

The area in Table A.5 that is closest to 0.17 is exactly 0.1700, and therefore $z_? = 0.44$.

Next, we know that

$$z_? = 0.44 = \frac{x_? - 100.0}{16.0}$$

Solving for $x_?$

$$x_? = (16.0 \times 0.44) + 100.0 = 7.04 + 100.0 = 107.04, \qquad \text{or } 107.0$$

Thus, the 67th percentile for this *IQ* distribution is 107.0.

12.15 For the *IQ* distribution in Problem 12.14, what *IQ* score is: (a) the 33rd percentile, (b) the 2nd decile?

Solution

(*a*) The 33rd percentile ($Q_{33/100} = P_{33}$) is the x value below which are 33% of the data. Therefore, we must solve this equation for $x_?$:

$$P(X < x_?) = P(X \leq x_?) = P\left(Z \leq \frac{x_? - 100.0}{16.0}\right) = P(Z \leq z_?) = 0.33$$

where

$$P(Z \leq z_?) = 0.33 = 0.5 - P(z_? \leq Z \leq 0)$$

Thus,

$$P(z_? \leq Z \leq 0) = 0.5 - 0.33 = 0.17$$

Therefore, $z_?$ is the negative version of the value in Problem 12.14.

$$z_? = -0.44$$

and thus

$$z_? = -0.44 = \frac{x_? - 100.0}{16.0}$$

and

$$x_? = [16.0 \times (-0.44)] + 100.0 = -7.04 + 100.0 = 92.96, \qquad \text{or } 93.0$$

Thus, the 33rd percentile for this *IQ* distribution is 93.0.

(*b*) The 2nd decile ($Q_{2/10} = D_2$) is the x value below which is 20% of the data. Therefore, we must solve this equation for $x_?$:

$$P(X < x_?) = P(X \leq x_?) = P\left(Z \leq \frac{x_? - 100.0}{16.0}\right) = P(Z \leq z_?) = 0.20$$

where

$$P(Z \leq z_?) = 0.20 = 0.50 - P(z_? \leq Z \leq 0)$$

Thus,

$$P(z_? \leq Z \leq 0) = 0.5 - 0.20 = 0.30$$

The area in Table A.5 that is closest to 0.30 is 0.2996, and so $z_? = -0.84$. Therefore,

$$z_? = -0.84 = \frac{x_? - 100.0}{16.0}$$

and

$$x_? = [16.0 \times (-0.84)] + 100.0 = -13.44 + 100.0 = 86.56, \qquad \text{or } 86.6$$

Thus, the 2nd decile for this *IQ* distribution is 86.6.

12.16 For the *IQ* distribution in Problems 12.14 and 12.15, what is the probability that a randomly selected person from the population will have an *IQ* score: (*a*) of 140, (*b*) exactly at the 67th percentile (107.0 from Problem 12.14)?

Solution

If we are treating this discrete *IQ* distribution "as if it were continuous" (see Problem 12.14), then we know for all continuous probability distributions [see Example 12.1(*b*)] that

$$P(X = x) = 0$$

and therefore that

$$P(X = 140) = P(X = 107.0) = 0$$

However, if it is here assumed that each of these exact values is actually the midpoint of an implied range of a measurement category (see Seciton 2.10, Volume 1), then it is possible to calculate for $P(X = 140)$: $P(139.5 \leq X \leq 140.5)$, and for $P(X = 107.0)$: $P(106.95 \leq X \leq 107.05)$.

(*a*) Using equation (12.7),

$$P(139.5 \leq Z \leq 140.5) = P\left(\frac{139.5 - 100.0}{16.0} \leq Z \leq \frac{140.5 - 100.0}{16.0}\right) = P(2.47 \leq Z \leq 2.53)$$

We know from Table A.5 that the area above $0 \leq z \leq 2.47$ is 0.4932 and the area above $0 \leq z \leq 2.53$ is 0.4943. Thus,

$$P(139.5 \leq X \leq 140.5) = P(2.47 \leq Z \leq 2.53) = 0.4943 - 0.4932 = 0.0011$$

(*b*)
$$P(106.95 \leq X \leq 107.05) = P\left(\frac{106.95 - 100.0}{16.0} \leq Z \leq \frac{107.05 - 100.0}{16.0}\right) = P(0.43 \leq Z \leq 0.44)$$

We know from Table A.5 that the area above $0 \leq z \leq 0.43$ is 0.1664 and the area above $0 \leq z \leq 0.44$ is 0.1700. Thus,

$$P(106.95 \leq Z \leq 107.05) = P(0.43 \leq Z \leq 0.44) = 0.1700 - 0.1664 = 0.0036$$

ONE-TAILED AND TWO-TAILED PROBABILITIES

12.17 If the normally distributed variable X has $\mu = 14.5$ and $\sigma = 2.1$, then what are z_α and x_α if $\alpha = 0.01$?

Solution

We know from equation (12.9) that

$$P(Z > z_\alpha) = \alpha = 0.01$$

Therefore, to find z_α we must find the z value associated with the area in Table A.5 that is closest to $0.5 - 0.01 = 0.49$:

$$P(0 \leq Z \leq z_\alpha) = 0.49$$

Here it is clear that $z_\alpha = 2.33$.

Using equation (12.12),

$$x_\alpha = 14.5 + (2.33 \times 2.1) = 14.5 + 4.893 = 19.393, \qquad \text{or } 19.4$$

12.18 For the normally distributed variable in Problem 12.17, with $\mu = 14.5$ and $\sigma = 2.1$, what are $-z_\alpha$ and $x_{1-\alpha}$ when $\alpha = 0.02$?

Solution

We know from equation (12.11) that

$$P(Z < -z_\alpha) = \alpha = 0.02$$

Therefore, to find $-z_\alpha$ we must find the z value associated with the area in Table A.5 that is closest to $0.5 - 0.02 = 0.48$:

$$P(-z_\alpha \leq Z \leq 0) = 0.48$$

This area is 0.4798 and so $-z_\alpha = -2.05$. Substituting this value in equation (12.12),

$$x_{1-\alpha} = 14.5 + (-2.05 \times 2.1) = 14.5 - 4.305 = 10.195, \qquad \text{or } 10.2$$

12.19 If X is a normally distributed variable with $\mu = 1.83$ and $\sigma = 0.15$, then if $\alpha = 0.01$ what are $z_{\alpha/2}$, $-z_{\alpha/2}$, $x_{\alpha/2}$, and $x_{1-\alpha/2}$?

Solution

We know from equation (12.16) that

$$P(Z > z_{\alpha/2}) = \alpha/2 = 0.01/2 = 0.005$$

Therefore, to find $z_{\alpha/2}$ we must find the z value associated with the area in Table A.5 that is closest to $0.5 - 0.005 = 0.495$:

$$P(0 \leq Z \leq z_{\alpha/2}) = 0.495$$

There are two equally close areas: 0.4949 with $z = 2.57$ and 0.4951 with $z = 2.58$. Therefore,

$$z_{\alpha/2} = \frac{2.57 + 2.58}{2} = 2.575$$

Because of the symmetry of the standard normal distribution, we know that

$$-z_{\alpha/2} = -2.575$$

Using equation (12.12),

$$x_{\alpha/2} = 1.83 + (2.575 \times 0.15) = 1.83 + 0.38625 = 2.21625, \qquad \text{or } 2.22$$
$$x_{1-\alpha/2} = 1.83 + (-2.575 \times 0.15) = 1.83 - 0.38625 = 1.44375, \qquad \text{or } 1.44$$

THE NORMAL APPROXIMATION TO THE BINOMIAL DISTRIBUTION

12.20 In Example 12.10(*a*) it was determined for the binomial variable, number of heads in 14 flips of a coin, that the probability of 9 flips is $P(X = 9) = 0.1222$. Determine $P(X = 9)$ for this variable using the normal approximation to the binomial.

Solution

Treating the value 9 as a measurement category with the implied range of 8.5 to 9.5, we want to find the area under the normal curve in Fig. 12-12 ($\mu = np = 7$, $\sigma = \sqrt{npq} = \sqrt{3.5} = 1.8708$) that is above the interval $8.5 \le x \le 9.5$. Using the version of equation (12.7) from Example 12.10(*b*),

$$P(8.5 \le X \le 9.5) = P\left(\frac{8.5 - np}{\sqrt{npq}} \le Z \le \frac{9.5 - np}{\sqrt{npq}}\right)$$
$$= P\left(\frac{8.5 - 7}{1.8708} \le Z \le \frac{9.5 - 7}{1.8708}\right)$$
$$= P(0.80 \le Z \le 1.34)$$

From Table A.5,

$$P(0 \le Z \le 0.80) = 0.2881 \qquad P(0 \le Z \le 1.34) = 0.4099$$

Therefore,

$$P(0.80 \le Z \le 1.34) = 0.4099 - 0.2881 = 0.1218$$

Comparing the true binomial result with the normal approximation, we can see that they are identical through the second decimal place:

$$P(X = 9) = 0.1222 \approx P(0.80 \le Z \le 1.34) = 0.1218$$

12.21 For the binomial variable, number of heads in 14 flips of a coin, use both the binomial and normal-approximation techniques (see Example 12.10) to determine the probability of getting at most 6 heads.

Solution

To determine the true binomial probability $P(X \le 6)$ we use the relevant terms from the binomial expansion in Example 12.10(a):

$$P(X=0) = q^{14} = (\tfrac{1}{2})^{14} = 0.000061$$

$$P(X=1) = 14q^{13}p = 14(\tfrac{1}{2})^{13}(\tfrac{1}{2}) = 0.000854$$

$$P(X=2) = 91q^{12}p^2 = 91(\tfrac{1}{2})^{12}(\tfrac{1}{2})^2 = 0.005554$$

$$P(X=3) = 364q^{11}p^3 = 364(\tfrac{1}{2})^{11}(\tfrac{1}{2})^3 = 0.022217$$

$$P(X=4) = 1001q^{10}p^4 = 1001(\tfrac{1}{2})^{10}(\tfrac{1}{2})^4 = 0.061096$$

$$P(X=5) = 2002q^9p^5 = 2002(\tfrac{1}{2})^9(\tfrac{1}{2})^5 = 0.122192$$

$$P(X=6) = 3003q^8p^6 = 3003(\tfrac{1}{2})^8(\tfrac{1}{2})^6 = 0.183289$$

Therefore,

$$\begin{aligned} P(X \le 6) &= 0.000061 + 0.000854 + 0.005554 + 0.022217 + 0.061096 \\ &\quad + 0.122192 + 0.183289 \\ &= 0.395263, \qquad \text{or } 0.3953 \end{aligned}$$

The normal-approximation solution for this problem can be determined by finding the area under the normal curve above either of these two intervals: $-0.5 \le x \le 6.5$ or $-\infty < x \le 6.5$. The first interval, $-0.5 \le x \le 6.5$, represents the exact interval in the binomial distribution (0 to 6) corrected for continuity at both ends. The second interval, $-\infty < x \le 6.5$, the one that would be used most typically, extends downward from the continuity-corrected upper boundary 6.5 to the lower limit of the normal distribution, $-\infty$.

To solve for $-0.5 \le x \le 6.5$, we use the standard-normal techniques from Section 12.12 with $\mu = np = 7$, $\sigma = \sqrt{npq} = \sqrt{3.5} = 1.8708$:

$$\begin{aligned} P(-0.5 \le X \le 6.5) &= P\left(\frac{-0.5 - np}{\sqrt{npq}} \le Z \le \frac{6.5 - np}{\sqrt{npq}}\right) \\ &= P\left(\frac{-0.5 - 7}{1.8708} \le Z \le \frac{6.5 - 7}{1.8708}\right) \\ &= P(-4.01 \le Z \le 0.27) \end{aligned}$$

From Table A.5

$$P(-4.01 \le Z \le 0) = 0.5000 \qquad P(-0.27 \le Z \le 0) = 0.1064$$

Therefore,

$$P(-4.01 \le Z \le -0.27) = 0.5000 - 0.1064 = 0.3936$$

To solve for $-\infty < x \le 6.5$, we know from the above result that

$$P(-\infty < X \le 6.5) = P(-\infty < Z \le 0.27)$$

and that

$$P(-\infty < Z \le -0.27) = 0.5000 - 0.1064 = 0.3936$$

It will almost always be true, as it is here, that the results for the two intervals are identical. Therefore, as it is easier to calculate the solution to the extremes of the normal distribution ($-\infty$ or ∞), this is the solution that is typically used.

Comparing the true binomial result with the normal approximation, we can see that they are again identical through the second decimal place:

$$P(X \le 6) = 0.3953 \approx P(-\infty < Z \le -0.27) = 0.3936$$

12.22 In a city where 48% of the registered voters are Republicans, a random sample of 200 registered voters are telephoned and each one is asked whether they are in favor of a new airport. Using normal-approximation techniques, what is the probability that fewer than 100 of the voters that are called will be Republicans?

Solution

Assuming this is a binomial experiment, then what is requested is $P(X < 100)$ in the binomial distribution where $\mu = np = 200 \times 0.48 = 96$, $\sigma^2 = npq = 200 \times 0.48 \times 0.52 = 49.92$, and $\sigma = \sqrt{npq} = \sqrt{49.92} = 7.0654$. As both np and nq are greater than 5 ($np = 96$, $nq = 104$), the normal approximation solution is appropriate (see Section 12.12).

All values of the binomial variable are integers, and so

$$P(X < 100) = P(X \leq 99)$$

Correcting for continuity [see Example 12.10(*b*)], the normal approximation is the area under the normal curve ($\mu = 96$, $\sigma^2 = 49.92$, $\sigma = 7.0654$) above the interval $-\infty < x \leq 99.5$:

$$\begin{aligned} P(-\infty < X \leq 99.5) &= P\left(-\infty < Z \leq \frac{99.5 - np}{\sqrt{npq}}\right) \\ &= P\left(-\infty < Z \leq \frac{99.5 - 96}{7.0654}\right) \\ &= P(-\infty < Z \leq 0.50) \end{aligned}$$

From Table A.5,

$$P(0 \leq Z \leq 0.50) = 0.1915$$

Thus,

$$P(-\infty < Z \leq 0.50) = 0.5000 + 0.1915 = 0.6915$$

Therefore,

$$P(X < 100) \approx 0.6915$$

12.23 A manufacturer receives electrical fuses in lots of 100,000. He has a sampling plan (see Section 11.11) that specifies that a random sample of 800 fuses should be tested from each lot, and that the lot should be accepted if the sample contains 10 or fewer defective fuses. Use normal-approximation techniques to determine the probability of accepting the lot (P_a) for a hypothetical proportion of defective fuses in the lot of $p = 0.01$.

Solution

Assuming this is a binomial experiment, then what is requested is $P_a = P(X \leq 10)$ in the binomial distribution where $\mu = np = 800 \times 0.01 = 8$, $\sigma^2 = npq = 800 \times 0.01 \times 0.99 = 7.92$, and $\sigma = \sqrt{npq} = \sqrt{7.92} = 2.8142$. As both np and nq are greater than 5 ($np = 8$, $nq = 792$), the normal-approximation solution is appropriate (see Section 12.12).

Correcting for continuity [see Example 12.10(*b*)], the normal approximation is the area under the normal curve ($\mu = 8$, $\sigma^2 = 7.92$, $\sigma = 2.8142$) above the interval $-\infty < x \leq 10.5$:

$$\begin{aligned} P(-\infty < X \leq 10.5) &= P\left(-\infty < Z \leq \frac{10.5 - np}{\sqrt{npq}}\right) \\ &= P\left(-\infty < Z \leq \frac{10.5 - 8}{2.8142}\right) \\ &= P(-\infty < Z \leq 0.89) \end{aligned}$$

From Table A.5,

$$P(0 \le Z \le 0.89) = 0.3133$$

and so

$$P(-\infty < Z \le 0.89) = 0.5000 + 0.3133 = 0.8133$$

Therefore,

$$P_a = P(X \le 10) \approx 0.8133$$

THE NORMAL APPROXIMATION TO THE POISSON DISTRIBUTION

12.24 The cable manufacturer in Example 12.11 has determined that for the 4-meter unit of cable there are $\lambda = 4.0$ defects per 4 meters. Use both the Poisson and the normal-approximate techniques to determine the probability of getting 17, 18, or 19 defects in $t = 4.5$ units of cable.

Solution

To determine the true Poisson probability $P(17 \le X \le 19)$ we use equation (11.26),

$$f(x) = \frac{\mu^x e^{-\mu}}{x!}$$

to find $f(17)$, $f(18)$, and $f(19)$ in the Poisson distribution where $\mu = \sigma^2 = \lambda t = (4.0)(4.5) = 18$, and $\sigma = \sqrt{\lambda t} = \sqrt{18} = 4.2426$:

$$f(17) = \frac{(18)^{17} e^{-18}}{17!} = 0.0936$$

$$f(18) = \frac{(18)^{18} e^{-18}}{18!} = 0.0936$$

$$f(19) = \frac{(18)^{19} e^{-18}}{19!} = 0.0887$$

From Example 12.10(a) we know that for a discrete variable such as this one,

$$\begin{aligned} P(17 \le X \le 19) &= P(X = 17) + P(X = 18) + P(X = 19) \\ &= f(17) + f(18) + f(19) \\ &= 0.0936 + 0.0936 + 0.0887 = 0.2759 \end{aligned}$$

As $\lambda t \ge 10$, we can use the normal-approximation technique from Section 12.13 with the continuity correction [see Example 12.10(b)] to find $P(16.5 \le X \le 19.5)$ in the normal distribution where $\mu = \sigma^2 = \lambda t = 18$ and $\sigma = \sqrt{18} = 4.2426$:

$$\begin{aligned} P(16.5 \le X \le 19.5) &= P\left(\frac{16.5 - \lambda t}{\sqrt{\lambda t}} \le Z \le \frac{19.5 - \lambda t}{\sqrt{\lambda t}}\right) \\ &= P\left(\frac{16.5 - 18}{4.2426} \le Z \le \frac{19.5 - 18}{4.2426}\right) \\ &= P(-0.35 \le Z \le 0.35) \end{aligned}$$

We know from Table A.5

$$P(-0.35 \le Z \le 0) = P(0 \le Z \le 0.35) = 0.1368$$

and therefore

$$P(-0.35 \le Z \le 0.35) = 2(0.1368) = 0.2736$$

Comparing the true Poisson result with the normal approximation, we see that they are identical through the second decimal place:

$$P(17 \leq X \leq 19) = 0.2759 \approx P(-0.35 \leq Z \leq 0.35) = 0.2736$$

The normal approximation is closer to the true Poisson value in this problem than it was in Example 12.11 because λt in this problem is three times larger (18 vs. 6). Recall from Section 12.13 that the larger the λt, the closer the normal approximation.

12.25 For the Geiger counter experiment in Example 11.25, the physicist determined that for the 10-second unit there are $\lambda = 5.5$ particles per 10 seconds. Use normal-approximation techniques to determine the probability of recording more than 73 particles in a 2-minute interval.

Solution

Because all values of the Poisson variable are integers,

$$P(X > 73) = P(X \geq 74) = P(74 \leq X)$$

Thus, correcting for continuity, the normal approximation is the area under the normal curve ($\mu = \sigma^2 = \lambda t = 5.5 \times 12 = 66$, $\sigma = \sqrt{\lambda t} = 8.1240$) above the interval $73.5 \leq x < \infty$:

$$P(73.5 \leq X < \infty) = 0.5000 - P\left(0 \leq Z \leq \frac{73.5 - \lambda t}{\sqrt{\lambda t}}\right)$$

$$= 0.5000 - P\left(0 \leq Z \leq \frac{73.5 - 66}{8.1240}\right)$$

$$= 0.5000 - P(0 \leq Z \leq 0.92)$$

From Table A.5

$$P(73.5 \leq X < \infty) = 0.5000 - 0.3212 = 0.1788$$

Therefore,

$$P(X > 73) \approx 0.1788$$

UNIFORM PROBABILITY DISTRIBUTIONS

12.26 For the experiment of rolling a die once, use uniform-probability techniques [see Example 12.12(*f*)] to find $P(X < 4)$.

Solution

Using equation (12.19) with $k = 6$,

$$f(x) = \frac{1}{k} = \frac{1}{6}$$

and

$$P(X < 4) = P(X = 1) + P(X = 2) + P(X = 3)$$

$$= f(1) + f(2) + f(3)$$

$$= \frac{1}{6} + \frac{1}{6} + \frac{1}{6} = \frac{3}{6} = 0.5$$

12.27 For the continuous random variable X in Example 12.13 that can assume values only in the interval $1 \leq x \leq 6$, if X has a continuous uniform probability distribution, then determine $P(X < 4)$.

Solution

As $f(x) = 0$ everywhere except in the interval $1 \le x \le 6$, and as this is a continuous probability distribution,

$$P(X < 4) = P(X \le 4) = P(1 \le X \le 4)$$

Therefore, using the equation from Example 12.13(*f*),

$$P(c \le X \le d) = \frac{d-c}{b-a}$$

with $d = 4$, $c = 1$, $b = 6$, and $a = 1$:

$$P(X < 4) = \frac{d-c}{b-a} = \frac{4-1}{6-1} = \frac{3}{5} = 0.6$$

12.28 In a study of bird navigation, the investigator places young birds in the center of a large circular cage and then determines their direction of flight from the center under different experimental conditions. The circumference of the cage is calibrated in degrees clockwise from due north, with 0° and 360° at due north. For each flight, the investigator determines the degrees clockwise from due north for the flight direction. In one experiment, the investigator provides no navigation clues and assumes therefore that the flight directions will be randomly determined. If she is correct, then the continuous random variable—degrees from due north—will be uniformly distributed over the interval $0 \le x \le 360$. Assuming she is correct, graph this distribution showing its density function $f(x)$ and $\mu \pm \sigma$, and determine the probability that a flight will be between 10° and 50° from due north.

Solution

From Section 12.15 we know that

$$f(x) = \frac{1}{b-a}, \quad \text{for } a \le x \le b, \quad \text{and } f(x) = 0 \quad \text{elsewhere}$$

$$\mu = \frac{b+a}{2}$$

$$\sigma = \sqrt{\frac{(b-a)^2}{12}}$$

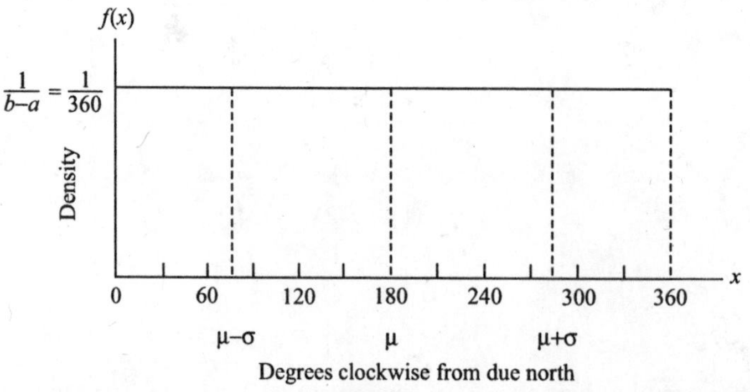

Fig. 12-19

For this problem,

$$f(x) = \frac{1}{360 - 0} = \frac{1}{360}, \text{ for } 0 \leq x \leq 360, \quad \text{and} \quad f(x) = 0 \text{ elsewhere}$$

$$\mu = \frac{360 + 0}{2} = 180$$

$$\sigma = \sqrt{\frac{(360 - 0)^2}{12}} = \sqrt{10{,}800} = 103.92$$

These values are shown on the graph of this distribution presented in Fig. 12-19.

From Example 12.13(*f*) we know that the probability that X will assume a value in the interval $c \leq x \leq d$ within the defining interval $a \leq x \leq b$ is $\frac{d - c}{b - a}$. Therefore, with $a = 0$, $b = 360$, $c = 10$, and $d = 50$,

$$P(10 \leq X \leq 50) = \frac{50 - 10}{360 - 0} = 0.11$$

12.29 You arrive at the 10th floor elevator of a building exactly 5 minutes before the start of a meeting on the 11th floor. It has been determined that the time spent waiting for an elevator on any floor of the building varies from 0 to 10 minutes, and that this continuous random variable (waiting time) is uniformly distributed over the interval $0 \leq x \leq 10$. If it takes the elevator 10 seconds to go from floor to floor and it will then take you 20 seconds to cross the 11th floor from the elevator to the meeting, what is the probability that you will be on time for the meeting?

Solution

With 30 seconds added to the interval for travel time, we have a new variable (time to meeting) that is uniformly distributed over the interval $0.5 \leq x \leq 10.5$. For this variable we want to determine $P(0.5 \leq X \leq 5)$. From Example 12.13(*f*) we know that the probability that X will assume a value in the interval $0.5 \leq x \leq 5$ within the defining interval $0.5 \leq x \leq 10.5$ is

$$P(0.5 \leq X \leq 5) = \frac{d - c}{b - a} = \frac{5 - 0.5}{10.5 - 0.5} = \frac{4.5}{10} = 0.45$$

12.30 An industrial psychologist has determined that it takes a worker between 9 and 15 minutes to complete a task on an automobile assembly line. If the continuous random variable—time to complete the task—is uniformly distributed over the interval $9 \leq x \leq 15$, then determine for this distribution: (*a*) $f(x)$, μ, σ, and the parameters, (*b*) $P(X < 13)$, (*c*) $P(4 < X < 7)$.

Solution

(*a*) Using equations (12.23), (12.24), and (12.26),

$$f(x) = \frac{1}{b - a} = \frac{1}{15 - 9} = \frac{1}{6}, \qquad \text{for } 9 \leq x \leq 15, \qquad \text{and} \qquad f(x) = 0 \qquad \text{elsewhere}$$

$$\mu = \frac{b + a}{2} = \frac{15 + 9}{2} = 12$$

$$\sigma = \sqrt{\frac{(b - a)^2}{12}} = \sqrt{\frac{(15 - 9)^2}{12}} = \sqrt{3} = 1.73$$

The parameters are $a = 9$ and $b = 15$.

(*b*) Using the equation from Example 12.13(*f*),

$$P(X < 13) = P(9 \leq X \leq 13) = \frac{d - c}{b - a} = \frac{13 - 9}{15 - 9} = 0.67$$

(*c*) $P(4 < X < 7) = 0$ because $f(x) = 0$ everywhere except in the interval $9 \leq x \leq 15$

THE EXPONENTIAL DISTRIBUTION

12.31 At the hospital in Example 12.15 on Sundays between 6 PM and 10 PM, an average of 5 emergency cases arrive per hour at the emergency room. For the exponential distribution of the random variable, time between arrivals, shown in Fig. 12-16, what is the probability that the time between one arrival and the next will be longer than 10 minutes?

Solution

As is true for any continuous probability distribution, the total area (probability) under the exponential curve (from 0 to ∞) is 1.0 [see Example 12.1(*f*)]. Thus,

$$P(X > x) = 1 - P(X \leq x)$$

We know from equation (12.31) that

$$P(X \leq x) = F(x) = 1 - e^{-\lambda x}$$

Therefore,

$$P(X > x) = 1 - (1 - e^{-\lambda x}) = e^{-\lambda x}$$

Thus, for $x =$ (10 minutes, or 0.1667 hours) and $\lambda = 5$,

$$P(X > 0.1667) = e^{-(5 \times 0.1667)} = e^{-0.8335} = 0.4345$$

Therefore, the probability is 0.4345 that the time between successive arrivals will be longer than 10 minutes.

12.32 For the emergency room in Problem 12.31, if the discrete random variable, number of arrivals, has a Poisson distribution, then what is the probability that the time to the next arrival from any arbitrary zero-point in the 6 PM to 10 PM period will be between 15 and 25 minutes?

Solution

This problem resembles the ones in Example 12.15(*b*) and Problem 12.31, except that now we are concerned with the time to the next arrival from any given instant in time rather than the time between consecutive arrivals. It is said that an exponentially distributed random variable is *memoryless*, which means that the probability of future events is independent of such factors as how long the Poisson process has been generating events or how recently an event has occurred. Thus, for this problem, the probability for time to next arrival is the same whether the zero-point is a previous arrival or an arbitrary instant in time.

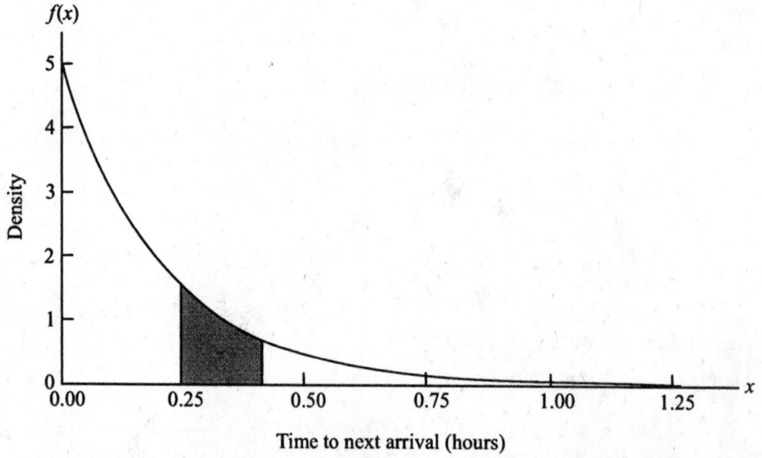

Fig. 12-20

Therefore, the exponential probability distribution for the continuous random variable time to next arrival with $\lambda = 5$ is again [see Example 12.15(*b*)]

$$f(x) = 5e^{-5x}, \quad \text{for} \quad x \geq 0, \quad \text{and} \quad f(x) = 0 \quad \text{for } x < 0$$

This exponential distribution is presented in Fig. 12-20 with the requested probability shown as the shaded area under the curve over the interval (15 minutes, or 0.25 hours) $\leq x \leq$ (25 minutes, or 0.4167 hours). The value of this probability can be determined by using equations (10.9) of Volume 1 and (12.31). Thus,

$$\begin{aligned} P(0.25 \leq X \leq 0.4167) &= F(0.4167) - F(0.25) \\ &= [1 - e^{-(5\times 0.4167)}] - [1 - e^{-(5\times 0.25)}] \\ &= [1 - e^{-2.0835}] - [1 - e^{-1.25}] \\ &= (1 - 0.1245) - (1 - 0.2865) = 0.1620 \end{aligned}$$

Therefore, the probability is 0.1620 that the time to the next arrival from any instant during the 6 PM to 10 PM interval will be between 15 and 25 minutes.

12.33 In normal use, it takes an average of 7.3 years before a type of television tube fails. If *time to failure* is exponentially distributed, what is the probability that such a tube will fail within 4 years from the start of use?

Solution

The exponential distribution is often used to model the time to failure (or *length of life*, or *lifetime*) of a system. This usage requires the assumption that the system has the memoryless property of the exponential distribution (see Problem 12.32). Here, it requires the assumption that the future lifetime of the system is independent of how long the system has been operating. While this is rarely true for equipment in the real world, the exponential distribution is a reasonable model if the average time to failure, as in this problem, is very long.

Assuming, then, that time to failure of the television tube is exponentially distributed, we know that

$$\mu = 1/\lambda = 7.3 \text{ years}$$

and thus that

$$\lambda = 1/7.3 = 0.1370$$

Therefore, using equation (12.31),

$$F(4) = P(X \leq 4) = 1 - e^{-(0.1370\times 4)} = 1 - e^{-0.5480} = 1 - 0.5781 = 0.4219$$

Thus, the probability is 0.4219 that such a tube will fail within 4 years of the start of use.

12.34 For the television tubes in Problem 12.33, what is the probability that four of them, in four independently operating television sets, will each fail within 4 years from the start of their use?

Solution

As we can assume that each failure is an independent event, we can solve this problem with the generalization of the special multiplication rule [equation (9.9), Volume 1]. Thus, as we know from Problem 12.33 that

$$P(X \leq 4) = 0.4219$$

and if we denote the four times to failure as X_1, X_2, X_3, and X_4, then

$$P[(X_1 \leq 4) \cap (X_2 \leq 4) \cap (X_3 \leq 4) \cap (X_4 \leq 4)] = (0.4219)^4 = 0.0317$$

Therefore, the probability is 0.0317 that four such tubes will independently fail within 4 years of the start of their use.

12.35 For the television tubes in Problems 12.33 and 12.34, it is known that the probability that a tube will fail in h years or less is 0.8. What is h?

Solution

From Problem 12.33 we know that

$$F(h) = P(X \leq h) = 1 - 1^{-0.1370h}$$

Therefore,

$$1 = e^{-0.1370h} = 0.8$$

and

$$e^{-0.1370h} = 0.2$$

We know from Section 1.10 in Volume 1 that

$$\text{if} \qquad \log_e n = x, \qquad \text{then} \qquad n = e^x$$

Therefore, here [see Problem 1.23(*b*), Volume 1]

$$\log_e 0.2 = -0.1370h$$
$$-1.6094 = -0.1370h$$

and so

$$h = \frac{-1.6094}{-0.1370} = 11.7474 \text{ years}$$

Supplementary Problems

THE NORMAL AND STANDARD NORMAL DISTRIBUTIONS

12.36 Using equation (12.1), calculate $f(x)$ for $X = 1$ for a normal distribution with the parameters $\mu = 2$ and $\sigma^2 = 1$.

Ans. 0.24197

12.37 For the continuous random variable X that is normally distributed with $\mu = 4.0$ sec and $\sigma = 0.4$ sec, transform the following $X = x$ values into $Z = z$ values: (*a*) $x = 5.3$ sec, (*b*) $x = 3.3$ sec.

Ans. (*a*) 3.25, (*b*) −1.75

12.38 For the continuous random variable X in Problem 12.37, transform the following $Z = z$ values back into $X = x$ values: (*a*) $z = -0.92$, (*b*) $z = 2.93$.

Ans. (*a*) 3.6 sec, (*b*) 5.2 sec

12.39 With regard to the criminal-justice study in Problem 12.13, how many of the next 100 arrested people would you expect to be tried in less than 200 days?

Ans. 30.85, or 31

12.40 From the results of the criminal-justice study in Problems 12.13 and 12.39, what are the odds against (see Problem 8.24 in Volume 1) the next arrested person being tried in less than 200 days?

Ans. $P(A)$ = probability that the arrested person will be tried in less than 200 days. $\frac{P(A')}{P(A)} = \frac{1 - 0.3085}{0.3085} = \frac{0.6915}{0.3085} \approx \frac{7}{3}$; the odds against the trial taking place in less than 200 days are approximately 7 to 3.

12.41 The QUICK-TUNE Company advertises a complete tune-up of your car for \$34.98. Furthermore, it guarantees that the tune-up will be free of charge if it is not completed in 30 minutes or less. The company knows that the time required for a tune-up is a normally distributed variable X with $\mu = 23.2$ min and $\sigma = 4.17$ min. If each tune-up actually costs QUICK-TUNE an average of \$24.00 (for parts, labor, advertising, etc.), then how much profit can the company expect to make on the next 200 tune-ups?

Ans. $P(X > 30 \text{ min} = 0.5 - 0.4484 = 0.0516$; the number of free tune-ups $= 0.0516 \times 200 = 10.32$, or 10; the cost of the free tune-ups $= 10 \times \$24 = \$240$; the profit from tune-ups that are not free $= 190 \times (\$34.98 - \$24.00) = \$2{,}086.20$; and the overall profit $= \$2{,}086.20 - \$240.00 = \$1{,}846.20$.

12.42 Each of the 380 students in a university psychology course can earn a total of 500 points in the course. This total-point score X is normally distributed and the professor is "grading on the curve." To him this means the following relationships between total scores and grades: A if the total is in the interval $x \geq (\mu + \sigma)$, B if in the interval $\mu \leq x < (\mu + \sigma)$, C if in the interval $(\mu - \sigma) \leq x < \mu$, D if in the interval $(\mu - 2\sigma) \leq x < (\mu - \sigma)$, and F if in the interval $x < (\mu - 2\sigma)$. If it turns out that the lowest possible scores for A and C are 448 and 352, respectively, then: (*a*) What are σ and μ? (*b*) How many students got Bs?

Ans. Treating this distribution "as if it were continuous": (*a*) $\sigma = 48$ and $\mu = 400$, (*b*) 129.69, or 130

ONE-TAILED AND TWO-TAILED PROBABILITIES

12.43 For the ground squirrels in Example 12.7, the variable body weight of males is normally distributed with a mean of 400 g and a standard deviation of 100 g. If $\alpha = 0.01$, then what are z_α and x_α?

Ans. $z_\alpha = 2.33$, $x_\alpha = 633$ g

12.44 For the weights of male ground squirrels in Problem 12.43, if $\alpha = 0.02$, then what are $-z_\alpha$ and $x_{1-\alpha}$?

Ans. $-z_\alpha = -2.05$, $x_{1-\alpha} = 195$ g

12.45 For the weights of male ground squirrels in Problem 12.43, if $\alpha = 0.05$, then what are $z_{\alpha/2}$, $-z_{\alpha/2}$, $x_{\alpha/2}$, and $x_{1-\alpha/2}$?

Ans. $z_{\alpha/2} = 1.96$, $-z_{\alpha/2} = -1.96$, $x_{\alpha/2} = 596$ g, $x_{1-\alpha/2} = 204$ g

THE NORMAL APPROXIMATION TO THE BINOMIAL DISTRIBUTION

12.46 For the binomial variable number of heads in 800 flips of a coin, use normal-approximation techniques to determine the probability of getting more than 415 heads.

Ans. ≈ 0.1357

12.47 You are a dermatologist who treats a specific skin condition with drug A that is known to cure the condition 64% of the time. Use normal approximation techniques to determine the probability that if drug A is used on the next 250 patients with this condition, it will cure more than 150 of them but fewer than 175.

Ans. ≈ 0.8663

12.48 A medical school receives 1,000 applications for the 130 places in its next first-year class. It must admit more than 130 students because typically only 60% of those admitted will actually join the class. If the school admits 200 applicants, then what is the probability that too many applicants—131 or more—will agree to join the class? Solve this problem with normal-approximation techniques.

Ans. ≈ 0.0643

THE NORMAL APPROXIMATION TO THE POISSON DISTRIBUTION

12.49 For the Geiger-counter experiment in Example 11.25 and Problem 12.25, the physicist calculates the average rate of recording particles in a 10-second interval to be $\lambda = 5.5$ particles. Using normal-approximation techniques, determine the probability of recording 66 particles in a 2-minute interval.

Ans. ≈ 0.0478

12.50 Thirty cars pass a crosswalk every hour. What is the probability that, for a particular 5-minute period, more than 6 cars will pass the crosswalk?

Ans. ≈ 0.0057

UNIFORM PROBABILITY DISTRIBUTIONS

12.51 For the experiment of rolling a die once, use uniform-probability techniques to find $P(5 \leq X \leq 9)$.

Ans. 0.3333

12.52 A continuous random variable X can assume values only in the interval $1 \leq x \leq 6$. If X has a continuous uniform probability distribution, then what is $P(5 \leq X \leq 9)$?

Ans. 0.2000

12.53 In the bird-navigation study in Problem 12.28, the investigator assumes that flight directions will be randomly determined and the continuous random variable—degrees from due north—will be uniformly distributed over the interval $0 \leq x \leq 360$. Assuming she is correct, determine the probability that a flight will be between 300° and 340° from due north.

Ans. 0.1111

12.54 The industrial psychologist in Problem 12.30 has determined that it takes a worker between 9 and 15 minutes to complete a task on an automobile assembly line. If the continuous random variable—time to complete the task—is uniformly distributed over the interval $9 \leq x \leq 15$, then determine for this distribution: (*a*) $P(12 < X < 14)$, (*b*) $P(X \geq 10)$.

Ans. (*a*) 0.3333, (*b*) 0.8333

THE EXPONENTIAL DISTRIBUTION

12.55 For the cable-defect experiment in Section 11.26, where the discrete random variable, number of defects, has a Poisson distribution with $\lambda = 4.0$ defects per 4 meters, what is the probability that two defects will be separated by more than 50 cm?

Ans. $e^{-0.5} = 0.6065$

12.56 For the car-passing study in Problem 12.50, where 30 cars pass a crosswalk every hour, if the discrete random variable, number of cars passing, has a Poisson distribution, then what is the probability that the time between one passing and the next will be longer than 5 minutes?

Ans. 0.0822

12.57 An ornithologist walks along a fenceline in junco habitat, and counts the number of junco nests that he can see from the fence. He counts 30 nests within a one-kilometer (1,000 meters) segment of the fence. If the discrete random variable, number of nests, has a Poisson distribution, then what is the probability that the distance between two nests will be 20 meters or less?

Ans. 0.4512

12.58 For the density of junco nests described in Problem 12.57, what is the probability that the distance from any particular point along the fenceline to the next nest will be between 10 and 30 meters?

Ans. 0.3342

CHAPTER 13

Sampling Distributions

13.1 SIMPLE RANDOM SAMPLING REVISITED

In our overview of statistics in Chapter 3 of Volume 1, we indicated that this science has two divisions: descriptive statistics (collecting, organizing, describing, and presenting data) and inferential statistics (making inferences about entire populations from sample information). We further indicated that inferential statistics has four theoretical components: probability theory, sampling theory, estimation theory, and hypothesis-testing theory. Of these elements of statistics, we have at this point completed introductions to both descriptive statistics (see Volume 1, Chapters 2 through 7) and probability theory (see Volume 1, Chapters 8 through 10, and Chapters 11 and 12 of this volume). We now go on to the remaining three components of inferential statistics: sampling theory (this chapter), estimation theory (starting with Chapter 14), and hypothesis-testing theory (starting with Chapter 16).

We briefly discussed aspects of sampling theory in Chapter 3 of Volume 1, with particular emphasis on methods of sampling, called sampling designs (see Section 3.15), that are required for inferential statistics. We indicated that there are inferential techniques, called random sampling or probability sampling, available for any version of the sampling designs (see Section 3.17), but that one of these versions, simple random sampling (see Section 3.18), is by far the most important—that indeed most methods in elementary inferential statistics are based on the assumption that the samples were taken with simple random sampling.

13.2 INDEPENDENT RANDOM VARIABLES

In Section 3.14 of Volume 1 we discussed the differences between mathematical statistics and general statistics. Mathematical statistics is an integrated, mathematical system of axioms and theorems. General statistics, by contrast, is a nonmathematical interpretation of this mathematical system developed for general, practical use by nonmathematicians. Thus, as would be expected, there is a fundamental, mathematical definition of simple random sampling, and various simplified nonmathematical interpretations of this definition (see Section 13.3).

An important component of the theoretical, mathematical definition of simple random sampling is the concept of *independent random variables*. We saw in probability theory (see Section 9.4, Volume 1) that two events A and B are independent when the occurrence of one does not affect the probability of whether or not the second will occur. Similarly, two random variables X and Y are independent if when X assumes a specific value x, this does not affect the probability of the specific value y that Y will assume.

For discrete random variables X, Y, and Z, if events $X = x$, $Y = y$, and $Z = z$ are independent for all x, y, and z, then these variables are independent, and from the generalization of the special multiplication rule [equation (9.9), Volume 1]

$$P(X = x, Y = y, Z = z) = P(X = x)P(Y = y)P(Z = z)$$

For continuous random variables X, Y, and Z, if the events $X \leq x$, $Y \leq y$, and $Z \leq z$ are independent of all x, y, and z, then

$$P(X \leq x, Y \leq y, Z \leq z) = P(X \leq x)P(Y \leq y)P(Z \leq z)$$

13.3 MATHEMATICAL AND NONMATHEMATICAL DEFINITIONS OF SIMPLE RANDOM SAMPLING

The theoretical, *mathematical definition of simple random sampling* from a population is stated in the language of random variables and probability distributions. Recall from Sections 10.5 and 10.6 of volume 1 that probability distributions are the mathematical models for population relative frequency distributions. Thus, if a population of measurements is generated by a random variable X, then the probability distribution for that variable is the mathematical model for that population distribution.

If we view the taking of a sample of size n from a population to be a statistical experiment with n trials, then the outcome of each trial is an observation on the population random variable X. Because each of the n observations is randomly determined (see Section 10.1 of Volume 1), the n observations correspond to a set of n random variables $X_1, X_2, \ldots, X_n$. These n random variables are said to form a simple random sample when two conditions are met: (1) the n random variables are independent (see Section 13.2), and (2) the n random variables all have the same probability distribution as the population random variable X. If these two conditions are met, then the set of n variables $X_1, X_2, \ldots, X_n$ is called a simple random sample, having specific values $X_1 = x_1$, $X_2 = x_2, \ldots, X_n = x_n$.

Another way in which the two conditions of the mathematical definition are stated is: (1) the n successive trials of the experiment are independent, and (2) the probability distribution of X remains constant over trials.

In Section 3.18 of Volume 1 we gave a common intuitive-level, *nonmathematical definition of simple random sampling* from a population:

> Simple random sampling is a method of sampling in which at every selection from the population all remaining elements (sampling units) in the population have the same probability of being included in the sample.

Two similar nonmathematical definitions found in general statistics books are:

> A sample of n elements from a population is a simple random sample if it is true that all possible samples of n elements from the population had the same probability of being selected.

> A sample of n elements from a popoulation is a simple random sample if it is true that all elements in the population had equal and independent probabilities of being selected.

These nonmathematical definitions are attempts to interpret the same fundamental mathematical definition. If the conditions specified in these nonmathematical definitions are satisfied, then, within limits that we will discuss in the following sections of this chapter, it can be accepted that the sampling is simple random sampling.

EXAMPLE 13.1 The first nine letters of the alphabet (A through I) are printed separately on otherwise identical cards, and these cards are placed in a bowl. If three cards are drawn blindly one at a time from the bowl, then this is sampling without replacement from a finite population (see Volume 1, Section 3.16). (*a*) By a nonmathematical definition, is this a simple random sample? (*b*) How many different three-letter samples could be drawn in this way from the nine letters? (*c*) What is the probability of each of these three-letter samples?

Solution

(*a*) If the three letters (cards) are drawn in such a way that on each selection all remaining letters have an equal probability of being selected (i.e., applying the first version of the nonmathematical definition given above), then such a sample is a simple random sample.

(*b*) As the order of selection does not matter, each such sample is one of the possible *combinations* of $N = 9$ distinct objects (letters) taken $n = 3$ at a time. Therefore, using equation (9.20) of Volume 1, there are these many possible three-letter simple random samples (combinations) from the nine letters:

$$_NC_n = \binom{N}{n} = \frac{N!}{n!(N-n)!} = \frac{9!}{3!(9-3)!} = \frac{9 \times 8 \times 7}{3 \times 2 \times 1} = 84$$

(*c*) For each of the 84 possible simple random samples, the specific letters can be drawn in any order. The probability of the first letter (L_1) will be

$$P(L_1) = \frac{3}{9}$$

The probability of the second letter (L_2) given that L_1 has been taken is

$$P(L_2|L_1) = \frac{2}{8}$$

And finally, the probability of the third letter (L_3) given that both L_1 and L_2 have been taken is

$$P(L_3|L_2 \cap L_1) = \frac{1}{7}$$

To find the probability of getting this sample ($L_1 \cap L_2 \cap L_3$) we use equation (9.5) of Volume 1:

$$P(L_1 \cap L_2 \cap L_3) = P(L_1)P(L_2|L_1)P(L_3|L_2 \cap L_1) = \frac{3}{9} \times \frac{2}{8} \times \frac{1}{7} = 0.011905$$

EXAMPLE 13.2 In Example 13.1 if, instead of taking the three-letter sample one letter at a time, each of the 84 possible samples had been printed separately on 84 otherwise identical cards and one card had been blindly selected, then: (*a*) By a nonmathematical definition, is this a simple random sample? (*b*) What is the probability of each of the 84 possible samples being the one selected?

Solution

(*a*) By the second version of a nonmathematical definition of a simple random sample given above, as all possible cards had an equal probability of being taken, this is a simple random sample.

(*b*) The probability of selecting each of the 84 possible three-letter samples is

$$\frac{1}{\binom{N}{n}} = \frac{1}{\binom{9}{3}} = \frac{1}{84} = 0.011905$$

This is the same probability that we got for taking the three letters one at a time. It illustrates the general rule for sampling from a finite population without replacement:

> Simple random samples can be taken either one at a time if all remaining population elements have the same probability of selection, or as an entire sample at once if all such samples have the same probability of selection.

13.4 ASSUMPTIONS OF THE SAMPLING TECHNIQUE

In order to make valid probability decisions using inferential techniques, certain assumptions must be satisfied (see Volume 1, Section 3.13). One assumption of the sampling technique that underlies all inferential techniques is the *assumption of independence*: the selection of one element from a population for a sample does not affect the probability of the selection of any other element. A second assumption important to inferential statistics is the *assumption of random sampling*: a simple random sample was taken from the population. These two assumptions are not the same. While independence of observations within the sample is required for all inferential techniques, there are inferential techniques available for forms of probability sampling other than simple random sampling (see Volume 1, Section 3.17).

When a simple random sample has been taken, it would seem that both assumptions have automatically been satisfied. Independence is required for a theoretical simple random sample (see Section 13.3) and this same condition of independence is stated in at least one common nonmathematical definition (the third version given in Section 13.3). While indeed the assumption of independence of observations is satisfied when taking a simple random sample either from an infinite population or from a finite population with replacement, this assumption is not satisfied when taking a simple random sample from a finite population without replacement (see Examples 13.1 and 13.2).

Simple random sampling from an infinitely large population is the ideal sampling situation, as it satisfies all the assumptions of the sampling technique. One can assume that: (1) the distribution of the population remains constant over sampling whether this sampling is with or without replacement, (2) on every selection from this constant population each remaining element of the population has an equal probability of being selected, (3) all possible combinations of elements in the population have an equal probability of being selected, and (4) all elements in the population have an equal and independent probability of being selected.

Simple random sampling from a finite population with replacement is treated as if it were simple random sampling from an infinite population. Because elements are replaced between selections, the distribution of the population remains constant and it can be assumed that all conditions given above for sampling from an infinite population are satisfied.

Simple random sampling from a finite population without replacement violates the independence assumption because the removal of one element changes the probability of all remaining elements. Inferential techniques, however, are robust (see Volume 1, Problem 3.14) with regard to this violation: if the finite population has a size N that is large compared to the sample size n, then the violation is not a problem. Some statistics books specify that sampling without replacement is not a problem unless n is more than 5% of N ($n > 0.05N$).

In subsequent problems in this and later chapters, *when the term random sample or sample is used it will mean simple random sample. Whether the sampling was defined mathematically or nonmathematically, whether it was from a finite or an infinite population, and whether it was taken with or without replacement, will be apparent from the context.*

13.5 THE RANDOM VARIABLE $\bar{X}$

Both a population and a sample taken from it have an arithmetic mean. The population mean is a parameter defined by equation (3.2) of Volume 1:

$$\mu = \frac{\sum_{i=1}^{N} x_i}{N}$$

and the sample mean is a statistic defined by equation (3.1) of Volume 1:

$$\bar{x} = \frac{\sum_{i=1}^{n} x_i}{n}$$

EXAMPLE 13.3 The following is a five-element population of numbers ($N = 5$): 0, 1, 2, 3, 4. (*a*) Using Table A.1 in the Appendix of Volume 1 and the technique from Example 3.5 of Volume 1 but with sampling with replacement, take five different two-number ($n = 2$) random samples from this population. (*b*) Determine the arithmetic mean of this population and of each of the five samples taken from it. (*c*) From the five sample means, determine the overall mean.

Solution

(*a*) We first determine a starting place in Table A.1 of Volume 1: the intersection of column 37 and row 17, the number 51. We then go down the left side of column 37 from this starting place, taking with replacement (i.e., accepting repeated numbers) five different pairs (samples) from this population as they appear: (2, 2), (4, 2), (0, 1), (3, 2), (2, 1).

(*b*) Using equation (3.2) of Volume 1, the arithmetic mean of the population is

$$\mu = \frac{0+1+2+3+4}{5} = 2.0$$

Using equation (3.1) of Volume 1, the arithmetic means of the samples are:

$$\bar{x}_1 = \frac{2+2}{2} = 2.0, \quad \bar{x}_2 = \frac{4+2}{2} = 3.0, \quad \bar{x}_3 = \frac{0+1}{2} = 0.5, \quad \bar{x}_4 = \frac{3+2}{2} = 2.5, \quad \bar{x}_5 = \frac{2+1}{2} = 1.5$$

(*c*) We indicated in Section 6.10 of Volume 1 that if a population has been sampled several times and arithmetic means have been calculated for each sample, then the best estimate of the population mean from these samples is the overall mean calculated with equation (6.19) of Volume 1:

$$\text{Overall mean} = \frac{\sum_{i=1}^{5} n_i\bar{x}_i}{\sum_{i=1}^{5} n_i}$$

$$= \frac{(2 \times 2.0) + (2 \times 3.0) + (2 \times 0.5) + (2 \times 2.5) + (2 \times 1.5)}{2+2+2+2+2} = 1.9$$

This example illustrates that, whereas a population of numbers has only one arithmetic mean μ, which is a constant, a series of random samples each of size n taken from this population has an arithmetic mean $\bar{x}$ for each sample, and the means vary over the series of samples. If we consider each sample mean as the randomly determined quantitative outcome of a statistical experiment, then $\bar{X}$ is a random variable (see Volume 1, Section 10.1). As with other random variables, we must distinguish between the random variable $\bar{X}$ and the real-number values $\bar{x}$ that it can assume. Thus, for the sampling problem in Example 13.3, $\bar{X}$ can assume 25 values (see Example 13.4) among which are: $\bar{x}_1 = 2.0$, $\bar{x}_2 = 3.0$, $\bar{x}_3 = 0.5$, $\bar{x}_4 = 2.5$, and $\bar{x}_5 = 1.5$.

13.6 THEORETICAL AND EMPIRICAL SAMPLING DISTRIBUTIONS OF THE MEAN

If a population from which a random sample is taken was generated by a discrete random variable X, then $\bar{X}$ (see Section 13.5) is also a discrete random variable. As with other such variables, $\bar{X}$ has a discrete probability distribution defined by a probability mass function $[f(\bar{x})]$ with a domain consisting of all possible values that $\bar{X}$ can assume ($\bar{X} = \bar{x}$) and a range consisting of the probabilities of occurrence assigned to these values $[P(\bar{X} = \bar{x})]$ (see Volume 1, Section 10.3).

If the sampled population was generated by a continuous random variable X, then $\bar{X}$ is also a continuous random variable. As with other such variables, $\bar{X}$ has a continuous probability distribution defined by a probability density function $[f(\bar{x})]$ with a domain consisting of all the infinite and uncountable values that $\bar{X}$ can assume ($\bar{X} = \bar{x}$) and a range consisting of the probability densities assigned to these values (see Volume 1, Section 10.4).

A *theoretical sampling distribution of the mean* is a probability distribution (discrete or continuous) consisting of the $f(\bar{x})$ values (probabilities or densities) assigned to all the values that $\bar{X}$ can assume. It is called a sampling distribution of the mean because it represents the means of repeated samples of a constant size n taken from the population. It is called a theoretical sampling distribution because it includes all possible means, and typically this inclusion requires mathematical derivation from a theoretical model.

An *empirical sampling distribution of the mean*, by contrast, is developed by actually taking repeated random samples of a constant size n from a population, calculating an arithmetic mean $\bar{X} = \bar{x}$ for each sample, and then constructing a relative frequency distribution of these means. Recall from Sections 10.5 and 10.6 in Volume 1 that probability distributions are used as mathematical models for population relative frequency distributions and that, as the sample size increases, the sample relative frequency distribution becomes more and more similar to the probability distribution. In sampling theory, probability distributions are used as mathematical models for empirical population sampling distributions, and as the number of empirically taken samples of size n increases toward the often impossible goal of "all possible samples" that could be taken from the population, the empirical sampling distribution of the mean approaches the theoretical sampling distribution of the mean.

Theoretical sampling distributions are available for most of the descriptive statistics presented in Chapters 6 and 7 in Volume 1, and they can be approximated by appropriate empirical sampling distributions. Thus, for example, the sample variance s^2 (see Volume 1, Section 7.7) of a random sample of constant size n from a population of size N is actually a random variable S^2 that can take on specific values $s^2(S^2 = s^2)$, and there is a theoretical sampling distribution of the variance that can be approximated by an empirical sampling distribution of the variance. In this chapter we concentrate on the sampling distribution of the mean, but we will also consider the *sampling distribution of the sample sum* (see Section 13.19), *the number of successes* (see Section 13.22), and *the proportion* (see Section 13.23). Other important sampling distributions, introduced in later chapters, include the *t distribution* (Chapter 14), the *chi-square distribution* (Chapter 15), the *F distribution* (Chapter 17), and the *sampling distribution of the difference between two means* (Chapter 17).

A typical statistical analysis involves a population parameter with an unknown value, and only one sample available for making inferences about the value of the parameter [i.e., an estimation problem or a hypothesis-testing problem (see Volume 1, Section 3.6)]. A value of a sample statistic is easily calculated to estimate the value of the parameter, but how good is this estimate—how close is it to the real value of the parameter? Is this sample a "typical" random sample or is it an extreme version? Do the values of the sample statistic vary widely with repeated sampling? These and other such questions are answered in inferential statistics by means of theoretical sampling distributions. Indeed, theoretical sampling distributions are the foundations of virtually all forms of statistical inference.

EXAMPLE 13.4 Use sampling with replacement to develop the discrete theoretical sampling distribution of the mean for random samples of size $n = 2$ from the population of numbers in Example 13.3: 0, 1, 2, 3, 4. Develop the distribution by completing the following steps: (*a*) list all such possible samples that can be taken from the population, along with the arithmetic mean of each, (*b*) summarize these arithmetic means in frequency and relative frequency distributions, (*c*) calculate the probability of selection for each mean and present the resulting sampling distribution in both a probability table and a probability histogram (see Volume 1, Section 10.3).

Solution

(*a*) From the counting rule: multiplication principle (see Volume 1, Section 9.12), we know that there are $(n_1 \times n_2 = 5 \times 5 = 25)$ possible random samples of size $n = 2$ from this population if sampling is done with replacement. These samples and their means [(sample) $\bar{x}$] are

[(0, 0) 0.0]	[(1, 0) 0.5]	[(2, 0) 1.0]	[(3, 0) 1.5]	[(4, 0) 2.0]
[(0, 1) 0.5]	[(1, 1) 1.0]	[(2, 1) 1.5]	[(3, 1) 2.0]	[(4, 1) 2.5]
[(0, 2) 1.0]	[(1, 2) 1.5]	[(2, 2) 2.0]	[(3, 2) 2.5]	[(4, 2) 3.0]
[(0, 3) 1.5]	[(1, 3) 2.0]	[(2, 3) 2.5]	[(3, 3) 3.0]	[(4, 3) 3.5]
[(0, 4) 2.0]	[(1, 4) 2.5]	[(2, 4) 3.0]	[(3, 4) 3.5]	[(4, 4) 4.0]

(*b*) The requested frequency and relative frequency distributions are given in Table 13.1, where $N_{\bar{x}}$ denotes the number of possible $\bar{x}$ values.

Table 13.1

Sample mean $\bar{x}_i$	Frequency f_i	Relative frequency $f_i/N_{\bar{x}}$
0.0	1	0.04
0.5	2	0.08
1.0	3	0.12
1.5	4	0.16
2.0	5	0.20
2.5	4	0.16
3.0	3	0.12
3.5	2	0.08
4.0	1	0.04
$\sum$	25	1.00

(*c*) Because in random sampling all possible samples have the same probability of being selected (see Section 13.3), each of the 25 possible samples has this probability of being selected: $1/25 = 0.04$. As these samples are mutually exclusive events, we know from Property (4) of the set theory interpretation of probability (see Volume 1, Section 8.6) that the probability of selecting any of the k samples $(S_1, S_2, \ldots, S_k)$ that have the same mean is

$$P(S_1 \cup S_2 \cup \cdots \cup S_k) = P(S_1) + P(S_2) + \cdots + P(S_k)$$

Therefore, to get the probability of a given mean, we add the probabilities of all samples that have that mean. Thus,

$$P(\bar{X} = 0.0) = 0.04$$
$$P(\bar{X} = 0.5) = 0.04 + 0.04 = 0.08$$
$$P(\bar{X} = 1.0) = 0.04 + 0.04 + 0.04 = 0.12$$

and so on. The probabilities so-calculated for each mean are presented as a theoretical sampling distribution in Table 13.2 and as a histogram in Fig. 13-1. Note that the relative frequency distribution

Table 13.2

Sample mean $\bar{x}$	Probability $f(\bar{x})$
0.0	0.04
0.5	0.08
1.0	0.12
1.5	0.16
2.0	0.20
2.5	0.16
3.0	0.12
3.5	0.08
4.0	0.04
$\sum$	1.00

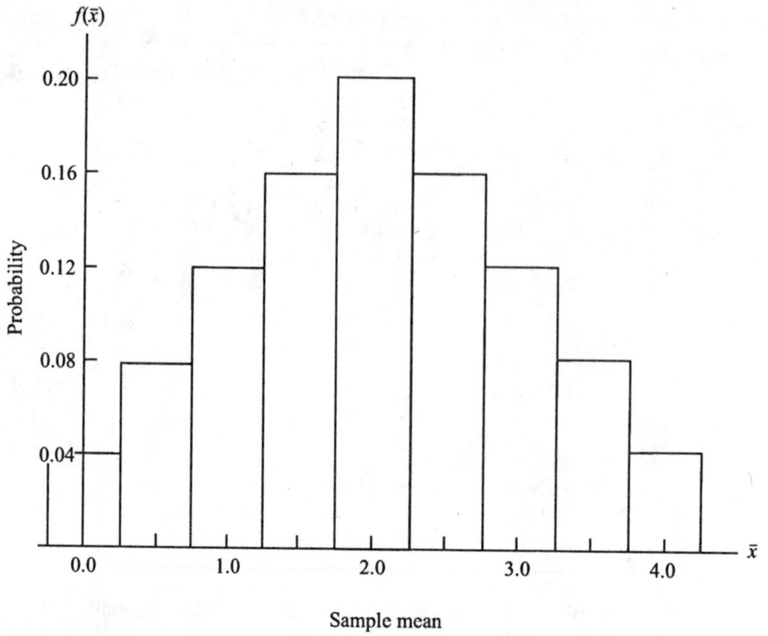

Fig. 13-1

(see Table 13.1) and the theoretical sampling distribution (see Table 13.2 and Fig. 13-1) are the same.

EXAMPLE 13.5 Use sampling without replacement to develop the discrete theoretical sampling distribution of the mean for random samples of size $n = 2$ from the population of numbers in Example 13.3: 0, 1, 2, 3, 4. Develop the distribution by completing the following steps: (*a*) list all such possible samples that can be taken from the population along with the arithmetic mean of each, (*b*) summarize these arithmetic means in frequency and relative frequency distributions, (*c*) calculate the probability of selection for each mean and present the resulting sampling distribution in both a probability table and a probability histogram.

Solution

(*a*) When random sampling without replacement from a finite population, the order of values is not considered. For example, in this problem the sample (0, 4) is considered to be identical to (4, 0). Thus, the total number of possible random samples of constant size n from a finite population of size N taken without replacement is determined by the counting rule: combinations [equation (9.20), Volume 1].

$$_NC_n = \binom{N}{n} = \frac{N!}{n!(N-n)!}$$

Solving for $N = 5$ and $n = 2$, the total number of possible samples is

$$_5C_2 = \binom{5}{2} = \frac{5!}{2!(5-2)!} = \frac{5 \times 4}{2 \times 1} = 10$$

These samples and their means [(sample) $\bar{x}$] are

[(0, 1) 0.5]	[(1, 3) 2.0]
[(0, 2) 1.0]	[(1, 4) 2.5]
[(0, 3) 1.5]	[(2, 3) 2.5]
[(0, 4) 2.0]	[(2, 4) 3.0]
[(1, 2) 1.5]	[(3, 4) 3.5]

(*b*) The requested frequency and relative frequency distributions are given in Table 13.3, where $N_{\bar{x}}$ is again the number of possible values of $\bar{x}$.

Table 13.3

Sample mean $\bar{x}_i$	Frequency f_i	Relative frequency $f_i/N_{\bar{x}}$
0.5	1	0.1
1.0	1	0.1
1.5	2	0.2
2.0	2	0.2
2.5	2	0.2
3.0	1	0.1
3.5	1	0.1
$\sum$	10	1.0

(*c*) The logic of the probability calculations is the same as in Example 13.4(*c*). Now the probability of each possible sample and, therefore, its mean is $1/10 = 0.1$, and thus

$$P(\bar{X} = 0.5) = 0.1$$
$$P(\bar{X} = 1.0) = 0.1$$
$$P(\bar{X} = 1.5) = 0.1 + 0.1 = 0.2$$

and so on. The probabilities so-calculated for each mean are presented as a theoretical sampling distribution of the mean in Table 13.4 and the probability histogram in Fig. 13-2. Again note, as in Example 13.4, that the relative frequency distribution (see Table 13.3) and theoretical sampling distribution (see Table 13.4 and Fig. 13-2) are the same.

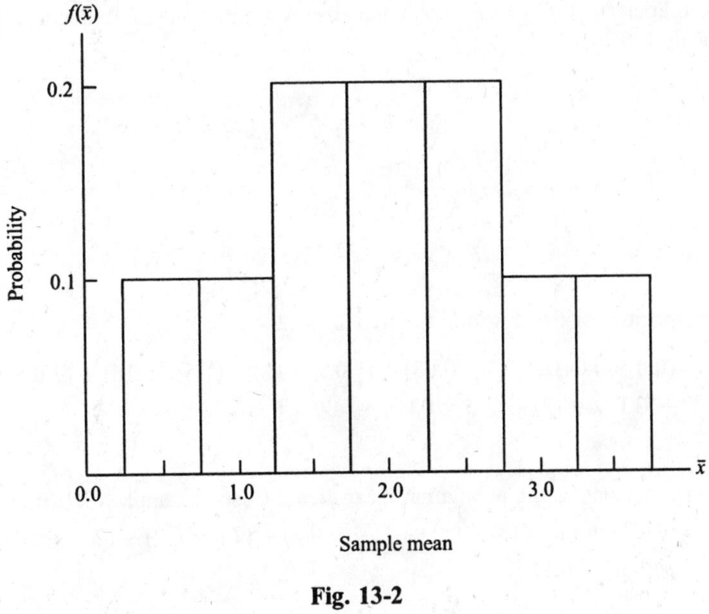

Fig. 13-2

Table 13.4

Sample mean $\bar{x}$	Probability $f(\bar{x})$
0.5	0.1
1.0	0.1
1.5	0.2
2.0	0.2
2.5	0.2
3.0	0.1
3.5	0.1
Σ	1.0

13.7 THE MEAN OF THE SAMPLING DISTRIBUTION OF THE MEAN

A theoretical sampling distribution of the mean is a probability distribution (discrete or continuous) consisting of the $f(\bar{x})$ values (probabilities or densities) assigned to all the values that $\bar{X}$ can assume (see Section 13.6). For any such theoretical sampling distribution of the mean, whether discrete or continuous, it can be proven mathematically that the mean $\mu_{\bar{x}}$ [or expected value $E(\bar{X})$] of the theoretical sampling distribution is always equal to the mean μ of the population from which the samples were taken. Thus,

$$E(\bar{X}) = \mu_{\bar{x}} = \mu \tag{13.1}$$

EXAMPLE 13.6 Using the definition of $E(X)$ from Section 10.9, Volume 1, show that $\mu_{\bar{x}} = \mu$ for the theoretical sampling distribution in: (*a*) Table 13.2, (*b*) Table 13.4.

Solution

(*a*) In Section 10.9 of Volume 1 we said

If X is a discrete random variable that can take on values $x_1, x_2, \ldots, x_k$ with the respective probabilities $f(x_1), f(x_2), \ldots, f(x_k)$, then the expected value of X, denoted by $E(X)$, is [Volume 1, equation (10.10)]

$$E(X) = \mu = \sum_{i=1}^{k} x_i f(x_i) = \sum_x x f(x)$$

Modifying the equation to solve for $E(\bar{X})$, we get

$$E(\bar{X}) = \mu_{\bar{x}} = \sum_{i=1}^{k} \bar{x}_i f(\bar{x}_i) = \sum_{\bar{x}} \bar{x} f(\bar{x}) \tag{13.2}$$

Using this equation for the distribution in Table 13.2,

$$\begin{aligned} E(\bar{X}) = \mu_{\bar{x}} &= (0.0 \times 0.04) + (0.5 \times 0.08) + (1.0 \times 0.12) + (1.5 \times 0.16) + (2.0 \times 0.20) + (2.5 \times 0.16) \\ &\quad + (3.0 \times 0.12) + (3.5 \times 0.08) + (4.0 \times 0.04) \\ &= 2.0 \end{aligned}$$

This value is the same as the population mean $\mu = 2.0$ [see Example 13.3(*b*)].

(*b*) $$\begin{aligned} E(\bar{X}) = \mu_{\bar{x}} &= (0.5 \times 0.1) + (1.0 \times 0.1) + (1.5 \times 0.2) + (2.0 \times 0.2) + (2.5 \times 0.2) + (3.0 \times 0.1) \\ &\quad + (3.5 \times 0.1) \\ &= 2.0 \end{aligned}$$

13.8 THE ACCURACY OF AN ESTIMATOR

Any sample statistic that gives an estimate of a population parameter is called an *estimator*. The typical symbols used to denote the parameter and its estimator are: θ (the Greek letter *theta*) for the parameter and $\hat{\theta}$ (read "theta-hat") for its estimator. Of the various symbols used to denote a specific estimate or value of $\hat{\theta}$, we will use $\hat{\theta}^*$.

In Section 2.14 of Volume 1 we said that in statistics the accuracy of a measurement is its closeness to the true measurement, and that this property is determined primarily by the presence or absence of systematic errors, or measurement bias (see Volume 1, Section 2.13). Similarly, the *accuracy of an estimator* $\hat{\theta}$ is determined by the closeness of the mean of its theoretical sampling distribution [expected value $E(\hat{\theta})$] to the population parameter θ that it is estimating. Thus, the accuracy of an estimator is measured by $|E(\hat{\theta}) - \theta|$, which is the absolute value of the distance between $E(\hat{\theta})$ and θ.

The term $E(\hat{\theta}) - \theta$ is called the *bias of the estimator* $\hat{\theta}$, and, as with measurement bias, this bias is considered to be a consequence of systematic errors. When $E(\hat{\theta}) = \theta$ or $E(\hat{\theta}) - \theta = 0$, the estimator is said to be *unbiased*, or to have the *property of unbiasedness*. Thus, $\hat{\theta}$ is a perfectly accurate estimator of θ when it is unbiased.

In Example 13.6 we demonstrated, by showing that $E(\bar{X}) = \mu$, that the estimator $\hat{\theta} = \bar{X}$ is a perfectly accurate (unbiased) estimator of the parameter $\theta = \mu$.

13.9 THE VARIANCE OF THE SAMPLING DISTRIBUTION OF THE MEAN: INFINITE POPULATION OR SAMPLING WITH REPLACEMENT

When sampling is from an infinite population or from a finite population with replacement, it can be proven mathematically that the variance of the sampling distribution of the mean for these samples is

$$E[(\bar{X} - \mu_{\bar{x}})^2] = \sigma_{\bar{x}}^2 = \frac{\sigma^2}{n} \tag{13.3}$$

for all possible random samples of size n from a population of size N that has a mean μ and a variance σ^2.

EXAMPLE 13.7 Using the definition of $E[(X - \mu)^2]$ from Section 10.11 of Volume 1, show for the theoretical sampling distribution of the mean in Table 13.2 that $\sigma_{\bar{x}}^2 = \dfrac{\sigma^2}{n}$.

Solution

In Section 10.11 of Volume 1 we said that

> If X is a discrete random variable that can take on the value $x_1, x_2, \ldots, x_k$ with respective probabilities $f(x_1), f(x_2), \ldots, f(x_k)$, then the variance of X is
>
> $$E[(X - \mu)^2] = \sigma^2 = \sum_x (x - \mu)^2 f(x)$$

Modifying this equation to solve for $E[(\bar{X} - \mu_{\bar{x}})^2]$, we get

$$E[(\bar{X} - \mu_{\bar{x}})^2] = \sigma_{\bar{x}}^2 = \sum_{\bar{x}} (\bar{x} - \mu_{\bar{x}})^2 f(\bar{x}) \tag{13.4}$$

Using this equation for the distribution in Table 13.2 with $\mu_{\bar{x}} = 2.0$ [see Example 13.6(*a*)],

$$\begin{aligned} E[(\bar{X} - \mu_{\bar{x}})^2] &= [(0.0 - 2.0)^2 0.04] + [(0.5 - 2.0)^2 0.08] + [(1.0 - 2.0)^2 0.12] \\ &\quad + [(1.5 - 2.0)^2 0.16] + [(2.0 - 2.0)^2 0.20] + [(2.5 - 2.0)^2 0.16] \\ &\quad + [(3.0 - 2.0)^2 0.12] + [(3.5 - 2.0)^2 0.08] + [(4.0 - 2.0)^2 0.04] \\ &= 1.00 \end{aligned}$$

To show that this value is equal to σ^2/n, we first calculate σ^2 for the population: 0, 1, 2, 3, 4, using equation (7.12) of Volume 1 with $\mu = 2.0$ [see Example 13.3(*b*)]:

$$\sigma^2 = \frac{\sum_{i=1}^{N}(x_i - \mu)^2}{N}$$
$$= \frac{(0 - 2.0)^2 + (1 - 2.0)^2 + (2 - 2.0)^2 + (3 - 2.0)^2 + (4 - 2.0)^2}{5} = 2.00$$

Therefore, as $n = 2$,

$$\sigma_{\bar{x}}^2 = \frac{\sigma^2}{n} = \frac{2.00}{2} = 1.00$$

13.10 THE VARIANCE OF THE SAMPLING DISTRIBUTION OF THE MEAN: FINITE POPULATION SAMPLED WITHOUT REPLACEMENT

If sampling is done without replacement from a finite population, then it can be proven mathematically that the variance of the sampling distribution of the mean for these samples is

$$E[(\bar{X} - \mu_{\bar{x}})^2] = \sigma_{\bar{x}}^2 = \frac{\sigma^2}{n} \times \frac{N - n}{N - 1} \tag{13.5}$$

for all possible samples of size n from a population of size N that has a mean μ and a variance σ^2. In this equation, the factor $\frac{N - n}{N - 1}$ is called the *square of the finite population correction factor.*

EXAMPLE 13.8 Using equation (13.4), show for the theoretical sampling distribution of the mean in Table 13.4 that $\sigma_{\bar{x}}^2 = \frac{\sigma^2}{n} \times \frac{N - n}{N - 1}$.

Solution

Equation (13.4) states that

$$E[(\bar{X} - \mu_{\bar{x}})^2] = \sigma_{\bar{x}}^2 = \sum_{\bar{x}}(\bar{x} - \mu_{\bar{x}})^2 f(\bar{x})$$

Therefore, for the distribution in Table 13.4 in which $\mu_{\bar{x}} = 2.0$ [see Example 13.6(*b*)],

$$\begin{aligned}\sigma_{\bar{x}}^2 &= [(0.5 - 2.0)^2 0.1] + [(1.0 - 2.0)^2 0.1] + [(1.5 - 2.0)^2 0.2] + [(2.0 - 2.0)^2 0.2] + [(2.5 - 2.0)^2 0.2] \\ &\quad + [(3.0 - 2.0)^2 0.1] + [(3.5 - 2.0)^2 0.1] \\ &= 0.75\end{aligned}$$

To show that this value is the same as $\frac{\sigma^2}{n} \times \frac{N - n}{N - 1}$, we use $n = 2$, $N = 5$, and the population variance $\sigma^2 = 2.00$ from Example 13.7

$$\sigma_{\bar{x}}^2 = \frac{\sigma^2}{n} \times \frac{N - n}{N - 1} = \frac{2.00}{2} \times \frac{5 - 2}{5 - 1} = 0.75$$

When sampling from a finite population without replacement, the variance of the sampling distribution of the mean can be calculated without the square of the finite population correction factor if the population size N is large compared to the sample size n. This is true because if n is held constant as N is increased, then $\frac{N - n}{N - 1}$ approaches 1.0 as a limit. For this reason, many statistics books state as a rule of thumb that it is not necessary to use the square of the correction factor when n is less or equal to 5% of N ($n \leq 0.05N$).

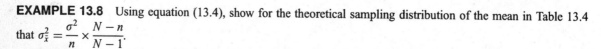

13.11 THE STANDARD ERROR OF THE MEAN

If a random sample is taken from a population and the specific value $\hat{\theta}^*$ of an estimator $\hat{\theta}$ (see Section 13.8) is calculated from this sample, then the difference between $\hat{\theta}^*$ and the parameter θ that it is estimating, $\hat{\theta}^* - \theta$, is called the *sampling error.* If the estimator is unbiased, then sampling error is also called *random error* because it is due to random fluctuations of the estimate from sample to sample. Thus, for such a random sample, if a value of the sample mean ($\bar{X} = \bar{x}$) is calculated to estimate the population parameter μ, then the difference between this estimate and μ (or, $\bar{x} - \mu$) is called sampling error or random error ($\bar{X}$ is an unbiased estimator of μ).

Recall from Section 7.9 of Volume 1 that the positive square root of the population variance ($\sqrt{\sigma^2} = \sigma$) is called the standard deviation because it is a measure of the standard, or typical, deviation of any measurement from its population mean ($x_i - \mu$, see Volume 1, Section 6.4). Similarly, the positive square root of the variance of the sampling distribution of the mean

$$\sqrt{E[(\bar{X} - \mu_{\bar{x}})^2]} = \sigma_{\bar{x}} = \sqrt{\sigma_{\bar{x}}^2} \tag{13.6}$$

is called the *standard error of the mean* because it is a measure of the standard, or typical, sampling error—the amount that a sample mean estimate can be expected to vary, from sample to sample, about the population mean.

When sampling from an infinite population or a finite population with replacement, we know that [equation (13.3)]

$$\sigma_{\bar{x}}^2 = \frac{\sigma^2}{n}$$

Therefore, for these sampling conditions the standard error of the mean is

$$\sigma_{\bar{x}} = \sqrt{\sigma_{\bar{x}}^2} = \sqrt{\frac{\sigma^2}{n}} = \frac{\sqrt{\sigma^2}}{\sqrt{n}} = \frac{\sigma}{\sqrt{n}} \tag{13.7}$$

EXAMPLE 13.9 For the theoretical sampling distribution of the mean in Table 13.2, determine the standard error of the mean both by taking the square root of the variance of the sampling distribution, $\sigma_{\bar{x}}^2$, and by using equation (13.7).

Solution

In Example 13.7, we found that $\sigma_{\bar{x}}^2 = 1.00$. Therefore, the standard error of the mean is

$$\sigma_{\bar{x}} = \sqrt{\sigma_{\bar{x}}^2} = \sqrt{1.00} = 1.00$$

Calculating $\sigma_{\bar{x}}$ using equation (13.7) with $\sigma = \sqrt{2.00}$ (see Example 13.7),

$$\sigma_{\bar{x}} = \frac{\sigma}{\sqrt{n}} = \frac{\sqrt{2.00}}{\sqrt{2}} = 1.00$$

For sampling without replacement from a finite population, we know that [equation (13.5)]

$$\sigma_{\bar{x}}^2 = \frac{\sigma^2}{n} \times \frac{N-n}{N-1}$$

and so, under these sampling conditions, the standard error of the mean is

$$\sigma_{\bar{x}} = \sqrt{\sigma_{\bar{x}}^2} = \sqrt{\frac{\sigma^2}{n} \times \frac{N-n}{N-1}} = \sqrt{\frac{\sigma^2}{n}}\sqrt{\frac{N-n}{N-1}} = \frac{\sigma}{\sqrt{n}} \times \sqrt{\frac{N-n}{N-1}} \tag{13.8}$$

where $\sqrt{\frac{N-n}{N-1}}$ is known as the *finite population correction factor.*

EXAMPLE 13.10 For the theoretical sampling distribution of the mean in Table 13.4, determine the standard error of the mean both by taking the square root of the variance of the sampling distribution, $\sigma_{\bar{x}}^2$, and by using equation (13.8).

Solution

In Example 13.8 we found that $\sigma_{\bar{x}}^2 = 0.75$. Therefore, the standard error of the mean is

$$\sigma_{\bar{x}} = \sqrt{\sigma_{\bar{x}}^2} = \sqrt{0.75} = 0.8660$$

Calculating $\sigma_{\bar{x}}$ using equation (13.8) and again with $\sigma = \sqrt{2.00}$ (see Example 13.7),

$$\sigma_{\bar{x}} = \frac{\sigma}{\sqrt{n}} \times \sqrt{\frac{N-n}{N-1}} = \frac{\sqrt{2.00}}{\sqrt{2}} \times \sqrt{\frac{5-2}{5-1}} = 1.00\sqrt{0.75} = 0.8660$$

All descriptive statistics have been developed as estimators of population parameters. Theoretical sampling distributions (for all possible same-size random samples) exist for most of these statistics. Because these statistics have been developed to be unbiased estimators of their parameters (see Section 13.8), the means of their theoretical sampling distributions are equal to the parameters that they estimate. The difference between any given calculation of a statistic and the parameter it is estimating is sampling error. Therefore, the standard deviation of a theoretical sampling distribution for any given statistic is called the standard error of that statistic—the amount that the statistic can be expected to vary about its parameter from sample to sample. As new theoretical sampling distributions are introduced in this and later chapters, the standard error of the given statistic with its unique calculation formula will be presented.

13.12 THE PRECISION OF AN ESTIMATOR

In Section 2.14 in Volume 1 we introduced two fundamental statistical properties of measurement: accuracy (the closeness of the measurement to the true measurement) and precision (the closeness of repeated measurements of the same thing). Similarly, two fundamental properties of an estimator $\hat{\theta}$ are its accuracy [measured by $|E(\hat{\theta}) - \theta|$ (see Section 13.8)] and its precision.

> If random samples of size n are taken repeatedly from a population of size N and values $\hat{\theta}^*$ of the estimator $\hat{\theta}$ are calculated for each sample in order to estimate the population parameter θ, then the *precision of the estimator* is determined by the variability or spread of the repeated estimates. The less variable (the closer together) the estimates, the more precise the estimator.

From this definition it can be seen that the standard error of the sampling distribution for an estimator $\hat{\theta}$ (see Section 13.11) is a measure of the precision of that estimator; the smaller the standard error, the more precise the estimator. Thus, the standard error of the mean $\sigma_{\bar{x}}$ is a measure of the precision of $\bar{X}$ as an estimator of μ; the smaller the $\sigma_{\bar{x}}$, the more precisely $\bar{X}$ estimates μ. If $\hat{\theta}$ is an unbiased estimator (see Section 13.8), as $\bar{X}$ is an unbiased estimator of μ, then it is said that a standard error measures *random error*—chance variation in a series of estimates that results from random sampling. If there are two unbiased estimators $\hat{\theta}_1$ and $\hat{\theta}_2$, then $\hat{\theta}_1$ is a more precise estimator if it has the smaller standard error.

The precision of $\bar{X}$ as an estimator of μ is measured by the standard error of the mean, and it can be seen for both versions of the $\sigma_{\bar{x}}$ formula [equations (13.7) and (13.8)], that if n were to be increased as σ was held constant, then $\sigma_{\bar{x}}$ would decrease and thus $\bar{X}$ would become a more precise estimator of μ. The reverse effect is true for σ. If n were to be held constant as σ was increased, then $\sigma_{\bar{x}}$ would increase and thus $\bar{X}$ would become less precise.

EXAMPLE 13.11 Taking random samples of size n from an infinite population that has a standard deviation $\sigma = 2.0$, show that $\bar{X}$ would be a more precise estimator of μ if sample size were increased from $n = 4$ to $n = 16$.

Solution

The precision of $\bar{X}$ as an estimator of μ is measured by the standard error of the mean $\sigma_{\bar{x}}$. For sampling from an infinite population, $\sigma_{\bar{x}} = \frac{\sigma}{n}$. Therefore, for $\sigma = 2.0$ and $n = 4$,

$$\sigma_{\bar{x}} = \frac{2.0}{\sqrt{4}} = \frac{2.0}{2} = 1.0$$

Increasing n from 4 to 16,

$$\sigma_{\bar{x}} = \frac{2.0}{\sqrt{16}} = \frac{2.0}{4} = 0.5$$

Thus, with a four-fold increase in sample size and a constant σ, $\sigma_{\bar{x}}$ decreases by 50%.

13.13 DETERMINING PROBABILITIES WITH A DISCRETE SAMPLING DISTRIBUTION OF THE MEAN

In Section 10.7 of Volume 1 we saw how the cumulative distribution function of a discrete random variable X can be used to find the probability that X will take on a value that is less than or equal to x. Similarly, the cumulative distribution function of the discrete random variable $\bar{X}$ gives the probability that $\bar{X}$ will take on a value that is less than or equal to $\bar{x}$. This function, denoted by $F(\bar{x})$, is defined for all real numbers $(-\infty < \bar{x} < \infty)$ by

$$F(\bar{x}) = P(\bar{X} \leq \bar{x}) \tag{13.9}$$

and for any real number a, $P(\bar{X} \leq a)$ can be calculated with the formula

$$F(a) = \sum_{\bar{x} \leq a} f(\bar{x}) \tag{13.10}$$

where the symbol $\sum_{\bar{x} \leq a} f(\bar{x})$ means take the sum of the values of $f(\bar{x})$ for all values of $\bar{x}$ that are less than or equal to a.

EXAMPLE 13.12 Given the population of numbers in Example 13.3: 0, 1, 2, 3, 4, and the discrete sampling distribution of the mean in Table 13.2, determine the probability that the mean $(\bar{X} = \bar{x})$ of a random sample of size $(n = 2)$ selected with replacement from this population will be at most 2.0.

Solution

We know from Equation (13.10) that

$$F(2.0) = \sum_{\bar{x} \leq 2.0} f(\bar{x})$$

Substituting the required values of $f(\bar{x})$ from Table 13.2,

$$\begin{aligned} F(2.0) &= f(0.0) + f(0.5) + f(1.0) + f(1.5) + f(2.0) \\ &= 0.04 + 0.08 + 0.12 + 0.16 + 0.20 \\ &= 0.60 \end{aligned}$$

13.14 DETERMINING PROBABILITIES WITH A NORMALLY DISTRIBUTED SAMPLING DISTRIBUTION OF THE MEAN

In theory, a population is said to be infinitely large and normally distributed if its continuous random variable X has a normal probability distribution (see Section 12.2). In applied problems, a population of any size is said to be normally distributed when its empirical frequency (or relative frequency) distribution can reasonably be fit by a normal curve. From the theoretical definition (and therefore it holds true for the applied definition), it can be proven mathematically that

> If all possible random samples of the same size n are drawn from an infinitely large, normally distributed population (mean μ, variance σ^2, standard deviation σ) and a value $\bar{x}$ of the continuous random variable $\bar{X}$ is calculated for each sample, then $\bar{X}$ will have a normally distributed sampling distribution with mean $\mu_{\bar{x}} = \mu$, variance $\sigma_{\bar{x}}^2 = \frac{\sigma^2}{n}$, and standard deviation $\sigma_{\bar{x}} = \frac{\sigma}{\sqrt{n}}$. This result will be exactly true for all samples of size n.

Such a normally distributed, continuous random variable $\bar{X}$ can be standardized with this version of the Z transformation [equation (12.3)],

$$Z = \frac{\bar{X} - \mu_{\bar{x}}}{\sigma_{\bar{x}}} \tag{13.11}$$

which converts the normal distribution of $\bar{X}$ into the standard normal distribution ($\mu_z = 0$ and $\sigma_z^2 = \sigma_z = 1$), defined by equation (12.5). Because sampling is from an infinitely large population, $\mu_{\bar{x}} = \mu$ and $\sigma_{\bar{x}} = \sigma/\sqrt{n}$ for the distribution of $\bar{X}$ (see Sections 13.7 and 13.9), and therefore the above version of the Z transformation is also presented in textbooks in the forms

$$Z = \frac{\bar{X} - \mu}{\sigma_{\bar{x}}} \tag{13.12}$$

and

$$Z = \frac{\bar{X} - \mu}{\sigma/\sqrt{n}} \tag{13.13}$$

EXAMPLE 13.13 A random sample ($n = 100$) is taken from a normally distributed population ($\mu = 20.0$, $\sigma = 1.0$). (*a*) What are the characteristics (i.e., the shape and parameters) of the distribution of the continuous random variable $\bar{X}$? (*b*) What is the probability that $\bar{X}$ will take on a value $\bar{x}$ in the interval $20.0 \leq \bar{x} \leq 20.2$?

Solution

(*a*) $\bar{X}$ is normally distributed with $\mu_{\bar{x}} = 20.0$ and $\sigma_{\bar{x}} = \frac{\sigma}{\sqrt{n}} = \frac{1.0}{\sqrt{100}} = 0.10$.

(*b*) If $\bar{X}$ is standardized with equation (13.12), we know that the resulting continuous Z variable has the standard normal distribution. Therefore, equation (12.7) can be modified to read

$$P(a \leq \bar{X} \leq b) = P\left(\frac{a - \mu_{\bar{x}}}{\sigma_{\bar{x}}} \leq Z \leq \frac{b - \mu_{\bar{x}}}{\sigma_{\bar{x}}}\right) = P(z_a \leq Z \leq z_b) \tag{13.14}$$

Using Table A.5 in the Appendix and equation (13.14),

$$\begin{aligned} P(20.0 \leq \bar{X} \leq 20.2) &= P\left(\frac{20.0 - 20.0}{0.10} \leq Z \leq \frac{20.2 - 20.0}{0.10}\right) \\ &= P(0.00 \leq Z \leq 2.00) \\ &= 0.4772 \end{aligned}$$

13.15 THE CENTRAL LIMIT THEOREM: SAMPLING FROM A FINITE POPULATION WITH REPLACEMENT

As we indicated in Section 13.6, theoretical sampling distributions are the foundations of virtually all forms of statistical inference. These tools, however, can only be used if their characteristics (shape, parameters) are known.

Section 13.14 clearly states the characteristics of a theoretical sampling distribution of the mean $\bar{X}$ given that the population being sampled is normally distributed. There we said that it can be mathematically proven that if all possible samples of size n are taken from a normally distributed population and $\bar{X} = \bar{x}$ is calculated for each sample, then the resulting continuous theoretical sampling distribution of the mean will be normally distributed. Further, we said that this will be exactly true for all samples of size n.

But what if, in the real world of applied statistics, the shape of the population distribution is unknown, or it it known to be skewed or multimodal, or if it is finite with a discrete random variable? Remarkably, for almost all such population distributions that will be encountered in the applied context, theoretical sampling distributions developed for such populations can be considered to be approximately normally distributed if the sample sizes n are "sufficiently large." (For what "sufficiently large" means in this context, see Section 13.18.) This is the essence of one of the most important theorems in inferential statistics, the *central limit theorem*. This theorem, first discovered by Pierre Simon de Laplace (see Section 12.2), states for sampling from finite populations with replacement that:

> It can be proven mathematically that if all possible random samples of size n are drawn with replacement from a finite population of size N that has finite parameters (μ, σ^2, σ) and if $\bar{X} = \bar{x}$ is calculated for each sample, then if n is sufficiently large, the resulting theoretical sampling distribution of the mean will be approximately normally distributed with parameters $\mu_{\bar{x}} = \mu$, $\sigma_{\bar{x}}^2 = \dfrac{\sigma^2}{n}$, and $\sigma_{\bar{x}} = \dfrac{\sigma}{\sqrt{n}}$.

Thus, no matter what the distribution-characteristics of the finite population being sampled, if the sample size n is sufficiently large, the resulting sampling distribution of the mean will be approximately normal, and this approximation gets better and better as n increases. This version of the theorem applies to any finite population that is sampled with replacement.

EXAMPLE 13.14 The experiment consists of the random selection of one number from the three-element population ($N = 3$): 3, 4, 5. The probability distribution for the random variable "number selected" is the discrete uniform probability distribution (see Section 12.14) shown in Fig. 13-3. Using techniques from Example 13.4, develop the discrete theoretical sampling distribution of the mean for: (*a*) randomly selecting two numbers, with replacement between each selection, (*b*) randomly selecting four numbers, with replacement between each selection. Then (*c*) for each distribution, determine $\mu_{\bar{x}}$ and $\sigma_{\bar{x}}$.

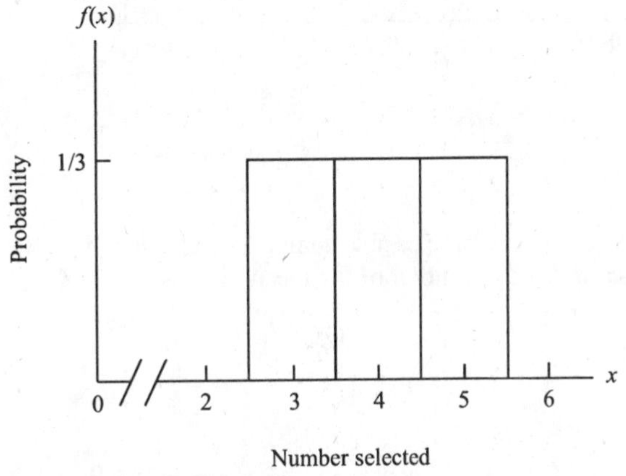

Fig. 13-3

Solution

(*a*) There are $(3 \times 3 = 9)$ possible samples of size $n = 2$, yielding five possible sample means. The theoretical sampling distribution of the mean for this problem is presented in Table 13.5 and in the histogram in Fig. 13-4.

Table 13.5

Sample mean $\bar{x}$	Probability $f(\bar{x})$
3.0	0.111111
3.5	0.222222
4.0	0.333333
4.5	0.222222
5.0	0.111111
$\sum$	0.999999

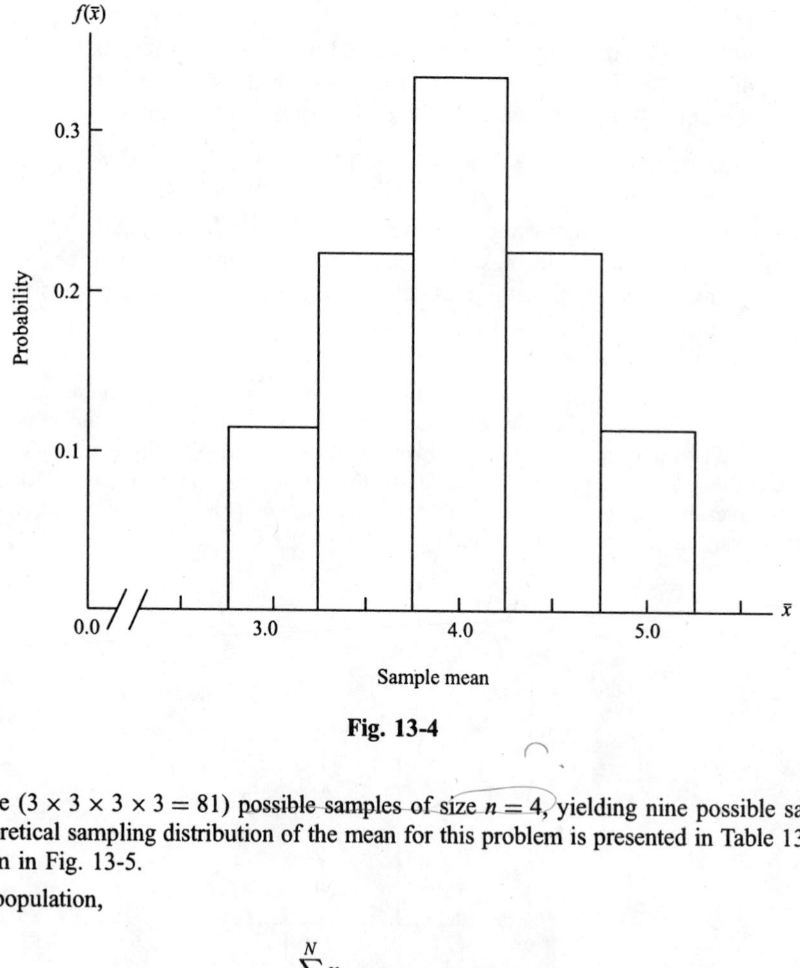

Fig. 13-4

(*b*) There are ($3 \times 3 \times 3 \times 3 = 81$) possible samples of size $n = 4$, yielding nine possible sample means. The theoretical sampling distribution of the mean for this problem is presented in Table 13.6 and in the histogram in Fig. 13-5.

(*c*) For the population,

$$\mu = \frac{\sum_{i=1}^{N} x_i}{N} = \frac{3+4+5}{3} = 4.0$$

and

$$\sigma = \sqrt{\frac{\sum_{i=1}^{N}(x_i - \mu)^2}{N}} = \sqrt{\frac{(3-4.0)^2 + (4-4.0)^2 + (5-4.0)^2}{3}} = 0.816497, \quad \text{or } 0.82$$

Table 13.6

Sample mean $\bar{x}$	Probability $f(\bar{x})$
3.00	0.012346
3.25	0.049383
3.50	0.123457
3.75	0.197531
4.00	0.234568
4.25	0.197531
4.50	0.123457
4.75	0.049383
5.00	0.012346
$\sum$	1.000002

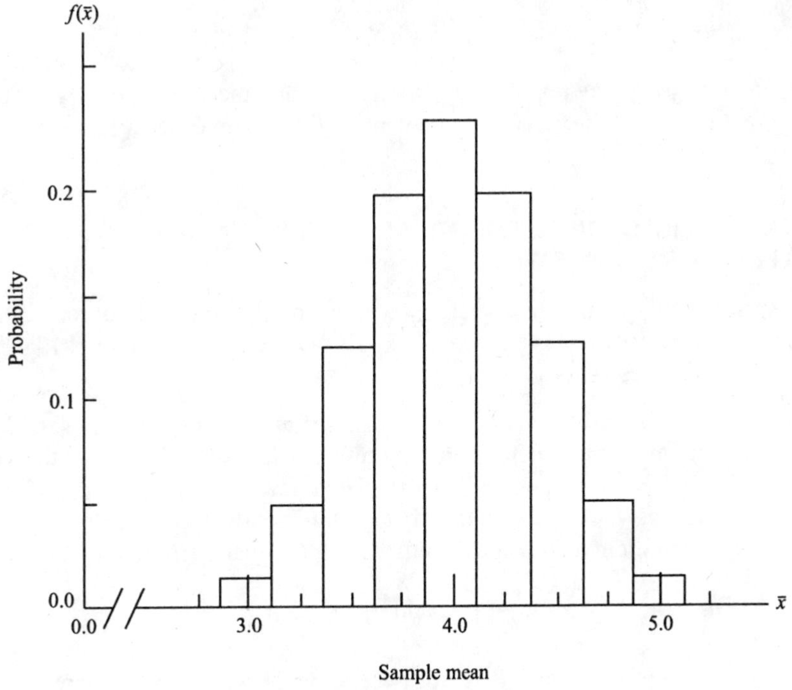

Fig. 13-5

Therefore, using equations (13.1) and (13.7) for the distribution in (*a*),

$$\mu_{\bar{x}} = \mu = 4.0$$

$$\sigma_{\bar{x}} = \frac{\sigma}{\sqrt{n}} = \frac{0.816497}{\sqrt{2}} = \frac{0.816497}{1.414214} = 0.577350, \quad \text{or } 0.58$$

and for the distribution in (*b*),

$$\mu_{\bar{x}} = \mu = 4.0$$

$$\sigma_{\bar{x}} = \frac{\sigma}{\sqrt{n}} = \frac{0.816497}{\sqrt{4}} = \frac{0.816497}{2} = 0.408249, \quad \text{or } 0.41$$

This example illustrates the truth of the central limit theorem. Here, sampling was done with replacement from a finite population ($N = 3$) that has a discrete uniform probability distribution (see Fig. 13-3). Even starting with such a distribution, as sample size increases from $n = 2$ to $n = 4$, the sampling distribution of the mean becomes increasingly similar to a normal distribution (unimodal, symmetric, bell-shaped; see Figs. 13-4 and 13-5). Note also that as n increases, $\sigma_{\bar{x}}$ decreases (from 0.58 to 0.41), which indicates, as would be expected for a normal distribution, that the probabilities become more concentrated near the mean.

13.16 THE CENTRAL LIMIT THEOREM: SAMPLING FROM AN INFINITE POPULATION

In Section 13.15 we described how the central limit theorem applies to samples from a finite population with replacement. In the following version, the theorem also applies to sampling from any form of infinitely large population:

> It can be proven mathematically that if all possible random samples of size n are drawn from an infinite population (with or without replacement) that has finite parameters (μ, σ^2, σ) and if $\bar{X} = \bar{x}$ is calculated for each sample, then if n is sufficiently large, the resulting theoretical sampling distribution of the mean will be approximately normally distributed with parameters $\mu_{\bar{x}} = \mu$, $\sigma_{\bar{x}}^2 = \frac{\sigma^2}{n}$, and $\sigma_{\bar{x}} = \frac{\sigma}{\sqrt{n}}$.

Note here that even though the population is infinitely large, the degree to which a normal distribution fits the sampling distribution of the mean is still determined by sample size n rather than by population size N.

13.17 THE CENTRAL LIMIT THEOREM: SAMPLING FROM A FINITE POPULATION WITHOUT REPLACEMENT

A third version of the central limit theorem applies to sampling without replacement from any form of finite population. In this version, as you would expect from Sections 13.10 and 13.11, the relation of N to n is specified. Thus, it states that:

> It can be proven mathematically that if all possible random samples of size n are drawn without replacement from a finite population of size N that has finite parameters (μ, σ^2, σ) and if $\bar{X} = \bar{x}$ is calculated for each sample, and if N is at least twice as large as n ($N \geq 2n$), then if n is sufficiently large, the resulting theoretical sampling distribution of the mean will be approximately normally distributed with parameters $\mu_{\bar{x}} = \mu$, $\sigma_{\bar{x}}^2 = \frac{\sigma^2}{n} \times \frac{N-n}{N-1}$, and $\sigma_{\bar{x}} = \frac{\sigma}{\sqrt{n}} \times \sqrt{\frac{N-n}{N-1}}$.

Recall from Section 13.10 that it is not necessary to use the finite population correction factor if $n \leq 0.05N$.

13.18 HOW LARGE IS "SUFFICIENTLY LARGE?"

In all three versions of the central limit theorem given above, it was stated that if n is "sufficiently large" then the theoretical sampling distribution of the mean will be approximately normally distributed. The term "sufficiently large" is used in defining the central limit theorem because there is no absolute rule: the sample size n that is required for applying the central limit theorem varies as a function of the shape of the population distribution. The closer the population distribution is to normal (unimodal, symmetric, bell-shaped), the smaller the sample size that is needed. For such "normal" populations, some statistics books state that samples as small as $n = 25$ or $n = 20$ are sufficiently large. The more skewed the population, the larger the sample that is required for sufficiency. A generally accepted rule of thumb for any type of population distribution is

> If $n \geq 30$, then the sample size is sufficiently large to apply the central limit theorem with reasonable accuracy.

Because of this generally accepted rule and the importance of the central limit theorem to inferential statistics, the number 30 is usually accepted as the boundary between two theoretical areas: *large-sample statistics* and *small-sample statistics*. If $n \geq 30$, then *large-sample methods* that require applications of the central limit theorem can be used. If $n < 30$, then *small-sample methods* are used, which are introduced in Chapters 14 and 16.

EXAMPLE 13.15 At a large university, the distribution of GPAs (overall grade point averages, see Problem 6.43 in Volume 1) for the 7,300 members of the senior class has parameters $\mu = 3.19$ and $\sigma = 0.24$. If a random sample of 36 seniors is taken without replacement, what is the probability that the sample mean GPA will be within $0.4\sigma_{\bar{x}}$ of μ?

Solution

Because $n \geq 30$ and $N \geq 2n$, the version of the central limit theorem for sampling from a finite population without replacement (see Section 13.17) can be applied here. As $n \leq 0.05N$, it is not necessary to use the finite population correction factor. Therefore, we can say that the distribution of $\bar{X}$ is approximately normal with parameters $\mu_{\bar{x}} = \mu = 3.19$ and $\sigma_{\bar{x}} = \dfrac{\sigma}{\sqrt{n}} = \dfrac{0.24}{\sqrt{36}} = 0.04$. Using this information we can get the approximate solution to this problem, which can be restated as

$$\begin{aligned} P(\mu - 0.4\sigma_{\bar{x}} \leq \bar{X} \leq \mu + 0.4\sigma_{\bar{x}}) &= P[3.19 - (0.4 \times 0.04) \leq \bar{X} \leq 3.19 + (0.4 \times 0.04)] \\ &= P(3.174 \leq \bar{X} \leq 3.206) \end{aligned}$$

Using an approximate version of equation (13.14),

$$P(a \leq \bar{X} \leq b) \approx P\left(\frac{a - \mu_{\bar{x}}}{\sigma_{\bar{x}}} \leq Z \leq \frac{b - \mu_{\bar{x}}}{\sigma_{\bar{x}}}\right) = P(z_a \leq Z \leq z_b) \tag{13.15}$$

we must solve

$$P(3.174 \leq \bar{X} \leq 3.206) \approx P\left(\frac{3.174 - 3.19}{0.04} \leq Z \leq \frac{3.206 - 3.19}{0.04}\right) = P(-0.40 \leq Z \leq 0.40)$$

Using the value from Table A.5 for $z = 0.40$,

$$P(3.174 \leq \bar{X} \leq 3.206) \approx 2(0.1554) = 0.3108$$

13.19 THE SAMPLING DISTRIBUTION OF THE SAMPLE SUM

All possible random samples of size n $(X_1, X_2, \ldots, X_n)$ are drawn from an infinitely large, normally distributed population (μ, σ^2, σ), and the sum of values (*sample sum*, denoted by Y) is calculated for each sample with the formula

$$Y = \sum_{i=1}^{n} X_i \tag{13.16}$$

which can have values

$$y = \sum_{i=1}^{n} x_i \tag{13.17}$$

For these sampling conditions, it can be proven mathematically that the *sampling distribution of the sample sum* (of the random variable Y) is exactly normally distributed with parameters $\mu_y = n\mu$, $\sigma_y^2 = n\sigma^2$, and $\sigma_y = \sqrt{n}\sigma$ (where σ_y is the *standard error of the sample sum*).

As is always the case with a normally distributed random variable, if Y is normally distributed then the Z transformation

$$Z = \frac{Y - \mu_y}{\sigma_y} \tag{13.18}$$

will convert its normal distribution into a standard normal distribution (see Section 12.7). Therefore, probabilities can be determined within the sampling distribution of the sample sum with this version of equation (12.7):

$$P(a \le Y \le b) = P\left(\frac{a - \mu_y}{\sigma_y} \le Z \le \frac{b - \mu_y}{\sigma_y}\right) = P(z_a \le Z \le z_b) \tag{13.19}$$

EXAMPLE 13.16 A fishing company that owns 15 boats has found from many years of experience that the catch/boat/day is normally distributed with $\mu = 500$ lb and $\sigma = 40$ lb. What is the probability, if nine boats are fishing on a given day, that the catch that day will be between 4,400 lb and 4,600 lb?

Solution

We are determining the probability that the sum of a sample of nine catches, $y = \sum_{i=1}^{9} x_i$, taken from a normally distributed population of daily catches will be between 4,400 lb and 4,600 lb. We know that the random variable daily catches X is normally distributed and that therefore the random variable sample sum Y is also normally distributed, with $\mu_y = n\mu = 9 \times 500$ lb $= 4{,}500$ lb and $\sigma_y = \sqrt{n}\sigma = \sqrt{9} \times 40$ lb $= 120$ lb. Therefore, using equaiton (13.19) we must determine

$$P(4{,}400 \text{ lb} \le Y \le 4{,}600 \text{ lb}) = P\left(\frac{4{,}400 \text{ lb} - 4{,}500 \text{ lb}}{120 \text{ lb}} \le Z \le \frac{4{,}600 \text{ lb} - 4{,}500 \text{ lb}}{120 \text{ lb}}\right)$$
$$= P(-0.83 \le Z \le 0.83)$$

Using the value from Table A.5 for $z = 0.83$,

$$P(4{,}400 \text{ lb} \le Y \le 4{,}600 \text{ lb}) = 2(0.2967) = 0.5934$$

13.20 APPLYING THE CENTRAL LIMIT THEOREM TO THE SAMPLING DISTRIBUTION OF THE SAMPLE SUM

For a theoretical sampling distribution of the sample sum (see Section 13.19), developed either by sampling with replacement from a finite population or by sampling from an infinite population, the following version of the central limit theorem applies:

> It can be proven mathematically that if all possible random samples of size n are drawn from either a finite population with replacement or an infinite population, where the population has finite parameters (μ, σ^2, σ), and if the sample sum $Y = y$ is calculated for each sample, then if n is sufficiently large, the resulting sampling distribution of the sample sum Y will be approximately normally distributed with parameters $\mu_y = n\mu$, $\sigma_y^2 = n\sigma^2$, and $\sigma_y = \sqrt{n}\sigma$.

Again, the term "sufficiently large" means $n \ge 30$ (see Section 13.18). Also, if Y is approximately normally distributed, and Y is standardized with equation (13.18), then the resulting distribution of Z will be approximately the standard normal distribution, and the following version of equation (13.19) will be the basic probability relationship between the Y and Z distributions:

$$P(a \le Y \le b) \approx P\left(\frac{a-\mu_y}{\sigma_y} \le Z \le \frac{b-\mu_y}{\sigma_y}\right) = P(z_a \le Z \le z_b) \qquad (13.20)$$

With some modifications, this version of the central limit theorem can also be used for sampling without replacement from a finite population. The modifications are (see Section 13.17): N must be at least twice as large as n ($N \ge 2n$) and, unless $n \le 0.05N$, σ_y should be calculated with the formula

$$\sigma_y = \sqrt{n}\sigma \times \sqrt{\frac{N-n}{N-1}} \qquad (13.21)$$

EXAMPLE 13.17 At a large computer-software company, the distribution of overtime hours for the 1,000 programmers for the past week has the parameters $\mu = 5.75$ hours and $\sigma = 0.48$ hours. If a random sample (without replacement) of 36 programmers is taken, what is the probability that the total of their overtime for the past week was between 202 hr and 210 hr?

Solution

As $n \ge 30$ and $N \ge 2n$, the central limit theorem indicates that the distribution of $Y = \sum_{i=1}^{36} X_i$ is approximately normal with parameters $\mu_y = n\mu = 36 \times 5.75\text{ hr} = 207.0\text{ hr}$ and, as $n \le 0.05N$, $\sigma_y = \sqrt{n}\sigma = \sqrt{36} \times 0.48\text{ hr} = 2.88\text{ hr}$. Using this information, we can get the approximate solution to this restatement of the problem,

$$P(202\text{ hr} \le Y \le 210\text{ hr})$$

From equation (13.20) we know that

$$P(202\text{ hr} \le Y \le 210\text{ hr}) \approx P\left(\frac{202\text{ hr} - 207.0\text{ hr}}{2.88\text{ hr}} \le Z \le \frac{210\text{ hr} - 207.0\text{ hr}}{2.88\text{ hr}}\right) = P(-1.74 \le Z \le 1.04)$$

Using the values from Table A.5 for $z = 1.74$ and $z = 1.04$,

$$P(202\text{ hr} \le Y \le 210\text{ hr}) \approx 0.4591 + 0.3508 = 0.8099$$

13.21 SAMPLING FROM A BINOMIAL POPULATION

A *binomial population* is one in which the component elements have been placed in one of two possible categories: yes/no, plus/minus, male/female, red/nonred, defective/nondefective, and so on. Any measurement population, whether discrete or continuous, can be transformed into a binomial population. Thus, for example, a population of adult male height measurements can be transformed into a binomial population by classifying each measurement either as below 67 in (height < 67 in) or as equal to or greater than 67 in (height ≥ 67 in).

Any set of n Bernoulli trials (see Section 11.2) can be considered to be a random sample of size n from a binomial population whose elements are classified as either a success or a failure. The constant probability of success on any individual trial p, assumed for Bernoulli trials, is identical to the *proportion of successes* in the binomial population:

$$p = \frac{\text{number of successes in the population}}{\text{size of the population}}$$

(In some statistics books this population proportion is denoted by π, the Greek letter *pi*.) You can also see, conversely, that a random sample of size n from a binomial population, taken under Bernoulli-trial conditions, can be considered to be Bernoulli trials.

If each failure-element in a binomial population is given the value zero and each success-element is given the value one, then the relative frequency distribution for the population is fit exactly by a binomial probability distribution (see Sections 11.5 to 11.9) that has these characteristics: (1) the discrete random variable X counts the number of successes ($X = 0$ or $X = 1$) that occur in an individual ($n = 1$) Bernoulli trial, (2) for these two possible outcomes of an individual trial, the probability function $f(x)$ assigns the probabilities $f(0) = 1 - p = q$ and $f(1) = p$, (3) the parameters of the distribution are $n = 1$ and p, (4) the mean of the distribution [equation (11.4)] is $\mu = np = 1 \times p = p$, (5) the variance of the distribution [equation (11.6)] is $\sigma^2 = npq = 1 \times p \times q = pq$, and (6) the standard deviation of the distribution [equation (11.7)] is $\sigma = \sqrt{\sigma^2} = \sqrt{pq}$.

The proportion of successes p is a binomial-population parameter. This parameter can be estimated by determining the proportion of successes in a random sample from the population. This sample proportion is a sample-statistic estimator (see Section 13.8) that is calculated with

$$\bar{P} = \frac{Y}{n} \tag{13.22}$$

where $\bar{P}$ is the random variable proportion of successes in the sample (denoted in some books by $\hat{P}$ or P'), Y is the binomial random variable number of successes in the sample, and n is the sample size. (For an explanation of why the symbol Y is used to denote both number of successes and sample sum see Section 13.24.) The random variable $\bar{P}$ can assume real number values $\bar{P} = \bar{p}$. The probability distribution for $\bar{P}$ is the same as for the binomial random variable Y, except for a change in scale. Thus it is true that if a is the number of successes in a sample of size n taken under Bernoulli-trial conditions from an infinite binomial population that has the proportion p of successes, then

$$P(Y = a) = P\left(\frac{Y}{n} = \frac{a}{n}\right) = P\left(\bar{P} = \frac{a}{n}\right) \tag{13.23}$$

EXAMPLE 13.18 An infinite binomial population has a proportion $p = 0.4$ of success-elements. A random sample ($n = 10$) is drawn from the population under Bernoulli-trial conditions. The binomial random variable Y, used to count the number of successes in the sample, can have values from $Y = 0$ to $Y = 10$. Use the binomial probability function [equation (11.2)] to determine the probability that the sample will include: (*a*) 3 successes, (*b*) a proportion of 0.3 successes, (*c*) 30% successes. Then determine the probability that: (*d*) $\bar{P}$ is at most 0.4, (*e*) $\bar{P}$ is at least 0.3.

Solution

(*a*) Because this sample is equivalent to a binomial experiment of n trials, we can solve the problem with this version of equation (11.2):

$$f(y) = \binom{n}{y} p^y q^{n-y}, \qquad \text{for } y = 0, 1, 2, \ldots, n$$

which in this instance is

$$f(3) = \binom{10}{3}(0.4)^3(0.6)^7 = \frac{10!}{3!(10-3)!}(0.4)^3(0.6)^7$$
$$= (120)(0.064)(0.027994) = 0.214994$$

(*b*) We know from equation (13.23) that if $a = 3$ and $n = 10$, then

$$P(Y = 3) = P\left(\frac{Y}{10} = \frac{3}{10}\right) = P(\bar{P} = 0.3) = 0.214994$$

(*c*) Proportions can be expressed as fractions, decimals, or percentages, and so

$$P(\bar{P} = 30\%) = P(\bar{P} = 0.3) = 0.214994$$

(*d*) Converting equation (13.23) into an inequality (see Volume 1, Section 1.23) and inserting $a = 4$ and $n = 10$,

$$P(\bar{P} \le 0.4) = P\left(\frac{Y}{10} \le \frac{4}{10}\right) = P(Y \le 4)$$

Using the value from Table A.3 in the Appendix for $a = 4$, $n = 10$, and $p = 0.4$,

$$P(\bar{P} \leq 0.4) = P(Y \leq 4) = F(4) = 0.6331$$

(*e*) Converting equation (13.23) into an inequality, and inserting $a = 3$ and $n = 10$,

$$P(\bar{P} \geq 0.3) = P\left(\frac{Y}{10} \geq \frac{3}{10}\right) = P(Y \geq 3)$$

As the possible values of Y are the whole numbers $y = 0, 1, 2, \ldots, 10$,

$$P(Y \geq 3) = 1 - P(Y \leq 2) = 1 - F(2)$$

Using the value from Table A.3 for $a = 2$, $n = 10$, and $p = 0.4$,

$$P(\bar{P} \geq 0.3) = 1 - F(2) = 1 - 0.1673 = 0.8327$$

13.22 SAMPLING DISTRIBUTION OF THE NUMBER OF SUCCESSES

For a random sample of size n taken under Bernoulli-trial conditions from an infinite binomial population that has a proportion of successes p, the probability of $Y = y$ successes, for $y = 0, 1, 2, \ldots, n$, can be determined with the binomial probability function [equation (11.2)]. Therefore, if all possible samples of size n are drawn from an infinite binomial population under Bernoulli-trial conditions and the number of successes is determined for each sample, then the resulting theoretical *sampling distribution of the number of successes* (or *sampling distribution of counts*, or *sampling distribution of number of occurrences*) is the binomial probability distribution (see Sections 11.5 to 11.9) with

$$E(Y) = \mu_y = np \tag{13.24}$$

$$\text{var}(Y) = \sigma_y^2 = npq \tag{13.25}$$

$$\text{st dev}(Y) = \sigma_y = \sqrt{npq} \tag{13.26}$$

This standard deviation is called the *standard error of the number of successes*. As with previous sampling distributions (see Section 13.6), there are linked empirical sampling distributions of the number of successes, which are relative frequency distributions of actual $Y = y$ values for a set of samples of size n. As p must be constant for Bernoulli trials, these formulas are valid for sampling from an infinte binomial population and from a finite binomial population with replacement. If the sampling is from a finite binomial population without replacement, but $n \leq 0.05N$, then: (1) we can assume p is "essentially" constant, and (2) it is not necessary to include the finite population correction factor in calculating σ_y^2 or σ_y.

13.23 SAMPLING DISTRIBUTION OF THE PROPORTION

If all possible samples of size n are drawn from an infinite binomial population under Bernoulli-trial conditions and the proportion of successes $\bar{P} = \bar{p}$ is determined for each sample, then the resulting theoretical *sampling distribution of the proportion* (or *sampling distribution of a proportion*, or *sampling distribution of proportions*) is the same as the sampling distribution of the number of successes (see Section 13.22) except for a change in scale. This change in scale, however, produces these new formulas for mean, variance, and standard deviation:

$$E(\bar{P}) = \mu_{\bar{p}} = p \tag{13.27}$$

$$\text{var}(\bar{P}) = \sigma_{\bar{p}}^2 = \frac{pq}{n} \tag{13.28}$$

$$\text{st dev}(\bar{P}) = \sigma_{\bar{p}} = \sqrt{\frac{pq}{n}} \tag{13.29}$$

This standard deviation is called the *standard error of the proportion*. Again, as with the sampling distribution of the number of successes, the formulas apply for sampling from an infinite binomial population, for sampling from a finite binomial population with replacement, and, if $n \leq 0.05N$, for sampling from a finite population without replacement. Also, as with the distribution of number of successes, there are linked empirical sampling distributions of the proportion.

EXAMPLE 13.19 In general, it is true that if Y is a random variable, a and b are constants, and $a > 0$, then $R = aY + b$ is another random variable. If so, the means, variances, and standard deviations of the two variables are related as follows:

$$E(R) - aE(Y) + b$$
$$\text{var}(R) = a^2 \times \text{var}(Y)$$
$$\text{st dev}(R) = a \times \text{st dev}(Y)$$

Use these relationships to show how the change in scale from the sampling distribution of the number of successes (see Section 13.22) to the sampling distribution of the proportion produced the change in formulas for means, variances, and standard deviations.

Solution

Equation (13.22) states that

$$\bar{P} = \frac{Y}{n}$$

which can also be written as

$$\bar{P} = n^{-1}Y + 0$$

Therefore, using in the above relationships: $R = \bar{P}$, $Y = Y$, $a = n^{-1}$, $b = 0$, and from Section 13.22, $E(Y) = np$, $\text{var}(Y) = npq$, and $\text{st dev}(Y) = \sqrt{npq}$,

$$E(\bar{P}) = n^{-1}(np) + 0 = \frac{1}{n}(np) + 0 = p$$

$$\text{var}(\bar{P}) = (n^{-1})^2(npq) = \left(\frac{1}{n}\right)\left(\frac{1}{n}\right)(npq) = \frac{pq}{n}$$

$$\text{st dev}(\bar{P}) = n^{-1}\sqrt{npq} = \frac{\sqrt{npq}}{n} = \frac{\sqrt{npq}}{\sqrt{n^2}} = \sqrt{\frac{pq}{n}}$$

13.24 APPLYING THE CENTRAL LIMIT THEOREM TO THE SAMPLING DISTRIBUTION OF THE NUMBER OF SUCCESSES

From Section 12.12 we can say that if sample size is "sufficiently large" ($np \geq 5$ and $nq \geq 5$) we can: (1) treat the binomial random variable Y as if it is approximately normally distributed with $\mu_y = np$, $\sigma_y^2 = npq$, and $\sigma_y = \sqrt{npq}$, and (2) accept that if Y is standardized with equation (13.18), the resulting Z variable has a distribution that is approximately a standard normal distribution. Now we can state further that the theoretical justification for this normal approximation is the central limit theorem as applied to the sample sum $\left(Y = \sum_{i=1}^{n} X_i\right)$ (see Section 13.20): the binomial random variable number of successes in the sample Y can be treated as a special case of the sample sum.

To understand this, recall the mathematical definition of a simple random sample (see Section 13.3): a set of n independent random variables $X_1, X_2, \ldots, X_n$ that each have the same probability distribution as the population being sampled. Here, the population is a binomial population composed of successes ($X = 1$) and failures ($X = 0$) on a single trial ($n = 1$) that is binomially distributed ($\mu = p$, $\sigma^2 = pq$, and $\sigma = \sqrt{pq}$). Thus, each independent random variable X_i in the sample has this distribution, and can assume only the values $X = 0$ and $X = 1$. Therefore, the binomial random variable number of successes in a sample Y is really a calculation of this sample statistic [equation (13.16)]: $Y = \sum_{i=1}^{n} X_i$, and from the central limit theorem applied to sums, we know that if n is "sufficiently large" then the sampling distribution of this statistic will be approximately normally distributed.

13.25 APPLYING THE CENTRAL LIMIT THEOREM TO THE SAMPLING DISTRIBUTION OF THE PROPORTION

As we indicated in Section 13.23, the sampling distribution of the proportion is the same as the binomially distributed sampling distribution of the number of successes, but with a change in scale. It is reasonable, then, to accept that: The sampling distribution of the proportion is approximately normally distributed if n is "sufficiently large" ($np \geq 5$ and $nq \geq 5$) with $\mu_{\bar{p}} = p$, $\sigma_{\bar{p}}^2 = \frac{pq}{n}$, and $\sigma_{\bar{p}} = \sqrt{\frac{pq}{n}}$, and that, under these conditions,

$$Z = \frac{\bar{P} - \mu_{\bar{p}}}{\sigma_{\bar{p}}} \tag{13.30}$$

will have a distribution that approximates a standard normal distribution. The theoretical justification for this is again the central limit theorem, but now as applied to the sample mean (see Sections 13.15 to 13.17). Thus, $\bar{P}$ is treated as a special case of the sample mean.

To understand this, recall that $\bar{P} = \frac{Y}{n}$ [equation (13.22)] and $Y = \sum_{i=1}^{n} X_i$ (see Section 13.24), and so

$$\bar{P} = \frac{\sum_{i=1}^{n} X_i}{n} \tag{13.31}$$

Thus $\bar{P}$ is actually the mean number of successes per sample draw (or trial).

Knowing that $\bar{P}$ is actually a sample mean, we can derive $\mu_{\bar{p}}$ from $\mu_{\bar{x}}$, $\sigma_{\bar{p}}^2$ from $\sigma_{\bar{x}}^2$, and $\sigma_{\bar{p}}$ from $\sigma_{\bar{x}}$. Thus, if the binomial population is infinite, or finite and sampling is with replacement, or finite and sampling is without replacement but $n \leq 0.05N$, then it is true that

$$\mu_{\bar{x}} = \mu = \mu_{\bar{p}}$$

$$\sigma_{\bar{x}}^2 = \frac{\sigma^2}{n} = \sigma_{\bar{p}}^2$$

$$\sigma_{\bar{x}} = \frac{\sigma}{\sqrt{n}} = \sigma_{\bar{p}}$$

We know that for the binomial population (see Section 13.21) $\mu = p$, $\sigma^2 = pq$, and $\sigma = \sqrt{pq}$, and therefore

$$\mu_{\bar{p}} = p$$

$$\sigma_{\bar{p}}^2 = \frac{pq}{n}$$

$$\sigma_{\bar{p}} = \frac{\sqrt{pq}}{\sqrt{n}} = \sqrt{\frac{pq}{n}}$$

which are the formulas we gave in Section 13.23 and derived differently in Example 13.19.

Note: In this section, we stated that the central limit theorem can be applied if $np \geq 5$ and $np \geq 5$, whereas earlier (in Section 13.18) we stated that the central limit theorem requires $n \geq 30$. Why is there this difference? It is permissible, when applying the central limit theorem to binomially distributed sampling distributions, to use the rule $np \geq 5$ and $nq \geq 5$ because these distributions become increasingly more symmetrical the closer that p is to 0.5 (see Section 12.12). Thus, if $p = 0.5$, a sample as small as

$n = 10$ will allow use of the theorem. However, by this rule, n must be increased as p gets farther from 0.5. Thus, for example, when $p = 0.1$, n must be at least 50.

13.26 DETERMINING PROBABILITIES WITH A NORMAL APPROXIMATION TO THE SAMPLING DISTRIBUTION OF THE PROPORTION

When samples are taken from a binomial population under Bernoulli-trial conditions, the sampling distribution of the proportion will be binomially distributed with $\mu_{\bar{p}} = p$, $\sigma_{\bar{p}}^2 = \frac{pq}{n}$, and $\sigma_{\bar{p}} = \sqrt{\frac{pq}{n}}$. If $np \geq 5$ and $nq \geq 5$, then we can say that the distribution is approximately normally distributed (see Section 13.25) and that equation (13.30), $Z = \frac{\bar{P} - \mu_{\bar{p}}}{\sigma_{\bar{p}}}$, will have approximately a standard normal distribution. Thus, it would seem that we could determine probabilities with the relationship

$$P(a \leq \bar{P} \leq b) \approx P\left(\frac{a - \mu_{\bar{p}}}{\sigma_{\bar{p}}} \leq Z \leq \frac{b - \mu_{\bar{p}}}{\sigma_{\bar{p}}}\right) = P(z_a \leq Z \leq z_b) \tag{13.32}$$

and this is the solution found in many statistics books. However, the random variable $\bar{P}$ is a discrete random variable and some books suggest, as with the normal approximation to the binomial distribution [see Example 12.10(*b*)], that a *continuity correction* should be used, particularly for small samples. The correction suggested is the appropriate addition or subtraction of $1/2n$. To demonstrate this correction, we use it in the following example and where appropriate in the remainder of this chapter. However, because it is rarely used and for simplicity of presentation, we will not use the correction factor in later chapters when we apply estimation theory (see Chapter 15) and hypothesis-testing theory (see Chapter 16) to proportions.

EXAMPLE 13.20 Just prior to an election, a poll indicated that a majority ($p = 0.51$) of the population of 100,000 registered voters in a city preferred candidate A for mayor. However, when an exit poll is taken of 100 actual voters, the proportion in this random sample that prefer A is $\bar{P} = 0.49$. Assuming that the proportion that favor A in the voting population is also $p = 0.51$, what is $P(0.40 \leq \bar{P} \leq 0.60)$?

Solution

If we accept that this is sampling from a binomial population under Bernoulli-trial conditions, then the sampling distribution of the proportion favoring A will be binomially distributed with $\mu_{\bar{p}} = p = 0.51$, $\sigma_{\bar{p}}^2 = \frac{pq}{n} = \frac{0.51 \times 0.49}{100} = 0.002499$, and $\sigma_{\bar{p}} = \sqrt{\frac{pq}{n}} = \sqrt{0.002499} = 0.049989999$, or 0.05. As $np = 51$ and $nq = 49$, we can say that this distribution is approximately normally distributed. To convert this distribution to a standard normal distribution by using a Z transformation, we will first apply a continuity correction of $1/2n$ to equation (13.32):

$$P\left(0.40 - \frac{1}{2n} \leq \bar{P} \leq 0.60 + \frac{1}{2n}\right) \approx \left(\frac{0.40 - 1/2n - 0.51}{0.05} \leq Z \leq \frac{0.60 + 1/2n - 0.51}{0.05}\right)$$

Inserting the value of the correction factor, $\frac{1}{2n} = \frac{1}{2(100)} = 0.005$, into the equation,

$$P(0.395 \leq \bar{P} \leq 0.605) \approx P\left(\frac{0.395 - 0.51}{0.05} \leq Z \leq \frac{0.605 - 0.51}{0.05}\right) = P(-2.30 \leq Z \leq 1.90)$$

Using the values from Table A.5 for $z = 2.30$ and $z = 1.90$,

$$P(0.40 \leq \bar{P} \leq 0.60) \approx 0.4893 + 0.4713 = 0.9606$$

Solved Problems

THE SAMPLING DISTRIBUTION OF THE MEAN

13.1 Sampling with replacement (accepting repeated numbers and repeated samples) from Table A.1 in the Appendix to Volume 1, using the procedures from Example 13.3, 100 two-number ($n = 2$) random samples were taken from the five-number population in Example 13.3: 0, 1, 2, 3, 4. The results are summarized in Table 13.7, which gives the frequency of selection of each of the 25 possible samples and the mean of each sample. From this information, develop an empirical sampling distribution of the mean for this sampling problem and present it in a summary table.

Table 13.7

[(Sample) $\bar{x}_i$]	Frequency f_i	[(Sample) $\bar{x}_i$]	Frequency f_i	[(Sample) $\bar{x}_i$]	Frequency f_i
[(0, 0) 0.0]	5	[(1, 3) 2.0]	4	[(3, 1) 2.0]	5
[(0, 1) 0.5]	6	[(1, 4) 2.5]	5	[(3, 2) 2.5]	5
[(0, 2) 1.0]	4	[(2, 0) 1.0]	3	[(3, 3) 3.0]	2
[(0, 3) 1.5]	3	[(2, 1) 1.5]	6	[(3, 4) 3.5]	2
[(0, 4) 2.0]	2	[(2, 2) 2.0]	4	[(4, 0) 2.0]	3
[(1, 0) 0.5]	7	[(2, 3) 2.5]	5	[(4, 1) 2.5]	1
[(1, 1) 1.0]	4	[(2, 4) 3.0]	4	[(4, 2) 3.0]	7
[(1, 2) 1.5]	3	[(3, 0) 1.5]	1	[(4, 3) 3.5]	5
				[(4, 4) 4.0]	4

Solution

An empirical sampling distribution of the mean is a relative frequency distribution. The empirical sampling distribution for this set of data is presented in Table 13.8. The relative-frequency values in this distribution approximate the probability values in the theoretical sampling distribution of the mean shown in Table 13.2, but because the number of samples is so small (100) compared with the available population of samples (∞), the approximation is not close.

Table 13.8

Sample mean $\bar{x}_i$	Relative frequency $f_i/n_{\bar{x}}$
0.0	0.05
0.5	0.13
1.0	0.11
1.5	0.13
2.0	0.18
2.5	0.16
3.0	0.13
3.5	0.07
4.0	0.04
$\sum$	1.00

13.2 Use sampling with replacement to develop the discrete sampling distribution of the mean for random samples of size $n = 2$ from the population of numbers ($N = 3$): 7, 10, 12. To do this: (*a*) List all such possible samples that can be taken from the population, along with the arithmetic mean of each, (*b*) summarize these arithmetic means in frequency and relative frequency distributions, (*c*) calculate the probability of selection for each mean and present the resulting sampling distribution in a probability table.

Solution

(*a*) From the counting rule: multiplication principle (see Volume 1, Section 9.12) we know that there are ($n_1 \times n_2 = 3 \times 3 = 9$) possible random samples of size $n = 2$. These samples and their means, [(sample) $\bar{x}$], are

$$[(7, 7)\ 7.0] \quad [(10, 7)\ 8.5] \quad [(12, 7)\ 9.5]$$
$$[(7, 10)\ 8.5] \quad [(10, 10)\ 10.0] \quad [(12, 10)\ 11.0]$$
$$[(7, 12)\ 9.5] \quad [(10, 12)\ 11.0] \quad [(12, 12)\ 12.0]$$

(*b*) The requested frequency and relative frequency distributions are given in Table 13.9, where $N_{\bar{x}}$ denotes the number of possible $\bar{x}$ values.

Table 13.9

Sample mean $\bar{x}_i$	Frequency f_i	Relative frequency $f_i/N_{\bar{x}}$
7.0	1	0.111111
8.5	2	0.222222
9.5	2	0.222222
10.0	1	0.111111
11.0	2	0.222222
12.0	1	0.111111
Σ	9	0.999999

(*c*) Using techniques from Example 13.4(*c*) and knowing that each of the nine possible samples has the probability of being selected of $\frac{1}{9}$, we get the theoretical sampling distribution shown in Table 13.10.

Table 13.10

Sample mean $\bar{x}$	Probability $f(\bar{x})$
7.0	0.111111
8.5	0.222222
9.5	0.222222
10.0	0.111111
11.0	0.222222
12.0	0.111111
Σ	0.999999

13.3 Use sampling without replacement to develop the discrete theoretical sampling distribution of the mean for random samples of size $n = 2$ from the three-number population in problem 13.2: 7, 10, 12. To do this: (*a*) List all such possible samples that can be taken from the population along with the arithmetic mean of each, (*b*) summarize these arithmetic means in frequency and relative frequency distributions, (*c*) calculate the probability of selection for each mean and present the resulting sampling distribution in a probability table.

Solution

(*a*) As in Example 13.5(*a*), the total number of possible random samples is determined with the counting rule: combinations [equation (9.20) in Volume 1]

$${}_3C_2 = \binom{3}{2} = \frac{3!}{2!(3-2)!} = 3$$

These samples and their means [(sample) $\bar{x}$], are

[(7, 10) 8.5] [(7, 12) 9.5] [(10, 12) 11.0]

(*b*) The requested frequency and relative frequency distributions are given in Table 13.11, where again $N_{\bar{x}}$ represents the number of possible $\bar{x}$ values.

Table 13.11

Sample mean $\bar{x}_i$	Frequency f_i	Relative frequency $f_i/N_{\bar{x}}$
8.5	1	0.333333
9.5	1	0.333333
11.0	1	0.333333
$\sum$	3	0.999999

(*c*) Using techniques from Example 13.4(*c*) and knowing that each of the possible samples has a probability of being selected of $\frac{1}{3}$, we get the theoretical sampling distribution shown in Table 13.12.

Table 13.12

Sample mean $\bar{x}$	Probability $f(\bar{x})$
8.5	0.333333
9.5	0.333333
11.0	0.333333
$\sum$	0.999999

13.4 A subdivision of a town has six homes, one with 1 bedroom, one with 2 bedrooms, one with 3 bedrooms, one with 4 bedrooms, one with 5 bedrooms, and one with 6 bedrooms. A potential buyer chooses, at random, two different homes to visit (i.e., sampling without replacement). (*a*) What is the total number of unique samples? (*b*) What is the probability that the mean number of bedrooms in a sample will be 4.0?

Solution

(*a*) As in Example 13.5(*a*), the total number of possible samples is determined by using the counting rule: combinations [equation (9.20), Volume 1],

$$ {}_3C_2 = \binom{6}{2} = \frac{6!}{2!(6-2)!} = 15 $$

(*b*) This is the list of all possible random samples and their means, [(sample) $\bar{x}$]:

[(1, 2) 1.5]				
[(1, 3) 2.0]	[(2, 3) 2.5]			
[(1, 4) 2.5]	[(2, 4) 3.0]	[(3, 4) 3.5]		
[(1, 5) 3.0]	[(2, 5) 3.5]	[(3, 5) 4.0]	[(4, 5) 4.5]	
[(1, 6) 3.5]	[(2, 6) 4.0]	[(3, 6) 4.5]	[(4, 6) 5.0]	[(5, 6) 5.5]

Two of these 15 means are equal to 4.0 bedrooms. Therefore, the probability of getting a sample in which the average is 4.0 is 2/15, or 0.1333.

THE MEAN, VARIANCE, AND STANDARD DEVIATION OF THE SAMPLING DISTRIBUTION OF THE MEAN

13.5 For the theoretical sampling distribution of the mean in Table 13.10, determine the mean, variance, and standard error of the mean.

Solution

Using equation (13.2),

$$ \mu_{\bar{x}} = \sum_{\bar{x}} \bar{x}f(\bar{x}) = 7.0\left(\frac{1}{9}\right) + 8.5\left(\frac{2}{9}\right) + 9.5\left(\frac{2}{9}\right) + 10.0\left(\frac{1}{9}\right) + 11.0\left(\frac{2}{9}\right) + 12.0\left(\frac{1}{9}\right) $$

$$ = 9.6667, \quad \text{or } 9.67 $$

Using equation (13.4),

$$ \sigma_{\bar{x}}^2 = \sum_{\bar{x}} (\bar{x} - \mu_{\bar{x}})^2 f(\bar{x}) $$

$$ = (7.0 - 9.67)^2\left(\frac{1}{9}\right) + (8.5 - 9.67)^2\left(\frac{2}{9}\right) + (9.5 - 9.67)^2\left(\frac{2}{9}\right) + (10.0 - 9.67)^2\left(\frac{1}{9}\right) $$

$$ + (11.0 - 9.67)^2\left(\frac{2}{9}\right) + (12.0 - 9.67)^2\left(\frac{1}{9}\right) $$

$$ = 2.1111, \quad \text{or } 2.111 $$

Using equation (13.6),

$$ \sigma_{\bar{x}} = \sqrt{\sigma_{\bar{x}}^2} = \sqrt{2.1111} = 1.4530, \quad \text{or } 1.45 $$

13.6 For the theoretical sampling distribution of the mean in Table 13.12, determine the mean, variance, and standard error of the mean.

Solution

Using equation (13.2),

$$ \mu_{\bar{x}} = \sum_{\bar{x}} \bar{x}f(\bar{x}) = 8.5\left(\frac{1}{3}\right) + 9.5\left(\frac{1}{3}\right) + 11.0\left(\frac{1}{3}\right) $$

$$ = 9.6667, \quad \text{or } 9.67 $$

Using equation (13.4),

$$\sigma_{\bar{x}}^2 = \sum_{\bar{x}} (\bar{x} - \mu_{\bar{x}})^2 f(\bar{x})$$

$$= (8.5 - 9.67)^2 \left(\frac{1}{3}\right) + (9.5 - 9.67)^2 \left(\frac{1}{3}\right) + (11.0 - 9.67)^2 \left(\frac{1}{3}\right)$$

$$= 1.0556, \qquad \text{or } 1.056$$

Using equation (13.6),

$$\sigma_{\bar{x}} = \sqrt{\sigma_{\bar{x}}^2} = \sqrt{1.0556} = 1.0274, \qquad \text{or } 1.03$$

13.7 Taking random samples of size n without replacement from a finite population of $N = 60$ with $\sigma = 2.0$, show that $\bar{X}$ would be a more precise estimator of μ if sample size were increased from $n = 4$ to $n = 16$.

Solution

Again, as in Example 13.11, we determine changes in precision with sample size by evaluating changes in $\sigma_{\bar{x}}$. Now, as sampling is without replacement from a finite population, and as both values of n are greater than 5% of N (see Section 13.10), we apply the finite-population correction factor, using equation (13.8) for $N = 60$, $\sigma = 2.0$, and $n = 4$:

$$\sigma_{\bar{x}} = \frac{2.0}{\sqrt{4}} \sqrt{\frac{60 - 4}{60 - 1}} = 1.0\sqrt{0.949153} = 0.974245, \qquad \text{or } 0.97$$

Increasing n from 4 to 16,

$$\sigma_{\bar{x}} = \frac{2.0}{\sqrt{16}} \sqrt{\frac{60 - 16}{60 - 1}} = 0.5\sqrt{0.745763} = 0.431788, \qquad \text{or } 0.43$$

Thus, a four-fold increase in sample size, while holding σ constant, decreases $\sigma_{\bar{x}}$ by over 55%.

13.8 For the empirical sampling distribution of the mean in Table 13.8, calculate the mean of the sample means (denoted by $\hat{\mu}_{\bar{x}}$, read mu–x-bar–hat) and the standard deviation of the sample means (denoted by $\hat{\sigma}_{\bar{x}}$, read sigma–x-bar–hat). To make these calculations, remove the relative frequency column from Table 13.8 and replace it with these four columns: frequency (f_i), frequency × mean ($f_i\bar{x}_i$), mean squared ($\bar{x}_i^2$), and frequency × mean squared ($f_i\bar{x}_i^2$). Then, make the calculations with these versions of equations (6.10) and (7.33) from Volume 1:

$$\hat{\mu}_{\bar{x}} = \frac{\sum_{i=1}^{k} f_i\bar{x}_i}{n_{\bar{x}}} \tag{13.33}$$

and

$$\hat{\sigma}_{\bar{x}} = \sqrt{\frac{\sum_{i=1}^{k} f_i\bar{x}_i^2 - \dfrac{\left(\sum_{i=1}^{k} f_i\bar{x}_i\right)^2}{n_{\bar{x}}}}{n_{\bar{x}} - 1}} \tag{13.34}$$

where $n_{\bar{x}}$ denotes the number of samples.

Solution

The requested table with the $\hat{\mu}_{\bar{x}}$ and $\hat{\sigma}_{\bar{x}}$ calculations is shown in Table 13.13. You can see that with only 100 samples out of the infinite number of possible samples, these estimates are only fair estimates of $\mu_{\bar{x}}$ [$\hat{\mu}_{\bar{x}} = 1.92$ versus $\mu_{\bar{x}} = 2.0$; see Example 13.6(*a*)] and $\sigma_{\bar{x}}$($\hat{\sigma}_{\bar{x}} = 1.06$ versus $\sigma_{\bar{x}} = 1.00$; see Example 13.9).

Table 13.13

Sample mean $\bar{x}_i$	Frequency f_i	$f_i\bar{x}_i$	$\bar{x}_i^2$	$f_i\bar{x}_i^2$
0.0	5	0.0	0.00	0.00
0.5	13	6.5	0.25	3.25
1.0	11	11.0	1.00	11.00
1.5	13	19.5	2.25	29.25
2.0	18	36.0	4.00	72.00
2.5	16	40.0	6.25	100.00
3.0	13	39.0	9.00	117.00
3.5	7	24.5	12.25	85.75
4.0	4	16.0	16.00	64.00
$\sum$	100	192.5		482.25

$$\mu_{\bar{x}} = \frac{\sum f_i\bar{x}_i}{n_{\bar{x}}} = \frac{192.5}{100} = 1.92$$

$$\hat{\sigma}_{\bar{x}}^2 = \sqrt{\frac{\sum f_i\bar{x}_i^2 - \frac{(\sum f_i x_i)^2}{n_{\bar{x}}}}{n_{\bar{x}} - 1}} = \sqrt{\frac{482.25 - \frac{(192.5)^2}{100}}{99}} = 1.0621, \qquad \text{or } 1.06$$

DETERMINING PROBABILITIES WITH A DISCRETE SAMPLING DISTRIBUTION OF THE MEAN

13.9 For the five-number population in Example 13.3: 0, 1, 2, 3, 4, and the discrete sampling distribution of the mean shown in Table 13.2, determine the probability that the mean $(\bar{X} = \bar{x})$ of a random sample of size $(n = 2)$ selected with replacement from this population will be more than 0.5 but at most 2.0.

Solution

The general rules for discrete-variable cumulative distribution functions from Section 10.7 of Volume 1 also apply to a discrete $\bar{X}$. Thus here, using equation (10.4) of Volume 1,

$$P(0.5 < \bar{X} \leq 2.0) = F(2.0) - F(0.5)$$

We know from Example 13.12 that $F(2.0) = 0.60$ for this distribution. Calculating $F(0.5)$,

$$F(0.5) = f(0.0) + f(0.5) = 0.04 + 0.08 = 0.12$$

Therefore,

$$P(0.5 < \bar{X} \leq 2.0) = 0.60 - 0.12 = 0.48$$

13.10 Given the five-number population in Example 13.3: 0, 1, 2, 3, 4 and the discrete sampling distribution of the mean in Table 13.4, determine the probability that the mean $(\bar{X} = \bar{x})$ of a random sample of size $(n = 2)$ selected without replacement from this population will be 0.5, 1.0, or 1.5.

Solution

Using equation (13.10) and values from Table 13.4

$$F(1.5) = \sum_{\bar{x} \leq 1.5} f(\bar{x})$$
$$= f(0.5) + f(1.0) + f(1.5) = 0.1 + 0.1 + 0.2 = 0.4$$

13.11 For the five-number population in Example 13.3: 0, 1, 2, 3, 4, and the discrete sampling distribution of the mean in Table 13.4, determine the probability that the mean ($\bar{X} = \bar{x}$) of a random sample of size ($n = 2$) selected without replacement from this population will be at least 1.5 but less than 4.5.

Solution

Converting equation (10.7) of Volume 1 for discrete $\bar{X}$,

$$P(1.5 \leq \bar{X} < 4.5) = F(4.5) - F(1.5) + f(1.5) - f(4.5)$$

and as

$$F(4.5) = F(3.5) = \sum_{\bar{x} \leq 3.5} f(\bar{x}) = 1.0$$
$$F(1.5) = 0.4$$
$$f(1.5) = 0.2$$
$$f(4.5) = 0.0$$

Therefore,

$$P(1.5 \leq \bar{X} < 4.5) = 1.0 - 0.4 + 0.2 - 0.0 = 0.8$$

13.12 For the three-number population in example 13.14: 3, 4, 5, and the sampling distribution of the mean in Table 13.5, determine the probability that the mean ($\bar{X} = \bar{x}$) of a random sample of size $n = 2$ selected with replacement from the population will be less than 5.0 but greater than 3.0.

Solution

Converting equation (10.6) of Volume 1 for discrete $\bar{X}$ and using values from Table 13.5,

$$P(3.0 < \bar{X} < 5.0) = F(5.0) - F(3.0) - f(5.0)$$
$$= 1.0 - 0.111111 - 0.111111 = 0.7778$$

13.13 For the discrete sampling distribution of the mean in Table 13.5, we know from Example 13.14(*c*) that $\mu_{\bar{x}} = 4.0$ and $\sigma_{\bar{x}} = 0.577350$, or 0.58. From this information, what is the probability that the random variable $\bar{X}$ will take on a value in the interval $\mu_{\bar{x}} \pm 1.5\sigma_{\bar{x}}$?

Solution

As was true for the discrete random variable X in Example 10.12 of Volume 1, this problem for the discrete random variable $\bar{X}$ has an approximate solution using a variation of Chebyshev's theorem and an exact solution. The variation of the theorem that applies to a sampling distribution of the mean is

> For any number $k \geq 1$, the probability that a random variable $\bar{X}$ with mean $\mu_{\bar{x}}$ and standard deviation $\sigma_{\bar{x}}$ will take on a value in the interval $\mu_{\bar{x}} \pm k\sigma_{\bar{x}}$ is at least $1 - \frac{1}{k^2}$.

Therefore, here, the probability is at least

$$1 - \frac{1}{k^2} = 1 - \frac{1}{(1.5)^2} = 1 - \frac{1}{2.25} = 1 - 0.444444 = 0.555556, \quad \text{or } 0.56$$

The exact solution requires a summation of the probabilities for all possible values of $\bar{X}$ in the interval $\mu_{\bar{x}} \pm 1.5\sigma_{\bar{x}}$:

$$\mu_{\bar{x}} \pm 1.5\sigma_{\bar{x}} = 4.0 \pm 1.5(0.577350), \text{ or } 4.0 \pm 0.866025, \qquad \text{or from 3.13 to 4.87}$$

As $\bar{X}$ can only take on the values 3.5, 4.0, and 4.5 in this interval, we can say from Table 13.5 that

$$\begin{aligned} P(-1.5\sigma_{\bar{x}} \leq \bar{X} \leq 1.5\sigma_{\bar{x}}) &= f(3.5) + f(4.0) + f(4.5) \\ &= 0.222222 + 0.333333 + 0.222222 \\ &= 0.777777, \qquad \text{or } 0.78 \end{aligned}$$

DETERMINING PROBABILITIES WITH A NORMALLY DISTRIBUTED SAMPLING DISTRIBUTION OF THE MEAN

13.14 A random sample ($n = 9$) is taken from a normally distributed population ($\mu = 0.75$, $\sigma = 0.15$). (*a*) What are the characteristics (shape, parameters) of the distribution of the continuous random variable $\bar{X}$? (*b*) What is the probability that $\bar{X}$ will take on a value $\bar{x}$ that is at most 0.80? (*c*) What is the probability that $\bar{X}$ will take on a value $\bar{x}$ that is at least 0.80?

Solution

(*a*) From Section 13.14 we know that $\bar{X}$ is normally distributed with $\mu_{\bar{x}} = \mu = 0.75$ and $\sigma_{\bar{x}} = \frac{\sigma}{\sqrt{n}} = \frac{0.15}{\sqrt{9}} = 0.05$.

(*b*) From Equation (13.14) we know that

$$\begin{aligned} P(\bar{X} \leq 0.80) &= P(-\infty < Z \leq 0.00) + P\left(0.00 \leq Z \leq \frac{0.80 - 0.75}{0.05}\right) \\ &= 0.5 + P(0.00 \leq Z \leq 1.00) \end{aligned}$$

Therefore, using the value from Table A.5 for $z = 1.00$,

$$P(\bar{X} \leq 0.80) = 0.5 + 0.3413 = 0.8413$$

(*c*) From equation (10.1) of Volume 1 we know that for a continuous probability distribution,

$$P(a < \bar{X} \leq b) = P(a \leq \bar{X} \leq b) = P(a < \bar{X} < b) = P(a \leq \bar{X} < b)$$

Therefore,

$$P(\bar{X} \geq 0.80) = 1 - P(\bar{X} \leq 0.80) = 1 - 0.8413 = 0.1587$$

13.15 A random sample ($n = 64$) is taken from a normally distributed population ($\sigma = 10.0$). If $P(X \leq 62.0) = 0.9452$, then what is $\mu_{\bar{x}}$?

Solution

From equation (13.14) and using the technique from Problem 12.11, we know that

$$P(\bar{X} \leq 62.0) = P(Z \leq z_?) = 0.9452$$

and that

$$\begin{aligned} P(Z \leq z_?) = 0.9452 &= P(-\infty < Z \leq 0) + P(0 \leq Z \leq z_?) \\ &= 0.5 + P(0 \leq Z \leq z_?) \end{aligned}$$

Therefore,

$$P(0 \leq Z \leq z_?) = 0.9452 - 0.5 = 0.4452$$

and thus from Table A.5

$$z_? = 1.60$$

Rearranging the terms in equation (13.11),

$$\bar{X} = \mu_{\bar{x}} + Z\sigma_{\bar{x}} \tag{13.35}$$

Using $\bar{X} = \bar{x} = 62.0$ and $\sigma_{\bar{x}} = \dfrac{10.0}{\sqrt{64}} = 1.25$ in equation (13.35),

$$\begin{aligned} 62.0 &= \mu_{\bar{x}} + (1.60 \times 1.25) \\ &= \mu_{\bar{x}} + 2.0 \end{aligned}$$

and thus

$$\mu_{\bar{x}} = 60.0$$

13.16 If the normally distributed random variable $\bar{X}$ has $\mu_{\bar{x}} = 5.5$ and $\sigma_{\bar{x}} = 0.45$, then what are z_α and $\bar{x}_\alpha$ if $\alpha = 0.025$?

Solution

Recall from Section 12.10 [equation (12.9)] that, when written with these symbols, α denotes the area in the upper tail of a probability distribution. Thus, for the continuous normally distributed variable $\bar{X}$,

$$P(\bar{X} > \bar{x}_\alpha) = P\left(Z > \frac{\bar{x}_\alpha - \mu_{\bar{x}}}{\sigma_{\bar{x}}}\right) = P(Z > z_\alpha) = \alpha \tag{13.36}$$

which for the standard normal distribution is the shaded area in Fig. 12-9. In this problem we are given that

$$P(Z > z_\alpha) = \alpha = 0.025$$

and that therefore

$$P(0 \le Z \le z_{0.025}) = 0.5 - 0.025 = 0.475$$

From Table A.5 we find that $z_{0.025} = 1.96$. Using equation (13.35),

$$\begin{aligned} \bar{x}_\alpha &= \mu_{\bar{x}} + z_\alpha \sigma_{\bar{x}} \\ &= 5.5 + (1.96 \times 0.45) = 5.5 + 0.882 = 6.382, \qquad \text{or } 6.4 \end{aligned}$$

13.17 For the carrot developed for growth in heavy clay soil (see Problems 12.8 to 12.12), assume that carrot-length X is normally distributed with $\mu = 11.5$ cm and $\sigma = 1.15$ cm. What is the probability for a random sample of 25 of these carrots that the mean $\bar{X}$ of the sample will be within 0.5 cm of μ in either direction?

Solution

Restating the problem, we must determine

$$P(\mu - 0.5 \text{ cm} \le \bar{X} \le \mu + 0.5 \text{ cm})$$

We know that $\mu_{\bar{x}} = \mu = 11.5$ cm and that $\sigma_{\bar{x}} = \dfrac{\sigma}{\sqrt{n}} = \dfrac{1.15 \text{ cm}}{\sqrt{25}} = 0.23$ cm. Thus, using equation (13.14), we must solve the relationship

$$\begin{aligned} &P(11.5 \text{ cm} - 0.5 \text{ cm} \le \bar{X} \le 11.5 \text{ cm} + 0.5 \text{ cm}) \\ &\quad = P\left(\frac{11.0 \text{ cm} - 11.5 \text{ cm}}{0.23 \text{ cm}} \le Z \le \frac{12.0 \text{ cm} - 11.5 \text{ cm}}{0.23 \text{ cm}}\right) \\ &P(11.0 \text{ cm} \le \bar{X} \le 12.0 \text{ cm}) = P(-2.17 \le Z \le 2.17) \end{aligned}$$

Using the value from Table A.5 for $z = 2.17$,

$$P(11.0 \text{ cm} \le \bar{X} \le 12.0 \text{ cm}) = 2(0.4850) = 0.9700$$

13.18 For the carrots in Problem 13.17, if a sample of 49 is taken to estimate μ, what is the probability that this estimate will be in error by at most 0.25 cm?

Solution

By error in this problem, we mean sampling error $\bar{x} - \mu$ (see Section 13.11). Therefore, we must determine the probability that the mean $\bar{x}$ of a sample of size $n = 49$ will take on a value within ± 0.25 cm of $\mu_{\bar{x}} = \mu = 11.5$ cm. We know that for $n = 49$, $\sigma_{\bar{x}} = \frac{\sigma}{\sqrt{n}} = \frac{1.15 \text{ cm}}{\sqrt{49}} = 0.164286$ cm. Thus, using equation (13.14), we must solve the relationship

$$P(11.5 \text{ cm} - 0.25 \text{ cm} \le \bar{X} \le 11.5 \text{ cm} + 0.25 \text{ cm})$$
$$= P\left(\frac{11.25 \text{ cm} - 11.5 \text{ cm}}{0.164286 \text{ cm}} \le Z \le \frac{11.75 \text{ cm} - 11.5 \text{ cm}}{0.164286 \text{ cm}}\right)$$
$$P(11.25 \text{ cm} \le \bar{X} \le 11.75 \text{ cm}) = P(-1.52 \le Z \le 1.52)$$

Using the value from Table A.5 for $z = 1.52$,

$$P(11.25 \text{ cm} \le \bar{X} \le 11.75 \text{ cm}) = 2(0.4357) = 0.8714$$

13.19 A cultural anthropologist has found, using radioactive-dating techniques, that the ages X of a unique type of bone-scraping tool are essentially normally distributed ($\mu = 12{,}500$ years, $\sigma = 400$ years). If, from thousands of these scraping tools, 150 random samples of four each ($n = 4$) are taken and dated, how many of these samples will have means that are 12,800 years old or older?

Solution

First we must determine $P(\bar{X} \ge 12{,}800 \text{ yr})$. We know that $\mu_{\bar{x}} = \mu = 12{,}500$ yr and $\sigma_{\bar{x}} = \frac{\sigma}{\sqrt{n}} = \frac{400 \text{ yr}}{\sqrt{4}} = 200$ yr. Therefore,

$$P(\bar{X} \ge 12{,}800 \text{ yr}) = P\left(Z \ge \frac{12{,}800 \text{ yr} - 12{,}500 \text{ yr}}{200 \text{ yr}}\right) = P(Z \ge 1.50)$$

Using the value from Table A.5 for $z = 1.50$,

$$P(Z \ge 1.50) = 0.5 - 0.4332 = 0.0668$$

Thus, the expected number of the 150 samples with mean ages that are 12,800 years old or older is

$$0.0668 \times 150 = 10.02, \qquad \text{or } 10.0$$

THE CENTRAL LIMIT THEOREM

13.20 For the distribution of *GPAs* ($\mu = 3.19$ and $\sigma = 0.24$) in Example 13.15, we found for a random sample of 36 seniors, taken without replacement, that $\mu_{\bar{x}} = \mu = 3.19$ and $\sigma_{\bar{x}} = \frac{\sigma}{\sqrt{n}} = 0.04$. For such samples of $n = 36$, what is a if $P(|\bar{X} - \mu| \le a) = 0.34$?

Solution

Restating the probability, we must solve the equation

$$P(\mu - a \leq \bar{X} \leq \mu + a) = 0.34$$

For this problem of sampling without replacement from a finite population, as $n \geq 30$ and $N \geq 2n$, we can apply the central limit theorem (see Section 13.17) and use equation (13.15):

$$P(\mu - a \leq \bar{X} \leq \mu + a) = 0.34 \approx P\left(\frac{\mu - a - (\mu_{\bar{x}} = \mu)}{\sigma_{\bar{x}}} \leq Z \leq \frac{\mu + a - (\mu_{\bar{x}} = \mu)}{\sigma_{\bar{x}}}\right)$$

$$\approx P\left(\frac{-a}{\sigma_{\bar{x}}} \leq Z \leq \frac{a}{\sigma_{\bar{x}}}\right)$$

The closest z value in Table A.5 for a probability of $\frac{0.34}{2} = 0.17$ is exactly 0.44. Therefore

$$\frac{a}{\sigma_{\bar{x}}} \approx 0.44$$

Knowing that $\sigma_{\bar{x}} = 0.04$,

$$a \approx 0.44 \times 0.04 = 0.0176$$

13.21 A manufacturer of cosmetics has 1,500 door-to-door salespeople who averaged μ =\$3,100 in sales last month, with a standard deviation of σ = \$350. If a random sample of 49 of these salespeople is taken without replacement, what is the probability that this group averaged less than \$3,000 last month?

Solution

As $n \geq 30$ and $N \geq 2n$, we can apply the version of the central limit theorem for sampling from a finite population without replacement (see Section 13.17) and can say that the distribution of $\bar{X}$ is approximately normal with parameters $\mu_{\bar{x}} = \mu$ =\$3,100 and, as $n \leq 0.05N$, $\sigma_{\bar{x}} = \frac{\sigma}{\sqrt{n}} = \frac{\$350}{\sqrt{49}} = \$50$. Using this information, we can get the approximate solution to the problem, which can be stated as

$$P(\bar{X} < \$3{,}000)$$

From equation (13.15) we can say that

$$P(\bar{X} < \$3{,}000) \approx P\left(Z < \frac{\$3{,}000 - \$3{,}100}{\$50}\right) = P(Z < -2.00)$$

Using the value in Table A.5 for $z = 2.00$,

$$P(\bar{X} < \$3{,}000) \approx 0.5 - 0.4772 = 0.0228$$

13.22 A standard anesthetic used in dentistry takes an average of μ = 290 sec (σ = 25 sec) from injection to the elimination of sensitivity in the injected area of the gums and teeth. For the next 32 patients of a given dentist, what is the probability (approximately) that they will average somewhere between 295 sec and 300 sec from injection to insensitivity.

Solution

Here, because $n \geq 30$ and because the experiment is infinitely repeatable, the version of the central limit theorem for sampling from an infinite population (see Section 13.16) can be applied. Therefore, we can say that the distribution of $\bar{X}$ is approximately normal with parameters $\mu_{\bar{x}} = \mu = 290$ sec and $\sigma_{\bar{x}} = \frac{\sigma}{\sqrt{n}} = \frac{25 \text{ sec}}{\sqrt{32}} = \frac{25 \text{ sec}}{5.656854} = 4.419418$ sec. Using this information, we can get the approximate solution to this restatement of the problem,

$$P(295 \text{ sec} \leq \bar{X} \leq 300 \text{ sec})$$

Using equation (13.15)

$$P(295 \text{ sec} \leq \bar{X} \leq 300 \text{ sec}) \approx P\left(\frac{295 \text{ sec} - 290 \text{ sec}}{4.419418 \text{ sec}} \leq Z \leq \frac{300 \text{ sec} - 290 \text{ sec}}{4.419418 \text{ sec}}\right)$$
$$\approx P(1.13 \leq Z \leq 2.26)$$

Using values from Table A.5 for $z = 1.13$ and $z = 2.26$,

$$P(295 \text{ sec} \leq \bar{X} \leq 300 \text{ sec}) \approx 0.4881 - 0.3708 = 0.1173$$

DETERMINING PROBABILITIES WITH A NORMALLY DISTRIBUTED SAMPLING DISTRIBUTION OF THE SAMPLE SUM

13.23 The fishing company in Example 13.16 has found for its 15 boats that the catch per boat per day is normally distributed with $\mu = 500$ lb and $\sigma = 40$ lb. If the company guarantees its major distributor a minimum daily catch of 4,200 lb, what is the probability that the company will not meet this minimum guarantee on a given day if only nine boats are fishing?

Solution

The essence of this problem is that we are taking a sample of $n = 9$ daily catches $(X = x)$ from a normally distributed population of daily catches. We take the sum $y = \sum_{i=1}^{9} x_i$ of these nine catches and then determine $P(Y < 4{,}200 \text{ lb})$. Because sampling is from a normal distribution, the sampling distribution of Y is also normally distributed (see Section 13.19) with $\mu_y = n\mu = 9 \times 500 \text{ lb} = 4{,}500 \text{ lb}$ and $\sigma_y = \sqrt{n}\sigma = \sqrt{9} \times 40 \text{ lb} = 120 \text{ lb}$. From equation (13.19), we can say that

$$P(Y < a) = P\left(Z < \frac{a - \mu_y}{\sigma_y}\right)$$

Therefore,

$$P(Y < 4{,}200 \text{ lb}) = P\left(Z < \frac{4{,}200 \text{ lb} - 4{,}500 \text{ lb}}{120 \text{ lb}}\right) = P(Z < -2.50)$$

Using the value from Table A.5 for $z = 2.50$,

$$P(Y < 4{,}200 \text{ lb}) = 0.5 - 0.4938 = 0.0062$$

DETERMINING PROBABILITIES WITH A NORMAL APPROXIMATION TO THE SAMPLING DISTRIBUTION OF THE SAMPLE SUM

13.24 For the computer-software company in Example 13.17, the distribution of overtime hours for the 1,000 programmers for the past week has the parameters $\mu = 5.75$ hr and $\sigma = 0.48$ hr. If a random sample (without replacement) of 64 programmers is taken, what is the probability that the total of their overtime for the past week was at most 375 hr?

Solution

As $n \geq 30$ and $N \geq 2n$, the central limit theorem (see Section 13.20) indicates that the distribution of $Y = \sum_{i=1}^{64} X_i$ is approximately normal with parameters $\mu_y = n\mu = 64 \times 5.75 \text{ hr} = 368.0 \text{ hr}$ and, as $n > 0.05N$, we must use equation (13.21):

$$\sigma_y = \sqrt{n}\sigma \times \sqrt{\frac{N-n}{N-1}} = \sqrt{64} \times 0.48 \text{ hr} \times \sqrt{\frac{1{,}000 - 64}{1{,}000 - 1}} = 3.72 \text{ hr}$$

Using this information we can get the approximate solution to this restatement of the problem,

$$P(Y \leq 375 \text{ hr})$$

From equation (13.20), we can say that

$$P(Y \leq 375 \text{ hr}) \approx P\left(Z \leq \frac{375 \text{ hr} - \mu_y}{\sigma_y}\right) = P\left(Z \leq \frac{375 \text{ hr} - 368.0 \text{ hr}}{3.72 \text{ hr}}\right) = P(Z \leq 1.88)$$

Using the value from Table A.5 for $z = 1.88$,

$$P(Y \leq 375 \text{ hr}) \approx 0.5 + 0.4699 = 0.9699$$

DETERMINING PROBABILTIES WITH A NORMAL APPROXIMATION TO THE SAMPLING DISTRIBUTION OF THE PROPORTION

13.25 The exit poll in Example 13.20, conducted on a random sample of 100 voters, indicates that the proportion of voters who preferred candidate A was $\bar{p} = 0.49$. Assuming that the proportion that favors A in the voting population was $p = 0.51$, what is $P(0.48 \leq \bar{P} \leq 0.53)$?

Solution

As in Example 13.20, we assume that the sampling distribution of the proportion favoring A is binomially distributed with $\mu_{\bar{p}} = 0.51$, $\sigma^2_{\bar{p}} = 0.002499$, and $\sigma_{\bar{p}} = 0.05$. Using the continuity correction, $\frac{1}{2n} = \frac{1}{2(100)} = 0.005$, this problem can be solved with equation (13.32):

$$P(0.48 - 0.005 \leq \bar{P} \leq 0.53 + 0.005) \approx P\left(\frac{0.48 - 0.005 - 0.51}{0.05} \leq Z \leq \frac{0.53 + 0.005 - 0.51}{0.05}\right)$$

$$P(0.475 \leq \bar{P} \leq 0.535) \approx P(-0.70 \leq Z \leq 0.50)$$

Using the values from Table A.5 for $z = 0.70$ and $z = 0.50$,

$$P(0.48 \leq \bar{P} \leq 0.53) \approx 0.2580 + 0.1915 = 0.4495$$

13.26 A computer manufacturer buys a type of circuit chip in lots of 10,000. He accepts the possibility that 3% of these chips will be defective, but rejects the lot if he finds in a sample of 200 from the lot that 5% or more are defective. What is the probability he will reject a lot?

Solution

If we accept that this is sampling from a binomial population under Bernoulli-trial conditions, then the sampling distribution of the proportion of defectives will be binomially distributed with $\mu_{\bar{p}} = p = 0.03$, $\sigma^2_{\bar{p}} = \frac{pq}{n} = \frac{0.03 \times 0.97}{200} = 0.0001455$, and $\sigma_{\bar{p}} = \sqrt{\frac{pq}{n}} = \sqrt{0.0001455} = 0.012062$. As $nq = 6$ and $nq = 194$, we can say that the sampling distribution of the proportion of defectives is approximately normally distributed (see Section 13.25) and that

$$Z = \frac{\bar{P} - \mu_{\bar{p}}}{\sigma_{\bar{p}}} = \frac{\bar{P} - 0.03}{0.012062}$$

will have an approximate standard normal distribution. Therefore, with the continuity correction of $\frac{1}{2n} = \frac{1}{400} = 0.0025$, we must solve [from equation (13.32)]

$$P(\bar{P} \geq 0.05 - 0.0025) = P(\bar{P} \geq 0.0475) \approx P\left(Z \geq \frac{0.05 - 0.0025 - 0.03}{0.012062}\right) = P(Z \geq 1.45)$$

Using the value from Table A.5 for $z = 1.45$,

$$P(\bar{P} \geq 0.05) \approx 0.5 - 0.4265 = 0.0735$$

13.27 A geologist working for an oil company has determined that oil can be found under a specific domed rock formation 54% of the time. What is the probability that, in the next 100 times the company drills under such a formation, they will find oil at least 53% of the time?

Solution

If we accept that this is sampling from a binomial population under Bernoulli-trial conditions, then the sampling distribution of the proportion of successful explorations will be binomially distributed with $\mu_{\bar{p}} = p = 0.54$, $\sigma_{\bar{p}}^2 = \frac{pq}{n} = \frac{0.54 \times 0.46}{100} = 0.002484$, $\sigma_{\bar{p}} = \sqrt{\frac{pq}{n}} = \sqrt{0.002484} = 0.49840$. As $np = 54$ and $nq = 46$, we can say that this sampling distribution of the proportion is approximately normally distributed (see Section 13.25) and that

$$Z = \frac{\bar{P} - \mu_{\bar{p}}}{\sigma_{\bar{p}}} = \frac{\bar{P} - 0.54}{0.049840}$$

will have approximately a standard normal distribution. Thus, with the continuity correction $\frac{1}{2n} = \frac{1}{200} = 0.005$, we must solve [from equation (13.32)]

$$P(\bar{P} \geq 0.53 - 0.005) = P(\bar{P} \geq 0.525) \approx P\left(Z \geq \frac{0.53 - 0.005 - 0.54}{0.049840}\right) = P(Z \geq -0.30)$$

Using the value from Table A.5 for $z = 0.30$,

$$P(\bar{P} \geq 0.53) \approx 0.5 + 0.1179 = 0.6179$$

Supplementary Problems

THE SAMPLING DISTRIBUTION OF THE MEAN

13.28 A construction company plans to build a new road connecting two towns. To find out how much traffic to expect, five random samples of 50 residents each are drawn without replacement from the joined populations of both towns (from telephone books), and each person is asked how many times a month they expect to drive round-trip between the two towns on the new road. These are the results for the five samples (times/month): $\bar{x}_1 = 6.5$, $\bar{x}_2 = 8.4$, $\bar{x}_3 = 7.3$, $\bar{x}_4 = 7.6$, $\bar{x}_5 = 6.8$. What is the overall mean of the samples?

Ans. 7.32 times per month

13.29 For the list of possible random samples and their means in Problem 13.4(*b*), calculate the probability of selection for each possible mean and present the resulting sampling distribution in a probability table.

Ans. The requested sampling distribution is shown in Table 13.14.

Table 13.14

Sample mean $\bar{x}$	Probability $f(\bar{x})$
1.5	0.066667
2.0	0.066667
2.5	0.133333
3.0	0.133333
3.5	0.200000
4.0	0.133333
4.5	0.133333
5.0	0.066667
5.5	0.066667
Σ	1.000000

13.30 A vast population of beetles (N essentially infinite) exhibits variation in the number of spots on the dorsal surface. The number can be 1, 2, or 3, with all three numbers occurring in equal proportions within the population. Determine the sampling distribution of the mean for possible random samples of size $n = 2$ taken with replacement from this population of spot numbers. Calculate the probability of selection for each possible sample mean and present the resulting sampling distribution in a probability table.

Ans. The requested sampling distribution is shown in Table 13.15.

Table 13.15

Sample mean $\bar{x}$	Probability $f(\bar{x})$
1.0	0.111111
1.5	0.222222
2.0	0.333333
2.5	0.222222
3.0	0.111111
Σ	0.999999

THE MEAN, VARIANCE, AND STANDARD DEVIATION OF THE SAMPLING DISTRIBUTION OF THE MEAN

13.31 What is the mean of the sampling distribution in Table 13.14?

Ans. 3.50

13.32 What is the standard error of the sampling distribution in Table 13.14?

Ans. 1.08

13.33 What is the mean of the sampling distribution in Table 13.15?

Ans. 2.00

13.34 What is the standard error of the sampling distribution in Table 13.15?

Ans. 0.58

DETERMINING PROBABILITIES WITH A DISCRETE SAMPLING DISTRIBUTION OF THE MEAN

13.35 For the sampling distribution in Table 13.14, what is the probability that the mean number of bedrooms in a sample will be more than 2.0?

Ans. 0.8667

13.36 For the sampling distribution in Table 13.15, what is the probability that the mean number of spots in a sample will be more than 1.5 but less than 3.0?

Ans. 0.5556

13.37 For the population of beetles described in Problem 13.30, and the values of $\mu_{\bar{x}}$ and $\sigma_{\bar{x}}$ from Problems 13.33 and 13.34, what is the probability that $\bar{X}$ will take on a value in the interval $\mu_{\bar{x}} \pm 1.25\sigma_{\bar{x}}$? Solve this problem by using: (*a*) Chebyshev's theorem, and (*b*) the exact solution (see Problem 13.13).

Ans. (*a*) At least 0.3600, (*b*) 0.7778

DETERMINING PROBABILITIES WITH A NORMALLY DISTRIBUTED SAMPLING DISTRIBUTION OF THE MEAN

13.38 A company that sells peanut butter states on the jar that each jar contains 18 ounces of peanut butter. To achieve this standard, they set their jar-filling machine to put 18.3 ounces in each jar. As a quality control, the machine is routinely tested by taking random samples ($n = 16$) of filled jars and weighing their contents. From thousands of such weighings, the company accepts that this contents-weight X is normally distributed with $\mu = 18.3$ oz and $\sigma = 0.12$ oz. The filling machine is readjusted if the mean of any sample $\bar{X} = \bar{x}$ is more than three standard deviations from $\mu_{\bar{x}}$. For any given sample, what is the probability that the filling machine will have to be readjusted?

Ans. 0.0026

13.39 In late summer, the body weights of male ground squirrels are known to be normally distributed with a population mean of 400 grams and standard deviation of 100 grams. A random sample of 50 squirrels is taken. What is the probability that the sample mean will be between 380 grams and 420 grams?

Ans. 0.8414

13.40 For a very large population of children, intelligence quotient scores (*IQ* scores) that are acquired by using the Stanford–Binet Intelligence Scale tend to be normally distributed with a population mean of 100.0 and standard deviation of 16.0. A random sample of 100 such scores is taken. What is the probability that the sample mean will take on a value greater than 102?

Ans. 0.1056

THE CENTRAL LIMIT THEOREM

13.41 In a population of 500 songbirds, the average number of eggs per nest is 3.2 and the standard deviation is 0.8. If a sample of 36 nests is taken, with replacement, what is the probability that the sample mean will be greater than 3.0 eggs?

Ans. ≈ 0.9332

13.42 If the population of songbirds described in Problem 13.41 had been sampled ($n = 36$) without replacement, what is the probability that the sample mean will be greater than 3.0 eggs?

Ans. ≈ 0.9406

DETERMINING PROBABILITIES WITH A NORMALLY DISTRIBUTED SAMPLING DISTRIBUTION OF THE SAMPLE SUM

13.43 For the fishing company described in Example 13.16 and Problem 13.23, if it had been true for the random sample $X_1, X_2, \ldots, X_9$ that the sampling distribution of X_3 was normally distributed with parameters $\mu_3 = 450$ lb and $\sigma_3 = 40$ lb, then what would be the probability that the total catch in one day for a sample of nine boats will be between 3,850 lb and 3,900 lb?

Ans. 0.0581

DETERMINING PROBABILITIES WITH A NORMAL APPROXIMATION TO THE SAMPLING DISTRIBUTION OF THE SAMPLE SUM

13.44 For the computer-software company in Example 13.17 and Problem 13.24, the distribution of overtime hours for the 1,000 programmers for the past week has the parameters $\mu = 5.75$ hr and $\sigma = 0.48$ hr. If a random sample (without replacement) of 49 programmers is taken, what is the probability that the total of their overtime for the past week is greater than or equal to 280 hr but at most 283 hr?

Ans. ≈ 0.3428

DETERMINING PROBABILITIES WITH A NORMAL APPROXIMATION TO THE SAMPLING DISTRIBUTION OF THE PROPORTION

13.45 If the computer manufacturer in Problem 13.26 doubles the random sample from each lot from 200 to 400 but still rejects the lot if 5% or more are defective, then what is the new probability that he will reject a lot?

Ans. ≈ 0.0139

13.46 A fisheries biologist knows from many studies of populations of bluegills in lakes that 44% of the fish are males. If he now takes a sample of 40 bluegills from a lake, what is the probability that the proportion of males will be between 42% and 46%?

Ans. ≈ 0.3182

CHAPTER 14

One-Sample Estimation of the Population Mean

14.1 ESTIMATION

Inferential statistics is the division of the science of statistics that provides the logic and techniques for making inferences (generalizations) about the characteristics of entire populations from the characteristics of samples taken from these populations (see Volume 1, Section 3.5). There are four theoretical components to inferential statistics: probability theory (see Chapters 8 through 10 of Volume 1 and Chapters 11 and 12 of this volume), sampling theory (see Chapter 13), estimation theory, and hypothesis-testing theory. In this chapter we begin work on inferential problems with an introduction to estimation theory as applied to one-sample estimation of the popuulation mean μ. Then in Chapter 15 we deal with one-sample estimation of the population variance σ^2 and standard deviation σ and of the binomial-population proportion p. We go on in Chapter 16 to introduce hypothesis-testing theory, again as applied to single samples. We deal with two-sample estimation and hypothesis-testing problems in Chapter 17, and then with multisample versions of these problems in Chapter 18.

Estimation theory provides techniques for estimating unknown population parameters from sample statistics. Recall that population parameters are numerical descriptive measures of some population characteristics, calculated empirically from an entire measurement population, while sample statistics (or statistics) are empirical numerical measures of some measurement-sample characteristic (see Volume 1, Section 3.4). Do not confuse empirical population parameters with probability distribution parameters, which are defining constants in theoretical distribution equations (see Section 11.9).

An estimator is any sample statistic $\hat{\theta}$ that gives an estimate of a population parameter θ (see Section 13.8). An estimate is any numerical value of an estimator $\hat{\theta}^*$ calculated from a specific sample. Thus, the sample mean $\bar{X}$ is an estimator of the popuulation μ, which for any given sample yields the specific estimate $\bar{X} = \bar{x}$. Because the specific estimate varies from sample to sample, estimators are random variables with theoretical and empirical distributions called sampling distributions (see Section 13.6).

One-sample estimation problems, in which a numerical approximation to a population parameter is determined from one sample taken from that population, are of importance in every area of modern life: estimating the voting or television viewing preferences of a population, estimating the size of a wild animal population, estimating the prevalence of a disease in a population, estimating miles per gallon under city-driving conditions for a population of new cars, and so on.

14.2 CRITERIA FOR SELECTING THE OPTIMAL ESTIMATOR

Mathematical statisticians use several criteria of "goodness of estimation" in selecting the optimal estimator $\hat{\theta}$ for a population parameter θ. Among these are: *unbiasedness, precision, efficiency, consistency,* and *sufficiency.*

In Section 13.8 we indicated that an estimator $\hat{\theta}$ is unbiased—has the property of unbiasedness—when the mean of its sampling distribution $E(\hat{\theta})$ is equal to the parameter being estimated: $E(\hat{\theta}) = \theta$. We also indicated that the absolute distance $|E(\hat{\theta}) - \theta|$, is called the accuracy of the estimator, and when $|E(\hat{\theta}) - \theta| = 0$ the estimator is said to be a perfectly accurate (unbiased) estimator of θ.

Unbiasedness, then, indicates that there are no systematic errors built into the estimator; that in the long run it will neither overestimate nor underestimate the parameter. But given that two or more estimators are unbiased, with no systematic errors, they can still differ in the spread or variability of their estimates—in the amount of random error included in the estimate. The properties of precision and efficiency of an estimator both deal with this variability in related but different ways.

In Section 13.12 we said that the precision of an estimator $\hat{\theta}$ is the variability or spread of repeated estimates $\hat{\theta}*$ of a parameter θ, and it is measured by the standard deviation (standard error) of its sampling distribution. Thus, one estimator is said to be more precise than another if it has a smaller standard error.

The efficiency of an estimator $\hat{\theta}$ also deals with the spread of estimation, but it is measured by what is called the *mean square error* (MSE) of the estimator, which is

$$\begin{aligned}(\text{MSE of } \hat{\theta}) &= (\text{variance of } \hat{\theta}) + (\text{bias of } \hat{\theta}) \\ (\text{MSE of } \hat{\theta}) &= \sigma^2_{\hat{\theta}} + [E(\hat{\theta}) - \theta]\end{aligned} \tag{14.1}$$

which indicates that MSE is equal to the variance of the sampling distribution of the estimator plus the bias of the estimator. Clearly, then, if the estimator is unbiased,

$$(\text{MSE of } \hat{\theta}) = \sigma^2_{\hat{\theta}}$$

Thus, the efficiency of an unbiased estimator is measured by the variance of its sampling distribution, and the efficiency of two or more unbiased estimators of the same parameter can be compared by comparing their variances: For two such estimators, the one with the smaller variance is said to be *more efficient*; for more than two, the one with the smallest variance is said to be *most efficient.*

The final two properties, consistency and sufficiency, are mathematical concepts that we can only loosely define here. An estimator $\hat{\theta}$ is said to be consisitent—to have the property of consistency—when its estimates gets closer and closer to the parameter θ it is estimating as sample size n increases toward population size N. For unbiased estimators, then, the properties of efficiency, precision, and consistency have the following relationship: The larger n becomes, the smaller $\sigma^2_{\bar{x}}$ and $\sigma_{\bar{x}}$ become, and so the estimator becomes more efficient and precise and the estimates become more closely packed (consistent) around the parameter. Finally, an estimator is said to be sufficient if it summarizes all information on a parameter that is available in a sample.

Both unbiasedness and efficiency are desirable properties of an estimator. If two or more estimators of a parameter θ are being considered and both are unbiased, then the most efficient estimator—the one with the smallest variance—is selected as optimal and called the *minimum variance unbiased estimator.* Thus, while there are many central-tendency estimators that could be used to estimate the population mean μ, such as the median, mode, and midrange (see Volume 1, Chapter 6), the sample mean $\bar{X}$ is the minimum variance unbiased estimator of μ. Similarly, of all the dispersion estimators (see Volume 1, Chapter 7) that could be used to estimate population variance σ^2, the sample variance S^2 is the minimum variance unbiased estimator of σ^2. (Recall from Section 7.7, Volume 1, that $n - 1$ is used in the denominator of the sample variance formula to achieve an unbiased estimate.) In addition to unbiasedness and efficiency, both $\bar{X}$ and S^2 also have the properties of consistency and sufficiency.

The sample standard deviation S is not a minimum variance unbiased estimator of its parameter, the population standard deviation σ; it is a slightly biased estimator. However, based on the other criteria of "goodness of estimation," the sample standard deviation is on balance still the optimal estimator of σ and you will find it routinely used for this purpose throughout this book.

14.3 THE ESTIMATED STANDARD ERROR OF THE MEAN $S_{\bar{x}}$

The optimal estimator of the standard error of the mean $\sigma_{\bar{x}}$ (see Section 13.11), is the *estimated standard error of the mean* $S_{\bar{x}}$, as defined by this formula for samples of size n from an infinite or unknown-sized population:

$$S_{\bar{x}} = \frac{S}{\sqrt{n}} \tag{14.2}$$

and by this formula if sampling without replacement from a finite population in which N is known and $n > 0.05N$ (see Sections 13.10 and 13.11):

$$S_{\bar{x}} = \frac{S}{\sqrt{n}}\sqrt{\frac{N-n}{N-1}} \tag{14.3}$$

For any given sample, the random variable $S_{\bar{x}}$ has the specific value $s_{\bar{x}}$. As S is a slightly biased estimator of σ, $S_{\bar{x}}$ is a slightly biased estimator of $\sigma_{\bar{x}}$. But $S_{\bar{x}}$ is the optimal estimator of $\sigma_{\bar{x}}$ (as S is the optimal estimator of σ) based on other criteria of "goodness of estimation."

14.4 POINT ESTIMATES

For any given random sample from a population of measurements, if a specific numerical value $\hat{\theta}^*$ is calculated for an estimator $\hat{\theta}$ to estimate a population parameter θ, then that single numerical value $\hat{\theta}^*$ is called a *point estimate* of the parameter θ. You can also think of it as a single point on the real number line (see Volume 1, Section 1.20).

EXAMPLE 14.1 Given the following information calculated from a random sample taken from an infinite population, determine point estimates $\hat{\theta}^*$ for the estimators $\bar{X}$, S^2, S, and $S_{\bar{x}}$: $n = 10$, $\sum x_i = 84.1$, and $\sum x_i^2 = 708.33$.

Solution

For the estimator $\bar{X}$ [see equation (3.1) of Volume 1 and Section 13.5],

$$\bar{X} = \frac{\sum X_i}{n}$$

and thus the point estimate is

$$\bar{x} = \frac{84.1}{10} = 8.41$$

For the estimator S^2 [see equation (7.17) of Volume 1 and Section 13.6],

$$S^2 = \frac{\sum X_i^2 - \frac{(\sum X_i)^2}{n}}{n-1}$$

and thus the point estimate is

$$s^2 = \frac{708.33 - \frac{(84.1)^2}{10}}{10 - 1} = \frac{708.33 - 707.281}{9} = 0.116556, \quad \text{or } 0.117$$

For the estimator S [see equation (7.24) of Volume 1],

$$S = \sqrt{S^2}$$

and thus the point estimate is

$$s = \sqrt{0.116556} = 0.341403, \quad \text{or } 0.34$$

(The rounding off guidelines for reporting $\bar{x}$, s^2, and s are from Section 7.11 of Volume 1.)

For sampling from an infinite population, the estimator of $S_{\bar{x}}$ is equation (14.2)

$$S_{\bar{x}} = \frac{S}{\sqrt{n}}$$

and thus the point estimate is

$$s_{\bar{x}} = \frac{0.341403}{\sqrt{10}} = \frac{0.341403}{3.16228} = 0.107961, \quad \text{or } 0.11$$

(A standard-error point estimate is reported as rounded off to two significant figures.)

14.5 REPORTING AND EVALUATING THE POINT ESTIMATE

Sample point estimates for variance, standard deviation, and standard error of the mean are typically presented in written reports or talks with the lower-case symbols (s^2, s, and $s_{\bar{x}}$). There is disagreement, however, as to how the sample-mean estimate should be reported. You will find either $\bar{X}$ or $\bar{x}$ used, depending on the conventions of the subject area or journal. This disagreement on the proper symbol for the mean is reflected in statistics books: some books use $\bar{X}$ throughout; some books use $\bar{x}$ throughout; and many, as here, use $\bar{x}$ in discussions of descriptive statistics (see Volume 1, Chapters 6 and 7), and then later, after introducing the concept of random variables (see Volume 1, Section 10.1), always make the distinction between the variable $\bar{X}$ and a specific value it can assume $\bar{x}$. This distinction allows such unambiguous symbolic statements as $P(\bar{x}_1, < \bar{X} < \bar{x}_2) = 0.95$, which states that the probability is 0.95 that the estimator of μ, the random variable $\bar{X}$, will assume a value between the specific estimates $\bar{x}_1$ and $\bar{x}_2$.

In reporting a point estimate of a population parameter, sufficient accompanying information should be given to allow judgement of the "quality" of the estimate: its accuracy and its precision. The accuracy of an estimate is determined by the amount of systematic error (or bias) that is included in the estimate. This systematic error can enter the estimation process in several ways: (1) with measurement techniques that systematically produce distortions in one direction (see Volume 1, Section 2.13), (2) with flawed, nonrandom sampling designs that lead to some form of sampling bias (see Volume 1, Section 3.22), or (3) by using a biased statistical estimator $\hat{\theta}$ (see Sections 13.8 and 14.2). The precision of an estimate is determined by the degree of random error present—how much the estimate $\hat{\theta}^*$ fluctuates randomly around the parameter θ from sample to sample (see Section 13.12).

If a sample mean $\bar{x}$ is given as the point estimate of the population mean μ, along with descriptions of the measurement and sampling techniques that were used, then the first two sources of systematic error described above can be evaluated, and knowing that $\bar{X}$ is an unbiased estimator of μ eliminates the third source. If, in addition, the sample size n and the standard error of the mean $\sigma_{\bar{x}}$ are reported (typically as $\bar{x} \pm \sigma_{\bar{x}}$), and μ is estimated by several different-sized samples, then the relative precision of the estimates can be determined by comparing the different values of $\sigma_{\bar{x}}$.

In a typical study, the population standard deviation σ is not known. However, if either $\bar{x} \pm s$ or $\bar{x} \pm s_{\bar{x}}$ is reported, along with sample size n, the population size N (if known), and descriptions of measurement and sampling techniques, then a statistically sophisticated reader or listener can use equation (14.2) or

(14.3) to convert s to $s_{\bar{x}}$ and vice versa. Thus, given either $\bar{x} \pm s$ or $\bar{x} \pm s_{\bar{x}}$, it is possible to: (1) evaluate the dispersion of the specific random sample being described, (2) see a point estimate s of the population standard deviation σ, and (3) see a point estimate $s_{\bar{x}}$ of the precision-measuring standard error of the mean $\sigma_{\bar{x}}$ (see Section 13.12). Moreover, this information can also be used to calculate an *interval estimate* for the population mean μ, which is the optimal and complete solution to any statistical estimation problem.

14.6 RELATIONSHIP BETWEEN POINT ESTIMATES AND INTERVAL ESTIMATES

An unknown population parameter θ can be estimated from a single random sample with either a point estimate or an interval estimate. A point estimate, as we have seen, is simply a numerical value $\hat{\theta}*$ calculated for the estimator $\hat{\theta}$ from the sample. While this value alone tells nothing about the quality of the estimate, supplementary information on quality can be provided: accuracy can be evaluated with descriptions of measurement and sampling techniques, and precision can be evaluated by providing either the standard error of the estimator (for $\bar{X}, \bar{x} \pm \sigma_{\bar{x}}$) or the estimate of the standard error (for $\bar{X}, \bar{x} \pm s_{\bar{x}}$).

At this point in the chapter we are still in descriptive statistics; we have a point-estimate value and some idea of its accuracy and precision, but we can not, as yet, go on from there to make the leap from sample to population. We can not attempt to relate the point estimate to its parameter—to give some indication of how close the estimate is to the parameter, or, put another way, to determine how much possible error there is in the estimate. To make such inferences about population parameters from sample information, we must now enter the realm of inferential statistics (see Volume 1, Section 3.5).

An interval estimate is a sample-to-population inference. With a known degree of certainty, an interval estimate places the population parameter θ within an interval $a \le \theta \le b$, where a and b are the lower and upper boundaries of an interval of values on the real number line. These boundary values of an interval are determined by three factors: (1) the sample point estimate $\hat{\theta}*$ (e.g., $\bar{x}$), (2) a sample statistic that relates the point estimate to the population parameter [e.g., the Z statistic, $Z = (\bar{X} - \mu)/\sigma_{\bar{x}}$ (see Section 13.14)], and (3) the sampling distribution of that statistic (e.g., if $\bar{X}$ is normally distributed, then the sampling distribution of this Z statistic is the standard normal). In this chapter we examine how such intervals are calculated from a single sample for the purpose of locating the population mean μ. These interval estimates are known as *confidence intervals for the population mean.*

14.7 DERIVING $P(\bar{x}_{1-\alpha/2} \le \bar{X} \le \bar{x}_{\alpha/2}) = P(-z_{\alpha/2} \le Z \le z_{\alpha/2}) = 1 - \alpha$

If all possible random samples of size n $(X_1, X_2, \ldots, X_n)$ are drawn from an infinitely large, normally distributed population (mean μ, variance σ^2, and standard deviation σ) and the value $\bar{x}$ of the continuous random variable $\bar{X}$ is calculated for each sample, then the following is true:

$$P(\bar{x}_{1-\alpha/2} \le \bar{X} \le \bar{x}_{\alpha/2}) = P(-z_{\alpha/2} \le Z \le z_{\alpha/2}) = 1 - \alpha \tag{14.4}$$

To understand how this probability statement is derived, we must go back to the general version of this statement given in Section 12.11 for the continuous normally distributed variable X [equation (12.18)]

$$P(x_{1-\alpha/2} \le X \le x_{\alpha/2}) = P(-z_{\alpha/2} \le Z \le z_{\alpha/2}) = 1 - \alpha$$

Interpretation of this statement requires these points, established in Chapter 12:

(1) For the variable X, α may represent either the upper or lower tail area of its normal distribution, either to the right of x_α or to the left of $x_{1-\alpha}$.

(2) If α is located entirely in one tail of the distribution and X is standardized by the Z transformation, $Z = \dfrac{X - \mu}{\sigma}$, then α represents either the upper or lower tail area of the standard normal distribution, either to the right of z_α or to the left of $-z_\alpha$.

(3) If α is divided equally between the two tails, and we denote these equal areas by $\alpha/2$, then

$$P(x_{1-\alpha/2} \leq X \leq x_{\alpha/2}) = 1 - \alpha$$

which states that the probability that X will assume a value in the interval between $x_{1-\alpha/2}$ and $x_{\alpha/2}$ is equal to the area of the distribution that lies between them: $1 - \alpha$.

(4) If X is standardized, then it is also true for the standard normal variable Z that

$$P(-z_{\alpha/2} \leq Z \leq z_{\alpha/2}) = 1 - \alpha$$

Now, we know (see Section 13.14) that if all possible random samples $(X_1, X_2, \ldots, X_n)$ of the same size n are drawn from an infinitely large normally distributed population (μ, σ^2, σ) and $\bar{x}$ is calculated for each sample, then the distribution of $\bar{X}$ (the sampling distribution of the mean) will be a normal distribution with $\mu_{\bar{x}} = \mu$ and $\sigma_{\bar{x}} = \frac{\sigma}{\sqrt{n}}$. Therefore, as with X above, it will also be true for $\bar{X}$ that

$$P(\bar{x}_{1-\alpha/2} \leq \bar{X} \leq \bar{x}_{\alpha/2}) = 1 - \alpha$$

which states that the probability that $\bar{X}$ will assume a value $\bar{x}$ in the interval between $\bar{x}_{1-\alpha/2}$ and $\bar{x}_{\alpha/2}$ is the area of the sampling distribution of $\bar{X}$ that lies above that interval: $1 - \alpha$. This relationship also holds if $\bar{X}$ is standardized by the Z transformation, and thus

$$P(\bar{x}_{1-\alpha/2} \leq \bar{X} \leq \bar{x}_{\alpha/2}) = P(-z_{\alpha/2} \leq Z \leq z_{\alpha/2}) = 1 - \alpha$$

EXAMPLE 14.2 For the standard normal distribution, find $z_{\alpha/2}$ and $-z_{\alpha/2}$ when $1 - \alpha = 0.90$.

Solution

When $1 - \alpha = 0.90$, $\alpha = 0.10$. We know that [equation (12.16)]: $P(Z > z_{\alpha/2}) = \alpha/2$. Therefore,

$$P(Z > z_{0.10/2}) = P(Z > z_{0.05}) = 0.05$$

Thus we must find in Table A.5 the z value with an area that is closest to

$$P(0 \leq Z \leq z_{0.05}) = 0.45$$

which is

$$z_{0.05} = 1.645$$

With the symmetry of the standard normal distribution,

$$-z_{0.05} = -1.645$$

14.8 DERIVING $P(\bar{X} - z_{\alpha/2}\sigma_{\bar{x}} \leq \mu \leq \bar{X} + z_{\alpha/2}\sigma_{\bar{x}}) = 1 - \alpha$

In the previous section, we saw that if all possible random samples of size n are drawn from an infinitely large, normally distributed population and the value $\bar{x}$ of the continuous random variable $\bar{X}$ is calculated for each sample, then [equation (14.4)]

$$P(\bar{x}_{1-\alpha/2} \leq \bar{X} \leq \bar{x}_{\alpha/2}) = P(-z_{\alpha/2} \leq Z \leq z_{\alpha/2}) = 1 - \alpha$$

From this relationship for these conditions, we can show that it is also true that

$$P(\bar{X} - z_{\alpha/2}\sigma_{\bar{x}} \leq \mu \leq \bar{X} + z_{\alpha/2}\sigma_{\bar{x}}) = 1 - \alpha \qquad (14.5)$$

This is done by making use of the rules for performing arithmetic operations within inequalities (see Volume 1, Section 1.23).

We start with the relationship

$$P(-z_{\alpha/2} \leq Z \leq z_{\alpha/2}) = 1 - \alpha$$

Substituting $Z = \dfrac{\bar{X} - \mu}{\sigma_{\bar{x}}}$ [equation (13.12)],

$$P\left(-z_{\alpha/2} \le \frac{\bar{X} - \mu}{\sigma_{\bar{x}}} \le z_{\alpha/2}\right) = 1 - \alpha$$

Multiplying the three components of the inequality by $\sigma_{\bar{x}}$, we get

$$P(-z_{\alpha/2}\sigma_{\bar{x}} \le \bar{X} - \mu \le z_{\alpha/2}\sigma_{\bar{x}}) = 1 - \alpha$$

Multiplying through the inequality by -1 changes the direction of the inequality and changes $\bar{X} - \mu$ into $\mu - \bar{X}$

$$P(z_{\alpha/2}\sigma_{\bar{x}} \ge \mu - \bar{X} \ge -z_{\alpha/2}\sigma_{\bar{x}}) = 1 - \alpha$$

which is equivalent to

$$P(-z_{\alpha/2}\sigma_{\bar{x}} \le \mu - \bar{X} \le z_{\alpha/2}\sigma_{\bar{x}}) = 1 - \alpha$$

Finally, we add $\bar{X}$ to each component of the inequality,

$$P(\bar{X} - z_{\alpha/2}\sigma_{\bar{x}} \le \mu \le \bar{X} + z_{\alpha/2}\sigma_{\bar{x}}) = 1 - \alpha$$

This derivation gives the probability version of an interval estimate (see Section 14.6) of the population mean μ for these conditions: single random sample of size n from an infinitely large, normally distributed population with a known standard deviation σ. It states that for any given *future* random sample of size n from this population, there is a probability of $1 - \alpha$ that the interval between $\bar{X} - z_{\alpha/2}\sigma_{\bar{x}}$ and $\bar{X} + z_{\alpha/2}\sigma_{\bar{x}}$ will contain the mean μ. Because $\bar{X}$ is a random variable, this interval is also a random variable.

EXAMPLE 14.3 A random sample ($n = 9$, $\bar{x} = 14.3$) is taken from an infinitely large, normally distributed population with known standard deviation $\sigma = 1.5$. If $1 - \alpha = 0.95$, then $\alpha = 0.05$ and $z_{\alpha/2} = z_{0.025}$. Using Table A.5 we find that the z value with an area that is closest to 0.025 is 1.96. Because under these conditions, $\sigma_{\bar{x}} = \sigma/\sqrt{n}$, equation (14.5) can be written as

$$P\left(\bar{X} - z_{\alpha/2}\frac{\sigma}{\sqrt{n}} \le \mu \le \bar{X} + z_{\alpha/2}\frac{\sigma}{\sqrt{n}}\right) = 1 - \alpha \qquad (14.6)$$

Substituting the above values in equation (14.6) we get

$$P\left[14.3 - \left(1.96 \times \frac{1.5}{\sqrt{9}}\right) \le \mu \le 14.3 + \left(1.96 \times \frac{1.5}{\sqrt{9}}\right)\right] = 0.95$$

$$P(13.32 \le \mu \le 15.28) = 0.95$$

What is wrong with the substitutions we just made and the final probability statement?

Solution

The probability statement is false. The unknown population mean μ is a single, fixed number—it does not vary from sample to sample. Therefore, it is either in the interval from 13.22 to 15.28 or it is not; it has an unknown probability of either zero or one of being in the interval.

The probability statement

$$P\left(\bar{X} - z_{\alpha/2}\frac{\sigma}{\sqrt{n}} \le \mu \le \bar{X} + z_{\alpha/2}\frac{\sigma}{\sqrt{n}}\right) = 1 - \alpha$$

is correct. It is a derived property of the relationship between a normal sampling distribution of the mean and the standard normal distribution. It states that, for the next random sample of size n taken from the population, there is a $1 - \alpha$ probability that the random interval from $\bar{X} - z_{\alpha/2}\sigma_{\bar{x}}$ to $\bar{X} + z_{\alpha/2}\sigma_{\bar{x}}$ will contain μ. It does not make this probability claim about any specific interval, and therefore, our mistake was to substitute a specific sample $\bar{x}$ value for the random variable $\bar{X}$ within the parentheses of the probability statement.

14.9 CONFIDENCE INTERVAL FOR THE POPULATION MEAN μ: KNOWN STANDARD DEVIATION σ, NORMALLY DISTRIBUTED POPULATION

In Section 14.6 we indicated that an interval estimate places the population parameter θ, with a known degree of certainty, within a specific interval $a \leq \theta \leq b$, where a and b are values on the real number line. We further stated the boundary values (a and b) are determined by: (1) the sample point estimate $\hat{\theta}^*$, (2) a sample statistic that relates $\hat{\theta}^*$ to the population parameter that θ is estimating, and (3) the sampling distribution of that statistic. In Section 14.8 we were able, using the Z statistic and its sampling distribution (the standard normal distribution) to place the population mean μ, with a known degree of certainty $(1 - \alpha)$, within a random interval in the probability statement [equation (14.5)]

$$P(\bar{X} - z_{\alpha/2}\sigma_{\bar{x}} \leq \mu \leq \bar{X} + z_{\alpha/2}\sigma_{\bar{x}}) = 1 - \alpha$$

But we found in Example 14.3 that we could not then go on to use a sample point estimate $\hat{\theta}^*$ ($\bar{x} = 14.3$) to calculate specific interval boundary values a and b within the parentheses of the probability statement. This dilemma is resolved by the calculation of a specific $(1 - \alpha)$ *100% confidence interval*, which provides the correct and complete interval estimate of μ.

To understand the concept of confidence intervals, consider the implications of equation (14.5). It indicates that if all possible samples of the same size n are taken from this population (infinitely large, normally distributed, known σ) and specific values for the random interval

$$\bar{X} - z_{\alpha/2}\sigma_{\bar{x}} \leq \mu \leq \bar{X} + z_{\alpha/2}\sigma_{\bar{x}}$$

are calculated for each sample, then $(1 - \alpha)100\%$ of these specific intervals

$$\bar{x} - z_{\alpha/2}\sigma_{\bar{x}} \leq \mu \leq \bar{x} + z_{\alpha/2}\sigma_{\bar{x}}$$

will contain μ. Therefore, we can state that we are $(1 - \alpha)100\%$ *confident* that in repeated sampling this method will produce μ-containing intervals $(1 - \alpha)100\%$ of the time. For this reason, any such specific interval is called a $(1 - \alpha)100\%$ confidence interval [also written as a $100(1 - \alpha)\%$ *confidence interval*]. Thus, if $\alpha = 0.05$ and $1 - \alpha = 0.95$, then any such interval would be a $(0.95)100\%$, or 95%, confidence interval, and we are 95% confident that this specific interval does contain μ. The confidence interval estimate is not a probability statement; rather, the value $(1 - \alpha)$ is an indication of the theoretical success rate of this method of estimation.

As with point estimates, there are estimators and specific estimates for the confidence intervals. The random interval above is the interval-estimator for μ under these conditions, and any specific interval calculated from this estimator is an estimate.

EXAMPLE 14.4 For the conditions in Example 14.3 ($n = 9$, $\bar{x} = 14.3$, $\sigma = 1.5$), if $1 - \alpha = 0.95$, what is the confidence-interval estimate?

Solution

For a 95% confidence interval, we know that $z_{\alpha/2} = z_{0.025}$. From Example 14.3 we know that $z_{0.025} = 1.96$. Thus, we can say, with a 95% level of confidence, that μ lies within the interval

$$\bar{x} - 1.96\sigma_{\bar{x}} \leq \mu \leq \bar{x} + 1.96\sigma_{\bar{x}}$$

Substituting $\bar{x} = 14.3$ and $\sigma_{\bar{x}} = \dfrac{\sigma}{\sqrt{n}} = \dfrac{1.5}{\sqrt{9}}$,

$$14.3 - (1.96)\left(\frac{1.5}{\sqrt{9}}\right) \leq \mu \leq 14.3 + (1.96)\left(\frac{1.5}{\sqrt{9}}\right)$$

$$13.32 \leq \mu \leq 15.28$$

and we can say we are 95% confident that μ lies between 13.32 and 15.28.

14.10 PRESENTING CONFIDENCE LIMITS

With the confidence interval we now have the specific interval $a \leq \theta \leq b$ for estimating μ, where $a = \bar{x} - z_{\alpha/2}\sigma_{\bar{x}}$ and $b = \bar{x} + z_{\alpha/2}\sigma_{\bar{x}}$. These values, the endpoints of the interval that we are $(1-\alpha)100\%$ confident contains μ, are called the interval's *confidence limits*. The confidence intervals can be presented in any one of the following forms:

(1) $\bar{x} - z_{\alpha/2}\sigma_{\bar{x}} \leq \mu \leq \bar{x} + z_{\alpha/2}\sigma_{\bar{x}}$ (as presented in Section 14.9)

(2) $L = \bar{x} - z_{\alpha/2}\sigma_{\bar{x}}$, $U = \bar{x} + z_{\alpha/2}\sigma_{\bar{x}}$, where L represents the lower end of the interval and U represents the upper end. Other symbols used are: L (for left end of the interval) and R (for right end), L_1 (for lower or left end) and L_2 (for upper or right end).

(3) $(\bar{x} - z_{\alpha/2}\sigma_{\bar{x}}, \bar{x} + z_{\alpha/2}\sigma_{\bar{x}})$

(4) $\bar{x} \pm z_{\alpha/2}\sigma_{\bar{x}}$

EXAMPLE 14.5 The following confidence interval for the population mean μ is presented in a journal article: $1.25\ \text{cm} \pm (1.96 \times 0.078\ \text{cm})$. For this interval, what are (is) the: (*a*) confidence limits, (*b*) *fiducial limits* (*c*) *confidence coefficient*, (*d*) *confidence level*, (*e*) *degree of confidence*, (*f*) *critical values*, and (g) interval?

Solution

(*a*) The confidence limits are

$$L = 1.25\ \text{cm} - (1.96 \times 0.078\ \text{cm}) = 1.097\ \text{cm} \qquad U = 1.25\ \text{cm} + (1.96 \times 0.078\ \text{cm}) = 1.403\ \text{cm}$$

(*b*) Some authors use the terms fiducial limits and confidence limits synonymously to refer to the end points of the confidence interval.

(*c*) The quantity $1-\alpha$ is called the confidence coefficient. Thus here, because $z_{\alpha/2} = 1.96$, we know from Example 14.3, that $\alpha/2 = 0.025$, $\alpha = 0.05$, and $1 - \alpha = 0.95$. Therefore, the confidence coefficient is 0.95.

(*d*) The confidence level is the confidence coefficient expressed as a percentage. Thus here the confidence level is 95%.

(*e*) The degree of confidence can refer to either the confidence coefficient or the confidence level. Thus here the degree of confidence is either 0.95 or 95%.

(*f*) The critical values are the $\pm z_{\alpha/2}$ values for the Z variable that are the boundary values for the area $1-\alpha$ in the standard normal distribution. Thus here the $\pm z_{\alpha/2}$ values are ± 1.96.

(g) The interval is the interval on the real number line between the confidence limits. Thus here it is the continuous interval between 1.097 cm and 1.403 cm.

14.11 PRECISION OF THE CONFIDENCE INTERVAL

So far in this book, we have presented two statistical definitions of the term precision (and a physical-sciences definition in Section 2.15 of Volume 1). First (see Volume 1, Section 2.14) we defined it as a statistical property of measurement: the closeness of repeated identical measurements of the same thing is the precision of that measurement. Then (see Section 13.12), we defined precision as a property of a statistical estimator $\hat{\theta}$: the variability of repeated estimates $\hat{\theta}^*$ of the parameter θ is the precision of the estimator $\hat{\theta}$, which is measured by the standard deviation (standard error) of the sampling distribution of $\hat{\theta}$. Now we define this same term as a property of a confidence-interval estimator.

> If random samples of size n are taken repeatedly from a population of size N and confidence intervals at the same confidence level are calculated for each sample, then the precision of the confidence-interval estimator is determined by the widths of these intervals: the narrower these widths, the more precise the interval estimator.

For the confidence-interval estimator in Section 14.9, $\bar{X} \pm z_{\alpha/2}\sigma_{\bar{x}}$, both $z_{\alpha/2}$ and $\sigma_{\bar{x}}$ are constants for a given confidence level and sample size. Therefore, the widths of all interval estimates are exactly

$2 \times (z_{\alpha/2}\sigma_{\bar{x}})$. Thus, this number defines the precision of the estimator; the smaller this number, the more precise the estimator.

While $2z_{\alpha/2}\sigma_{\bar{x}}$ is the exact measure of the precision of the estimator $\bar{X} \pm z_{\alpha/2}\sigma_{\bar{x}}$, many statistics books present $z_{\alpha/2}\sigma_{\bar{x}}$ as the measure of the precision of any specific confidence-interval estimate $\bar{x} \pm z_{\alpha/2}\sigma_{\bar{x}}$. This measure is called the *margin of error of the estimate of* μ, or simply the *margin of error*, because we are $(1-\alpha)100\%$ confident that the absolute value of the sampling error (see Section 13.11), $|\bar{x}-\mu|$, will not be greater than $z_{\alpha/2}\sigma_{\bar{x}}$. This measure will be denoted by E:

$$E = z_{\alpha/2}\sigma_{\bar{x}} \tag{14.7}$$

The smaller the E, the more precise the estimate. You will also find other symbols used for this quantity in statistics books, including $A, B, e, e_{\alpha/2}, r$ and δ.

EXAMPLE 14.6 In Example 14.4 we determined the following 95% confidence interval for a random sample ($n = 9$, $\bar{x} = 14.3$) taken from an infinitely large normally distributed population ($\sigma = 1.5$):

$$\bar{x} \pm z_{\alpha/2}\sigma_{\bar{x}}$$

$$14.3 \pm (1.96)\left(\frac{1.5}{\sqrt{9}}\right)$$

$$14.3 \pm 0.98$$

Now determine the 90% and 99% confidence intervals for the same data. Compare these three intervals to see how an increase in confidence level affects the precision of a confidence-interval estimate.

Solution

The precision of the 95% confidence-interval estimate of μ is [equation (14.7)] $E = 0.98$. Using the $z_{\alpha/2}$ value for $1-\alpha = 0.90$ from Example 14.2, 1.645, the 90% confidence interval is

$$14.3 \pm (1.645)\left(\frac{1.5}{\sqrt{9}}\right)$$

$$14.3 \pm 0.82$$

and thus for the 90% interval,

$$E = 0.82$$

Finding $z_{\alpha/2}$ value for $1-\alpha = 0.99$ ($\alpha = 0.01$)

$$P(Z > z_{\alpha/2}) = P(Z > z_{0.005}) = 0.005$$

The z value with an area closest to 0.005 in Table A.5 is 2.575. Therefore,

$$\mu \pm z_{\alpha/2}\sigma_{\bar{x}} = 14.3 \pm (2.575)\left(\frac{1.5}{\sqrt{9}}\right) = 14.3 \pm 1.29$$

and thus, for this 99% interval,

$$E = 1.29$$

From these results, you can see that with $\bar{x}$ and $\sigma_{\bar{x}}$ held constant, the confidence interval for μ increases in width as the confidence level increases from 90% to 95% to 99%, and thus the precision of the interval estimate (as measured by E) is decreased. In essence, there is a trade-off: For increasing certainty of containing the parameter, you have to accept a decrease in the precision of the interval estimate.

The 90%, 95%, and 99% confidence intervals are the most commonly used intervals, but any level of confidence interval can be used. The goal is to achieve an optimal balance between the level of confidence and the precision of the interval estimate.

The precision of the confidence interval estimate is also affected by sample size. Thus, for an estimate of μ, $\bar{x} \pm z_{\alpha/2}\sigma_{\bar{x}}$, as the sample size increases, the estimate becomes more precise because the margin of error of the estimate ($E = z_{\alpha/2}\sigma_{\bar{x}}$) decreases.

EXAMPLE 14.7 Four random samples of varying size are taken from the population in Examples 14.3, 14.4, and 14.6 ($\sigma = 1.5$). Assuming that the sample mean remains the same at $\bar{x} = 14.3$ for all four samples, determine the effect on the 95% confidence interval of an increase in sample size from $n = 9$ to $n = 18$ to $n = 36$ to $n = 900$.

Solution

We know from Example 14.6 that for $n = 9$, the 95% confidence interval for μ is 14.3 ± 0.98. Increasing the sample size from $n = 9$ to $n = 18$, we find that

$$\bar{x} \pm z_{\alpha/2}\sigma_{\bar{x}}$$

$$14.3 \pm (1.96)\left(\frac{1.5}{\sqrt{18}}\right)$$

$$14.3 \pm 0.69$$

For $n = 36$ we find that

$$14.3 \pm (1.96)\left(\frac{1.5}{\sqrt{36}}\right)$$

$$14.3 \pm 0.49$$

and for $n = 900$,

$$14.3 \pm (1.96)\left(\frac{1.5}{\sqrt{900}}\right)$$

$$14.3 \pm 0.10$$

Thus, as sample size increases from 9 to 18 to 36 to 900, the margin of error of the estimate of μ decreases from 0.98 to 0.69 to 0.49 to 0.10. This demonstrates that for a given confidence level with known σ, the confidence-interval estimate can be made more precise by increasing sample size.

14.12 DETERMINING SAMPLE SIZE WHEN THE STANDARD DEVIATION IS KNOWN

How large should a sample be? This is an important question for any research program, because the taking and analyzing of each sample measurement costs money, time, and other resources. The object, therefore, should be to use the sample size that achieves the goals of the research without wasting resources.

If a goal of the research is to determine a confidence-interval estimate of an unknown population mean μ, then the necessary sample size to achieve this goal is a function of the "quality" of the interval estimate that is required. This required quality-of-estimate has two components: (1) the degree of precision, and (2) the level of confidence. Both components can be found in equation (14.7): $E = z_{\alpha/2}\sigma_{\bar{x}}$, where E is a measure of the precision of the estimate and $z_{\alpha/2}$ is the critical value associated with the confidence level of the estimate. Therefore, if desired values for E and $z_{\alpha/2}$ can be determined in advance, if σ is known, and if $\frac{\sigma}{\sqrt{n}}$ is substituted for $\sigma_{\bar{x}}$ in equation (14.7),

$$E = z_{\alpha/2}\frac{\sigma}{\sqrt{n}}$$

then by solving this equation for sample size n, we can determine in advance the necessary sample size to achieve these quality-of-estimate requirements. The general solution of this equation for sample size is as follows:

(1) Square both sides of the equation:

$$E^2 = \frac{z_{\alpha/2}^2\sigma^2}{n}$$

(2) Solve for n:

$$n = \frac{z_{\alpha/2}^2 \sigma^2}{E^2}$$

or

$$n = \left(\frac{z_{\alpha/2}\sigma}{E}\right)^2 \tag{14.8}$$

Thus, if σ is known and you can decide in advance the desired values for E (the margin of error of the estimate that you can tolerate) and $z_{\alpha/2}$ (the level of confidence that you require), then this solution for n can be used to determine the sample size needed to achieve this quality-of-estimate.

EXAMPLE 14.8 You design an experiment that involves taking a random sample from an infinitely large, normally distributed population with known standard deviation $\sigma = 1.5$. Your experiment requires a confidence-interval estimate that will give 95% confidence that the margin of error of the estimate of μ is $E = 1.0$. How large should the sample be?

Solution

Using equation (14.8) and substituting $\sigma = 1.5$, $z_{\alpha/2} = 1.96$, $E = 1.0$,

$$n = \left(\frac{1.96 \times 1.5}{1.0}\right)^2$$
$$= 8.64$$

Because sample size must be an integer, this value of n should be rounded upward to the nearest integer. Thus, the required sample size is $n = 9$.

14.13 CONFIDENCE INTERVAL FOR THE POPULATION MEAN μ: KNOWN STANDARD DEVIATION σ, LARGE SAMPLE ($n \geq 30$) FROM ANY POPULATION DISTRIBUTION

Often you cannot be certain that the finite population you are sampling from is normally distributed. In such a case, if $n \geq 30$ and the population size N is "at least twice as large" as the sample size (see Sections 13.15 to 13.18), then you can say from the central limit theorem that the sampling distribution of $\bar{X}$ is approximately a normal distribution. When this is true and $\bar{X}$ is standardized with the Z transformation [equation (13.12)],

$$Z = \frac{\bar{X} - \mu}{\sigma_{\bar{x}}}$$

the resulting distribution of Z is approximately the standard normal distribution. Because of this approximate normality of $\bar{X}$ and Z, and the fact that you know σ, you can use the techniques of Section 14.9 to find the *approximate 95% confidence interval for* μ.

EXAMPLE 14.9 You are a highway engineer studying whether a busy, curving, downhill section of the interstate highway needs to be widened. You measured (with a radar gun) the speed of 85 vehicles going past the halfway point of this section, and for this sample you get a mean speed of $\bar{x} = 66.3$ mph. If from previous studies you know that $\sigma = 8.3$ mph, then what is the approximate 95% confidence interval for the population mean speed μ past that halfway point?

Solution

You do not know whether the finite population of these speeds is normally distributed, but because $n \geq 30$ and N is "at least twice as large" as 85, you can say from the central limit theorem that the sampling distribution of $\bar{X}$ is approximately normally distributed. From Example 14.3, we know that $z_{\alpha/2} = z_{0.025} = 1.96$. This is sampling without replacement, but for this busy road it must be true that $n \leq 0.05N$, so we can use equation (13.7),

$$\sigma_{\bar{x}} = \frac{\sigma}{\sqrt{n}} = \frac{8.3 \text{ mph}}{\sqrt{85}} = 0.900261 \text{ mph}$$

Substituting these value and $\bar{x} = 66.3$ mph in $\bar{x} \pm z_{\alpha/2}\sigma_{\bar{x}}$ we get this approximate 95% confidence interval for μ:

$$66.3 \text{ mph} \pm (1.96 \times 0.900261 \text{ mph})$$
$$66.3 \text{ mph} \pm 1.76 \text{ mph}$$

14.14 DETERMINING CONFIDENCE INTERVALS FOR THE POPULATION MEAN μ WHEN THE POPULATION STANDARD DEVIATION σ IS UNKNOWN

So far in this chapter, we have accepted the unrealistic condition that while the population mean μ is not known we do somehow know the population standard deviation σ. We did this in order to introduce confidence intervals with the familiar standard normal techniques. The more realistic condition is that both μ and σ are unknown and the only information we have about the population comes from a single random sample. Fortunately, under these conditions there are statistical techniques available for estimating μ from sample information. The techniques come from two areas: *large sampling theory* if the sample is large ($n \geq 30$), and *small sampling theory* (or *exact sampling theory*) if the sample is small ($n < 30$).

With a large sample, we can assume that: (1) whatever the form of the population distribution, the sampling distribution of the mean will be approximately normal (Sections 13.15 through 13.18), and (2) the estimated standard error of the mean $S_{\bar{x}}$ will be a reasonable estimator of the standard error of the mean $\sigma_{\bar{x}}$ (see Section 14.3). If these assumptions are valid, then the sampling distribution of the ratio $\frac{\bar{X} - \mu}{S_{\bar{x}}}$ can be approximated by the sampling distribution of the Z transformation, $Z = \frac{\bar{X} - \mu}{\sigma_{\bar{x}}}$ (which forms the standard normal distribution) and the confidence intervals for μ can be approximated with the techniques used in Section 14.9. We will deal further with these large-sample techniques—when and how they can be used—in Sections 14.23 and 14.24. In Sections 14.15 through 14.22, we concentrate on how to estimate μ when the population is normally distributed, σ is unknown, and $n < 30$.

When $n < 30$, the standard normal distribution is not a good approximation for the sampling distribution of the ratio $\frac{\bar{X} - \mu}{S_{\bar{x}}}$, and the approximation becomes increasingly bad as n decreases from 30 to smaller numbers. However, if we can assume that the population being sampled is normally distributed, then it turns out that the ratio $\frac{\bar{X} - \mu}{S_{\bar{x}}}$ has an exact, known sampling distribution called the *t distribution* or *Student's t distribution*.

14.15 THE t DISTRIBUTION

If the sample size n is less than 30, the population standard deviation σ is unknown, and the population distribution can be assumed to be normal, then the boundaries a and b of a confidence interval $a \leq \mu \leq b$ are determined by means of: (1) the sample point estimate ($\bar{x}$), (2) the *t statistic* (or *T statistic*), and (3) the sampling distribution of that statistic, known as the *t distribution*.

The t statistic is the random variable

$$T = \frac{\bar{X} - \mu}{S_{\bar{x}}} \tag{14.9}$$

that can assume specific values

$$t = \frac{\bar{x} - \mu}{s_{\bar{x}}} \tag{14.10}$$

The t distribution comes from small sampling theory, which states that

> If all possible samples of size n are taken from a normally distributed population with mean μ and standard deviation σ, and if values $t = \frac{\bar{x} - \mu}{s_{\bar{x}}}$ of the random variable $T = \frac{\bar{X} - \mu}{S_{\bar{x}}}$ are calculated for each sample, then the t values will have a continuous probability distribution (sampling distribution) called the t distribution.

As with the probability distributions described in previous chapters, the t distribution is defined by a specific and unique probability function. The continuous probability density functions for the t distribution, which we will not derive, is

$$f(t) = c\left(1 + \frac{t^2}{\nu}\right)^{-(\nu+1)/2} \tag{14.11}$$

where $t = \frac{\bar{x} - \mu}{s_{\bar{x}}}$

$\nu = n - 1$ (the symbol ν is the lower-case Greek letter *nu*)

$c =$ a constant that is a function of ν; it is used to make the total area in the t distribution equal to one

It can be seen that this probability function has the values t of the variable T, and two constants, ν and c, where c is a function of ν. Therefore, ν is the parameter of the t distribution, just as n and p are the parameters of the binomial distribution (see Section 11.9) and μ and σ^2 (or μ and σ) are the parameters of the normal distribution (see Section 12.3). This parameter ν is called the *number of degrees of freedom* or simply *degrees of freedom*, for reasons we will discuss in Section 14.17. The symbol ν is the most common symbol for degrees of freedom, but you will also find: *df*, *d.f.*, *DF*, *d*, *r*, and others.

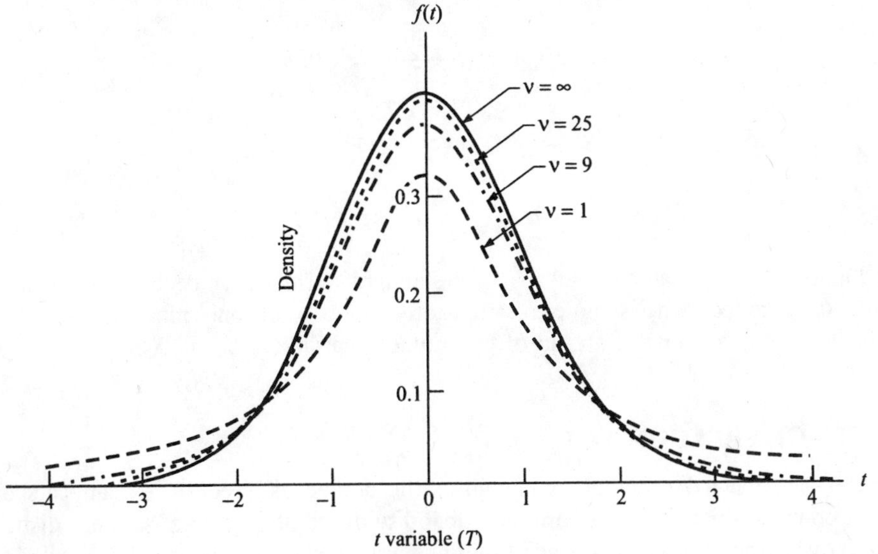

Fig. 14-1

As with previous distributions, such as the binomial and the normal, the t distribution is not a single distribution but rather a family of distributions, one for each integer value of the degrees of freedom ($\nu = n - 1$). Four of the infinitely many distributions, for $\nu = 1, 9, 25$, and ∞, are shown superimposed in Fig. 14-1. It can be seen that each distribution is bell-shaped and symmetric around a mean of zero. It is also true, but not seen, that each distribution extends continuously from $-\infty$ to ∞.

As we have indicated, the probability function for the t distribution was mathematically derived under the assumption that sampling was from a normally distributed population. Fortunately, however, t-distribution techniques have been found to be *robust* (see Problem 3.14 in Volume 1) in that they give valid results unless there are extreme departures from normality.

14.16 RELATIONSHIP BETWEEN THE t DISTRIBUTION AND THE STANDARD NORMAL DISTRIBUTION

It can be proven mathematically that at infinite degrees of freedom ($\nu = \infty$) the t distribution and the standard normal distribution (see Section 12.6) are identical. Thus, the curve for the t distribution when $\nu = \infty$, shown in Fig. 14-1, is the standard normal curve. As the degrees of freedom decrease from infinity, the t curves remain bell-shaped and symmetric around a mean of zero, but they become progressively flatter than the standard normal, with more area added to the tails. Below $\nu = 30$, the t distribution is quite different from the standard normal distribution.

The increasing spread of the t distribution with decreases in ν is reflected in the standard deviation of the t distribution:

$$\sigma = \sqrt{\frac{\nu}{\nu - 2}} \quad \text{when} \quad \nu \geq 3 \tag{14.12}$$

Thus, while the standard deviation of the standard normal distribution is always $\sigma = 1$, the standard deviation of the t distribution when $\nu < \infty$ is always greater than one and becomes increasingly so as ν decreases. This increase in the standard deviation with decreases in degrees of freedom is shown in the following series:

$$\text{For } \nu = 500, \sigma = \sqrt{\frac{500}{500 - 2}} = 1.002$$

$$\text{For } \nu = 50, \sigma = \sqrt{\frac{50}{50 - 2}} = 1.021$$

$$\text{For } \nu = 30, \sigma = \sqrt{\frac{30}{30 - 2}} = 1.035$$

$$\text{For } \nu = 15, \sigma = \sqrt{\frac{15}{15 - 2}} = 1.074$$

$$\text{For } \nu = 5, \sigma = \sqrt{\frac{5}{5 - 2}} = 1.291$$

The t distribution shows greater spread than the standard normal as ν decreases because, while the standard normal only reflects the sample-to-sample fluctuations of one random variable, $\bar{X}$, the t distribution reflects the fluctuations of a ratio of two random variables, $\bar{X}$ and $S_{\bar{x}}$.

14.17 DEGREES OF FREEDOM

The parameter ν in the t distribution is known as the degree of freedom. It reappears often in the remainder of this book as a parameter of various probability distributions, because these distributions are interlinked and derived from one another. Each time the parameter ν appears, it will be called the number of degrees of freedom, or simply degrees of freedom, but it will not always be calculated by the same formula as in the t distribution ($v = n - 1$). Therefore, each time v appears, you need to identify and keep in mind the specific calculation formula for v associated with the specific distribution.

To fully understand why the name "degrees of freedom" is given to the parameter v would require understanding concepts from mathematical statistics that are beyond the scope of this book. Unfortunately, there is no simple, intuitive-level explanation for the concepts that would cover all appearances of the parameter v in different probability distributions. There is, however, an intuitive-level explanation for how this term applies to the t distribution.

One can think of the number of degrees of freedom associated with a statistic as the number of unrestricted, free-to-vary values that are used in calculating the statistic. Thus, for example, when the statistic is the sum of the n values in a sample, $\sum_{i=1}^{n} X_i$, there are no restrictions on this calculation—any n values can be selected for it and, therefore, there are n degrees of freedom associated with the statistic.

When the statistic of interest is the standard deviation for the sample

$$S = \sqrt{\frac{\sum_{i=1}^{n}(X_i - \bar{X})^2}{n - 1}}$$

there is one restriction on the n values in a specific calculation: the values must have a mean of $\bar{X} = \bar{x}$. Having calculated $\bar{x}$ first, we have lost one degree of freedom in the calculation of $S = s$. Thus, the degrees of freedom associated with the sample standard deviation (as well as the sample variance) is $n - 1$. This value $n - 1$ can be seen in the denominator of the S (and S^2) statistic, which is why this denominator is often called the degrees of freedom and why the formula for S is sometimes written as

$$S = \sqrt{\frac{\sum_{i=1}^{n}(X_i - \bar{X})^2}{df}}$$

In calculating specific values of the random variable T,

$$t = \frac{\bar{x} - \mu}{s_{\bar{x}}} = \frac{\bar{x} - \mu}{s/\sqrt{n}}$$

there is again only one restriction on the n values used in the calculation: the sample mean $\bar{x}$. It determines the restrictions placed on both the numerator and the denominator calculations. Again, the n values used to calculate the t value must have a mean of $\bar{x}$, and so the calculation of this statistic has one restriction, and the degree of freedom associated with this t statistic are $v = n - 1$.

14.18 THE TERM "STUDENT'S *t* DISTRIBUTION"

William Sealy Gosset (1876–1937) was a British statistician who worked for the Guinness Brewery in Dublin, Ireland. While doing quality-control research for the brewery, he recognized the need for small-sample statistical inferences. Among his many contributions was the discovery of the t distribution. Because the brewery had a policy that prohibited publication of employee research, Gossett secretly published his discovery of the t distribution in a 1908 paper under the pen name "Student." It is for this reason that the t distribution is called *Student's t distribution*.

14.19 CRITICAL VALUES OF THE *t* DISTRIBUTION

In Section 12.10 we indicated for the standard normal distribution that [equation (12.9)] $P(Z > z_\alpha) = \alpha$; that the area (probability) under the standard normal curve to the right of z_α is α. This value z_α is thus a *critical value* [see Example 14.5(*f*)] for the standard normal distribution. It is also called a *critical boundary value* because it is the boundary point between the areas $1 - \alpha$ to the left and α to its right. We also indicated in Section 12.10 [equation (12.11)] that, due to the symmetry of the standard normal distribution, $P(Z < -z_\alpha) = \alpha$. The t distribution has comparable critical values. Thus, for the t distribution with ν degrees of freedom,

$$P(T > t_{\alpha,\nu}) = \alpha \tag{14.13}$$

where T is the random variable $T = \dfrac{\bar{X} - \mu}{S_{\bar{x}}}$ and $t_{\alpha,\nu}$ denotes the boundary between α on its right and $1 - \alpha$ on its left in a t distribution with ν degrees of freedom. This relationship between area and the one-tailed critical value is illustrated in Fig. 14-2(*a*). Like the standard normal distribution, the t distribution is symmetric and so

$$P(T < -t_{\alpha,\nu}) = \alpha \tag{14.14}$$

where $-t_{\alpha,\nu}$ denotes the boundary between α to its left and $1 - \alpha$ to its right. The relationship between this one-tailed critical value and area for the t distribution with ν degrees of freedom is shown in Fig. 14-2(*b*).

In our examination of the standard normal distribution, we also dealt with two-tailed probabilities, in which α is divided equally between the two tails. We showed that [equation (12.18)]

$$P(-z_{\alpha/2} \le Z \le z_{\alpha/2}) = 1 - \alpha$$

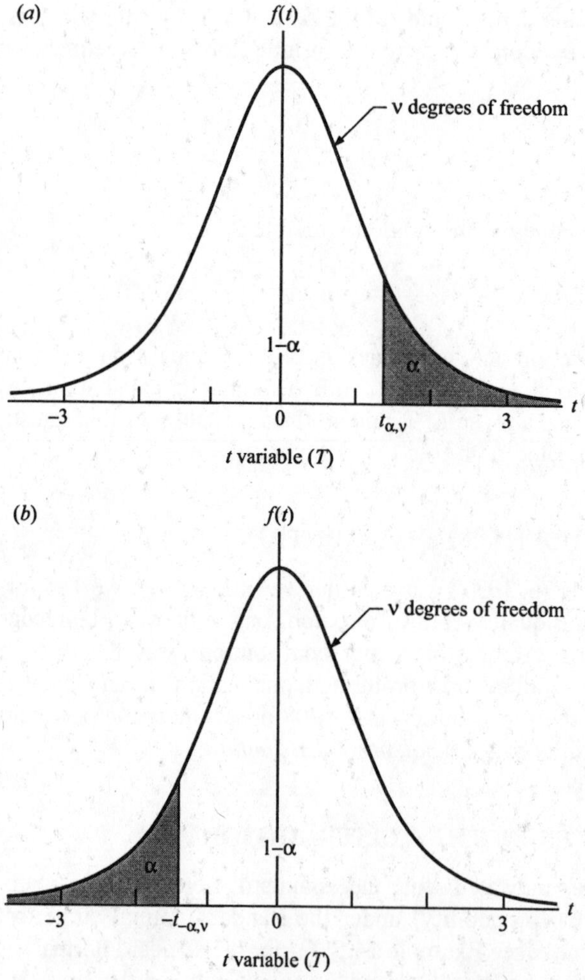

Fig. 14-2

which means: the probability that the random variable Z will assume a value betwen $-z_{\alpha/2}$ and $z_{\alpha/2}$ is equal to $1 - \alpha$. The values of $-z_{\alpha/2}$ and $z_{\alpha/2}$ are thus critical two-tailed values. Similarly, for the t distribution with ν degrees of freedom,

$$P(-t_{\alpha/2,\nu} \leq T \leq t_{\alpha/2,\nu}) = 1 - \alpha \tag{14.15}$$

which means: the probability that the random variable $T = \dfrac{\bar{X} - \mu}{S_{\bar{x}}}$ will assume a value between $-t_{\alpha/2,\nu}$ and $t_{\alpha/2,\nu}$ is equal to $1 - \alpha$. The values of $-t_{\alpha/2,\nu}$ and $t_{\alpha/2,\nu}$ are two-tailed critical values for a t distribution with ν degrees of freedom. This relationship between areas and two-tailed critical values for the t distribution is illustrated in Fig. 14-3.

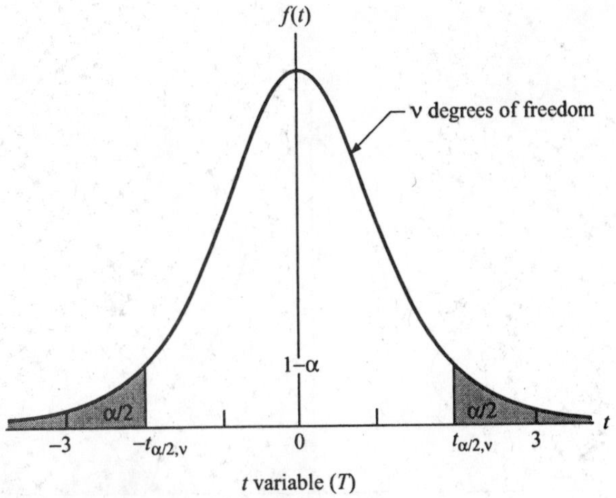

Fig. 14-3

14.20 TABLE A.6: CRITICAL VALUES OF THE *t* DISTRIBUTION

Table A.6 in the Appendix (*Critical Values of the t Distribution*) gives positive critical values of $t_{\alpha,\nu}$ and $t_{\alpha/2,\nu}$ for selected t distributions ($\nu = 1, \ldots, 30, 40, 60, 120, \infty$). This is a new form of table: other tables, presented in previous chapters, give area (probability) within a certain defined region of a probability distribution. In Table A.6 each row represents a different t distribution as determined by its particular value of ν. The values in the left-hand column are degrees of freedom ν and the values in rows are the critical values that cut off a specific area in the right (positive) tail of the distribution. The area cut off to the right is identified by the α value in the t_α symbol at the top of each column.

Table 14.1 contains a section of Table A.6 showing five t distributions: $\nu = 21, 22, 23, 24$, and 25. The first column of critical values consists of critical $t_{0.10}$ values in each distribution that cut off $\alpha = 0.10$ to the right. The second column consists of critical $t_{0.05}$ values that cut off $\alpha = 0.05$ to the right, and so on. Because the t distribution is symmetric about a mean of zero,

$$P(T < -t_{\alpha,\nu}) = P(T > t_{\alpha,\nu}) = \alpha \tag{14.16}$$

which means that in a given t distribution with ν degrees of freedom, the area to the left of $-t_{\alpha,\nu}$ is equal to the area to the right of $t_{\alpha,\nu}$, and each area is equal to α. Thus, while Table A.6 gives only positive critical values, it can be used to find negative critical values as well because $-t_{\alpha,\nu}$ is identical to $t_{\alpha/\upsilon}$ except for sign.

EXAMPLE 14.10 Use the section of Table A.6 shown in Table 14.1 to find $t_{\alpha,\nu} = t_{0.025,25}$ and $-t_{\alpha,\nu} = -t_{0.025,25}$.

Solution

For a t distribution with $\nu = 25$ degrees of freedom, the value $t_{0.025,25} = 2.060$ (circled value in Table 14.1) cuts off $\alpha = 0.025$ to its right (see Fig. 14-4). Because of equation (14.16): $-t_{0.025,25} = -2.060$.

Table 14.1

	t_α					
ν	$t_{0.10}$	$t_{0.05}$	$t_{0.025}$	$t_{0.01}$	$t_{0.005}$	$t_{0.0005}$
21	1.323	1.721	2.080	2.518	2.831	3.819
22	1.321	1.717	2.074	2.508	2.819	3.792
23	1.319	1.714	2.069	2.500	2.807	3.767
24	1.318	1.711	2.064 (circled)	2.492	2.797	3.745
25	1.316	1.708	2.060	2.485	2.787	3.725

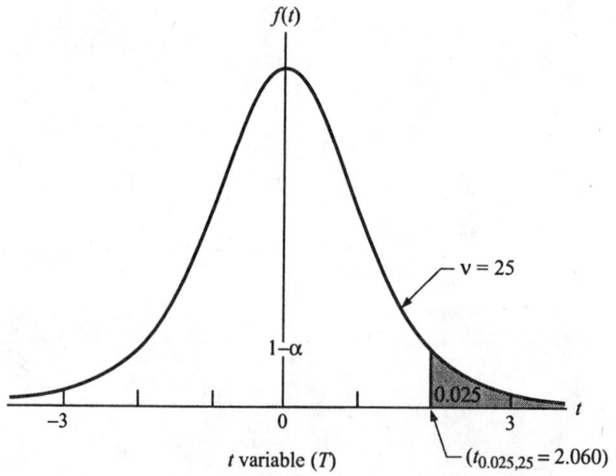

Fig. 14-4

Table A.6 is designed not only to find one-tailed critical values, but also to find two-tailed critical values, where α is divided equally between the two tails of the distribution, with $\alpha/2$ within each tail. We saw above how each row in Table A.6 represents a different t distribution (determined by ν) and each column represents a positive critical $t_{\alpha,\nu}$ value that cuts off the area α in the right tail. In this table, each value in a column is also a $t_{\alpha/2}$ for the particular ν value.

EXAMPLE 14.11 Use the section of Table A.6 shown in Table 14.2 to find $t_{\alpha/2,\nu} = t_{0.05/2,25}$ and $-t_{\alpha/2,\nu} = -t_{0.025/2,25}$.

Solution

The problem is to find a critical value in the t distribution with $\nu = 25$ degrees of freedom that cuts off an area of $\alpha/2 = 0.05/2 = 0.025$ to its right. Going in Table 14.2 to the $\nu = 25$ row and following it to the $t_{0.05/2}$ column, we find the value of 2.060 (circled). This value divides the distribution into an area equal to $\alpha/2$ (i.e., 0.025) on its right and $1 - \alpha/2$ on its left. This is the same value we found in Example 14.10 for $t_{\alpha,\nu} = t_{0.025,25}$, because both critical values cut off 0.025 in the positive tail of the distribution. Because the t distribution is symmetric around zero, $t_{\alpha/2,\nu}$ and $-t_{\alpha/2,\nu}$ are the same except for sign, and therefore $-t_{0.05/2,25} = -2.060$. The relationship between t_α and $t_{\alpha/2}$ for a given t distribution is illustrated for $t_{0.025,25}$ and $t_{0.05/2,25}$ in Fig. 14-5.

Table 14.2

	$t_{\alpha/2}$					
	$t_{0.20/2}$	$t_{0.10/2}$	$t_{0.05/2}$	$t_{0.02/2}$	$t_{0.01/2}$	$t_{0.001/2}$
	t_{α}					
ν	$t_{0.10}$	$t_{0.05}$	$t_{0.025}$	$t_{0.01}$	$t_{0.005}$	$t_{0.0005}$
21	1.323	1.721	2.080	2.518	2.831	3.819
22	1.321	1.717	2.074	2.508	2.819	3.792
23	1.319	1.714	2.069	2.500	2.807	3.767
24	1.318	1.711	2.064	2.492	2.797	3.745
25	1.316	1.708	2.060	2.485	2.787	3.725

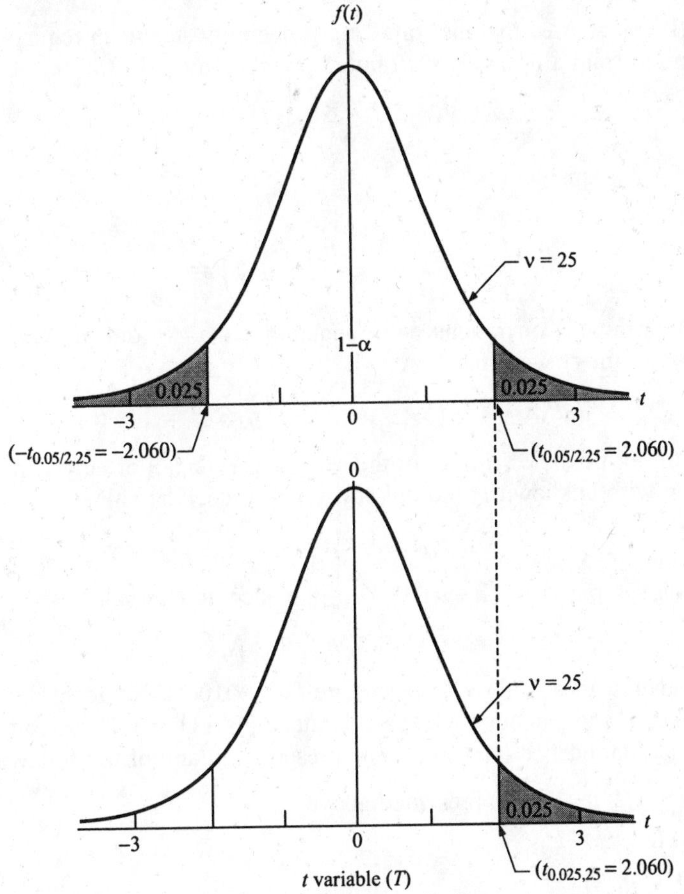

Fig. 14-5

14.21 CONFIDENCE INTERVAL FOR THE POPULATION MEAN μ: STANDARD DEVIATION σ NOT KNOWN, SMALL SAMPLE ($n < 30$) FROM A NORMALLY DISTRIBUTED POPULATION

We now examine the confidence interval for the population mean of a normally distributed population when the standard deviation is not known and the sample size is less than 30. For such a small sample, we cannot assume that: (1) the sampling distribution of the mean will be approximately normal, nor that (2) the estimated standard error of the mean $S_{\bar{x}}$ will be a reasonable estimator of the standard error of the mean $\sigma_{\bar{x}}$. Thus, we cannot transform the sampling distribution of the mean into the standard normal distribution and use $\pm z_{\alpha/2}$ as critical values. Instead, under these conditions we use $\pm t_{\alpha/2,\nu}$ as critical values and the exactly correct specific interval estimate of the population mean μ, the $(1-\alpha)100\%$ confidence interval, is calculated with

$$\bar{x} - t_{\alpha/2,\nu}s_{\bar{x}} \le \mu \le \bar{x} + t_{\alpha/2,\nu}s_{\bar{x}} \tag{14.17}$$

To understand why this is true, recall that in Section 14.15 we indicated that for any sample of size n:

> If all possible samples of size n are taken from a normally distributed population with mean μ and standard deviation σ, and if values $t = \dfrac{\bar{x}-\mu}{s_{\bar{x}}}$ of the random variable $T = \dfrac{\bar{X}-\mu}{S_{\bar{x}}}$ are calculated for each sample, then the t values will have a continuous probability distribution called the t distribution. Further, this t distribution has the parameter (degrees of freedom) $\nu = n - 1$.

Then in Section 14.19 we showed that the following probability statement [equation (14.15)] was exactly true for any size sample from a normally distributed population:

$$P(-t_{\alpha/2,\nu} \le T \le t_{\alpha/2,\nu}) = 1 - \alpha$$

Substituting $\dfrac{\bar{X}-\mu}{S_{\bar{x}}}$ for T [equation (14.9)],

$$P\left(-t_{\alpha/2,\nu} \le \frac{\bar{X}-\mu}{S_{\bar{x}}} \le t_{\alpha/2,\nu}\right) = 1 - \alpha$$

Performing the same arithmetic operations with inequalities that we did in Section 14.8, we derive this probability version of an interval estimate

$$P(\bar{X} - t_{\alpha/2,\nu}S_{\bar{x}} \le \mu \le \bar{X} + t_{\alpha/2,\nu}S_{\bar{x}}) = 1 - \alpha \tag{14.18}$$

Thus we can say that if all possible samples of the same size n (small or large) are taken from a normally distributed population with unknown μ and unknown σ, and specific values for the random interval

$$\bar{X} - t_{\alpha/2,\nu}S_{\bar{x}} \le \mu \le \bar{X} + t_{\alpha/2,\nu}S_{\bar{x}}$$

are calculated for each sample, then $(1-\alpha)100\%$ of the specific intervals

$$\bar{x} - t_{\alpha/2,\nu}s_{\bar{x}} \le \mu \le \bar{x} + t_{\alpha/2,\nu}s_{\bar{x}}$$

will contain the population mean μ. We are therefore $(1-\alpha)100\%$ confident that any given interval so determined will contain μ, and that any such specific interval is a $(1-\alpha)100\%$ confidence interval. Again, as in Section 14.10, the confidence interval can be presented in any of the following forms:

(1) $\bar{x} - t_{\alpha/2,\nu}s_{\bar{x}} \le \mu \le \bar{x} + t_{\alpha/2,\nu}s_{\bar{x}}$ (as presented above)

(2) $L = \bar{x} - t_{\alpha/2,\nu}s_{\bar{x}}$, $U = \bar{x} + t_{\alpha/2,\nu}s_{\bar{x}}$

(3) $(\bar{x} - t_{\alpha/2,\nu}s_{\bar{x}}, \bar{x} + t_{\alpha/2,\nu}s_{\bar{x}})$

(4) $\bar{x} \pm t_{\alpha/2,\nu}s_{\bar{x}}$

EXAMPLE 14.12 A random sample of size $n = 16$ is taken from a normally distributed population with unknown μ and σ. If the sample has a mean $\bar{x} = 27.9$ and standard deviation $s = 3.23$, then what is the 95% confidence interval for μ?

Solution

As this is a small sample, we use t distribution confidence interval

$$\bar{x} \pm t_{\alpha/2,\nu}s_{\bar{x}}$$

for this we need

$$s_{\bar{x}} = \frac{s}{\sqrt{n}} = \frac{3.23}{\sqrt{16}} = 0.807500$$

and a $t_{\alpha/2,\nu}$ value from Table A.6 for the confidence level. For a 95% confidence level, $1 - \alpha = 0.95$, $\alpha = 0.05$, and $\alpha/2 = 0.05/2$. As $\nu = n - 1 = 16 - 1 = 15$, we get

$$t_{\alpha/2,\nu} = t_{0.05/2,15} = 2.131$$

and thus the 95% confidence interval is

$$27.9 \pm (2.131 \times 0.08075)$$
$$27.9 \pm 1.72$$

14.22 DETERMINING SAMPLE SIZE: UNKNOWN STANDARD DEVIATION, SMALL SAMPLE FROM A NORMALLY DISTRIBUTED POPULATION

In Section 14.11, for the case where the population standard deviation σ is known, we defined the margin of error of the estimate of μ as [equation (14.7)]: $E = z_{\alpha/2}\sigma_{\bar{x}}$. From this definition, we showed in Section 14.12 that the sample size required to achieve a desired E value can be determined with equation (14.8): $n = \left(\frac{z_{\alpha/2}\sigma}{E}\right)^2$.

If the population is normal, σ is unknown, and $n < 30$, the determination of the required sample size to achieve a desired E is a more complex problem. Now the appropriate specific confidence interval is $\bar{x} \pm t_{\alpha/2}s_{\bar{x}}$ (see Section 14.21) and for this interval the margin of error of the estimation of μ is defined as

$$E = t_{\alpha/2,\nu}s_{\bar{x}} \tag{14.19}$$

Both components, $t_{\alpha/2,\nu}$ and $s_{\bar{x}}$, depend on the specific sample and thus it is only appropriate to determine E with this formula after the fact—after the sample has been taken and the confidence interval has been calculated. Because both components vary from sample to sample, we *cannot* use

$$n = \left(\frac{t_{\alpha/2,\nu}s}{E}\right)^2$$

to determine the future sample size necessary to achieve a desired E value. Instead, it is suggested that to get a rough idea of what n should be, a sample standard deviation s from a previous study should be substituted into this approximate formula

$$n \approx \left(\frac{z_{\alpha/2}s}{E}\right)^2 \tag{14.20}$$

This approximate solution generally underestimates n because it uses $z_{\alpha/2}$, which is equivalent to $t_{\alpha/2,\infty}$ (see Section 14.16), and these are, for a given α, the smallest possible $t_{\alpha/2}$ values.

EXAMPLE 14.13 For the 95% confidence interval in Example 14.12, for the sample where $\bar{x} = 27.9$ and $s = 3.23$, how large a sample n should be taken in a repetition of the study to get a margin of error of $E = 1.25$ for the estimate of μ?

Solution

To find the n needed to achieve $E = 1.25$, we substitute $s = 3.23$, $z_{\alpha/2} = z_{0.05/2} = 1.96$, and $E = 1.25$ in equation (14.20),

$$n \approx \left(\frac{1.96 \times 3.23}{1.25}\right)^2 = 25.7$$

Thus, to have a reasonable chance of achieving $E = 1.25$, the size of the next sample should be at least 26.

EXAMPLE 14.14 Had the study in Example 14.13 been done with the sample size ($n = 26$), would the desired $E = 1.25$ have been achieved for the 95% confidence interval? If not, what sample size would have achieved this level?

Solution

If n had been 26, then

$$s_{\bar{x}} = \frac{s}{\sqrt{n}} = \frac{3.23}{\sqrt{26}} = 0.633455$$

$$t_{\alpha/2,\nu} = t_{0.05/2,25} = 2.060$$

and thus

$$E = t_{\alpha/2,\nu} s_{\bar{x}} = 2.060 \times 0.633455 = 1.30492, \quad \text{or } 1.30$$

which is close to, but larger than, $E = 1.25$. To find the appropriate sample size, we calculate E for larger samples.

For $n = 27$,

$$E = t_{0.05/2,26} s_{\bar{x}} = 2.056 \times \frac{3.23}{\sqrt{27}} = 1.27804, \quad \text{or } 1.28$$

For $n = 28$,

$$E = t_{0.05/2,27} s_{\bar{x}} = 2.052 \times \frac{3.23}{\sqrt{28}} = 1.25257, \quad \text{or } 1.25$$

for $n = 29$,

$$E = t_{0.05/2,28} s_{\bar{x}} = 2.048 \times \frac{3.23}{\sqrt{29}} = 1.22838, \quad \text{or } 1.23$$

As it took a sample size of 28 to achieve $E = 1.25$, we can see that the approximate formula, which determined a sample size of 26, underestimated the appropriate size by 2. Because of this underestimation, it is suggested that to achieve a desired E value add 10% to 15% to the approximate n.

14.23 CONFIDENCE INTERVAL FOR THE POPULATION MEAN μ: STANDARD DEVIATION σ NOT KNOWN, LARGE SAMPLE ($n \geq 30$) FROM A NORMALLY DISTRIBUTED POPULATION

For a sample of any size n ($n \geq 30$ or $n < 30$) taken from a population that is normally distributed with unknown standard deviation, t-distribution techniques provide the theoretically correct, exact solution for finding the confidence interval for the population mean. Thus, exact confidence intervals can be calculated with $\bar{x} \pm t_{\alpha/2,\nu} s_{\bar{x}}$.

For a large sample ($n \geq 30$), however, statistics books do not agree on the best way to determine the confidence interval. The problem with the exact solution, involving the t distribution, is that the exact $t_{\alpha/2,\nu}$ value may not be readily available for samples in which $n \geq 30$. Table A.6, which is typical of general statistics books, only gives $t_{\alpha/2}$ values for $\nu = 1, \ldots, 30, 40, 60, 120$, and ∞. While more complete tables of t distributions are available, as well as computer and calculator programs that yield exact $t_{\alpha/2,\nu}$ values, it is often necessary to use approximate t values when $n \geq 30$. Two suggestions for approximate values are: (1) use the t value in the given table for the next lowest available degree of freedom, and (2) *interpolate* between available t values in the table.

EXAMPLE 14.15 For Table A.6 using these two suggestions, determine the approximate value for $t_{0.05/2,50}$.

Solution

Following suggestion (1), the t value in Table A.6 for the next lowest available degrees of freedom is

$$t_{0.05/2,50} \approx t_{0.05/2,40} = 2.021$$

Following suggestion (2), we use the technique of *linear interpolation*. First, parallel scales, one for degrees of freedom and the other for $t_{0.05/2,\nu}$ values, have been formed in Fig. 14-6. Degrees of freedom $\nu = 50$ is at the position on the degrees-of-freedom scale (marked by a cross) that is $(10/20 = \frac{1}{2})$ of the distance from $\nu = 40$ to $\nu = 60$. Therefore, $t_{0.05/2,50}$ is also $\frac{1}{2}$ of the distance between 2.021 and 2.000 on the $t_{0.05/2,\nu}$ scale (also marked with a cross). Thus,

$$t_{0.05/2,50} \approx \tfrac{1}{2}(2.021 - 2.000) + 2.000 = 2.0105, \quad \text{or } 2.011$$

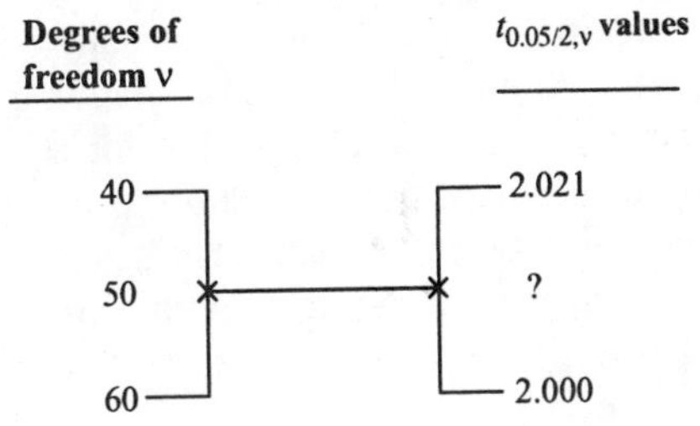

Fig. 14-6

As a simpler alternative to using approximate t values for $n \geq 30$, some statistics books offer the following rule of thumb:

> If σ is unknown and the population being sampled is normally distributed, then when $n \geq 30$ (or, in some books, $n > 30$), always use $\bar{x} \pm z_{\alpha/2}s_{\bar{x}}$

This alternative solution is also an approximate $(1 - \alpha)100\%$ confidence interval, but the authors who recommend it think it is justifiable to use z values to approximate the exact t values under these conditions because: (1) if the population is normal, then the sampling distribution of the mean will always be normal, (2) for $n \geq 30$ the estimated standard error of the mean $S_{\bar{x}}$ will be a reasonable estimator of the standard error of the mean $\sigma_{\bar{x}}$, and (3) above $n = 30$, there is little difference between $z_{\alpha/2}$ and $t_{\alpha/2,\nu}$ values for the same α.

EXAMPLE 14.16 A random sample of $n = 41$ is taken from a normally distributed population with unknown σ. The mean of the sample is $\bar{x} = 12.3$ and the standard deviation is $s = 0.90$. From this information, estimate the population mean μ by determining both $\bar{x} \pm z_{0.05/2}s_{\bar{x}}$ and $\bar{x} \pm t_{0.05/2,\nu}s_{\bar{x}}$.

Solution

From the rule of thumb described above, we know that under the conditions of this problem we can estimate μ with the approximate 95% confidence interval $\bar{x} \pm z_{0.05/2}s_{\bar{x}}$. Here

$$\bar{x} = 12.3$$

$$z_{0.05/2} = 1.96$$

$$s_{\bar{x}} = \frac{s}{\sqrt{n}} = \frac{0.90}{\sqrt{41}} = 0.140556$$

and thus the approximate 95% confidence interval is

$$12.3 \pm (1.96 \times 0.140556)$$

$$12.3 \pm 0.275$$

We also know from the discussion above that the theoretically correct, exact 95% confidence interval for this problem is $\bar{x} \pm t_{0.05/2,\nu} s_{\bar{x}}$. Table A.6 gives the exact value: $t_{0.05/2,40} = 2.021$. Therefore, the exact 95% confidence interval is

$$12.3 \pm (2.021 \times 0.140556)$$

$$12.3 \pm 0.284$$

Note: While the intervals are very similar, the exact interval is wider and thus claims less precision. It is said to be a more *conservative estimate of* μ.

14.24 CONFIDENCE INTERVAL FOR THE POPULATION MEAN μ: STANDARD DEVIATION σ NOT KNOWN, LARGE SAMPLE ($n \geq 30$) FROM A POPULATION THAT IS NOT NORMALLY DISTRIBUTED

Exact t-distribution techniques require sampling from a normally distributed population. With a large sample ($n \geq 30$), however, even with the population standard deviation σ unknown, there is no need for the t distribution with its assumption of normality. We know that for a large sample: (1) the central limit theorem indicates that the sampling distribution of the mean will be approximately normal, and (2) the estimated standard error of the mean $S_{\bar{x}}$ will be a reasonable estimator of the standard error of the mean $\sigma_{\bar{x}}$. Therefore, the approximate confidence interval for a large sample from a population that is not normally distributed can be formed by using $\bar{x} \pm z_{\alpha/2} s_{\bar{x}}$.

EXAMPLE 14.17 A chain of convenience stores that feature 24-hours-per-day service is evaluating a location for a new store. One measure, taken for 60 consecutive nights, is traffic flow (the number of vehicles passing the location in either direction) from 10 PM to 5 AM. The sample of $n = 60$ has $\bar{x} = 238.2$ and $s = 31.32$. Because of heavier traffic on weekends, the population of traffic-flow values appears skewed rather than normal. Not knowing the value of σ, determine a 95% confidence interval for the mean μ of this population.

Solution

With a sample size of 60, we can calculate the approximate 95% confidence interval using $\bar{x} \pm z_{\alpha/2} s_{\bar{x}}$. Here $\bar{x} = 238.2$, $z_{0.05/2} = 1.96$, and as $n \leq 0.05N$,

$$s_{\bar{x}} = \frac{s}{\sqrt{n}} = \frac{31.32}{\sqrt{60}} = 4.04339$$

Therefore, the approximate 95% confidence interval is

$$238.2 \pm (1.96 \times 4.04339)$$

$$238.2 \pm 7.93$$

14.25 CONFIDENCE INTERVAL FOR THE POPULATION MEAN μ: SMALL SAMPLE ($n < 30$) FROM A POPULATION THAT IS NOT NORMALLY DISTRIBUTED

When a small sample ($n < 30$) is taken from a population that is not normally distributed, there is no standard, satisfactory solution to the problem of estimation. Table 14.3 is a summary of what has been said so far in this chapter. It shows the appropriate confidence interval (exact or approximate) to be used as a function of whether σ is known, whether the population is normal, and the sample size. Note the two rows of question marks—both involve a small sample from a population that is not normally distributed. For such a sample, neither Z-distribution nor t-distribution techniques are appropriate.

One technique that can be used, but rarely is used, involves Chebyshev's theorem (see Volume 1, Section 7.15).

> For any number $k \geq 1$, and a set of data $x_1, x_2, \ldots, x_n$ (or $x_1, x_2, \ldots, x_N$), the proportion of the measurements that lies within k standard deviation of their mean will be at least $1 - \dfrac{1}{k^2}$.

Table 14.3

Population	Sample size	Confidence interval	Exact or approximate	Defining section
Known σ				
Normal	$n \geq 30$	$\bar{x} \pm z_{\alpha/2}\sigma_{\bar{x}}$	Exact	14.9
Normal	$n < 30$	$\bar{x} \pm z_{\alpha/2}\sigma_{\bar{x}}$	Exact	14.9
Not normal	$n \geq 30$	$\bar{x} \pm z_{\alpha/2}\sigma_{\bar{x}}$	Approximate	14.13
Not normal	$n < 30$	?	?	?
Unknown σ				
Normal	$n \geq 30$	$\bar{x} \pm t_{\alpha/2,\nu}s_{\bar{x}}$	Exact for exact t	14.23
		or		
		$\bar{x} \pm z_{\alpha/2}s_{\bar{x}}$	Approximate	14.23
Normal	$n < 30$	$\bar{x} \pm t_{\alpha/2,\nu}s_{\bar{x}}$	Exact	14.21
Not normal	$n \geq 30$	$\bar{x} \pm z_{\alpha/2}s_{\bar{x}}$	Approximate	14.24
Not normal	$n < 30$	?	?	?

This theorem yields the following probability statement for a sampling distribution of the population mean:

$$P(|\bar{X} - \mu| \leq k\sigma_{\bar{x}}) \geq 1 - \frac{1}{k^2}$$

which states that the probability that the population mean μ is within $k\sigma_{\bar{x}}$ distance of any sample mean $\bar{x}$ is at least $1 - \frac{1}{k^2}$. Therefore, for any size sample from any type of population, if σ is known then one can be at least $1 = \frac{1}{k^2}$ confident that μ is located within the approximate interval

$$x \pm k\sigma_{\bar{x}}$$

and if σ is unknown, one can be at least $1 - \frac{1}{k^2}$ confident that μ is located within the approximate interval

$$\bar{x} \pm ks_{\bar{x}}$$

EXAMPLE 14.18 A new type of heart operation is being performed at a hospital. For the 20 such operations that have been completed, the average length-of-stay in the hospital is $\bar{x} = 14.3$ days ($s = 2.84$ days). Because of complications from the operation, it seems that the population of length-of-stay measures is not normally distributed, but rather positively skewed. Not knowing σ, use the Chebyshev interval to determine the at-least-90% approximate confidence interval for the population mean μ.

Solution

First we set $1 - \frac{1}{k^2}$ equal to 0.90 and solve for k:

$$1 - \frac{1}{k^2} = 0.90$$

$$\frac{1}{k^2} = 0.10$$

$$0.10k^2 = 1$$

$$k = \sqrt{10} = 3.16228$$

Not knowing the value of σ, we substitute this k value into $\bar{x} \pm ks_{\bar{x}}$, where

$$\bar{x} = 14.3 \text{ days}$$

$$s_{\bar{x}} = \frac{s}{\sqrt{n}} = \frac{2.84 \text{ days}}{\sqrt{20}} = 0.635043 \text{ days}$$

Thus, the at-least-90% approximate confidence interval for μ is

$$14.3 \text{ days} \pm (3.16228 \times 0.635043 \text{ days})$$

$$14.3 \text{ days} \pm 2.01 \text{ days}$$

Had we been able to assume that the population is normal, and thus been able to use t-distribution techniques, we would have gotten this exact and more precise 90% confidence interval:

$$14.3 \text{ days} \pm [(t_{0.10/2,19} = 1.729) \times (0.635043 \text{ days})]$$

$$14.3 \text{ days} \pm 1.10 \text{ days}$$

Solved Problems

POINT ESTIMATES

14.1 A clothing manufacturer receives a unique population of 150 red, 10 cm diameter, leather buttons for a set of band uniforms. To determine whether the buttons are really 10 cm in diameter, a random sample of nine is taken without replacement, and these are their diameters, to the nearest millimeter: 9.9, 10.0, 10.0, 10.1, 9.9, 10.1, 10.0, 10.0, 9.9. From this information, determine point estimates for $\bar{X}$, S, and $S_{\bar{x}}$

Solution

$$\bar{X} = \frac{\sum X_i}{n}$$

$$\bar{x} = \frac{89.9 \text{ cm}}{9} = 9.98889 \text{ cm, or } 9.99 \text{ cm}$$

$$S = \sqrt{\frac{\sum X_i^2 - \frac{(\sum X_i)^2}{n}}{n-1}}$$

$$s = \sqrt{\frac{898.05 \text{ cm}^2 - \frac{(89.9 \text{ cm})^2}{9}}{9-1}} = \sqrt{\frac{898.05 \text{ cm}^2 - 898.0011 \text{ cm}^2}{8}} = 0.0781825 \text{ cm, or } 0.078 \text{ cm}$$

Because this is sampling without replacement from a finite population and $n > 0.05N$, we use equation (14.3),

$$S_{\bar{x}} = \frac{S}{\sqrt{n}}\sqrt{\frac{N-n}{N-1}}$$

$$s_{\bar{x}} = \frac{0.0781825 \text{ cm}}{\sqrt{9}}\sqrt{\frac{150-9}{150-1}} = 0.0260608 \text{ cm} \times 0.972784 = 0.0253515 \text{ cm, or } 0.025 \text{ cm}$$

CONFIDENCE INTERVAL FOR THE POPULATION MEAN: KNOWN STANDARD DEVIATION, NORMAL DISTRIBUTION

14.2 For the standard normal distribution, find $z_{\alpha/2}$ and $-z_{\alpha/2}$ when $1 - \alpha = 0.99$.

Solution

When $1 - \alpha = 0.99$, $\alpha = 0.01$. Therefore,

$$P(Z > z_{\alpha/2}) = P(Z > z_{0.01/2}) = P(Z > z_{0.005}) = 0.005$$

Now we must find the z value associated with the closest area in Table A.6 to

$$P(0 \leq Z \leq z_{0.005}) = 0.495$$

which is

$$z_{0.005} = 2.575$$

and thus

$$-z_{0.005} = -2.575$$

14.3 A random sample is taken from an infinitely large, normally distributed population with known standard deviation $\sigma = 1.5$. Before taking the sample you had wanted to be 98% confident that the margin of error of the estimate of μ would be [equation (14.7)] $E = 0.85$. How large a sample should you have taken?

Solution

We know $1 - \alpha = 0.98$, $\alpha = 0.02$, and $\alpha/2 = 0.01$. Therefore, we determine from Table A.6 the z value for the area that is closest to 0.49, which is: $z_{\alpha/2} = z_{0.01} = 2.33$. Substituting this value, $E = 0.85$, and $\sigma = 1.5$, into equation (14.8),

$$n = \left(\frac{2.33 \times 1.5}{0.85}\right)^2 = 16.91$$

which is rounded up to $n = 17$. Thus, to be 98% confident that the margin of error of the estimate will be 0.85 we needed a sample size of $n = 17$.

14.4 The 95% confidence interval for the mean μ of a very large normally distributed population is presented in a journal article as $1.25 \text{ cm} \pm (1.96 \times 0.078 \text{ cm})$. The sample size is reported as $n = 25$, and it is said that the population standard deviation σ, not presented, was used in this calculation. How large a sample would have been required to achieve 99% confidence that the margin of error of the estimate would be $E = 0.1$ cm?

Solution

First, knowing that $n = 25$, we need to determine the value of σ from the 95% confidence interval:

$$1.25 \text{ cm} \pm (1.96 \times 0.078 \text{ cm})$$

$$z_{\alpha/2}\sigma_{\bar{x}} = 1.96 \times 0.078 \text{ cm}$$

As $n \leq 0.05N$, we can use equation (13.7) to find σ:

$$\sigma_{\bar{x}} = \frac{\sigma}{\sqrt{n}} = 0.078 \text{ cm}$$

$$\sigma = 0.078 \text{ cm}\sqrt{25} = 0.39 \text{ cm}$$

Next, substituting $\sigma = 0.39$ cm, $E = 0.1$ cm, and the critical value for the 99% confidence level, $z_{\alpha/2} = z_{0.005} = 2.575$ into equation (14.8),

$$n = \left(\frac{2.575 \times 0.39 \text{ cm}}{0.1 \text{ cm}}\right)^2 = 100.85$$

which rounds up to $n = 101$. Thus, to be 99% confident that the margin of error of the estimate is 0.1 cm, a sample size of $n = 101$ was required.

14.5 You have developed a new fast-growing onion for a seed company, and now you want to determine the average time μ (in days) from planting the seed to its maturity (appearance of a developed bulb, tops bent over, etc.). Assume that you know, from preliminary studies, that these times are normally distributed with $\sigma = 8.3$ days. How large a sample of time-to-maturity measurements would you have to take in order to develop a 95% confidence interval for μ that would have a precision of $E = 2$ days?

Solution

Substituting $\sigma = 8.3$ days, $z_{0.025} = 1.96$, and $E = 2$ days into equation (14.8),

$$n = \left(\frac{1.96 \times 8.3 \text{ days}}{2 \text{ days}}\right)^2 = 66.16$$

which rounded up to the next largest integest is $n = 67$.

14.6 You do the onion study in Problem 14.5, taking a sample of 67 time-to-maturity measurements, and get a sample mean of $\bar{x} = 71.2$ days. For these measurements, what is the 95% confidence interval?

Solution

We know that $n = 67$ and $\sigma = 8.3$ days. Therefore,

$$\sigma_{\bar{x}} = \frac{\sigma}{\sqrt{n}} = \frac{8.3 \text{ days}}{\sqrt{67}} = 1.01401 \text{ days}$$

Substituting this value, $z_{0.025} = 1.96$, and $\bar{x} = 71.2$ days into $\bar{x} \pm z_{\alpha/2}\sigma_{\bar{x}}$, we find that the 95% confidence interval is

$$71.2 \text{ days} \pm (1.96 \times 1.01401 \text{ days})$$

$$71.2 \text{ days} \pm 1.99 \text{ days}$$

14.7 A sociologist is studying the television-viewing habits of pre-teens, defined as children between 10 and 12 years old, in the urban and rural areas of a state. A random sample of $n = 50$ rural pre-teens, taken without replacement from the $N = 39{,}200$ available, yields a mean watching-time in one week of $\bar{x} = 12.5$ hours. Assuming that the watching-times for the pre-teen population that week were normally distributed, and that it is known that $\sigma = 2.2$ hours, then what is the 96% confidence interval for μ, the mean watching-time for pre-teens that week in hours?

Solution

As $1 - \alpha = 0.96$, $\alpha = 0.04$ and $\alpha/2 = 0.02$. From Table A.5, we find that the z value for the area that is closest to 0.48 is $z_{\alpha/2} = z_{0.02} = 2.05$. While we are sampling from a finite population without replacement, as $n \leq 0.05N$, we can use equation (13.7) to calculate $\sigma_{\bar{x}}$:

$$\sigma_{\bar{x}} = \frac{\sigma}{\sqrt{n}} = \frac{2.2 \text{ hr}}{\sqrt{50}} = 0.311127 \text{ hr}$$

Substituting this value, $z_{0.02} = 2.05$, and $\bar{x} = 12.5$ hr into $\bar{x} \pm z_{\alpha/2}\sigma_{\bar{x}}$, the 96% confidence interval is

$$12.5 \text{ hr} \pm (2.05 \times 0.311127 \text{ hr})$$

$$12.5 \text{ hr} \pm 0.64 \text{ hr}$$

14.8 For the study in Problem 14.7, how large a sample size n would have halved the resulting E value in the 96% interval?

Solution

The E value was 0.64 hr, and so we want to find the n needed to achieve $E = 0.32$ hr. Because we can use $\sigma_{\bar{x}} = \frac{\sigma}{\sqrt{n}}$, we can solve the problem with equation (14.8),

$$n = \left(\frac{2.05 \times 2.2 \text{ hr}}{0.32 \text{ hr}}\right)^2 = 198.63$$

which rounds up to $n = 199$. Thus, to halve the E value a sample that was four times as large was required.

14.9 One of the listed ingredients in a 6-fluid-ounce container of a daytime colds medicine is 200 mg of guaifenesin. As a quality control, the manufacturer takes a daily sample of n of these containers and analyzes the contents of each for guaifenesin and the other components. A 99.9% confidence interval is then determined for the population mean μ for each component. If the company knows that the guaifenesin weights are normally distributed with $\sigma = 0.11$ mg, then how large a sample size n is needed if the manufacturer wants $E = 0.05$ mg for the 99.9% confidence interval for guaifenesin?

Solution

As $1 - \alpha = 0.999$, $\alpha = 0.001$, and $\alpha/2 = 0.0005$. Therefore, we determine from Table A.5 the z value for the closest area to 0.4995. As there are six z values associated with 0.4995, we take their average:

$$z_{\alpha/2} = z_{0.0005} = \frac{3.27 + 3.28 + 3.29 + 3.30 + 3.31 + 3.32}{6} = 3.295$$

Substituting this value, $E = 0.05$ mg and $\sigma = 0.11$ mg into equation (14.8):

$$n = \left(\frac{3.295 \times 0.11 \text{ mg}}{0.05 \text{ mg}}\right)^2 = 52.55$$

which rounds up to $n = 53$.

CONFIDENCE INTERVAL FOR THE POPULATION MEAN: KNOWN STANDARD DEVIATION, LARGE SAMPLE FROM ANY DISTRIBUTION

14.10 You are the highway engineer described in Example 14.9, who found a mean speed of $\bar{x} = 66.3$ mph for 85 vehicles going past a section of highway. From previous studies you know that $\sigma = 8.3$ mph. You decide to redo the speed-study with a smaller sample, and are willing to let the E value in your 95% confidence interval be twice as large as the $E = 1.76$ mph in Example 14.9. How large a sample n do you need to take?

Solution

Because $\bar{X}$ is assumed to be approximately normally distributed and we can use $\sigma_{\bar{x}} = \frac{\sigma}{\sqrt{n}}$ (see Example 14.9), we solve this problem with an approximation of equation (14.8):

$$n \approx \left(\frac{z_{\alpha/2}\sigma}{E}\right)^2 \tag{14.21}$$

Substituting $z_{\alpha/2} = z_{0.025} = 1.96$, $\sigma = 8.3$ mph, and $E = (2 \times 1.76 \text{ mph} = 3.52 \text{ mph})$ in this equation,

$$n \approx \left(\frac{1.96 \times 8.3 \text{ mph}}{3.52 \text{ mph}}\right)^2 = 21.36$$

It would seem then that the answer, after rounding up, would be a sample of 22. However, as we must invoke the central limit theorem here, the minimum sample size n must be at least 30.

14.11 You work for an airline and are studying the time it takes for passengers to get their baggage after leaving a plane. You know that this population of times is not normally distributed, but rather is somewhat positively skewed, and that $\sigma = 6.4$ min. You take a random sample of 45 measurements and get a mean time of $\bar{x} = 26.7$ min. What is the approximate 99% confidence interval for the population mean time μ?

Solution

Because $n \geq 30$ and N is "at least twice as large" as 85, you can say from the central limit theorem that $\bar{X}$ is approximately normally distributed, and as it must be true that $n \leq 0.05N$, we can calculate $\sigma_{\bar{x}}$ with equation (13.7):

$$\sigma_{\bar{x}} = \frac{\sigma}{\sqrt{n}} = \frac{6.4 \text{ min}}{\sqrt{45}} = 0.954056 \text{ min}$$

Substituting this value, $\bar{x} = 26.7$ min, and $z_{\alpha/2} = z_{0.005} = 2.575$ into $\bar{x} \pm z_{\alpha/2}\sigma_{\bar{x}}$, you get this approximate 99% confidence interval for μ:

$$26.7 \text{ min} \pm (2.575 \times 0.954056 \text{ min})$$

$$26.7 \text{ min} \pm 2.46 \text{ min}$$

THE t DISTRIBUTION

14.12 Use Table A.6 to find: (*a*) $t_{\alpha,\nu} = t_{0.10,6}$, and (*b*) $-t_{\alpha,\nu} = -t_{0.01,15}$.

Solution

(*a*) $t_{\alpha,\nu} = t_{0.10,6} = 1.440$, (*b*) $-t_{\alpha,\nu} = -t_{0.01,15} = -2.602$

14.13 Use Table A.6 to find: (*a*) $-t_{\alpha/2,\nu} = -t_{0.001/2,60}$, and (*b*) $t_{\alpha,\nu} = t_{0.0005,40}$.

Solution

(*a*) $-t_{\alpha/2,\nu} = -t_{0.001/2,60} = 3.460$, (*b*) $t_{\alpha,\nu} = t_{0.0005,40} = 3.551$

14.14 Use Table A.6 to determine what happens to $t_{\alpha,\nu} = t_{0.025,\nu}$ for the following increases in degrees of freedom: 5, 15, 30, 60, 120, ∞.

Solution

$$t_{0.025,5} = 2.571$$
$$t_{0.025,15} = 2.131$$
$$t_{0.025,30} = 2.042$$
$$t_{0.025,60} = 2.000$$
$$t_{0.025,120} = 1.980$$
$$t_{0.025,\infty} = 1.960$$

It can be seen that for a given α value ($\alpha = 0.025$ here), the value of $t_{\alpha,v}$ decreases as degrees of freedom v increases. This occurs because, as v increases, the area under the curve of the distribution shifts from the tails toward the mean (see Fig. 14-1), and so less distance is required from the mean to the $t_{\alpha,v}$ boundary. As we indicated in Section 14.16, at $v = \infty$ the t distribution becomes the standard normal distribution, and this can be seen in the $v = \infty$ row of Table A.6. Thus, in this problem, $t_{0.025,\infty} = 1.960$ and in Table A.5 you can see that the value that cuts off $\alpha = 0.025$ to its right is $z_{0.025} = 1.96$.

14.15 Use Table A.6 to determine what happens to $t_{\alpha,15}$ as α decreases as follows: 0.025, 0.01, 0.005, 0.0005.

Solution

$$t_{0.025,15} = 2.131$$
$$t_{0.01,15} = 2.602$$
$$t_{0.005,15} = 2.947$$
$$t_{0.0005,15} = 4.073$$

Here it can be seen that, for a given distribution, the $t_{\alpha,v}$ value increases as α decreases.

14.16 Use Table A.6 to find $t_{1-\alpha,v} = t_{0.99,18}$.

Solution

The following is true for the t distribution:

$$t_{1-\alpha,v} = -t_{\alpha,v} \tag{14.22}$$

which states that the t value that has an area of $1 - \alpha$ to its right, $t_{1-\alpha,v}$, is the same as the t value that has α to its left, $-t_{\alpha,v}$, for a given t distribution with v degrees of freedom and a given α value. We know from Table A.6 that

$$t_{\alpha,v} = t_{0.01,18} = 2.552$$

Therefore,

$$-t_{\alpha,v} = -t_{0.01,18} = -2.552$$

and thus

$$t_{1-\alpha,v} = t_{0.99,18} = -2.552$$

CONFIDENCE INTERVAL FOR THE POPULATION MEAN: UNKNOWN STANDARD DEVIATION, SMALL SAMPLE FROM A NORMAL DISTRIBUTION

14.17 A random sample of size $n = 16$ is taken from a normally distributed population with unknown μ and σ. If the sample has a mean $\bar{x} = 27.9$ and standard deviation $s = 3.23$, then what is the 99% confidence interval for the data?

Solution

As this is a small sample, the t distribution confidence interval is appropriate (see Section 14.21): $\bar{x} \pm t_{\alpha/2,v} s_{\bar{x}}$. For a 99% confidence level, $1 - \alpha = 0.99$, $\alpha = 0.01$, and $\alpha/2 = 0.01/2$. Since $v = n - 1 = 15$, we find in Table A.6 that: $t_{\alpha/2,v} = t_{0.01/2,15} = 2.947$. Sampling from a normal distribution, we know that [equation (14.2)] $s_{\bar{x}} = \frac{s}{\sqrt{n}} = \frac{3.23}{\sqrt{16}} = 0.80750$, and so the 99% confidence interval is

$$27.9 \pm (2.947 \times 0.8075)$$
$$27.9 \pm 2.38$$

14.18 An anthropologist who specializes in human evolution discovers seven adult *Homo erectus* skeletons in an area of Africa where they have never been found before. One measure he takes is cranial capacity (the brain space in the skull), measured in cubic centimeters, cm^3. He gets these results: 925, 892, 900, 875, 910, 906, and 899. Determine the 95% confidence interval for the mean μ of the population from which this sample was taken.

Solution

It is typically true that cranial capacity is normally distributed, so we will assume it here. While this is sampling without replacement from a finite population, because we do not know the size of the population in relation to the sample we will use equation (14.2), $s_{\bar{x}} = \frac{s}{\sqrt{n}}$, in the appropriate 95% confidence interval, $\bar{x} \pm t_{\alpha/2,\nu}\left(\frac{s}{\sqrt{n}}\right)$. The components of the confidence interval are

$$\bar{x} = \frac{\sum x_i}{n} = \frac{6{,}307\ \text{cm}^3}{7} = 901.0\ \text{cm}^3$$

$$s = \sqrt{\frac{\sum(x_i - \bar{x})^2}{n-1}} = \sqrt{\frac{1{,}444\ \text{cm}^6}{6}} = 15.5134\ \text{cm}^3$$

$$\sqrt{n} = \sqrt{7} = 2.64575$$

$$t_{\alpha/2,\nu} = t_{0.05/2,6} = 2.447$$

Therefore, the 95% confidence interval for μ is

$$901.0\ \text{cm}^3 \pm \left[2.447 \times \left(\frac{15.5134\ \text{cm}^3}{2.64575}\right)\right]$$

$$901.0\ \text{cm}^3 \pm 14.35\ \text{cm}^3$$

14.19 How many more skulls would the anthropologist described in Problem 14.18 have to find in order to achieve $E = 10.0\ \text{cm}^3$ for his 95% confidence interval?

Solution

Using the standard deviation, $s = 15.5134\ \text{cm}^3$, calculated in Problem 14.18, $z_{0.05/2} = 1.96$, and $E = 10.0\ \text{cm}^3$ in equation (14.20),

$$n \approx \left(\frac{1.96 \times 15.5134\ \text{cm}^3}{10.0\ \text{cm}^3}\right)^2 = 9.25$$

Rounding up to $n = 10$ and adding 15% (see Example 14.14) to make $n = 12$, he needs to find at least five more skulls to be reasonably certain of getting $E = 10.0\ \text{cm}^3$.

14.20 An aircraft manufacturing company receives a lot of 400 ball bearings that must each be 1.000 cm in diameter. Employees take a random sample of 25, and accept the lot only if $\bar{x}$ of the sample is 1.000 cm and the 99.9% confidence interval calculated from the sample has an E of 0.001 cm or less. The sample data are summarized in Table 14.4. Will the lot be accepted?

Solution

Using equation (6.9) of Volume 1,

$$\bar{x} = \frac{\sum f_i x_i}{\sum f_i} = \frac{25.001\ \text{cm}}{25} = 1.00004\ \text{cm}$$

Table 14.4

Diameter (cm) x_i	Frequency f_i	$f_i x_i$ (cm)	x_i^2 (cm^2)	$f_i x_i^2$ (cm^2)
0.998	2	1.996	0.996004	1.992008
0.999	4	3.996	0.998001	3.992004
1.000	12	12.000	1.000000	12.000000
1.001	5	5.005	1.002001	5.010005
1.002	2	2.004	1.004004	2.008008
$\sum$	25	25.001 cm		25.002025 cm^2

Assuming this population of diameters is normally distributed, then the appropriate 99.9% confidence interval would be $\bar{x} \pm t_{0.001/2,24} s_{\bar{x}}$. From Table A.6, $t_{0.001/2,24} = 3.745$. Using equation (7.35) of Volume 1,

$$s = \sqrt{\frac{\sum f_i x_i^2 - n\bar{x}^2}{n-1}} = \sqrt{\frac{(25.002025\ \text{cm})^2 - 25(1.00004\ \text{cm})^2}{24}} = 0.001020\ \text{cm}$$

As this is sampling from a finite population without replacement, and as $n > 0.05N$, we calcualte $s_{\bar{x}}$ with equation (14.3):

$$s_{\bar{x}} = \frac{s}{\sqrt{n}}\sqrt{\frac{N-n}{N-1}} = \frac{0.001020\ \text{cm}}{\sqrt{25}}\sqrt{\frac{400-25}{400-1}} = 0.000198\ \text{cm}$$

Therefore, the 99.9% confidence interval is

$$1.00004\ \text{cm} \pm (3.745 \times 0.000198\ \text{cm})$$
$$1.00004\ \text{cm} \pm 0.000742\ \text{cm}$$

Thus, $E = 0.000742$ cm, which meets the requirement of "E of 0.001 cm or less." Both criteria are met and the lot is accepted.

CONFIDENCE INTERVAL FOR THE POPULATION MEAN: UNKNOWN STANDARD DEVIATION, LARGE SAMPLE FROM A NORMAL DISTRIBUTION

14.21 A psychologist is studying the development of motor skills in babies who are addicted to drugs at birth. One of the standard measures she takes is the age of the baby when it is able to sit with support. For 50 such babies, she finds $\bar{x} = 129.4$ days and $s = 15.26$ days. Not knowing σ, determine the 99% confidence interval for μ by using both $\bar{x} \pm z_{0.01/2} s_{\bar{x}}$ and $\bar{x} \pm t_{0.01/2,\nu} s_{\bar{x}}$.

Solution

Developmental times for motor skills are typically normally distributed, so we can assume it is true here. If so, then as $n \geq 30$ and we do not know σ, the rule of thumb in Section 14.23 indicates that an approximate solution to this problem is $\bar{x} \pm z_{\alpha/2} s_{\bar{x}}$. Here

$$\bar{x} = 129.4\ \text{days}$$
$$z_{0.01/2} = 2.575$$

and, as this is theoretically an infinitely repeatable experiment,

$$s_{\bar{x}} = \frac{s}{\sqrt{n}} = \frac{15.26\ \text{days}}{\sqrt{50}} = 2.15809\ \text{days}$$

Thus, the approximate 99% confidence interval is

$$129.4 \text{ days} \pm (2.575 \times 2.15809 \text{ days})$$
$$129.4 \text{ days} \pm 5.56 \text{ days}$$

To determine the exactly correct 99% confidence interval $\bar{x} \pm t_{0.01/2,\nu} s_{\bar{x}}$, we need the exact $t_{0.01/2,49}$ value. This value is not available from Table A.6, but two suggested methods for approximating the exact t value are demonstrated in Example 14.15.

Following suggestion (1), the t value in Table A.6 for the next lowest available degree of freedom is $t_{0.01/2,40} = 2.704$. Therefore, the approximate 99% confidence interval is

$$129.4 \text{ days} \pm (2.704 \times 2.15809 \text{ days})$$
$$129.4 \text{ days} \pm 5.84 \text{ days}$$

Following suggestion (2) and using linear interpolation, we form parallel scales (see Fig. 14-7), one for degrees of freedom and the other for $t_{0.01/2,\nu}$ values. As degrees of freedom $\nu = 49$ is 9/20 of the distance from $\nu = 40$ to $\nu = 60$ (marked by a cross), therefore $t_{0.01/2,49}$ is also 9/20 of the distance between 2.704 and 2.660 on the $t_{0.01/2,\nu}$ scale (also marked with a cross). Thus

$$t_{0.01/2,49} \approx 2.704 - \left[\frac{9}{20} \times (2.704 - 2.660 = 0.044)\right] = 2.684$$

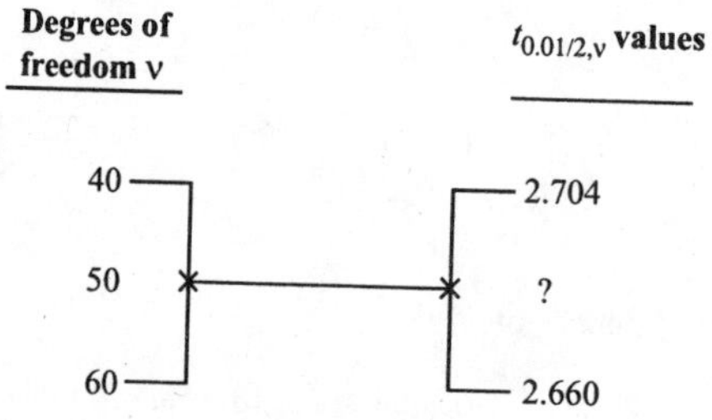

Fig. 14-7

Using this interpolated value, the approximate 99% confidence interval is

$$129.4 \text{ days} \pm (2.684 \times 2.15809 \text{ days})$$
$$129.4 \text{ days} \pm 5.79 \text{ days}$$

14.22 A random sample of $n = 70$ is taken from a normally distributed population with unknown μ and σ. The mean of the sample is 22 and the standard deviation is 8. Estimate μ by using $\bar{x} \pm z_{\alpha/2} s_{\bar{x}}$ to determine an approximate 95% confidence interval.

Solution

$$\bar{x} = 22$$
$$z_{0.05/2} = 1.96$$
$$s_{\bar{x}} = \frac{s}{\sqrt{n}} = \frac{8}{\sqrt{70}} = 0.956183$$

The approximate 95% confidence interval is

$$22 \pm (1.96 \times 0.956183)$$
$$22 \pm 1.87$$

CONFIDENCE INTERVAL FOR THE POPULATION MEAN: UNKNOWN STANDARD DEVIATION, DISTRIBUTION NOT NORMAL

14.23 A health insurance company is interested in knowing the average age of residents in a town of 50,000 people. Neither the mean nor the standard deviation of the population of ages is known. The company assumes that this population is not normally distributed, but rather positively skewed. A random sample of 100 residents is taken and the results are: mean age $\bar{x} = 40$ years, and standard deviation $s = 15$ years. Determine the approximate 95% confidence interval for this population.

Solution

With a sample as large as 100, we can calculate the approximate 95% confidence interval using $\bar{x} \pm z_{\alpha/2} s_{\bar{x}}$. Here

$$\bar{x} = 40 \text{ yr}$$

$$z_{0.05/2} = 1.96$$

and, as $n \leq 0.05N$,

$$s_{\bar{x}} = \frac{s}{\sqrt{n}} = \frac{15 \text{ yr}}{\sqrt{100}} = 1.5 \text{ yr}$$

Therefore, the approximate 95% confidence interval is

$$40 \text{ yr} \pm (1.96 \times 1.5 \text{ yr})$$

$$40 \text{ yr} \pm 2.94 \text{ yr}$$

14.24 A marine biologist wants to know the body sizes of an endangered species of dolphin. Neither the population mean nor the population standard deviation is known for this species. The biologist knows that the species has failed to reproduce in the past ten years, and so she assumes that the size distribution is negatively skewed, with more larger adults than would be the case if the distribution were normal. She is only able to measure 10 animals, finding a mean length $\bar{x} = 2.667$ meters with a standard deviation of 0.820 meters. Use the Chebyshev interval (see Section 14.25) to determine the at-least-95% approximate confidence interval for the population mean μ.

Solution

The first step is to find k:

$$1 - \frac{1}{k^2} = 0.95$$

$$\frac{1}{k^2} = 0.05$$

$$k^2 = 20$$

$$k = 4.47214$$

Next, this k value is substituted into $\bar{x} \pm k s_{\bar{x}}$, where

$$\bar{x} = 2.667 \text{ m}$$

$$s_{\bar{x}} = \frac{s}{\sqrt{n}} = \frac{0.820 \text{ m}}{\sqrt{10}} = 0.259307 \text{ m}$$

and at-least-95% approximate confidence interval for μ is

$$2.667 \text{ m} \pm (4.47214 \times 0.259307 \text{ m})$$

$$2.667 \text{ m} \pm 1.1597 \text{ m}$$

Supplementary Problems

POINT ESTIMATES

14.25 A random sample ($n = 12$) is taken from an infinite population and the following sums are calculated: $\sum_{i=1}^{12} x_i = 64$ and $\sum_{i=1}^{12} x_i^2 = 362$. What are the point estimates for the estimators $\bar{X}$, S^2, S, and $S_{\bar{x}}$?

Ans. $\bar{x} = 5.3$, $s^2 = 1.88$, $s = 1.4$, $s_{\bar{x}} = 0.4$

CONFIDENCE INTERVAL: KNOWN STANDARD DEVIATION, NORMAL DISTRIBUTION

14.26 A random sample ($n = 12$, $\bar{x} = 5.3$) is taken from an infinitely large, normally distributed population with known standard deviation $\sigma = 1.4$. For $1 - \alpha = 0.95$, what is the confidence-interval estimate?

Ans. $4.51 \le \mu \le 6.09$

14.27 For the fast-growing onions in Problem 14.6, with the sample of 67 time-to-maturity measurements that has a mean $\bar{x} = 71.2$ days, if you can assume these times are normally distributed with $\sigma = 8.3$ days, then what is the 97% confidence interval for the population mean μ?

Ans. 71.2 days $\pm$ 2.20 days

14.28 If in the onion study in Problem 14.27, the data were from a sample of 82 times-to-maturity measurements, what is the 97% confidence interval for the population mean μ?

Ans. 71.2 days $\pm$ 1.99 days

14.29 A random sample ($n = 25$, $\bar{x} = 80$) is taken from an infinitely large, normally distributed population with known standard deviation $\sigma = 10$. For 95% and 99% confidence intervals, find the margin of error of the estimates.

Ans. For the 95% confidence interval, $E = 3.92$; for the 99% confidence interval, $E = 5.15$

14.30 Two random samples ($n = 20$ and $n = 40$) are taken from an infinitely large, normally distributed population with known standard deviation $\sigma = 10$. Both samples have the same mean $\bar{x} = 100$. What are the 99% confidence intervals for the two samples?

Ans. For $n = 20$, 100 ± 5.76; for $n = 40$, 100 ± 4.07

CONFIDENCE INTERVALS: KNOWN STANDARD DEVIATION, LARGE SAMPLE FROM ANY DISTRIBUTION

14.31 You are a developer and want to know the average cost of a home in your district of approximately 200,000 homes. You take a random sample of 60 homes and get a mean $\bar{x} = \$65{,}000$. From previous studies, you know that the population of cost-per-home measurements is positively skewed with a standard deviation $\sigma = \$7{,}000$. What is the approximate 95% confidence interval for the population mean μ?

Ans. \$65,000 $\pm$ \$1,771.2

14.32 In the study of homes in Problem 14.31, if your sample of 60 homes came from a population of 800 homes, and again, $\bar{x} = \$65{,}000$ and $\sigma = \$7{,}000$, then what is the approximate 95% confidence interval for the population mean μ?

Ans. \$65,000 $\pm$ \$1,704.6

THE t DISTRIBUTION

14.33 Use Table A.6 to find $t_{\alpha/2,\nu} = t_{0.01/2,8}$.

Ans. 3.355

14.34 Use Table A.6 to find $-t_{\alpha/2,\nu} = -t_{0.20/2,18}$.

Ans. -1.330

CONFIDENCE INTERVAL: UNKNOWN STANDARD DEVIATION, SMALL SAMPLE FROM A NORMAL DISTRIBUTION

14.35 A random sample of size $n = 20$ is taken from a normally distributed population with an unknown μ and σ. If the sample has a mean $\bar{x} = 8.36$ and a standard deviation $s = 0.92$, then what is the 95% confidence interval for μ?

Ans. 8.36 ± 0.431

14.36 For the 95% confidence interval in Problem 14.35, using $s = 0.92$, find the approximate n needed to achieve a margin of error of $E = 0.25$ for the estimate of μ.

Ans. $n \approx 52.02$, or at least 53

14.37 A random sample of size $n = 16$ is taken from a normally distributed population with unknown μ and σ. If the sample has a mean $\bar{x} = 27.9$ and standard deviation $s = 3.23$, then what is the 90% confidence interval for the data?

Ans. 27.9 ± 1.42

14.38 Sixteen female volunteers used a new diet pill before each meal for six months. Weight loss in pounds during the six months was calcualted for the 16-person sample, and t-distribution techniques were used to calculate this 98% confidence interval for the mean weight loss μ: 8.3 lb $\pm$ 0.162625 lb. What are $\bar{x}$ and s for this sample?

Ans. $\bar{x} = 8.3$ lb, $s = 0.25$ lb

14.39 If the study of diet pills described in Problem 14.38 is repeated, how large should the sample be in order to achieve $E = 0.10$ lb for a 98% confidence interval?

Ans. At least 40

CONFIDENCE INTERVAL: UNKNOWN STANDARD DEVIATION, LARGE SAMPLE FROM A NORMAL DISTRIBUTION

14.40 A random sample of $n = 91$ is taken from a normally distributed population with unknown μ and σ. The mean of the sample is $\bar{x} = 600$ and the standard deviation is $s = 120$. Determine the approximate 95% confidence interval by using the t distribution and interpolation.

Ans. 600 ± 25.0

14.41 For the random sample and population in Problem 14.40, determine the approximate 95% confidence interval by using the standard normal distribution.

Ans. 600 ± 24.7

CONFIDENCE INTERVAL: UNKNOWN STANDARD DEVIATION, DISTRIBUTION NOT NORMAL

14.42 You want to know the average height μ of a population of oak trees in a vast woodland. You assume that the distribution of heights is negatively skewed rather than normal, with more adult trees at their maximum height than would be the case if the distribution were normal. You measure the heights of 60 trees ($n \leq 0.05N$) and find: $\bar{x} = 20.5$ meters and $s = 7.81$ meters. What is the approximate 95% confidence interval for μ?

Ans. 20.5 m $\pm$ 1.98 m

14.43 You are measuring body weight in a population of desert mice. In the past year this population seems to have more than doubled, and because of this rapid increase you assume the population is not normally distributed on body weight; there will be an abnormal number of young and thus light individuals (a positive skew). You do not know either μ or σ of this population of body weights. To estimate μ, you measure body weight for a sample of 20 mice and find: $\bar{x} = 17.01$ g and $s = 5.671$ g. Use Chebyshev's interval to determine the at-least-90% approximate confidence interval for μ.

Ans. 17.01 g $\pm$ 4.010 g

CHAPTER 15

One-Sample Estimation of the Population Variance, Standard Deviation, and Proportion

15.1 OPTIMAL ESTIMATORS OF VARIANCE, STANDARD DEVIATION, AND PROPORTION

In Chapter 14 we presented a variety of confidence-interval solutions to the statistical problem of estimating the population mean μ from a single sample. These solutions were based on two fundamental distributions: the normal distribution and the t distribution. Now in this chapter we use single samples to determine confidence-interval estimates for three other parameters: the variance σ^2 and standard deviation σ of a normally distributed population, and the proportion p of a binomial population. As in Chapter 14, we place each of these population parameters θ within an interval $a \leq \theta \leq b$, where a and b are the lower and upper boundaries of an interval of values on the real number line. These boundary values are determined by (see Section 14.6): (1) the sample point estimate $\hat{\theta}^*$, (2) a sample statistic that relates the point estimate to the population parameter, and (3) the sampling distribution of that statistic.

In Section 14.2 we reviewed the criteria for selecting the optimal estimator $\hat{\theta}$ for a population parameter θ: unbiasedness, precision, efficiency, consistency, and sufficiency. We indicated in that section that the optimal estimator for the population variance σ^2 is the sample variance S^2 and the optimal estimator for the population standard deviation σ is the sample standard deviation S (although it is a slightly biased). We also know that any specific sample estimate $S^2 = s^2$ is a point estimate of σ^2, and any specific sample estimate $S = s$ is a point estimate of σ. We now say that the optimal estimator for the binomial parameter p is the sample proportion $\bar{P}$ (see Sections 13.21 and 15.13), and that any specific sample value $\bar{P} = \bar{p}$ is a point estimate of p.

15.2 THE CHI-SQUARE STATISTIC AND THE CHI-SQUARE DISTRIBUTION

The first goal of this chapter is to develop confidence intervals for the population variance σ^2 from information contained within a single random sample from a normally distributed population. To obtain confidence-interval boundary values for this parameter we need: (1) a point estimate s^2 of the sample S^2, (2) a sample statistic that relates S^2 to σ^2, and (3) a sampling distribution of that statistic.

The sample statistic generally used for this purpose is the *chi-square statistic*,

$$X^2 = \frac{(n-1)S^2}{\sigma^2} \tag{15.1}$$

where X is the upper case of the Greek letter *chi* and the symbol X^2 is read "kai-square." This statistic can assume specific values

$$\chi^2 = \frac{(n-1)s^2}{\sigma^2} \tag{15.2}$$

where χ is the lower case of *chi* and χ^2 is also read "kai-square."

The chi-square statistic is a random variable with a sampling distribution called the *chi-square distribution* (or *χ^2 distribution*). We know from sampling theory that

> If all possible samples of size n are taken from a normally distributed population with variance σ^2, and if specific values $\chi^2 = \dfrac{(n-1)s^2}{\sigma^2}$ of the random variable $X^2 = \dfrac{(n-1)S^2}{\sigma^2}$ are calculated for each sample, then the χ^2 values will have a continuous probability distribution (sampling distribution) called the chi-square distribution.

As with previous continuous probability distributions (see Sections 12.2, 12.15, 12.16, and 14.15), the chi-square distribution is defined by a specific and unique probability density function. This function, which we will not derive, is

$$f(\chi^2) = c(\chi^2)^{(\nu/2)-1}e^{-\chi^2/2} \tag{15.3}$$

where $\chi^2 = \dfrac{(n-1)s^2}{\sigma^2}$

$e = 2.71828\ldots$ (see Volume 1, Problem 1.23)

$\nu = n - 1$

$c =$ a constant (which is a function of ν) that is required to make the total area under the chi-square distribution equal to 1

This function has the same single parameter ν as the t distribution (denoted also by d, df, $d.f.$, DF, r, and others) and is again called the *number of degrees of freedom*, or simply *degrees of freedom* (see Section 14.15 and 14.17). As with the t distribution, $\nu = n - 1$ because there is one restriction on the calculation of χ^2, which is the calculation of the sample mean $\bar{x}$. As indicated in Section 14.17, because of the interlinking of probability distributions, this parameter ν will appear often in this book.

As with previous continuous probability distributions, the chi-square distribution is not just one distribution but a family of continuous distributions, known collectively as the chi-square distribution. There is a unique distribution for each integer value of the number of degrees of freedom ($\nu = n - 1$). Of these infinitely many distributions, four ($\nu = 1, 3, 5, 10$) are shown superimposed in Fig. 15-1.

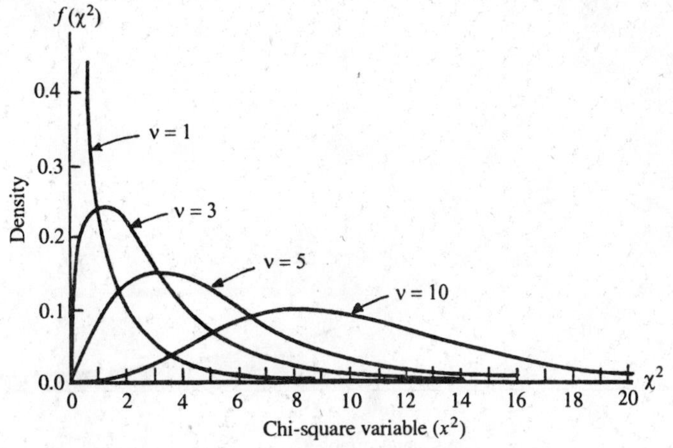

Fig. 15-1

The chi-square distribution is very different from the t distribution and the standard normal distribution, as you can see from examining Fig. 15-1. While the latter two distributions are symmetric about a mean of zero, the chi-square distribution is asymmetric (positively skewed) with no χ^2 values less than zero. As the degrees of freedom increase above $v = 2$, the chi-square distribution becomes unimodal and more and more symmetric, but never about a mean of zero. As a matter of fact, the mean is the number of degrees of freedom: $\mu = v = n - 1$. Three other descriptive parameters of the chi-square distribution are: the variance, $\sigma^2 = 2v = 2(n-1)$; the standard deviation, $\sigma = \sqrt{2v} = \sqrt{2(n-1)}$; and (when $v > 2$), the mode, $v - 2 = n - 3$.

15.3 CRITICAL VALUES OF THE CHI-SQUARE DISTRIBUTION

In Section 12.10, we stated for the continuous normally distributed random variable X and the standard-normal variable Z that [equation (12.9)]

$$P(X > x_\alpha) = P(Z > z_\alpha) = \alpha$$

Then, in Section 14.19 we stated for the T random variable that [equation (14.13)]

$$P(T > t_{\alpha,v}) = \alpha$$

Similarly, we now state for the random variable X^2,

$$P(X^2 > \chi^2_{\alpha,v}) = \alpha \tag{15.4}$$

where $\chi^2_{\alpha,v}$ denotes the critical value (or critical boundary value) in the chi-square distribution with v degrees of freedom that has α on its right and $1 - \alpha$ on its left. This relationship between area and critical value is illustrated in Fig. 15-2.

The standard normal distribution and the t distribution are symmetric around a mean value of zero, and so the critical values cutting off the same α in the positive and negative tails of the distribution are, respectively: $-z_\alpha$ and z_α for the standard normal, $-t_{\alpha,v}$ and $t_{\alpha,v}$ for the t distribution. The chi-square distribution, by contrast, is not symmetric about its mean, and for $n > 1$ its mean is never zero. Therefore, for the chi-square distribution the critical value that cuts off α to the left, in the negative tail, is $\chi^2_{1-\alpha,v}$ and thus

$$P(X^2 < \chi^2_{1-\alpha,v}) = \alpha \tag{15.5}$$

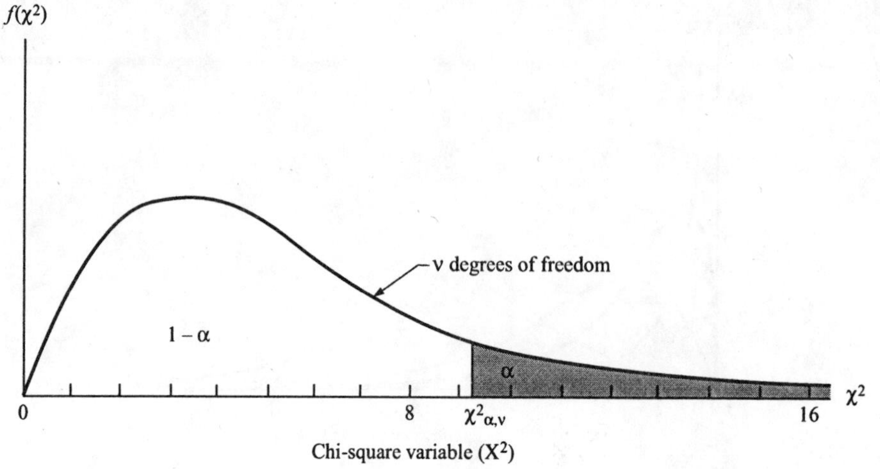

Fig. 15-2

This relationship between area and critical value is illustrated in Fig. 15-3.

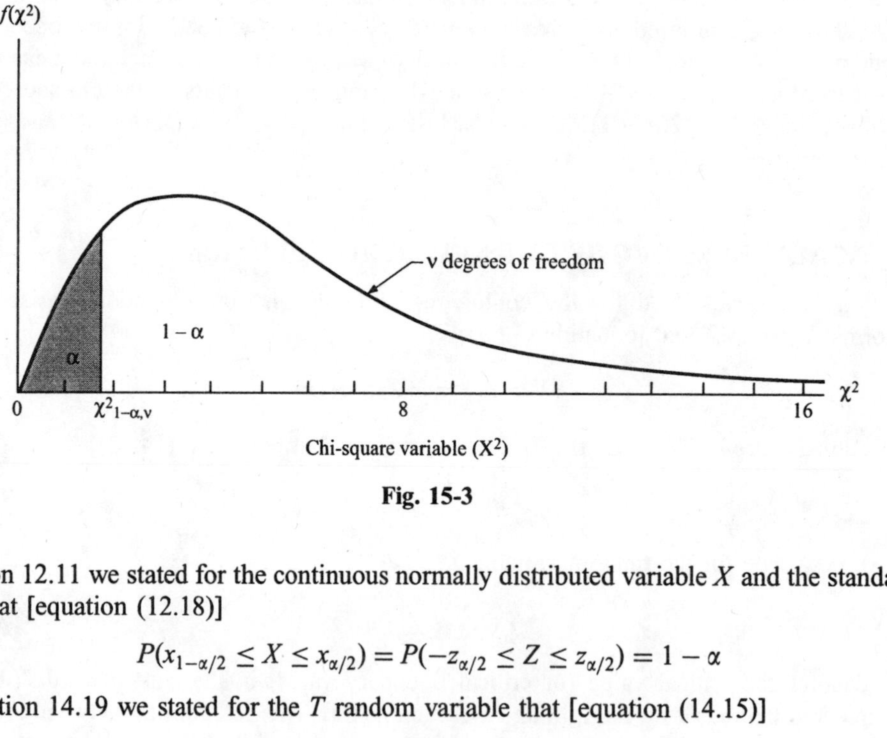

Fig. 15-3

In Section 12.11 we stated for the continuous normally distributed variable X and the standard normal variable Z that [equation (12.18)]

$$P(x_{1-\alpha/2} \leq X \leq x_{\alpha/2}) = P(-z_{\alpha/2} \leq Z \leq z_{\alpha/2}) = 1 - \alpha$$

Then, in Section 14.19 we stated for the T random variable that [equation (14.15)]

$$P(-t_{\alpha/2,\nu} \leq T \leq t_{\alpha/2,\nu}) = 1 - \alpha$$

Now, for the X^2 random variable, we state that

$$P(\chi^2_{1-\alpha/2,\nu} \leq X^2 \leq \chi^2_{\alpha/2,\nu}) = 1 - \alpha \tag{15.6}$$

where $\chi^2_{\alpha/2,\nu}$ denotes the critical value for the chi-square distribution with ν degrees of freedom cutting off an area $\alpha/2$ in the right tail and $\chi^2_{1-\alpha/2,\nu}$ denotes the critical value for the same chi-square distribution, cutting off an area $\alpha/2$ in the left tail. This relationship between areas and critical values is illustrated in Fig. 15-4.

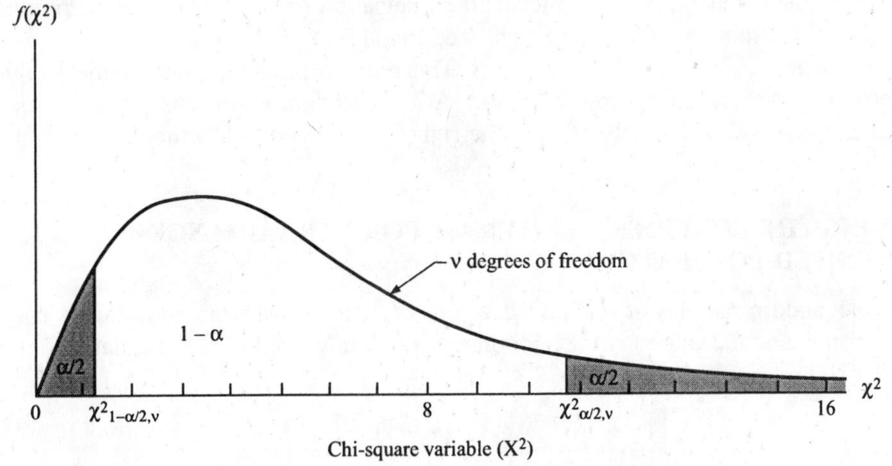

Fig. 15-4

15.4 TABLE A.7: CRITICAL VALUES OF THE CHI-SQUARE DISTRIBUTION

Table A.7 in the Appendix (*Critical Values of the Chi-Square Distribution*) gives critical $\chi^2_{\alpha,\nu}$ values for selected chi-square distributions ($\nu = 1, \ldots, 30, 40, 50, 60, 70, 80, 90,$ and 100). Each row in the table represents a different chi-square distribution, identified by its degrees of freedom ν in the left-hand column. The values in each row are critical values $\chi^2_{\alpha,\nu}$ for the given chi-square distribution, which cut off a specific area α to the right. This area is identified by the α value in the χ^2_α symbol at the top of each column. Table 15.1, which is a section of Table A.7, shows the critical values for $\nu = 6, 7, 8, 9,$ and 10. The first column gives $\chi^2_{0.995}$ values that cut off $\alpha = 0.995$ to their right, and the last column gives $\chi^2_{0.005}$ values that cut off $\alpha = 0.005$ to their right.

Table 15.1

ν	χ^2_α										
	$\chi^2_{0.995}$	$\chi^2_{0.990}$	$\chi^2_{0.975}$	$\chi^2_{0.950}$	$\chi^2_{0.900}$	$\chi^2_{0.500}$	$\chi^2_{0.100}$	$\chi^2_{0.050}$	$\chi^2_{0.025}$	$\chi^2_{0.010}$	$\chi^2_{0.005}$
6	0.676	0.872	1.24	1.64	2.20	5.35	10.64	12.59	14.45	16.81	18.55
7	0.989	1.24	1.69	2.17	2.83	6.35	12.02	14.07	16.01	18.48	20.28
8	1.34	1.65	2.18	2.73	3.49	7.34	13.36	15.51	17.53	20.09	21.96
9	1.73	2.09	2.70	3.33	4.17	8.34	14.68	16.92	19.02	21.67	23.59
10	2.16	2.56	3.25	3.94	4.87	9.34	15.99	18.31	20.48	23.21	25.19

EXAMPLE 15.1 Use Table 15.1 to find $\chi^2_{\alpha,\nu} = \chi^2_{0.050,10}$ and $\chi^2_{1-\alpha,\nu} = \chi^2_{1-0.050,10}$.

Solution

To find $\chi^2_{0.050,10}$, we use the $\chi^2_{0.050}$ column and the $\nu = 10$ row. The correct value is 18.31 (circled in the table); it cuts off an area equal to $\alpha = 0.05$ to its right. The table only gives χ^2_α, and so to find $\chi^2_{1-\alpha}$ we first convert it to its χ^2_α equivalent. Thus, to find $\chi^2_{1-0.050,10}$ we need to locate the $\chi^2_{0.950}$ value for $\nu = 10$. Using the $\chi^2_{0.950}$ column and the $\nu = 10$ row, we find 3.94 (circled in the table); it cuts off an area equal to $\alpha = 0.950$ to its right (or 0.050 to its left).

For a given α value, $\chi^2_{\alpha,\nu}$ increases as ν increases. This relationship between critical value and degrees of freedom can be seen by moving down one of the columns of Table A.7. The relationship exists because as ν increases, both the mean ($\mu = \nu$) and the standard deviation ($\sigma = \sqrt{2\nu}$) of the distribution increase, and the mass of the distribution shifts to the right (see Fig. 15-1).

For a given ν value, $\chi^2_{\alpha,\nu}$ increases as α decreases. This relationship between the critical value and α can be seen by moving along one of the rows of Table A.7. The relationship exists because as α defines a smaller area, the critical value that cuts off α to the right gets farther and farther to the right.

15.5 DERIVING THE CONFIDENCE INTERVAL FOR THE VARIANCE σ^2 OF A NORMALLY DISTRIBUTED POPULATION

If all possible random samples of size n ($X_1, X_2, \ldots, X_n$) are drawn from an infinitely large, normally distributed population and the value s^2 of the continuous random variable S^2 is calculated for each sample, then

$$P\left[\frac{(n-1)S^2}{\chi^2_{\alpha/2,\nu}} \leq \sigma^2 \leq \frac{(n-1)S^2}{\chi^2_{1-\alpha/2,\nu}}\right] = 1 - \alpha \tag{15.7}$$

To show that this relationship is true, we begin with equation (15.6),

$$P(\chi^2_{1-\alpha/2,\nu} \leq \mathrm{X}^2 \leq \chi^2_{\alpha/2,\nu}) = 1 - \alpha$$

Substituting the random variable $\mathrm{X}^2 = \frac{(n-1)S^2}{\sigma^2}$ [equation (15.1)] into this equation, we get

$$P\left[\chi^2_{1-\alpha/2,\nu} \leq \frac{(n-1)S^2}{\sigma^2} \leq \chi^2_{\alpha/2,\nu}\right] = 1 - \alpha$$

Dividing each term in the inequality by $(n-1)S^2$, which does not change the direction of the inequality (see Volume 1, Section 1.23),

$$P\left[\frac{\chi^2_{1-\alpha/2,\nu}}{(n-1)S^2} \leq \frac{1}{\sigma^2} \leq \frac{\chi^2_{\alpha/2,\nu}}{(n-1)S^2}\right] = 1 - \alpha$$

Finally, inverting each term reverses the direction of the inequality

$$P\left[\frac{(n-1)S^2}{\chi^2_{1-\alpha/2,\nu}} \geq \sigma^2 \geq \frac{(n-1)S^2}{\chi^2_{\alpha/2,\nu}}\right] = 1 - \alpha$$

which can also be written as

$$P\left[\frac{(n-1)S^2}{\chi^2_{\alpha/2,\nu}} \leq \sigma^2 \leq \frac{(n-1)S^2}{\chi^2_{1-\alpha/2,\nu}}\right] = 1 - \alpha$$

Thus, if specific values of the random interval

$$\frac{(n-1)S^2}{\chi^2_{\alpha/2,\nu}} \leq \sigma^2 \leq \frac{(n-1)S^2}{\chi^2_{1-\alpha/2,\nu}}$$

are calculated for each sample, then $(1-\alpha)100\%$ of these specific values

$$\frac{(n-1)s^2}{\chi^2_{\alpha/2,\nu}} \leq \sigma^2 \leq \frac{(n-1)s^2}{\chi^2_{1-\alpha/2,\nu}} \tag{15.8}$$

will contain σ^2. Therefore, any such specific interval is called a $(1-\alpha)100\%$ *confidence interval for* σ^2.

These techniques for finding the $(1-\alpha)100\%$ confidence interval for σ^2 can only be used for populations that are normally distributed; they are not robust against departures from normality.

15.6 PRESENTING CONFIDENCE LIMITS

In Section 14.10 we indicated that the $(1-\alpha)100\%$ confidence interval for the population mean μ (known σ, normal population) can be presented in any one of the following forms:

(1) $\bar{x} - z_{\alpha/2}\sigma_{\bar{x}} \leq \mu \leq \bar{x} + z_{\alpha/2}\sigma_{\bar{x}}$

(2) $L = \bar{x} - z_{\alpha/2}\sigma_{\bar{x}},\ U = \bar{x} + z_{\alpha/2}\sigma_{\bar{x}}$

(3) $(\bar{x} - z_{\alpha/2}\sigma_{\bar{x}}, \bar{x} + z_{\alpha/2}\sigma_{\bar{x}})$

(4) $\bar{x} \pm z_{\alpha/2}\sigma_{\bar{x}}$

The $(1-\alpha)100\%$ confidence intervals for the population variance σ^2 can only be presented in three of these forms:

$$(1)\quad \frac{(n-1)s^2}{\chi^2_{\alpha/2,\nu}} \leq \sigma^2 \leq \frac{(n-1)s^2}{\chi^2_{1-\alpha/2,\nu}}$$

$$(2)\quad L = \frac{(n-1)s^2}{\chi^2_{\alpha/2,\nu}},\qquad U = \frac{(n-1)s^2}{\chi^2_{1-\alpha/2,\nu}}$$

$$(3)\quad \left[\frac{(n-1)s^2}{\chi^2_{\alpha/2,\nu}}, \frac{(n-1)s^2}{\chi^2_{1-\alpha/2,\nu}}\right]$$

The fourth form cannot be used because:

(1) While the Z statistic $\left(Z = \dfrac{\bar{X}-\mu}{\sigma_{\bar{x}}}\right)$ relates the point estimate to its parameter by subtraction, the chi-square statistic $\left[X^2 = \dfrac{(n-1)S^2}{\sigma^2}\right]$ makes this relationship by a ratio $\left(\dfrac{S^2}{\sigma^2}\right)$;

(2) While with the Z technique the confidence interval is created by adding and subtracting an error factor from the point estimate $(\bar{x} \pm z_{\alpha/2}\sigma_{\bar{x}})$, with the chi-square technique the confidence interval is created by multiplying the point estimate by an error factor $\left[\dfrac{(n-1)}{\chi^2} \times s^2\right]$;

(3) While the standard normal distribution is symmetric about a mean of zero, thus allowing the symmetric form $\bar{x} \pm z_{\alpha/2}\sigma_{\bar{x}}$, the chi-square distribution is asymmetric.

EXAMPLE 15.2 In Example 14.12, for a random sample ($n = 16$, $\bar{x} = 27.9$, and $s = 3.23$) taken from a normally distributed population (unknown μ and σ), we found that the 95% confidence interval for the population mean μ was 27.9 ± 1.72. For this same sample, for the population variance σ^2, what is: (*a*) its 95% confidence interval, (*b*) the 99% confidence interval?

Solution

(*a*) We have to determine

$$\left[\frac{(n-1)s^2}{\chi^2_{\alpha/2,\nu}}, \frac{(n-1)s^2}{\chi^2_{1-\alpha/2,\nu}}\right]$$

for the specific values

$$s^2 = (3.23)^2 = 10.4329$$
$$\nu = n - 1 = 16 - 1 = 15$$
$$\alpha/2 = 0.025$$
$$1 - \alpha/2 = 0.975$$

Therefore, from Table A.7,

$$\chi^2_{\alpha/2,\nu} = \chi^2_{0.025,15} = 27.49$$
$$\chi^2_{1-\alpha/2,\nu} = \chi^2_{0.975,15} = 6.26$$

Thus, the 95% confidence interval for σ^2 is

$$\left(\frac{15 \times 10.4329}{27.49}, \frac{15 \times 10.4329}{6.26}\right) = (5.69, 25.00)$$

(b) The s^2 and ν values are the same but now: $\alpha/2 = 0.005$ and $1 - \alpha/2 = 0.995$. Therefore, from Table A.7,

$$\chi^2_{\alpha/2,\nu} = \chi^2_{0.005,15} = 32.80$$
$$\chi^2_{1-\alpha/2,\nu} = \chi^2_{0.995,15} = 4.60$$

Thus, the 99% confidence interval for σ^2 is

$$\left(\frac{15 \times 10.4329}{32.80}, \frac{15 \times 10.4329}{4.60}\right) = (4.77, 34.02)$$

15.7 PRECISION OF THE CONFIDENCE INTERVAL FOR THE VARIANCE

Because confidence-interval estimates for the population mean μ can be written in the symmetric form $\bar{x} \pm$ (margin of error), the precision of any specific interval estimate is measured by margin-of-error values [$E = z_{\alpha/2}\sigma_{\bar{x}}$ (see Section 14.11), $E = t_{\alpha/2,\nu}s_{\bar{x}}$ (see Section 14.22)]. Such E values can not be calculated for the confidence-interval estimates of σ^2 (see Section 15.6), but we can return to the original definition (see Section 14.11) and use the width of any specific interval estimate as the measure of precision of that estimate:

$$\text{Precision} = (\text{upper boundary}) - (\text{lower boundary}) \tag{15.9}$$

EXAMPLE 15.3 For the sample in Example 15.2, determine the precision of: (*a*) the 95% confidence interval, (*b*) the 99% confidence interval.

Solution

(*a*) For the 95% interval, precision $= 25.00 - 5.69 = 19.31$.

(*b*) For the 99% interval, precision $= 34.02 - 4.77 = 29.25$.

This demonstrates that for a given sample, the precision of the interval estimate of σ^2 decreases (interval width increases) with increases in $(1 - \alpha)100\%$.

EXAMPLE 15.4 What happens to the precision of the 95% confidence interval in Example 15.2, if we hold s^2 constant at 10.4329 while increasing the sample size from $n = 16$ to: (*a*) $n = 31$, (*b*) $n = 61$?

Solution

(*a*) For $n = 31$,

$$s^2 = 10.4329$$
$$\nu = n - 1 = 31 - 1 = 30$$

and from Table A.7,

$$\chi^2_{\alpha/2,\nu} = \chi^2_{0.025,30} = 46.98$$
$$\chi^2_{1-\alpha/2,\nu} = \chi^2_{0.975,30} = 16.79$$

Thus, the 95% confidence interval for σ^2 is

$$\left[\frac{(n-1)s^2}{\chi^2_{\alpha/2,\nu}}, \frac{(n-1)s^2}{\chi^2_{1-\alpha/2,\nu}}\right] = \left(\frac{30 \times 10.4329}{46.98}, \frac{30 \times 10.4329}{16.79}\right) = (6.66, \ 18.64)$$

Therefore, for this interval,

$$\text{Precision} = 18.64 - 6.66 = 11.98$$

(*b*) For $n = 61$,

$$s^2 = 10.4329$$
$$\nu = n - 1 = 61 - 1 = 60$$

and from Table A.7,

$$\chi^2_{\alpha/2,\nu} = \chi^2_{0.025,60} = 83.30$$
$$\chi^2_{1-\alpha/2,\nu} = \chi^2_{0.975,60} = 40.48$$

Thus, the 95% confidence interval for σ^2 is

$$\left(\frac{60 \times 10.4329}{83.30}, \frac{60 \times 10.4329}{40.48}\right) = (7.51, \ 15.46)$$

Therefore, for this interval,

$$\text{Precision} = 15.46 - 7.51 = 7.95$$

This demonstrates that the precision of an interval estimate of σ^2 increases (interval width decreases) as sample size n increases.

15.8 DETERMINING SAMPLE SIZE NECESSARY TO ACHIEVE A DESIRED QUALITY-OF-ESTIMATE FOR THE VARIANCE

In Chapter 14 we presented techniques for determining in advance the necessary sample size to achieve a desired quality-of-estimate in a confidence-interval estimate of μ (see Sections 14.12 and 14.22). These techniques involved solving the equation [E = (margin of error)] for n. Unfortunately, while there are various techniques for pre-determining sample size n for confidence intervals for σ^2, they are not as clear and simple.

Because the exact chi-square technique does not produce a symmetric confidence interval of the form $s^2 \pm$ (margin of error), it is not possible to produce an exact equation for n. However, if it is true that all samples (preliminary and future) are large ($n \geq 100$), then there is an approximate technique for pre-determining n using the normal approximation of the sampling distribution of S^2 (see Section 15.10). Other than that, given a preliminary point estimate s^2 and knowing the desired quality-of-estimate (confidence level and roughly the desired width of the interval), a series of confidence intervals for different sample sizes (see Example 15.4) could be calculated until the desired quality is achieved. Also, it would generally be true that μ and σ^2 would be estimated simultaneously, and thus the necessary sample size would be determined for the estimation of μ.

15.9 USING NORMAL-APPROXIMATION TECHNIQUES TO DETERMINE CONFIDENCE INTERVALS FOR THE VARIANCE

It can be seen in Fig. 15-1 that, as the degrees of freedom ν increases, the chi-square distributions become more and more symmetric. It can be proven mathematically that at large ν, the chi-square distribution approaches the normal distribution. Unfortunately, the typical practical application does not involve a sample that is large enough to allow a normal approximation of a chi-square distribution.

For a more reasonable sample size $[(\nu = n - 1) > 30]$, however, it can be shown that the sampling distribution for the random variable $\sqrt{2X^2} - \sqrt{2\nu - 1}$ is essentially the standard normal distribution $(\mu = 0, \sigma^2 = \sigma = 1)$. Therefore, for $\nu > 30$,

$$Z \approx \sqrt{2X^2} - \sqrt{2\nu - 1}$$

Rearranging terms, the equation becomes

$$X^2 \approx \tfrac{1}{2}(Z + \sqrt{2\nu - 1})^2 \tag{15.10}$$

This equation can be used to calculate approximate chi-square values for determining confidence intervals for σ^2 when $\nu > 30$.

EXAMPLE 15.5 In Example 15.4 we found for $\alpha = 0.05$ and $n = 61$ that

$$\chi^2_{\alpha/2,\nu} = \chi^2_{0.025,60} = 83.30$$
$$\chi^2_{1-\alpha/2,\nu} = \chi^2_{0.975,60} = 40.48$$

Find these values again, using the approximate technique described above.

Solution

For these conditions, we can use equation (15.10), and therefore it is true that

$$\chi^2_{\alpha/2} \approx \tfrac{1}{2}(z_{\alpha/2} + \sqrt{2\nu - 1})^2$$

and

$$\chi^2_{1-\alpha/2,\nu} \approx \tfrac{1}{2}(-z_{\alpha/2} + \sqrt{2\nu - 1})^2$$

For $\alpha = 0.05$, we find in Table A.5 that $z_{\alpha/2} = z_{0.025} = 1.96$ and thus $-z_{\alpha/2} = -z_{0.025} = -1.96$. Substituting these values, as well as $\nu = n - 1 = 61 - 1 = 60$, we find that

$$\chi^2_{0.025,60} \approx \tfrac{1}{2}[z_{0.025} + \sqrt{(2 \times 60) - 1}]^2 = \tfrac{1}{2}(1.96 + \sqrt{119})^2 = 82.80$$
$$\chi^2_{0.975,60} \approx \tfrac{1}{2}[-z_{0.025} + \sqrt{(2 \times 60) - 1}]^2 = \tfrac{1}{2}(-1.96 + \sqrt{119})^2 = 40.04$$

Comparing these results with those found in Example 15.4 (83.30, 40.48), you can see that when $\nu > 30$, this normal approximation gives a reasonably close approximation of χ^2 values.

15.10 USING THE SAMPLING DISTRIBUTION OF THE SAMPLE VARIANCE TO APPROXIMATE A CONFIDENCE INTERVAL FOR THE POPULATION VARIANCE

If samples from a normally distributed population are very large $(n \geq 100)$, then the sampling distribution of the random variable S^2 (the sample variance) can be used to approximate a $(1 - \alpha)100\%$ confidence interval for σ^2. Without mathematical derivation, we simply state here that

> If samples are very large $(n \geq 100)$ and from a normally distributed population, then the sampling distribution of S^2 is essentially normal with mean $\mu_{s^2} = \sigma^2$ and standard deviation (standard error) $\sigma_{s^2} = \sigma^2 \sqrt{\frac{2}{n}}$.

It follows from this statement that, under these conditions, the $(1 - \alpha)100\%$ confidence interval for σ^2 can be approximated by

$$s^2 \pm z_{\alpha/2}\sigma^2 \sqrt{\frac{2}{n}} \tag{15.11}$$

and, by using the point estimate s^2 to estimate σ^2, this becomes

$$s^2 \pm z_{\alpha/2}s^2\sqrt{\frac{2}{n}} \tag{15.12}$$

EXAMPLE 15.6 If for the sample in Example 15.4, s^2 remains 10.4329 but n is increased to 350, then use equation (15.12) to determine the approximate 95% confidence interval for σ^2.

Solution

From Table A.5 we find that $z_{0.05/2} = 1.96$. Therefore, the approximate 95% confidence interval for σ^2 is

$$10.4329 \pm \left(1.96 \times 10.4329 \times \sqrt{\frac{2}{350}}\right)$$

$$10.43 \pm 1.55$$

or

$$(8.88, 11.98)$$

An advantage of using this approximate confidence interval is that it provides an approximate margin-of-error equation. Thus, for equation (15.11),

$$E \approx z_{\alpha/2}\sigma^2\sqrt{\frac{2}{n}} \tag{15.13}$$

Solving this equation for n,

$$n \approx \left(\frac{\sqrt{2}z_{\alpha/2}\sigma^2}{E}\right)^2$$

Substituting s^2 for σ^2, we can determine approximate future sample size to achieve a desired quality-of-estimate with

$$n \approx \left(\frac{\sqrt{2}z_{\alpha/2}s^2}{E}\right)^2 \tag{15.14}$$

EXAMPLE 15.7 If we want to repeat the study described in Example 15.6 in order to get an approximate 95% confidence interval with $E = 1.00$ instead of $E = 1.55$, use equation (15.14) with $s^2 = 10.4329$ to determine how large a sample will be needed.

Solution

Substituting $E = 1.00$, $z_{0.05/2} = 1.96$, and $s^2 = 10.4329$ in the equation, we get,

$$n \approx \left(\frac{\sqrt{2} \times 1.96 \times 10.4329}{1.00}\right)^2 = 836.28, \quad \text{or } 837$$

Thus, to decrease the margin of error from $E = 1.55$ to $E = 1.00$, we would need to increase the sample size from 350 to at least 837.

15.11 CONFIDENCE INTERVAL FOR THE STANDARD DEVIATION σ OF A NORMALLY DISTRIBUTED POPULATION

The exact $(1 - \alpha)100\%$ confidence interval for the population standard deviation σ is calculated by taking the positive square roots of the lower and upper limits of the confidence interval for the variance σ^2 (Section 15.6):

$$\left[\sqrt{\frac{(n-1)s^2}{\chi^2_{\alpha/2,\nu}}}, \sqrt{\frac{(n-1)s^2}{\chi^2_{1-\alpha/2,\nu}}}\right] \tag{15.15}$$

EXAMPLE 15.8 Before going to a doctor for a physical examination, you use a blood-pressure monitor to take 21 measurements of your blood pressure. The 21 diastolic-pressure measurements (in mmHg) are: 77, 85, 84, 81, 82, 78, 81, 79, 84, 83, 80, 80, 83, 81, 79, 81, 80, 79, 82, 78, 82. First use the frequency distribution technique from Problem 7.15 of Volume 1 to determine the sample standard deviation s. Then find the exact 95% confidence interval for σ of the population of diastolic-pressure measurements, assuming this population is normally distributed.

Solution

The calculation of the sample standard deviation, $s = 2.16576$ mmHg, is shown at the bottom of Table 15.2. Therefore, $s^2 = 4.69052\ \text{mmHg}^2$. We also know that $n - 1 = 21 - 1 = 20$. From Table A.7 we find that

$$\chi^2_{\alpha/2,\nu} = \chi^2_{0.05/2,20} = 34.17$$

$$\chi^2_{1-\alpha/2,\nu} = \chi^2_{1-0.05/2,20} = 9.59$$

Table 15.2

Diastolic pressure (mmHg) x_i	Frequency f_i	$f_i x_i$ (mmHg)	$(x_i - \bar{x})$ (mmHg)	$(x_i - \bar{x})^2$ (mmHg^2)	$f_i(x_i - \bar{x})^2$ (mmHg^2)
77	1	77	−3.9	15.21	15.21
78	2	156	−2.9	8.41	16.82
79	3	237	−1.9	3.61	10.83
80	3	240	−0.9	0.81	2.43
81	4	324	0.1	0.01	0.04
82	3	246	1.1	1.21	3.63
83	2	166	2.1	4.41	8.82
84	2	168	3.1	9.61	19.22
85	1	85	4.1	16.81	16.81
Σ	21	1,699 mmHg			93.81 mmHg^2

$$\bar{x} = \frac{\Sigma f_i x_i}{n} = \frac{1{,}699\ \text{mmHg}}{21} = 80.9\ \text{mmHg}$$

$$s = \sqrt{\frac{\Sigma f_i(x_i - \bar{x})^2}{n-1}} = \sqrt{\frac{93.81\ \text{mmHg}^2}{20}} = 2.16576\ \text{mmHg}$$

Substituting these values into equation (15.15), we get this exact 95% confidence interval for σ:

$$\left(\sqrt{\frac{20 \times 4.69052\ \text{mmHg}^2}{34.17}},\ \sqrt{\frac{20 \times 4.69052\ \text{mmHg}^2}{9.59}}\right) = (1.66\ \text{mmHg},\ 3.13\ \text{mmHg})$$

15.12 USING THE SAMPLING DISTRIBUTION OF THE SAMPLE STANDARD DEVIATION TO APPROXIMATE A CONFIDENCE INTERVAL FOR THE POPULATION STANDARD DEVIATION

The $(1 - \alpha)100\%$ confidence interval for the population standard deviation σ can be approximated by using the sampling distribution of the random variable S (the sample standard deviation). The technique is similar to the procedures used in Section 15.10, where the sampling distribution of the sample variance S^2

was used to approximate a confidence interval for the population variance σ^2 [equation (15.12)]. Here, again without mathematical derivation, we state that

> If samples are very large ($n \geq 100$) and from a normally distributed population, then the sampling distribution of S is essentially normal with mean $\mu_s = \sigma$ and standard deviation (standard error) $\sigma_s = \dfrac{\sigma}{\sqrt{2n}}$.

It follows from these conditions that the $(1 - \alpha)100\%$ confidence interval for σ can be approximated by

$$s \pm z_{\alpha/2} \frac{\sigma}{\sqrt{2n}}$$

Using the point estimate s to estimate σ, any specific approximate confidence interval is

$$s \pm z_{\alpha/2} \frac{s}{\sqrt{2n}} \tag{15.16}$$

EXAMPLE 15.9 In Example 15.6 using equation (15.12), we determined for a sample ($n = 350$, $s^2 = 10.4329$) from a normally distributed population, that the approximate 95% confidence interval for the variance is (8.88, 11.98). Determine the approximate 95% confidence interval for σ of this population: (*a*) by taking the positive square root of these approximate limits, (*b*) by using equation (15.16).

Solution

(*a*) $(\sqrt{8.88}, \sqrt{11.98}) = (2.98, 3.46)$

(*b*) Substituting $s = \sqrt{10.4329} = 3.23$, $z_{\alpha/2} = z_{0.05/2} = 1.96$, and $2n = 2(350) = 700$ into equation (15.16),

$$3.23 \pm \left(1.96 \times \frac{3.23}{\sqrt{700}}\right)$$

$$3.23 \pm 0.24$$

or

$$(2.99, 3.47)$$

15.13 THE OPTIMAL ESTIMATOR FOR THE PROPORTION p OF A BINOMIAL POPULATION

In Section 13.21, we indicated that the proportion of successes p in a binomial population can be estimated with the random variable $\bar{P}$, which is the proportion of successes in a random sample from the population. This variable is defined by the formula [equation (13.22)]

$$\bar{P} = \frac{Y}{n}$$

where Y is the binomial random variable number of successes in the sample, and n is sample size. $\bar{P}$ is an unbiased estimator of p because the mean of its sampling distribution is p [equation (13.27)]: $E(\bar{P}) = \mu_{\bar{p}} = p$. For this and other reasons, $\bar{P}$ is considered the optimal estimator of p. Therefore, for any given sample the specific $\bar{P} = \bar{p}$ value calculated from the sample is the optimal point estimate of p.

EXAMPLE 15.10 An infinitely large binomial population has an unknown proportion p of success-elements. A random sample of $n = 150$ elements is taken from the population under Bernoulli-trial conditions (see Section 11.2) and there are $y = 82$ success-elements in the sample. What is the optimal point estimate $\hat{\theta}^*$ of the parameter p?

Solution

$$\bar{p} = \frac{y}{n} = \frac{82}{150} = 0.546667, \quad \text{or } 0.55$$

15.14 DERIVING THE APPROXIMATE CONFIDENCE INTERVAL FOR THE PROPORTION p OF A BINOMIAL POPULATION

We know from Section 13.23 that if all possible random samples of size n are drawn under Bernoulli-trial conditions from an infinitely large binomial population that has the proportion p of success-elements, and if the sample proportion $\bar{P} = \bar{p}$ is determined for each sample, then the resulting theoretical sampling distribution of the proportion will be binomially distributed with mean [equation (13.27)] $\mu_{\bar{p}} = p$ and standard deviation (standard error of the proportion) [equation (13.29)]

$$\sigma_{\bar{p}} = \sqrt{\frac{pq}{n}}$$

where $q = 1 - p$. We also know from Section 13.25, that if n is "sufficiently large" ($np \geq 5$ and $nq \geq 5$), then the sampling distribution of the proportion is approximately normal with again $\mu_{\bar{p}} = p$ and $\sigma_{\bar{p}} = \sqrt{\frac{pq}{n}} = \sqrt{\frac{p(1-p)}{n}}$. Therefore, under these conditions the random variable [equation (13.30)]

$$Z = \frac{\bar{P} - \mu_{\bar{p}}}{\sigma_{\bar{p}}} = \frac{\bar{P} - p}{\sqrt{\dfrac{p(1-p)}{n}}}$$

will have a distribution that is approximately a standard normal distribution. From this information, we can derive the equation for *an approximate* $(1 - \alpha)100\%$ *confidence interval for the binomial proportion p*.

We begin with equation (12.18),

$$P(-z_{\alpha/2} \leq Z \leq z_{\alpha/2}) = 1 - \alpha$$

and then substitute equation (13.30) for Z,

$$P\left[-z_{\alpha/2} \leq \frac{\bar{P} - p}{\sqrt{\dfrac{p(1-p)}{n}}} \leq z_{\alpha/2}\right] \approx 1 - \alpha$$

Multiplying each term of the inequality by $\sqrt{\frac{p(1-p)}{n}}$ and then subtracting $\bar{P}$ from each term, we get

$$P\left[-\bar{P} - z_{\alpha/2}\sqrt{\frac{p(1-p)}{n}} \leq -p \leq -\bar{P} + z_{\alpha/2}\sqrt{\frac{p(1-p)}{n}}\right] \approx 1 - \alpha$$

Finally, multiplying through the inequality by -1 we get

$$P\left[\bar{P} + z_{\alpha/2}\sqrt{\frac{p(1-p)}{n}} \geq p \geq \bar{P} - z_{\alpha/2}\sqrt{\frac{p(1-p)}{n}}\right] \approx 1 - \alpha$$

which can also be written as

$$P\left[\bar{P} - z_{\alpha/2}\sqrt{\frac{p(1-p)}{n}} \leq p \leq \bar{P} + z_{\alpha/2}\sqrt{\frac{p(1-p)}{n}}\right] \approx 1 - \alpha \tag{15.17}$$

For a "sufficiently large" sample taken under Bernoulli-trial conditions from an infinitely large binomial population, if specific values of the random interval

$$\bar{P} - z_{\alpha/2}\sqrt{\frac{p(1-p)}{n}} \leq p \leq \bar{P} + z_{\alpha/2}\sqrt{\frac{p(1-p)}{n}}$$

are calculated for all samples of size n, then approximately $(1-\alpha)100\%$ of these sample intervals

$$\bar{p} - z_{\alpha/2}\sqrt{\frac{p(1-p)}{n}} \leq p \leq \bar{p} + z_{\alpha/2}\sqrt{\frac{p(1-p)}{n}} \tag{15.18}$$

will contain p. Therefore, any such specific interval is called an approximate $(1-\alpha)100\%$ confidence interval for the population proportion p.

This approximate confidence interval can be presented (see Section 14.10) in any one of the following forms:

(1) $\bar{p} - z_{\alpha/2}\sqrt{\frac{p(1-p)}{n}} \leq p \leq \bar{p} + z_{\alpha/2}\sqrt{\frac{p(1-p)}{n}}$

(2) $L \approx \bar{p} - z_{\alpha/2}\sqrt{\frac{p(1-p)}{n}}, \; U \approx \bar{p} + z_{\alpha/2}\sqrt{\frac{p(1-p)}{n}}$

(3) $\left[\bar{p} - z_{\alpha/2}\sqrt{\frac{p(1-p)}{n}}, \; \bar{p} + z_{\alpha/2}\sqrt{\frac{p(1-p)}{n}}\right]$

(4) $\bar{p} \pm z_{\alpha/2}\sqrt{\frac{p(1-p)}{n}}$

15.15 ESTIMATING THE PARAMETER p

In Section 15.14 we used normal-approximation techniques to develop an approximate $(1-\alpha)100\%$ confidence interval for the binomial proportion p: $\bar{p} \pm z_{\alpha/2}\sqrt{\frac{p(1-p)}{n}}$. There is, however, a significant problem with this confidence interval: To calculate the confidence limits for a given sample, you have to know the population parameter p that is being estimated. The problem of not knowing p has two standard solutions: the *point-estimate solution* and the *conservative solution.*

In the point-estimate solution, if n is "sufficiently large," then the sample point estimate $\bar{p}$ is a satisfactory substitute for the parameter p in the confidence limits, which are then written as

$$\bar{p} \pm z_{\alpha/2}\sqrt{\frac{\bar{p}(1-\bar{p})}{n}} \tag{15.19}$$

The conservative solution makes use of the fact that it can be mathematically proven that regardless of the value of p, the largest possible value of the term $p(1-p)$ is $\frac{1}{4}$ (i.e., when $p = 0.5$ and $1-p = 0.5$). Therefore, if n is not "sufficiently large" or the most conservative possible solution is required, then $\frac{1}{4}$ is substituted for the term $p(1-p)$, and the confidence interval is written as

$$\bar{p} \pm z_{\alpha/2}\sqrt{\frac{1/4}{n}}$$

or

$$\bar{p} \pm z_{\alpha/2}\sqrt{\frac{1}{4n}} \tag{15.20}$$

The conservative solution provides a confidence interval with the maximum possible width, and so it should be stated that the confidence level for the interval is *at least* $(1-\alpha)100\%$.

EXAMPLE 15.11 For the sample in Example 15.10, calculate the approximate 95% confidence interval for the unknown population proportion p using the normal-approximation technique with: (*a*) the point-estimate solution, and (*b*) the conservative solution.

Solution

(*a*) Substituting $n = 150$, $\bar{p} = 0.546667$, and $z_{\alpha/2} = z_{0.05/2} = 1.96$ into equation (15.19),

$$0.546667 \pm \left[1.96 \times \sqrt{\frac{0.546667(1 - 0.546667)}{150}}\right]$$

$$0.55 \pm 0.0797$$

(*b*) Substituting $n = 150$ and $\bar{p} = 0.546667$ into equation (15.20),

$$0.546667 \pm \left(1.96 \times \sqrt{\frac{1}{4 \times 150}}\right)$$

$$0.55 \pm 0.0800$$

As one would expect, the margin of error for the conservative solution (0.0800) is somewhat larger than the margin of error for the point-estimate solution (0.0797).

15.16 DECIDING WHEN n IS "SUFFICIENTLY LARGE," p NOT KNOWN

When determining probabilities with a normal approximation to the sampling distribution of the proportion, we said that sample size n was "sufficiently large" to use this technique when both $np \geq 5$ and $nq \geq 5$ (see Section 15.14). But this assumed that we knew the population parameter p and were only approximating one distribution with another. When p is not known, however, to calculate a confidence interval for p we must not only approximate a binomial distribution with a normal distribution, but also approximate p with its sample estimate $\bar{p}$ or the maximum possible value of $p(1 - p)$ (see Section 15.15).

For unknown p, statistics books differ on whether n is "sufficiently large" when $np \geq 5$ and $nq \geq 5$. Some books say yes, even with the double approximation, but most books suggest more caution. Some of the more conservative "sufficiently large" n values that have been suggested are: $np \geq 10$ and $nq \geq 10$, $np \geq 15$ and $nq \geq 15$, $n \geq 30$ [which is the same rule used for applying the central limit theorem (see Section 13.18)], and, most conservatively, only when $n \geq 100$.

15.17 APPROXIMATE CONFIDENCE INTERVALS FOR THE BINOMIAL PARAMETER p WHEN SAMPLING FROM A FINITE POPULATION WITHOUT REPLACEMENT

The approximate confidence-interval formulas in Sections 15.14 and 15.15 were derived with the assumption that the binomial population being sampled was infinitely large. These formulas hold true also for sampling from a finite binomial population with replacement. They are not, however, applicable when sampling from a finite binomial population without replacement. If $n > 0.05N$, then the point-estimate solution and the conservative solution (see Section 15.15) should include the finite population correction factor (see Section 13.11), becoming

$$\bar{p} \pm z_{\alpha/2}\sqrt{\frac{\bar{p}(1-\bar{p})}{n}}\sqrt{\frac{N-n}{N-1}} \tag{15.21}$$

and

$$\bar{p} \pm z_{\alpha/2}\sqrt{\frac{1}{4n}}\sqrt{\frac{N-n}{N-1}} \tag{15.22}$$

For these conditions, when $n \leq 0.05N$ the finite population correction factor is not needed.

15.18 THE EXACT CONFIDENCE INTERVAL FOR THE BINOMIAL PARAMETER p

All of the $(1-\alpha)100\%$ confidence intervals for the binomial parameter p that use the technique of normal approximation (see Sections 15.14, 15.15, and 15.17) are approximate formulas. Exact techniques also exist, involving the binomial distribution (see Section 11.5) and the hypergeometric distribution (see Section 11.21), but they are complex and rarely presented in introductory statistics books.

15.19 PRECISION OF THE APPROXIMATE CONFIDENCE-INTERVAL ESTIMATE OF THE BINOMIAL PARAMETER p

In determining the precision of a confidence interval for the population mean with known σ (see Section 14.11), we indicated that for any specific confidence-interval estimate, $\bar{x} \pm z_{\alpha/2}\sigma_{\bar{x}}$, the precision of the estimate is measured by the margin of error: $E = z_{\alpha/2}\sigma_{\bar{x}}$. (The smaller the margin of error, the more precise the estimate.) Similarly for the binomial parameter p, the *precision of the approximate confidence-interval estimate* (see Section 15.14)

$$\bar{p} \pm z_{\alpha/2}\sqrt{\frac{p(1-p)}{n}}$$

is also measured by the approximate margin of error

$$E \approx z_{\alpha/2}\sqrt{\frac{p(1-p)}{n}} \tag{15.23}$$

Because p is not known, we know from Section 15.15 that the actual approximate $(1-\alpha)100\%$ confidence interval for p is either the point-estimate solution [equation (15.19)], with precision measured by

$$E \approx z_{\alpha/2}\sqrt{\frac{\bar{p}(1-\bar{p})}{n}} \tag{15.24}$$

or the conservative solution [equation (15.20)], with precision measured by

$$E \approx z_{\alpha/2}\sqrt{\frac{1}{4n}} \tag{15.25}$$

15.20 DETERMINING SAMPLE SIZE FOR THE CONFIDENCE INTERVAL OF THE BINOMIAL PARAMETER p

In our study of confidence intervals for the population mean, we found that the sample size required depends upon the desired quality-of-estimate, which includes both the degree of precision and the level of confidence (see Section 14.12). If σ is known, both properties of the confidence interval are found in the equation for the margin of error for the mean: $E = z_{\alpha/2}\sigma_{\bar{x}} = z_{\alpha/2}\frac{\sigma}{\sqrt{n}}$. Solving this equation for n, we found the sample size required for a particular level of confidence $(1-\alpha)$ and degree of precision (E) [equation (14.8)]. Similarly for the approximate $(1-\alpha)100\%$ confidence-interval estimate of the binomial parameter p, both components of quality—level of confidence and degree of precision—are found in the margin of error

$$E \approx z_{\alpha/2}\sqrt{\frac{p(1-p)}{n}}$$

and solving this equation for n, the sample size required,

$$n \approx \left[\frac{z_{\alpha/2}\sqrt{p(1-p)}}{E}\right]^2 \tag{15.26}$$

In practice, because p is not known, we use either of the solutions from Section 15.15 to determine the sample size n. For the point-estimate solution [equation (15.19)], the margin of error is

$$E \approx z_{\alpha/2}\sqrt{\frac{\bar{p}(1-\bar{p})}{n}}$$

and solving this equation for n, the sample size required is

$$n \approx \left[\frac{z_{\alpha/2}\sqrt{\bar{p}(1-\bar{p})}}{E}\right]^2 \tag{15.27}$$

For the conservative solution [equation (15.20)], the margin of error is

$$E \approx z_{\alpha/2}\sqrt{\frac{1}{4n}}$$

and solving this equation for n, the sample size required is

$$n \approx \left(\frac{z_{\alpha/2}}{2E}\right)^2 \tag{15.28}$$

EXAMPLE 15.12 In Example 15.11, we found approximate 95% confidence-interval estimates of p for the sample in Example 15.10. We found a point-estimate solution of 0.55 ± 0.0797 and a conservative solution of 0.55 ± 0.0800. Determine for both solutions how large a sample size n would be required if we want to repeat the study and get an approximate 95% confidence interval with a margin of error of $E = 0.05$.

Solution

Using equation (15.27) and inserting $z_{\alpha/2} = z_{0.05/2} = 1.96$, $E = 0.05$, and $\bar{p} = 0.546667$ (from Example 15.10), the required sample size is

$$n \approx \left[\frac{1.96\sqrt{0.546667(1-0.546667)}}{0.05}\right]^2 = 380.813, \quad \text{or } 381$$

Using equation (15.28) and inserting the same $z_{0.05/2}$ and E values, the required sample size is

$$n \approx \left(\frac{1.96}{2 \times 0.05}\right)^2 = 384.160, \quad \text{or } 385$$

If there is just one prior point-estimate $\bar{p}$ of p, then this should be used in the point-estimate version [equation (15.27)] to determine the sample size needed for a repeat of the study. If there is more than one prior $\bar{p}$ value, then it is recommended that:

(1) If the range of prior $\bar{p}$ values is either entirely below or entirely above 0.5, then choose the prior $\bar{p}$ value that is closest to 0.5 to calculate n with equation (15.27).

(2) If the range of prior $\bar{p}$ values includes a value of 0.5, then use equation (15.28) to calculate n.

EXAMPLE 15.13 In Problem 14.5 you determined for the fast-growing onion the sample size needed to get a desired level of precision for the average time-to-maturity in days. Now you are studying the proportion p of seeds that germinate. From preliminary studies you have three point-estimates $\bar{p}$: 0.75, 0.78, and 0.85. You want to repeat this study to get an approximate 95% confidence interval for p that will have a margin of error $E = 0.02$ or less. How large a sample n of seeds will you need to test?

Solution

Following recommendation (1), we substitute $\bar{p} = 0.75$, $z_{0.05/2} = 1.96$, and $E = 0.02$ into equation (15.27):

$$n \approx \left[\frac{1.96\sqrt{0.75(1-0.75)}}{0.02}\right]^2 = 1{,}800.75, \quad \text{or } 1{,}801$$

The two equations for calculating sample size n [equations (15.27) and (15.28)] are based on the assumption that sampling is from an infinitely large population, or at least a very large one (say, $N > 25{,}000$). If, however, the population is not very large, then both formulas overestimate the n that is required. To deal with this problem, a two-step process is recommended:

(1) Calculate n, using either equation (15.27) or (15.28).

(2) Then modify n for the smaller population by using the formula

$$\text{Modified sample size} \approx \frac{n}{1 + \dfrac{n}{N}} \tag{15.29}$$

where n is the sample size determined in step (1) and N is the size of the population being sampled.

15.21 APPROXIMATE CONFIDENCE INTERVAL FOR THE PERCENTAGE OF A BINOMIAL POPULATION

Proportions are converted to percentages by multiplying them by 100%. An approximate $(1-\alpha)100\%$ confidence interval can be calculated for the percentage $p \times 100\%$ of a binomial population by determining an approximate confidence interval for the population proportion p and then multiplying the components of this interval by 100%. Such confidence intervals for percentage are commonly used to present the results of voting polls (see Problems 15.18 through 15.23).

EXAMPLE 15.14 For the fast-growing onion (see Example 15.13), you take a sample of 1,000 seeds and find that 760 of them germinate ($p = 0.76$). Given that this sample is "sufficiently large" and is taken under Bernoulli-trial conditions, find the approximate 95% confidence interval for the population percentage $p \times 100\%$ that will germinate.

Solution

First, we substitute $\bar{p} = 0.760$, $z_{0.05/2} = 1.96$, and $n = 1{,}000$ into equation (15.19) to get the approximate 95% confidence interval for the population proportion:

$$0.76 \pm 1.96\sqrt{\frac{0.76(1-0.76)}{1{,}000}}$$

$$0.76 \pm 0.026$$

Next we multiply the components of this interval by 100% to get the approximate 95% confidence interval for the population proportion:

$$(0.76 \times 100\%) \pm (0.026 \times 100\%)$$

$$76\% \pm 2.6\%$$

15.22 APPROXIMATE CONFIDENCE INTERVAL FOR THE TOTAL NUMBER IN A CATEGORY OF A BINOMIAL POPULATION

The approximate confidence interval for the proportion p of a binomial population can be converted to an approximate confidence interval for the *total number of "successes"* by multiplying the components of the interval by the population size N.

EXAMPLE 15.15 In Example 15.14 we calculated an approximate 95% confidence interval for the proportion p of seeds that germinate in a population of onion seeds. For a sample of 1,000 seeds, we found the approximate 95% confidence interval for p to be 0.76 ± 0.026. If the seed company has a population of 100,000 of these seeds, what is an approximate 95% confidence interval for the total number of seeds that germinate in this population?

Solution

To convert a confidence interval for the proportion p into a confidence interval for the total number in the population, we multiply the components of the interval by population size (100,000):

$$(0.76 \times 100{,}000) \pm (0.026 \times 100{,}000)$$

$$76{,}000 \pm 2{,}600$$

15.23 THE CAPTURE-RECAPTURE METHOD FOR ESTIMATING POPULATION SIZE N

The *capture-recapture method* is used to estimate the size of a population that cannot be counted, because it is too large, too mobile, too hidden, too spread-out, or for some other reason. The method is commonly used to estimate wild-animal populations, but has also been used for such populations as drug addicts in a city. The method has two stages:

(1) A sample is taken from the population and the elements are marked in some way and then released back into the population. We denote the size of this sample by n_1.

(2) After "sufficient time" for the n_1 elements of the sample to disperse back into the population, a second sample is taken of size n_2. In this sample, there are r recaptured (i.e., marked) elements from the first sample.

If we now assume that the proportion of recaptured elements in the second sample,

$$\bar{p} = \frac{r}{n_2}$$

is a point estimate of the proportion of marked elements in the population,

$$p = \frac{n_1}{N}$$

then we can say that

$$\frac{r}{n_2} \approx \frac{n_1}{N}$$

Solving this for N, we get this approximate estimate of population size:

$$N \approx \frac{n_1 n_2}{r} \tag{15.30}$$

EXAMPLE 15.16 The state of Minnesota wants to estimate the size of its wolf population by using the capture-recapture method. Picking capture sites at random, a sample of 65 wolves is captured, marked with ear tags, and released. One month later, again picking sites at random, a second sample of 85 wolves is captured, of which three are recaptures (i.e., individuals with ear tags from the first sample). Approximately how large is the Minnesota wolf population N?

Solution

Using equation (15.30), the capture-recapture method for estimating N, and the values $n_1 = 65, n_2 = 85, r = 3$

$$N \approx \frac{65 \times 85}{3} = 1{,}841.67, \quad \text{or } 1{,}842$$

Solved Problems

TABLE A.7: CRITICAL VALUES OF THE CHI-SQUARE DISTRIBUTION

15.1 Use Table A.7 to find $\chi^2_{\alpha/2,\nu} = \chi^2_{0.100/2,10}$ and $\chi^2_{1-\alpha/2,\nu} = \chi^2_{1-0.100/2,10}$.

Solution

Unlike Table A.6 for the t distribution, Table A.7 does not directly give the critical boundary values involving $\alpha/2$. Instead, it is necessary to first convert the $\chi^2_{\alpha/2,\nu}$ and $\chi^2_{1-\alpha/2,\nu}$ values to equivalent $\chi^2_{\alpha,\nu}$ values. Thus, here

$$\chi^2_{\alpha/2,\nu} = \chi^2_{0.100/2,10} = \chi^2_{0.050,10} = 18.31$$

and

$$\chi^2_{1-\alpha/2,\nu} = \chi^2_{1-0.100/2,10} = \chi^2_{1-0.050,10} = \chi^2_{0.950,10} = 3.94$$

15.2 Use Table A.7 to find: (*a*) $\chi^2_{\alpha,\nu} = \chi^2_{0.005,27}$, (*b*) $\chi^2_{1-\alpha,\nu} = \chi^2_{1-0.025,17}$, (*c*) $\chi^2_{\alpha/2,\nu} = \chi^2_{0.010/2,100}$.

Solution

(*a*) $\chi^2_{\alpha,\nu} = \chi^2_{0.005,27} = 49.64$

(*b*) $\chi^2_{1-\alpha,\nu} = \chi^2_{1-0.025,17} = \chi^2_{0.975,17} = 7.56$

(*c*) $\chi^2_{\alpha/2,\nu} = \chi^2_{0.010/2,100} = \chi^2_{0.005,100} = 140.2$

15.3 Use Table A.7 to determine what happens to $\chi^2_{\alpha,\nu} = \chi^2_{0.025,\nu}$ for the following increases in degrees of freedom: 5, 10, 30, 50, 100.

Solution

$$\chi^2_{0.025,5} = 12.83$$
$$\chi^2_{0.025,10} = 20.48$$
$$\chi^2_{0.025,30} = 49.98$$
$$\chi^2_{0.025,50} = 71.42$$
$$\chi^2_{0.025,100} = 129.6$$

15.4 Use Table A.7 to determine what happens to $\chi^2_{\alpha,20}$ as α decreases as follows: 0.100, 0.050, 0.025, 0.010, 0.005.

Solution

$$\chi^2_{0.100,20} = 28.41$$
$$\chi^2_{0.050,20} = 31.41$$
$$\chi^2_{0.025,20} = 34.17$$
$$\chi^2_{0.010,20} = 35.57$$
$$\chi^2_{0.005,20} = 40.00$$

CONFIDENCE INTERVAL FOR THE VARIANCE

15.5 A random sample ($n = 16, \bar{x} = 27.9$, and $s = 3.23$) is taken from a normally distributed population. What is the 90% confidence interval for the population variance σ^2?

Solution

The confidence limits for σ^2 are [form (3), Section 15.6]

$$\left[\frac{(n-1)s^2}{\chi^2_{\alpha/2,\nu}}, \frac{(n-1)s^2}{\chi^2_{1-\alpha/2,\nu}}\right]$$

where here

$$s^2 = (3.23)^2 = 10.4329$$
$$\nu = n - 1 = 16 - 1 = 15$$

For $1 - \alpha = 0.90$, $\alpha = 0.10$, $\alpha/2 = 0.05$, and $1 - \alpha/2 = 0.95$. Therefore, from Table A.7,

$$\chi^2_{\alpha/2,\nu} = \chi^2_{0.05,15} = 25.00$$
$$\chi^2_{1-\alpha/2,\nu} = \chi^2_{0.95,15} = 7.26$$

Thus, the 90% confidence interval for σ^2 is

$$\left(\frac{15 \times 10.4329}{25.00}, \frac{15 \times 10.4329}{7.26}\right) = (6.26,\ 21.56)$$

15.6 In Example 15.4, we found for $s^2 = 10.4329$ and $n = 61$ that the exact 95% confidence interval for σ^2 was (7.51, 15.46). Then, in Example 15.6, holding s^2 at 10.4329, increasing n to 350, and using the sampling distribution of S^2, we found that the approximate 95% confidence interval for σ^2 was (8.88, 11.98). Now, with again $s^2 = 10.4329$ and $n = 350$, use the normal-approximation technique from Section 15.9 to get another version of the approximate 95% confidence interval for σ^2.

Solution

First, we substitute these values into equation (15.10): $z_{0.025} = 1.96$, $-z_{0.025} = -1.96$, $s^2 = 10.4329$, and ($\nu = n - 1 = 350 - 1 = 349$), to get

$$\chi^2_{0.025,349} \approx \tfrac{1}{2}[z_{0.025} + \sqrt{(2 \times 349) - 1}]^2 = \tfrac{1}{2}(1.96 + \sqrt{697})^2 = 402.17$$
$$\chi^2_{0.975,349} \approx \tfrac{1}{2}[-z_{0.025} + \sqrt{(2 \times 349) - 1}]^2 = \tfrac{1}{2}(-1.96 + \sqrt{697})^2 = 298.68$$

Then, these approximate chi-square values are substituted into the confidence limits, to get this version of the approximate 95% confidence interval for σ^2:

$$\left(\frac{349 \times 10.4329}{402.17}, \frac{349 \times 10.4329}{298.68}\right) = (9.05,\ 12.19)$$

Note that this approximate confidence interval is fairly close to the approximate interval in Example 15.6. Also note that, by increasing n from 61 to 350, the precision [here width of interval (see Section 15.7)] was increased (width decreased) from $(15.46 - 7.51 = 7.95)$ to $(11.98 - 8.88 = 3.10)$ in Example 15.6, and to $(12.19 - 9.05 = 3.14)$ in this problem.

15.7 To study memory consolidation during learning, a psychologist plans to inject a stimulating drug into rats either before or after maze-learning trials. He first studies a noninjected control group (see Volume 1, Section 3.10) of 41 rats, measuring for each rat the total number of maze-learning errors (wrong turns) before the rat achieves the criterion of an errorless run through the maze. His results in errors-to-criterion are $\bar{x} = 13.2$ with $s^2 = 5.19$. If it is assumed that the population of errors-to-criterion measurements is normally distributed, then determine the exact 95% confidence intervals for both μ and σ^2 of the population.

Solution

For μ, we know from Sections 14.21 and 14.23 that under these conditions the exact confidence interval to use is $\bar{x} \pm t_{\alpha/2,\nu} s_{\bar{x}}$. For this problem we know that

$$s_{\bar{x}} = \frac{s}{\sqrt{n}} = \frac{\sqrt{5.19}}{\sqrt{41}} = 0.355788$$

and from Table A.6 we find that

$$t_{\alpha/2,\nu} = t_{0.05/2,40} = 2.021$$

Therefore, the exact 95% confidence interval for μ is

$$13.2 \pm (2.021 \times 0.355788)$$
$$13.2 \pm 0.72$$

or

$$(12.48,\ 13.92)$$

To determine the exact 95% confidence interval for σ^2, we substitute: $n - 1 = 40$, $s^2 = 5.19$, and from Table A.7,

$$\chi^2_{\alpha/2,\nu} = \chi^2_{0.05/2,40} = 59.34$$
$$\chi^2_{1-\alpha/2,\nu} = \chi^2_{1-0.05/2,40} = 24.43$$

into the confidence limits (see Section 15.6):

$$\left(\frac{40 \times 5.19}{59.34}, \frac{40 \times 5.19}{24.43}\right) = (3.50,\ 8.50)$$

15.8 Working for a food company, you are asked to determine the average "total fat" (in grams) in a standard package of potato chips. You analyze 101 packages and get these results: $\bar{x} = 18.2$ g, $s^2 = 0.56\ \text{g}^2$. If it is assumed that the population of total-fat measurements is normally distributed, then determine the 90% confidence intervals for both μ and σ^2 of the population.

Solution

For μ, as an exact t value is not available in Table A.6 for $\nu = n - 1 = 100$, we will use the approximate confidence interval (see Section 14.23) $\bar{x} \pm z_{\alpha/2} s_{\bar{x}}$. For this problem, we know that

$$s_{\bar{x}} = \frac{s}{\sqrt{n}} = \frac{\sqrt{0.56\ \text{g}^2}}{\sqrt{101}} = 0.0744618\ \text{g}$$

and from Table A.5 we find

$$z_{\alpha/2} = z_{0.10/2} = 1.645$$

Therefore, the approximate confidence interval for μ is

$$18.2\text{ g} \pm (1.645 \times 0.0744618\text{ g})$$
$$18.2\text{ g} \pm 0.12\text{ g}$$

or

$$(18.08\text{ g},\ 18.32\text{ g})$$

To determine the exact 90% confidence interval for σ^2, we substitute $n - 1 = 100$, $s^2 = 0.56\text{ g}^2$, and from Table A.7,

$$\chi^2_{\alpha/2,\nu} = \chi^2_{0.10/2,100} = 124.3$$
$$\chi^2_{1-\alpha/2,\nu} = \chi^2_{1-0.10/2,100} = 77.93$$

into the confidence limits (see Section 15.6):

$$\left(\frac{100 \times 0.56\text{ g}^2}{124.3},\ \frac{100 \times 0.56\text{ g}^2}{77.93}\right) = (0.45\text{ g}^2,\ 0.72\text{ g}^2)$$

15.9 A bulb manufacturer wants to improve the average life (200 hr) of his three-way light bulbs. A new version is developed and you test 400 of them, getting these life-of-bulb results: $\bar{x} = 286.2\text{ hr}$, $s^2 = 26.32\text{ hr}^2$. Assuming the population of life-of-bulb measurements is normally distributed, use equation (15.12) to determine the approximate 99% confidence interval for σ^2.

Solution

Substituting into equation (15.12) the values $s^2 = 26.32\text{ hr}^2$, $n = 400$, and, from Table A.5, $z_{0.01/2} = 2.575$, the approximate 99% confidence interval for σ^2 is

$$26.32\text{ hr}^2 \pm \left(2.575 \times 26.32\text{ hr}^2 \times \sqrt{\frac{2}{400}}\right)$$
$$26.32\text{ hr}^2 \pm 4.79\text{ hr}^2$$

or

$$(21.53\text{ hr}^2,\ 31.11\text{ hr}^2)$$

15.10 To repeat the study in Problem 15.9 and get an approximate 99% confidence interval with a margin of error of $E = 4.00\text{ hr}^2$, how large a sample would be required?

Solution

Using equation (15.14) and the values: $z_{\alpha/2} = z_{0.01/2} = 2.575$, $s^2 = 26.32\text{ hr}^2$, and $E = 4.00\text{ hr}^2$, we find

$$n \approx \left(\frac{\sqrt{2} \times 2.575 \times 26.32\text{ hr}^2}{4.00\text{ hr}^2}\right)^2 = 574.16, \quad \text{or } 575$$

Thus, to decrease the margin of error from $E = 4.79\text{ hr}^2$ to $E = 4.00\text{ hr}^2$, we need to increase sample size from 400 to at least 575.

CONFIDENCE INTERVAL FOR THE STANDARD DEVIATION

15.11 In Problem 15.8 we found that the exact 90% confidence interval for σ^2 of the total-fat-measurement population was $(0.45\text{ g}^2, 0.72\text{ g}^2)$. What is the exact 90% confidence interval for σ of this population?

Solution

Using equation (15.15), the exact 90% confidence interval for σ is

$$(\sqrt{0.45\ \text{g}^2},\ \sqrt{0.72\ \text{g}^2}) = (0.67\ \text{g},\ 0.85\ \text{g})$$

15.12 In Problem 15.9, we determined that the approximate 99% confidence interval for the variance σ^2 of the normally distributed population of life-of-bulb measurements was $(21.53\ \text{hr}^2,\ 31.11\ \text{hr}^2)$. Determine the approximate 99% confidence interval for σ of this population by: (*a*) taking the positive square root of these approximate limits, (*b*) using equation (15.16).

Solution

(*a*) $(\sqrt{21.53\ \text{hr}^2},\ \sqrt{31.11\ \text{hr}^2}) = (4.64\ \text{hr},\ 5.58\ \text{hr})$

(*b*) Using equation (15.16) and

$$s = \sqrt{26.32\ \text{hr}^2} = 5.13030\ \text{hr}$$

$$z_{\alpha/2} = z_{0.01/2} = 2.575$$

$$2n = 2 \times 400 = 800$$

the approximate 99% confidence interval is

$$5.13\ \text{hr} \pm \left(2.575 \times \frac{5.13030\ \text{hr}}{\sqrt{800}}\right)$$

$$5.13\ \text{hr} \pm 0.47\ \text{hr}$$

or

$$(4.66\ \text{hr},\ 5.60\ \text{hr})$$

CONFIDENCE INTERVAL FOR THE PROPORTION OF A BINOMIAL POPULATION

15.13 In Example 15.13, you determined, for the fast-growing onion, that for the proportion p of seeds that germinate, you will need to test at least 1,801 seeds to get an approximate 95% confidence interval with $E = 0.02$ or less. You do the germination study with 1,801 seeds and 1,423 of them germinate. For these results determine an approximate 95% confidence interval for p. Does this interval meet the maximum tolerable margin of error of $E = 0.02$?

Solution

The study gives this point estimate of p:

$$\bar{p} = \frac{1{,}423}{1{,}801} = 0.790117$$

The sample size satisfies the strictest conditions for using the normal-approximation technique (see Sections 15.15 and 15.16):

$$(n\bar{p} = 1{,}423.0) > 15, \qquad [n(\bar{q} = 1 - \bar{p}) = 378.0] > 15$$

and

$$(n = 1{,}801) > 100$$

As n is "sufficiently large," we use the point-estimate solution. Substituting $n = 1{,}801$, $z_{0.05/2} = 1.96$, and $\bar{p} = 0.790117$ into equation (15.19), we get this approximate 95% confidence interval for p:

$$0.790117 \pm \left[1.96 \times \sqrt{\frac{0.790117(1 - 0.790117)}{1,801}}\right]$$

$$0.79 \pm 0.019$$

As 0.019 is less than 0.02, a sample size of 1,801 provides the acceptable margin or error of $E = 0.02$.

15.14 A car manufacturer is receiving a new type of electronic part in lots (see Section 11.11) of 3,000. The company wants to determine an approximate 90% confidence interval for the proportion p of defective parts, with a margin of error of $E = 0.04$ or less. If the first lot received is treated as a population, how large a sample n from the lot should be tested?

Solution

As there are no prior point estimates of p, the conservative solution should be used. Substituting $z_{0.10/2} = 1.645$ and $E = 0.04$ into equation (15.28), we get

$$n \approx \left(\frac{1.645}{2 \times 0.04}\right)^2 = 422.816, \quad \text{or } 423$$

Because this population is not large, following the recommendation in Section 15.20, we modify the sample size with equation (15.29):

$$\text{Modified sample size} \approx \frac{423}{1 + \dfrac{423}{3{,}000}} = 370.727, \quad \text{or } 371$$

15.15 The study in Problem 15.14 is done, and of the sample of 371 parts, 18 are defective. From these results, determine an approximate 90% confidence interval for the proportion p of parts in the population (lot) that are defective. Does the sample size and confidence interval provide the desired margin of error $E \leq 0.04$?

Solution

The study gives this point estimate of p:

$$\bar{p} = \frac{18}{371} = 0.0485175$$

The sample size satisfies the strictest conditions (see Problem 15.13) for using the normal-approximation technique,

$$(n\bar{p} = 18.0) > 15, \qquad [n(\bar{q} = 1 - \bar{p}) = 353.0] > 15$$

and

$$(n = 371) > 100$$

As n is "sufficiently large" we use the point-estimate solution (see Section 15.15), but because $(n/N = 371/3{,}000 = 0.123677) > 0.05$, we must use equation (15.21). Substituting $n = 371$, $N = 3{,}000$, $z_{0.10/2} = 1.645$, and $\bar{p} = 0.0485175$ into this equation, we get

$$0.0485175 \pm \left[1.645 \times \sqrt{\frac{0.0485175(1 - 0.0485175)}{371}} \times \sqrt{\frac{3{,}000 - 371}{3{,}000 - 1}}\right]$$

$$0.049 \pm 0.0172$$

The margin of error, $E \approx 0.0172$, is less than the maximum acceptable $E = 0.04$.

15.16 In Problem 15.15, we found that using a sample size of 371 gave a margin of error of $E \approx 0.0172$, which was less than the maximum acceptable $E = 0.04$. These results indicate that if we repeat the study we can use a smaller sample. For the same level of confidence (90%), using $\bar{p} = 0.0485175$ from Problem 15.15, what is the minimum sample size n needed that will give us $E = 0.04$?

Solution

Using equation (15.28) for finding n with the point-estimate solution and inserting the specific values $z_{\alpha/2} = z_{0.10/2} = 1.645$, $E = 0.04$, and $\bar{p} = 0.0485175$, we find that the required sample size is

$$n \approx \left[\frac{1.645\sqrt{0.0485175(1 - 0.0485175)}}{0.04}\right]^2 = 78.07$$

Thus, we would need a sample of at least 79 parts to attain our desired quality of estimate. This would satisfy the least conservative requirement from Section 15.16 to use the point-estimate solution: $n \geq 30$. To satisfy the more conservative requirement of $np \geq 10$, however, would require a minimum n of 206.

CONFIDENCE INTERVAL FOR THE PERCENTAGE AND TOTAL OF A BINOMIAL POPULATION

15.17 In Problem 15.15 we got the approximate 90% confidence interval for the proportion of parts in the population (lot) p that are defective as: 0.049 ± 0.0172. Using the results from this sample, determine an approximate 92% confidence interval for the percentage of parts $p \times 100\%$ that are defective in this population.

Solution

First we need to determine the approximate 92% confidence interval for p. Again, we calculate the confidence interval using the point-estimate solution with the finite population correction factor [equation (15.21)]. In Table A.5 we find that the z value associated with the closest area to $[0.5 - (\alpha/2 = 0.08/2 = 0.04) = 0.46]$ is $z_{\alpha/2} = z_{0.08/2} = 1.75$. Substituting this value, $n = 371$, $N = 3{,}000$, and $\bar{p} = 0.0485175$ (see Problem 15.15) into the equation,

$$0.0485175 \pm \left[1.75 \times \sqrt{\frac{0.0485175(1 - 0.0485175)}{371}} \times \sqrt{\frac{3{,}000 - 371}{3{,}000 - 1}}\right]$$

$$0.049 \pm 0.0183$$

Multiplying the components of this interval by 100% (see Section 15.21), we get the approximate 92% confidence interval for the population percentage $p \times 100\%$:

$$(0.049 \times 100\%) \pm (0.0183 \times 100\%)$$

$$4.9\% \pm 1.83\%$$

15.18 A new candidate is running for president. He asks a polling organization to conduct a nationwide, random-digit-dialing telephone poll (see Volume 1, Problem 3.25) to determine the percentage of potential voters who would vote for him over the incumbent president. How large a sample of adult Americans should the agency poll if they want to get an approximate 95% confidence interval with a margin of error of $E = 3.0\%$ or less for this percentage ($p \times 100\%$) of the population of potential voters?

Solution

As there are no previous point estimates $\bar{p}$ available, the polling organization should substitute $z_{\alpha/2} = z_{0.05/2} = 1.96$ and $E = 0.03$ into equation (15.28):

$$n \approx \left(\frac{1.96}{2 \times 0.03}\right)^2 = 1{,}067.11, \quad \text{or } 1{,}068$$

15.19 As suggested in Problem 15.18, the polling organization questions a sample of 1,068 voters and finds that 384 would vote for the new candidate, 545 would vote for the incumbent, and 139 are undecided. From these results, determine an approximate 95% confidence interval for the percentage in the population ($p \times 100\%$) of potential voters who would vote for the new candidate.

Solution

The first step is to determine an approximate 95% confidence interval for the proportion p of such voters. The results show a point estimate of

$$\bar{p} = \frac{384}{1{,}068} = 0.359551$$

The sample n satisfies the strictest conditions for using the normal-approximation technique (see Section 15.16), and as n is "sufficiently large" and it is undoubtedly true that $n \leq 0.05N$, equation (15.19) will be used. Substituting $n = 1{,}068$, $z_{0.05/2} = 1.96$ and $\bar{p} = 0.359551$ into this equation, we get this approximate 95% confidence interval for p:

$$0.359551 \pm \left[1.96 \times \sqrt{\frac{0.359551(1 - 0.359551)}{1{,}068}}\right]$$

$$0.36 \pm 0.029$$

Multiplying the components of this interval by 100% (see Section 15.21), we get the approximate 95% confidence interval for $p \times 100\%$:

$$(0.36 \times 100\%) \pm (0.029 \times 100\%)$$

$$36\% \pm 2.9\%$$

15.20 The candidate in Problems 15.18 and 15.19 wanted to know the percentage of potential voters who would vote for him over the incumbent president. In answering this question, is the following a correct summary of the poll results in Problem 15.19?

> In a telephone poll of 1,068 adult Americans, 36% indicated they would vote for the new candidate over the incumbent. This result has a margin of error of ± 2.9 percent at the 95% level of confidence, which, in theory, means that 19 out of 20 times that such a polling result is achieved, it will differ from the true national voter preference $p \times 100\%$ by no more than (+) or (−) the margin of error.

Solution

The summary is essentially correct except for the phrase "...a margin of error of ± 2.9 percent." This is an incorrect statement. The margin of error is ± 2.9 percentage points. Percentage points are units of a percentage scale, and the margin of error is thus 2.9 of these units in both directions on the scale from the point estimate $\bar{p} = 36\%$. A margin of error of "2.9 percent" would mean a distance on the scale of $(0.029 \times 36 = 1.04)$ percentage points in both directions from $\bar{p}$.

15.21 Why do most polling organizations consider a sample of 1,500 to be a "sufficiently large" sample for a national poll?

Solution

Most polling organizations accept the following as a practical standard goal: achieve an approximate 95% confidence interval for population percentage $p \times 100\%$ that has a margin of error of at most three percentage points. From the results of Problems 15.18 and 15.19, you can see that, regardless of the size of the population being sampled, this goal can generally be achieved with a sample of 1,500.

15.22 A town council wants to poll a random sample of the town's 2,000 registered voters on the question: Should the town purchase land for a park? If the council wants to achieve an approximate 95% confidence interval for the percentage $p \times 100\%$ of registered voters who favor the purchase, with a margin of error of at most three percentage points, then how large a sample should be polled?

Solution

As there are no prior point estmates of p, equation (15.28) should be used. Substituting $z_{0.05/2} = 1.96$ and $E = 0.03$ into this equation, we get

$$n \approx \left(\frac{1.96}{2 \times 0.03}\right)^2 = 1{,}067.11, \quad \text{or } 1{,}068$$

Because this is not a poll of a large population, we can reduce the sample by substituting $n = 1{,}068$ and $N = 2{,}000$ into the formula [equation (15.29)] for determining modified sample size:

$$\text{Modified sample size} \approx \frac{1{,}068}{1 + \dfrac{1{,}068}{2{,}000}} = 696.22, \quad \text{or } 697$$

15.23 The poll in Problem 15.22 has been taken and 382 of the 697 sampled registered voters say yes, the land should be purchased. From this result, determine an approximate 95% confidence interval for the percentage $p \times 100\%$ of the town's registered voters who would be in favor of the purchase.

Solution

First we need to determine the approximate 95% confidence interval for the population proportion p. The poll gives this point estimate:

$$\bar{p} = \frac{382}{697} = 0.548063$$

The sample size satisfies the conditions for using normal-approximation techniques (see Section 15.16) but, because $(n/N = 697/2{,}000 = 0.35) > 0.05$, it is necessary to use equation (15.21). Substituting $z_{0.05/2} = 1.96$, $n = 697$, $N = 2{,}000$, and $\bar{p} = 0.548063$ into this equation, we get

$$0.548063 \pm \left[1.96 \times \sqrt{\frac{0.548063(1 - 0.548063)}{697}} \times \sqrt{\frac{2{,}000 - 697}{2{,}000 - 1}}\right]$$

$$0.55 \pm 0.0298$$

Multiplying the components of this interval by 100% (see Section 15.21), we get this approximate 95% confidence interval for $p \times 100\%$:

$$(0.55 \times 100\%) \pm (0.0298 \times 100\%)$$

$$55\% \pm 2.98\%$$

As requested by the town council (see Problem 15.22), the approximate 95% interval has a margin of error of "at most three percentage points."

15.24 For the population (lot) of 3,000 parts in Problem 15.14, what is an approximate 92% confidence interval for the total number of defective parts in the population?

Solution

In Problem 15.17 we found that the approximate 92% confidence interval for the proportion p of defectives in the population was 0.049 ± 0.0183. This confidence interval can be converted into an approximate 92% confidence interval for the total number of defective parts by multiplying the components of the interval by population size $N = 3{,}000$. Thus,

$$(0.049 \times 3{,}000) \pm (0.0183 \times 3{,}000)$$

$$147 \pm 54.9$$

15.25 For the population of 2,000 registered voters in Problems 15.22 and 15.23, what is an approximate 95% confidence interval for the total number of registered voters that favor the purchase?

Solution

Using the same technique as in Problem 15.24, we multiply the components of the approximate 95% interval for p in Problem 15.23 by the population size $N = 2{,}000$, and get this approximate 95% confidence interval:

$$(0.55 \times 2{,}000) \pm (0.0298 \times 2{,}000)$$
$$1{,}100 \pm 59.6$$

THE CAPTURE-RECAPTURE METHOD FOR ESTIMATING POPULATION SIZE

15.26 A wheat farmer wants to estimate the number of grasshoppers in his field before the application of a pesticide. He chooses at random a plot that is small enough to be within the hopping range of a grasshopper. Using a hand-held "sweep net," he takes five long sweeps of the area. When he empties the net, he finds he has collected 164 grasshoppers, which he marks with enamel paint and releases back into the plot. The following day, he repeats the procedure and finds that he has captured 183 grasshoppers, of which 13 carry the paint mark from the previous sample. What is the approximate size of the grasshopper population in this plot?

Solution

Using equation (15.30) with $n_1 = 164$, $n_2 = 183$, and $r = 13$,

$$N \approx \frac{(164)(183)}{13} = 2{,}308.6, \quad \text{or } 2{,}309$$

15.27 The manager of a city park wants to know how many pre-school children use the park on week-day mornings. During four randomly chosen 15-minute intervals on a week-day morning, he takes the names of all the different pre-schoolers that enter the park gates: 26 children. His second sample, done in the same way on a second week-day morning, consists of 32 children, of whom 17 were in his first sample. Approximately how many pre-school children visit the park on week-day mornings?

Solution

Using equation (15.30) with $n_1 = 26$, $n_2 = 32$, and $r = 17$, we get

$$N \approx \frac{(26)(32)}{17} = 48.9, \quad \text{or } 49$$

Supplementary Problems

TABLE A.7: CRITICAL VALUES OF THE CHI-SQUARE DISTRIBUTION

15.28 Use Table A.7 to find $\chi^2_{1-\alpha/2,\nu} = \chi^2_{1-0.100/2,50}$.

Ans. 34.76

15.29 Use Table A.7 to find $\chi^2_{\alpha,\nu} = \chi^2_{0.500,21}$.

Ans. 20.34

15.30 Use Table A.7 to find $\chi^2_{1-\alpha,\nu} = \chi^2_{1-0.500,40}$.

Ans. 39.34

CONFIDENCE INTERVAL FOR THE VARIANCE

15.31 An insect biologist is interested in the body size of beetles in a population. He takes a random sample of 20 beetles and measures their wing lengths in millimeters, finding $\bar{x} = 32.4$ mm, $s = 4.02$ mm. Assuming the population of wing lengths is normally distributed, what is the 95% confidence interval for the population variance σ^2?

Ans. (9.35 mm, 34.46 mm)

15.32 Another, larger sample ($n = 40$) of beetles is taken from the population described in Problem 15.31, and now $s = 3.90$ mm. Use the normal-approximation technique (see Section 15.9) to find the approximate 95% confidence interval for the population variance σ^2.

Ans. (10.29 mm, 25.54 mm)

15.33 A third, even larger sample ($n = 200$) is taken from the population described in Problem 15.31. This time $s = 3.48$ mm. Use equation (15.12) to determine the approximate 95% confidence interval for the population variance σ^2.

Ans. (9.74 mm, 14.48 mm)

CONFIDENCE INTERVAL FOR THE STANDARD DEVIATION

15.34 The body weights of male ground squirrels are known to be normally distributed. You take a random sample of 12 male ground squirrels, weigh each squirrel, and get the following weights in grams: 380, 385, 400, 375, 420, 415, 412, 401, 405, 411, 410, 383. Find the exact 95% confidence interval [equation (15.15)] for the population standard deviation σ.

Ans. (10.79 g, 25.86 g)

15.35 For the body weights of ground squirrels in Problem 15.34, suppose you took a larger sample ($n = 120$), and found $\bar{x} = 400.0$ g and $s = 14.0$ g. Use the sampling distribution of the sample standard deviation [equation (15.16)] to determine the approximate 95% confidence interval for the population standard deviation σ.

Ans. (12.23 g, 15.77 g)

APPROXIMATE CONFIDENCE INTERVAL FOR THE PROPORTION OF A BINOMIAL POPULATION

15.36 A random sample ($n = 120$) of blue gills is taken, with replacement, from a large lake known to hold a population of approximately 2,000 of these fish, and the proportion of males in the sample was found to be $\bar{p} = 0.45$. Use the normal approximation technique to find the approximate 95% confidence interval for the unknown population proportion p, with: (*a*) the point-estimate solution, (*b*) the conservative solution.

Ans. (*a*) 0.45 ± 0.0890, (*b*) 0.45 ± 0.0895

15.37 For the population of approximately 2,000 blue gills in Problem 15.36, suppose that the sample ($n = 120$, $\bar{p} = 0.45$ of males) was taken without replacement. Use the normal approximation technique to find the approximate 95% confidence interval for the unknown population proportion p, with: (*a*) the point-estimate solution, (*b*) the conservative solution.

Ans. (*a*) 0.45 ± 0.0863, (*b*) 0.45 ± 0.0868

15.38 In Example 15.11(*a*), using the point-estimate solution with $\bar{p} = 0.546667$, we found an approximate confidence interval for p of 0.55 ± 0.0797. How large a sample size n would be required if we want to repeat the study and get, again using the point-estimate solution, an approximate 95% confidence interval with $E = 0.03$?

Ans. 1,058

15.39 In Example 15.11(*b*), using the conservative solution with $\bar{p} = 0.546667$, we found an approximate confidence interval for p of 0.55 ± 0.0800. How large a sample size n would be required if we want to repeat the study and get, again using the conservative solution, an approximate 95% confidence interval with $E = 0.03$?

Ans. 1,068

CONFIDENCE INTERVAL FOR THE PERCENTAGE AND TOTAL IN A BINOMIAL POPULATION

15.40 A car salesman is interested in knowing the percentage of the 320 seventeen-year-olds in his region who own their own cars. He takes a random sample, without replacement, of 50 seventeen-year-olds and finds that 18 of them own their own cars. What is the approximate 90% confidence interval for the percentage of this binomial population?

Ans. $36\% \pm 10.3\%$

15.41 A medical researcher wants to know the effect of running on percent body fat. She takes a random sample of 80 male runners from a population of 18,000 male runners and divides them into two categories: men who run more than 50 miles a week and men who run less than 50 miles a week. She finds that of this sample, 16 run more than 50 miles a week. What is the approximate 95% confidence interval for the percentage $p \times 100\%$ of male runners who run more than 50 miles a week?

Ans. $20\% \pm 8.8\%$

15.42 For the study of seventeen-year-olds in Problem 15.40, what is the approximate 90% confidence interval for the total number who own cars?

Ans. 115.2 ± 32.96

15.43 For the study of runners in Problem 15.41, what is the approximate 95% confidence interval for the total number who run more than 50 miles per week?

Ans. $3{,}600 \pm 1{,}584$

THE CAPTURE-RECAPTURE METHOD FOR ESTIMATING POPULATION SIZE

15.44 Red-winged blackbirds congregate in huge flocks during the winter on midwestern wheat farms. A wheat farmer wants to know how many of these birds roost in the trees of his woodlot. He sets out baited traps, at random times and places in the woodlot. He captures 28 birds and marks them with leg bands. Four days later, he uses the same trapping procedure and captures 22 birds, of which 6 have leg bands. What is the approximate size of the flock in his woodlot?

Ans. 103 birds

15.45 A conservationist concerned about the decline of frogs wants to monitor the frog population in a pond. Part of his plan involves estimating the number of tadpoles in the pond each year. At randomly chosen times of the day and places in the pond, he nets 120 tadpoles, marks them with a small dot of waterproof paint, and then releases them. Two days later, he takes a second sample, capturing 99 tadpoles of which 18 are marked. What is the approximate number of tadpoles in this pond?

Ans. 660

CHAPTER 16

One-Sample Hypothesis Testing

16.1 STATISTICAL HYPOTHESIS TESTING

Inferential statistics has four theoretical components, of which we have already introduced three: probability theory, sampling theory, and estimation theory. In this chapter we deal with the last component: hypothesis-testing theory. We do this by examining how the theory is applied to *one-sample tests of hypotheses about population parameters*: the mean μ, the variance σ^2, the standard deviation σ, and the proportion p. Then in Chapter 17 we introduce two-sample techniques for solving both estimation and hypothesis-testing problems, and in Chapter 18 we deal with multisample techniques for solving both types of problems.

While both estimation and hypothesis testing use empirical sample evidence to make inferences about unknown population characteristics, the forms of the inferences are quite different in the two areas. Consider the unknown population parameter θ. In a statistical estimation problem, the sample information is used to estimate the value of θ by placing it, with a known degree of "confidence," within the boundaries of a specific interval (see Chapters 14 and 15). In a statistical hypothesis-testing problem, by contrast, a pair of *statistical hypotheses* is formed that give competing, alternative assumptions about θ, and the sample information is used to decide, with a known degree of "probability," which one of the competing assumptions should be accepted as correct.

16.2 THE NULL HYPOTHESIS AND THE ALTERNATIVE HYPOTHESIS

In Section 3.6 in Volume 1 we defined a *statistical hypothesis* as:

> An assumption (or guess) about unknown properties of one or more measurement populations, typically either about their parameters or about how they are spread (distributed) from smallest to largest values.

Now, at this more advanced stage of our study, we can say that this assumption is not directly about the measurement population, but rather about the mathematical models that are used to describe the population: random variables (see Sections 10.1 and 10.2 in Volume 1) and their probability distributions (see Sections 10.3 and 10.4 in Volume 1). This chapter deals with the unknown parameters θ of such models.

In every hypothesis-testing problem, there is a pair of competing statistical hypotheses: the *null hypothesis* and the *alternative hypothesis*. The null hypothesis, denoted by H_0, is typically a clear statement of equality: The unknown population parameter θ is equal to some specific constant value θ_0. In symbolic form, this hypothesis is written

$$H_0\colon \theta = \theta_0$$

The null hypothesis is also called the *no-difference hypothesis* or the *null-difference hypothesis*, because it states that there is no (null) difference between θ and θ_0.

The alternative hypothesis, denoted by H_1 (also by H_a or H_A), is an assumption about θ that differs from H_0. The alternative hypothesis occurs in one of four general forms.

(1) $H_1\colon \theta \neq \theta_0$. This form states that θ is not equal to θ_0. It is called a *two-sided alternative* because it deals with possible differences from θ_0 on either side of θ_0. As it deals with differences in either direction, this hypothesis is also called a *nondirectional alternative*.

(2) $H_1\colon \theta < \theta_0$. This form states that θ is less than θ_0. It is called a *one-sided alternative* because it deals only with possible differences from θ_0 on one side of θ_0. As the concern is with values to the left side of θ_0, or less than θ_0, this hypothesis is also called a *left directional alternative* (or a *less-than directional alternative*).

(3) $H_1\colon \theta > \theta_0$. This form states that θ is greater than θ_0. It is also called a one-sided alternative, and, as the concern here is only with values to the right of θ_0, or greater than θ_0, this hypothesis is called a *right directional alternative* (or a *greater-than directional alternative*).

(4) $H_1\colon \theta = \theta_1$. This form states that θ is actually equal to some specific value θ_1 other than θ_0. We will not use this alternative in our study of hypothesis testing, but it will be of importance in determining the *power of a hypothesis test* (see Section 16.18).

Some statistical hypotheses are simple and others are composite. A *simple statistical hypothesis* states unambiguously that the parameter θ is equal to some specific constant. Both the null hypothesis ($H_0\colon \theta = \theta_0$) and the fourth alternative hypothesis listed above ($H_1\colon \theta = \theta_1$) are simple hypotheses. By contrast, a *composite statistical hypothesis* is a combination of an unspecified number of simple hypotheses. Of the hypotheses listed above, $H_1\colon \theta \neq \theta_0$, $H_1\colon \theta > \theta_0$, and $H_1\colon \theta > \theta_0$ are composite hypotheses. Thus, for example, $H_1\colon \theta \neq \theta_0$ states that θ is not equal to θ_0, which means that it is equal to some other unspecified specific value.

16.3 TESTING THE NULL HYPOTHESIS

At the start of a one-sample hypothesis test, there is sufficient information about the unknown population parameter θ to allow selection of one of the following pairs of statistical hypotheses for testing:

(1) $H_0\colon \theta = \theta_0, \quad H_1\colon \theta \neq \theta_0$

(2) $H_0\colon \theta = \theta_0, \quad H_1\colon \theta < \theta_0$

(3) $H_0\colon \theta = \theta_0, \quad H_1\colon \theta > \theta_0$

The pair chosen depends on a variety of factors (see Section 16.11).

In the logic of statistical hypothesis testing, while the test always begins with this selection of a pair of hypotheses, it is the null hypothesis H_0 that is actually tested. A random sample of size n is taken from the population of interest, a point estimate $\hat{\theta}^*$ of the unknown parameter θ is calculated from the sample, and then a procedure called a *hypothesis test* is used to compare $\hat{\theta}^*$ with the null's hypothesized value θ_0. The comparison procedure varies as a function of the selected alternative hypothesis H_1, but whatever procedure is used leads to one of the following decisions:

(1) If $\hat{\theta}^*$ is so similar to θ_0 that by the rules of the test it is judged to be "*consistent with*" θ_0, then the *null hypothesis H_0 is accepted* and, consequently, the *alternative hypothesis H_1 is rejected*.

(2) If $\hat{\theta}^*$ is so different from θ_0 that by the rules of the test it is judged to be "*inconsistent with*" θ_0, then the *null hypothesis* H_0 *is rejected* and, consequently, the *alternative hypothesis* H_1 *is accepted.*

The logic of a hypothesis test is an argument based on *deductive reasoning* (see Section 3.7 and Problem 3.6 in Volume 1) that is done in mathematical form. The logic begins with the null hypothesis as its starting premise and then examines the logical consequences of this premise—what must also be true if the null is true. In particular, it determines the *conditional probability* (see Section 9.2 in Volume 1): Given that H_0: $\theta = \theta_0$ is true, what is the probability of getting a point estimate at least as different from the value hypothesized by the null (θ_0) as the one calculated from the sample ($\hat{\theta}^*$)? Or, in symbolic form

$$P\,(\text{point estimate at least as different from } \theta_0 \text{ as } \hat{\theta}^* | H_0 \text{ is true}) \tag{16.1}$$

This conditional probability is determined by using a *test statistic*, which is a sample statistic (see Section 14.1) with these properties: (1) it allows comparison of the sample point estimate ($\hat{\theta}^*$) and the null's hypothesized value (θ_0), and (2) it is associated with a probability distribution that is known under the assumption that H_0 is true. In general, all the sample statistics used in Chapters 14 and 15 can be used for hypothesis testing, only instead of mathematically manipulating the statistic to place the unknown parameter θ within an interval, now the specific value of θ that is hypothesized by H_0 (i.e., θ_0) is placed in the statistic for comparison with the point estimate $\hat{\theta}^*$.

16.4 TWO-SIDED VERSUS ONE-SIDED HYPOTHESIS TESTS

A hypothesis test may be two-sided or one-sided, depending on which alternative hypothesis H_1 is selected (see Section 16.2) to pair with the null hypothesis H_0: $\theta = \theta_0$. In a *two-sided hypothesis test*, the nondirectional, two-sided alternative H_1: $\theta \neq \theta_0$ is selected. In a *one-sided hypothesis test*, either one of the directional, one-sided alteratives is selected. If H_1: $\theta < \theta_0$ is selected, then the one-sided test is called a *left directional test* (or a *less-than directional test*), and if H_1: $\theta > \theta_0$ is selected, then the one-sided test is called a *right directional test* (or a *greater-than directional test*).

16.5 TESTING HYPOTHESES ABOUT THE POPULATION MEAN μ: KNOWN STANDARD DEVIATION σ, NORMALLY DISTRIBUTED POPULATION

To understand the concepts involved in hypothesis testing, we will consider in our discussions beginning here and continuing through Section 16.18 the familiar example of random sampling from an infinitely large, normally distributed population with known standard deviation σ and unknown mean μ. (The assumption of a known population standard deviation is unrealistic in most situations, but it allows us to develop concepts using the familiar Z statistic and its standard normal distribution.)

Suppose you are interested in knowing whether the unknown population mean μ is equal to the specific value μ_0, and choose the two-sided hypothesis test: testing the null hypothesis, H_0: $\mu = \mu_0$, against the two-sided alternative hypothesis, H_1: $\mu \neq \mu_0$. Assuming the null is true, you know that (see Section 13.14)

> If all possible random samples of size n are drawn from an infinitely large, normally distributed population (mean μ_0, standard deviation σ_0) and a value $\bar{x}$ of the continuous random variable $\bar{X}$ is calculated for each sample, then $\bar{X}$ will have a normally distributed sampling distribution with mean $\mu_{\bar{x}} = \mu_0$ and standard deviation (standard error) $\sigma_{\bar{x}} = \dfrac{\sigma_0}{\sqrt{n}}$.

And further you can assume (see Section 13.14) that if the normally distributed variable $\bar{X}$ is standardized with this version of the Z transformation [equation (13.12)]

$$Z = \frac{\bar{X} - \mu_0}{\sigma_{\bar{x}}} \tag{16.2}$$

then the sampling distribution of $\bar{X}$ will be converted into the standard normal distribution, with $\mu_z = 0$ and $\sigma_z = 1$. Clearly, then, this Z statistic meets the two criteria for a test statistic (see Section 16.3): (1) it allows comparison of the point estimate ($\bar{x}$) with the null's hypothesized parameter (μ_0) by expressing the distance between them in standard-error units (divided by $\sigma_{\bar{x}}$), and (2) it is associated with a probability distribution (the standard normal distribution) that is known under the assumption that H_0 is true.

The Z statistic can be used to measure the likelihood that H_0 is true. If we denote the specific value of the Z statistic calculated for a given sample as z^*, then: If $z^* = 0$, the sample mean $\bar{x}$ must equal μ_0, and thus H_0: $\mu = \mu_0$ is very likely to be true. When, however, z^* is a large number, in either the positive or the negative direction from zero, $z^* = a$ or $z^* = -a$, then there is a considerable distance between $\bar{x}$ and μ_0, and thus H_0: $\mu = \mu_0$ is not likely to be true. This likelihood is quantitatively evaluated by determining a value for equation (16.1) by either calculating a P value (see Section 16.6) or by using a decision rule (see Section 16.10).

16.6 THE *P* VALUE

The *P value of a hypothesis test* is the conditional probability of observing a test-statistic value at least as extreme as the one calculated from the sample, given that H_0 is true. Consider a two-sided test, where H_0: $\mu = \mu_0$ and H_1: $\mu \neq \mu_0$. Here, as the concern is with observed differences on either side of μ_0, one must consider both positive and negative extreme z values, $z^* = a$ and $z^* = -a$. Therefore, it is necessary to simultaneously determine the probability of such extreme values in both directions, by using the standard normal distribution to calculate this P value, or simply P:

$$P \text{ value} = P = P[Z \geq (z^* = a) \text{ or } Z \leq (z^* = -a)|H_0 \text{ is true}] \qquad (16.3)$$

This P value is illustrated in Fig. 16-1, where the sum of the shaded areas in the right and left tails of the standard normal distribution equals the P value. The P value for such a two-sided test can be shown by the *general addition rule* (see Section 9.6 in Volume 1) to equal the following:

$$P \text{ value} = P = P[Z \geq (z^* = a)|H_0 \text{ is true}] + P[Z \leq (z^* = -a)|H_0 \text{ is true}]$$

And because the standard normal distribution is symmetric, this can be written as

$$P = 2[P(Z \geq (z^* = a)|H_0 \text{ is true})] \qquad (16.4)$$

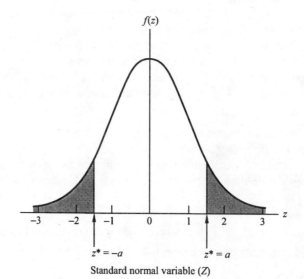

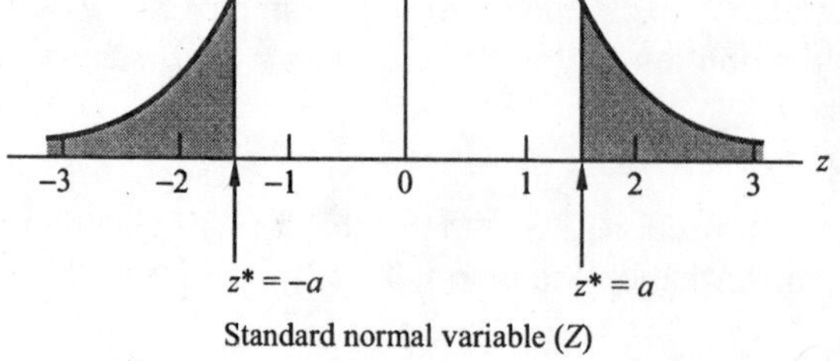

Fig. 16-1

For a left directional test, with hypotheses H_0: $\mu = \mu_0$ and H_1: $\mu < \mu_0$, the test is only performed if the observed z value is negative: $z^* = -a$. If instead z^* is positive, with the sample mean thus larger than the hypothesized mean μ_0, then, by convention, the null hypothesis is accepted. Thus, if z^* is negative, only extreme values in the negative direction are considered, and the P value for the test is

$$P \text{ value} = P = P[Z \leq (z^* = -a)|H_0 \text{ is true}] \tag{16.5}$$

This probability is illustrated in Fig. 16-2(a), where the shaded area in the left tail of the standard normal distribution is the P value.

For a right directional test, with hypotheses H_0: $\mu = \mu_0$ and H_1: $\mu > \mu_0$, the test is only performed if the observed z value is positive: $z^* = a$. If instead z^* is negative, with the sample mean thus smaller than the hypothesized mean μ_0, then again by convention, the null hypothesis is accepted. Thus if z^* is positive, only extreme values in the positive direction are considered, and the P value for the test is

$$P \text{ value} = P = P[Z \geq (z^* = a)|H_0 \text{ is true}] \tag{16.6}$$

This probability is illustrated in Fig. 16-2(b), where the shaded area in the right tail of the standard normal distribution is the P value.

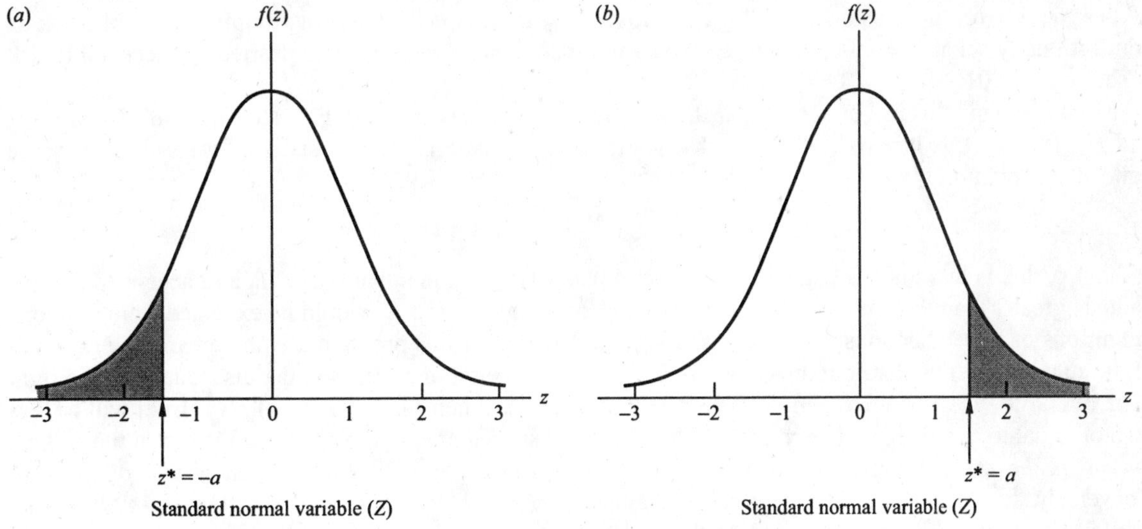

Fig. 16-2

16.7 TYPE I ERROR VERSUS TYPE II ERROR

A hypothesis test concludes with a decision: H_0 is accepted or H_0 is rejected. This decision is an inference about the unknown population characteristic, based on incomplete information from a sample, and so there is always the risk of an incorrect decision. The four possible outcomes to such a test, summarized in Table 16.1, are

(1) An incorrect decision: H_0 is actually true but it is rejected. This error is called a *Type I error*.

(2) A correct decision: H_0 is false and it is rejected.

(3) A correct decision: H_0 is true and it is accepted.

(4) An incorrect decision: H_0 is actually false, but it is accepted. This error is called a *Type II error*.

Table 16.1

	Actual state of the population	
Decision	H_0 is true	H_0 is false
Reject H_0	Type I error	Correct decision
Accept H_0	Correct decision	Type II error

16.8 CRITICAL VALUES AND CRITICAL REGIONS

A P value (see Section 16.6) can be thought of as a descriptive statistic that measures how much support the data give to the null hypothesis: the smaller the P value, the less the support. But what level of support is considered so small that the null hypothesis should be rejected?

Statisticians answer this question by considering the risk of error involved in the decision, specifically the risk of a Type I error: rejecting H_0 when it is true. They know that, for a given sample, the smaller the P value the smaller the probability that H_0 is true, and therefore the smaller the probability of making a Type I error. Considering this, it has been agreed that the risk (probability) of a Type I error should be the determining factor in the acceptance or rejection of H_0. If P is less than or equal to an accepted maximum risk of a Type I error, denoted by α ($P \leq \alpha$), then H_0 is rejected. On the other hand, if $P > \alpha$, then the risk of a Type I error is considered too great and so H_0 is accepted. This maximum acceptable risk is conventionally set at $\alpha = 0.05$, although when a more *conservative decision* is desired the acceptable risk is set at $\alpha = 0.01$.

To understand this use of α, consider the specific example diagramed in Fig. 16-3(*a*). With H_0: $\mu = \mu_0$ and H_1: $\mu > \mu_0$, this is a right directional test. As the Z statistic is the test statistic, we use the P value defined by equation (16.6):

$$P = P[Z \geq (z^* = a)|H_0 \text{ is true}]$$

If this P value is less than or equal to a predetermined α ($P \leq \alpha$), then we reject H_0 and accept H_1. If this value is greater than the predetermined α ($P > \alpha$), then we accept H_0. As would be expected from previous definitions of α (see Sections 12.10, 12.11, 14.19, and 15.3), for this problem α is the area in the right tail of the standard normal distribution shown in Fig. 16-3(*a*)—the set of z values in the distribution to the right of z_α. It is true for all positive sample z^* values, that if $z^* > z_\alpha$, then $P[Z \geq (z^* = a)|H_0$ is true] will be less than or equal to α and H_0 will be rejected. Therefore, the shaded area to the right of z_α is called the *critical region of the test* (or the *rejection region of the test*) and z_α is called the *critical value of the test*. Conversely, for all positive and negative z^* values, if $z^* \leq z_\alpha$, then $p[Z \geq (z^* = a)|H_0$ is true] will be greater than α and H_0 will be accepted, so the unshaded area to the left of z_α is called the *acceptance region of the test*. (Recall from Section 16.6, that by convention in a right directional test, H_0 is automatically accepted if z^* is negative.) From the diagram you can see that once α is set, it becomes the probability of a Type I error in the test because it represents the relative frequency of z^* values falling in the critical region *by chance* when H_0 is true.

The conditions for a left directional test, using Z as the test statistic, are shown in Fig. 16-3(*b*). Here H_0 is tested with the P value defined by equation (16.5)

$$P = P[Z \leq (z^* = -a)|H_0 \text{ is true}]$$

Again if $P \leq \alpha$ we reject H_0, and if $P > \alpha$ we accept it. Now α is the set of z values in the standard normal distribution to the left of $-z_\alpha$. Thus, for all negative z^* values, if $z^* < -z_\alpha$, then

$$P = P[Z \leq (z^* = -a)|H_0 \text{ is true}]$$

will be less than or equal to α and H_0 will be rejected. Therefore, the shaded area to the left of $-z_\alpha$ in Fig. 16-3(*b*) is the critical region of the test and $-z_\alpha$ is the critical value of the test. Conversely, for all positive or negative z^* values, if $z^* \geq -z_\alpha$, then $P = P[Z \leq (z^* = -a)|H_0$ is true] will be greater than α and H_0 will

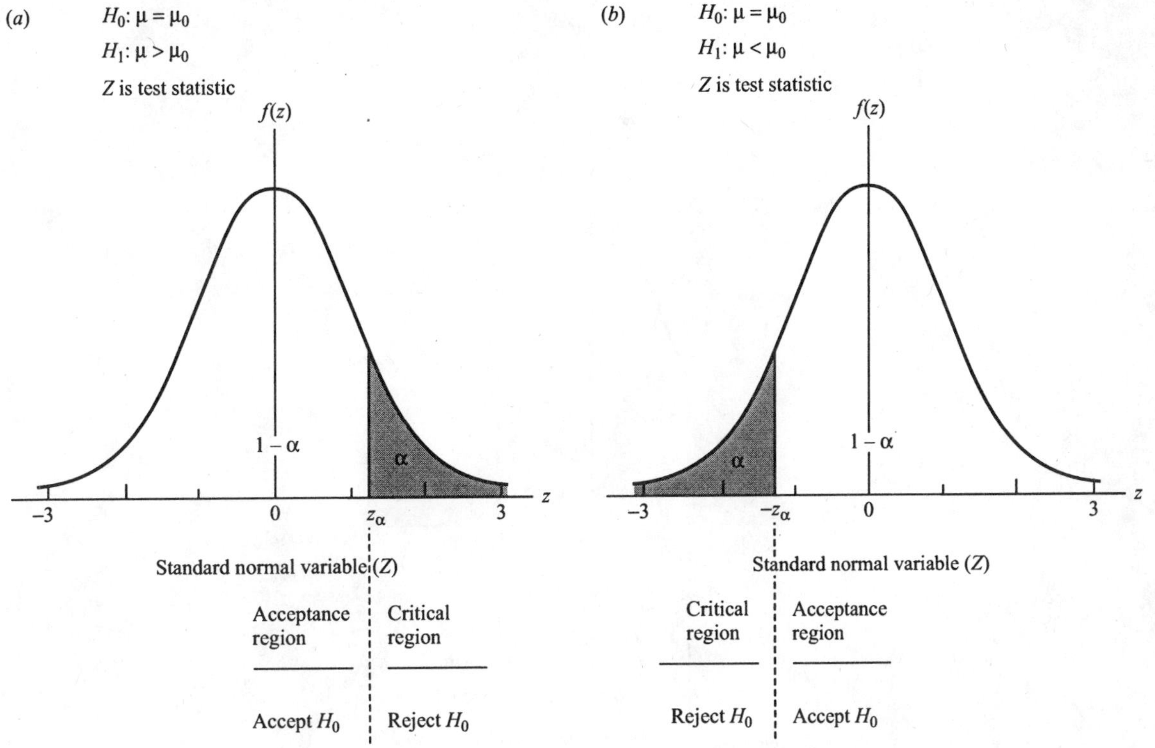

Fig. 16-3

be accepted, so the unshaded area to the right of $-z_\alpha$ in Fig. 16-3(*b*) is the acceptance region. (Recall from Section 16.6 that by convention in a left directional test, H_0 is automatically accepted if z^* is positive.) Again, α is the probability of a Type I error.

Finally, the conditions for a two-sided test, using Z as the test statistic, are shown in Fig. 16-4. Here we are not concerned with direction [i.e., in whether z^* is larger or smaller than the mean of the standard normal distribution (zero)], but only in whether z^* is different from the mean. Therefore, we test H_0 with the P value defined by equation (16.4):

$$P = 2[P(Z \geq (z^* = a)|H_0 \text{ is true})]$$

As before, if $P \leq \alpha$ we reject H_0 and if $P > \alpha$ we accept it, but now $\alpha = \alpha/2 + \alpha/2$ because it is divided evenly between the two tails of the standard normal distribution, with $\alpha/2$ in each tail. For this two-sided test, α is the set of z values in the distribution both to the right of $z_{\alpha/2}$ and to the left of $-z_{\alpha/2}$ (the shaded areas in Fig. 16-4). If $z^* > z_{\alpha/2}$ or $z^* < -z_{\alpha/2}$, then $P = 2[(Z \geq (z^* = a)|H_0$ is true)] will be less than or equal to α, and H_0 will be rejected. The sum of the two tail areas is the critical region of the test and both $z_{\alpha/2}$ and $-z_{\alpha/2}$ are critical values of the test. Conversely, if z^* is in the interval $-z_{\alpha/2} \leq z^* \leq z_{\alpha/2}$, then $P = 2[P(Z \geq (z^* = a)|H_0 \text{ is true})]$ will be greater than α and H_0 will be accepted. Therefore, the area over this interval (the unshaded area in Fig. 16-4) is the acceptance region of the test.

The terms *one-tailed hypothesis test* and *two-tailed hypothesis test* refer to the locations of the critical regions in the sampling distribution of the test statistic. In a one-sided test, the critical region is entirely in one tail of the distribution (see Fig. 16-3), and for this reason such a test is also called a one-tailed test. In a two-sided test, the critical region is divided evenly between the two tails (see Fig. 16-4), and so such a test is called a two-tailed test. One-sided tests that are right directional [see Fig. 16-3(*a*)] are also called *right-tailed tests* or *upper one-tailed tests*; those that are left directional [see Fig. 16-3(*b*)] are also called *left-tailed tests* or *lower one-tailed tests*.

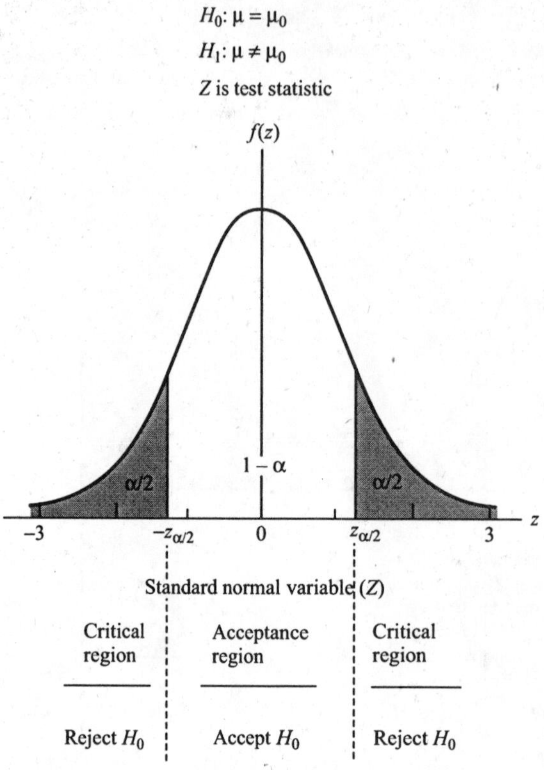

Fig. 16-4

16.9 THE LEVEL OF SIGNIFICANCE

In Section 16.8 we indicated that α is the probability of a Type I error (the probability of rejecting the null hypothesis when it is actually true). We now say that α is also the *level of significance of the hypothesis test*, because it is used to evaluate the *significance of the sample result*, to distinguish *significant* (or *real*) *differences* from what the null hypothesizes. If the difference between the point estimate $\hat{\theta}^*$ and the hypothesized parameter θ_0 is so great that $P \leq \alpha$ and H_0 is rejected, then the result is said to be *statistically significant*. If $P > \alpha$ and H_0 is accepted, then the result is said to be *not statistically significant*. Thus α is the boundary between statistical significance and nonsignificance, and for this reason it is called the *level of significance of the hypothesis test* (or the *significance level of the test*). In the standard normal distributions shown in Figs. 16-3 and 16-4, the critical regions are also the statistically significant regions, and the acceptance regions are also the not statistically significant regions.

As indicated in Section 16.8, α is set before an experiment at either 0.05 or 0.01. When $\alpha = 0.05$ is selected, for example, the researcher reports in the methods section of the report that "the statistical hypothesis test was carried out at the 0.05 level of significance" (or the "5% level of significance"). If $P \leq 0.05$ and H_0 is rejected, then the researcher reports that "the result is significant at the 0.05 level of significance." If $P > 0.05$ and H_0 is accepted, then the researcher reports that "the result is not statistically significant at the 0.05 level of significance."

The terms "statistically significant" and "not statistically significant" apply to sample results only, not to H_0, H_1, or the parameters they indicate. Thus, one would say that the "sample results are statistically significant," or "the z^* value is statistically significant" but not that "H_0 is statistically significant" or "μ_0 is statistically significant." A statement of statistical significance, however, does say that H_0 is rejected.

There are degrees of statistical significance. Thus, $P \leq 0.05$ is said to be a "significant result" and $P \leq 0.01$ is said to be a "highly significant result." While $\alpha = 0.05$ and $\alpha = 0.01$ are the generally accepted boundaries between significance and nonsignificance, researchers often report the highest level of significance for the data: $P < 0.05$, $P < 0.02$, $P < 0.01$, $P < 0.001$, and so on. This is why, when possible, the actual P value for the data is reported because it is the highest level of significance (i.e., smallest P) at which H_0 can be rejected. For this reason, the P value is called the *observed level of significance* (or the *descriptive level of significance*, or the *attained level of significance*). Reporting the actual P value allows the readers to make their own judgements about the significance of the results.

16.10 DECISION RULES FOR STATISTICAL HYPOTHESIS TESTS

In Section 16.8 we presented the fundamental decision-law of hypothesis testing: If $P \leq \alpha$, then reject H_0; if $P > \alpha$, then accept H_0. When the components of a hypothesis test—H_0, H_1, the test statistic, and the significance level α—are selected before a test is conducted, this selection automatically converts this general law into a specific *decision rule* for the test. Such a specific rule can be stated in either of two equivalent forms: for P values and their relationships to the significance levels of the tests, or for test-statistic values and their relationships to critical values.

To understand decision rules, we will first develop them for the right-tailed test illustrated in Fig. 16-3(*a*), with Z as the test statistic. The critical z values for a given α level are obtained from Table A.5. Thus, if $\alpha = 0.05$ is selected as the significance level for this test, then these two equivalent decision rules result:

Reject H_0 *if* $P \leq 0.05$

or

Reject H_0 *if* $z^* > (z_\alpha = z_{0.05} = 1.645)$

These two rules are equivalent, because it will always be true that if $z^* > 1.645$, then $P \leq 0.05$ (see Section 16.8). When $\alpha = 0.01$ is selected as the significance level, then these are the two equivalent rules

Reject H_0 *if* $P \leq 0.01$

or

Reject H_0 *if* $z^* > (z_\alpha = z_{0.01} = 2.33)$

For the left-tailed test illustrated in Fig. 16-3(*b*), when $\alpha = 0.05$ is selected, the two equivalent decision rules are

Reject H_0 *if* $P \leq 0.05$

or

Reject H_0 if $z^* < (-z_\alpha = -z_{0.05} = -1.645)$

And when $\alpha = 0.01$ is selected, the equivalent rules are

Reject H_0 *if* $P \leq 0.01$

or

Reject H_0 *if* $z^* < (-z_\alpha = -z_{0.01} = -2.33)$

For the two-tailed test illustrated in Fig. 16-4, when $\alpha = 0.05$ is selected, the two equivalent rules are

Reject H_0 *if* $P \leq 0.05$

or

$$\textit{Reject } H_0 \textit{ if } z^* > (z_{\alpha/2} = z_{0.05/2} = 1.96) \textit{ or if } z^* < (-z_{\alpha/2} = -z_{0.05/2} = -1.96)$$

And if $\alpha = 0.01$ is selected, then the two equivalent rules are

$$\textit{Reject } H_0 \textit{ if } P \leq 0.01$$

or

$$\textit{Reject } H_0 \textit{ if } z^* > (z_{\alpha/2} = z_{0.01/2} = 2.575) \textit{ or if } z^* < (-z_{\alpha/2} = -z_{0.01/2} = -2.575)$$

16.11 SELECTING STATISTICAL HYPOTHESES

Single-sample hypothesis-testing methods are also called *detection methods* because they can be used to detect changes in established parameters. Thus they could be used in the hypothesis-testing stage of research (see Volume 1, Section 3.8) to detect whether hypothesized increases or decreases in a parameter have occurred. For example, does a new gasoline additive really increase miles-per-gallon? These methods are also used in the exploratory stage of research (see Volume 1, Section 3.8) to detect whether any change has occurred, regardless of direction. For example, does a new blood-pressure drug have an effect on body temperature? The techniques could also be used in industrial quality control to routinely monitor production parameters. For example, do the company's potato chips match the parameters listed on the bag (e.g., 6 g saturated fat per serving)?

During the hypothesis-testing stage of research, the researcher usually is looking for differences, and so the research hypothesis is typically placed in the statistical alternative hypothesis H_1. In this context, then, the researcher hopes the test will lead to a rejection of H_0 in favor of H_1. Because of this bias, the researcher is expected to be very cautious about Type I errors (rejecting H_0 when it is true). If detection of a change has important consequences, then the *most conservative* test should be used, which gives the least risk of Type I error. This would be the two-tailed test with $\alpha = 0.01$, because it requires the largest test-statistic value to achieve a rejection of H_0. By the same reasoning, the *least conservative* test in terms of Type I error would be a one-tailed test with $\alpha = 0.05$.

The more conservative, two-tailed test is the norm for all forms of statistical hypothesis-testing, and the more liberal one-tailed test is the exception. A one-tailed test, however, is appropriate when: (1) only one direction of change is important (e.g., whether a new appetite suppressant actually produces weight loss), or (2) the research hypothesis predicts a particular direction of change (e.g., cancer tumors will be decreased by a new treatment). A one-tailed test is not appropriate for exploratory research or quality-control monitoring when change in either direction is examined. If a one-tailed test is done and H_0 is rejected, then the conclusion can be directional (e.g., "There is evidence that weight decreased."). If, however, a two-tailed test is done and H_0 is rejected, then the conclusion should be nondirectional (e.g., "There is evidence that weight changed"). A significant two-tailed result can be used only to "suggest" a direction of change.

16.12 THE PROBABILITY OF A TYPE II ERROR

In Sections 16.9 and 16.10 we showed that in statistical hypothesis testing, concern about Type I error is the determining factor in the decision to accept or reject the null hypothesis. A maximum risk of Type I, α, is decided upon, and if $P \leq \alpha$, H_0 is rejected. In any such statistical decision, however, there is always a second possible error: Type II error (see Section 16.7). Let us now consider its influence on the hypothesis test.

The probability of such a Type II error is denoted by β (the Greek lowercase letter *beta*). Thus the probabilities of the four possible outcomes of a hypothesis test (see Table 16.1), summarized in Table 16.2, are:

(1) $\alpha = P(\text{Type I error}) = P(\text{rejecting } H_0 | H_0 \text{ is true})$
(2) $1 - \alpha = P(\text{correctly accepting } H_0) = P(\text{accepting } H_0 | H_0 \text{ is true})$
(3) $\beta = P(\text{Type II error}) = P(\text{accepting } H_0 | H_0 \text{ is false})$
(4) $1 - \beta = P$ (correctly rejecting H_0) $= P(\text{rejecting } H_0 | H_0 \text{ is false})$

Table 16.2

	Actual state of the population	
Decision	H_0 is true	H_0 is false
Reject H_0	Type I error Probability: α	Correct decision Probability: $1 - \beta$
Accept H_0	Correct decision Probability: $1 - \alpha$	Type II error Probability: β

While α and $1 - \alpha$ are known, set by the researcher prior to doing the test, β and $1 - \beta$ can not be determined without knowing the actual value of the population parameter θ being investigated. While this is never the case in inferential statistics, the relationship between α and β is known to be inverse: the larger the α, the smaller the β, and vice versa. This relationship is true because the larger the α, the smaller the acceptance region (see Section 16.8), and therefore the smaller the probability β of accepting a false null. This inverse relationship between α and β is another factor that must be considered in selecting α. The researcher must evaluate the relative seriousness of the two types of error, and realize that if α is set to minimize the risk of one type of error (e.g., $\alpha = 0.01$ to minimize Type I) then this will increase the risk of the other type.

16.13 CONSUMER'S RISK AND PRODUCER'S RISK

In our study of the binomial distribution, we described *consumer's risk* and *producer's risk* in lot-acceptance sampling (see Sections 11.11 and 11.12), and defined these risks as follows:

> If we call the receiver of the lot the consumer, then consumer's risk is the probability of accepting a lot that has a higher p (proportion of defectives) than the consumer can tolerate. If we call the supplier of the lot the producer, then the producer's risk is the probability of a lot being rejected that is actually in conformity with the consumer's requirements.

A lot-acceptance sampling plan (see Section 11.11) can make use of hypothesis-testing techniques. Thus, for example, if the consumer has requested a lot of 1,000 rods, each with a diameter of 8 mm, then when the lot arrives the sampling plan could call for testing, at the α level of significance, these hypotheses: H_0: $\mu = 8$ mm, H_1: $\mu \neq 8$ mm. Here the producer's risk is the probability of a Type I error (rejecting a true null hypothesis), which is α, and the consumer's risk is the probability of a Type II error (accepting a false null hypothesis), which is β.

16.14 WHY IT IS NOT POSSIBLE TO PROVE THE NULL HYPOTHESIS

The null hypothesis H_0 is a guess about an unknown characteristic of a population. Because this characteristic remains unknown (unless the entire population is measured), there can never be absolute certainty that H_0 is correct. Instead, probability decisions are made about H_0 using hypothesis-testing techniques in which this question is examined: If H_0 is correct, then what is the probability of getting the particular sample evidence? As we have seen, the outcome of a hypothesis test is the acceptance or rejection of H_0. If H_0 is accepted, it only means that there is insufficient evidence to reject H_0. It does not prove H_0 correct because there is always the unknown probability β of a Type II error (accepting a false null). Similarly, if H_0 is rejected, it does not prove that H_0 is incorrect because there is always the known probability α of a Type I error (rejecting a true null).

16.15 CLASSICAL INFERENCE VERSUS BAYESIAN INFERENCE

The elements of inferential statistics presented in this book are components of *classical inference*. So far in our introduction to inferential statistics in Chapters 14, 15, and now 16, we have examined how one-sample problems involving population parameters are solved in the two areas of classical inference: estimation and hypothesis testing. We have seen how, in these problems, we always deal with a population with an unknown parameter θ that is assumed to have a constant value. Random samples from this population yield point estimates $\hat{\theta}^*$, which are specific values of a random variable $\hat{\theta}$ that is an estimator of θ. From this sample information, we use estimation techniques to determine with a degree of confidence that a calculated interval of $\hat{\theta}$ values contains θ, and we use hypothesis-testing techniques to solve questions of the form: If θ_0 is the value of the unknown parameter, then what is the probability of getting $\hat{\theta}^*$ as a point estimate? Both estimation and hypothesis-testing techniques are based on *objective probabilities* (see Section 8.7 in Volume 1), which are probabilities determined with classical or relative frequency probability functions.

While classical inference is the most widely used form of statistical inference, there is another important form of statistical inference (see Section 9.9 in Volume 1) known as *Bayesian inference*, or *Bayesian decision analysis* (or *statistical decision analysis*). This form of inference was developed to aid the process of decision making when there are various possible alternative courses of action and the information necessary for choosing among the alternatives is incomplete or uncertain. In Bayesian inference, unknown parameters are considered as random variables rather than as constants. By assigning subjective probabilities (see Section 8.7 in Volume 1) to possible values of these random variables, potential benefits and harms from the different courses of action can be determined. This form of inference is called Bayesian inference because Bayes' theorem (see Section 9.9 in Volume 1) is used to revise the assigned subjective probabilities as new sample information is acquired.

To understand how these two forms of inference differ and how both can be useful in a business context, let us again make use of the example of carrots developed to grow well in heavy clay soil (see Problem 12.8). Using classical inference, the seed company assumes that under defined, constant growth conditions this new kind of carrot has a population of length measurements with an unknown but constant mean μ. Using estimation techniques, they can achieve a degree of confidence that a calculated interval of $\bar{X}$ contains μ, and using hypothesis-testing techniques they can test hypotheses about μ, such as $\mu = \mu_0$, at the α level of significance.

If we now shift the carrot example from population characteristics to marketing, then Bayesian inference can come into play. In a simple example, it could be used in deciding how many seed packets of the carrots the company should prepare for sale. If demand is low and they have prepared too many packets, then they will lose money; if demand is high and they have prepared too few, then they will also lose money. Demand, as measured by potential packet sales, is a parameter θ that is treated as a random variable with different possible levels (say 10,000, 20,000, or 30,000). Each level is assigned a subjective probability, which is an educated guess about demand, and with these and known costs of production it is possible to use Bayesian techniques to estimate potential profits and losses from the alternative courses of action (e.g., different numbers of seed packets produced). These estimates allow a rational production decision despite uncertain information. To improve this information, sample market surveys could be taken and then the Bayes' theorem used to revise the subjective probabilities.

While this book deals exclusively with classical inference, a presentation of Bayesian inference can be found in any business statistics textbook.

16.16 PROCEDURE FOR TESTING THE NULL HYPOTHESIS

The following sequence of steps is used with the Z statistic to solve one-sample hypothesis-testing problems concerned with the unknown population parameter θ:

(1) Choose a null hypothesis H_0 and an alternative hypothesis H_1 (see Sections 16.2 and 16.11).

(2) Choose a level of signficance α (see Sections 16.9 and 16.11).

(3) Decide on the test statistic (see Section 16.3). From this and α, determine the decision rule for the test, stated either in terms of P values or critical values (see Section 16.10).

(4) Take a random sample from the population and from it calculate a value for the test statistic and, when possible, a P value.

(5) From the sample results and the decision rule, decide whether to reject or accept the null hypothesis (see Section 16.10).

EXAMPLE 16.1 As a chemist working for a battery manufacturer, you are given the problem of developing an improved battery for a calculator that will last "significantly longer" than the current battery. You know that measures of the current battery's lifetime in the calculator are normally distributed with $\mu = 100.3$ min and $\sigma = 6.25$ min. You develop an improved battery that theoretically should last longer, and from preliminary tests you decide that you can assume its lifetime measures are also normally distributed with $\sigma = 6.25$ min. To do a test of H_0: $\mu = 100.3$ min, you take a sample of $n = 15$ lifetimes of the improved battery in the calculator and find that $\bar{x} = 105.6$ min. Do a two-tailed test of H_0 using $\alpha = 0.01$ and a decision rule stated in terms of P values. Present the solution in the sequence of steps listed above.

Solution

(1) H_0: $\mu = 100.3$ min, $\quad H_1$: $\mu \neq 100.3$ min

(2) $\alpha = 0.01$

(3) As the population is normally distributed and σ is known, we use the Z statistic [equation (16.2)]. With $\alpha = 0.01$, the two-tailed decision rule stated for P values (see Section 16.10) is

$$\text{Reject } H_0 \text{ if } P \leq 0.01$$

(4) The specific value of the test statistic is

$$z^* = \frac{\bar{x} - \mu_0}{\sigma_{\bar{x}}} = \frac{105.6 \text{ min} - 100.3 \text{ min}}{6.25 \text{ min}/\sqrt{15}} = 3.284, \quad \text{or } 3.28$$

To determine the P value, we use equation (16.4):

$$P = 2[P(Z \geq (z^* = a)|H_0 \text{ is true})]$$

As Z is a continuous random variable, this formula is the same as

$$P = 2[P(Z > (z^* = a)|H_0 \text{ is true})]$$

From Table A.5 we find that the area (probability) in the standard normal distribution above the interval $0 \leq z \leq 3.28$ is 0.4995. Therefore, as the total area to the right of zero is 0.5,

$$P = 2[P(Z > 3.28|H_0 \text{ is true})]$$
$$= 2(0.5 - 0.4995) = 0.001$$

(5) As $P < 0.01$, we reject H_0 and accept H_1. There is a significant difference at the 0.01 level of significance between the sample average lifetime and the hypothesized average lifetime, and the results suggest that the improved battery lasts longer in the calculator.

EXAMPLE 16.2 You repeat the battery study in Example 16.1, increasing the sample size to $n = 20$, and now find $\bar{x} = 105.0$ min. Again assuming the lifetime measures for the improved battery are normally distributed with $\sigma = 6.25$ min, you do a one-tailed test of H_0: $\mu = 100.3$ min, using $\alpha = 0.05$ and a decision rule stated in terms of critical values. Present the solution in the sequence of steps listed above.

Solution

(1) H_0: $\mu = 100.3$ min. Because only an increase in lifetimes is important and there are theoretical reasons to believe they will increase, you use this right-tailed alternative hypothesis: H_1: $\mu > 100.3$ min

(2) $\alpha = 0.05$

(3) Using the Z statistic with $\alpha = 0.05$, the right-tailed decision rule stated in terms of critical values (see Section 16.10) is

$$\text{Reject } H_0 \text{ if } z^* > 1.645$$

(4) The value of the Z statistic is

$$z^* = \frac{\bar{x} - \mu_0}{\sigma_{\bar{x}}} = \frac{105.0 \text{ min} - 100.3 \text{ min}}{6.25 \text{ min}/\sqrt{20}} = 3.363, \quad \text{or } 3.36$$

To determine the P value, we use this equivalent version of equation (16.6):

$$P = P(Z > 3.36 | H_0 \text{ is true})$$

Finding the P value with the method used in Example 16.1 and the appropriate value from Table A.5:

$$P = 0.5 - 0.4996 = 0.0004$$

(5) As $z^* > 1.645$, we reject H_0 and accept H_1. This result is confirmed by the fact that the P value is less than 0.05. Thus, the company can be informed that the evidence evaluated at the 0.05 level of significance indicates that the new battery has a longer lifetime in the calculator.

16.17 HYPOTHESIS TESTING USING $\bar{X}$ AS THE TEST STATISTIC

The random variable $\bar{X}$ can be used directly (rather than transformed to a Z) as a test statistic when a random sample is taken from a normally distributed population with an unknown mean μ but a known standard deviation σ. To see how this is done, consider the right-tailed test with H_0: $\mu = \mu_0$ and H_1: $\mu > \mu_0$. First, we know from equation (13.36) that

$$P(\bar{X} > \bar{x}_\alpha) = P\left(Z > \frac{\bar{x}_\alpha - \mu_{\bar{x}}}{\sigma_{\bar{x}}}\right) = P(Z > z_\alpha) = \alpha$$

From this you can see that

$$z_\alpha = \frac{\bar{x}_\alpha - \mu_{\bar{x}}}{\sigma_{\bar{x}}}$$

Substituting μ_0 for $\mu_{\bar{x}}$ and solving for $\bar{x}_\alpha$, we get

$$\bar{x}_\alpha = \mu_0 + z_\alpha \sigma_{\bar{x}} \tag{16.7}$$

Therefore, if we determine a specific sample value of $\bar{X}$, which we will denote by $\bar{x}^*$, the decision rule for this right-tailed test stated for critical values is

$$\text{Reject } H_0 \text{ if } \bar{x}^* > (\bar{x}_\alpha = \mu_0 + z_\alpha \sigma_{\bar{x}})$$

With similar derivations, we can produce critical-value decision rules for the left-tailed test and the two-tailed test. Without showing these derivations, we will simply state that the rule for the left-tailed test is

$$\text{Reject } H_0 \text{ if } \bar{x}^* < (\mu_0 - z_\alpha \sigma_{\bar{x}})$$

and the rule for the two-tailed test is

$$\text{Reject } H_0 \text{ if } \bar{x}^* > (\bar{x}_{\alpha/2} = \mu_0 + z_{\alpha/2}\sigma_{\bar{x}}) \qquad \text{or if} \qquad \bar{x}^* < (\bar{x}_{1-\alpha/2} = \mu_0 - z_{\alpha/2}\sigma_{\bar{x}})$$

EXAMPLE 16.3 Repeat the right-tailed test in Example 16.2 using $\bar{X}$ as the test statistic. Present the solution in the sequence of steps given in Section 16.16.

Solution

(1) H_0: $\mu = 100.3$ min, $\quad H_1$: $\mu > 100.3$ min

(2) $\alpha = 0.05$

(3) Because the population is normally distributed and σ is known, we can use $\bar{X}$ as the test statistic. With $\alpha = 0.05$ and from Table A.5, $z_\alpha = z_{0.05} = 1.645$, the right-tailed decision rule stated in terms of critical values is

$$\text{Reject } H_0 \text{ if} \quad \bar{x}^* > \left[\bar{x}_\alpha = \bar{x}_{0.05} = \mu_0 + 1.645\sigma_{\bar{x}} = 100.3 \text{ min} + 1.645\left(\frac{6.25 \text{ min}}{\sqrt{20}}\right) = 102.6 \text{ min}\right]$$

(4) The value of the $\bar{X}$ statistic is $\bar{x}^* = 105.0$ min and the P value is the same as in Example 16.2: $P = 0.0004$.

(5) As $\bar{x}^* > 102.6$ min, we again reject H_0 and accept H_1, at the 0.05 level of significance, and this is again confirmed by the fact that $P < 0.05$.

16.18 THE POWER OF A TEST, OPERATING CHARACTERISTIC CURVES, AND POWER CURVES

The probability of correctly rejecting a false null, $1 - \beta$ (see Section 16.12), is called the *power of a hypothesis test*. While the actual power of a test cannot be determined without knowing the population parameter θ, one can often determine β, and therefore $1 - \beta$, for a range of possible alternative values of θ. If we denote these possible alternative values by θ_x, then these calculated values of β and $1 - \beta$ are denoted by $\beta(\theta_x)$ and $1 - \beta(\theta_x)$.

A plot of $\beta(\theta_x)$ for a given α and sample size n is called an *operating characteristic curve* (or *OC curve*) and a plot of $1 - \beta(\theta_x)$ for the same constant features is called a *power curve* (or *power function*). These curves are used to examine the sensitivity of a test to a false null over the range of possible alternative values θ_x, and they also reveal the affects on $\beta(\theta_x)$ and $1 - \beta(\theta_x)$ of possible changes in α or n. In Problems 16.5 through 16.9 we will determine such curves for population means [plots of $\beta(\mu_x)$ and $1 - \beta(\mu_x)$].

EXAMPLE 16.4 The battery manufacturer (see Examples 16.1, 16.2, and 16.3) wants the improved battery to last in the calculator at least an average of 5 minutes longer than the current battery, or at least an average of 105.3 min. For the right-tailed test in Examples 16.2 and 16.3, where $n = 20$ and $\alpha = 0.05$, what is the probability of a Type II error if the mean of the population of "lifetimes" for the improved battery is actually 105.3 min rather than the 100.3 min hypothesized by the null? Again assume that the population standard deviation is $\sigma = 6.25$ min, whether the population mean is 100.3 min or 105.3 min.

Solution

The conditions of the problem produce two possible sampling distributions of the mean $\bar{X}$ that are shown together in Fig. 16-5: The lower distribution is defined by the null H_0: $\mu = \mu_0 = 100.3$ min, and has a mean $\mu_{\bar{x}} = \mu_0 = 100.3$ min and a standard error $\sigma_{\bar{x}} = \dfrac{\sigma}{\sqrt{n}} = \dfrac{6.25 \text{ min}}{\sqrt{20}}$; and the upper distribution is defined by the simple alternative hypothesis H_1: $\mu = \mu_1 = 105.3$ min, with a mean $\mu_{\bar{x}} = \mu_1 = 105.3$ min and the same standard error. We know from Example 16.3 that the critical value for $\alpha = 0.05$ in the lower, null-defined distribution is $\bar{x}_{0.05} = 102.6$ min. We can now see that if the mean of the population is actually 105.3 min, then the probability of a Type II error (accepting a false null) is the gray area to the left of 102.6 min in the upper

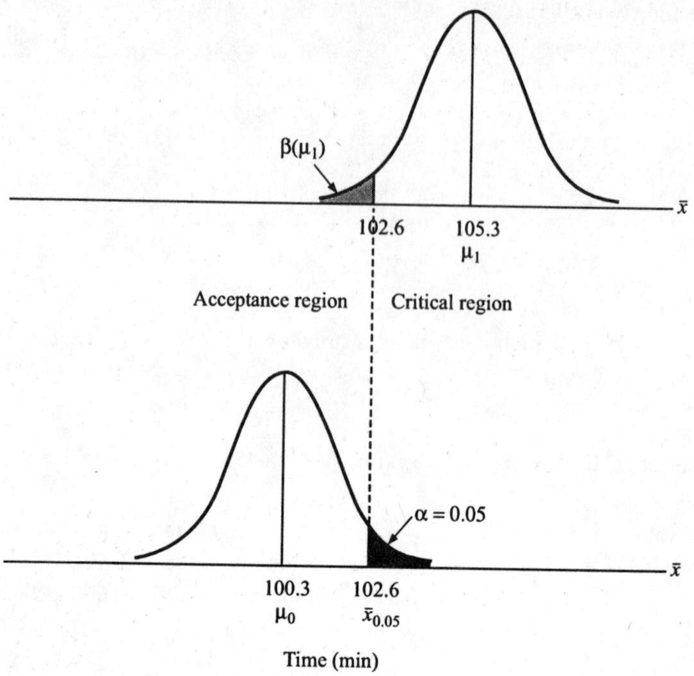

Fig. 16-5

sampling distribution, which is $\beta(\mu_1) = \beta(105.3)$ (see Section 16.12). This is true because this gray area represents all possible $\bar{x}$ values in the upper distribution that are in the "acceptance region" of the test.

To find $\beta(105.3)$ we use the Z transformation on the upper distribution to find this z_1 value (where the subscript 1 indicates the alternative distribution):

$$z_1 = \frac{102.6 \text{ min} - 105.3 \text{ min}}{6.25 \text{ min}/\sqrt{20}} = -1.932, \quad \text{or } -1.93$$

Taking this value to Table A.5, we find that

$$\beta(105.3) = 0.5 - 0.4732 = 0.0268$$

This result indicates that for this right-tailed test at $\alpha = 0.05$, if the population mean is actually 105.3 min, then there is a 2.68% chance of making a Type II error.

EXAMPLE 16.5 For the right-tailed test in Example 16.4, what is the power of the test if the population mean is actually $\mu = \mu_1 = 105.3$ min?

Solution

The power of a hypothesis test is $1 - \beta(\theta_x)$. Therefore, here, the power of the test is

$$1 - \beta(\mu_1) = 1 - \beta(105.3) = 1 - 0.0268 = 0.9732$$

This result indicates for this test, if μ is actually 105.3 min, then the test will correctly reject the false null 97.32% of the time.

16.19 TESTING HYPOTHESES ABOUT THE POPULATION MEAN μ: STANDARD DEVIATION σ NOT KNOWN, SMALL SAMPLE ($n < 30$) FROM A NORMALLY DISTRIBUTED POPULATION

So far in this chapter, we have dealt with one-sample hypothesis testing under the familiar but unrealistic conditions: any size sample from a normally distributed population that has an unknown μ but a known σ. Now we will deal with one-sample hypothesis testing under more typical conditions: small sample ($n < 30$) from a normally distributed population where both μ and σ are unknown. Under these conditions, while the overall logical structure of one-sample hypothesis testing remains the same, elements of the procedures must be changed because, with an unknown σ and a small sample, it is no longer appropriate to use $Z = \frac{\bar{X} - \mu_0}{\sigma_{\bar{x}}}$ as the test statistic.

Now, as was true for estimating μ under these conditions (see Section 14.21), the appropriate test statistic is the t statistic [equation (14.9)] with μ_0 substituted for μ:

$$T = \frac{\bar{X} - \mu_0}{S_{\bar{x}}} = \frac{\bar{X} - \mu_0}{S/\sqrt{n}} \tag{16.8}$$

which can assume specific values

$$t = \frac{\bar{x} - \mu_0}{s_{\bar{x}}} = \frac{\bar{x} - \mu_0}{s/\sqrt{n}} \tag{16.9}$$

This statistic meets the two criteria (see Section 16.3) for a test statistic: (1) it allows comparison of the sample point estimate ($\bar{x}$) and the null-hypothesized value of the parameter (μ_0), and (2) under the assumption that H_0 is true, the t statistic has a known probability distribution: the t distribution, with $\nu = n - 1$ (see Section 14.15).

16.20 THE P VALUE FOR THE t STATISTIC

We will denote the specific value of the t statistic calculated for any given sample of size n as t^*. Therefore, the P value of a hypothesis test (see Section 16.6) using the t statistic is the conditional probability of obtaining a t^*, in a t distribution with $\nu = n - 1$, that is at least as extreme as the one calculated for the sample, given that H_0: $\mu = \mu_0$ is true. Here, then, is how the P values are calculated for the three alternative hypotheses, H_1: $\mu \neq \mu_0$, H_1: $\mu < \mu_0$, and H_1: $\mu > \mu_0$.

For the two-tailed test with H_0: $\mu = \mu_0$ and H_1: $\mu \neq \mu_0$, we must look in the appropriate t distribution at both positive and negative extreme values, $t^* = a$ and $t^* = -a$, and thus the P value is

$$P = P[T \geq (t^* = a) \text{ or } T \leq (t^* = -a) | H_0 \text{ is true}]$$

And, since the t distribution is symmetric, this can be written as (see Section 16.6)

$$P = 2[P(t \geq \langle t^* = a \rangle | H_0 \text{ is true})] \tag{16.10}$$

For the left-tailed test with H_0: $\mu = \mu_0$ and H_1: $\mu < \mu_0$, we are only concerned with negative extreme t^* values, and so the P value is

$$P = P[T \leq (t^* = -a) | H_0 \text{ is true}] \tag{16.11}$$

For the right-tailed test with H_0: $\mu = \mu_0$ and H_1: $\mu > \mu_0$, we are only concerned with positive extreme t^* values, and so the P value is

$$P = P[T \geq (t^* = a) | H_0 \text{ is true}] \tag{16.12}$$

Table A.6 (*Critical Values of the t Distribution*) is limited in both the t distributions it gives and the t_α and $t_{\alpha/2}$ values it provides for a given distribution, and therefore it is not possible to use it to find exact P values. However, Table A.6 can be used to get an approximate P value or to bracket P values within a range of P values. (Many statistics programs for calculators and computers do give exact P values.)

EXAMPLE 16.6 A sample ($n = 20, \bar{x} = 4.0, s = 0.83$) is taken from a normally distributed population that has an unknown μ and unknown σ. If the t statistic is to be used with this sample to do a right-tailed test of H_0: $\mu = 3.6$, then approximate the P value for the observed t^* by using Table A.6 and (*a*) interpolation, (*b*) bracketing.

Solution

(*a*) Using equation (16.9), with $\bar{x} = 4.0$, $\mu_0 = 3.6$, and $s_{\bar{x}} = \frac{s}{\sqrt{n}} = \frac{0.83}{\sqrt{20}} = 0.1856$, we find that

$$t^* = \frac{4.0 - 3.6}{0.1856} = 2.1552, \quad \text{or } 2.155$$

From Table A.6 we can see that this t^* value for the ($\nu = n - 1 = 20 - 1 = 19$) distribution is between $t_{0.025,19} = 2.093$ and $t_{0.01,19} = 2.539$. Thus, the P value [equation (16.12)]

$$P(T \geq 2.155 | H_0 \text{ is true})$$

is somewhere between 0.025 and 0.01. We can approximate this value by using the standard linear interpolation sequence (see Example 14.15). First, parallel scales are formed, one for t^* values and the other for P values (see Fig. 16-6). As $t^* = 2.155$ is 0.0621/0.446 of the distance between $t^* = 2.093$ and $t^* = 2.539$, the associated P value is 0.062/0.446 of the distance between $P = 0.025$ and $P = 0.01$. Therefore,

$$P \approx 0.025 - \left[\frac{0.062}{0.446} \times (0.025 - 0.01 = 0.015)\right] = 0.0229, \quad \text{or } 0.023$$

(*b*) From part (*a*) it can be seen that the P value is in the range between 0.025 and 0.01, which is typically written

$$0.01 < P < 0.025$$

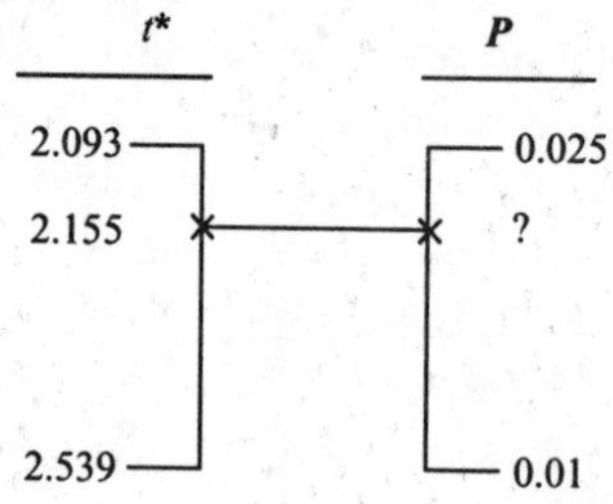

Fig. 16-6

16.21 DECISION RULES FOR HYPOTHESIS TESTS WITH THE *t* STATISTIC

Because for the t statistic it is only possible to approximate or bracket P values using Table A.6 (see Section 16.20), we will only present critical-value decision rules. Also, unlike the critical-value decision rules for the Z statistic (see Section 16.10), which give a specific critical value, $\pm z_\alpha$ or $z_{\alpha/2}$, for any α level, the critical-value decision rules for the t statistic give a different critical value, $\pm t_{\alpha,\nu}$ or $\pm t_{\alpha/2,\nu}$, for each sample size and thus degrees of freedom ($\nu = n - 1$). Therefore, we give here the general forms for the decision rules.

For the right-tailed test:

$$\text{Reject } H_0 \text{ if } t^* > t_{\alpha,\nu}$$

For the left-tailed test:

$$\text{Reject } H_0 \text{ if } t^* < -t_{\alpha,\nu}$$

And, for the two-tailed test:

$$\text{Reject } H_0 \text{ if } t^* > t_{\alpha/2,\nu} \quad \text{or} \quad t^* < -t_{\alpha/2,\nu}$$

EXAMPLE 16.7 For the sample in Example 16.6 ($n = 20$, $\bar{x} = 4.0$, $s = 0.83$), taken from a normally distributed population with an unknown μ and unknown σ, do a right-tailed test of H_0: $\mu = 3.6$, using $\alpha = 0.05$ and a critical-value decision rule. Present the solution in the series of steps from Section 16.16.

Solution

(1) H_0: $\mu = 3.6$, H_1: $\mu > 3.6$

(2) $\alpha = 0.05$

(3) As the population is normally distributed and σ is not known, we use the t statistic [equation (16.8)]. With $\alpha = 0.05$, ($\nu = n - 1 = 20 - 1 = 19$), and the $t_{0.05,19}$ value from Table A.6, the right-tailed decision rule is: Reject H_0 if $t^* > (t_{0.05,19} = 1.729)$.

(4) From Example 16.6: $t^* = 2.155$. From Table A.6 we can see that this t^* value for the $\nu = 19$ distribution is between $t_{0.025}$ and $t_{0.01}$. Thus, by bracketing (see Section 16.20), the P value is in the range: $0.01 < P < 0.025$.

(5) As $t^* > 1.729$, we reject H_0 and accept H_1. This result is confirmed by the fact that $P < 0.05$.

16.22 β, $1 - \beta$, POWER CURVES, AND *OC* CURVES

There are techniques for using Table A.6 to approximate β values and thus $1 - \beta$ values, but for the exact values required for power and *OC* curves it is necessary to use statistics programs for calculators and computers that generate t values for any t distribution.

16.23 TESTING HYPOTHESES ABOUT THE POPULATION MEAN μ: LARGE SAMPLE ($n \geq 30$) FROM ANY POPULATION DISTRIBUTION

Sometimes you do not know, and cannot reasonably assume, that the population is normally distributed. However, when the sample is large ($n \geq 30$) you can say from the central limit theorem that the sampling distribution of $\bar{X}$ is approximately normally distributed (see Section 13.18). [Also, if sampling from a finite population without replacement, population size N must be "at least twice as large" as sample size n (see Section 13.17).] If this is true, then when $\bar{X}$ is standardized with the Z transformation [equation (16.2)], the resulting distribution of Z is approximately the standard normal distribution (see Section 13.14). The next step in testing the hypothesis depends on whether the population standard deviation σ is known or unknown.

When σ is known, the techniques described in Sections 16.5 through 16.17 can be used to test the null hypothesis H_0: $\mu = \mu_0$.

EXAMPLE 16.8 In Example 14.9 we determined the approximate 95% confidence interval for the mean μ of the population of speeds for a downhill section of interstate highway, and found it to be 66.3 mph $\pm$ 1.76 mph. This interval was determined for a sample of $n = 85$ vehicles going $\bar{x} = 66.3$ mph. We knew that the population standard deviation was $\sigma = 8.3$ mph, but did not know if the population was normally distributed. We now want to know if the vehicles on this stretch of highway are going "significantly" faster than the speed limit, 65.0 mph. We use the sample and population information to do a right-tailed test of H_0: $\mu = 65.0$ mph at $\alpha = 0.05$, using a critical-value decision rule. Present the solution in the sequence of steps from Section 16.16.

Solution

(1) H_0: $\mu = 65.0$ mph, H_1: $\mu > 65.0$ mph

(2) $\alpha = 0.05$

(3) Because σ is known, the sample is large ($n \geq 30$), and N is "at least twice as large" as n, we can apply the central limit theorem and assume that $\bar{X}$ is approximately normally distributed, and use the Z test statistic. With $n = 85$ and $z_\alpha = z_{0.05} = 1.645$, the right-tailed decision rule stated for critical values is: Reject H_0 if $z^* > 1.645$.

(4) The value of the Z statistic is

$$z^* = \frac{\bar{x} - \mu_0}{\sigma_{\bar{x}}} = \frac{66.3 \text{ mph} - 65.0 \text{ mph}}{\frac{8.3 \text{ mph}}{\sqrt{85}}} = 1.444, \quad \text{or } 1.44$$

From Table A.5, the approximate P value is

$$P \approx P[Z \geq (z^* = a)|H_0 \text{ true}] = P(Z > 1.44) = 0.5 - 0.4251 = 0.0749$$

(5) As $z^* < 1.645$, we accept H_0. This decision is confirmed by the fact that the approximate P value is greater than 0.05. Thus, there is no evidence at the 0.05 level of significance that the vehicles are traveling faster than the speed limit.

When σ is not known but one can assume that the population is normally distributed, if the sample is large, the null hypothesis can be tested by: (1) the exact solution, using the t distribution if exact t values are available, (2) the approximate solution, using the t distribution if such t values must be approximated, or (3) the approximate solution, using the Z distribution. These three techniques are described in Section 14.23 for solving estimation problems.

When σ is not known and the population is clearly not normally distributed, if the sample is large, the null hypothesis can be tested by the approximate solution with the Z distribution and using $S_{\bar{x}}$ as an estimate of $\sigma_{\bar{x}}$. This technique is described in Section 14.24 for solving estimation problems.

16.24 ASSUMPTIONS OF ONE-SAMPLE PARAMETRIC HYPOTHESIS TESTING

The hypothesis-testing techniques described so far in this chapter are *parametric statistical techniques* based on *parametric assumptions*. They are called this because both the statistical hypotheses being tested and many of the assumptions deal with parameters. In Section 3.13 in Volume 1 we stated that

> Parametric statistical techniques (or parametric statistics) are based on very precise and restrictive assumptions about the characteristics of the measurement populations and the measurement samples being investigated. These assumptions, called parametric assumptions, state required features of the populations being studied, such as the nature of their parameters and the shapes of their distributions, and indicate the type of sample that must be taken.

Now, at this point in our discussion of hypothesis testing, we can state further that these assumptions are the defining properties of the specific mathematical models that are the foundations of the tests. To use the mathematical models and achieve meaningful probability decisions, the defining assumptions of the models must be satisified.

For the mathematical model described in Section 16.5, in which the Z statistic is used to find an exact solution, it is assumed that the population being studied is normally distributed and that its standard deviation σ is known. It is also assumed for this model that the population is of interval-level or ratio-level measurements (see Volume 1, Sections 2.6 and 2.7), and that a simple random sample (see Section 13.3) of any size n has been taken that satisfies the assumption of independence (see Section 13.4). It is further assumed, for this model, that if sampling has been done from a finite population without replacement and if $n > 0.05N$, then the finite population correction factor will be used in calculating $\sigma_{\bar{x}}$ (see Section 13.11). Finally, for this and any other statistical test, it is always assumed that every effort has been made to minimize measurement bias (see Volume 1, Section 2.13) and sampling bias (see Volume 1, Section 3.22), and that an unbiased statistical estimator has been used (see Section 14.2).

For the model used in Section 16.19, in which the t statistic is used to find an exact solution, it is again assumed that the population being studied is normally distributed, but now it is assumed that σ is not known and that the sample is small ($n < 30$). All other assumptions that apply to the model using the Z statistic described above also apply here.

The models described in Section 16.23, in which the Z and the t statistics are used to find exact and approximate solutions, have in common the assumption that a large sample ($n \geq 30$) has been taken from the population. If this is true, then where it is assumed that σ is known but the population distribution is not known, the central limit theorem assures that the random variable $\bar{X}$ is approximately normally distributed and that, therefore, Z will have approximately the standard normal distribution. When σ is not known, but the population is assumed to be normally distributed, the exact or the approximate solution using the t statistic can be used, as can the approximate solution using the Z statistic. When σ is not known and the population cannot be assumed to be normally distributed, the approximate solution using the Z statistic can be used. The other assumptions that apply to the models in the previous section also apply here.

16.25 WHEN THE ASSUMPTIONS ARE VIOLATED

In general, if one can be reasonably certain that the assumptions of the hypothesis test have been satisfied and if $P \leq \alpha$, then one can know that a sample result this extreme is not due to flaws in technique but instead must be due either to a very unusual random event if H_0 is true or to the fact that H_0 is false. But what if there are serious violations of the assumptions of the test?

For the *assumption of normality* (assuming normally distributed populations), the tests we have dealt with so far in this chapter are considered to be *robust* (see Section 14.15). This means that moderate deviations from normality do not seriously affect the results. In a large-sample situation ($n \geq 30$), the assumption can be ignored because the central limit theorem allows use of the approximate Z solution (see Section 16.23). However, in a small-sample situation with unknown σ, the exact t solution is required (see Section 16.19) and if the deviation from normality is severe this solution should not be used unless it is possible to *transform* the data (see Section 3.13 in Volume 1).

Therefore, the first step in analyzing such small-sample data is to examine the shape of the sample distribution. A relative frequency distribution (see Volume 1, Section 4.3) or a stem-and-leaf display (see Volume 1, Section 5.10) will quickly show if the distribution is symmetrical or skewed, unimodal or multimodal. Another method is to plot the cumulative percentage distribution of the sample (see Problem 4.18 in Volume 1) on *normal probability paper*: A cumulative percentage distribution of a normal distribution plotted on this paper is a straight line. There are also a variety of "goodness of fit" tests (see Section 20.3) in which sample frequencies are compared with expected frequencies for a normal distribution.

If these tests indicate there are severe deviations from normality, then the next step (see Fig. 3-3 in Volume 1) is to attempt a transformation of the data. In such a transformation the common linear measurement scale (see Volume 1, Section 2.1) that was used to take the data is transformed (changed) into another measurement scale. The object is to find a scale that will satisfy the violated assumptions. There are no set rules for transformations, but you will find many suggestions in statistics books appropriate for different types of violations. Thus, for example, if the sample distribution is positively skewed (see Problem 5.6 in Volume 1), then a *logarithmic transformation* is suggested: each measurement value in the sample is changed to its logarithm (typically to the base 10). Or if the data are discrete measurements (see Volume 1, Section 2.8), these tend to have a Poisson distribution (see Section 11.27), and taking the square root of each sample value can make such a distribution approximately normal.

If the transformation is successful and the assumptions of the test are essentially satisfied, then hypothesis testing can be done on the transformed data. The transformation must then be reported in the presentation of the results.

If the original data seriously violate the parametric assumptions and no transformation can be found to satisfy the assumptions, then no parametric test should be done. Therefore, it will not be possible to test such parametric hypotheses as H_0: $\mu = \mu_0$. However, other aspects of the data can be analyzed with nonparametric tests that do not have such restrictive assumptions (see Chapter 20).

While the term "parametric assumptions" is typically used with reference to hypothesis tests, the estimation techniques in Chapters 14 and 15, because they are used to estimate parameters, are also part of parametric inferential statistics. Each technique has specific, restrictive assumptions (requirements) for achieving a legitimate confidence interval for the parameter.

16.26 TESTING HYPOTHESES ABOUT THE VARIANCE σ^2 OF A NORMALLY DISTRIBUTED POPULATION

Hypotheses about the variance of a population can be evaluated with single samples, in which the null hypothesis H_0: $\sigma^2 = \sigma_0^2$ is tested against one of three alternative hypotheses (see Section 16.3): H_1: $\sigma^2 > \sigma_0^2$, H_1: $\sigma^2 < \sigma_0^2$, or H_1: $\sigma^2 \neq \sigma_0^2$. We know that the sample variance S^2 is the minimum variance unbiased estimator of σ^2 (see Section 14.2) and that any specific sample estimate $S^2 = s^2$ is a point estimate of σ^2. We also know from Section 15.2 that the appropriate test statistic for the population variance (when there is a single sample and the population is normally distributed) is the chi-square statistic [equation (15.1)] with σ_0^2 substituted for σ^2:

$$X^2 = \frac{(n-1)S^2}{\sigma_0^2} \tag{16.13}$$

which can assume specific values:

$$\chi^2 = \frac{(n-1)s^2}{\sigma_0^2} \tag{16.14}$$

This chi-square statistic meets the two criteria (see Section 16.3) for a test statistic: (1) it allows comparison of the point estimate (s^2) and the null-hypothesized value (σ_0^2), and (2) it is associated with a probability distribution (the chi-square distribution with degrees of freedom $\nu = n - 1$, see Section 15.2) that is known under the assumption that H_0 is true.

We will denote the specific value of X^2 calculated for a given sample as χ^{2*}. Therefore, the P value of a hypothesis test (see Section 16.6) that uses X^2 as the test statistic is the conditional probability of observing, when H_0 is true, a χ^2 value that is at least as extreme as χ^{2*} in a particular chi-square distribution defined by its degrees of freedom ($\nu = n - 1$). These are the probability statements for the three pairs of statistical hypotheses.

For the right-tailed test with H_0: $\sigma^2 = \sigma_0^2$ and H_1: $\sigma^2 > \sigma_0^2$, the P value is

$$P = P(X^2 \geq \chi^{2*} | H_0 \text{ is true}) \tag{16.15}$$

For the left-tailed test with H_0: $\sigma^2 = \sigma_0^2$ and H_1: $\sigma^2 < \sigma_0^2$, the P value is

$$P = P(X^2 \leq \chi^{2*} | H_0 \text{ is true}) \tag{16.16}$$

For the two-tailed test with H_0: $\sigma^2 = \sigma_0^2$ and H_1: $\sigma^2 \neq \sigma_0^2$, the probability statement is not straightforward, because the distribution of X^2 is asymmetric with only positive values. One possible solution has these steps:

(1) Determine whether χ^{2*} is greater than or less than the mean of the chi-square distribution $\mu = \nu = n - 1$ (see Section 15.2).

(2) If $\chi^{2*} > \mu$, then the P value is

$$P = 2[P(X^2 \geq \chi^{2*} | H_0 \text{ is true})] \tag{16.17}$$

(3) If $\chi^{2*} < \mu$, then the P value is

$$P = 2[P(X^2 \leq \chi^{2*} | H_0 \text{ is true})] \tag{16.18}$$

As with the t statistic (see Section 16.19), with the X^2 statistic it is typically only possible to approximate or bracket P values using Table A.7 (*Critical Values for the Chi-Square Distribution*). Therefore, we will only present critical-value decision rules. Also, as with the t statistic, because critical values for the X^2 statistic depend on both α and $(\nu = n - 1)$, we give here the general form of the decision rules.

For the right-tailed test:

$$\textit{Reject } H_0 \textit{ if } \chi^{2*} > \chi^2_{\alpha,\nu}$$

For the left-tailed test:

$$\textit{Reject } H_0 \textit{ if } \chi^{2*} < \chi^2_{1-\alpha,\nu}$$

And for the two-tailed test:

$$\textit{Reject } H_0 \textit{ if } \chi^{2*} > \chi^2_{\alpha/2,\nu} \qquad \textit{or if} \qquad \chi^{2*} < \chi^2_{1-\alpha/2,\nu}$$

EXAMPLE 16.9 A sample ($n = 16$) is taken from a normally distributed population with an unknown σ^2. If the sample variance is $s^2 = 2.86$, do a right-tailed test of H_0: $\sigma^2 = 2.50$, using $\alpha = 0.01$ and a critical-value decision rule. Present the solution in the series of steps from Section 16.16.

Solution

(1) H_0: $\sigma^2 = 2.50$, $\quad H_1$: $\sigma^2 > 2.50$

(2) $\alpha = 0.01$

(3) As the population is normally distributed, we use the X^2 statistic [equation (16.13)]. With $\alpha = 0.01$, $(\nu = n - 1 = 16 - 1 = 15)$, and the $\chi^2_{0.01,15}$ value from Table A.7, the right-tailed decision rule is: Reject H_0 if $\chi^{2*} > (\chi^2_{0.01,15} = 30.58)$.

(4) The value of the X^2 statistic is

$$\chi^{2*} = \frac{(n-1)s^2}{\sigma_0^2} = \frac{(16-1)2.86}{2.50} = 17.160, \quad \text{or } 17.16$$

From Table A.7, we can see that this χ^{2*} value for the $\nu = 15$ distribution is between $\chi^2_{0.50,15}$ and $\chi^2_{0.10,15}$. Thus, by bracketing, the P value is in the range: $0.10 < P < 0.50$.

(5) As $\chi^{2*} < 30.58$, we accept H_0. This result is confirmed by the fact that $P > 0.01$.

16.27 TESTING HYPOTHESES ABOUT THE STANDARD DEVIATION σ OF A NORMALLY DISTRIBUTED POPULATION

When it is the population standard deviation σ that is being investigated, the null hypothesis will be H_0: $\sigma = \sigma_0$, and the three alternatives will be H_1: $\sigma > \sigma_0$, H_1: $\sigma < \sigma_0$, and H_0: $\sigma \neq \sigma_0$. As the null statement that "σ equals some value σ_0" implies an equality of the squares of σ and this value, the variances, the same test statistic X^2 and decision procedures that were used in Section 16.26 can be used here.

EXAMPLE 16.10 A sample ($n = 28$) is taken from a normally distributed population with an unknown standard deviation σ. If the sample standard deviation is $s = 4.91$, do a right-tailed test of H_0: $\sigma = 3.50$, using $\alpha = 0.05$ and a critical-value decision rule. Present the solution in the sequence of steps from Section 16.16.

Solution

(1) H_0: $\sigma = 3.50$, $\quad H_1$: $\sigma > 3.50$

(2) $\alpha = 0.05$

(3) As the population is normally distributed, we use the X^2 statistic [equation (16.13)]. With $\alpha = 0.05$, $(\nu = n - 1 = 28 - 1 = 27)$, and the $\chi^2_{0.05,27}$ value from Table A.7, the right-tailed decision rule is: Reject H_0 if $\chi^{2*} > (\chi^2_{0.05,27} = 40.11)$.

(4) The value of the X^2 statistic is

$$\chi^{2*} = \frac{(n-1)s^2}{\sigma_0^2} = \frac{(28-1)(4.91)^2}{(3.50)^2} = 53.136, \quad \text{or } 53.14$$

From Table A.7, we can see that this χ^{2*} value for the $\nu = 27$ distribution is larger than $\chi^2_{0.005,27}$, and therefore the P value is in the range: $P < 0.005$.

(5) As $\chi^{2*} > 40.11$, we reject H_0 and accept H_1. This result is confirmed by the fact that $P < 0.05$.

16.28 TESTING HYPOTHESES ABOUT THE PROPORTION p OF A BINOMIAL POPULATION: LARGE SAMPLES

Hypotheses about the proportion p of a binomial population are tested either by normal-approximation techniques or by binomial-distribution techniques, with the choice depending on sample size. In this section, we examine techniques used for large samples, and then in Section 16.29 we will deal with small-sample techniques.

Consider the situation where a sample of n elements is taken under Bernoulli-trial conditions from an infinitely large binomial population (see Section 13.21) that has an unknown proportion p of success-elements. If it is hypothesized that this proportion has the value p_0, then what test statistic should be used to test H_0: $p = p_0$ against one of the three alternatives H_1: $p > p_0$, H_1: $p < p_0$, or H_1: $p \neq p_0$?

We know from Section 13.25, that if H_0: $p = p_0$ is true and if n is "sufficiently large" ($np_0 \geq 5$ and $nq_0 \geq 5$), then the sampling distribution of the proportion is approximately normally distributed with $\mu_{\bar{p}} = p_0$ and $\sigma_{\bar{p}} = \sqrt{\frac{p_0 - (1 - p_0)}{n}}$. Therefore, under these conditions the random variable Z [equation (13.30)] with p_0 substituted for $\mu_{\bar{p}}$

$$Z = \frac{\bar{P} - \mu_{\bar{p}}}{\sigma_{\bar{p}}} = \frac{\bar{P} - p_0}{\sqrt{\frac{p_0(1-p_0)}{n}}} \tag{16.19}$$

which can assume specific values

$$z = \frac{\bar{p} - p_0}{\sqrt{\frac{p_0(1-p_0)}{n}}} \tag{16.20}$$

has a distribution that is approximately the standard normal distribution. Thus, for such large-sample testing of hypotheses about the proportion, this Z statistic, which meets the two criteria of Section 16.3, is the appropriate test statistic. Therefore, the procedures for determining P values (see Section 16.6) and decision rules (see Section 16.10) for the Z statistic can be used here.

EXAMPLE 16.11 A sample of $n = 100$ is taken under Bernoulli-trial conditions from an infinitely large binomial population that has an unknown proportion p of success elements, and the value $\bar{p} = 0.49$ is obtained. Do a right-tailed test of H_0: $p = 0.40$, using $\alpha = 0.05$, and a critical-value decision rule. Present the solution in the sequence of steps from Section 16.16.

Solution

(1) H_0: $p = 0.40$, $\quad H_1$: $p > 0.40$

(2) $\alpha = 0.05$

(3) As ($np_0 = 100 \times 0.40 = 40$) > 5 and ($nq_0 = 100 \times 0.60 = 60$) > 5, we use the Z statistic [equation (16.19)], which has approximately the standard normal distribution. With $\alpha = 0.05$, the right-tailed decision rule is: Reject H_0 if $z^* > 1.645$.

(4) The value of the Z statistic is

$$z^* = \frac{\bar{p} - p_0}{\sqrt{\frac{p_0(1-p_0)}{n}}} = \frac{0.49 - 0.40}{\sqrt{\frac{0.40(1-0.40)}{100}}} = 1.837, \quad \text{or } 1.84$$

and the approximate P value from Table A.7 is

$$P \approx P[Z \geq (z^* = a)|H_0 \text{ is true}] = P(Z > 1.84) = 0.5 - 0.4671 = 0.0329$$

(5) As $z^* > 1.645$, we reject H_0 and accept H_1. This result is confirmed by the fact that the approximate P value is less than 0.05.

16.29 TESTING HYPOTHESES ABOUT THE PROPORTION p OF A BINOMIAL POPULATION: SMALL SAMPLES

When a small sample is taken from a binomial population and both np_0 and nq_0 are not greater than or equal to 5, then the normal-approximation technique from Section 16.28 cannot be used. Instead, we use the binomial random variable Y, number of successes in the sample, as the test statistic, and this variable can be defined by this version of equation (13.22):

$$Y = n\bar{P} \tag{16.21}$$

which can assume specific values

$$y = n\bar{p} \tag{16.22}$$

The variable Y has a known probability distribution if H_0 is true—the binomial distribution (see Section 11.5)—and thus we can go directly to this distribution to determine exact P values in a hypothesis test.

EXAMPLE 16.12 You think a coin may be weighted to give a larger proportion of heads than tails. You flip the coin seven times and get six heads. If success is getting a head, then the infinite binomial population for this coin has an unknown proportion p of success elements. Using this sample, do the right-tailed test, at $\alpha = 0.05$, of H_0: $p = 0.5$. Present the results in the sequence of steps from Section 16.16.

Solution

(1) H_0: $p = 0.5$, $\quad H_1$: $p > 0.5$

(2) $\alpha = 0.05$

(3) As ($np_0 = 7 \times 0.5 = 3.5$) < 5 and ($nq_0 = 7 \times 0.5 = 3.5$) < 5, we use Y as the test statistic. The right-tailed decision rule is: Reject H_0 if $P \leq 0.5$, and P is directly calculated with this equation with the symbol y^* used for the specific sample value of Y:

$$P = P(Y \geq y^*|H_0 \text{ is true})$$

(4) For this sample $y^* = 6$, and for this problem we know from Table 11.2 that

$$P = P(Y \geq 6|H_0 \text{ is true}) = 0.0547 + 0.0078 = 0.0625$$

(5) As $P > 0.05$ we accept H_0. There is no evidence, at the 0.05 level of significance, that the coin is weighted to give a larger proportion of heads than tails.

Solved Problems

TESTING HYPOTHESES ABOUT THE POPULATION MEAN μ: KNOWN STANDARD DEVIATION σ, NORMALLY DISTRIBUTED POPULATION

16.1 The company that sells carrot seeds for heavy, clay soil conducts a yearly quality-control test to see, among other things, if it can still say that the average length of carrots from the seeds will be 11.5 cm (see Problem 12.8). Assigned this test, you take a random sample of 40 of these carrots from a field of mature carrots and find that their average length is $\bar{x} = 11.8$ cm. Assuming that the population of length measurements is still normally distributed with $\sigma = 1.15$ cm, you do a two-tailed test of H_0: $\mu = 11.5$ cm at the $\alpha = 0.05$ level of significance, using a critical-value decision rule (see Section 16.10). Present the solution in the sequence of steps from Section 16.16.

Solution

(1) H_0: $\mu = 11.5$ cm, $\quad H_1$: $\mu \neq 11.5$ cm

(2) $\alpha = 0.05$

(3) As the population is normally distributed and σ is known, we can use the Z statistic [equation (16.2)]. With $\alpha = 0.05$, the two-tailed decision rule is: Reject H_0 if $z^* > 1.96$ or if $z^* < -1.96$.

(4) The value of the Z statistic is

$$z^* = \frac{\bar{x} - \mu_0}{\sigma_{\bar{x}}} = \frac{11.8 \text{ cm} - 11.5 \text{ cm}}{1.15 \text{ cm}/\sqrt{40}} = 1.6499, \quad \text{or } 1.65$$

To determine the P value, we use equation (16.4):

$$P = 2[P(Z \geq (z^* = a)|H_0 \text{ is true})]$$

From Table A.5, we find that the area (probability) in the standard normal distribution above the interval $0 \leq z \leq 1.65$ is 0.4505. Therefore,

$$P = 2(0.5 - 0.4505) = 0.0990$$

(5) As $-1.96 < z^* < 1.96$, we accept H_0. This result is confirmed by the fact that $P > 0.05$. These results inform the company that as H_0: $\mu = 11.5$ cm cannot be rejected, they can continue to state in their advertising that $\mu = 11.5$ cm.

16.2 There is reason to believe that the heavy-soil carrots in Problem 16.1 will not grow as long in sandy soil, i.e., will not average 11.5 cm. You test this by growing these carrots in sandy soil, taking a random sample of 50 mature carrots, and finding that their average length is $\bar{x} = 11.1$ cm. Assuming that the population of length measurements is still normally distributed with $\sigma = 1.15$ cm, do a left-tailed test of H_0: $\mu = 11.5$ cm, using $\alpha = 0.01$, and a critical-value decision rule (see Section 16.10). Present the solution in the sequence of steps from Section 16.16.

Solution

(1) H_0: $\mu = 11.5$ cm, $\quad H_1$: $\mu < 11.5$ cm

(2) $\alpha = 0.01$

(3) Using the Z statistic with $\alpha = 0.01$, the left-tailed decision rule is: Reject H_0 if $z^* < -2.33$.

(4) The value of the Z statistic is

$$z^* - \frac{\bar{x} - \mu_0}{\sigma_{\bar{x}}} = \frac{11.1 \text{ cm} - 11.5 \text{ cm}}{1.15 \text{ cm}/\sqrt{50}} = -2.4595, \quad \text{or } -2.46$$

To determine the P value we use this equivalent version of equation (16.5):

$$P = P(Z < -2.46|H_0 \text{ is true})$$

Finding the P value with the method used in Example 16.1 and the appropriate value from Table A.5,

$$P = 0.5 - 0.4931 = 0.0069$$

(5) As $z^* < -2.33$, we reject H_0 and accept H_1. This result is confirmed by the fact that $P < 0.01$. There is thus evidence at the 0.01 level of significance that the average length of carrots in sandy soil is less than 11.5 cm.

16.3 Statistical decisions were made in Examples 16.1 and 16.2, and in Problems 16.1 and 16.2. Which possible error could have been made with these decisions: Type I or Type II?

Solution

In Examples 16.1 and 16.2, and in Problem 16.2, H_0 was rejected, and therefore it is possible that Type I errors were made (see Table 16.1). In Problem 16.1, H_0 was accepted, and therefore a Type II error may have been made.

16.4 Repeat the two-tailed test in Problem 16.1 but this time use $\bar{X}$ as the test statistic. Present the solution in the sequence of steps from Section 16.16.

Solution

(1) H_0: $\mu = 11.5\text{ cm}$, $\quad H_1$: $\mu \neq 11.5\text{ cm}$

(2) $\alpha = 0.05$

(3) As the population is normally distributed and σ is known, we can use $\bar{X}$ as the test statistic (see Section 16.17). With $\alpha = 0.05$ and from Table A.5: $z_{\alpha/2} = z_{0.05/2} = 1.96$, the two-tailed decision rule stated in terms of critical values is

Reject H_0 if

$$\bar{x}^* > \left[\bar{x}_{0.05/2} = \mu_0 + z_{0.05/2}\sigma_{\bar{x}} = 11.5\text{ cm} + 1.96\left(\frac{1.15\text{ cm}}{\sqrt{40}}\right) = 11.86\text{ cm}\right]$$

or if

$$\bar{x}^* < \left[\bar{x}_{1-0.05/2} = \mu_0 - z_{0.05/2}\sigma_{\bar{x}} = 11.5\text{ cm} - 1.96\left(\frac{1.15\text{ cm}}{\sqrt{40}}\right) = 11.14\text{ cm}\right]$$

(4) The value of the $\bar{X}$ statistic is $\bar{x}^* = 11.8\text{ cm}$ and the P value is the same as in Problem 16.1, $P = 0.0990$.

(5) As $11.14\text{ cm} < \bar{x}^* < 11.86\text{ cm}$, we again accept H_0. This result is confirmed by the fact that $P > 0.05$.

β, $1 - \beta$, POWER CURVES, AND *OC* CURVES

16.5 In Example 16.5, for $n = 20$, $\sigma = 6.25\text{ min}$, and $\alpha = 0.05$, we found that if $\mu_1 = 105.3\text{ min}$ is the true population mean, then the probability that this right-tailed test would reject H_0: $\mu = 100.3\text{ min}$, is $1 - \beta(105.3) = 0.9732$. Under the same conditions, what is the probability of rejecting H_0 if the true population mean is: (*a*) 101.3 min, (*b*) 100.3 min, (*c*) 99.3 min?

Solution

(*a*) The conditions of the problem are shown in Fig. 16-7. Here, while the lower, null-defined distribution remains the same as in Fig. 16-5, the upper distribution defined by H_1: $\mu = \mu_1 = 101.3\text{ min}$ has shifted to the left so that most of it (the gray area) is in the acceptance region of the test. To find $\beta(101.3)$, we first determine this z_1 value:

$$z_1 = \frac{102.6\text{ min} - 101.3\text{ min}}{6.25\text{ min}/\sqrt{20}} = 0.930, \quad \text{or } 0.93$$

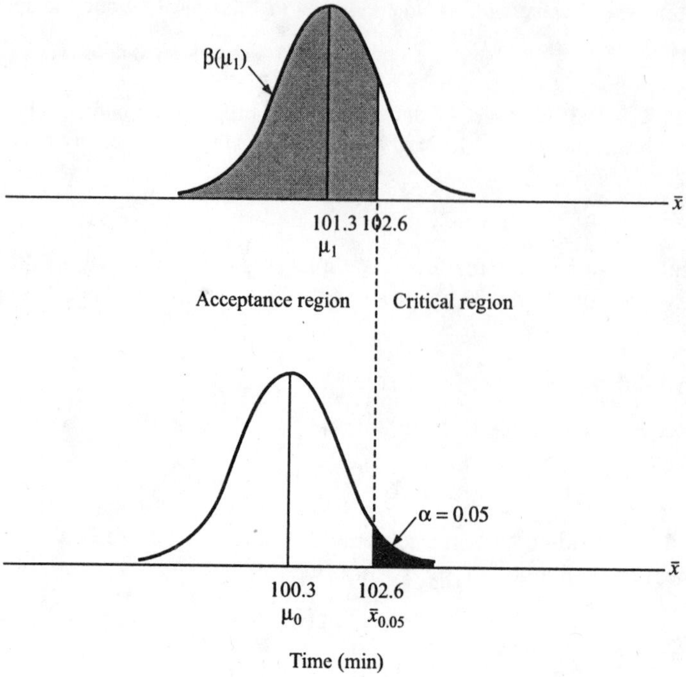

Fig. 16-7

Therefore, from Table A.5, the probability of a Type II error is

$$\beta(101.3) = 0.5 + 0.3238 = 0.8238$$

and thus the probability of rejecting H_0 (correctly) is

$$1 - \beta(101.3) = 1 - 0.8238 = 0.1762$$

(*b*) Here the true mean is the mean of the test distribution defined by the null and therefore the probability of rejecting H_0 (incorrectly, a Type I error) is the black area in the lower distribution in Fig. 16-7, the significance level of the test $\alpha = 0.05$.

(*c*) Here the true mean $\mu_1 = 99.3$ min is less than the null-defined mean $\mu = 100.3$ min and therefore rejecting H_0 and accepting H_1: $\mu > 100.3$ min is also a Type I error. However, now, as you can see from the top distribution in Fig. 16-8, the percent of the true distribution in the critical region of the test is less than α, and therefore the probability of a Type I error is less than α. This problem demonstrates that: *In a one-tailed test, α is actually the maximum possibility of making a Type I error, and this maximum is only true when the true mean is the null-defined μ_0*. If in a right-tailed test $\mu_1 < \mu_0$, then the probability of a Type I error is less than α, and we denote this by $\alpha(\mu_1)$. Here, to find $\alpha(\mu_1) = \alpha(99.3)$, we first determine this z_1 value,

$$z_1 = \frac{102.6 \text{ min} - 99.3 \text{ min}}{6.25 \text{ min}/\sqrt{20}} = 2.361, \quad \text{or } 2.36$$

and then from Table A.5 we find

$$\alpha(99.3) = 0.5 - 0.4909 = 0.0091$$

Thus, the probability of rejecting H_0 (incorrectly, making a Type I error) is 0.0091.

16.6 In Examples 16.4 and 16.5, and Problem 16.5, we determined probabilities for accepting or rejecting H_0: $\mu = 100.3$ min given different values for the true population mean μ_x. These probabilities are shown in Table 16.3. Complete the table, still assuming the same right-tailed test under the same conditions.

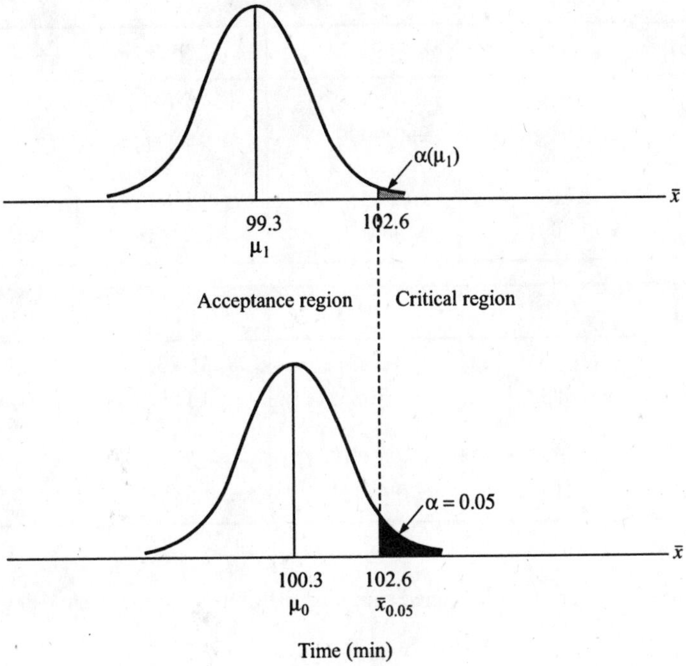

Fig. 16-8

Table 16.3

True mean (min)	97.3	98.3	99.3	100.3	101.3
P(accepting H_0)	$1 - \alpha$ (97.3) =	$1 - \alpha$ (98.3) =	$1 - \alpha$ (99.3) = 0.9909	$1 - \alpha$ = 0.95	β (101.3) = 0.8238
P(rejecting H_0)	α (97.3) =	α (98.3) =	α (99.3) = 0.0091	α = 0.05	$1 - \beta$ (101.3) = 0.1762

True mean (min)	102.3	103.3	104.3	105.3	106.3
P(accepting H_0)	β (102.3) =	β (103.3) =	β (104.3) =	β (105.3) = 0.0268	β (106.3) =
P(rejecting H_0)	$1 - \beta$ (102.3) =	$1 - \beta$ (103.3) =	$1 - \beta$ (104.3) =	$1 - \beta$ (105.3) = 0.9732	$1 - \beta$ (106.3) =

Solution

The completed table is presented in Table 16.4.

16.7 Redo Table 16.4 with all the conditions the same for the right-tailed test except that now the sample size n has been doubled from 20 to 40.

Solution

The completed table is presented in Table 16.5. To show how these values are determined, we will do the calculations for true-means 99.3 min and 101.3 min. The first step for these calculations is to determine a new

Table 16.4

True mean (min)	97.3	98.3	99.3	100.3	101.3
P(accepting H_0)	$1-\alpha$ (97.3) $= 0.9999$	$1-\alpha$ (98.3) $= 0.9990$	$1-\alpha$ (99.3) $= 0.9909$	$1-\alpha$ $= 0.95$	β (101.3) $= 0.8238$
P(rejecting H_0)	α (97.3) $= 0.0001$	α (98.3) $= 0.0010$	α (99.3) $= 0.0091$	α $= 0.05$	$1-\beta$ (101.3) $= 0.1762$

True mean (min)	102.3	103.3	104.3	105.3	106.3
P(accepting H_0)	β (102.3) $= 0.5832$	β (103.3) $= 0.3085$	β (104.3) $= 0.1112$	β (105.3) $= 0.0268$	β (106.3) $= 0.0040$
P(rejecting H_0)	$1-\beta$ (102.3) $= 0.4168$	$1-\beta$ (103.3) $= 0.6915$	$1-\beta$ (104.3) $= 0.8888$	$1-\beta$ (105.3) $= 0.9732$	$1-\beta$ (106.3) $= 0.9960$

critical value, $\bar{x}_{0.05}$, for the null-defined sampling distribution of the mean using the procedure from Example 16.3. Thus,

$$\bar{x}_{0.05} = \mu_0 + 1.645\sigma_{\bar{x}} = 100.3 \text{ min} + 1.645\left(\frac{6.25 \text{ min}}{\sqrt{40}}\right) = 101.93 \text{ min}$$

Next, to find $\alpha(99.3)$ we use the technique from Problem 16.5(*c*) and first determine

$$z_1 = \frac{101.93 \text{ min} - 99.3 \text{ min}}{6.25 \text{ min}/\sqrt{40}} = 2.661, \quad \text{or } 2.66$$

and then from Table A.5 we find

$$\alpha(99.3) = 0.5 - 0.4961 = 0.0039$$

and thus

$$1 - \alpha(99.3) = 1 - 0.0039 = 0.9961$$

Table 16.5

True mean (min)	97.3	98.3	99.3	100.3	101.3
P(accepting H_0)	$1-\alpha$ (97.3) $= 1$	$1-\alpha$ (98.3) $= 0.9999$	$1-\alpha$ (99.3) $= 0.9961$	$1-\alpha$ $= 0.95$	β (101.3) $= 0.7389$
P(rejecting H_0)	α (97.3) $= 0.0000$	α (98.3) $= 0.0001$	α (99.3) $= 0.0039$	α $= 0.05$	$1-\beta$ (101.3) $= 0.2611$

True mean (min)	102.3	103.3	104.3	105.3	106.3
P(accepting H_0)	β (102.3) $= 0.3557$	β (103.3) $= 0.0823$	β (104.3) $= 0.0082$	β (105.3) $= 0.0003$	β (106.3) $= 0.0000$
P(rejecting H_0)	$1-\beta$ (102.3) $= 0.6443$	$1-\beta$ (103.3) $= 0.9177$	$1-\beta$ (104.3) $= 0.9918$	$1-\beta$ (105.3) $= 0.9997$	$1-\beta$ (106.3) $= 1$

To find $\beta(101.3)$ we use the technique from Problem 16.5(*a*) and first determine

$$z_1 = \frac{101.93 \text{ min} - 101.3 \text{ min}}{6.25 \text{ min}/\sqrt{40}} = 0.638, \quad \text{or } 0.64$$

Consulting Table A.5,

$$\beta(101.3) = 0.5 + 0.2389 = 0.7389$$

and thus

$$1 - \beta(101.3) = 1 - 0.7389 = 0.2611$$

16.8 From Tables 16.4 and 16.5, construct power curves (see Section 16.18) on the same axes for the $n = 20$ and $n = 40$ conditions.

Solution

The requested power curves are presented in Fig. 16-9. The horizontal axis shows possible values for the true population mean μ_x and the vertical axis shows the probability of rejecting the null hypothesis H_0: $\mu = 100.3$ min. For completeness, such curves typically show the probability of rejection both for when H_0 should be rejected ($\mu_x > 100.3$ min) and for when H_0 should be accepted ($\mu_x \leq 100.3$ min). When H_0 should be rejected, the vertical distance from any specific μ_x point on the horizontal axis to the curve for a test is the power of that test (see Section 16.18), $1 - \beta(\mu_x)$. Therefore, when H_0 should be rejected, the probability of a Type II error for any specific μ_x, $\beta(\mu_x)$, is the vertical distance above μ_x from the power curve to the 1.0 line. This is shown for $\beta(101.3)$ in Fig. 16-9. When H_0 should be accepted, the vertical distance from a specific μ_x on the horizontal axis to the curve for a test is the probability of a Type I error in that test, $\alpha(\mu_x)$, with $\alpha = 0.05$ at $\mu_x = \mu_0 = 100.3$ min. Therefore, where H_0 should be accepted, the vertical distance from the power curve for a test to the 1.0 line for any specific μ_x, $1 - \alpha(\mu_x)$, is the probability of correctly accepting H_0 in that test.

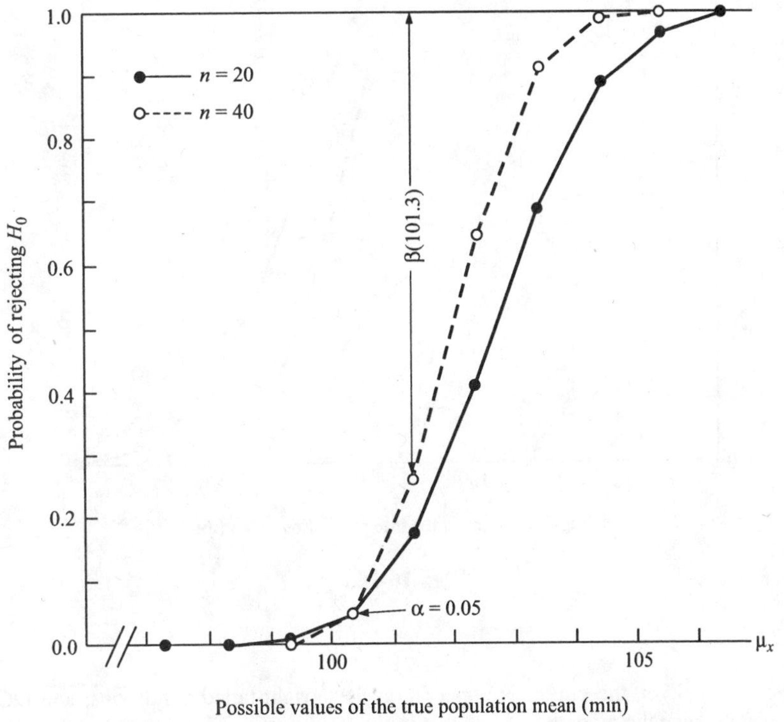

Fig. 16-9

The two curves shown in Fig. 16-9 are specific to these test conditions: right-tailed test, $\alpha = 0.05$, $n = 20$ or 40, normally distributed sampling distribution of $\bar{X}$. Such *S-shaped curves* are typical power curves for right-tailed tests, whereas *reverse-S-shaped curves* are typical for left-tailed tests. The power curves for two-tailed tests combine these two types of curves.

16.9 From Tables 16.4 and 16.5, construct *OC* curves (operating characteristic curves, see Section 16.18) on the same axes for the $n = 20$ and $n = 40$ conditions.

Solution

The requested *OC* curves are presented in Fig. 16-10. Again, as with the power curves in Fig. 16-9, the horizontal axis shows possible values of the true population mean μ_x. Now, however, the vertical axis shows the probability of accepting the null hypothesis H_0: $\mu = 100.3$ min. Again, for completeness, the curves show the probability for acceptance both for when H_0 should be rejected and also for when H_0 should be accepted. These curves are *complementary* to the curves in Fig. 16-9. Therefore, when H_0 should be rejected, the vertical distance from any μ_x on the horizontal axis to the curve is now $\beta(\mu_x)$, and the vertical distance from this intersection to the 1.0 line is now $1 - \beta(\mu_x)$. This is shown for $1 - \beta(103.3)$ in Fig. 16.10. Similarly, when H_0 should be accepted, the vertical distance from any μ_x on the horizontal axis to the curve is $1 - \alpha(\mu_x)$.

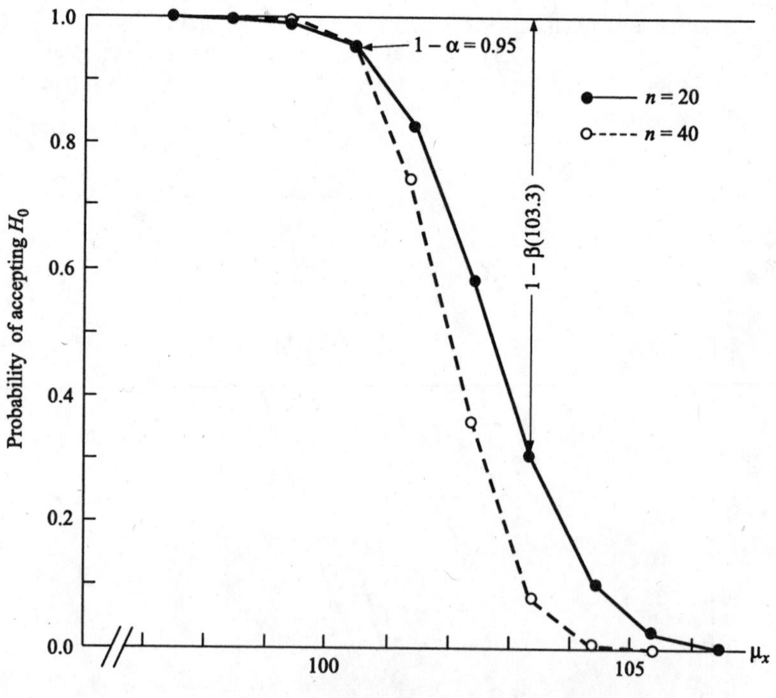

Fig. 16-10

Again as in Fig. 16-9, the curves are specific to these right-tailed conditions, and *OC* curves for such conditions typically have the reverse-S-shape that is shown here. For a left-tailed test the *OC* curves would be S-shaped. Again, the *OC* curves for a two-tailed test would combine both of these curves.

16.10 How are the probabilities of a Type I or a Type II error affected by changes in sample size?

Solution

From the tables and curves in Problems 16.6 through 16.9, it can be seen that if all other test conditions are kept constant and sample size is increased, then the probabilities of both types of error, $\alpha(\mu_x)$ and $\beta(\mu_x)$, will simultaneously decrease. This is true for all μ_x values but μ_0, where α remains constant.

16.11 How are the probabilities of a Type I or a Type II error affected by the distance between an alternative μ_x and the null-defined μ_0?

Solution

From the tables and curves in Problems 16.6 through 16.9, it can be seen that if all other test conditions are kept constant, and the distance between an alternative μ_x and μ_0 is increased, then in this right-tailed test if μ_x is to the left of μ_0, $\alpha(\mu_x)$ will decrease, and if μ_x is to the right of μ_0, $\beta(\mu_x)$ will decrease.

16.12 How are the probabilities of a Type I and Type II error affected by decreasing α?

Solution

If all other test conditions are kept constant, and α is decreased, then $\alpha(\mu_x)$ will be decreased for all μ_x values where H_0 should be accepted, and $\beta(\mu_x)$ will be increased for all μ_x values where H_0 should be rejected. The only way to avoid this increase in $\beta(\mu_x)$ with a decrease in α is to increase sample size.

TESTING HYPOTHESES ABOUT THE POPULATION MEAN: STANDARD DEVIATION NOT KNOWN, SMALL SAMPLE FROM A NORMALLY DISTRIBUTED POPULATION

16.13 For a sample of $n = 25$, what are the decision rules for one-sample hypothesis tests of H_0: $\mu = \mu_0$, where t is the test statistic, if $\alpha = 0.05$ and (*a*) H_1: $\mu > \mu_0$, (*b*) H_1: $\mu < \mu_0$, (*c*) H_1: $\mu \neq \mu_0$?

Solution

Because it is only possible to approximate or bracket P values using Table A.6 (see Section 16.20), we will use critical-value decision rules (see Section 16.21).

(*a*) For this right-tailed test where $\nu = n - 1 = 25 - 1 = 24$,

$$\text{Reject } H_0 \text{ if } t^* > (t_{\alpha,\nu} = t_{0.05,24} = 1.711)$$

(*b*) For this left-tailed test where $\nu = 24$,

$$\text{Reject } H_0 \text{ if } t^* < (-t_{\alpha,\nu} = -t_{0.05,24} = -1.711)$$

(*c*) For this two-tailed test where $\nu = 24$,

$$\text{Reject } H_0 \text{ if } t^* > (t_{\alpha/2,\nu} = t_{0.05/2,24} = 2.064) \quad \text{or if} \quad t^* < (-t_{\alpha/2,\nu} = -t_{0.05/2,24} = -2.064)$$

16.14 For the test conditions in Problem 16.13, what are the decision rules if $\alpha = 0.01$?

Solution

(*a*) For this right-tailed test where $\nu = 24$,

$$\text{Reject } H_0 \text{ if } t^* > (t_{\alpha,\nu} = t_{0.01,24} = 2.492)$$

(*b*) For this left-tailed test where $\nu = 24$,

$$\text{Reject } H_0 \text{ if } t^* < (-t_{\alpha,\nu} = -t_{0.01,24} = -2.492)$$

(c) For this two-tailed test where $\nu = 24$,

$$\text{Reject } H_0 \text{ if } t^* > (t_{\alpha/2,\nu} = t_{0.01/2,24} = 2.797) \quad \text{or if} \quad t^* < (-t_{\alpha/2,\nu} = -t_{0.01/2,24} = -2.797)$$

16.15 You are a biologist studying a species of Great-Plains soldier beetle. You discover a population of this species living in the mountains 3,000 feet above the plains and take a variety of measurements for $n = 20$ male beetles to see if mountain-males differ from plains-males. One measure is the length of a black spot on the wings. You know for plains-males that spot length is normally distributed with $\mu = 3.14$ mm. From the mountain-male sample, you find for spot length that $\bar{x} = 3.23$mm with $s = 0.214$ mm. Assuming spot length is normally distributed for mountain-males, do a two-tailed test at $\alpha = 0.05$ of H_0: $\mu = 3.14$ mm. Present the solution in the sequence of steps from Section 16.16.

Solution

(1) H_0: $\mu = 3.14$ mm, H_1: $\mu \neq 3.14$ mm

(2) $\alpha = 0.05$

(3) Using the t statistic [equation (16.8)], with $\alpha = 0.05$ and ($\nu = n - 1 = 20 - 1 = 19$), the two-tailed decision rule (see Section 16.21) is:

$$\text{Reject } H_0 \text{ if } t^* > (t_{0.05/2,19} = 2.093) \quad \text{or if} \quad t^* < (-t_{0.05/2,19} = -2.093)$$

(4) The value of the t statistic is

$$t^* = \frac{3.23 \text{ mm} - 3.14 \text{ mm}}{0.214 \text{ mm}/\sqrt{20}} = 1.8808, \quad \text{or } 1.881$$

The P value for $\nu = 19$ is in the range (see Section 16.20)

$$(2 \times 0.025) < P < (2 \times 0.05), \quad \text{or} \quad 0.05 < P < 0.10$$

(5) As $-2.093 < t^* < 2.093$, we accept H_0. This result is confirmed by the fact that the P value is in the range $0.05 < P < 0.10$. There is not a significant difference at the 0.05 level of significance between the sample average spot length and the hypothesized average spot length.

16.16 Before doing the test in Problem 16.15, you had the hypothesis that the mountain-males would have longer spots as an evolved way of increasing heat absorption. Therefore, you could have done a right-tailed test of H_0: $\mu = 3.14$ mm. Do this test at $\alpha = 0.05$, presenting the solution in the sequence of steps from Section 16.16.

Solution

(1) H_0: $\mu = 3.14$ mm, H_1: $\mu > 3.14$ mm

(2) $\alpha = 0.05$

(3) Using the t statistic with $\nu = 19$ and $\alpha = 0.05$, the right-tailed decision rule is: Reject H_0 if $t^* > 1.729$.

(4) Again $t^* = 1.881$, but now for this right-tailed test the P value for $\nu = 19$ is in the range of $0.025 < P < 0.05$.

(5) As $t^* > 1.729$, we now reject H_0 and accept H_1. This result is confirmed by the fact that the P value is in the range $0.025 < P < 0.05$. Here we can say that the sample mean spot length is significantly longer than the hypothesized mean spot length at the 0.05 level of significance, and these results indicate that mountain-males have a longer average spot length.

16.17 A standard dental anesthetic eliminates sensation on the average $\mu = 10.5$ min after injection. There is a new version of this anesthetic, which the manufacturer claims will act "significantly faster." You are a dentist and you use this new version with 10 patients, getting these times from injection to elimination of sensation (in minutes): 9.3, 9.5, 9.2, 9.0, 9.3, 9.5, 9.4, 9.3, 9.2, 9.1. As the previous times-to-effect were normally distributed, it is reasonable to assume a normal distribution for the new anesthetic. Because you are concerned only with a decrease in times-to-effect, use the sample information and a t statistic to do a left-tailed test of H_0: $\mu = 10.5$ min at $\alpha = 0.01$. Present the solution in the sequence of steps from Section 16.16.

Solution

(1) H_0: $\mu = 10.5$ min, H_1: $\mu < 10.5$ min

(2) $\alpha = 0.01$

(3) Using the t statistic with $\alpha = 0.01$ and ($\nu = n - 1 = 10 - 1 = 9$), the left-tailed decision rule is:

$$\text{Reject } H_0 \text{ if } t^* < -2.821$$

(4) For this sample

$$\bar{x} = \frac{\sum x_i}{n} = \frac{92.8 \text{ min}}{10} = 9.28 \text{ min}$$

$$s = \sqrt{\frac{\sum(x_i - \bar{x})^2}{n-1}} = 0.1619 \text{ min}$$

Therefore, the value of the t statistic is

$$t^* = \frac{9.28 \text{ min} - 10.5 \text{ min}}{0.1619 \text{ min}/\sqrt{10}} = -23.8294, \quad \text{or } -23.829$$

The P value for ($\nu = 9$) is in the range $P < 0.0005$.

(5) As $t^* < -2.821$, we reject H_0 and accept H_1. This result is confirmed by the fact that the P value is in the range of $P < 0.0005$. We can say that the evidence evaluated at the 0.01 level of significance indicates that the new anesthetic does act faster.

16.18 If the sample in Problem 16.17 had been (in minutes): 10.5, 10.7, 11.0, 10.7, 10.6, 10.7, 10.8, 10.9, 10.5, 11.0, then what would have been the result of the same left-tailed test of H_0: $\mu = 10.5$ min?

Solution

A left-tailed test can only have a significant result, a rejection of H_0, if the sample mean is less than the hypothesized population mean (see Section 16.6). Here the sample mean is $\bar{x} = 10.74$ min and thus H_0 must be accepted—there is insufficient evidence to reject H_0 and claim that the new anesthetic acts faster.

TESTING HYPOTHESES ABOUT THE VARIANCE AND STANDARD DEVIATION OF A NORMALLY DISTRIBUTED POPULATION

16.19 For a sample of $n = 19$, what are the critical-value decision rules (see Section 16.26) for one-sample hypothesis tests of H_0: $\sigma^2 = \sigma_0^2$, where X^2 is the test statistic, $\alpha = 0.05$, and (*a*) H_1: $\sigma^2 > \sigma_0^2$, (*b*) H_1: $\sigma^2 < \sigma_0^2$, (*c*) H_1: $\sigma^2 \neq \sigma_0^2$?

Solution

(*a*) For this right-tailed test where $\nu = 19 - 1 = 18$,

$$\text{Reject } H_0 \text{ if } \chi^{2*} > (\chi^2_{\alpha,\nu} = \chi^2_{0.05,18} = 28.87)$$

(*b*) For this left-tailed test where $\nu = 18$,

$$\text{Reject } H_0 \text{ if } \chi^{2*} < (\chi^2_{1-\alpha,\nu} = \chi^2_{0.95,18} = 9.39)$$

(c) For this two-tailed test where $\nu = 18$,

$$\text{Reject } H_0 \text{ if } \chi^{2*} > (\chi^2_{\alpha/2,\nu} = \chi^2_{0.025,18} = 31.53) \quad \text{or if} \quad \chi^{2*} < (\chi^2_{1-\alpha/2,\nu} = \chi^2_{0.975,18} = 8.23)$$

16.20 For the study of soldier beetles described in Problem 16.15, suppose that you know for the plains-males that spot length is normally distributed with $\mu = 3.14$ mm and $\sigma^2 = 0.0505\,\text{mm}^2$. For the mountain-male sample of $n = 20$, you found for spot length that $\bar{x} = 3.23$ mm, $s = 0.214$ mm, and $s^2 = 0.0458\,\text{mm}^2$. Assuming that spot length is normally distributed for the mountain-males, do a two-tailed test at $\alpha = 0.05$ using a critical-value decision rule, of H_0: $\sigma^2 = 0.0505\,\text{mm}^2$. Present the solution in the sequence of steps from Section 16.16.

Solution

(1) H_0: $\sigma^2 = 0.0505\,\text{mm}^2$, $\quad H_1$: $\sigma^2 \neq 0.0505\,\text{mm}^2$

(2) $\alpha = 0.05$

(3) Using the X^2 statistic with $\alpha = 0.05$ and ($\nu = n - 1 = 20 - 1 = 19$), the two-tailed decision rule (see Section 16.26) is:

$$\text{Reject } H_0 \text{ if } \chi^{2*} > (\chi^2_{0.05/2,19} = 32.85) \quad \text{or if} \quad \chi^{2*} < (\chi^2_{1-0.05/2,19} = 8.91)$$

(4) The value of the X^2 statistic is [equation (16.14)]

$$\chi^{2*} = \frac{(n-1)s^2}{\sigma_0^2} = \frac{(20-1)0.0458\,\text{mm}^2}{0.0505\,\text{mm}^2} = 17.2317, \quad \text{or } 17.23$$

As $\chi^{2*} < (\mu = \nu = 19)$, the P value from Table A.7 is in the crude range (see Section 16.26) of $(2 \times 0.1) < P < (2 \times 0.5)$, or $0.2 < P < 1.0$.

(5) As $8.91 < \chi^{2*} < 32.85$, we accept H_0. This result is confirmed by the fact that the P value is in the range $0.2 < P < 1.0$. Thus, at the $\alpha = 0.05$ level of significance, there is no evidence that the two populations have different variances.

16.21 You have developed a new brake light for a type of car, and you believe this light will decrease both the mean and variance of reaction times to the car's brake light. From standard tests with the current light, you know that the population of reaction times (one time per person) is normally distributed with $\mu = 0.33$ sec and $\sigma^2 = 0.00284\,\text{sec}^2$. Using the same standard test, you take a sample of reaction times ($n = 51$, one time per person) with the new light and get $\bar{x} = 0.25$ sec and $s^2 = 0.00182\,\text{sec}^2$. Assuming the times for the new light are also normally distributed, do a left-tailed test of H_0: $\sigma^2 = 0.00284\,\text{sec}^2$. Do the test at $\alpha = 0.05$ and present the solution in the sequence of steps from Section 16.16.

Solution

(1) H_0: $\sigma^2 = 0.00284\,\text{sec}^2$, $\quad H_1$: $\sigma^2 < 0.00284\,\text{sec}^2$

(2) $\alpha = 0.05$

(3) Using the X^2 statistic with $\nu = 50$ and Table A.7, the left-tailed decision rule is (see Section 16.26): Reject H_0 if $\chi^{2*} < (\chi^2_{0.95,50} = 34.76)$.

(4) The value of the X^2 statistic is [equation (16.14)]

$$\chi^{2*} = \frac{(51-1)0.00182\,\text{sec}^2}{0.00284\,\text{sec}^2} = 32.0423, \quad \text{or } 32.04$$

From Table A.7, the P value for $\nu = 50$ is in the range of $0.01 < P < 0.025$.

(5) As $\chi^{2*} < 34.76$, we reject H_0 and accept H_1. This result is confirmed by the fact that the P value is in the range of $0.01 < P < 0.025$. Thus, we can say that the evidence evaluated at the 0.05 level of significance indicates that the new light produces a smaller variance in reaction time.

16.22 In the "nutrition facts" printed on a 355 ml can of diet soda, it is stated that there are only 35 mg of sodium. To legitimately claim this amount, the soda is maintained at $\mu = 34.5$ mg of sodium with $\sigma = 0.24$ mg. In regular quality-control tests, 10 cans are selected at random from the production line, and, among other tests, if the standard deviation of the sample is significantly greater (at $\alpha = 0.05$) than 0.24 mg, the production line is stopped and the soda mixing process is readjusted. If in one such test $s = 0.29$ mg, determine whether readjustment is necessary. Present the solution in the sequence of steps from Section 16.16.

Solution

(1) H_0: $\sigma = 0.24$ mg, H_1: $\sigma > 0.24$ mg

(2) $\alpha = 0.05$

(3) The null hypothesis stated for "σ equals some value σ_0" implies an equality of the squares of σ and this value, here H_0: $\sigma^2 = (0.24 \text{ mg})^2 = 0.0576 \text{ mg}^2$. Therefore, the same test statistic X^2 and decision procedures that were used for the variance (see Section 16.26) can be used here. With $\nu = 10 - 1 = 9$, from Table A.7, the right-tailed decision rule is: Reject H_0 if $\chi^{2*} > (\chi^2_{0.05,9} = 16.92)$.

(4) The value of the X^2 statistic is

$$\chi^{2*} = \frac{(n-1)s^2}{\sigma_0^2} = \frac{(10-1)(0.29 \text{ mg})^2}{(0.24 \text{ mg})^2} = 13.1406, \quad \text{or } 13.14$$

From Table A.7, the P value for $\nu = 9$ is in the range of $0.1 < P < 0.5$.

(5) As $\chi^{2*} < 16.92$, we accept H_0. This result is confirmed by the fact that the P value is in the range $0.1 < P < 0.5$. There is no evidence, at the 0.05 level of significance, that the sample standard deviation is greater than the required $\sigma = 0.24$ mg. Thus, no readjustment of the mixing process is necessary.

16.23 From the information in Problem 16.22, do a two-tailed test of H_0: $\sigma = 0.24$ mg, at $\alpha = 0.05$. Present the solution in the sequence of steps from Section 16.16.

Solution

(1) H_0: $\sigma = 0.24$ mg, H_1: $\sigma \neq 0.24$ mg

(2) $\alpha = 0.05$

(3) Using the X^2 statistic with $\alpha = 0.05$ and $\nu = 9$, the two-tailed decision rule is (see Section 16.26): Reject H_0 if $\chi^{2*} > 19.02$ or if $\chi^{2*} < 2.70$.

(4) As in Problem 16.22, $\chi^{2*} = 13.14$, and as $\chi^{2*} > (\mu = n - 1 = 9)$ (see Section 16.26), the P value is in the crude range of $(2 \times 0.1) < P < (2 \times 0.5)$, or $0.2 < P < 1.0$.

(5) As $2.70 < \chi^{2*} < 19.02$, we accept H_0. Again, this result is confirmed by the fact that the P value is in the range $0.2 < P < 1.0$. Thus, again, there is no evidence, at the 0.05 level of significance, that readjustment is necessary.

TESTING HYPOTHESES ABOUT THE PROPORTION OF A BINOMIAL POPULATION

16.24 The chairman of a university psychology department takes a random sample of 75 of the 1,727 students majoring in his department, and asks each of them: Which of the elective courses offered by the department should be retained? He decides that if significantly fewer than 20% of the majors want the course, then it will be eliminated. If the result for *Psychology 403* is that 11 of 75 want it retained, then determine its fate by doing a left-tailed test of H_0: $p = 0.20$ at $\alpha = 0.01$. Use a critical-value decision rule and present the results in the sequence of steps from Section 16.16.

Solution

(1) H_0: $p = 0.20$, H_1: $p < 0.20$

(2) $\alpha = 0.01$

(3) Considering the current majors to be a population of $N = 1{,}727$, $n = 75/1{,}727N$, or $0.043N$, and therefore $n < 0.05N$ and we can consider p essentially constant despite sampling without replacement (see Section 11.2) and it is not necessary to multiply $\sigma_{\bar{p}}$ by the finite population correction factor (see Section 13.11). Thus, as $(np_0 = 75 \times 0.2 = 15) > 5$ and $(nq_0 = 75 \times 0.8 = 60) > 5$, the Z test statistic [equation (16.19)] has approximately a standard normal distribution. From Table A.5, $z_{0.01} = 2.33$, and so the decision rule is: Reject H_0 if $z^* < -2.33$.

(4) As $p_0 = 0.2$ and $\bar{p} = 11/75 = 0.147$, the value of the Z statistic is

$$z^* = \frac{0.147 - 0.20}{\sqrt{\dfrac{0.20(1 - 0.20)}{75}}} = -1.148, \quad \text{or} \; -1.15$$

and the approximate P value from Table A.5 is

$$P \approx P[Z \leq (z^* = -a)|H_0 \text{ is true}] = P(Z < -1.15) = 0.5 - 0.3749 = 0.1251$$

(5) As $z^* > -2.33$ we accept H_0 at the 0.01 level of significance. This result is confirmed by the fact that the approximate P value is greater than 0.01. There is no evidence that the interest in *Psychology 403* is less than 20%; the course is retained.

16.25 You think a coin may be an unfair coin, weighted to give more heads or more tails than if it were fair. You flip the coin seven times and get six heads. Do a two-tailed test of H_0: $p = 0.5$ at $\alpha = 0.5$. Use a critical-value decision rule and present the solution in the sequence of steps from Section 16.16.

Solution

(1) H_0: $p = 0.5$, $\quad H_1$: $p \neq 0.5$

(2) $\alpha = 0.05$

(3) Using the small-sample binomial technique from Section 16.29 and dividing α evenly between the two tails of the distribution, the decision rule is (see Example 16.12): Reject H_0 if y^* is 0 or 7.

(4) $y^* = 6$

(5) As $0 < y^* < 7$, we accept H_0 at the 5% level of significance.

16.26 A pharmaceutical company claims that a new over-the-counter drug will grow hair on the heads of 60% of the men who try it. From complaints they receive, a consumer group thinks this percentage is too high. The group tries the drug on 8 men of the same age and for a fixed amount of time, and finds that only 3 of the 8 men grow hair. For this sample, do a left-tailed test of H_0: $p = 0.6$ at $\alpha = 0.05$, using a P-value decision rule and presenting the results in the sequence of steps from Section 16.16.

Solution

(1) H_0: $p = 0.6$, $\quad H_1$: $p < 0.6$

(2) $\alpha = 0.05$

(3) Using the small-sample binomial technique from Section 16.29, the P value is

$$P = P(Y \leq y^*|H_0 \text{ is true})$$

and the decision rule is: Reject H_0 if $P < 0.05$.

(4) For this sample $y^* = 3$, and the binomial distribution for H_0: $p = 0.6$ is shown in Table 16.6. From this table,

$$P = P(Y \leq 3 | H_0 \text{ is true}) = 0.123863 + 0.041288 + 0.007864 + 0.000655 = 0.173670$$

Table 16.6

Number who grow hair y	Probability $f(y) = \binom{n}{y} p^y q^{n-y}$
0	$f(0) = \binom{8}{0}(0.6)^0(0.4)^8 = 0.000655$
1	$f(1) = \binom{8}{1}(0.6)^1(0.4)^7 = 0.007864$
2	$f(2) = \binom{8}{2}(0.6)^2(0.4)^6 = 0.041288$
3	$f(3) = \binom{8}{3}(0.6)^3(0.4)^5 = 0.123863$
4	$f(4) = \binom{8}{4}(0.6)^4(0.4)^4 = 0.232243$
5	$f(5) = \binom{8}{5}(0.6)^5(0.4)^3 = 0.278692$
6	$f(6) = \binom{8}{6}(0.6)^6(0.4)^2 = 0.209019$
7	$f(7) = \binom{8}{7}(0.6)^7(0.4)^1 = 0.089580$
8	$f(8) = \binom{8}{8}(0.6)^8(0.4)^0 = 0.016796$
Σ	1.000000

(5) As $P > 0.05$ we accept H_0. There is no evidence at the 5% level of significance that the claimed proportion is too high.

16.27 For the sample in Problem 16.26, do a two-tailed test of H_0: $p = 0.6$ at $\alpha = 0.05$. Use a critical-value decision rule, and present the solution in the sequence of steps from Section 16.16.

Solution

(1) H_0: $p = 0.6$, $\quad H_1$: $p \neq 0.6$

(2) $\alpha = 0.05$

(3) As in Problem 16.26, the binomial test should be used and for this 0.05 is divided evenly between the two tails of the distribution. Using Table 16.6, the decision rule is: Reject H_0 if y^* is 0, 1, or 8.

(4) Again $y^* = 3$. For this two-tailed test, we do not calculate the P value because of the asymmetry of the distribution.

(5) As $1 < y^* < 8$, we again accept H_0.

Supplementary Problems

TESTING HYPOTHESES ABOUT THE POPULATION MEAN

16.28 In mid-August, the population of body weights of male ground squirrels is known to be normally distributed with $\mu = 400$ g and $\sigma = 100$ g. To determine if this weight has already been achieved by July, you take a random sample of 25 male ground squirrels in mid-July, weigh them, and find that $\bar{x} = 350$ g. Assuming that the mid-July weights are normally distributed with $\sigma = 100$ g, do a two-tailed test of H_0: $\mu = 400$ g at the 0.05 level of significance. State the decision rule in terms of critical values, give the value of the test statistic and the P value, and then state whether you accept or reject H_0.

Ans. Reject H_0 if $z^* > 1.96$ or if $z^* < -1.96$, $z^* = -2.50$, $P < 0.0124$, reject H_0

16.29 The population of body lengths of blue-bellied lizards on the mainland is known to be normally distributed with $\mu = 60$ mm and $\sigma = 15$ mm. To determine if the body lengths of a population of the same species on a nearby island, formed by colonists from the mainland, has remained the same size, you take a random sample of nine lizards from this island population and find that $\bar{x} = 65$ mm. Assuming that the island lengths are normally distributed with $\sigma = 15$ mm, do a two-tailed test of: H_0: $\mu = 60$ mm using $\alpha = 0.05$. State the decision rule in terms of critical values, give the value of the test statistic and the P value, and then state whether you accept or reject H_0.

Ans. Reject H_0 if $z^* > 1.96$ or if $z^* < -1.96$, $z^* = 1.00$, $P = 0.317$, accept H_0

16.30 For the length population of blue-bellied lizards in Problem 16.29, suppose that you repeat the study (at $\alpha = 0.05$) with a much larger sample ($n = 101$), and again find that for the island sample $\bar{x} = 65$ mm. Assuming that the body lengths of the island population are normally distributed with $\sigma = 15$ mm, do a two-tailed test of H_0: $\mu = 60$ mm. State the decision rule in terms of critical values, give the value of the test statistic and the P value, and then state whether you accept or reject H_0.

Ans. Reject H_0 if $z^* > 1.96$ or if $z^* < -1.96$, $z^* = 3.35$, $P = 0.0008$, reject H_0

16.31 Do a two-tailed test of H_0: $\mu = 400$ g for the sample of $n = 25$ ground squirrels in Problem 16.28, using $\bar{X}$ as the test statistic and $\alpha = 0.01$. State the decision rule in terms of critical values, give the value of the test statistic, and then state whether you accept or reject H_0.

Ans. Reject H_0 if $\bar{x}^* > \left[400\text{ g} + 2.575\left(\frac{100\text{ g}}{\sqrt{25}}\right) = 451.5\text{ g}\right]$ or if

$\bar{x}^* < \left[400\text{ g} - 2.575\left(\frac{100\text{ g}}{\sqrt{25}}\right) = 348.5\text{ g}\right]$, $\bar{x}^* = 350$ g, accept H_0

16.32 You have developed a new milk substitute for feeding young calves, and want to know whether the calves gain more weight during their first month after birth on this substitute than on cow's milk. On cow's milk, the population of weight-gains during the first month is known to be normally distributed with $\mu = 30$ lb and $\sigma = 12$ lb. You put 36 calves on the milk-substitute diet and find that their average weight-gain in their first month is $\bar{x} = 40$ lb. Do a right-tailed test of H_0: $\mu = 30$ lb using $\bar{X}$ as the test statistic and $\alpha = 0.05$. Assume that weight-gain on the new diet is normally distributed with $\sigma = 12$ lb. State the decision rule in terms of critical values, give the value of the test statistic, and then state whether you accept or reject H_0.

Ans. Reject H_0 if $\bar{x}^* > \left[30\text{ lb} + 1.645\left(\frac{12\text{ lb}}{\sqrt{36}}\right) = 33.29\text{ lb}\right]$, $\bar{x}^* = 40$ lb, reject H_0

β, $1-\beta$, POWER CURVE, AND *OC* CURVE

16.33 For the milk-substitute study in Problem 16.32, what is the probability of a Type II error if the mean weight-gain of calves on the milk substitute is actually 35 lb rather than 30 lb? What is the power of the test? Assume $\sigma = 12$ lb remains the same whether the calves are fed cow's milk or milk substitute.

Ans. Probability of a Type II error, $\beta(35) = 0.1949$; power of the test, $1 - \beta(35) = 0.8051$

16.34 For the milk-substitute study in Problems 16.32 and 16.33, if $\alpha = 0.01$ had been used in the test, then what would have been the probability of a Type II error if the mean weight-gain was actually 36 lb rather than 30 lb? What is the power of the test? Again assume $\sigma = 12$ lb remains the same whether the calves are fed cow's milk or milk substitute.

Ans. Probability of a Type II error, $\beta(36) = 0.2514$; power of the test, $1 - \beta(36) = 0.7486$

TESTING HYPOTHESES ABOUT THE POPULATION MEAN: STANDARD DEVIATION NOT KNOWN, SMALL SAMPLE FROM A NORMALLY DISTRIBUTED POPULATION

16.35 A medical researcher believes that life at high altitudes may have a long-term effect on heart rate in older women. She knows that the average resting heart rate in all 70-year-old women is normally distributed with an average of $\mu = 74$ beats per minute. To explore the possible effect of altitude, she takes a random sample of 25 women, from a population of 70-year-old women who live above 9,000 feet. She finds that their average heart rate is $\bar{x} = 68$ beats per minute, with $s = 10$ beats per minute. Do a two-tailed test, at $\alpha = 0.05$, of H_0: $\mu = 74$ beats per minute. Give the value of the test statistic. State whether you accept or reject H_0 and the approximate probability (by bracketing) of getting this sample mean given that H_0 is true.

Ans. $t^* = -3.00$, reject H_0, $0.001 < P < 0.01$

16.36 A nutritionist has developed a new sports drink, made of glucose and various ions, and wants to know whether it will improve the running times in 10-kilometer races. He knows that for the large race run in his city last year, the population of running times for 30-year-old men was normally distributed with $\mu = 40$ min. To determine the effect of the sports drink, he takes a random sample of 20 such men who ran this race and has them take specified amounts of his drink before and during their next 10-kilometer race. The results: mean running time $\bar{x} = 38$ min, $s = 5$ min. Do a left-tailed test, at $\alpha = 0.05$, of H_0: $\mu = 40$ min. Give the value of the test statistic. State whether you accept or reject H_0 and the approximate probability (by bracketing) of getting this sample mean given that H_0 is true.

Ans. $t^* = -1.789$, reject H_0, $0.025 < P < 0.05$

16.37 The nutritionist in Problem 16.36 now wants to test his sports drink on women. In last year's 10 km race in his city, the population of running times for 30-year-old women was normally distributed with $\mu = 43$ min. He randomly selects 20 such female runners who ran this race, and has them take specified amounts of his drink before and during their next 10 km race. The results: $\bar{x} = 42$ min, $s = 6$ min. Do a left-tailed test, at $\alpha = 0.05$, of H_0: $\mu = 43$ min. Give the value of the test statistic. State whether you accept or reject H_0 and give the approximate probability (by bracketing) of getting this sample given that H_0 is true.

Ans. $t^* = -0.745$, accept H_0, $P > 0.10$

TESTING HYPOTHESES ABOUT THE VARIANCE AND STANDARD DEVIATION OF A NORMALLY DISTRIBUTED POPULATION

16.38 From Problem 16.28, we know that in mid-August, the body weights of male ground squirrels are normally distributed with $\mu = 400$ g and $\sigma^2 = 10{,}000\ \text{g}^2$. You are interested in knowing whether this weight is more variable when the ground squirrels live in more marginal habitats, where the quality and quantity of food vary more from place to place. You randomly select and weigh 51 male ground squirrels from the more marginal habitats and find: $\bar{x} = 350\,\text{g}$, $s^2 = 11{,}025\,\text{g}^2$. Do a right-tailed test (at $\alpha = 0.05$) of H_0: $\sigma^2 = 10,000\,\text{g}^2$. Give the value of the test statistic. State whether you accept or reject H_0 and give the approximate probability (by bracketing) of getting this sample weight given that H_0 is true.

Ans. $\chi^{2*} = 55.125$, accept H_0, $0.1 < P < 0.5$

16.39 From Problems 16.29 and 16.30, we know that the population of lengths of blue-bellied lizards on the mainland is normally distributed with $\mu = 60\,\text{mm}$ and $\sigma^2 = 225\,\text{mm}^2$. For the sample of lengths ($n = 101$) from the island population in Problem 16.30, we found that $\bar{x} = 65\,\text{mm}$ and $s^2 = 100\,\text{mm}^2$. Do a two-tailed test (at $\alpha = 0.05$) of H_0: $\sigma^2 = 225\,\text{mm}^2$. Give the value of the test statistic. State whether you accept or reject H_0 and the approximate probability (by bracketing) of getting this sample result given that H_0 is true.

Ans. $\chi^{2*} = 44.444$, reject H_0, $P < 0.01$

16.40 For the milk-substitute experiment in Problem 16.32, the variance in weight-gain of one-month-old calves fed on cow's milk is $\sigma^2 = 144\,\text{lb}^2$. You have reason to believe that one-month-old calves who were fed the substitute may be less variable (have a smaller standard deviation) in their weight-gain than the calves who were fed cow's milk. You take a new random sample of 30 one-month-old calves who were fed the milk substitute and measure their weight-gain, getting a sample variance $s^2 = 81\,\text{lb}^2$. Do a left-tailed test, at $\alpha = 0.05$, of H_0: $\sigma = 12\,\text{lb}$. Give the value of the test statistic. State whether you accept or reject H_0, and give the probability (by bracketing) of getting this sample result given that H_0 is true.

Ans. $\chi^{2*} = 16.31$, reject H_0, $0.025 < P < 0.05$

TESTING HYPOTHESES ABOUT THE PROPORTION OF A BINOMIAL POPULATION

16.41 A fisheries biologist wants to know the sex ratio of small-mouth bass in a large lake. He knows that males and females are about equal in number at the time of hatching, but thinks that males do not survive as well as females, and wants to know whether there are, in fact, fewer adult males than females in the lake. He takes a random sample of 100 adult bass to test H_0: $p = 0.5$ against H_1: $p < 0.5$, where p is the proportion of males in the lake. Give the critical-value decision rule for this test when $\alpha = 0.01$.

Ans. Reject H_0 if $z^* < (-z_\alpha = -z_{0.01} = -2.33)$

16.42 For the study of small-mouth bass in Problem 16.41, the biologist finds that 45 of the 100 fish ($\bar{p} = 0.45$) in his sample are males. Do the left-tailed test, at $\alpha = 0.01$, of H_0: $p = 0.5$ using the critical-value decision rule.

Ans. $z^* = -1.01$, accept H_0 because $z^* > -2.33$

16.43 You are interested in knowing the sex ratio of tide-pool sculpins, and have reason to believe that there are fewer males than females. You randomly select a tide pool and examine all the sculpins, finding that 3 are males and 6 are females. Do a left-tailed test (at $\alpha = 0.05$) of H_0: $p = 0.5$. What is the probability of getting this sample result given that the null is true? Do you accept or reject the null hypothesis?

Ans. $P = P(Y \leq 3 | H_0 \text{ is true}) = 0.254$, accept H_0

CHAPTER 17

Two-sample Estimation and Hypothesis Testing

17.1 INDEPENDENT SAMPLES VERSUS PAIRED SAMPLES

In the previous three chapters, we examined one-sample parametric inferential statistics: estimation of population parameters (Chapters 14 and 15) and testing of hypotheses about these parameters (Chapter 16). Now we go on to examine two-sample parametric estimation and hypothesis testing.

In the typical two-sample problem, there are two random variables, X_1 and X_2, that have the same type of unknown parameter (e.g., both have unknown means). The investigator wants to know how these parameters differ, and takes a sample of observations from each variable (population) to use for estimating this unknown difference or for testing hypotheses about it. In such two-sample problems, each specific value in a sample is denoted by a symbol with two subscripts, x_{ij}, where i represents the variable and j the specific value in the sample sequence. Thus, x_{12} is the second value in the sample from variable X_1.

Of the many factors that must be considererd in selecting the appropriate two-sample techniques for inferential problems, one of the most important is whether the samples are independent or paired. The samples are called *independent samples* if taking observations for one sample in no way affects the probabilities of taking observations for the other sample (see Section 9.1 in Volume 1). The samples are called *paired samples* (or *dependent samples* or *matched samples*) if the observations are taken in pairs, which in this context means that an observation for one sample in some way determines an observation taken for the other sample.

To understand these concepts, consider the problem of testing a new pupil-widening liquid for eye examinations that the manufacturer claims will act faster than the standard liquid. This claim can be tested with either independent or paired samples. In the independent case, two separate groups of subjects are randomly selected and one group receives the standard liquid while the other group receives the new liquid. In the paired case, only one group of subjects is selected and each person receives both liquids, the standard liquid in one eye and the new liquid in the other. In the first case, the samples are independent because the taking of a standard-liquid observation in no way affects the taking of a new-liquid observation. In the second case, the samples are paired because an observation for one sample is paired with an observation for the other sample—the samples are not both randomly determined.

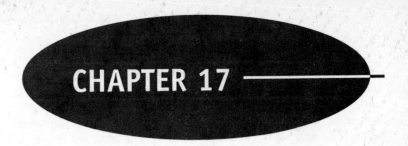

There are advantages and disadvantages to both types of sampling. The independent case, where both samples are randomly determined, is often the only possible sampling technique. In the paired case, the pairing allows better control of extraneous variables (see Section 3.10 in Volume 1). Thus, in the experiment with the two eye liquids, applying both liquids to the same person controls random differences between the samples in extraneous variables related to age, health, or other differences among individuals that may affect their response to the eye liquids.

We will begin our examination of two-sample inferential techniques by dealing with independent samples. Thus, in Sections 17.2 through 17.10, we will present independent-samples methods for estimating the difference between two population means ($\mu_1 - \mu_2$), and for testing hypotheses about this difference. Then, in Sections 17.11 and 17.12, we present comparable methods for paired samples.

17.2 THE OPTIMAL ESTIMATOR OF THE DIFFERENCE BETWEEN TWO POPULATION MEANS ($\mu_1 - \mu_2$)

You are studying the relationships between two normally distributed populations. The first population has an unknown mean μ_1 and a known standard deviation σ_1, and the second has an unknown mean μ_2 and a known standard deviation σ_2. To estimate the difference between the unknown means, $\mu_1 - \mu_2$, you take independent random samples from the two populations, of sizes n_1 and n_2. For these samples, what is the optimal estimator of the difference?

To answer this question we go back to the definition of an estimator. Thus, in Section 14.1 we said that an estimator is any sample statistic $\hat{\theta}$ that gives an estimate of a population parameter θ, and an estimate is any numerical value of an estimator $\hat{\theta}^*$ calculated from a specific sample. These definitions can now be extended to this two-sample case.

Thus, we can say that if $\bar{X}_1$ is the random variable representing the means of random samples of size n_1 drawn from the first population and $\bar{X}_2$ is the random variable representing the means of random samples of size n_2 drawn from the second population, and these samples are independent, then the two-sample statistic $\bar{X}_1 - \bar{X}_2$ is an *estimator of the difference between the population means*, $\mu_1 - \mu_2$. Further, it can be proven mathematically that $\bar{X}_1 - \bar{X}_2$ is the optimal, unbiased estimator (see Section 14.2) of $\mu_1 - \mu_2$.

We can also say that in any specific instance where two such independent samples are taken and the sample means are calculated, $\bar{X}_1 = \bar{x}_1$ and $\bar{X}_2 = \bar{x}_2$, then the difference between the sample means $\bar{x}_1 - \bar{x}_2$ is a *point estimate of the difference between the population means* $\mu_1 - \mu_2$.

17.3 THE THEORETICAL SAMPLING DISTRIBUTION OF THE DIFFERENCE BETWEEN TWO MEANS

In Section 13.6 we said:

> A theoretical sampling distribution of the mean is a probability distribution (discrete or continuous) consisting of the $f(\bar{x})$ values (probabilities or densities) assigned to all the values that $\bar{X}$ can assume.

Similarly, now in the two-sample case we can say that: A probability distribution, discrete or continuous, that gives the assigned probability or density for all values the two-sample statistic $\bar{X}_1 - \bar{X}_2$ can assume is called a *theoretical sampling distribution of the difference between two means* (or a *theoretical sampling distribution of the differences of means*). Further, without attempting proof, we can say that if the random variable X_1 is normally distributed with mean μ_1 and standard deviation σ_1 and the random variable X_2 is normally distributed with mean μ_2 and standard deviation σ_2, and if values of $\bar{X}_1 - \bar{X}_2$ are calculated for all possible combinations of independent random samples of sizes n_1 and n_2 from the two populations, then the sampling distribution of the difference between the two means will be normally distributed with mean

$$\mu_{\bar{x}_1 - \bar{x}_2} = \mu_1 - \mu_2 \tag{17.1}$$

variance

$$\sigma^2_{\bar{x}_1-\bar{x}_2} = \frac{\sigma_1^2}{n_1} + \frac{\sigma_2^2}{n_2} \tag{17.2}$$

and standard deviation

$$\sigma_{\bar{x}_1-\bar{x}_2} = \sqrt{\frac{\sigma_1^2}{n_1} + \frac{\sigma_2^2}{n_2}} \tag{17.3}$$

The standard deviation of a theoretical sampling distribution for a given statistic is called the standard error of that statistic (see Section 13.11), and so equation (17.3) is called the *standard error of the difference between two means.*

17.4 CONFIDENCE INTERVAL FOR THE DIFFERENCE BETWEEN MEANS ($\mu_1 - \mu_2$): STANDARD DEVIATIONS (σ_1 AND σ_2) KNOWN, INDEPENDENT SAMPLES FROM NORMALLY DISTRIBUTED POPULATIONS

If we want to place a population parameter θ within an interval $a \leq \theta \leq b$ with a known degree of certainty, we need: (1) a sample point estimate $\hat{\theta}^*$, (2) a sample statistic that relates the point estimate $\hat{\theta}^*$ to the population parameter θ, and (3) the sampling distribution of that statistic (see Section 14.6). At this point in our discussion of how to estimate the difference between two population means, $\mu_1 - \mu_2$, we know the optimal estimator $\bar{X}_1 - \bar{X}_2$, which yields the point estimate $\bar{x}_1 - \bar{x}_2$ for independent samples of sizes n_1 and n_2, and we know that if X_1 and X_2 are normally distributed, then the sampling distribution of $\bar{X}_1 - \bar{X}_2$ is normally distributed with mean $\mu_{\bar{x}_1-\bar{x}_2} = \mu_1 - \mu_2$ and standard deviation $\sigma_{\bar{x}_1-\bar{x}_2} = \sqrt{\frac{\sigma_1^2}{n_1} + \frac{\sigma_2^2}{n_2}}$.

This tells us that when independent samples are taken from normally distributed populations with unknown means but known standard deviations, then the following Z statistic,

$$Z = \frac{(\bar{X}_1 - \bar{X}_2) - (\mu_1 - \mu_2)}{\sigma_{\bar{x}_1-\bar{x}_2}} = \frac{(\bar{X}_1 - \bar{X}_2) - (\mu_1 - \mu_2)}{\sqrt{\frac{\sigma_1^2}{n_1} + \frac{\sigma_2^2}{n_2}}} \tag{17.4}$$

which can assume specific values

$$z = \frac{(\bar{x}_1 - \bar{x}_2) - (\mu_1 - \mu_2)}{\sqrt{\frac{\sigma_1^2}{n_1} + \frac{\sigma_2^2}{n_2}}} \tag{17.5}$$

satisfies requirements (2) and (3) above. It relates the point estimate $\bar{x}_1 - \bar{x}_2$ to the population parameter $\mu_1 - \mu_2$ and, because $\bar{X}_1 - \bar{X}_2$ is normally distributed, we know that the sampling distribution of this Z statistic is the standard normal distribution.

Therefore, using the same logic sequence that we used to derive the $(1-\alpha)100\%$ confidence interval for μ (see Sections 14.7 through 14.10), we get these four ways of presenting the specific values for the $(1-\alpha)100\%$ confidence interval for $\mu_1 - \mu_2$:

(1) $(\bar{x}_1 - \bar{x}_2) - z_{\alpha/2}\sigma_{\bar{x}_1-\bar{x}_2} \leq \mu_1 - \mu_2 \leq (\bar{x}_1 - \bar{x}_2) + z_{\alpha/2}\sigma_{\bar{x}_1-\bar{x}_2}$

(2) $L = (\bar{x}_1 - \bar{x}_2) - z_{\alpha/2}\sigma_{\bar{x}_1-\bar{x}_2}, \quad U = (\bar{x}_1 - \bar{x}_2) + z_{\alpha/2}\sigma_{\bar{x}_1-\bar{x}_2}$

(3) $[(\bar{x}_1 - \bar{x}_2) - z_{\alpha/2}\sigma_{\bar{x}_1-\bar{x}_2}, (\bar{x}_1 - \bar{x}_2) + z_{\alpha/2}\sigma_{\bar{x}_1-\bar{x}_2}]$

(4) $(\bar{x}_1 - \bar{x}_2) \pm z_{\alpha/2}\sigma_{\bar{x}_1-\bar{x}_2}$

EXAMPLE 17.1 Independent random samples are taken from two normally distributed populations that have unknown means, μ_1 and μ_2, and known standard deviations. For the first population, $\sigma_1 = 0.73$ and the sample values are $n_1 = 25$ and $\bar{x}_1 = 6.9$. For the second population, $\sigma_2 = 0.89$ and the sample values are $n_2 = 20$ and $\bar{x}_2 = 6.7$. What is the 95% confidence interval for $\mu_1 - \mu_2$?

Solution

Using the fourth form of presentation above plus equation (17.3) for the standard error, we get

$$(\bar{x}_1 - \bar{x}_2) \pm z_{\alpha/2}\sqrt{\frac{\sigma_1^2}{n_1} + \frac{\sigma_2^2}{n_2}}$$

From Table A.5: $z_{0.05/2} = 1.96$. Therefore, the 95% confidence interval is

$$(6.9 - 6.7) \pm 1.96\sqrt{\frac{(0.73)^2}{25} + \frac{(0.89)^2}{20}}$$

$$0.2 \pm 0.48$$

17.5 TESTING HYPOTHESES ABOUT THE DIFFERENCE BETWEEN MEANS ($\mu_1 - \mu_2$): STANDARD DEVIATIONS (σ_1 AND σ_2) KNOWN, INDEPENDENT SAMPLES FROM NORMALLY DISTRIBUTED POPULATIONS

Every two-sample hypothesis-testing problem involves a pair of competing statistical hypotheses: the null hypothesis H_0 and the alternative hypothesis H_1, just as was true for one-sample hypothesis-testing (see Sections 16.2 and 16.3). Again, there are two-tailed and one-tailed hypothesis tests, and the one-tailed tests are either right-tailed or left-tailed (see Sections 16.4 and 16.8).

In all cases of two-sample hypothesis testing with independent samples, the null hypothesizes that a specific difference exists between the two means. If we denote this difference with the symbol δ_0 (where δ is the lowercase Greek letter *delta*), then in symbolic form the null hypothesis is written

$$H_0\colon \mu_1 - \mu_2 = \delta_0$$

While δ_0 can be any specific value, typically the interest is in the more general question: Do μ_1 and μ_2 differ? With that question, the null hypothesis is that they do not differ, and so $\delta_0 = 0$. This version of the null hypothesis is written either as $H_0\colon \mu_1 - \mu_2 = 0$ or as $H_0\colon \mu_1 = \mu_2$.

In this brief introduction to two-sample hypothesis testing, we consider only the case where $\delta_0 = 0$, which yields these possible statistical hypotheses for testing:

For a two-tailed test, either

$$H_0\colon \mu_1 - \mu_2 = 0, \qquad H_1\colon \mu_1 - \mu_2 \neq 0$$

or

$$H_0\colon \mu_1 = \mu_2, \qquad H_1\colon \mu_1 \neq \mu_2$$

For a right-tailed test, either

$$H_0\colon \mu_1 - \mu_2 = 0, \qquad H_1\colon \mu_1 - \mu_2 > 0$$

or

$$H_0\colon \mu_1 = \mu_2, \qquad H_1\colon \mu_1 > \mu_2$$

For a left-tailed test, either

$$H_0\colon \mu_1 - \mu_2 = 0, \qquad H_1\colon \mu_1 - \mu_2 < 0$$

or

$$H_0\colon \mu_1 = \mu_2, \qquad H_1\colon \mu_1 < \mu_2$$

In Section 16.3 we said that what is being determined in a statistical hypothesis test is the conditional probability: Given that H_0 is true, what is the probability of getting a point estimate $\hat{\theta}^*$ at least as different from the hypothesized population parameter θ_0 as $\hat{\theta}^*$? Here, where the null hypothesis is that $\mu_1 - \mu_2 = \delta_0 = 0$, we are determining the conditional probability

$$P\,[\text{point estimate at least as different from 0 as } (\bar{x}_1 - \bar{x}_2) | H_0 \text{ is true}]$$

As with one-sample hypothesis-testing (see Section 16.3), determination of the conditional probability requires a test statistic that: (1) allows comparison of the sample point estimate and the null's hypothesized value of the population parameter, and (2) is associated with a probability distribution that is known under the assumption that H_0 is true. For independent samples from two normally distributed populations with known standard deviations, this version of the Z statistic [equation (17.4)] can be used for testing H_0: $\mu_1 - \mu_2 = 0$:

$$Z = \frac{(\bar{X}_1 - \bar{X}_2) - (\mu_1 - \mu_2 = 0)}{\sigma_{\bar{x}_1 - \bar{x}_2}} = \frac{(\bar{X}_1 - \bar{X}_2) - 0}{\sqrt{\dfrac{\sigma_1^2}{n_1} + \dfrac{\sigma_2^2}{n_2}}} \tag{17.6}$$

This statistic satisfies requirement (1) above by comparing $(\bar{x}_1 - \bar{x}_2)$ with 0, and it satisfies requirement (2) because if both X_1 and X_2 are normally distributed then this Z statistic has the standard normal distribution when H_0 is true.

For two-sample tests using this Z statistic, we use the same decision rules for P values and for critical values that were used for one-sample tests with the Z statistic (see Section 16.10). Also, in the following example and then in all subsequent hypothesis-testing problems in this book, *we will again present the solution in the standard sequence of steps from Section 16.16.*

EXAMPLE 17.2 For the conditions in Example 17.1, do a two-tailed test of H_0: $\mu_1 - \mu_2 = 0$, using $\alpha = 0.05$ and a critical-value decision rule.

Solution

(1) H_0: $\mu_1 - \mu_2 = 0$, $\quad H_1$: $\mu_1 - \mu_2 \neq 0$

(2) $\alpha = 0.05$

(3) As both populations are normally distributed, both σ_1 and σ_2 are known, and the samples are independent, we can use the Z statistic [equation (17.6)]. With $\alpha = 0.05$, using the appropriate value from Table A.5, the decision rule is: Reject H_0 if $z^* > (z_{0.05/2} = 1.96)$ or if $z^* < (-z_{0.05/2} = -1.96)$.

(4) The value of the Z statistic is

$$z^* = \frac{(6.9 - 6.7) - 0}{\sqrt{\dfrac{(0.73)^2}{25} + \dfrac{(0.89)^2}{20}}} = 0.810, \quad \text{or } 0.81$$

To determine the P value, we use equation (16.4),

$$P = 2[P(Z \geq (z^* = 0.81) | H_0 \text{ is true})]$$

which is equivalent to

$$P = 2[P(Z > 0.81 | H_0 \text{ is true})]$$

and thus with the appropriate value from Table A.5,

$$P = 2(0.5 - 0.2910) = 0.4180$$

(5) As $-1.96 < z^* < 1.96$, we accept H_0 at the 0.05 level of significance. This result is confirmed by the fact that $P > 0.05$.

17.6 THE ESTIMATED STANDARD ERROR OF THE DIFFERENCE BETWEEN TWO MEANS

To this point in the chapter, we have made the unrealistic assumption that while the two population means are unknown, the two population standard deviations are known. Now, we begin to deal with the more typical situation where both sets of parameters are unknown. Under these conditions, to do estimation and hypothesis testing we need to use an estimate of the standard error of the difference between two means [equation (17.3)] calculated from the samples that is called the *estimated standard error of the difference between two means* (denoted by $S_{\bar{x}_1-\bar{x}_2}$ for the variable and $s_{\bar{x}_1-\bar{x}_2}$ for calculated values). This estimated value is determined in three different ways, depending on sampling conditions and technique requirements.

For independent sampling with replacement, or for sampling from infinite or unknown-sized populations, $S_{\bar{x}_1-\bar{x}_2}$ can be calculated with the formula

$$S_{\bar{x}_1-\bar{x}_2} = \sqrt{\frac{S_1^2}{n_1} + \frac{S_2^2}{n_2}} \tag{17.7}$$

where S_1^2 and S_2^2 are sample variances and n_1 and n_2 are sample sizes. Under these conditions, equation (17.7) is the optimal estimator of $\sigma_{\bar{x}_1-\bar{x}_2}$. This equation can also be written as

$$S_{\bar{x}_1-\bar{x}_2} = \sqrt{S_{\bar{x}_1}^2 + S_{\bar{x}_2}^2} \tag{17.8}$$

where $S_{\bar{x}_1}$ and $S_{\bar{x}_2}$ are standard errors of the mean calculated for each sample.

For independent sampling without replacement from finite populations, in which the population sizes N_1 and N_2 are known and $n > 0.05N$ for both populations, the finite population correction factor should be included in equation (17.7):

$$S_{\bar{x}_1-\bar{x}_2} = \sqrt{\left[\frac{S_1^2}{n_1}\left(\frac{N_1-n_1}{N_1-1}\right)\right] + \left[\frac{S_2^2}{n_2}\left(\frac{N_2-n_2}{N_2-1}\right)\right]} \tag{17.9}$$

A third version of $S_{\bar{x}_1-\bar{x}_2}$ is needed when the techniques being used (see Sections 17.7 and 17.8) require the assumption of equal population standard deviations and variances: $\sigma_1 = \sigma_2$ and $\sigma_1^2 = \sigma_2^2$. This assumption is called the *assumption of homogeneity of variance* (or the *assumption of homoscedasticity*). We will examine later in the chapter how this assumption can be tested (see Sections 17.21 and 17.22), but for now we can say that if the variances can be assumed to be equal ($\sigma_1^2 = \sigma_2^2 = \sigma^2$), then equation (17.3) becomes

$$\sigma_{\bar{x}_1-\bar{x}_2} = \sqrt{\frac{\sigma^2}{n_1} + \frac{\sigma^2}{n_2}} = \sqrt{\sigma^2\left(\frac{1}{n_1} + \frac{1}{n_2}\right)} \tag{17.10}$$

In this equation, the *common population variance* σ^2 can best be estimated by combining the two sample variances in a formula called the *pooled estimate of the common population variance*, which we will denote for the variable with the symbol S_p^2:

$$S_p^2 = \frac{(n_1-1)S_1^2 + (n_2-1)S_1^2}{n_1+n_2-2} \tag{17.11}$$

Substituting this equation for σ^2 in equation (17.10), and modifying for samples, gives

$$S_{\bar{x}_1-\bar{x}_2} = \sqrt{\left[\frac{(n_1-1)S_1^2 + (n_2-1)S_2^2}{n_1+n_2-2}\right]\left(\frac{1}{n_1} + \frac{1}{n_2}\right)} \tag{17.12}$$

or, using the S_p^2 notation,

$$S_{\bar{x}_1-\bar{x}_2} = \sqrt{S_p^2\left(\frac{1}{n_1}+\frac{1}{n_2}\right)} = S_p\sqrt{\frac{1}{n_1}+\frac{1}{n_2}} \tag{17.13}$$

These formulas can assume specific values

$$s_{\bar{x}_1-\bar{x}_2} = \sqrt{\left[\frac{(n_1-1)s_1^2+(n_2-1)s_2^2}{n_1+n_2-2}\right]\left(\frac{1}{n_1}+\frac{1}{n_2}\right)} = s_p\sqrt{\frac{1}{n_1}+\frac{1}{n_2}} \tag{17.14}$$

17.7 CONFIDENCE INTERVAL FOR THE DIFFERENCE BETWEEN MEANS ($\mu_1 - \mu_2$): STANDARD DEVIATIONS NOT KNOWN BUT ASSUMED EQUAL ($\sigma_1 = \sigma_2$), SMALL ($n_1 < 30$ AND $n_2 < 30$) INDEPENDENT SAMPLES FROM NORMALLY DISTRIBUTED POPULATIONS

When small samples ($n_1 < 30$ and $n_2 < 30$) are taken from two normally distributed populations with unknown means μ_1 and μ_2 and unknown standard deviations σ_1 and σ_2, the Z statistic [equation (17.4)] cannot be used to calculate confidence intervals, because the population variances are components of the equation.

If, however, homogeneity of variance (see Section 17.6) can be assumed, then the t distribution (see Section 14.15) can be used to give a theoretically correct, exact solution. The statistic used under these conditions is

$$T = \frac{(\bar{X}_1-\bar{X}_2)-(\mu_1-\mu_2)}{S_{\bar{x}_1-\bar{x}_2}} = \frac{(\bar{X}_1-\bar{X}_2)-(\mu_1-\mu_2)}{\sqrt{\left[\frac{(n_1-1)S_1^2+(n_2-1)S_2^2}{n_1+n_2-2}\right]\left(\frac{1}{n_1}+\frac{1}{n_2}\right)}} \tag{17.15}$$

where the denominator is equation (17.12). This statistic can assume specific values

$$t = \frac{(\bar{x}_1-\bar{x}_2)-(\mu_1-\mu_2)}{s_{\bar{x}_1-\bar{x}_2}} = \frac{(\bar{x}_1-\bar{x}_2)-(\mu_1-\mu_2)}{\sqrt{\left[\frac{(n_1-1)s_1^2+(n_2-1)s_2^2}{n_1+n_2-2}\right]\left(\frac{1}{n_1}+\frac{1}{n_2}\right)}} \tag{17.16}$$

This statistic satisfies the three criteria for interval estimation because there is: (1) a sample point estimate $(\bar{x}_1 - \bar{x}_2)$, (2) a sample statistic that relates the point estimate to the population parameter $(\mu_1 - \mu_2)$, and (3) a known sampling distribution of that statistic under the conditions of this problem (a t distribution with $\nu = n_1 + n_2 - 2$ degrees of freedom).

Using this t statistic and the logic sequence from Sections 14.7 through 14.10, a $(1-\alpha)100\%$ confidence interval for the difference between two population means $\mu_1 - \mu_2$ can be derived. As in Section 17.4, the confidence intervals using this t statistic can be presented in four ways:

(1) $(\bar{x}_1-\bar{x}_2) - t_{\alpha/2,\nu}s_{\bar{x}_1-\bar{x}_2} \leq \mu_1-\mu_2 \leq (\bar{x}_1-\bar{x}_2) + t_{\alpha/2,\nu}s_{\bar{x}_1-\bar{x}_2}$

(2) $L = (\bar{x}_1-\bar{x}_2) - t_{\alpha/2,\nu}s_{\bar{x}_1-\bar{x}_2}, \quad U = (\bar{x}_1-\bar{x}_2) + t_{\alpha/2,\nu}s_{\bar{x}_1-\bar{x}_2}$

(3) $[(\bar{x}_1-\bar{x}_2) - t_{\alpha/2,\nu}s_{\bar{x}_1-\bar{x}_2}, \quad (\bar{x}_1-\bar{x}_2) + t_{\alpha/2,\nu}s_{\bar{x}_1-\bar{x}_2}]$

(4) $(\bar{x}_1-\bar{x}_2) \pm t_{\alpha/2,\nu}s_{\bar{x}_1-\bar{x}_2}$

EXAMPLE 17.3 To investigate how sleep affects memory, a psychologist tested human subjects for retention of details from a documentary movie on arctic wildlife under two conditions: (1) the movie was shown at 7 PM, the subjects had their normal night including sleep, then at 7 AM the next day they were each given a 50-question multiple-choice exam on the movie; (2) the movie was shown at 7 AM, the subjects had their normal day not including sleep, then at 7 PM the same day they were each given the 50-question exam. The samples are independent, with 15 subjects in each group, and the results are: group (1), $n_1 = 15$, $\bar{x}_1 = 37.2$ correct, $s_1^2 = 3.33$; group (2), $n_2 = 15$, $\bar{x}_2 = 35.6$ correct, $s_2^2 = 3.24$. Assuming the populations for the two conditions are normally distributed and that $\sigma_1^2 = \sigma_2^2$, calculate a 95% confidence interval for $\mu_1 - \mu_2$.

Solution

This problem can be solved using equation (17.15). Therefore, the confidence interval is

$$(\bar{x}_1 - \bar{x}_2) \pm t_{\alpha/2,\nu} s_{\bar{x}_1 - \bar{x}_2}$$

where $(\bar{x}_1 - \bar{x}_2) = 37.2 - 35.6 = 1.6$. From Table A.6, for a t distribution with $(\nu = n_1 + n_2 - 2 = 15 + 15 - 2 = 28)$, we find that $t_{\alpha/2,\nu} = t_{0.05/2,28} = 2.048$. Using these values in equation (17.12), we get

$$s_{\bar{x}_1 - \bar{x}_2} = \sqrt{\left[\frac{(14 \times 3.33) + (14 \times 3.24)}{28}\right]\left(\frac{1}{15} + \frac{1}{15}\right)} = 0.6618$$

Therefore, the 95% confidence interval is

$$1.6 \pm (2.048 \times 0.6618)$$
$$1.6 \pm 1.36$$

17.8 TESTING HYPOTHESES ABOUT THE DIFFERENCE BETWEEN MEANS ($\mu_1 - \mu_2$): STANDARD DEVIATIONS NOT KNOWN BUT ASSUMED EQUAL ($\sigma_1 = \sigma_2$), SMALL ($n_1 < 30$ AND $n_2 < 30$) INDEPENDENT SAMPLES FROM NORMALLY DISTRIBUTED POPULATIONS

All sets of statistical hypotheses from Section 17.5 can be used when the population standard deviations and variances are not known but homogeneity of variance can be assumed. To test the null hypothesis, the appropriate sample statistic is the t statistic [equation (17.15)] with $\mu_1 - \mu_2 = 0$,

$$T = \frac{(\bar{X}_1 - \bar{X}_2) - (\mu_1 - \mu_2 = 0)}{\sqrt{\left[\frac{(n_1 - 1)S_1^2 + (n_2 - 1)S_2^2}{n_1 + n_2 - 2}\right]\left(\frac{1}{n_1} + \frac{1}{n_2}\right)}} \tag{17.17}$$

which can assume specific values

$$t = \frac{(\bar{x}_1 - \bar{x}_2) - 0}{\sqrt{\left[\frac{(n_1 - 1)s_1^2 + (n_2 - 1)s_2^2}{n_1 + n_2 - 2}\right]\left(\frac{1}{n_1} + \frac{1}{n_2}\right)}} \tag{17.18}$$

This statistic can be used to determine the required conditional probability,

$$P\,[\text{point estimate at least as different from 0 as } (\bar{x}_1 - \bar{x}_2) | H_0 \text{ is true}]$$

because it meets the two criteria for a test statistic: (1) it allows comparison of the point estimate $(\bar{x}_1 - \bar{x}_2)$ with the null's hypothesized value $(\mu_1 - \mu_2 = 0)$ by means of the distance between them expressed in standard-error units $(s_{\bar{x}_1 - \bar{x}_2})$, and (2) it is associated with a probability distribution (the t distribution with $\nu = n_1 + n_2 - 2$ degrees of freedom) that is known under the assumption that H_0 is true.

The critical-value decision rules developed for one-sample hypothesis-testing (see Section 16.21) can be used here with appropriate degrees of freedom.

EXAMPLE 17.4 For the memory study in Example 17.3, do a two-tailed test of H_0: $\mu_1 - \mu_2 = 0$, using $\alpha = 0.05$ and a critical-value decision rule.

Solution

(1) H_0: $\mu_1 - \mu_2 = 0$, H_1: $\mu_1 - \mu_2 \neq 0$

(2) $\alpha = 0.05$

(3) Because we can assume normally distributed populations, $\sigma_1^2 = \sigma_2^2$, and that the samples are independent, we can use equation (17.17). Thus, with $\alpha = 0.05$, ($\nu = n_1 + n_2 - 2 = 15 + 15 - 2 = 28$), and the appropriate value from Table A.6, the two-tailed decision rule is: Reject H_0 if $t^* > (t_{0.05/2,28} = 2.048)$ or if $t^* < (-t_{0.05/2,28} = -2.048)$.

(4) The value of the t statistic is

$$t^* = \frac{1.6 - 0}{0.6618} = 2.4176, \quad \text{or } 2.418$$

The approximate P value for $\nu = 28$ is in the range [see Example 16.6(*b*)]

$$(2 \times 0.01) < P < (2 \times 0.025) \quad \text{or} \quad 0.02 < P < 0.05$$

(5) As $t^* > 2.048$, we reject H_0 and accept H_1. This result is confirmed by the fact that the approximate P value is in the range $0.02 < P < 0.05$. There is thus a significant difference at the 0.05 level between the two-sample difference and zero, and the results suggest that the sleep group [group (1)] had, on the average, better test scores.

17.9 CONFIDENCE INTERVAL FOR THE DIFFERENCE BETWEEN MEANS ($\mu_1 - \mu_2$): STANDARD DEVIATIONS (σ_1 AND σ_2) NOT KNOWN, LARGE ($n_1 \geq 30$ AND $n_2 \geq 30$) INDEPENDENT SAMPLES FROM ANY POPULATION DISTRIBUTIONS

When large ($n_1 \geq 30$ and $n_2 \geq 30$) independent samples are taken from populations with unknown standard deviations, then either a t or a Z statistic can be used to determine $(1 - \alpha)100\%$ confidence intervals, depending on what can be assumed about the population variances and distributions.

If, under these conditions, homogeneity of variance and normal distributions can be assumed, then, theoretically, exact confidence intervals can be determined with the t statistic [equation (17.15)]. However, in practice, exact t values are typically not available for large samples from tables such as Table A.6. Therefore, for these conditions the choice will usually be between two approximate solutions: (1) using an approximate t value (see Section 14.23), or (2) because sample sizes are large and thus the sample standard deviations are reasonable estimates of their population standard deviations, this Z statistic, which has equation (17.7) in the denominator,

$$Z = \frac{(\bar{X}_1 - \bar{X}_2) - (\mu_1 - \mu_2)}{\sqrt{\frac{S_1^2}{n_1} + \frac{S_2^2}{n_2}}} \tag{17.19}$$

can be used to get an approximate confidence interval.

If large samples are taken, σ_1 and σ_2 are not known, and the populations can not be assumed to be normally distributed, then it is still possible to use equation (17.19) to determine approximate confidence intervals, because under these conditions the central limit theorem (see Sections 13.15 through 13.18) assures that the sampling distributions of $\bar{X}_1$ and $\bar{X}_2$ are approximately normally distributed, and from this it can be proven that equation (17.19) has approximately the standard normal distribution.

EXAMPLE 17.5 Independent random samples are taken from two populations that have unknown standard deviations and unknown distributions. For population (1) with unknown mean μ_1, the sample results are $n_1 = 45$, $\bar{x}_1 = 2.16$, and $s_1 = 0.358$. For population (2) with unknown mean μ_2, the sample results are $n_2 = 40$, $\bar{x}_2 = 1.98$, and $s_2 = 0.352$. What is the approximate 95% confidence interval for $\mu_1 - \mu_2$?

Solution

Because the samples are large ($n_1 \geq 30$ and $n_2 \geq 30$), equation (17.19) can be used with this modification of the confidence interval from Section 17.4, to find an approximate 95% confidence interval

$$(\bar{x}_1 - \bar{x}_2) \pm z_{\alpha/2} s_{\bar{x}_1 - \bar{x}_2}$$

where $(\bar{x}_1 - \bar{x}_2) = 2.16 - 1.98 = 0.18$, and, for equation (17.7),

$$s_{\bar{x}_1 - \bar{x}_2} = \sqrt{\frac{s_1^2}{n_1} + \frac{s_2^2}{n_2}} = \sqrt{\frac{(0.358)^2}{45} + \frac{(0.352)^2}{40}} = 0.0771$$

From Table A.5: $z_{\alpha/2} = z_{0.05/2} = 1.96$. Therefore, the approximate 95% confidence interval for $\mu_1 - \mu_2$ is

$$0.18 \pm (1.96 \times 0.0771)$$
$$0.18 \pm 0.151$$

17.10 TESTING HYPOTHESES ABOUT THE DIFFERENCE BETWEEN MEANS ($\mu_1 - \mu_2$): STANDARD DEVIATIONS (σ_1 AND σ_2) NOT KNOWN, LARGE ($n_1 \geq 30$ AND $n_2 \geq 30$) INDEPENDENT SAMPLES FROM ANY POPULATION DISTRIBUTIONS

When large ($n_1 \geq 30$ and $n_2 \geq 30$) independent samples are taken from populations with unknown standard deviations, then, as with estimation in Section 17.9, either a t or a Z statistic can be used to test hypotheses, depending on what can be assumed about the population variances and distributions. If homogeneity of variance and normal distributions can be assumed, then the same t and Z statistics can be used as in Section 17.9, with $\mu_1 - \mu_2 = 0$. If the populations can not be assumed to be normally distributed, then the Z statistic with $\mu_1 - \mu_2 = 0$ can be used.

EXAMPLE 17.6 For the conditions in Example 17.5, do a two-tailed test of H_0: $\mu_1 - \mu_2 = 0$, using $\alpha = 0.05$ and a critical-value decision rule.

Solution

(1) H_0: $\mu_1 - \mu_2 = 0$, $\quad H_1$: $\mu_1 - \mu_2 \neq 0$

(2) $\alpha = 0.05$

(3) Under the conditions of this problem, the Z statistic [equation (17.19)] can be used with $\mu_1 - \mu_2 = 0$. With $n_1 = 45$, $n_2 = 40$, and $\alpha = 0.05$, the two-tailed decision rule is: Reject H_0 if $z^* > (z_{0.05/2} = 1.96)$ or if $z^* < (-z_{0.05/2} = -1.96)$.

(4) The value of the Z statistic is

$$z^* = \frac{(2.16 - 1.98) - 0}{\sqrt{\frac{(0.358)^2}{45} + \frac{(0.352)^2}{40}}} = 2.334, \quad \text{or } 2.33$$

From Table A.5, the approximate P value [equation (16.4)] is

$$P \approx 2[P(Z \geq (z^* = a)|H_0 \text{ is true})] = 2[P(Z > 2.33)] = 2(0.5 - 0.4901) = 0.0198$$

(5) As $z^* > 1.96$, we reject H_0 and accept H_1. This result is confirmed by the fact that the approximate P value is less than 0.05. There is thus a significant difference at the 0.05 level of significance between the sample difference and zero, and the results suggest that μ_1 is larger than μ_2.

17.11 CONFIDENCE INTERVAL FOR THE DIFFERENCE BETWEEN MEANS ($\mu_1 - \mu_2$): PAIRED SAMPLES

Recall from Section 17.1 that the term "paired samples" means that an observation for one sample in some way determines an observation taken for the other sample. When such paired samples are being used, they require different two-sample estimation techniques from the ones we have described so far in this chapter. When determining a confidence interval for the difference between means from two populations ($\mu_1 - \mu_2$), using paired samples, the appropriate technique is the *paired-samples model*, which has these components: (1) a *random sample of n differences* that has a mean $\bar{d}$, (2) the *population of differences*, with mean μ_d, from which the sample was taken, and (3) a *sampling distribution of the mean difference* for difference-samples of size n, which has a mean $\mu_{\bar{d}} = \mu_d$.

We begin our examination of the paired-samples model with the random variables X_1 and X_2 that describe the two populations under consideration. Paired samples are formed by taking n paired observations of the two variables. If we denote each value in a pair by x_{ij}, where the subscript i refers to the variable and the subscript j refers to the specific value in the sample sequence (see Section 17.1), then the paired sample is

$$(x_{11}, x_{21}), (x_{12}, x_{22}), \ldots, (x_{1n}, x_{2n})$$

Thus, for example, the values (x_{11}, x_{21}) are the first pair of values taken in the sample, a value from variable X_1 and its paired value from variable X_2.

Next, for each of the j pairs, we determine the *difference between* x_{1j} and x_{2j}, which we denote by d_j. Thus

$$x_{11} - x_{21} = d_1, \qquad x_{12} - x_{22} = d_2, \ldots, x_{1n} - x_{2n} = d_n$$

This sample of differences has the mean

$$\bar{d} = \frac{\sum_{j=1}^{n} d_j}{n} \tag{17.20}$$

and the standard deviation

$$s_d = \sqrt{\frac{\sum_{j=1}^{n} (d_j - \bar{d})^2}{n-1}} \tag{17.21}$$

which can be written as this computational formula [comparable to equation (7.28) in Volume 1]:

$$s_d = \sqrt{\frac{\sum_{j=1}^{n} d_j^2 - n\bar{d}^2}{n-1}} \tag{17.22}$$

It is assumed that this sample of differences is a random sample from a population of differences for paired samples of size n that has an unknown mean

$$\mu_d = \frac{\sum_{j=1}^{N} d_j}{N} = \mu_1 - \mu_2 \tag{17.23}$$

and an unknown standard deviation

$$\sigma_d = \sqrt{\frac{\sum_{j=1}^{N} (d_j - \mu_d)^2}{N}} \tag{17.24}$$

It is further assumed that this population of differences is normally distributed.

A theoretical sampling distribution of the mean difference can be formed by taking all possible random samples of size n from the population of differences and calculating a mean difference $\bar{d}$ for each sample. This sampling distribution, described by the random variable $\bar{D}$, is normally distributed because the population of differences is normally distributed (see Section 13.14), and it has the mean

$$\mu_{\bar{d}} = \mu_d = \mu_1 - \mu_2$$

and standard deviation, or *standard error of the mean difference* (see Section 13.11)

$$\sigma_{\bar{d}} = \frac{\sigma_d}{\sqrt{n}} \tag{17.25}$$

When σ_d is unknown, S_d is the optimal estimator of σ_d, and so the *estimated standard error of the mean difference* (see Section 14.3) can be calculated with this formula for specific values:

$$s_{\bar{d}} = \frac{s_d}{\sqrt{n}} \tag{17.26}$$

From this discussion you can see that when the paired-samples model is used, the problem becomes the one-sample problem of how to estimate the mean difference (μ_d) using $\bar{d}$ rather than the two-sample problem of how to estimate the difference between means ($\mu_1 - \mu_2$) using $\bar{x}_1 - \bar{x}_2$. In this one-sample format, therefore, the optimal estimator of μ_d is $\bar{D}$, and any specific sample value $\bar{D} = \bar{d}$ is a point estimate of μ_d.

To calculate a $(1 - \alpha)100\%$ confidence interval for the difference between population means from paired samples, we use this t statistic:

$$T = \frac{\bar{D} - \mu_d}{S_{\bar{d}}} \tag{17.27}$$

which can assume specific values

$$t = \frac{\bar{d} - \mu_d}{s_{\bar{d}}} \tag{17.28}$$

It can be proven that this t statistic has a t distribution with $\nu = n - 1$ degrees of freedom, where $n =$ (number of pairs). Therefore, the exact solution is the one-sample t solution, described in Section 14.21, with $\bar{d}$ substituted for $\bar{x}$, μ_d substituted for μ, and $s_{\bar{d}}$ substituted for $s_{\bar{x}}$. Thus, the exact $(1 - \alpha)100\%$ confidence interval for μ_d can be presented in any one of the following forms:

(1) $\bar{d} - t_{\alpha/2,\nu} s_{\bar{d}} \le \mu_d \le \bar{d} + t_{\alpha/2,\nu} s_{\bar{d}}$

(2) $L = \bar{d} - t_{\alpha/2,\nu} s_{\bar{d}}, \quad U = \bar{d} + t_{\alpha/2,\nu} s_{\bar{d}}$

(3) $[\bar{d} - t_{\alpha/2,\nu} s_{\bar{d}}, \quad \bar{d} + t_{\alpha/2,\nu} s_{\bar{d}}]$

(4) $\bar{d} \pm t_{\alpha/2,\nu} s_{\bar{d}}$

This t solution is the exact solution for any sample size n, but if $n \ge 30$, then this Z statistic,

$$Z = \frac{\bar{D} - \mu_d}{S_{\bar{d}}} \tag{17.29}$$

has approximately the standard normal distribution, because $S_{\bar{d}}$ is a reasonable estimator of $\sigma_{\bar{d}}$. Therefore, when $n \ge 30$, an approximate solution to finding the confidence interval for the difference between two population means is the one-sample Z solution (see Sections 14.10 and 14.23), with $\bar{d}$ substituted for $\bar{x}$, μ_d substituted for μ, and $s_{\bar{d}}$ substituted for $s_{\bar{x}}$. This approximate $(1 - \alpha)100\%$ confidence interval for μ_d can be presented in any one of the following forms:

(1) $\bar{d} - z_{\alpha/2} s_{\bar{d}} \le \mu_d \le \bar{d} + z_{\alpha/2} s_{\bar{d}}$

(2) $L = \bar{d} - z_{\alpha/2} s_{\bar{d}}, \quad U = \bar{d} + z_{\alpha/2} s_{\bar{d}}$

(3) $[\bar{d} - z_{\alpha/2}s_{\bar{d}}, \bar{d} + z_{\alpha/2}s_{\bar{d}}]$

(4) $\bar{d} \pm z_{\alpha/2}s_{\bar{d}}$

EXAMPLE 17.7 Ten male patients with high blood pressure are put on an exercise-and-diet regimen designed to lower blood pressure. The results for each patient for systolic pressure (in mmHg) at the start of the regimen (x_{1j}) and after six months (x_{2j}) are shown in Table 17.1. From this set of data, determine a 99% confidence interval for μ_d (the mean of the differences between the start and six months later), assuming the population of differences is normally distributed.

Table 17.1

Patient j	Start x_{1j} (mmHg)	Six month x_{2j} (mmHg)
1	141	142
2	169	165
3	158	150
4	180	176
5	147	143
6	160	157
7	175	170
8	163	157
9	148	143
10	163	162

Table 17.2

Patient j	Start x_{1j} (mmHg)	Six months x_{2j} (mmHg)	d_j (mmHg)	d_j^2 (mmHg)^2
1	141	142	− 1	1
2	169	165	4	16
3	158	150	8	64
4	180	176	4	16
5	147	143	4	16
6	160	157	3	9
7	175	170	5	25
8	163	157	6	36
9	148	143	5	25
10	163	162	1	1
Σ			39 mmHg	209 (mmHg)^2

$$\bar{d} = \frac{\sum d_j}{n} = \frac{39 \text{ mm}}{10} = 3.9 \text{ mmHg}$$

$$s_d = \sqrt{\frac{\sum d_j^2 - n\bar{d}^2}{n-1}} = \sqrt{\frac{209 \text{ (mmHg)}^2 - [10 \times (3.9 \text{ mmHg})^2]}{10-1}} = 2.5144 \text{ mmHg}$$

$$s_{\bar{d}} = \frac{s_d}{\sqrt{n}} = \frac{2.5144 \text{ mmHg}}{\sqrt{10}} = 0.7951 \text{ mmHg}$$

Solution

The exact solution is

$$\bar{d} \pm t_{\alpha/2,\nu} s_{\bar{d}}$$

To determine $\bar{d}$ and $s_{\bar{d}}$, we add two columns to Table 17.1: a difference column ($d_j = x_{1j} - x_{2j}$) and a difference-squared column (d_j^2). The modified table with these columns and the resulting calculations of $\bar{d}$, s_d, and $s_{\bar{d}}$, using equations (17.20), (17.22), and (17.26), are shown in Table 17.2.

From Table A.6 with $\nu = 10 - 1 = 9$, $t_{0.01/2,9} = 3.250$. Therefore, the 99% confidence interval is

$$3.9 \text{ mmHg} \pm (3.250 \times 0.7951 \text{ mmHg})$$
$$3.9 \text{ mmHg} \pm 2.58 \text{ mmHg}$$

17.12 TESTING HYPOTHESES ABOUT THE DIFFERENCE BETWEEN MEANS ($\mu_1 - \mu_2$): PAIRED SAMPLES

Every two-sample hypothesis-testing problem involving paired samples has a pair of statistical hypotheses, H_0 and H_1, just as with one-sample hypothesis-testing and independent-samples hypothesis-testing, and, as before, there are both two-tailed and one-tailed tests. In these tests, the null hypothesis is that a specific difference δ_0 exists between the two means, $\mu_1 - \mu_2$ (see Section 17.5). For paired samples, $\mu_1 - \mu_2 = \mu_d$ [equation (17.23)], and so H_0 can be written symbolically either as H_0: $\mu_1 - \mu_2 = \delta_0$ or as H_0: $\mu_d = \delta_0$.

Again, as in Section 17.5, we will only consider the case where $\delta_0 = 0$, which yields these possible statistical hypotheses for testing:

For two-tailed tests, either

$$H_0\colon \mu_1 - \mu_2 = 0, \qquad H_1\colon \mu_1 - \mu_2 \neq 0$$

or

$$H_0\colon \mu_d = 0, \qquad H_1\colon \mu_d \neq 0$$

For right-tailed tests, either

$$H_0\colon \mu_1 - \mu_2 = 0, \qquad H_1\colon \mu_1 - \mu_2 > 0$$

or

$$H_0\colon \mu_d = 0, \qquad H_1\colon \mu_d > 0$$

For left-tailed tests, either

$$H_0\colon \mu_1 - \mu_2 = 0, \qquad H_1\colon \mu_1 - \mu_2 < 0$$

or

$$H_0\colon \mu_d = 0, \qquad H_1\colon \mu_d < 0$$

When using paired samples to test H_0: $\mu_d = 0$, if it can be assumed that the population of differences is normally distributed, then the exact solution can be found with this t statistic [equation (17.27)] with $\mu_d = 0$:

$$T = \frac{\bar{D} - (\mu_d = 0)}{S_{\bar{d}}} \tag{17.30}$$

which can assume specific values

$$t = \frac{\bar{d} - (\mu_d = 0)}{s_{\bar{d}}} \tag{17.31}$$

This statistic can be used to determine this version of the required conditional probability statement (see Section 17.5)

$$P\text{ (point estimate at least as different from 0 as } \bar{d}|H_0 \text{ is true)}$$

because it meets the two criteria (see Section 16.3) of a test statistic: (1) it compares $\bar{d}$ and $\mu_d = 0$ by means of the distance between them expressed in standard-errror units, and (2) it has a known probability distribution (the t distribution with $\nu = n - 1$ degrees of freedom, where $n =$ number of pairs) under the assumption that H_0 is true. For this hypothesis test, P values and decision rules used for one-sample hypothesis-testing (see Sections 16.20 and 16.21) can be used with appropriate degrees of freedom.

When $n \geq 30$, an approximate solution for paired-samples hypothesis-testing can be found using the Z statistic [equation (17.29)] with $\mu_d = 0$:

$$Z = \frac{\bar{D} - (\mu_d = 0)}{S_{\bar{d}}} \tag{17.32}$$

which can assume specific values

$$z = \frac{\bar{d} - (\mu_d = 0)}{s_{\bar{d}}} \tag{17.33}$$

This Z statistic also meets the two criteria of a test statistic: (1) it compares $\bar{d}$ and zero, and (2) it has approximately the standard normal distribution under the assumption that H_0 is true. For this hypothesis test, the P values and decision rules for one-sample hypothesis-testing (see Sections 16.6 and 16.10) can be used.

EXAMPLE 17.8 For the blood-pressure study in Example 17.7, do a right-tailed test of H_0: $\mu_d = 0$, using $\alpha = 0.01$ and a critical-value decision rule.

Solution

(1) H_0: $\mu_d = 0$, $\quad H_1$: $\mu_d > 0$

(2) $\alpha = 0.01$

(3) As the samples are paired and we are assuming that the population of differences (d_j) is normally distributed, we can use the t statistic [equation (17.30)]. Thus, with $- 0$, $\alpha = 0.01$, $\nu = n - 1 = 10 - 1 = 9$, and the appropriate value from Table A.6, the right-tailed decision rule is: Reject H_0 if $t^* > (t_{0.01,9} = 2.821)$.

(4) The value of the t statistic is

$$t^* = \frac{3.9 \text{ mmHg}}{0.7951 \text{ mmHg}} = 4.9050, \quad \text{or } 4.905$$

The P value for $\nu = 9$ is in the range $P < 0.0005$.

(5) As $t^* > 2.821$, we reject H_0 and accept H_1. This result is confirmed by the fact that the P value is less than 0.01. Thus we can say that the evidence evaluated at the 0.01 level of significance indicates that, on the average, there was a decrease in systolic pressure after six months on the diet–exercise regimen.

17.13 ASSUMPTIONS OF TWO-SAMPLE PARAMETRIC ESTIMATION AND HYPOTHESIS TESTING ABOUT MEANS

In Section 16.24, we examined the assumptions of one-sample parametric estimation and hypothesis testing. We indicated there that these assumptions are the defining properties of the mathematical models that form the base of each technique: the required characteristics of the populations being studied and of the samples that are taken from them. We said that the techniques are called parametric because they estimate parameters and test hypotheses about parameters, and because many of their assumptions deal with parameters. The two-sample estimation and hypothesis-testing techniques for differences between means, described in Sections 17.4 through 17.12, are called parametric techniques for the same reasons and, as you have seen, their mathematical models have many of the same assumptions as the one-sample models. In addition, there are new assumptions unique to two-sample problems.

For the model in Sections 17.4 and 17.5, it is assumed that the two populations being studied are normally distributed interval-level or ratio-level measurements, and that the population standard deviations are known. It is assumed that the samples are independent (see Section 17.1) random samples of any sizes. All other sampling assumptions that apply to the model in Section 16.5 also apply here, and to other models to be discussed in this section.

For the model in Sections 17.7 and 17.8, it is again assumed that both populations being studied are normally distributed interval-level or ratio-level measurements, but now while the population standard deviations are not known they, and the variances, are assumed to be equal: homogeneity of variance (see Section 17.6). The samples are again assumed to be independent random samples of any size.

The models in Sections 17.9 and 17.10 have in common the assumption that large ($n_1 \geq 30$ and $n_2 \geq 30$) independent samples have been taken from populations of interval-level or ratio-level measurements, and that the population standard deviations are not known. If homogeneity of variance and normal distributions can be assumed, then exact or approximate t techniques or approximate Z techniques can be used for estimation and hypothesis testing. If normality can not be assumed under these conditions, then there is an approximate technique based on the central limit theorem.

The model in Sections 17.11 and 17.12 has quite different assumptions from the previous two-sample models. Now, because the samples are paired, we can no longer assume independent random samples. However, by converting each pair to a difference and assuming the resulting sample of differences is a random sample from a normally distributed population of differences, we can use an exact one-sample t solution for estimation and hypothesis testing. Alternatively, if (number of differences) ≥ 30, we can assume that $s_{\bar{d}}$ is a reasonable estimate of $\sigma_{\bar{d}}$ and therefore use an approximate Z solution.

17.14 WHEN THE ASSUMPTIONS ARE VIOLATED

In discussing the assumptions of one-sample parametric estimation of means and hypothesis testing about means (see Section 16.24) we indicated that, aside from a variety of sampling requirements, there were three fundamental considerations: (1) whether the population could be assumed to be normally distributed, (2) whether σ was known, and (3) the size of the sample. Now, in the more complex two-sample situation, there are four fundamental considerations: (1) whether both populations can be assumed to be normally distributed, (2) whether both σ_1 and σ_2 are known, (3) whether it can be assumed that $\sigma_1 = \sigma_2$ and thus $\sigma_1^2 = \sigma_2^2$ (homogeneity of variance), and (4) the size of both samples.

The first step with two-sample problems, as with one-sample problems, is to analyze the sample data for how well they satisfy the assumptions. In Section 16.25 we gave ways for evaluating the normal-distribution assumption. In Section 17.21 we will show how to test for homogeneity of variance, but we can now say that independent-samples t techniques are considered more robust to assumption violations than is the homogeneity test, particularly if the sample sizes are equal, $n_1 = n_2$. The homogeneity assumption does not apply to paired-samples tests.

If it is determined that there are severe deviations from the assumptions, then, as in one-sample techniques, the next step is to attempt a transformation of the data (see Section 16.25). Again, there are no set rules for transformations but many suggestions are appropriate for different violations. Thus, for example, if the distributions are positively skewed, then a logarithmic transformation will tend to both make the distributions more symmetric and also to equalize the variances. In general, if the standard deviations are proportional to the means, then a logarithmic transformation may work, and if the variances are proportional to the means, then a square root transformation should be tried. The square root transformation can improve both normality and homogeneity of variance for counted data. If the distributions are negatively skewed, or the variances tend to decrease as the means increase, then squaring the data values should be tried.

Again, as with one-sample techniques, if the transformation is successful, then estimation and hypothesis testing can be done on the transformed data. Again, this fact must be indicated in the presentation of the results.

If the original data seriously violate the assumptions of all available parametric procedures, and no transformation can be found to satisfy the assumptions, then it will not be possible to determine the $(1-\alpha)100\%$ confidence interval for $\mu_1 - \mu_2$ or to test H_0: $\mu_1 - \mu_2 = 0$. Again, however, as with one-sample procedures, other aspects of the data can be analyzed with nonparametric procedures (see Chapter 20).

17.15 COMPARING INDEPENDENT-SAMPLING AND PAIRED-SAMPLING TECHNIQUES ON PRECISION AND POWER

In many situations, there will be a choice between paired-sampling techniques and independent-sampling techniques for solving estimation and hypothesis-testing problems. In general, if correct pairing can be achieved (see Section 17.1) and the number of pairs n that would be used is equal to the size of each independent sample that would be used ($n_1 = n_2 = n$), then under these conditions, paired-sampling techniques are preferable. This is because, for the same α level, the confidence interval for paired values will be more precise (narrower, see Section 14.11), and also a paired-samples hypothesis test will be more powerful than a comparable independent-samples test (more likely to reject a false null, see Section 16.18).

17.16 THE *F* STATISTIC

Suppose you are studying the relationships between two normally distributed populations. The first has unknown parameters μ_1, σ_1^2, and σ_1, and the second has unknown parameters μ_2, σ_2^2, and σ_2. To make statistical inferences about comparisons between these parameters, you take independent random samples from the two populations, of sizes n_1 and n_2. From this chapter you know that to make inferences comparing the two population means, you would estimate and test hypotheses about their differences, $\mu_1 - \mu_2$, using the sample difference $\bar{x}_1 - \bar{x}_2$ and either t or Z techniques. But what statistical techniques would you use under the conditions of this problem to make inferences comparing the two population variances, σ_1^2 and σ_2^2?

To compare population variances under these conditions, statistical inferences are not made about the differences between the variances, $\sigma_1^2 - \sigma_2^2$, but rather about the *ratio of the variances*, σ_1^2/σ_2^2. And, as S_1^2 is the optimal estimator of σ_1^2 and S_2^2 is the optimal estimator of σ_2^2 (see Section 14.2), so also is the ratio S_1^2/S_2^2 the optimal estimator of σ_1^2/σ_2^2. Thus, any specific ratio of sample variances $S_1^2/S_2^2 = s_1^2/s_2^2$ is a point estimate of the population ratio σ_1^2/σ_2^2.

To estimate and test hypotheses about σ_1^2/σ_2^2, we need a sample statistic that relates any specific point estimate s_1^2/s_2^2 to σ_1^2/σ_2^2, and has a known sampling distribution. For this we will use this F statistic

$$F = \frac{S_1^2/\sigma_1^2}{S_2^2/\sigma_2^2} = \frac{S_1^2\sigma_2^2}{S_2^2\sigma_1^2} \tag{17.34}$$

which can assume specific values

$$f = \frac{s_1^2/\sigma_1^2}{s_2^2/\sigma_2^2} = \frac{s_1^2\sigma_2^2}{s_2^2\sigma_1^2} \tag{17.35}$$

This statistic, for the sampling conditions we have posed, has a known sampling distribution called the *F distribution* (see Section 17.17).

In this F statistic it is arbitrary which population and its sample is labeled 1, and thus placed in the numerator. However, it is easier to use the critical-values tables for the F distribution (see Section 17.19) when the larger sample variance is labeled S_1^2 and placed in the numerator, and so some statistics books recommend this procedure. In this book, we use techniques that do not require placing the larger sample variance in the numerator.

17.17 THE F DISTRIBUTION

It is known from sampling theory that:

> Given two independent chi-square random variables (see Sections 13.2 and 15.2), X_1^2 and X_2^2, then the ratio of these continuous variables with each divided by its respective degrees of freedom, ν_1 and ν_2, is a continuous F *random variable*
>
> $$F = \frac{X_1^2/\nu_1}{X_2^2/\nu_2} \tag{17.36}$$
>
> that has an F distribution with two forms of degrees of freedom: ν_1 for the numerator of the F ratio, and ν_2 for the denominator. This statistic can assume specific values
>
> $$f = \frac{\chi_1^2/\nu_1}{\chi_2^2/\nu_2} \tag{17.37}$$

Futhermore, for the sampling conditions presented in Section 17.16, independent sampling from normal distributions, the following variables are independent chi-square variables (see Section 15.2):

$$X_1^2 = \frac{(n_1 - 1)S_1^2}{\sigma_1^2}, \quad \text{with } \nu_1 = n_1 - 1 \text{ degrees of freedom}$$

$$X_2^2 = \frac{(n_2 - 1)S_2^2}{\sigma_2^2}, \quad \text{with } \nu_2 = n_2 - 1 \text{ degrees of freedom}$$

Therefore, this F statistic, which is both equations (17.34) and (17.36),

$$F = \frac{X_1^2/\nu_1}{X_2^2/\nu_2} = \frac{\dfrac{(n_1 - 1)S_1^2}{\sigma_1^2(n_1 - 1)}}{\dfrac{(n_2 - 1)S_2^2}{\sigma_2^2(n_2 - 1)}} = \frac{S_1^2/\sigma_1^2}{S_2^2/\sigma_2^2} = \frac{S_1^2\sigma_2^2}{S_2^2\sigma_1^2}$$

has an F distribution with numerator degrees of freedom $\nu_1 = n_1 - 1$ and denominator degrees of freedom $\nu_2 = n_2 - 1$. You can see from this statistic why the F distribution is also known as the *variance ratio distribution*.

As with all previous probability distributions, the F distribution is defined by a specific and unique probability function. The continuous probability density function for the F distribution, which we will not derive, is

$$f(f) = cf^{\left(\frac{\nu_1}{2}\right)-1}\left(1 + \frac{\nu_1 f}{\nu_2}\right)^{-\left(\frac{\nu_1+\nu_2}{2}\right)} \tag{17.38}$$

where $f = \dfrac{\chi_1^2/\nu_1}{\chi_2^2/\nu_2} = \dfrac{s_1^2/\sigma_1^2}{s_2^2/\sigma_2^2}$

ν_1 = the degrees of freedom for the numerator of the F statistic

ν_2 = the degrees of freedom for the denominator of the F statistic

c = a constant that is a function of ν_1 and ν_2 that is needed to make the total area under the F distribution equal to 1

While the t and chi-square distributions have the single degrees-of-freedom parameter ν (see Sections 14.15 and 15.2), the F distribution has two degrees-of-freedom parameters, ν_1 and ν_2. This order of presentation, with the numerator degrees of freedom stated first, is a necessary convention for reasons that will soon become apparent.

As with previous probability distributions, the F distribution is not just one distribution but a family of continuous probability distributions, one for each combination of positive integer values of degrees of freedom. These infinitely many distributions are known collectively as the F distribution. Two such distributions (one for $\nu_1 = 2$, $\nu_2 = 2$ and the other for $\nu_1 = 9$, $\nu_2 = 9$) are shown superimposed in Fig. 17-1.

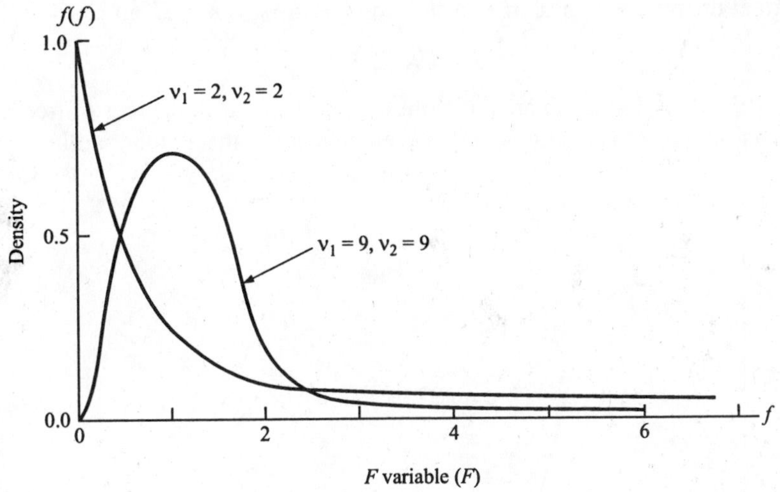

Fig. 17-1

Because an F random variable is the ratio of two independent chi-square random variables, each divided by its respective degrees of freedom, it is not surprising that the F distribution (see Fig. 17-1) resembles the chi-square distribution (see Fig. 15-1). Both distributions are continuous, asymmetric (positively skewed) distributions with only positive values. Also, as the chi-square distribution becomes more and more symmetric as ν increases, so does the F distribution as both ν_1 and ν_2 increase. The mean of the F distribution is

$$\mu = \frac{\nu_2}{\nu_2 - 2}, \qquad \text{for } \nu_2 > 2 \tag{17.39}$$

which approaches 1 as ν_2 increases. The variance of the F distribution is

$$\sigma^2 = \frac{2\nu_2^2(\nu_1 + \nu_2 - 2)}{\nu_1(\nu_2 - 2)^2(\nu_2 - 4)}, \qquad \text{for } \nu_2 > 4 \tag{17.40}$$

and the standard deviation is $\sqrt{\sigma^2}$.

The F distribution is named after the English statistician *Ronald Aylmer Fisher* (1890–1962), who derived and tabulated this distribution as part of his development of the *analysis of variance* (see Chapter 18). It was originally called the variance-ratio distribution, but later Fisher's fellow statisticians renamed it the F distribution in his honor. Besides the F distribution and the analysis of variance, Fisher made many other important contributions to statistics, including pioneering work on experimental design, correlation (see Chapter 19), and the theory of hypothesis testing.

17.18 CRITICAL VALUES OF THE F DISTRIBUTION

In Section 15.3 we stated for the random variable

$$X^2 = \frac{(n-1)S^2}{\sigma^2}$$

which has a chi-square distribution with $\nu = n - 1$ when sampling is done from a normal distribution, that [equation (15.4)]

$$P(X^2 > \chi^2_{\alpha,\nu}) = \alpha$$

Similarly, we now state for the random variable F [equations (17.34) and (17.36)] which, for independent sampling from normal distributions, has an F distribution with $\nu_1 = n_1 - 1$ and $\nu_2 = n_2 - 1$, that

$$P(F > f_{\alpha,\nu_1,\nu_2}) = \alpha \tag{17.41}$$

where f_{α,ν_1,ν_2} denotes the critical value in an F distribution with ν_1 and ν_2 degrees of freedom that has α on its right and $1 - \alpha$ on its left. This relationship between area and critical value is illustrated in Fig. 17-2.

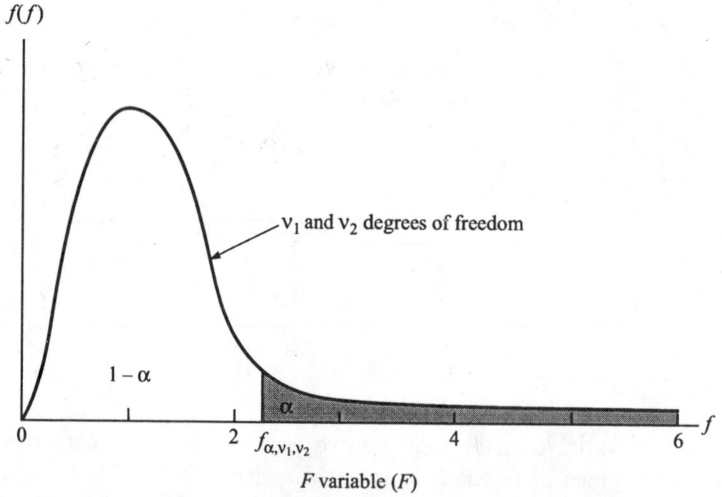

Fig. 17-2

In Section 15.3 we further stated for the random variable X^2, which has an asymmetric distribution, that [equation (15.5)]

$$P(X^2 < \chi^2_{1-\alpha,\nu}) = \alpha$$

Similarly, we now state for the random variable F that

$$P(F < f_{1-\alpha,\nu_1,\nu_2}) = \alpha \tag{17.42}$$

where $f_{1-\alpha,\nu_1,\nu_2}$ denotes the critical value in an F distribution with ν_1 and ν_2 degrees of freedom that has $1 - \alpha$ on its right and α on its left. This relationship between area and critical value is illustrated in Fig. 17-3.

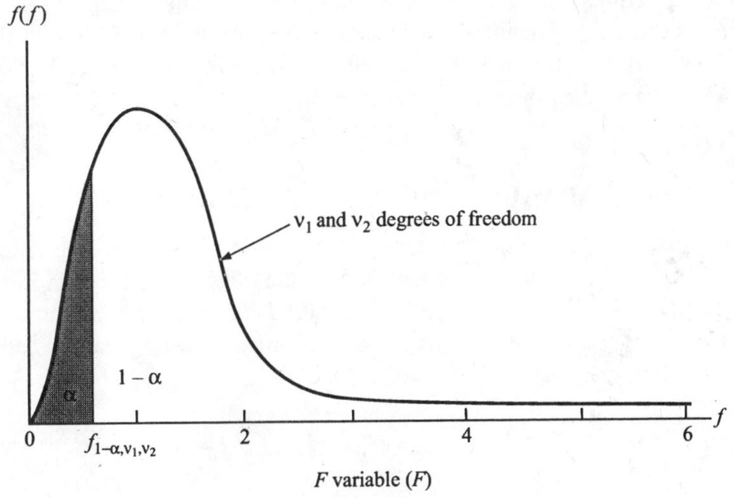

Fig. 17-3

The relationship between $f_{1-\alpha,\nu_1,\nu_2}$ and f_{α,ν_2,ν_1} is reciprocal,

$$f_{1-\alpha,\nu_1,\nu_2} = \frac{1}{f_{\alpha,\nu_2,\nu_1}} \tag{17.43}$$

and so is known as the *reciprocal rule* (or *reciprocal property*) for $f_{1-\alpha,\nu_1,\nu_2}$. Note that the reciprocal f_α value has the order of the degrees of freedom reversed: (ν_1, ν_2) becomes (ν_2, ν_1). This reversal will be important when we begin to use Table A.8 in the Appendix: *Critical Values of the F Distribution* (see Section 17.19).

Finally, in Section 15.3, we stated for the random variable X^2 that

$$P(\chi^2_{1-\alpha/2,\nu} \leq X^2 \leq \chi^2_{\alpha/2,\nu}) = 1 - \alpha$$

Similarly, we now state for the random variable F that

$$P(f_{1-\alpha/2,\nu_1,\nu_2} \leq F \leq f_{\alpha/2,\nu_1,\nu_2}) = 1 - \alpha \tag{17.44}$$

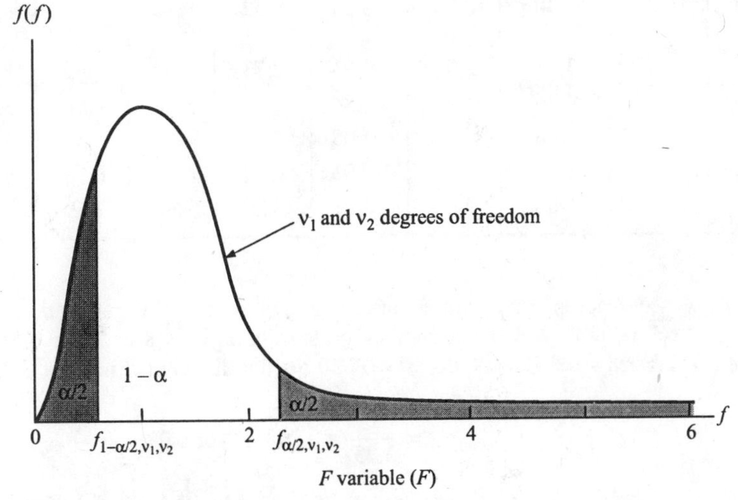

Fig. 17-4

where $f_{\alpha/2,\nu_1,\nu_2}$ denotes the critical value in an F distribution with ν_1 and ν_2 degrees of freedom that has the area $\alpha/2$ on its right, and $f_{1-\alpha/2,\nu_1,\nu_2}$ denotes the critical value for the same F distribution that has the area $\alpha/2$ on its left. This relationship between areas and critical values is illustrated in Fig. 17-4. The reciprocal rule [equation (17.43)] also applies to two-tailed values.

17.19 TABLE A.8: CRITICAL VALUES OF THE *F* DISTRIBUTION

Table A.8 gives critical f_{α,ν_1,ν_2} values for selected F distributions, and five α levels (0.100, 0.050, 0.025, 0.010, 0.005). The F distributions are identified by the degrees of freedom in their numerator (top columns: $\nu_1 = 1, \ldots, 10, 12, 15, 20, 24, 30, 40, 60, 120, \infty$) and denominator (side column: $\nu_2 = 1, \ldots, 30, 40, 60, 120, \infty$). Table A.8 gives only f_α values, but $f_{1-\alpha}$ values can be found by using the reciprocal rule [equation (17.43)].

EXAMPLE 17.9 Use Table A.8 to find $f_{\alpha,\nu_1,\nu_2} = f_{0.050,7,8}$ and $f_{1-\alpha,\nu_1,\nu_2} = f_{1-0.050,7,8}$.

Solution

A section of Table A.8 that includes the circled solutions to this problem is shown in Table 17.3. To find $f_{0.050,7,8}$, go to the column labeled $\nu_1 = 7$ and then down this column to the five-line (one for each α level) row labeled $\nu_2 = 8$, where for $\alpha = 0.050$ we find the circled number 3.50. Therefore, $f_{0.050,7,8} = 3.50$ is the critical value in the F distribution with $\nu_1 = 7$ and $\nu_2 = 8$ that has $\alpha = 0.050$ on its right.

To find $f_{1-0.050,7,8}$, we use equation (17.43). Here

$$f_{1-0.050,7,8} = \frac{1}{f_{0.050,8,7}}$$

Table 17.3

		ν_1								
ν_2	α	1	2	3	4	5	6	7	8	9
7	0.100	3.59	3.26	3.07	2.96	2.88	2.83	2.78	2.75	2.72
	0.050	5.59	4.74	4.35	4.12	3.97	3.87	3.79	(3.73)	3.68
	0.025	8.07	6.54	5.89	5.52	5.29	5.12	4.99	4.90	4.82
	0.010	12.25	9.55	8.45	7.85	7.46	7.19	6.99	6.84	6.72
	0.005	16.24	12.40	10.88	10.05	9.52	9.16	8.89	8.68	8.51
8	0.100	3.46	3.11	2.92	2.81	2.73	2.67	2.62	2.59	2.56
	0.050	5.32	4.46	4.07	3.84	3.69	3.58	(3.50)	3.44	3.39
	0.025	7.57	6.06	5.42	5.05	4.82	4.65	4.53	4.43	4.36
	0.010	11.26	8.65	7.59	7.01	6.63	6.37	6.18	6.03	5.91
	0.005	14.69	11.04	9.60	8.81	8.30	7.95	7.69	7.50	7.34

To find $f_{0.050,8,7}$ we accept that with ν_2 stated first, it is now, by convention (see Section 17.17), considered to be "ν_1" in Table A.8. Therefore, we go to column $\nu_1 = 8$ in Table 17.3, and then down the column to the row labeled $\nu_2 = 7$, where for $\alpha = 0.050$ we find the circled number 3.73. Thus,

$$f_{1-0.050,7,8} = \frac{1}{3.73} = 0.2681, \quad \text{or } 0.27$$

Therefore, $f_{1-0.050,7,8} = 0.27$ is the critical value in the F distribution with $\nu_1 = 7$ and $\nu_2 = 8$ that has $\alpha = 0.050$ on its left.

17.20 CONFIDENCE INTERVAL FOR THE RATIO OF VARIANCES (σ_1^2/σ_2^2): PARAMETERS (σ_1^2, σ_1, μ_1 AND σ_2^2, σ_2, μ_2) NOT KNOWN, INDEPENDENT SAMPLES FROM NORMALLY DISTRIBUTED POPULATIONS

For independent random sampling from normal distributions, we know that the random variable F [equations (17.34) and (17.36)] has an F distribution with $\nu_1 = n_1 - 1$ and $\nu_2 = n_2 - 1$ (see Section 17.17). From equation (17.44), we know that for such an F distribution,

$$P(f_{1-\alpha/2,\nu_1,\nu_2} \leq F \leq f_{\alpha/2,\nu_1,\nu_2}) = 1 - \alpha$$

From this probability statement, we can derive a confidence interval for the ratio of variances σ_1^2/σ_2^2. First, equation (17.34) is placed in equation (17.44):

$$P\left(f_{1-\alpha/2,\nu_1,\nu_2} \leq \frac{S_1^2\sigma_2^2}{S_2^2\sigma_1^2} \leq f_{\alpha/2,\nu_1,\nu_2}\right) = 1 - \alpha$$

Multiplying each term by S_2^2/S_1^2 we get

$$P\left[\frac{S_2^2}{S_1^2}(f_{1-\alpha/2,\nu_1,\nu_2}) \leq \frac{\sigma_2^2}{\sigma_1^2} \leq \frac{S_2^2}{S_1^2}(f_{\alpha/2,\nu_1,\nu_2})\right] = 1 - \alpha$$

Inverting each term we get

$$P\left[\frac{S_1^2}{S_2^2}\left(\frac{1}{f_{1-\alpha/2,\nu_1,\nu_2}}\right) \geq \frac{\sigma_1^2}{\sigma_2^2} \geq \frac{S_1^2}{S_2^2}\left(\frac{1}{f_{\alpha/2,\nu_1,\nu_2}}\right)\right] = 1 - \alpha$$

which can be written

$$P\left[\frac{S_1^2}{S_2^2}\left(\frac{1}{f_{\alpha/2,\nu_1,\nu_2}}\right) \leq \frac{\sigma_1^2}{\sigma_2^2} \leq \frac{S_1^2}{S_2^2}\left(\frac{1}{f_{1-\alpha/2,\nu_1,\nu_2}}\right)\right] = 1 - \alpha$$

Finally, using the reciprocal rule [equation (17.43)],

$$P\left[\frac{S_1^2}{S_2^2}\left(\frac{1}{f_{\alpha/2,\nu_1,\nu_2}}\right) \leq \frac{\sigma_1^2}{\sigma_2^2} \leq \frac{S_1^2}{S_2^2}\left(\frac{1}{\frac{1}{f_{\alpha/2,\nu_2,\nu_1}}}\right)\right] = 1 - \alpha$$

and thus

$$P\left[\frac{S_1^2}{S_2^2}\left(\frac{1}{f_{\alpha/2,\nu_1,\nu_2}}\right) \leq \frac{\sigma_1^2}{\sigma_2^2} \leq \frac{S_1^2}{S_2^2}(f_{\alpha/2,\nu_2,\nu_1})\right] = 1 - \alpha \tag{17.45}$$

Under the conditions of independent random sampling from normally distributed populations, the F statistic [equations (17.34) and (17.36)] satisfies the criteria for interval estimation (see Section 14.6) because there is: (1) a sample point estimate (s_1^2/s_2^2) of the population parameter (σ_1^2/σ_2^2), (2) a sample statistic (F) that relates the point estimate to the population parameter, and (3) a known sampling distribution under these conditions (the F distribution with $\nu_1 = n_1 - 1$ and $\nu_2 = n_2 - 1$).

We know from equation (17.45) that if specific values of the random interval

$$\frac{S_1^2}{S_2^2}\left(\frac{1}{f_{\alpha/2,\nu_1,\nu_2}}\right) \leq \frac{\sigma_1^2}{\sigma_2^2} \leq \frac{S_1^2}{S_2^2}(f_{\alpha/2,\nu_2,\nu_1})$$

are calculated for each sample, then $(1 - \alpha)100\%$ of these specific intervals

$$\frac{s_1^2}{s_2^2}\left(\frac{1}{f_{\alpha/2,\nu_1,\nu_2}}\right) \leq \frac{\sigma_1^2}{\sigma_2^2} \leq \frac{s_1^2}{s_2^2}(f_{\alpha/2,\nu_2,\nu_1})$$

will contain σ_1^2/σ_2^2. Therefore, any such specific interval is a $(1-\alpha)100\%$ confidence interval for σ_1^2/σ_2^2. As with the $(1-\alpha)100\%$ confidence interval for a single population variance (see Section 15.6), this confidence interval for the ratio between two population variances can be written in three forms:

(1) $$\frac{s_1^2}{s_2^2}\left(\frac{1}{f_{\alpha/2,\nu_1,\nu_2}}\right) \leq \frac{\sigma_1^2}{\sigma_2^2} \leq \frac{s_1^2}{s_2^2}\,(f_{\alpha/2,\nu_2,\nu_1})$$

(2) $$L = \frac{s_1^2}{s_2^2}\left(\frac{1}{f_{\alpha/2,\nu_1,\nu_2}}\right), \qquad U = \frac{s_1^2}{s_2^2}\,(f_{\alpha/2,\nu_2,\nu_1})$$

(3) $$\left[\frac{s_1^2}{s_2^2}\left(\frac{1}{f_{\alpha/2,\nu_1,\nu_2}}\right), \frac{s_1^2}{s_2^2}\,(f_{\alpha/2,\nu_2,\nu_1})\right]$$

EXAMPLE 17.10 For the memory study in Example 17.3, calculate an approximate 95% confidence interval for σ_1^2/σ_2^2.

Solution

In Example 17.3, independent samples ($n_1 = 15$, $s_1^2 = 3.33$, and $n_2 = 15$, $s_2^2 = 3.24$) were taken from two normally distributed populations. Therefore, we can use the $(1-\alpha)100\%$ confidence interval

$$\left[\frac{s_1^2}{s_2^2}\left(\frac{1}{f_{\alpha/2,\nu_1,\nu_2}}\right), \frac{s_1^2}{s_2^2}\,(f_{\alpha/2,\nu_2,\nu_1})\right]$$

where $\frac{s_1^2}{s_2^2} = \frac{3.33}{3.24}$. Going to Table A.8 for the critical values, however, we find two things: (1) it does not give critical values involving $\alpha/2$, and (2) it does not have values for an F distribution with $\nu_1 = n_1 - 1 = 14$ and $\nu_2 = n_2 - 1 = 14$. The first problem is easy to solve, simply convert $f_{\alpha/2}$ and $f_{1-\alpha/2}$ values into the equivalent f_α and $f_{1-\alpha}$ values. The second problem is more difficult. There are more complete F tables available, as well as calculator and computer programs for F distributions, but here we are restricted to using Table A.8. With such a restriction, there are two recommended solutions: *interpolation* and *next-lower* ν_1 *and* ν_2 *values*. We will demonstrate interpolation in Problem 17.20, but here we will use the next-lower values technique.

Table A.8 has $\nu_2 = 14$ but not $\nu_1 = 14$. Thus taking the next-lower value, we use the distribution for $\nu_1 = 12$ and $\nu_2 = 14$. Therefore,

$$f_{\alpha/2,\nu_1,\nu_2} = f_{0.050/2,14,14} \approx f_{0.025,12,14} = 3.05$$

To determine $f_{\alpha/2,\nu_2,\nu_1}$, we accept that with ν_2 stated first it is now, by convention, assumed to be "ν_1" (see Example 17.9) , so we again use $\nu_1 = 12$ for the numerator value. Therefore,

$$f_{\alpha/2,\nu_2,\nu_1} = f_{0.050/2,14,14} \approx f_{0.025,12,14} = 3.05$$

Therefore, the approximate 95% confidence interval for σ_1^2/σ_2^2 is

$$\left[\frac{3.33}{3.24}\left(\frac{1}{3.05}\right), \frac{3.33}{3.24}\,(3.05)\right] = (0.337, 3.135)$$

17.21 TESTING HYPOTHESES ABOUT THE RATIO OF VARIANCES (σ_1^2/σ_2^2): PARAMETERS (σ_1^2, σ_1, μ_1 AND σ_2^2, σ_2, μ_2) NOT KNOWN, INDEPENDENT SAMPLES FROM NORMALLY DISTRIBUTED POPULATIONS

Every variance-ratio hypothesis-testing problem involves H_0 and H_1 and, as when testing hypotheses about other parameters, there are both two-tailed and one-tailed tests. In these tests, the null hypothesis indicates that the ratio of the variances σ_1^2/σ_2^2 is equal to a specific value δ_0 (see Section 17.5). Thus, H_0 can be written symbolically

$$H_0\colon \sigma_1^2/\sigma_2^2 = \delta_0$$

While δ_0 can be any value, we will consider only the case where $\delta_0 = 1$ (i.e., the variances are equal), which yields these posssible statistical hypotheses for testing.

For two-tailed tests,

$$H_0\colon \sigma_1^2/\sigma_2^2 = 1, \qquad H_1\colon \sigma_1^2/\sigma_2^2 \neq 1$$

which can also be written as

$$H_0\colon \sigma_1^2 = \sigma_2^2, \qquad H_1\colon \sigma_1^2 \neq \sigma_2^2$$

For right-tailed tests, either

$$H_0\colon \sigma_1^2/\sigma_2^2 = 1, \qquad H_1\colon \sigma_1^2/\sigma_2^2 > 1$$

or

$$H_0\colon \sigma_1^2 = \sigma_2^2, \qquad H_1\colon \sigma_1^2 > \sigma_2^2$$

For left-tailed tests, either

$$H_0\colon \sigma_1^2/\sigma_2^2 = 1, \qquad H_1\colon \sigma_1^2/\sigma_2^2 < 1$$

or

$$H_0\colon \sigma_1^2 = \sigma_2^2, \qquad H_1\colon \sigma_1^2 < \sigma_2^2$$

For independent sampling from normally distributed populations, the null hypothesis is tested with the F statistic [equation (17.34)], which, under these conditions, if we accept that $H_0\colon \sigma_1^2/\sigma_2^2 = 1$ is true, becomes

$$F = \frac{S_1^2}{S_2^2} \tag{17.46}$$

This statistic has an F distribution with $\nu_1 = n_1 - 1$ and $\nu_2 = n_2 - 1$, and can assume specific values

$$f = \frac{s_1^2}{s_2^2} \tag{17.47}$$

The F statistic can be used to determine the required conditional probability

$$P\,(\text{point estimate at least as different from 1 as } s_1^2/s_2^2 | H_0 \text{ is true})$$

because it meets the two criteria (see Section 16.3) of a test statistic: (1) it allows comparison of the point estimate (s_1^2/s_2^2) with the null's hypothesized ratio $(\sigma_1^2/\sigma_2^2 = 1)$, and (2) it has a probability distribution (the F distribution with ν_1 and ν_2 degrees of freedom) that is known when H_0 is true.

When $F = S_1^2/S_2^2$ is used as the test statistic, the specific value for a given sample is denoted as $f^* = s_1^2/s_2^2$. Therefore, the P value of a hypothesis test (see Section 16.6) using F as the test statistic is the conditional probability of obtaining a value in an F distribution, where $\nu_1 = n_1 - 1$ and $\nu_2 = n_2 - 1$, that is at least as extreme as f^* when the null hypothesis is true. For a right-tailed test, the P value is

$$P = P(F \geq f^* | H_0 \text{ is true}) \tag{17.48}$$

and for a left-tailed test, the P value is

$$P = P(F \leq f^* | H_0 \text{ is true}) \tag{17.49}$$

For a two-tailed test, the P value is not straightforward, because the F distribution is asymmetric. Therefore, we use the solution for chi-square from Section 16.26, which has these steps:

(1) Determine whether f^* is greater than or less than the mean of the F distribution [equation (17.39)].

(2) If $f^* > \mu$, then the P value is

$$P = 2[P(F \geq f^* | H_0 \text{ is true})] \tag{17.50}$$

(3) If $f^* < \mu$, then the P value is

$$P = 2[P(F \leq f^* | H_0 \text{ is true})] \tag{17.51}$$

EXAMPLE 17.11 For independent samples ($n_1 = n_2 = 9$) from two normally distributed populations, what are the critical-value decision rules if H_0: $\sigma_1^2/\sigma_2^2 = 1$, where F is the test statistic, if $\alpha = 0.05$ and (*a*) H_1: $\sigma_1^2/\sigma_2^2 > 1$, (*b*) H_1: $\sigma_1^2/\sigma_2^2 < 1$, (*c*) H_1: $\sigma_1^2/\sigma_2^2 \neq 1$?

Solution

(*a*) For this right-tailed test, where $\nu_1 = \nu_2 = 8$: Reject H_0 if $f^* > (f_{\alpha,\nu_1,\nu_2} = f_{0.05,8,8} = 3.44)$.

(*b*) For this left-tailed test, where $\nu_1 = \nu_2 = 8$: Reject H_0 if

$$f^* < \left(f_{1-\alpha,\nu_1,\nu_2} = f_{1-0.05,8,8} = \frac{1}{f_{0.05,8,8}} = \frac{1}{3.44} = 0.29 \right)$$

(*c*) For this two-tailed test, where $\nu_1 = \nu_2 = 8$: Reject H_0 if $f^* > (f_{\alpha/2,\nu_1,\nu_2} = f_{0.05/2,8,8} = f_{0.025,8,8} = 4.43)$ or if

$$f^* < \left(f_{1-\alpha/2,\nu_1,\nu_2} = f_{1-0.05/2,8,8} = f_{1-0.025,8,8} = \frac{1}{f_{0.025,8,8}} = \frac{1}{4.43} = 0.23 \right)$$

EXAMPLE 17.12 For the independent samples in Example 17.11, with $n_1 = n_2 = 9$, the sample variances are $s_1^2 = 4.23$ and $s_2^2 = 1.56$. Do a right-tailed test of H_0: $\sigma_1^2/\sigma_2^2 = 1$, using $\alpha = 0.05$ and a critical-value decision rule.

Solution

(1) H_0: $\sigma_1^2/\sigma_2^2 = 1$, H_1: $\sigma_1^2/\sigma_2^2 > 1$

(2) $\alpha = 0.05$

(3) As we can assume independent samples from normal distributions, we can use the F statistic [equation (17.46)]. Thus, the right-tailed decision rule is: Reject H_0 if $f^* > (f_{\alpha,\nu_1,\nu_2} = f_{0.05,8,8} = 3.44)$

(4) The value of the F statistic is

$$f^* = \frac{s_1^2}{s_2^2} = \frac{4.23}{1.56} = 2.7115, \quad \text{or } 2.71$$

From Table A.8, for $\nu_1 = 8$ and $\nu_2 = 8$, we find that the P value is in the range $0.05 < P < 0.10$.

(5) As $f^* < 3.44$, we accept H_0. This result is confirmed by the fact that the P value is in the range $0.05 < P < 0.10$.

17.22 WHEN TO TEST FOR HOMOGENEITY OF VARIANCE

For independent samples, homogeneity of variance is assumed for two-sample estimation and hypothesis testing when t techniques (see Sections 17.7 and 17.8) are used. We have seen in Section 17.21 how this assumption can be tested using the *F test of the difference between two variances*. Should this test be done before each use of the t technique?

The F test of the difference between two variances (or the *variance ratio test*, or simply the *F test*) should be used to test for homogeneity of variance only when it is reasonably certain that the populations being independently sampled are truly normally distributed. This is because the F test is more sensitive (i.e., less robust) to departures from normality than the t techniques are to inhomogeneity of variance. However, if the populations can at least be assumed to be unimodal, then this problem with the F test will be minimized when the samples are of equal size.

If the assumption of normal populations is met, an F test is done, and H_0 is rejected, then one cannot assume homogeneity of variance. The next step, as we indicated in Section 17.14, is to attempt a transformation. If after transformation, the populations remain normally distributed and H_0 is accepted with a new F test, then homogeneity of variance can be assumed and t techniques can be used on the transformed data. If after transformation, the populations are no longer normal or H_0 is still rejected, then nonparametric procedures (see Chapter 20) are available for testing other aspects of the data.

When the assumption of normal distributions is met, an F test is done, and H_0 is accepted, it does not prove homogeneity of variance but it does allow acceptance of the assumption.

17.23 THE OPTIMAL ESTIMATOR OF THE DIFFERENCE BETWEEN PROPORTIONS $(p_1 - p_2)$: LARGE INDEPENDENT SAMPLES

Suppose you are studying the relationships between two infinitely large binomial populations (see Section 13.21) that are binomial on the same characteristic—that is, all elements of the two populations can be classified as having that characteristic (success-elements) or not (failure-elements). The proportions of success-elements in the two populations, denoted by p_1 and p_2, are unknown, and you want to estimate the difference between these two unknown proportions $(p_1 - p_2)$. To do this, you take independent random samples under Bernoulli-trial conditions from each of the populations—n_1 elements from the first, of which y_1 are success-elements, and n_2 elements from the second, of which y_2 are success-elements.

We know that when considering each population separately, the random variable proportion of success in the sample $\left(\bar{P} = \frac{Y}{n}\right)$ is an unbiased estimator of the proportion p (see Section 15.13) in the population. If we denote $\bar{P}_1 = \frac{Y_1}{n_1}$ as the unbiased estimator of p_1 and $\bar{P}_2 = \frac{Y_2}{n_2}$ as the unbiased estimator of p_2, then we now state (without attempting to prove it) that the optimal, unbiased estimator of $p_1 - p_2$ is

$$\bar{P}_1 - \bar{P}_2 = \frac{Y_1}{n_1} - \frac{Y_2}{n_2} \tag{17.52}$$

which can assume specific values

$$\bar{p}_1 - \bar{p}_2 = \frac{y_1}{n_1} - \frac{y_2}{n_2} \tag{17.53}$$

For any given pair of samples from the two populations, the specific value $\bar{P}_1 - \bar{P}_2 = \bar{p}_1 - \bar{p}_2$ is a point estimate of $p_1 - p_2$.

17.24 THE THEORETICAL SAMPLING DISTRIBUTION OF THE DIFFERENCE BETWEEN TWO PROPORTIONS

From Section 13.23 we know that if all possible samples of size n are drawn from an infinitely large binomial population under Bernoulli-trial conditions and the proportion of successes $\bar{P} = \bar{p}$ is determined for each sample, then the resulting theoretical sampling distribution of the proportion will have mean $\mu_{\bar{p}} = p$, variance $\sigma_{\bar{p}}^2 = \frac{pq}{n}$, and standard deviation $\sigma_{\bar{p}} = \sqrt{\frac{pq}{n}}$, where p is the proportion of successes in the population and $q = 1 - p$. Further, from Section 13.25, we know that if n is sufficiently large ($np \geq 5$ and $nq \geq 5$), this theoretical sampling distribution will be approximately normally distributed.

We now state, without attempting to prove it, that, for the sampling conditions in Section 17.23, if all possible combinations of samples of n_1 and n_2 are independently drawn from the two binomial populations under Bernoulli-trial conditions and the difference between proportions of successes is determined for each combination, $\bar{p}_1 - \bar{p}_2$, then the resulting *theoretical sampling distribution of the difference between two proportions* (or *theoretical sampling distribution of the differences of proportions*) will have these formulas for mean, variance, and standard deviation:

$$\mu_{\bar{p}_1-\bar{p}_2} = p_1 - p_2 \tag{17.54}$$

$$\sigma^2_{\bar{p}_1-\bar{p}_2} = \frac{p_1q_1}{n_1} + \frac{p_2q_2}{n_2} \tag{17.55}$$

$$\sigma_{\bar{p}_1-\bar{p}_2} = \sqrt{\frac{p_1q_1}{n_1} + \frac{p_2q_2}{n_2}} \tag{17.56}$$

where equation (17.56) is called the *standard error of the difference between two proportions*. Further, we state here that when both n_1 and n_2 are sufficiently large, this theoretical sampling distribution can be assumed to be approximately a normal distribution.

When are n_1 and n_2 sufficiently large? For unknown p_1 and p_2, some statistics books say that n_1 and n_2 are sufficiently large when $n_1\bar{p}_1 > 5$, $n_1\bar{q}_1 > 5$, $n_2\bar{p}_2 > 5$, and $n_2\bar{q}_2 > 5$. Others say that all four values should be greater than 10, or 20, or 30. Finally, the most conservative books say that n_1 and n_2 are sufficiently large only when they are both equal to or larger than 100 (see Section 15.16).

We can also state that, under the conditions of large samples taken under Bernoulli-trial conditions from two binomial populations, the random variable

$$Z = \frac{(\bar{P}_1 - \bar{P}_2) - (p_1 - p_2)}{\sqrt{\frac{p_1q_1}{n_1} + \frac{p_2q_2}{n_2}}} \tag{17.57}$$

has a distribution that is approximately the standard normal distribution.

17.25 APPROXIMATE CONFIDENCE INTERVAL FOR THE DIFFERENCE BETWEEN PROPORTIONS FROM TWO BINOMIAL POPULATIONS ($p_1 - p_2$): LARGE INDEPENDENT SAMPLES

With the information from Sections 17.23 and 17.24, we can now develop the $(1 - \alpha)100\%$ confidence interval for the difference between two proportions. We know from equation (12.18) that for the standard normal distribution,

$$P(-z_{\alpha/2} \le Z \le z_{\alpha/2}) = 1 - \alpha$$

Substituting equation (17.57) into equation (12.18) we get

$$P\left[-z_{\alpha/2} \le \frac{(\bar{P}_1 - \bar{P}_2) - (p_1 - p_2)}{\sqrt{\frac{p_1q_1}{n_1} + \frac{p_2q_2}{n_2}}} \le z_{\alpha/2}\right] \approx 1 - \alpha$$

Multiplying each term of the inequality by $\sqrt{\frac{p_1q_1}{n_1} + \frac{p_2q_2}{n_2}}$, and then subtracting $(\bar{P}_1 - \bar{P}_2)$ and multiplying by -1, we get

$$P\left[(\bar{P}_1 - \bar{P}_2) - z_{\alpha/2}\sqrt{\frac{p_1q_1}{n_1} + \frac{p_2q_2}{n_2}} \le p_1 - p_2 \le (\bar{P}_1 - \bar{P}_2) + z_{\alpha/2}\sqrt{\frac{p_1q_1}{n_1} + \frac{p_2q_2}{n_2}}\right] \approx 1 - \alpha \tag{17.58}$$

Having established this relationship, the description of an approximate $(1 - \alpha)100\%$ confidence interval should follow directly. However, as was true for single-sample estimation of a population proportion, to calculate an approximate confidence interval one needs to know the two population proportions, p_1 and p_2, that are being estimated. We solve the problem in the same way as with single-sample estimation (see Section 15.15), with the point-estimate solution and the conservative solution.

In the point-estimate solution, if both n_1 and n_2 are "sufficiently large" (see Section 17.24), then the point estimates $\bar{p}_1$, $\bar{q}_1$, $\bar{p}_2$, and $\bar{q}_2$ are satisfactory substitutes for p_1, q_1, p_2 and q_2 in the confidence limits. These limits can then be written in the four standard forms of the approximate interval:

(1) $(\bar{p}_1 - \bar{p}_2) - z_{\alpha/2}\sqrt{\frac{\bar{p}_1\bar{q}_1}{n_1} + \frac{\bar{p}_2\bar{q}_2}{n_2}} \le p_1 - p_2 \le (\bar{p}_1 - \bar{p}_2) + z_{\alpha/2}\sqrt{\frac{\bar{p}_1\bar{q}_1}{n_1} + \frac{\bar{p}_2\bar{q}_2}{n_2}}$

(2) $L \approx (\bar{p}_1 - \bar{p}_2) - z_{\alpha/2}\sqrt{\frac{\bar{p}_1\bar{q}_1}{n_1} + \frac{\bar{p}_2\bar{q}_2}{n_2}}, \qquad U \approx (\bar{p}_1 - \bar{p}_2) + z_{\alpha/2}\sqrt{\frac{\bar{p}_1\bar{q}_1}{n_1} + \frac{\bar{p}_2\bar{q}_2}{n_2}}$

(3) $\left[(\bar{p}_1 - \bar{p}_2) - z_{\alpha/2}\sqrt{\frac{\bar{p}_1\bar{q}_1}{n_1} + \frac{\bar{p}_2\bar{q}_2}{n_2}}, (\bar{p}_1 - \bar{p}_2) + z_{\alpha/2}\sqrt{\frac{\bar{p}_1\bar{q}_1}{n_1} + \frac{\bar{p}_2\bar{q}_2}{n_2}}\right]$

(4) $(\bar{p}_1 - \bar{p}_2) \pm z_{\alpha/2}\sqrt{\frac{\bar{p}_1\bar{q}_1}{n_1} + \frac{\bar{p}_2\bar{q}_2}{n_2}}$

The conservative solution makes use of the fact that it can be proven that regardless of the value of p, the largest possible value of the term is $p(1-p) = pq$ is $\frac{1}{4}$. Therefore, if both n_1 and n_2 are not "sufficiently large" or the most conservative possible solution is required, then $\frac{1}{4}$ is substituted for both p_1q_1 and p_2q_2 in the confidence limits, which in the fourth form above, become

$$(\bar{p}_1 - \bar{p}_2) \pm z_{\alpha/2}\sqrt{\frac{1}{4n_1} + \frac{1}{4n_2}} \tag{17.59}$$

These two types of confidence intervals are true for sampling from infinite populations or for sampling from finite populations with replacement, and for sampling from finite populations without replacement when $n \le 0.05N$ for both populations. If in the last case, $n > 0.05N$ for either population, then there are similar confidence limits formulas using the finite population correction factor (see Section 15.17).

EXAMPLE 17.13 You take independent random samples ($n_1 = 200$, $n_2 = 200$) from two infinitely large binomial populations under Bernoulli-trial conditions. You find that $y_1 = 105$ and $y_2 = 90$. What is the approximate 95% confidence interval for $p_1 - p_2$ using: (*a*) the point-estimate solution, and (*b*) the conservative solution?

Solution

(*a*) The point estimates of p_1, q_1, p_2, and q_2 are

$$\bar{p}_1 = \frac{y_1}{n_1} = \frac{105}{200} = 0.525, \qquad \bar{q}_1 = 1 - 0.525 = 0.475$$

$$\bar{p}_2 = \frac{y_2}{n_2} = \frac{90}{200} = 0.450, \qquad \bar{q}_2 = 1 - 0.450 = 0.550$$

As n_1 and n_2 both meet the most conservative requirement for sample size ($n \ge 100$), we can use the normal-approximation technique. Using Table A.5, $z_{\alpha/2} = z_{0.05/2} = 1.96$. Therefore, the approximate 95% confidence interval, using the point-estimate solution, is

$$(\bar{p}_1 - \bar{p}_2) \pm z_{\alpha/2}\sqrt{\frac{\bar{p}_1\bar{q}_1}{n_1} + \frac{\bar{p}_2\bar{q}_2}{n_2}}$$

$$(0.525 - 0.450) \pm 1.96\sqrt{\frac{(0.525 \times 0.475)}{200} + \frac{(0.450 \times 0.550)}{200}}$$

$$0.075 \pm 0.0977$$

(*b*) Using the conservative solution [equation (17.59)],

$$(0.525 - 0.450) \pm 1.96\sqrt{\frac{1}{4(200)} + \frac{1}{4(200)}}$$

$$0.075 \pm 0.0980$$

17.26 TESTING HYPOTHESES ABOUT THE DIFFERENCE BETWEEN PROPORTIONS FROM TWO BINOMIAL POPULATIONS ($p_1 - p_2$): LARGE INDEPENDENT SAMPLES

Every hypothesis-testing problem about a difference between proportions involves a null hypothesis H_0 and an alternative hypothesis H_1, and may be either a two-tailed or a one-tailed test. In these tests, the null hypothesis indicates that the difference between population proportions, $p_1 - p_2$, is equal to a specific value δ_0 (see Section 17.5). Thus, H_0 can be written symbolically as $H_0: p_1 - p_2 = \delta_0$. While δ_0 can be any value, we consider here only the case where $\delta_0 = 0$, which yields these possible statistical hypotheses for testing:

For two-tailed tests

$$H_0: p_1 - p_2 = 0, \qquad H_1: p_1 - p_2 \neq 0$$

which can also be written as

$$H_0: p_1 = p_2, \qquad H_1: p_1 \neq p_2$$

For right-tailed tests, either

$$H_0: p_1 - p_2 = 0, \qquad H_1: p_1 - p_2 > 0$$

or

$$H_0: p_1 = p_2, \qquad H_1: p_1 > p_2$$

For left-tailed tests, either

$$H_0: p_1 - p_2 = 0, \qquad H_1: p_1 - p_2 < 0$$

or

$$H_0: p_1 = p_2, \qquad H_1: p_1 < p_2$$

Now we need to find a statistic for testing the null hypothesis. We know from Section 17.24 that if we assume sample sizes n_1 and n_2 are sufficiently large, then the Z statistic [equation (17.57)] will have a distribution that is approximately the standard normal distribution. It can be used, therefore, to determine the required conditional probability

$$P\,(\text{point estimate at least as different from 0 as } \bar{p}_1 - \bar{p}_2 | H_0 \text{ is true})$$

because it meets the two conditions of a test statistic: (1) it allows comparison of the point estimate $(\bar{p}_1 - \bar{p}_2)$ with the null's hypothesized value $(p_1 - p_2 = 0)$, and (2) it has a probability distribution (the standard normal) that is known under the assumption that H_0 is true.

To calculate a specific z^* value of the Z statistic, the point-estimate and conservative solutions (see Sections 17.25) can be used for the denominator of equation (17.57), but when testing $H_0: p_1 - p_2 = 0$ the *pooled-estimate solution* is recommended. In this solution, it is assumed that H_0 is true, that $p_1 = p_2 = p$, and that the best estimate of p is $\bar{p}$, which is the total number of success-elements in the samples divided by the total number of elements in the samples:

$$\bar{p} = \frac{y_1 + y_2}{n_1 + n_2} = \frac{n_1\bar{p}_1 + n_2\bar{p}_2}{n_1 + n_2} \tag{17.60}$$

As $q = 1 - p$, the best estimate of q is $\bar{q} = 1 - \bar{p}$. Letting $p_1 - p_2 = 0$, and putting these estimates in the Z statistic, we get this formula for calculating Z values for two specific samples:

$$z^* = \frac{(\bar{p}_1 - \bar{p}_2) - (p_1 - p_2 = 0)}{\sqrt{\dfrac{\bar{p}\bar{q}}{n_1} + \dfrac{\bar{p}\bar{q}}{n_2}}} = \frac{(\bar{p}_1 - \bar{p}_2)}{\sqrt{\bar{p}\bar{q}\left(\dfrac{1}{n_1} + \dfrac{1}{n_2}\right)}} \tag{17.61}$$

All the decision rules for P values and critical values that were used in one-sample testing of $H_0: p_1 - p_2 = 0$ (see Section 16.10) can be used here for two-sample testing.

EXAMPLE 17.14 For the conditions in Example 17.13, do a two-tailed test of H_0: $p_1 - p_2 = 0$, using $\alpha = 0.05$ and a critical-value decision rule.

Solution

(1) H_0: $p_1 - p_2 = 0$, H_1: $p_1 - p_2 \neq 0$

(2) $\alpha = 0.05$

(3) As the independent samples are sufficiently large ($n_1 = n_2 = 200$), we can use the Z statistic and this two-tailed decision rule: Reject H_0 if $z^* > (z_{\alpha/2} = z_{0.050/2} = 1.96)$ or if $z^* < (-z_{\alpha/2} = -z_{0.050/2} = -1.96)$.

(4) Using equation (17.60),

$$\bar{p} = \frac{y_1 + y_2}{n_1 + n_2} = \frac{105 + 90}{200 + 200} = 0.4875$$
$$\bar{q} = 1 - \bar{p} = 1 - 0.4875 = 0.5125$$

and these values from Example 17.13,

$$\bar{p}_1 = 0.525, \qquad \bar{p}_2 = 0.450$$

the value of the Z statistic is

$$z^* = \frac{(0.525 - 0.450)}{\sqrt{(0.4875)(0.5125)\left(\frac{1}{200} + \frac{1}{200}\right)}} = 1.500, \quad \text{or } 1.50$$

Using Table A.5, the approximate P value [equation (16.4)] is

$$P \approx 2[P(Z \geq (z^* = a)|H_0 \text{ is true})] = 2[P(Z > 1.50)] = 2(0.5 - 0.4332) = 0.1336$$

(5) As $-1.96 < z^* < 1.96$, we accept H_0. This result is confirmed by the fact that the approximate P value is greater than 0.05.

Solved Problems

CONFIDENCE INTERVALS AND HYPOTHESIS TESTS FOR THE DIFFERENCE BETWEEN MEANS: KNOWN STANDARD DEVIATIONS, INDEPENDENT SAMPLES FROM NORMALLY DISTRIBUTED POPULATIONS

17.1 For each of the following examples, first indicate whether the samples are independent or paired, and then explain your choice: (*a*) To decide between two locations for a shopping center, a developer takes random samples of household incomes from both locations; (*b*) to test whether an exercise program reduces high blood pressure in a group of patients at a clinic, blood pressure is measured for each patient before and after the exercise program; (*c*) to determine whether front and rear legs are the same length in male deer, both right legs (front and back) are measured in a random sample of male deer; (*d*) to determine whether front-leg lengths are the same in male and female deer, the right front legs are measured in random samples of male and female deer; (*e*) to compare two barnacle-resistant paints for ship hulls, both paints are applied to each of a group of ships on adjacent sections of their hulls, and the accumulated barnacles are then counted after one year on all paint sections.

Solution

(*a*) Independent samples; taking observations in one location in no way affects the probabilities of observations in the other location.

(*b*) Paired samples; the post-exercise observations are not randomly determined.

(*c*) Paired samples; once one leg is measured the other leg measurement is not randomly determined.

(*d*) Independent samples; taking a male length in no way affects the probability of taking a female length, and vice versa.

(*e*) Paired samples; once a barnacle count is taken for one paint section on a ship, the count for the other section is not randomly determined.

17.2 A forester is interested in knowing the effect of elevation on the heights of redwood trees. He measures the heights of $n_1 = 100$ adult trees at sea level (population 1, with a known standard deviation of $\sigma_1 = 30\,\text{ft}$) and $n_2 = 73$ adult trees at 3,000 ft above sea level (population 2, with a known standard deviation of $\sigma_2 = 45\,\text{ft}$). The results are $\bar{x}_1 = 320\,\text{ft}$ and $\bar{x}_2 = 255\,\text{ft}$. What is the 95% confidence interval for $\mu_1 - \mu_2$?

Solution

Using equation (17.3), the confidence interval is (see Section 17.4)

$$(\bar{x}_1 - \bar{x}_2) \pm z_{\alpha/2}\sqrt{\frac{\sigma_1^2}{n_1} + \frac{\sigma_2^2}{n_2}}$$

Substituting the sample values and using $z_{0.05/2} = 1.96$

$$(320\text{ ft} - 255\text{ ft}) \pm 1.96\sqrt{\frac{(30\text{ ft})^2}{100} + \frac{(45\text{ ft})^2}{73}}$$

$$65\text{ ft} \pm (1.96 \times 6.0613\text{ ft})$$

$$65\text{ ft} \pm 11.9\text{ ft}$$

17.3 Independent random samples are taken from two normally distributed populations that have unknown means, μ_1 and μ_2, and known standard deviations. For the first population, $\sigma_1 = 0.73$ and the sample values are $n_1 = 25$, $\bar{x}_1 = 7.3$. For the second population, $\sigma_2 = 0.89$ and the sample values are $n_2 = 20$, $\bar{x}_2 = 6.7$. Do a right-tailed test of H_0: $\mu_1 - \mu_2 = 0$ using $\alpha = 0.01$ and a decision rule stated in terms of P values.

Solution

(1) H_0: $\mu_1 - \mu_2 = 0$, $\quad H_1$: $\mu_1 - \mu_2 > 0$

(2) $\alpha = 0.01$

(3) Using the Z statistic [equation (17.6)] with $\alpha = 0.01$, the right-tailed decision rule is: Reject H_0 if $P \leq 0.01$.

(4) The value of the Z statistic is

$$z^* = \frac{(7.3 - 6.7) - 0}{\sqrt{\frac{(0.73)^2}{25} + \frac{(0.89)^2}{20}}} = 2.431, \quad \text{or } 2.43$$

To determine the P value, we use equation (16.6),

$$P = P[Z \geq (z^* = a)|H_0 \text{ is true}]$$
$$= P(Z > 2.43) = 0.5 - 0.4925 = 0.0075$$

(5) As $P < 0.01$, we reject H_0 and accept H_1. Therefore, it can be said that the two-sample difference is significantly greater than zero at the 0.01 level of significance, and this indicates that μ_1 is greater than μ_2.

CONFIDENCE INTERVALS AND HYPOTHESIS TESTS FOR THE DIFFERENCE BETWEEN MEANS: STANDARD DEVIATIONS NOT KNOWN BUT ASSUMED EQUAL, SMALL INDEPENDENT SAMPLES FROM NORMALLY DISTRIBUTED POPULATIONS

17.4 To investigate the effects of a stimulant drug on rat maze-learning, a psychologist tested two groups of male rats. Group 1 is the control group, in which each rat is given a single daily maze-learning trial until it reaches a criterion of learning, which is passing through the maze without an error (i.e., without making a wrong turn), with each rat injected with a neutral saline solution after each daily trial. Group 2 is the experimental group, in which each rat is treated in the same way as the control group except that after each daily trial it is injected with the stimulant drug in the same saline solution. The performance measure taken for each rat was the total number of errors made on all trials before the criterion of learning was achieved. The samples were independent, with 10 subjects in each group, and the results were: group 1, $n_1 = 10$, $\bar{x}_1 = 19.5$, $s_1^2 = 3.59$; group 2, $n_2 = 10$, $\bar{x}_2 = 15.8$, $s_2^2 = 3.37$. Assuming the populations for both conditions are normally distributed and that there is homogeneity of variance (see Section 17.6), calculate a 98% confidence interval for $\mu_1 - \mu_2$.

Solution

This problem can be solved using the $(1 - \alpha)100\%$ confidence interval from Section 17.7. First, the estimated standard error is calculated with equation (17.14):

$$s_{\bar{x}_1-\bar{x}_2} = \sqrt{\left[\frac{(10-1)3.59 + (10-1)3.37}{18}\right]\left(\frac{1}{10}+\frac{1}{10}\right)} = 0.8343$$

We know that $(\bar{x}_1 - \bar{x}_2) = 19.5 - 15.8 = 3.7$. From Table A.6 for a t distribution with $(\nu = n_1 + n_2 - 2 = 10 + 10 - 2 = 18)$: $t_{\alpha/2,\nu} = t_{0.02/2,18} = 2.552$. Therefore, the 98% confidence interval is

$$3.7 \pm (2.552 \times 0.8343)$$

$$3.7 \pm 2.13$$

17.5 To investigate the effects of the hormone melatonin on insomnia, a doctor at a sleep-disorder clinic gives different pre-sleep doses of melatonin to two groups of patients and measures for each patient the time from taking the melatonin pill to falling asleep (determined by brain waves). Group 1 receives a 5 mg dose and group 2 receives a 15 mg dose. The samples are independent and the results are: group 1, $n_1 = 10$, $\bar{x}_1 = 14.8$ min, $s_1^2 = 4.36\text{ min}^2$; group 2, $n_2 = 12$, $\bar{x}_2 = 10.2$ min, $s_2^2 = 4.66\text{ min}^2$. Assuming the populations for both conditions are normally distributed and there is homoscedasticity (see Section 17.6), calculate a 99% confidence interval for $\mu_1 - \mu_2$.

Solution

This problem can be solved using the $(1 - \alpha)100\%$ confidence interval from Section 17.7. First, the estimated standard error is calculated with equation (17.14):

$$s_{\bar{x}_1-\bar{x}_2} = \sqrt{\left[\frac{(10-1)4.36\text{ min}^2 + (12-1)4.66\text{ min}^2}{20}\right]\left(\frac{1}{10}+\frac{1}{10}\right)} = 0.9108\text{ min}$$

We know that $(\bar{x}_1 - \bar{x}_2) = 14.8\text{ min} - 10.2\text{ min} = 4.6\text{ min}$. From Table A.6 for a t distribution, with $\alpha = 0.01$ and $(\nu = n_1 + n_2 - 2 = 10 + 12 - 2 = 20)$: $t_{\alpha/2,\nu} = t_{0.01/2,20} = 2.845$. Therefore, the 99% confidence interval is

$$4.6\text{ min} \pm (2.845 \times 0.9108\text{ min})$$

$$4.6\text{ min} \pm 2.59\text{ min}$$

17.6 Consider again the memory study in Examples 17.3 and 17.4. Before doing the test, the psychologist had the hypothesis that the group who saw the movie at 7 PM (group 1) would perform better on the memory test than the group who saw the movie at 7 AM (group 2). Therefore, a right-tailed test of H_0: $\mu_1 - \mu_2 = 0$ could have been done. Do this test at $\alpha = 0.01$ using a critical-value decision rule.

Solution

(1) H_0: $\mu_1 - \mu_2 = 0$, $\quad H_1$: $\mu_1 - \mu_2 > 0$

(2) $\alpha = 0.01$

(3) As we can assume normal distributions and homogeneity of variance, and the samples are independent, we can use the t statistic [equation (17.17)]. With $\alpha = 0.01$ and $\nu = 28$, from Table A.6 the right-tailed decision rule is: Reject H_0 if $t^* > (t_{0.01,28} = 2.467)$.

(4) As $t^* = 2.418$ (see Example 17.4), the P value is in the range $0.01 < P < 0.025$.

(5) As $t^* < 2.467$, we accept H_0. This result is confirmed by the fact that the P value is in the range $0.01 < P < 0.025$. Thus, unlike the significant two-tailed result at $\alpha = 0.05$ in Example 17.4, with a right-tailed test at $\alpha = 0.01$, there is no evidence that group (1) performed better than group (2).

17.7 For the maze-learning study in Problem 17.4, do a two-tailed test of H_0: $\mu_1 - \mu_2 = 0$, using $\alpha = 0.01$ and a critical-value decision rule.

Solution

(1) H_0: $\mu_1 - \mu_2 = 0$, $\quad H_1$: $\mu_1 - \mu_2 \neq 0$

(2) $\alpha = 0.01$

(3) As we can assume normal distributions and homogeneity of variance, and the samples are independent, we can use the t statistic [equation (17.17)]. With $\nu = 10 + 10 - 2 = 18$ and $\alpha = 0.01$, from Table A.6 the two-tailed decision rule is: Reject H_0 if $t^* > (t_{0.01/2,18} = 2.878)$ or if $t^* < (-t_{0.01/2,18} = -2.878)$.

(4) Using $s_{\bar{x}_1 - \bar{x}_2} = 0.8343$ from Problem 17.4, the value of the t statistic is

$$t^* = \frac{3.7 - 0}{0.8343} = 4.4349, \quad \text{or } 4.435$$

The P value for $\nu = 18$ is in the range of $P < (2 \times 0.0005)$.

(5) As $t^* > 2.878$, we reject H_0 and accept H_1. This result is confirmed by the fact that the P value is in the range $P < 0.001$. There is thus a significant difference at the 0.01 level of significance between the two-sample difference and zero, and the results suggest that the experimental group (group 2) had, on the average, fewer trials to criterion.

17.8 Before doing the test described in Problem 17.7, the psychologist had the hypothesis that the experimental group (group 2) would have, on the average, fewer trials to criterion. Therefore, a right-tailed test of H_0: $\mu_1 - \mu_2 = 0$ could have been done. Do this test at $\alpha = 0.01$ using a critical-value decision rule.

Solution

(1) H_0: $\mu_1 - \mu_2 = 0$, $\quad H_1$: $\mu_1 - \mu_2 > 0$

(2) $\alpha = 0.01$

(3) Using the t statistic with $\nu = 18$ and $\alpha = 0.01$, from Table A.6 the right-tailed decision rule is: Reject H_0 if $t^* > (t_{0.01,18} = 2.552)$.

(4) As in Problem 17.7, $t^* = 4.435$, but now for this right-tailed test the P value for $\nu = 18$ is in the range $P < 0.0005$.

(5) As $t^* > 2.552$, we reject H_0 and accept H_1. This result is confirmed by the fact that the P value is in the range $P < 0.0005$. Thus, we can say that the evidence evaluated at the 0.01 level of significance indicates that, on the average, there were fewer trials to criterion for the stimulant-injected experimental group.

17.9 For the melatonin study in Problem 17.5, do a two-tailed test of H_0: $\mu_1 - \mu_2 = 0$ using $\alpha = 0.02$ and a critical-value decision rule.

Solution

(1) H_0: $\mu_1 - \mu_2 = 0$, $\quad H_1$: $\mu_1 - \mu_2 \neq 0$

(2) $\alpha = 0.02$

(3) As we can assume normally distributed populations and homoscedasticity, and the samples are independent, we can use the t statistic [equation (17.17)]. With $\alpha = 0.02$ and $(\nu = n_1 + n_2 - 2 = 10 + 12 - 2 = 20)$, from Table A.6 the two-tailed decision rule is: Reject H_0 if $t^* > (t_{0.02/2,20} = 2.528)$ or if $t^* < (-t_{0.02/2,20} = -2.528)$.

(4) Using $s_{\bar{x}_1 - \bar{x}_2} = 0.9108$ min from Problem 17.5, the value of the t statistic is

$$t^* = \frac{4.6 \text{ min} - 0 \text{ min}}{0.9108 \text{ min}} = 5.0505, \quad \text{or } 5.051$$

The P value for $\nu = 20$ is in the range $P < (2 \times 0.0005)$, or $P < 0.001$.

(5) As $t^* > 2.528$, we reject H_0 and accept H_1. This result is confirmed by the fact that the P value is less than 0.001. There is thus a significant difference, at the 0.02 level of significance, between the two-sample difference and zero, and the results suggest that the 15 mg group fell asleep faster than the 5 mg group.

17.10 Before doing the test in Problem 17.9, the doctor's hypothesis was that the 15 mg group (group 2) would, on the average, fall asleep faster than the 5 mg group (group 1). Therefore, a right-tailed test of H_0: $\mu_1 - \mu_2 = 0$ could have been done. Do this test at $\alpha = 0.025$ using a critical-value decision rule.

Solution

(1) H_0: $\mu_1 - \mu_2 = 0$, $\quad H_1$: $\mu_1 - \mu_2 > 0$

(2) $\alpha = 0.025$

(3) Using the t statistic with $\nu = 20$ and $\alpha = 0.025$, from Table A.6 the right-tailed decision rule is: Reject H_0 if $t^* > (t_{0.025,20} = 2.086)$.

(4) As in Problem 17.9, $t^* = 5.051$, but now for this right-tailed test the P value for $\nu = 20$ is in the range $P < 0.0005$.

(5) As $t^* > 2.086$, we reject H_0 and accept H_1. This result is confirmed by the fact that the P value is less than 0.0005. We can say that the evidence evaluated at the 0.025 level of significance indicates that, on the average, the 15 mg group fell asleep faster than the 5 mg group.

CONFIDENCE INTERVALS AND HYPOTHESIS TESTS FOR THE DIFFERENCE BETWEEN MEANS: STANDARD DEVIATIONS NOT KNOWN, LARGE INDEPENDENT SAMPLES FROM ANY POPULATION DISTRIBUTIONS

17.11 In an attempt to develop larger carp, a biologist has discovered how to produce a genetically engineered (transgenic) carp that contains the growth hormone gene of a larger species of fish. She produces 61 of these transgenic carp and weighs them when they are 1 year old, getting these results: $\bar{x}_1 = 1.69$ lb, $s_1 = 0.254$ lb. Simultaneously, she grows 61 standard carp under the same conditions as the transgenic carp, getting these sample results at 1 year of age: $\bar{x}_2 = 1.57$ lb, $s_2 = 0.250$ lb. Assuming that both populations are normally distributed, which would be typical for such weight results, and that there is homogeneity of variance, what is the 95% confidence interval for $\mu_1 - \mu_2$?

Solution

Under the conditions of this problem, there is an exact t solution using Table A.6 and the confidence interval from Section 17.7. First, we calculate $s_{\bar{x}_1-\bar{x}_2}$ using equation (17.14):

$$s_{\bar{x}_1-\bar{x}_2} = \sqrt{\left[\frac{(61-1)(0.254\text{ lb})^2 + (61-1)(0.250\text{ lb})^2}{61+61-2}\right]\left(\frac{1}{61}+\frac{1}{61}\right)} = 0.0456\text{ lb}$$

We know that $(\bar{x}_1 - \bar{x}_2) = 1.69$ lb $- 1.57$ lb $= 0.12$ lb, and from Table A.6 for a t distribution with $\nu = 61 + 61 - 2 = 120$: $t_{\alpha/2,\nu} = t_{0.05/2,120} = 1.980$. Therefore, the 95% confidence interval for $\mu_1 - \mu_2$ is

$$0.12\text{ lb} \pm (1.980 \times 0.0456\text{ lb})$$

$$0.12\text{ lb} \pm 0.090\text{ lb}$$

17.12 You have been asked by the manager of an airport to evaluate which of two airlines does better in meeting their scheduled departure times. For each airline, you measure for 30 randomly selected flights: the time (in minutes) between scheduled departure and actual departure. You cannot assume that the populations of times are normally distributed or that there is homogeneity of variance. Your independent-sampling results are: airline (1), $\bar{x}_1 = 12.4$ min, $s_2 = 3.72$ min; airline (2), $\bar{x}_2 = 11.7$ min, $s_2 = 3.60$ min. What is the 99% confidence interval for $\mu_1 - \mu_2$?

Solution

While you cannot assume normal distributions, you do have large samples ($n_1 = 30$ and $n_2 = 30$) and so you can use equation (17.19) to get an approximate 99% confidence interval. First the estimated standard error is calculated [equation (17.7)]:

$$s_{\bar{x}_1-\bar{x}_2} = \sqrt{\frac{(3.72\text{ min})^2}{30} + \frac{(3.60\text{ min})^2}{30}} = 0.945\text{ min}$$

We know that $(\bar{x}_1 - \bar{x}_2) = 12.4$ min $- 11.7$ min $= 0.7$ min, and from Table A.5: $z_{0.01/2} = 2.575$. Therefore, the approximate 99% confidence interval for $\mu_1 - \mu_2$ is

$$0.7\text{ min} \pm (2.575 \times 0.945\text{ min})$$

$$0.7\text{ min} \pm 2.43\text{ min}$$

17.13 Before doing the study in Problem 17.11, the biologist hypothesized that the transgenic carp would, on the average, weigh more at 1 year age than the standard carp. Therefore, for the conditions in Problem 17.11, do a right-tailed test of H_0: $\mu_1 - \mu_2 = 0$, using $\alpha = 0.05$ and a critical-value decision rule.

Solution

(1) $H_0\colon \mu_1 - \mu_2 = 0, \qquad H_1\colon \mu_1 - \mu_2 > 0$

(2) $\alpha = 0.05$

(3) Under the conditions of this problem, the t statistic [equation (17.17)] can be used. For a t distribution with ($\nu = n_1 + n_2 - 2 = 61 + 61 - 2 = 120$), we find in Table A.6 that, for $\alpha = 0.05$, the right-tailed decision rule is: Reject H_0 if $t^* > (t_{0.05,120} = 1.658)$.

(4) The value of the t statistic is

$$t^* = \frac{(1.69\text{ lb} - 1.57\text{ lb}) - 0}{\sqrt{\left[\frac{(61-1)(0.254\text{ lb})^2 + (61-1)(0.250\text{ lb})^2}{61+61-2}\right]\left(\frac{1}{61}+\frac{1}{61}\right)}} = 2.6298, \quad \text{or } 2.630$$

From Table A.6, the P value for $\nu = 120$ is in the range $0.0005 < P < 0.005$.

(5) As $t^* > 1.658$, we reject H_0 and accept H_1. This result is confirmed by the fact that the P value is in the range $0.0005 < P < 0.005$. Thus, we can say that the evidence evaluated at the 0.05 level of significance indicates that, on the average, the transgenic fish weigh more than the standard fish when they are 1 year old.

17.14 For the conditions in Problem 17.12, do a two-tailed test of $H_0\colon \mu_1 - \mu_2 = 0$, using $\alpha = 0.01$ and a critical-value decision rule.

Solution

(1) $H_0\colon \mu_1 - \mu_2 = 0, \qquad H_1\colon \mu_1 - \mu_2 \neq 0$

(2) $\alpha = 0.01$

(3) Under the conditions of this problem, the Z statistic [equation (17.19)] has approximately the standard normal distribution. Therefore, with $n_1 = 30$, $n_2 = 30$, and $\alpha = 0.01$, the approximate two-tailed decision rule is: Reject H_0 if $z^* > (z_{0.01/2} = 2.575)$ or if $z^* < (-z_{0.01/2} = -2.575)$.

(4) The value of the Z statistic is

$$z^* = \frac{(12.4\text{ min} - 11.7\text{ min}) - 0}{\sqrt{\frac{(3.72\text{ min})^2}{30} + \frac{(3.60\text{ min})^2}{30}}} = 0.741, \quad \text{or } 0.74$$

From Table A.5, the approximate P value is [equation (16.4)]

$$P \approx 2[P(Z \geq (z^* = a)|H_0 \text{ is true})] = 2[P(Z > 0.74)] = 2(0.5 - 0.2704) = 0.4592$$

(5) As $-2.575 < z^* < 2.575$, we accept H_0. This result is confirmed by the fact that the approximate P value is greater than 0.01. There is no evidence at the 0.01 level of significance that the airlines differ in their on-time departures.

CONFIDENCE INTERVALS AND HYPOTHESIS TESTS FOR THE DIFFERENCE BETWEEN MEANS: PAIRED SAMPLES

17.15 The doctor in the melatonin study (see Problems 17.5 and 17.9) discovers that by the accident of random selection, the average age of his 15 mg group was younger than the average age of his 5 mg group. Worried that this extraneous variable (see Volume 1, Section 3.10) could have affected his results (the 15 mg group fell asleep faster), he decides to repeat the study using the paired-samples model. To do this, he first matches 12 pairs of patients on age, gender, general health, and other factors that might affect sleep, and then randomly assigns the pair members to either the 5 mg or 15 mg group. As before, the time from dose to falling asleep is measured for all patients, with the variable X_1 representing the 5 mg times, and the variable X_2 representing the 15 mg times. A time difference is calculated for each pair, $d_j = x_{1j} - x_{2j}$ (in minutes): $d_1 = 4.9$, $d_2 = 4.6$, $d_3 = 5.1$, $d_4 = 4.5$, $d_5 = 7.1$, $d_6 = 3.2$, $d_7 = 5.4$, $d_8 = 3.9$, $d_9 = 5.9$, $d_{10} = 4.6$, $d_{11} = 2.9$, $d_{12} = 4.7$. From these data, determine a 95% confidence interval for μ_d (the mean of the differences between the 5 mg and 15 mg times), assuming the population of differences is normally distributed.

Solution

Using the equations from Section 17.11, the first step is to determine $\sum d_j = 56.8$ min and $\sum d_j^2 = 282.92\ \text{min}^2$. Next, using these values we determine

$$\bar{d} = \frac{\sum d_j}{n} = \frac{56.8\ \text{min}}{12} = 4.73\ \text{min}$$

$$s_d = \sqrt{\frac{\sum d_j^2 - n\bar{d}^2}{n-1}} = \sqrt{\frac{282.92\ \text{min}^2 - [12 \times (4.73\ \text{min})^2]}{12-1}} = 1.1459\ \text{min}$$

$$s_{\bar{d}} = \frac{s_d}{\sqrt{n}} = \frac{1.1459\ \text{min}}{\sqrt{12}} = 0.3308\ \text{min}$$

For the conditions of the problem we can use the exact t solution from Section 17.11:

$$\bar{d} \pm t_{\alpha/2,\nu} s_{\bar{d}}$$

where, from Table A.6, $t_{0.05/2,11} = 2.201$. Therefore, the 95% confidence interval is

$$4.73\ \text{min} \pm (2.201 \times 0.3308\ \text{min})$$
$$4.73 \pm 0.728\ \text{min}$$

17.16 A scientist at a pharmaceutical company has discovered a substance in dandelions that in preliminary studies seems to reduce total blood-plasma cholesterol (in mg/dl) in mice when added to their food. She does a paired-samples model study of this effect by taking 35 pairs of male mice, each pair from the same litter at 10 weeks of age, and randomly assigns one member of each pair to one of two groups: control (X_1), which are fed the normal mouse diet for 20 days, and experimental (X_2), which are fed the normal diet with the dandelion substance added for 20 days. At the end of 20 days, the total plasma cholesterol is measured for all animals, and the difference (control minus experimental) is calculated for each pair, $d_j = x_{1j} - x_{2j}$. The results are $\bar{d} = -0.53$ mg/dl and $s_d = 1.895$ mg/dl. Determine a 95% confidence interval for μ_d (the population mean of the differences between the control and experimental cholesterol levels), assuming the population of differences is normally distributed.

Solution

With $(n = 35) > 30$, we could use either the exact t solution or the approximate Z solution from Section 17.12. As the exact t values are not available from Table A.6, we will use the approximate Z solution, $\bar{d} \pm z_{\alpha/2} s_{\bar{d}}$, where $\bar{d} = -0.53$ mg/dl and $s_{\bar{d}} = \frac{s_d}{\sqrt{n}} = \frac{1.895\ \text{mg/dl}}{\sqrt{35}} = 0.3203$ mg/dl. From Table A.5: $z_{0.05/2} = 1.96$. Therefore, the approximate 95% confidence interval is

$$-0.53\ \text{mg/dl} \pm (1.96 \times 0.3203\ \text{mg/dl})$$
$$-0.53\ \text{mg/dl} \pm 0.628\ \text{mg/dl}$$

17.17 For the melatonin study in Problem 17.15, do a right-tailed test of H_0: $\mu_d = 0$, using $\alpha = 0.05$ and a critical-value decision rule.

Solution

(1) H_0: $\mu_d = 0$, H_1: $\mu_d > 0$

(2) $\alpha = 0.05$

(3) As the samples are paired and we are assuming that the population of differences (d_j) is normally distributed, we can use the t statistic [equation (17.30)]. Thus, with $\alpha = 0.05$, ($\nu = n - 1 = 12 - 1 = 11$), we find from Table A.6 that the right-tailed decision rule is: Reject H_0 if $t^* > (t_{0.05,11} = 1.796)$.

(4) The value of the t statistic is

$$t^* = \frac{4.73 \text{ min} - 0}{0.3308 \text{ min}} = 14.2987, \quad \text{or } 14.299$$

The P value for $\nu = 11$ is in the range $P < 0.0005$.

(5) As $t^* > 1.796$, we reject H_0 and accept H_1. This result is confirmed by the fact that the P value is less than 0.0005. There is thus a significant difference at the 0.05 level of significance between the paired-samples difference and zero, and the results indicate that the 15 mg group fell asleep faster than the 5 mg group. These results are in agreement with the independent-samples study (see Problems 17.9 and 17.10).

17.18 For the cholesterol study in Problem 17.16, do a two-tailed test of H_0: $\mu_d = 0$, using $\alpha = 0.05$ and a critical-value decision rule.

Solution

(1) H_0: $\mu_d = 0$, H_1: $\mu_d \neq 0$

(2) $\alpha = 0.05$

(3) As the samples are paired and large [$(n = 35) > 30$], and we are assuming that the population of differences (d_j) is normally distributed, we can use either the t or Z solution from Section 17.12. As with the confidence interval in Problem 17.16, we will use the approximate Z solution because the exact t values are not available in Table A.6. Thus, with $\alpha = 0.05$ and the appropriate value from Table A.5, the two-tailed decision rule is: Reject H_0 if $z^* > (z_{0.05/2} = 1.96)$ or if $z^* < (-z_{0.05/2} = -1.96)$.

(4) The value of the Z statistic is

$$z^* = \frac{-0.53 \text{ mg/dl} - 0}{0.3203 \text{ mg/dl}} = -1.6537, \quad \text{or } -1.65$$

From Table A.5, the approximate P value is

$$P \approx 2[P(Z \geq \langle z^* = a\rangle | H_0 \text{ is true})] = 2[P(Z > 1.65)] = 2(0.5 - 0.4505) = 0.0990$$

(5) As $-1.96 > z^* < 1.96$, we accept H_0. This result is confirmed by the fact that the approximate P value is greater than 0.05. There is thus no evidence at the 0.05 level of significance that the dandelion substance affects total cholesterol levels.

CRITICAL VALUES OF THE F DISTRIBUTION

17.19 Use Table A.8 to find $f_{\alpha/2,\nu_1,\nu_2} = f_{0.010/2,4,6}$ and $f_{1-\alpha,\nu_1,\nu_2} = f_{1-0.010/2,4,6}$.

Solution

First convert $f_{\alpha/2}$ and $f_{1-\alpha/2}$ values to equivalent f_α values. Thus,

$$f_{0.010/2,4,6} = f_{0.005,4,6} = 12.03$$

and using the reciprocal rule [equation (17.43)] and the technique from Example 17.9,

$$f_{1-0.010/2,4,6} = f_{1-0.005,4,6} = \frac{1}{f_{0.005,6,4}} = \frac{1}{21.97} = 0.0455, \quad \text{or } 0.05$$

17.20 Use the interpolation technique (see Example 17.10) to find $f_{\alpha,\nu_1,\nu_2} = f_{0.050,11,7}$.

Solution

$f_{0.050,11,7}$ is not in Table A.8 but we do find $f_{0.050,10,7} = 3.64$ and $f_{0.050,12,7} = 3.57$. Following the standard linear interpolation sequence (see Example 14.15), first, parallel scales, one for ν_1 and the other for $f_{0.05,\nu_1,7}$ values have been formed in Fig. 17-5. Then, as $\nu_1 = 11$ is at the position on the ν_1 scale (marked by a cross) that is $\frac{1}{2}$ the distance from $\nu_1 = 10$ to $\nu_1 = 12$, therefore $f_{0.05,11,7}$ is also $\frac{1}{2}$ the distance between 3.64 and 3.57 on the $f_{0.05,\nu_1,7}$ scale (also marked with a cross). Thus, the approximate F value is

$$f_{0.050,11,7} \approx 3.64 - [0.5 \times (3.64 - 3.57 = 0.07)]$$
$$\approx 3.605, \quad \text{or } 3.60$$

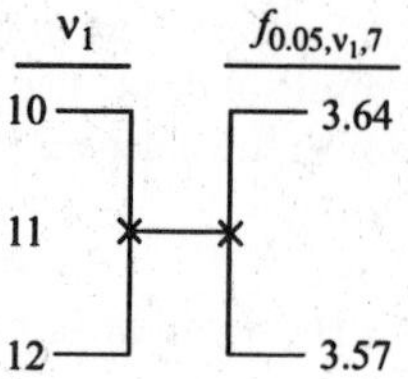

Fig. 17-5

17.21 Use Table A.8 to find: (*a*) $f_{\alpha,\nu_1,\nu_2} = f_{0.050,20,13}$, (*b*) $f_{1-\alpha,\nu_1,\nu_2} = f_{1-0.025,120,60}$, (*c*) $f_{1-\alpha,\nu_1,\nu_2} = f_{1-0.050/2,41,32}$. If the critical values are not in Table A.8, use the next-lower ν_1 and ν_2 values technique (see Example 17.10).

Solution

(*a*) $f_{0.050,20,13} = 2.46$

(*b*) Using the reciprocal rule [equation (17.43)],

$$f_{1-0.025,120,60} = \frac{1}{f_{0.025,60,120}} = \frac{1}{1.53} = 0.6536, \quad \text{or } 0.65$$

(*c*) As the value is not in the table,

$$f_{1-0.050/2,41,32} \approx f_{1-0.025,40,30} = \frac{1}{f_{0.025,30,40}} = \frac{1}{1.94} = 0.5155, \quad \text{or } 0.52$$

17.22 Use Table A.8 to determine what happens to $f_{0.050,\nu_1,\nu_2}$ as: (*a*) ν_2 is increased from 3 to 6 to 12 while ν_1 is held at 3, (*b*) ν_1 is increased from 3 to 6 to 12 while ν_2 is held at 3, and (*c*) ν_1 and ν_2 are simultaneously increased from 3 to 6 to 12.

Solution

(*a*) $f_{0.050,3,3} = 9.28$, $f_{0.050,3,6} = 4.76$, $f_{0.050,3,12} = 3.49$

(*b*) $f_{0.050,3,3} = 9.28$, $f_{0.050,6,3} = 8.94$, $f_{0.050,12,3} = 8.74$

(*c*) $f_{0.050,3,3} = 9.28$, $f_{0.050,6,6} = 4.28$, $f_{0.050,12,12} = 2.69$

From these results you can see that for the same α level, the larger the degrees of freedom, the smaller the critical value.

17.23 Use Table A.8 to determine what happens to $f_{\alpha,10,10}$ as α decreases as follows: 0.100, 0.050, 0.025, 0.010, 0.005.

Solution

$f_{0.100,10,10} = 2.32$, $f_{0.050,10,10} = 2.98$, $f_{0.025,10,10} = 3.72$,
$f_{0.010,10,10} = 4.85$, $f_{0.005,10,10} = 5.85$

From these results you can see that for the same ν_1 and ν_2 values, as α decreases, the critical value increases.

17.24 Verify the following relationships between the F distribution and the t, the standard normal, and the chi-square distributions using $\alpha = 0.050$: (*a*) $f_{\alpha,\nu_1=1,\nu_2} = (t_{\alpha/2,\nu=\nu_2})^2$, with $\nu_2 = 5$, (*b*) $f_{\alpha,\nu_1=1,\nu_2=\infty} = (z_{\alpha/2})^2$, (*c*) $f_{\alpha,\nu_1,\nu_2=\infty} = \dfrac{\chi^2_{\alpha,\nu=\nu_1}}{\nu_1}$, with $\nu_1 = 10$.

Solution

(*a*) From Table A.8, $f_{0.050,1,5} = 6.61$
From Table A.6, $(t_{0.050/2,5})^2 = (2.571)^2 = 6.6100$, or 6.61

(*b*) From Table A.8, $f_{0.050,1,\infty} = 3.84$
From Table A.5, $(z_{0.050/2})^2 = (1.96)^2 = 3.8416$, or 3.84

(*c*) From Table A.8, $f_{0.050,10,\infty} = 1.83$
From Table A.7, $\dfrac{\chi^2_{0.050,10}}{10} = \dfrac{18.31}{10} = 1.831$, or 1.83

CONFIDENCE INTERVALS AND HYPOTHESIS TESTING FOR THE RATIO OF VARIANCES: PARAMETERS NOT KNOWN, INDEPENDENT SAMPLES FROM NORMALLY DISTRIBUTED POPULATIONS

17.25 For the maze-learning study in Problem 17.4, calculate a 99% confidence interval for σ_1^2/σ_2^2.

Solution

In Problem 17.4, independent samples ($n_1 = 10$, $s_1^2 = 3.59$, and $n_2 = 10$, $s_2^2 = 3.37$) were taken from two normally distributed populations. Therefore, we can use here the $(1-\alpha)100\%$ confidence interval from Section 17.20,

$$\left[\frac{s_1^2}{s_2^2}\left(\frac{1}{f_{\alpha/2,\nu_1,\nu_2}}\right), \frac{s_1^2}{s_2^2}(f_{\alpha,\nu_2,\nu_1})\right]$$

where $\dfrac{s_1^2}{s_2^2} = \dfrac{3.59}{3.37}$. From Table A.8: $f_{\alpha/2,\nu_1,\nu_2} = f_{0.010/2,9,9} = 6.54$ and $f_{\alpha/2,\nu_2,\nu_1} = f_{0.010/2,9,9} = 6.54$. Therefore, the 99% confidence interval for σ_1^2/σ_2^2 is

$$\left[\frac{3.59}{3.37}\left(\frac{1}{6.54}\right), \frac{3.59}{3.37}(6.54)\right] = (0.163, 6.967)$$

17.26 For the melatonin study described in Problem 17.5, calculate at 90% confidence interval for σ_1^2/σ_2^2.

Solution

In Problem 17.5, independent samples ($n_1 = 10$, $s_1^2 = 4.36\,\text{min}^2$ and $n_2 = 12$, $s_2^2 = 4.66\,\text{min}^2$) were taken from two normally distributed populations. Therefore, we can use here the $(1-\alpha)100\%$ confidence interval from Section 17.20, with $\dfrac{s_1^2}{s_2^2} = \dfrac{4.36\,\text{min}^2}{4.66\,\text{min}^2}$. From Table A.8 we get the exact value $f_{\alpha/2,\nu_1,\nu_2} = f_{0.100/2,9,11} = 2.90$ and the approximate value, using the next-lower ν_1 and ν_2 values technique (see Example

17.10) $f_{\alpha/2,\nu_2,\nu_1} = f_{0.100/2,11,9} \approx f_{0.050,10,9} = 3.14$. Therefore, the approximate 90% confidence interval for σ_1^2/σ_2^2 is

$$\left[\frac{4.36\ \text{min}^2}{4.66\ \text{min}^2}\left(\frac{1}{2.90}\right), \frac{4.36\ \text{min}^2}{4.66\ \text{min}^2}(3.14)\right] = (0.323, 2.938)$$

17.27 Independent samples are taken from two normally distributed populations with unknown parameters. The sample values are $n_1 = n_2 = 16$, $s_1^2 = 0.41$, and $s_2^2 = 1.36$. Do a left-tailed test at $\alpha = 0.025$ of H_0: $\sigma_1^2/\sigma_2^2 = 1$ using a critical-value decision rule.

Solution

(1) H_0: $\sigma_1^2/\sigma_2^2 = 1$, $\quad H_1$: $\sigma_1^2/\sigma_2^2 < 1$

(2) $\alpha = 0.025$

(3) As we can assume independent samples from normal distributions, we can use the F statistic [equation (17.46)] and so, from Table A.8, the left-tailed decision rule [see Example (17.11(*b*)] is:

$$\text{Reject } H_0 \text{ if } f^* < \left(f_{1-0.025,15,15} = \frac{1}{f_{0.025,15,15}} = \frac{1}{2.86} = 0.3497, \text{ or } 0.35\right)$$

(4) The value of the F statistic is

$$f^* = \frac{s_1^2}{s_2^2} = \frac{0.41}{1.36} = 0.3015, \quad \text{or } 0.30$$

The P value [equation (17.49)] is $P = P(F \leq 0.030|H_0 \text{ is true})$. From step (3) we know that $f_{1-0.025,15,15} = 0.35$. From Table A.8, we find that

$$f_{1-0.01,15,15} = \frac{1}{f_{0.01,15,15}} = \frac{1}{3.52} = 0.2841, \quad \text{or } 0.28$$

Therefore, as $f^* = 0.30$, the P value is in the range $0.01 < P < 0.025$.

(5) As $f^* < 0.35$, we reject H_0 and accept H_1. This result is confirmed by the fact that the P value is in the range $0.01 < P < 0.025$.

17.28 In the maze-learning study described in Problem 17.4, homogeneity of variance was assumed. (In that study, $n_1 = 10$, $s_1^2 = 3.59$, $n_2 = 10$, and $s_2^2 = 3.37$.) Do a two-tailed test of this assumption, using $\alpha = 0.05$ and a critical-value decision rule.

Solution

(1) H_0: $\sigma_1^2/\sigma_2^2 = 1$, $\quad H_1$: $\sigma_1^2/\sigma_2^2 \neq 1$

(2) $\alpha = 0.05$

(3) As we can assume independent samples from normal distributions, we can use the F statistic [equation (17.46)]. Using Table A.8, the two-tailed decision rule [see Example (17.11(*c*)] is:

$$\text{Reject } H_0 \text{ if } f^* > (f_{0.05/2,9,9} = 4.03) \quad \text{or if} \quad f^* < \left(f_{1-0.05/2,9,9} = \frac{1}{f_{0.05/2,9,9}} = \frac{1}{4.03} = 0.2481, \text{ or } 0.25\right)$$

(4) The value of the F statistic is

$$f^* = \frac{s_1^2}{s_2^2} = \frac{3.59}{3.37} = 1.0653, \quad \text{or } 1.07$$

To define the range of the P value, we use the technique from Section 17.21. First, we find the mean,

$$\mu = \frac{\nu_2}{\nu_2 - 2} = \frac{9}{9 - 2} = 1.29$$

As $f^* < \mu$, the P value [equation (17.51)] is $P = 2[P(F \leq 1.07|H_0 \text{ is true})]$. From Table A.8

$$f_{1-0.100,9,9} = \frac{1}{f_{0.100,9,9}} = \frac{1}{2.44} = 0.4098$$

Thus we can say that the P value is in the range: $P > (2 \times 0.1)$, or $P > 0.2$.

(5) As $0.25 < f^* < 4.03$, we accept H_0. This result is confirmed by the fact that the P value is greater than 0.2. There is thus no evidence at the 0.05 level of significance that the variances differ, and we can accept the assumption of homogeneity of variance.

17.29 In the melatonin study in Problem 17.5, homogeneity of variance was assumed. (In that study, $n_1 = 10$, $s_1^2 = 4.36\,\text{min}^2$, $n_2 = 12$, $s_2^2 = 4.66\,\text{min}^2$.) Do a two-tailed test of that assumption, using $\alpha = 0.01$ and a critical-value decision rule.

Solution

(1) H_0: $\sigma_1^2/\sigma_2^2 = 1$, $\quad H_1$: $\sigma_1^2/\sigma_2^2 \neq 1$

(2) $\alpha = 0.01$

(3) As we can assume independent samples from normal distributions, we can use the F statistic [equation (17.46)]. Thus, with $\alpha = 0.01$ and $\nu_1 = 10 - 1 = 9$, and $\nu_2 = 12 - 1 = 11$, using the next-lower values techniques (see Example 17.10) with Table A.8, the approximate two-tailed decision rule [see Example 17.11(*c*)] is:

$$\text{Reject } H_0 \text{ if } f^* > (f_{0.010/2,9,11} = 5.54)$$

$$\text{or if} \quad f^* < \left(f_{1-0.010/2,9,11} = \frac{1}{f_{0.010/2,11,9}} \approx \frac{1}{f_{0.010/2,10,9}} = \frac{1}{6.42} = 0.1558, \text{ or } 0.16\right)$$

(4) The value of the F statistic is

$$f^* = \frac{s_1^2}{s_2^2} = \frac{4.36\text{ min}^2}{4.66\text{ min}^2} = 0.9356, \quad \text{or } 0.94$$

Using the technique from Section 17.21 to place the P value in a range, we find that

$$\mu = \frac{\nu_2}{\nu_2 - 2} = \frac{11}{11 - 2} = 1.2222, \quad \text{or } 1.22$$

As f^* is less than the mean, the P value [equation (17.51)] is $P = 2[P(F \leq 0.94|H_0 \text{ is true})]$. Again, using the next-lower values technique with Table A.8,

$$f_{1-0.100,9,11} = \frac{1}{f_{0.100,11,9}} \approx \frac{1}{f_{0.100,10,9}} = \frac{1}{2.42} = 0.4132, \quad \text{or } 0.41$$

Thus, we can say that the P value is in the range of $P > (2 \times 0.1)$, or $P > 0.2$.

(5) As $0.16 < f^* < 5.54$, we accept H_0. This result is confirmed by the fact that the P value is greater than 0.2. Thus, there is no evidence at the 0.01 level of significance that the variances differ, and we can accept the assumption of homogeneity of variance.

APPROXIMATE CONFIDENCE INTERVALS AND HYPOTHESIS TESTS FOR THE DIFFERENCE BETWEEN PROPORTIONS FROM TWO BINOMIAL POPULATIONS: LARGE INDEPENDENT SAMPLES

17.30 Two districts of a large city are being considered for a new stadium. A poll is taken of 1,000 registered voters in each district to estimate the unknown proportions, p_1 and p_2, of registered voters who favor having the stadium in their district. The results are: district 1, 572 in favor; district 2, 533 in favor. From these results, determine an approximate 99% confidence for $p_1 - p_2$ using (*a*) the point-estimate solution, and (*b*) the conservative solution (see Section 17.25).

Solution

(*a*) As n_1 and n_2 both meet the most conservative sample-size requirement ($n \geq 100$), we can use the normal-approximation technique (see Section 17.24). Further, as there are more than 100,000 voters in each district, $n \leq 0.05N$, and so there is no need for the finite-population correction factor. The point estimates of p_1, q_1, p_2, and q_2 are

$$\bar{p}_1 = \frac{y_1}{n_1} = \frac{572}{1{,}000} = 0.572, \qquad \bar{q}_1 = 1 - \bar{p}_1 = 1 - 0.572 = 0.428$$

$$\bar{p}_2 = \frac{y_2}{n_2} = \frac{553}{1{,}000} = 0.553, \qquad \bar{q}_2 = 1 - \bar{p}_2 = 1 - 0.553 = 0.447$$

Using Table A.5: $z_{\alpha/2} = z_{0.01/2} = 2.575$. The approximate 99% confidence interval using the point-estimate solution is

$$(\bar{p}_1 - \bar{p}_2) \pm z_{\alpha/2}\sqrt{\frac{\bar{p}_1\bar{q}_1}{n_1} + \frac{\bar{p}_2\bar{q}_2}{n_2}}$$

$$(0.572 - 0.553) \pm 2.575\sqrt{\frac{(0.572 \times 0.428)}{1{,}000} + \frac{(0.553 \times 0.447)}{1{,}000}}$$

$$0.019 \pm 0.0571$$

(*b*) Using the conservative solution [equation (17.59)]

$$(0.572 - 0.553) \pm 2.575\sqrt{\frac{1}{4(1{,}000)} + \frac{1}{4(1{,}000)}}$$

$$0.019 \pm 0.0576$$

17.31 You are conducting a clinical test of a new cholesterol-reducing drug with 1,000 men who have high cholesterol levels. For six months, you give 500 of these men (group 1) a daily pill that contains a standard dose of the drug. For the other 500 men (group 2), for six months you give a daily *placebo* (the same pill but without the drug). One of the many measures that you take is the incidence of headaches during the study, and these are the results: 6.2% of group 1 experienced headaches, 3.9% of group 2 experienced headaches. Convert these percentages to proportions. Then, using p_1 and p_2 to represent the unknown population proportions for these groups, determine an approximate 95% confidence interval for $p_1 - p_2$. Find this confidence interval using (*a*) the point-estimate solution, and (*b*) the conservative solution.

Solution

(*a*) As n_1 and n_2 both meet the most conservative requirement for sample size ($n \geq 100$), we can use the normal-approximation technique (see Section 17.24). Further, as the hypothetical populations for the groups in the experiment are very large, there is no need for the finite-population correction factor. The point estimates of p_1, q_1, p_2, and q_2 are: $\bar{p}_1 = 0.062$, $\bar{q}_1 = 0.938$, $\bar{p}_2 = 0.039$, $\bar{q}_2 = 0.961$. Therefore, as from Table A.5: $z_{\alpha/2} = z_{0.05/2} = 1.96$, the approximate 95% confidence interval using the point-estimate solution is

$$(\bar{p}_1 - \bar{p}_2) \pm z_{\alpha/2}\sqrt{\frac{\bar{p}_1\bar{q}_1}{n_1} + \frac{\bar{p}_2\bar{q}_2}{n_2}}$$

$$(0.062 - 0.039) \pm 1.96\sqrt{\frac{(0.062 \times 0.938)}{500} + \frac{(0.039 \times 0.961)}{500}}$$

$$0.023 \pm 0.0271$$

(*b*) Using the conservative solution [equation (17.59)],

$$(0.062 - 0.039) \pm 1.96\sqrt{\frac{1}{4(500)} + \frac{1}{4(500)}}$$
$$0.023 \pm 0.0620$$

17.32 For the stadium poll in Problem 17.30, do a two-tailed test of H_0: $p_1 - p_2 = 0$ using $\alpha = 0.01$ and a *P*-value decision rule.

Solution

(1) H_0: $p_1 - p_2 = 0$, H_1: $p_1 - p_2 \neq 0$

(2) $\alpha = 0.01$

(3) As the independent samples are sufficiently large ($n_1 = n_2 = 1{,}000$), we can use the Z statistic [equation (17.57)] and this two-tailed decision rule: Reject H_0 if $P \leq 0.01$.

(4) Using equation (17.60),

$$\bar{p} = \frac{y_1 + y_2}{n_1 + n_2} = \frac{572 + 553}{1{,}000 + 1{,}000} = 0.5625$$
$$\bar{q} = 1 - \bar{p} = 1 - 0.5625 = 0.4375$$

and these values from Problem 17.30,

$$\bar{p}_1 = 0.572, \qquad \bar{p}_2 = 0.553$$

the value of the Z statistic [equation (17.61)] is

$$z^* = \frac{(0.572 - 0.553)}{\sqrt{(0.5625)(0.4375)\left(\frac{1}{1{,}000} + \frac{1}{1{,}000}\right)}} = 0.856, \quad \text{or } 0.86$$

Using Table A.5, the approximate P value [equation (16.4)] is

$$P \approx 2[P(Z \geq \langle z^* = a \rangle | H_0 \text{ is true})] = 2[P(Z > 0.86)] = 2(0.5 - 0.3051) = 0.3898$$

(5) As the approximate P value is greater than 0.01, we accept H_0. Thus, there is no evidence at the 0.01 level of significance that the proportions differ between the two districts.

17.33 For the cholesterol study in Problem 17.31, do a two-tailed test of H_0: $p_1 - p_2 = 0$, using $\alpha = 0.05$ and a critical-value decision rule.

Solution

(1) H_0: $p_1 - p_2 = 0$, H_1: $p_1 - p_2 \neq 0$

(2) $\alpha = 0.05$

(3) As the independent samples are sufficiently large ($n_1 = n_2 = 500$), we can use the Z statistic [equation (17.57)] and, using Table A.5, this two-tailed decision rule: Reject H_0 if $z^* > (z_{0.05/2} = 1.96)$ or if $z^* < (-z_{0.05/2} = -1.96)$.

(4) Using equation (17.60),

$$\bar{p} = \frac{y_1 + y_2}{n_1 + n_2} = \frac{n_1\bar{p}_1 + n_2\bar{p}_2}{n_1 + n_2} = \frac{(500 \times 0.062) + (500 \times 0.039)}{500 + 500} = 0.0505$$
$$\bar{q} = 1 - \bar{p} = 1 - 0.0505 = 0.9495$$

and these values from Problem 17.31,

$$\bar{p}_1 = 0.062, \qquad \bar{p}_2 = 0.039$$

the value of the Z statistic [equation (17.61)] is

$$z^* = \frac{(0.062 - 0.039)}{\sqrt{(0.0505)(0.9495)\left(\frac{1}{500} + \frac{1}{500}\right)}} = 1.661, \quad \text{or } 1.66$$

Using Table A.5, the approximate P value [equation (16.4)] is

$$P \approx 2[P(Z \geq (z^* = a)|H_0 \text{ is true})] = 2[P(Z > 1.66)] = 2(0.5 - 0.4515) = 0.0970$$

(5) As $-1.96 < z^* < 1.96$, we accept H_0. This result is confirmed by the fact that the approximate P value is greater than 0.05. Thus, there is no evidence at the 0.05 level of significance that the proportions differ between the two groups.

17.34 Before doing the clinical test in Problem 17.31, you had the hypothesis that the group-1 subjects would have a larger proportion of headaches. Therefore, a right-tailed test of H_0: $p_1 - p_2 = 0$ could have been done. Do this test, using $\alpha = 0.05$ and a critical-value decision rule.

Solution

(1) H_0: $p_1 - p_2 = 0$, $\quad H_1$: $p_1 - p_2 > 0$

(2) $\alpha = 0.05$

(3) We can again use the Z statistic [equation (17.57)], and using Table A.5, this right-tailed decision rule: Reject H_0 if $z^* > (z_{0.050} = 1.645)$.

(4) From Problem 17.33, $z^* = 1.66$. Using Table A.5, the approximate P value [equation 16.6)] is

$$P \approx P[Z \geq (z^* = a)|H_0 \text{ is true}] = P(Z > 1.66) = 0.5 - 0.4515 = 0.0485$$

(5) As $z^* > 1.645$, we reject H_0 and accept H_1. This result is confirmed by the fact that the approximate P value is less than 0.05. Thus, using the one-tailed test, we can say that the evidence evaluated at the 0.05 level of significance indicates that the drug group had a larger proportion of headaches than the placebo group.

Supplementary Problems

CONFIDENCE INTERVALS AND HYPOTHESIS TESTS FOR THE DIFFERENCE BETWEEN MEANS: KNOWN STANDARD DEVIATIONS, INDEPENDENT SAMPLES FROM NORMALLY DISTRIBUTED POPULATIONS

17.35 A biologist is studying two populations of ring-necked snakes, and wants to know whether they are morphologically different. He counts the number of scale rows, which is known to be normally distributed in both populations with standard deviations of $\sigma_1 = 1.4$ in population 1 and $\sigma_2 = 1.2$ in population 2. He takes independent random samples of $n_1 = 35$ and $n_2 = 40$ from the two populations, and finds that $\bar{x}_1 = 17.0$ and $\bar{x}_2 = 16.3$. What is the 95% confidence interval for $\mu_1 - \mu_2$?

Ans. 0.7 ± 0.59

17.36 For the two populations of ring-necked snakes in Problem 17.35, do a two-tailed test, at $\alpha = 0.05$, of H_0: $\mu_1 - \mu_2 = 0$. State whether you accept or reject H_0, and give the probability of getting this z^* value given that H_0 is true.

Ans. Reject H_0 because $z^* = 2.31 > z_{\alpha/2} = 1.96$, $P = 0.021$

17.37 A marketing researcher is interested in knowing whether urban families differ from rural families in the number of times per month that they shop for groceries. Assuming that the frequency of shopping is normally distributed in both populations, the researcher takes independent random samples of urban families ($n_1 = 50$ families, $\sigma_1 = 2.3$ times per month) and rural families ($n_2 = 50$ families, $\sigma_2 = 2.8$ times per month), and finds that for the urban families, $\bar{x}_1 = 8.6$ times per month, and for the rural families, $\bar{x}_2 = 7.4$ times per month. What is the 95% confidence interval for $\mu_1 - \mu_2$?

Ans. 1.2 ± 1.00

17.38 For the marketing research described in Problem 17.37, do a right-tailed test, at $\alpha = 0.05$, of H_0: $\mu_1 - \mu_2 = 0$. State whether you accept or reject H_0, and give the probability of getting this z^* value given that H_0 is true.

Ans. Reject H_0 because $z^* = 2.34 > z_\alpha = 1.645$, $P = 0.0096$

CONFIDENCE INTERVALS AND HYPOTHESIS TESTS FOR THE DIFFERENCE BETWEEN MEANS: STANDARD DEVIATIONS NOT KNOWN BUT ASSUMED EQUAL, SMALL INDEPENDENT SAMPLES FROM NORMALLY DISTRIBUTED POPULATIONS

17.39 A conservationist is interested in knowing whether polar bears in the wild have lower rates of reproduction than polar bears in zoos. He measures the number of cubs produced per female during the peak reproductive years, between 15 and 30 years of age, in zoos ($n_1 = 24$, $\bar{x}_1 = 19.1$, $s_1 = 2.3$) and in a wild Alaskan population ($n_2 = 18$, $\bar{x}_2 = 16.3$, $s_2 = 4.1$). This measure of reproductive rate is normally distributed and is assumed to have the same variance in both populations. What is the 95% confidence interval for the difference between means?

Ans. 2.8 ± 2.01

17.40 Before doing the study in Problem 17.39, the researcher had reason to believe that the reproductive rate in wild polar bears is lower than in captive polar bears. Do a right-tailed test, at $\alpha = 0.05$, of H_0: $\mu_1 - \mu_2 = 0$. State whether you accept or reject H_0, and give the approximate probability of getting this t^* value given that H_0 is true.

Ans. Reject H_0 because $t^* = 2.814 > t_{0.05,40} = 1.684$, $0.005 < P < 0.005$

17.41 A gerontologist wants to know whether time of day has an effect on learning ability in elderly people. To form two groups, she takes two independent random samples of men over 75 years of age. The subjects in both groups read a chapter in a psychology book and then take a 50-question multiple-choice exam on the material. Group 1 ($n_1 = 12$) reads the chapter and takes the exam at 8 AM and group 2 ($n_2 = 12$) reads the chapter and takes the exam at 6 PM. The ability to learn is measured by the number of correct answers on the exam. The results: $\bar{x}_1 = 42$ correct, $s_1 = 2.0$, $\bar{x}_2 = 39$ correct, $s_2 = 3.3$. Assuming that the learning measures of both groups are normally distributed with homogeneity of variance, what is the 95% confidence interval for $\mu_1 - \mu_2$?

Ans. 3.0 ± 2.31

17.42 For the memory study in Problem 17.41, do a two-tailed test at $\alpha = 0.05$ of H_0: $\mu_1 - \mu_2 = 0$. State whether you accept or reject H_0, and give the approximate probability of getting this t^* value given that H_0 is true.

Ans. Reject H_0 because $t^* = 2.693 > t_{0.05/2,22} = 2.074$, $0.01 < P < 0.02$

CONFIDENCE INTERVALS AND HYPOTHESIS TESTS FOR THE DIFFERENCE BETWEEN MEANS: STANDARD DEVIATIONS NOT KNOWN, LARGE INDEPENDENT SAMPLES FROM ANY POPULATION DISTRIBUTIONS

17.43 The owner of a restaurant plans to open a second restaurant in another community, and wants to know how many customers to expect there compared with the number he gets in his first restaurant. He believes that the number of times people eat out in a restaurant each month does not form a normal distribution. He takes independent random samples of residents in the two communities, asking each person how often they eat out each month. His results: $n_1 = 120$, $\bar{x}_1 = 6.5$ times/month, $s_1 = 2.1$ times/month, and $n_2 = 120$, $\bar{x}_2 = 5.8$ times/month, $s_2 = 1.8$ times/month. What is the 95% confidence interval for $\mu_1 - \mu_2$?

Ans. 0.7 ± 0.49

17.44 For the restaurant customers in Problem 17.43, do a two-tailed test, at $\alpha = 0.05$, of H_0: $\mu_1 - \mu_2 = 0$. State whether you accept or reject H_0, and give the approximate probability of getting this z^* value given that H_0 is true.

Ans. Reject H_0 because $z^* = 2.77 > z_{0.05/2} = 1.96$, $P \approx 0.006$

17.45 A population geneticist wants to know whether two populations of lady bugs, in two valleys, are genetically different. One measure of possible difference is the number of dark spots on the wings, which he knows is not normally distributed in either population. He takes independent random samples, of 60 lady bugs each, from the two populations and finds: $\bar{x}_1 = 3.8$ spots, $s_1 = 1.2$ spots, and $\bar{x}_2 = 3.6$ spots, $s_2 = 1.3$ spots. What is the 95% confidence interval of $\mu_1 - \mu_2$?

Ans. 0.2 ± 0.45

17.46 For the lady-bug study in Problem 17.45, use a two-tailed test, at $\alpha = 0.05$, of H_0: $\mu_1 - \mu_2 = 0$. State whether you accept or reject H_0, and give the approximate probability of getting this z^* value given that H_0 is true.

Ans. Accept H_0 because $-1.96 < z^* = 0.88 < 1.96$, $P \approx 0.38$

CONFIDENCE INTERVALS AND HYPOTHESIS TESTS FOR THE DIFFERENCE BETWEEN MEANS: PAIRED SAMPLES

17.47 A dairy farmer wants to know whether a new hormone will increase the milk production of his cows. He takes a random sample of 22 cows and keeps daily records of how much milk each cow produces for 2 weeks just before the hormonal therapy begins and then again for 2 weeks just after 6 months of therapy. For each cow, he then subtracts the average milk total before therapy from the average milk total after therapy. The results are $\bar{d} = 1.23$ gal, $s_d = 0.68$ gal. Assuming that the population of differences is normally distributed, what is the 95% confidence interval for μ_d?

Ans. 1.23 gal $\pm$ 0.302 gal

17.48 For the milk-production study in Problem 17.47, do a right-tailed test, at $\alpha = 0.01$, of H_0: $\mu_d = 0$. State whether you accept or reject H_0, and give the approximate probability of getting this t^* value given that H_0 is true.

Ans. Reject H_0 because $t^* = 8.484 > t_{0.01,21} = 2.518$, $P < 0.005$

17.49 A manufacturer of hiking boots wants to know whether his new-style boots (population 1) last longer than the boots he now sells (population 2). He takes a random sample of 35 hikers and has each hiker wear the new-style boot on one foot (which foot is chosen at random) and the present boot on the other foot, and then keeps track of how many miles it takes for each boot to reach a certain level of deterioration. He calculates the differences in miles for the two boots worn by each hiker (present subtracted from new), finding an average difference $\bar{d} = 5$ miles with $s_d = 5$ miles. Assuming that the population of differences is normally distributed, use the approximate Z solution to determine the 95% confidence interval for μ_d.

Ans. 5 miles $\pm$ 1.7 miles

17.50 For the hiking-boot study in Problem 17.49, do a right-tailed test, at $\alpha = 0.05$, of H_0: $\mu_d = 0$. Use the approximate Z solution. State whether you accept or reject H_0, and give the approximate probability of getting this z^* value given that H_0 is true.

Ans. Reject H_0 because $z^* = 5.916 > z_{0.05} = 1.645$, $P \approx 0$

CRITICAL VALUES OF THE F DISTRIBUTION

17.51 Use Table A.8 to find the approximate value of $f_{\alpha,\nu_1,\nu_2} = f_{0.010,24,33}$. Use both techniques of approximation: interpolation and next-lower ν_1 and ν_2 values (see Example 17.10 and Problem 17.20).

Ans. Using interpolation $f_{0.010,24,33} \approx 2.47 - [0.3 \times (2.47 - 2.29 = 0.18)] = 2.4160$, or 2.42. Using next-lower values, $f_{0.010,24,33} \approx f_{0.010,24,30} = 2.47$

17.52 Use Table A.8 to find $f_{\alpha/2,\nu_1,\nu_2} = f_{0.100/2,15,17}$.

Ans. $f_{0.100/2,15,17} = f_{0.050,15,17} = 2.31$

17.53 Use Table A.8 to find $f_{1-\alpha/2,\nu_1,\nu_2} = f_{1-0.010/2,12,24}$.

Ans. $f_{1-0.010/2,12,24} = f_{1-0.005,12,24} = \dfrac{1}{f_{0.005,24,12}} = \dfrac{1}{4.43} = 0.2257$, or 0.23

17.54 Use Table A.8 to find $f_{\alpha,\nu_1,\nu_2} = f_{0.100,40,37}$ by means of the next-lower ν_1 and ν_2 values techniques (see Example 17.10).

Ans. $f_{0.100,40,37} \approx f_{0.100,40,30} = 1.57$

CONFIDENCE INTERVALS AND HYPOTHESIS TESTS FOR THE RATIO OF VARIANCES: PARAMETERS NOT KNOWN, INDEPENDENT SAMPLES FROM NORMALLY DISTRIBUTED POPULATIONS

17.55 A biologist wants to know whether elevation has an effect on variability of body size in a species of dragonfly. As an initial step toward finding an answer, she takes independent, random samples of $n_1 = 41$ from a low-elevation site and $n_2 = 41$ from a high-elevation site, and finds for body lengths that $s_1^2 = 0.15\,\text{mm}^2$ and $s_2^2 = 0.12\,\text{mm}^2$. Assuming that body lengths are normally distributed in both populations, what is the 95% confidence interval for the ratio of population variances σ_1^2/σ_2^2?

Ans. $(0.665, 2.350)$

17.56 For the dragonfly study in Problem 17.55, do a two-tailed test, at $\alpha = 0.05$, of the hypothesis: H_0: $\sigma_1^2/\sigma_2^2 = 1$. State whether you accept or reject H_0, and give the approximate probability of getting this f^* value given that H_0 is true.

Ans. Accept H_0 because $f^* = 1.25 < f_{0.05/2,40,40} = 1.88$, $P > 0.20$

APPROXIMATE CONFIDENCE INTERVALS AND HYPOTHESIS TESTS FOR THE DIFFERENCE BETWEEN PROPORTIONS FROM TWO BINOMIAL POPULATIONS: LARGE INDEPENDENT SAMPLES

17.57 A psychologist wants to know whether there are more left-handed people in the sciences than in the humanities. He takes random samples of 160 professors in science departments (population 1) and 160 professors in humanities departments (population 2). If p is the proportion that are left handed, and q is the proportion that are not, then the results are: $\bar{p}_1 = 0.32$, $\bar{q}_1 = 0.68$, $\bar{p}_2 = 0.28$, and $\bar{q}_2 = 0.72$. Using the point-estimate solution, what is the approximate 95% confidence interval for the difference between proportions $p_1 - p_2$?

Ans. 0.04 ± 0.100

17.58 For the handedness study in Problem 17.57, use the conservative solution to find the approximate 95% confidence interval for the difference between proportions.

Ans. 0.04 ± 0.110

17.59 For the handedness study in Problem 17.57, do a two-tailed test, at $\alpha = 0.05$, of H_0: $p_1 - p_2 = 0$. State whether you accept or reject H_0, and the approximate probability of getting this z^* value given that H_0 is true.

Ans. Accept H_0 because $-z_{0.05/2} = -1.96 < z^* = 0.781 < z_{0.05/2} = 1.96$, $P \approx 0.435$

CHAPTER 18

Multisample Estimation and Hypothesis Testing

18.1 MULTISAMPLE INFERENCES

In Chapters 14 through 17, we examined parametric one-sample and two-sample estimation and hypothesis testing. Now, in this chapter, we go on to introduce a very important and complex area of inferential statistics: *multisample estimation and hypothesis testing*. This chapter will focus on multisample inferences about population means and variances; later, in Chapter 20, as part of our discussion of nonparametric techniques, we will deal with multisample inferences about population proportions (see Section 20.5).

To understand the difference between previous inferential problems and multisample inferential problems, consider this example which we will follow through much of this chapter:

> You are developing a new variety of wheat plant to be grown in computer-controlled growth chambers during space flights. To maximize the use of the growth chambers, this plant must combine short stature and high yield. After years of crossbreeding, you have developed three types of wheat that are your final candidates: variety 1, variety 2, and variety 3. Among other experiments with these plants, you are growing five plants from each variety in a growth chamber and measuring the height (in inches) of each plant at maturity (130 days after germination).

While in the previous chapters on inferential statistics we dealt with at most two populations at a time, in multisample work we deal simultaneously with three or more populations. Thus, in the example we are analyzing three independent populations, one for each variety, having means μ_1, μ_2, and μ_3, and variances σ_1^2, σ_2^2, and σ_3^2. From the samples taken from these populations, we want to solve estimation and hypothesis-testing problems about these population parameters. To do this, we can not use previously developed techniques, but instead must now introduce a new technique called the *analysis of variance*.

18.2 THE ANALYSIS OF VARIANCE

The analysis of variance, commonly abbreviated as ANOVA (or ANOV, or AOV), is a technique for using sample information to test hypotheses about differences among k population means, where $k > 2$.

The technique was developed by R. A. Fisher (see Section 17.17), and it is now a large area of inferential statistics. In this chapter we can only briefly introduce the most basic forms of ANOVA.

While the technique is for testing hypotheses about population means, its components can also be used to determine confidence intervals for the population means (see Sections 18.16 and 18.24) and to evaluate differences among population variances (see Sections 18.17 and 18.24).

For the results of a study to be analyzable by ANOVA, there must have been one or more active independent variables, called *factors*, possibly affecting the dependent variable being measured. Thus, in the example in Section 18.1, there is one factor (variety of wheat) that is possibly affecting the dependent variable (height of plant). The categories of a factor that are used in the study are called *treatments* (or *levels*). Thus, in the example, there are three treatments for the factor: variety 1, variety 2, and variety 3. The factors can be at any level of measurement [in the example the factor is nominal level (see Volume 1, Section 2.4)], but to use parametric ANOVA the dependent variable must be at interval or ratio level (see Volume 1, Sections 2.6 and 2.7).

The technique evaluates differences in population means by examining the *sources of variation* in the sample data. In essence, it determines whether any of the variation in the sample means is due to differences in treatments (whether the samples were actually taken from populations with different means), or whether the differences in sample means are simply due to the random variation that would occur if the sampling had been done from identical populations (or the same population).

18.3 ANOVA: ONE-WAY, TWO-WAY, OR MULTIWAY

In the wheat experiment we have been following, there is only one independent variable, or factor: varieties of wheat. It is therefore said that the measurement data taken in the study (height of plant) can be *classified* only under one criterion: variety of wheat. The ANOVA done on the data is therefore called a *one-way ANOVA* (or *single-factor ANOVA*, or *one-factor ANOVA*, or *single-classification ANOVA*).

It is often the case, however, that to accomplish more with a single experiment, the experiment is designed to simultaneously investigate the effects of two or more independent factors on the dependent variable. If a two-factor design is used and the data can thus be classified under two criteria, then the analysis used is called a *two-way ANOVA*; if the design includes three factors, then the analysis is called a *three-way ANOVA*; and so on. In general, if there are more than two factors, then the analysis is called a *multiway ANOVA*.

For our wheat experiment, a design that would require a two-way ANOVA might simultaneously investigate the effects of both wheat variety and growth chamber temperature on plant height. A design that would require a three-way ANOVA, might add a third factor to the experiment, say amount of light in the growth chamber, or amount of a specific nutrient in the growth liquid.

In this chapter, which is a brief introduction to the logic and procedures of ANOVA, we will deal only with one-way ANOVA.

18.4 ONE-WAY ANOVA: FIXED EFFECTS OR RANDOM EFFECTS

A one-way ANOVA is called a *fixed-effects ANOVA* if the treatments for the factor being investigated have been selected nonrandomly as the only treatments of interest. A one-way ANOVA is called a *random-effects ANOVA* if the treatments are a random sample from a larger collection of treatments for the factor. If it is a fixed-effects design, conclusions from the study must be limited to the specific treatments used. If it is a random-effects design, then conclusions can be more general, dealing with the larger collection of treatments from which the sample of treatments was taken.

Different techniques are required for these two forms of ANOVA, and in this introductory chapter we deal only with fixed-effects techniques. Our wheat-variety experiment could have been either model, but we will assume that the three varieties being studied are the only varieties of interest, and thus that the results should be analyzed with a fixed-effects ANOVA.

18.5 ONE-WAY, FIXED-EFFECTS ANOVA: THE ASSUMPTIONS

For the results of an experiment (exploratory, controlled, or natural; see Volume 1, Sections 3.9 through 3.11) to be analyzed with a one-way, fixed-effects *ANOVA*, the experiment must have one independent variable (factor) and one dependent variable (see Section 18.3), and the treatments for the factor must have been non-randomly selected as the only treatments of interest (see Section 18.4). In addition, these assumptions must be satisfied:

(1) Independent random samples were taken from k populations of interval-level or ratio-level measurements, and these samples can be equal in size ($n_1 = n_2 = \cdots = n_k = n$) or unequal. (In Sections 18.6 through 18.13 we will give procedures for use with equal-sized samples, and then in Sections 18.18 through 18.22 we will give general procedures that can be used with either equal or unequal sample sizes.)

(2) Each of the k populations is normally distributed, with means $\mu_1, \mu_2, \ldots, \mu_k$, and variances $\sigma_1^2, \sigma_2^2, \ldots, \sigma_k^2$.

(3) The k population variances are equal: $\sigma_1^2 = \sigma_2^2 = \cdots = \sigma_k^2$. It is thus assumed that there is homogeneity of variance (see Section 17.6): that all the population variances are equal to a common variance σ^2.

18.6 EQUAL-SAMPLES, ONE-WAY, FIXED-EFFECTS ANOVA: H_0 AND H_1

The ANOVA is a technique for testing statistical hypotheses about population means. For the one-way fixed-effects ANOVA there is, as always, a pair of competing statistical hypotheses: the null (H_0) and the alternative (H_1). The null is always written

$$H_0\colon \mu_1 = \mu_2 = \cdots = \mu_k$$

The alternative can be written in various ways:

H_1: The k means are not all equal.
H_1: At least two of the means are not equal.
H_1: Not all means are equal.
H_1: H_0 is not true.

A normal distribution is completely determined by its parameters μ and σ^2 (see Section 12.3). Therefore, here, as we are assuming normal distributions and a common variance σ^2 (see Section 18.5), what we are really testing is whether the samples have been taken from identical populations (or the same population).

18.7 EQUAL-SAMPLES, ONE-WAY, FIXED-EFFECTS ANOVA: ORGANIZING THE DATA

We will assume that data have been collected for a study in which there was one factor with k treatments, and one dependent variable. We will further assume that k random samples of measurements were taken for the dependent variable, one for each treatment, with each sample of size n, producing a data total of nk observations. We will denote each observation by the symbol x_{ij}, where i represents the treatments from 1 to k, and j represents the specific value from 1 to n in the sequence for sample i. These nk data values are shown in the typical summary organization for one-way ANOVA in Table 18.1, where the rows represent the samples, and the columns represent values in each sample at that position in the sample sequence. Thus, for example, the first row shows the sample sequence from 1 to n for sample 1 (treatment 1), x_{11} to x_{1n}, and the column on the left shows the first data value in each of the k samples, x_{11} to x_{k1}.

The sum of the values in each row, called the *total* in ANOVA and denoted by T (capital T even though it is not a variable), is shown in the total column to the right of each row. Thus, for example, the

Table 18.1

Factor	Dependent variable							Total	Mean
1	x_{11}	x_{12}	$\cdots$	x_{1j}	$\cdots$	x_{1n}		$T_{1.}$	$\bar{x}_{1.}$
2	x_{21}	x_{22}	$\cdots$	x_{2j}	$\cdots$	x_{2n}		$T_{2.}$	$\bar{x}_{2.}$
$\vdots$	$\vdots$	$\vdots$		$\vdots$		$\vdots$		$\vdots$	$\vdots$
i	x_{i1}	x_{i2}	$\cdots$	x_{ij}	$\cdots$	x_{in}		$T_{i.}$	$\bar{x}_{i.}$
$\vdots$	$\vdots$	$\vdots$		$\vdots$		$\vdots$		$\vdots$	$\vdots$
k	x_{k1}	x_{k2}	$\cdots$	x_{kj}	$\cdots$	x_{kn}		$T_{k.}$	$\bar{x}_{k.}$
								$T_{..}$	$\bar{x}_{..}$

symbol $T_{1.}$, with its subscript (1.), means it is the sum of all observations for the first treatment. It is calculated with the formula

$$T_{1.} = \sum_{j=1}^{n} x_{1j} \tag{18.1}$$

and for the ith treatment, $T_{i.}$ is calculated with the formula

$$T_{i.} = \sum_{j=1}^{n} x_{ij} \tag{18.2}$$

The symbol at the bottom of the total column, $T_{..}$, means it is the sum of the nk observations in all samples, and it is calculated with the formula

$$T_{..} = \sum_{i=1}^{k} \sum_{j=1}^{n} x_{ij} \tag{18.3}$$

where the double summation sign means: First sum over all sample values from 1 to n for each treatment, and then sum over all treatments from 1 to k.

The mean of the values in each row is shown in the mean column to the right of the total column. Thus, for example, the symbol $\bar{x}_{1.}$ indicates it is the mean of all observations for the first treatment. It is calculated with the formula

$$\bar{x}_{1.} = \frac{\sum_{j=1}^{n} x_{1j}}{n} \tag{18.4}$$

and for the ith treatment, $\bar{x}_{i.}$ is calculated with the formula

$$\bar{x}_{i.} = \frac{\sum_{j=1}^{n} x_{ij}}{n} \tag{18.5}$$

The symbol at the bottom of the mean column, $\bar{x}_{..}$, indicates it is the mean of all nk observations, called the *overall mean* (see Volume 1, Section 6.10) (or the *grand mean*, or the *grand average*), and it is calculated with the formula

$$\bar{x}_{..} = \frac{\sum_{i=1}^{k} \sum_{j=1}^{n} x_{ij}}{nk} \tag{18.6}$$

EXAMPLE 18.1 In the example we have been following, you have performed the experiment of growing the five plants for each wheat variety, measuring the height of each plant (to the nearest inch) at maturity. These are the results: variety 1 (17, 18, 17, 16, 18); variety 2 (21, 19, 18, 19, 20); variety 3 (18, 21, 20, 21, 19). Organize the data into a summary table like Table 18.1.

Solution

The requested table, with totals and means calculated, is shown in Table 18.2.

Table 18.2

Wheat variety	Height (in)					Total	Mean
1	17	18	17	16	18	86 in	17.2 in
2	21	19	18	19	20	97 in	19.4 in
3	18	21	20	21	19	99 in	19.8 in
						282 in	18.8 in

18.8 EQUAL-SAMPLES, ONE-WAY, FIXED-EFFECTS ANOVA: THE BASIC RATIONALE

At this point in our discussion of one-way, fixed-effects ANOVA, we know that equal-sized random samples are taken from k independent, normally distributed populations that have a common variance, σ^2. We also know that we will somehow use this sample information in the ANOVA to test: H_0: $\mu_1 = \mu_2 = \cdots = \mu_k$.

The way this is done is to determine, from the data, two independent point estimates of σ^2 and compare them by using an F test (see Section 17.21). The first estimate, which will be the denominator of the F ratio, is called the *within-samples estimate* (or *error estimate*) which we will denote by s_W^2. This estimate is determined by calculating a variance for each of the k samples with respect to their own sample mean ($\bar{x}_{i.}$), and then pooling these variances. This estimate of σ^2 is then a measure of *within-samples random variation* (or *random error*).

The second estimate of σ^2, which will be the numerator of the F ratio, is called the *among-samples estimate*, which we will denote by s_A^2. This estimate is determined by first calculating the standard deviation of the sample means $\bar{x}_{i.}$ with respect to the overall mean $\bar{x}_{..}$. As this standard deviation is an estimated standard error of the mean, $s_{\bar{x}}$, we know that $s_{\bar{x}} = \dfrac{s_A}{\sqrt{n}}$ (see Section 14.3). Thus, $s_A = \sqrt{n}s_{\bar{x}}$, and $s_A^2 = ns_{\bar{x}}^2$. This second estimate of σ^2 is also a measure of within-samples random variation, but in addition it measures the variation among sample means that could be due to treatment differences.

If the null is true, then a specific value of the F ratio calculated from the sample data,

$$f^* = \frac{s_A^2}{s_W^2} \tag{18.7}$$

should be close to 1.0. If, on the other hand, the null is false, then this value will be significantly larger than 1.0. This is the basic rationale of the one-way ANOVA: comparing an estimate of σ^2 that is sensitive to the truth-or-falsehood of the null (s_A^2) to an estimate that is not sensitive to the null (s_W^2). This test will answer the question: Is the variation among the sample means due to random sampling variation that would occur when sampling from identical populations, or is the variation among the means too great to be attributed simply to such within-samples random variation?

18.9 $SST = SSA + SSW$

If all k samples in Table 18.1 are treated as one *total sample* with nk values, then the variation in this total can be measured with what is called the *total sum of squares* (see Volume 1, Section 7.5) denoted by SST. This is calculated with the formula

$$SST = \sum_{i=1}^{k}\sum_{j=1}^{n}(x_{ij} - \bar{x}..)^2 \tag{18.8}$$

It is the sum of the squared deviations of all kn values from the overall mean [equation (18.6)]. All ANOVAs begin with such an SST which is then mathematically split into component parts that measure different sources of variation in the data. Thus, here in the one-way fixed-effects ANOVA, SST can be mathematically split into two components:

$$SST = SSA + SSW \tag{18.9}$$

$$\sum_{i=1}^{k}\sum_{j=1}^{n}(x_{ij} - \bar{x}..)^2 = n\sum_{i=1}^{k}(\bar{x}_{i.} - \bar{x}..)^2 + \sum_{i=1}^{k}\sum_{j=1}^{n}(x_{ij} - \bar{x}_{i.})^2 \tag{18.10}$$

The first component

$$SSA = n\sum_{i=1}^{k}(\bar{x}_{i.} - \bar{x}..)^2 \tag{18.11}$$

is called the *among-samples sum of squares* (or *among-groups sum of squares*, or *between-groups sum of squares*, or *treatment sum of squares*, or *factor sum of squares*). It is the numerator of the variance equation (see Section 7.7 in Volume 1) for s_A^2 from Section 18.8, the among-samples estimate of the common variance σ^2. As we indicated, it is a measure of within-samples random variation plus the variation among sample means with respect to the overall mean that could be due to treatment differences.

The second component

$$SSW = \sum_{i=1}^{k}\sum_{j=1}^{n}(x_{ij} - \bar{x}_{i.})^2 \tag{18.12}$$

is called the *within-samples sum of squares* (or *within-groups sum of squares*, or *error sum of squares*). It is the numerator of the variance equation (see Section 7.7 in Volume 1) for s_W^2, the within-samples estimate of the common variance σ^2, which we indicated is a measure of within-samples variation around their respective sample means, independent of treatment conditions.

Equations (18.9) and (18.10) are called the *sum-of-squares identity* (see Volume 1, Section 1.12), and because of this identity, SSW is typically not calculated directly. Instead, SST and SSA are calculated and then SSW is calculated with the formula

$$SSW = SST - SSA \tag{18.13}$$

EXAMPLE 18.2 For the data in Table 18.2, first calculate SST, SSA, and SSW using equations (18.8), (18.11), and (18.12), and then use these values to show that equations (18.9), (18.10), and (18.13) are correct.

Solution

$$SST = \sum_{i=1}^{3}\sum_{j=1}^{5}(x_{ij} - \bar{x}..)^2 = 34.4\ \text{in}^2$$

$$SSA = 5\sum_{i=1}^{3}(\bar{x}_{i.} - \bar{x}..)^2 = 19.6\ \text{in}^2$$

$$SSW = \sum_{i=1}^{3}\sum_{j=1}^{5}(x_{ij} - \bar{x}_{i.})^2 = 14.8\ \text{in}^2$$

Testing equations (18.9) and (18.10),

$$34.4\ \text{in}^2 = 19.6\ \text{in}^2 + 14.8\ \text{in}^2$$

and therefore for equation (18.13),

$$14.8\ \text{in}^2 = 34.4\ \text{in}^2 - 19.6\ \text{in}^2$$

18.10 COMPUTATIONAL FORMULAS FOR *SST* AND *SSA*

In Chapter 7 of Volume 1, we gave computational formulas for calculating variances and standard deviations (see Sections 7.6, 7.8, 7.9, 7.10, 7.12, and 7.13). There are also algebraically equivalent, simpler to use, computational formulas for the sum-of-squares formulas in Section 18.9. These computational formulas use totals and means defined for Table 18.1. thus, for equation (18.8), the computational formula is

$$SST = \sum_{i=1}^{k}\sum_{j=1}^{n} x_{ij}^2 - \frac{T_{..}^2}{kn} \tag{18.14}$$

And for equation (18.11), the computational formula is

$$SSA = \frac{\sum_{i=1}^{k} T_{i.}^2}{n} - \frac{T_{..}^2}{kn} \tag{18.15}$$

Equation (18.13) is then used to calculate *SSW*.

EXAMPLE 18.3 In Example 18.2, *SST*, *SSA*, and *SSW* were calculated for the data in Table 18.2. Recalculate these values by using equations (18.13), (18.14), and (18.15).

Solution

$$SST = \sum_{i=1}^{3}\sum_{j=1}^{5} x_{ij}^2 - \frac{T_{..}^2}{kn} = 5{,}336\ \text{in}^2 - (79{,}524\ \text{in}^2/15) = 34.4\ \text{in}^2$$

$$SSA = \frac{\sum_{i=1}^{3} T_{i.}^2}{n} - \frac{T_{..}^2}{kn} - (26{,}606\ \text{in}^2/5) - (79{,}524\ \text{in}^2/15) = 19.6\ \text{in}^2$$

$$SSW = SST - SSA = 34.4\ \text{in}^2 - 19.6\ \text{in}^2 = 14.8\ \text{in}^2$$

18.11 DEGREES OF FREEDOM AND MEAN SQUARES

In Section 18.8 we said that the null hypothesis $H_0\colon \mu_1 = \mu_2 = \cdots = \mu_k$ can be tested in an ANOVA with specific observed values of the F ratio (equation 18.7)

$$f^* = \frac{s_A^2}{s_W^2}$$

where the numerator is the among-samples point estimate of the common variance σ^2 and the denominator is the within-samples point estimate. Then, in Section 18.9, we said that the total sum of squares, *SST*, can be broken down into the numerator of s_A^2, *SSA*, plus the numerator of s_W^2, *SSW*.

To complete the F ratio we must now determine the denominators of these two variance estimates. To do this we go back to the original definitions of population and sample variances. Thus, equations (7.12) and (7.13) in Volume 1 define the population variance as

$$\sigma^2 = \frac{\sum_{i=1}^{N}(x_i - \mu)^2}{N} = \frac{SS}{N}$$

The sum of squares divided by population size produces a population variance. For the sample variance, however, to get an unbiased estimate of the population variance it is necessary to divide the sample sum of squares by degrees of freedom (df), $n - 1$ [see equation (7.16) in Volume 1 and Section 14.17 of this volume]

$$s^2 = \frac{\sum_{i=1}^{n}(x_i - \bar{x})^2}{n-1} = \frac{SS}{df}$$

To generalize from this: To get an unbiased sample estimate of a population variance, it is necessary to divide the sample sum of squares by the appropriate number of degrees of freedom. In the ANOVA, such a variance estimate is called a *mean square* (short for *mean of the squared deviations from the group mean*).

At this point in the book we have seen that in mathematical statistics, degrees of freedom, denoted by df or ν, is the parameter of a probability distribution (see Sections 14.15, 15.2, and 17.17). However, we have also indicated that degrees of freedom can be interpreted (see Section 14.17) as the number of unrestricted, free-to-vary values that are used in the calculation of a statistic.

Using this second interpretation, we can see that for the among-samples estimate, the appropriate degrees of freedom are $k - 1$. This is true because there are k squared deviations in SSA, and having calculated $\bar{x}_{..}$ first, this means that to obtain the given value of SSA, only $k - 1$ of the squared deviations are unrestricted. Dividing SSA [equation (18.11)] by $k - 1$, we get this equation for the *mean square among* estimate of the common population variance, denoted by MSA:

$$MSA = \frac{SSA}{k-1} = \frac{\sum_{i=1}^{k}(\bar{x}_{i.} - \bar{x}_{..})^2}{k-1} \tag{18.16}$$

You can see from this, as was indicated in Section 18.8, that MSA is indeed $ns_{\bar{x}}^2$. MSA is an unbiased estimate of σ^2 if H_0 is true, and it overestimates σ^2 if H_1 is true.

For the within-samples estimate, the appropriate degrees of freedom are $k(n - 1)$ or $kn - k$. This is true because there is a mean calculated for each sample, and thus to obtain the given sample sum of squares, only $n - 1$ of the squared deviations from the sample mean are unrestricted. As there are k samples, there are thus $k(n - 1)$ degrees of freedom associated with SSW [equation (18.12)]. Dividing SSW by $k(n - 1)$, we get this equation for the *mean square within* estimate of σ^2, denoted by MSW:

$$MSW = \frac{SSW}{k(n-1)} = \frac{\sum_{i=1}^{k}\sum_{j=1}^{n}(x_{ij} - \bar{x}_{i.})^2}{k(n-1)} \tag{18.17}$$

Here you can see that as for each sample i,

$$\sum_{j=1}^{n}(x_{ij} - \bar{x}_{i.})^2 = (n-1)s_i^2$$

it is thus true, as was indicated in Section 18.8, that MSW is indeed determined by pooling the k sample variances (see Section 17.6). MSW is an unbiased estimate σ^2 whether or not H_0 is true.

Finally, a third estimate of σ^2 can be found by dividing the total sum of squares, SST [equation (18.8)], by the appropriate degree of freedom: $kn - 1$. This number is appropriate because to calculate SST after $\bar{x}_{..}$

has been calculated, $kn - 1$ of the squared deviations are free to vary. Dividing SST by $kn - 1$, we get this equation for the *mean square total* estimate of the common population variance, denoted by MST:

$$MST = \frac{SST}{kn-1} = \frac{\sum_{i=1}^{k}\sum_{j=1}^{n}(x_{ij} - \bar{x}..)^2}{kn-1} \tag{18.18}$$

It should be noted that the sum-of-squares identity [equations (18.9) and (18.10)] also holds for the degrees of freedom associated with each sum of squares. Thus,

$$df(\text{total}) = df(\text{among}) + df(\text{within}) \tag{18.19}$$

$$kn - 1 = (k-1) + k(n-1) \tag{18.20}$$

$$= k - 1 + kn - k = kn - 1$$

EXAMPLE 18.4 Using the values for SSA, SSW, and SST from Examples 18.2 and 18.3, calculate MSA, MSW, and MST.

Solution

Using equation (18.16),

$$MSA = \frac{SSA}{k-1} = \frac{19.6\text{ in}^2}{3-1} = 9.80\text{ in}^2$$

Using equation (18.17),

$$MSW = \frac{SSW}{k(n-1)} = \frac{14.8\text{ in}^2}{3(5-1)} = 1.23\text{ in}^2$$

Using equation (18.18),

$$MST = \frac{SST}{kn-1} = \frac{34.4\text{ in}^2}{(3\times 5)-1} = 2.46\text{ in}^2$$

18.12 THE F TEST

The ANOVA is completed by using the techniques from Section 17.21 to do an F test. In that section, we used as a test statistic the random variable

$$F = \frac{S_1^2}{S_2^2}$$

which can assume specific values

$$f = \frac{s_1^2}{s_2^2}$$

to test the null hypothesis: H_0: $\sigma_1^2/\sigma_2^2 = 1$. We were able to do this because the statistic has an F distribution with degrees of freedom $\nu_1 = n_1 - 1$ in the numerator, and $\nu_2 = n_2 - 1$ in the denominator, allowing us to determine critical-value decision rules and P values (see Section 17.21).

Now in the ANOVA we use this test statistic,

$$F = \frac{\dfrac{n\sum_{i=1}^{k}(\bar{X}_{i.} - \bar{X}_{..})^2}{k-1}}{\dfrac{\sum_{i=1}^{k}\sum_{j=1}^{n}(x_{ij} - \bar{X}_{i.})^2}{k(n-1)}} \tag{18.21}$$

which can assume specific values

$$f = \frac{\dfrac{n\sum_{i=1}^{k}(\bar{x}_{i.} - \bar{x}_{..})^2}{k-1}}{\dfrac{\sum_{i=1}^{k}\sum_{j=1}^{n}(x_{ij} - \bar{x}_{i.})^2}{k(n-1)}} = \frac{MSA}{MSW} \tag{18.22}$$

to test the null hypothesis H_0: $\mu_1 = \mu_2 = \cdots = \mu_k$. We can do this because this statistic has an F distribution with degrees of freedom $\nu_1 = k - 1$ for the numerator, and $\nu_2 = k(n-1)$ for the denominator. As MSA is always placed in the numerator of the F ratio and as we are only interested in whether MSA is larger than MSW, the F test is always a right-tailed test that has the critical-value decision rule [see Example 17.11(a)]

$$\text{Reject } H_0 \text{ if } f^* > f_{\alpha,\nu_1,\nu_2} \tag{18.23}$$

and the P value [equation (17.50)]

$$P = P(F \geq f^* | H_0 \text{ is true}) \tag{18.24}$$

where F represents the statistic, f_{α,ν_1,ν_2} represents a critical F value, and f^* represents a specific value of the F statistic calculated for the given samples.

EXAMPLE 18.5 For the wheat-variety example we have been following, do a right-tailed test of $H_0: \mu_1 = \mu_2 = \mu_3$, at $\alpha = 0.05$, using a critical-value decision rule. In this and all subsequent problems in this chapter, present the solution in the typical sequence of steps for hypothesis testing (see Section 16.16).

Solution

(1) H_0: $\mu_1 = \mu_2 = \mu_3$, H_1: The three means are not all equal.

(2) $\alpha = 0.05$

(3) As we can assume independent sampling from normal distributions with homogeneity of variance, we can use the above F statistic. Thus, using Table A.8 for $\nu_1 = k - 1 = 3 - 1 = 2$ and $\nu_2 = k(n-1) = 3(5-1) = 12$, the right-tailed decision rule is: Reject H_0 if $f^* > (f_{0.05,2,12} = 3.89)$.

(4) The value of the F statistic is

$$f^* = \frac{MSA}{MSW} = \frac{9.80 \text{ in}^2}{1.23 \text{ in}^2} = 7.97$$

From Table A.8 the P value is in the range $0.005 < P < 0.01$.

(5) As $f^* > 3.89$, we reject H_0 and accept H_1. This result is confirmed by the fact that the P value is in the range $0.005 < P < 0.01$. There is thus evidence at the 0.05 level of significance that not all of the three means are equal; i.e., that the samples come from different populations.

18.13 THE ANOVA TABLE

Table 18.3 is called an *ANOVA table* or *analysis of variance table*. It is the standard form for presenting the results of an ANOVA. Note that, as should be true from the sum-of-squares identity [equations (18.9) and (18.10)], the sum-of-squares and the degrees-of-freedom columns add up to the total.

Table 18.3

Source of variation	Sum of squares	Degrees of freedom	Mean square	F
Among-samples	SSA	$k-1$	$MSA = \frac{SSA}{k-1}$	$F = \frac{MSA}{MSW}$
Within-samples	SSW	$k(n-1)$	$MSW = \frac{SSW}{k(n-1)}$	
Total	SST	$kn-1$		

EXAMPLE 18.6 Present the results of the ANOVA in Example 18.5 in an ANOVA table.

Solution

The requested ANOVA table is shown in Table 18.4. Note that measurement units are not given in an ANOVA table.

Table 18.4

Source of variation	Sum of squares	Degrees of freedom	Mean square	F
Among-samples	19.6	2	9.80	7.97
Within-samples	14.8	12	1.23	
Total	34.4	14		

18.14 MULTIPLE COMPARISON TESTS

At the completion of a one-way, fixed-effects ANOVA either H_0: $\mu_1 = \mu_2 = \cdots = \mu_k$ has been accepted, or H_0 has been rejected and H_1: The k means are not all equal, has been accepted. If H_0 has been accepted, then the analysis is complete: there are no detectable differences among the k sample means. If, on the other hand, H_1 is accepted, then differences do exist between subgroups of means, and a further analysis is required to isolate these differences.

This analysis can not be done simply by performing a series of two-sample tests (see Chapter 17) on all possible sample pairs. This procedure would be invalid because it increases the risk of *Type I error* (see Section 16.7) for the multisample hypothesis H_0. While each pairwise comparison would have an α risk, with multiple simultaneous comparisons the risk for the multisample H_0 would be greater than α.

To solve this problem, a variety of tests have been developed that are called *multiple comparison tests*. These tests isolate the identical and different means, within a set of means that have ANOVA-determined significant differences. There is no general agreement on which of these tests is best, so we have chosen one of the most widely accepted tests, *Duncan's multiple-range test*, to illustrate these procedures.

18.15 DUNCAN'S MULTIPLE-RANGE TEST

Duncan's multiple-range test is performed if the ANOVA has produced a rejection of H_0. It has the same assumptions as the ANOVA, and requires equal sample sizes. (In Section 18.23 we will present an extension of the test for unequal sample sizes.) In essence, the test compares the range of any subset p of the sample means $\bar{x}_1, \bar{x}_2, \ldots, \bar{x}_k$, with a calculated statistic called the *least significant range*, denoted by R_p. If the range of the subset is less than R_p, then all the sample means in the subset are considered to be equal, as are thus all the associated population means. If the range of the subset is greater than R_p, then the sample means at the extremes of the range are considered to be significantly different, and thus their associated population means are considered to be different.

The tests should be done in a standard order. First, the range from the largest to smallest mean is compared with the appropriate R_p value. Then the range from the largest to second smallest; next from largest to third smallest; and so on, until the comparison is for the range from largest to second largest. Next, the comparison should be for the range from second largest to smallest, then from second largest to second smallest, and so on. These range comparisons with R_p are continued until all relationships between the means have been determined.

The statistic R_p is calculated with the formula

$$R_p = r_p\sqrt{\frac{MSW}{n}} \tag{18.25}$$

where r_p is a value called the *least significant studentized range*, *MSW* is the mean square within from the ANOVA, and n is the sample size. The r_p values are obtainable from Table A.9 in the Appendix (*Least Significant Studentized Ranges* r_p) for: subgroup sizes $p = 2, 3, \ldots, 6$; degrees of freedom (for the *MSW*) $\nu = 1, 2, \ldots, 20, 24, 30, 40, 60, 120, \infty$; and for $\alpha = 0.05$ and $\alpha = 0.01$.

EXAMPLE 18.7 In Example 18.5, we rejected H_0: $\mu_1 = \mu_2 = \mu_3$ at $\alpha = 0.05$. For these data and the same significance level, use Duncan's multiple-range test to determine differences between these means.

Solution

Calculations for Duncan's multiple-range test are done without measurement units.

(1) First, the $k = 3$ sample means are arranged in a linear order from smallest to largest:

$\bar{x}_1$	$\bar{x}_2$	$\bar{x}_3$
17.2	19.4	19.8

(2) Next, using $MSW = 1.23$ from Example 18.4, and r_p values from Table A.9 for $\alpha = 0.05$ and $\nu = 12$, R_p values are calculated using equation (18.25) and presented in a table.

p	2	3
r_p	3.082	3.225
R_p	1.529	1.600

(3) The range is determined for the subgroup of $p = 3$ values that includes the largest and smallest sample

means

$$\bar{x}_3 - \bar{x}_1 = 19.8 - 17.2 = 2.6$$

Therefore, as $2.6 > R_3 = 1.600$, we conclude that $\bar{x}_3$ and $\bar{x}_1$ are significantly different and thus that $\mu_3 > \mu_1$.

(4) Because there is a significant difference in step (3), we must now test pairs within this range. First

$$\bar{x}_3 - \bar{x}_2 = 19.8 - 19.4 = 0.4$$

and as $0.4 < R_2 = 1.529$, we conclude that $\bar{x}_3$ and $\bar{x}_2$ are not significantly different, and thus $\mu_3 = \mu_2$. Next

$$\bar{x}_2 - \bar{x}_1 = 19.4 - 17.2 = 2.2$$

and as $2.2 > R_2 = 1.529$, we conclude that $\bar{x}_2$ and $\bar{x}_1$ are significantly different, and thus $\mu_2 > \mu_1$.

(5) These conclusions are customarily summarized by drawing a line under adjacent means in the linear order in step (1) that are not significantly different:

$$\underline{\bar{x}_1} \quad \underline{\bar{x}_2 \quad \bar{x}_3}$$

and from these results, we can conclude that

$$\mu_1 < \mu_2 = \mu_3$$

18.16 CONFIDENCE-INTERVAL CALCULATIONS FOLLOWING MULTIPLE COMPARISONS

If an ANOVA has rejected H_0: $\mu_1 = \mu_2 = \cdots = \mu_k$, and a multiple comparison test has isolated differences among the k sample means, then it is possible to determine confidence intervals for individual population means and for differences between the means. Thus, if one sample mean $\bar{x}_{i\cdot}$ has been shown to be significantly different from all the other sample means, then the $(1-\alpha)100\%$ confidence interval for μ_i can be determined with the formula

$$\bar{x}_{i.} \pm t_{\alpha/2,\nu}\sqrt{\frac{MSW}{n_i}} \tag{18.26}$$

where MSW is the mean square within from the ANOVA, $n_i = n$, the sample size for each sample in the ANOVA, and degrees of freedom ν for the $t_{\alpha/2,\nu}$ is the degrees of freedom for the MSW in the ANOVA.

If the multiple comparison test has not found significant differences between two or more sample means, then first an overall mean is calculated for these means using equation (6.19) from Volume 1,

$$\bar{x}_w = \frac{\sum n_i\bar{x}_{i.}}{\sum n_i}$$

where the summation is over all the samples with means judged to be the same. Then a $(1-\alpha)100\%$ confidence interval for μ_w can be determined with the formula

$$\bar{x}_w \pm t_{\alpha/2,\nu}\sqrt{\frac{MSW}{\sum n_i}} \tag{18.27}$$

where MSW and ν are the same as before, and the summation is again over the samples with equal means.

Finally, if two of the sample means, say $\bar{x}_{i.}$ and $\bar{x}_{k.}$, have been found to be significantly different, then a $(1-\alpha)100\%$ confidence interval for $\mu_i - \mu_k$ can be determined using the following formula:

$$(\bar{x}_{i.} - \bar{x}_{k.}) \pm t_{\alpha/2,\nu}\sqrt{\frac{MSW}{n_i} + \frac{MSW}{n_k}} \tag{18.28}$$

where MSW and ν are the same as before, and n_i and n_k are the sample sizes for the two samples. For equal sample sizes the formula becomes

$$(\bar{x}_{i.} - \bar{x}_{k.}) \pm t_{\alpha/2,\nu}\sqrt{\frac{2(MSW)}{n}} \tag{18.29}$$

EXAMPLE 18.8 In Example 18.7 we concluded that $\mu_1 < \mu_2 = \mu_3$. For these data, calculate a 95% confidence interval for: (*a*) μ_1, (*b*) the overall mean μ_w for μ_2 and μ_3, and (*c*) $\mu_2 - \mu_1$.

Solution

(a) Using equation (18.26),

$$\bar{x}_{i.} \pm t_{\alpha/2,\nu}\sqrt{\frac{MSW}{n_i}}$$

where from Table 18.2, $\bar{x}_{1.} = 17.2$ in and $n_i = n = 5$. From Table A.6, $t_{\alpha/2,\nu} = t_{0.05/2,12} = 2.179$. And, from Example 18.4: $MSW = 1.23\text{ in}^2$. Therefore, the 95% confidence interval for μ_1 is

$$17.2\text{ in} \pm 2.179\sqrt{\frac{1.23\text{ in}^2}{5}}$$

$$17.2\text{ in} \pm 1.08\text{ in}$$

(*b*) Using equation (18.27),

$$\bar{x}_w \pm t_{\alpha/2,\nu}\sqrt{\frac{MSW}{\sum n_i}}$$

where the values are the same as in (*a*) except $\sum n_i = 2 \times 5 = 10$, and using equation (6.19) of Volume 1,

$$\bar{x}_w = \frac{\sum n_i\bar{x}_{i.}}{\sum n_i} = \frac{(5 \times 19.4\text{ in}) + (5 \times 19.8\text{ in})}{10} = 19.6\text{ in}$$

Therefore, the 95% confidence interval for μ_w is

$$19.6\text{ in} \pm 2.179\sqrt{\frac{1.23\text{ in}^2}{10}}$$

$$19.6\text{ in} \pm 0.76\text{ in}$$

(*c*) Using equation (18.29),

$$(\bar{x}_{i.} - \bar{x}_{k.}) \pm t_{\alpha/2,\nu}\sqrt{\frac{2(MSW)}{n}}$$

$$(19.4\text{ in} - 17.2\text{ in}) \pm 2.179\sqrt{\frac{(2 \times 1.23\text{ in}^2)}{5}}$$

$$2.2\text{ in} \pm 1.53\text{ in}$$

18.17 TESTING FOR HOMOGENEITY OF VARIANCE

In Section 18.5, we indicated that one of the assumptions of the one-way, fixed-effects ANOVA is homogeneity of variance; that all the population variances are equal to a common variance σ^2. In Section 17.21, we tested for homogeneity of variance in the two-sample case by using the variance-ratio test. This test can not be used in the multisample case, but there are a variety of multisample tests such as Cochran's test, the maximum F ratio test, and the test we will discuss because it is the most commonly used—*Bartlett's test.*

Bartlett's test has the usual pair of competing statistical hypotheses: the null

$$H_0\colon \sigma_1^2 = \sigma_2^2 = \cdots = \sigma_k^2$$

and the alternative, which is typically written as

$$H_1\colon \text{The } k \text{ variances are not all equal.}$$

The test statistic used is the random variable B, which has approximately the chi-square distribution (see Section 15.2) with $\nu = k - 1$ degrees of freedom, if, as we do in ANOVA, it can be assumed that the k samples come from independent normal distributions.

To determine values for B, $B = b$, and do the test, we begin by calculating the variance, s_i^2, for each of the k samples. Next, we pool these variances with the formula

$$s_p^2 = \frac{\sum_{i=1}^{k}(n_i - 1)s_i^2}{N - k} \tag{18.30}$$

where n_i is sample size, and

$$N = \sum_{i=1}^{k} n_i \tag{18.31}$$

(Note that this use of the symbol N to denote the sum of all sample sizes is different from its use heretofore to denote population size.)

Next, a value of the variable B is calculated with the formula

$$b = 2.3026\frac{q}{h} \tag{18.32}$$

where

$$q = (N - k)\ \log s_p^2 - \sum_{i=1}^{k}(n_i - 1)\ \log s_i^2 \tag{18.33}$$

and

$$h = 1 + \frac{1}{3(k-1)}\left(\sum_{i=1}^{k}\frac{1}{n_i - 1} - \frac{1}{N - k}\right) \tag{18.34}$$

This version of Bartlett's test utilizes common logarithms [to the base 10, see Problem 1.23(*a*) in Volume 1], but there are also versions of this test that use natural logarithms [to the base e, see Problem 1.23(*b*) in Volume 1].

The quantity q is zero when there is homogeneity of variance, and increases with increasing differences among the sample variances. Therefore, this is a right-tailed test with this critical-value decision rule

$$\text{Reject } H_0 \text{ if } b^* > \chi^2_{\alpha,\nu}$$

where b^* is the observed value of B and $\nu = k - 1$.

EXAMPLE 18.9 For the data in Table 18.2, test for homogeneity of variance at $\alpha = 0.05$ using Bartlett's test.

Solution

Calculations for Bartlett's test are done without using measurement units. Using equation (7.16) in Volume 1, the sample variances are $s_1^2 = 0.70$, $s_2^2 = 1.30$, $s_3^2 = 1.70$. Using equation (18.31) with $k = 3$,

$$N = \sum_{i=1}^{3} n_i = 3(5) = 15$$

Then, using equation (18.30),

$$s_p^2 = \frac{\sum_{i=1}^{3}(n_i - 1)s_i^2}{15 - 3} = \frac{14.8}{12} = 1.233$$

Next, using equation (18.33),

$$q = (N - k)\ \log s_p^2 - \sum_{i=1}^{3}(n_i - 1)\ \log s_i^2$$
$$= (12 \times 0.0910) - 0.7580 = 0.3340$$

And then, using equation (18.34),

$$h = 1 + \frac{1}{6}\left(\sum_{i=1}^{3}\frac{1}{n_i - 1} - \frac{1}{15 - 3}\right) = 1.1111$$

Therefore, using equation (18.32),

$$b^* = 2.3026 \times \frac{0.3340}{1.1111} = 0.692$$

The test for homogeneity of variance can now be summarized as follows:

(1) H_0: $\sigma_1^2 = \sigma_2^2 = \sigma_3^2$, H_1: The three variances are not all equal.

(2) $\alpha = 0.05$.

(3) Using the B statistic with a χ^2 value from Table A.7 for $\alpha = 0.05$ and $(\nu = k - 1 = 3 - 1 = 2)$, the critical-value decision rule is

$$\text{Reject } H_0 \text{ if } b^* > (\chi^2_{0.05,2} = 5.99)$$

(4) The value of the B statistic is $b^* = 0.692$, and thus from Table A.7 we can see that a comparable χ^{2*} value for the $\nu = 2$ distribution would be between $\chi^2_{0.900}$ and $\chi^2_{0.500}$. Therefore, the P value is in the range $0.5 < P < 0.9$.

(5) As $b^* < 5.99$, we accept H_0; there is homogeneity of variance. This is confirmed by the fact that $P > 0.05$.

18.18 ONE-WAY, FIXED-EFFECTS ANOVA: EQUAL OR UNEQUAL SAMPLE SIZES

In Sections 18.6 through 18.13, in our initial presentation of the one-way, fixed-effects ANOVA, we gave a procedure that requires equal sample sizes: $n_1 = n_2 = \cdots = n_k = n$. Now, in Sections 18.18 through 18.22, we present a general procedure for this ANOVA that can be used with equal or unequal sample sizes.

For this general procedure, the other assumptions from Section 18.5 remain the same: one independent variable and one dependent variable, treatments have been nonrandomly selected as the only treatments of interest, independent random samples have been taken from k normally distributed populations that have means $\mu_1, \mu_2, \ldots, \mu_k$, and variances $\sigma_1^2, \sigma_2^2, \ldots, \sigma_k^2$, and there is homogeneity of variance: $\sigma_1^2 = \sigma_2^2 = \cdots = \sigma_k^2 = \sigma^2$.

In this general procedure, the fundamental elements of the test remain the same: the statistical hypotheses (see Section 18.6), the organization of the data (see Section 18.7), the basic rationale (see Section 18.8), and the specifics of the technique (see Sections 18.9 through 18.13). Various formulas must be changed, however, to allow for unequal sample sizes.

18.19 GENERAL-PROCEDURE, ONE-WAY, FIXED-EFFECTS ANOVA: ORGANIZING THE DATA

The summary organization of the data remains the same as in Table 18.1, but the formulas for the descriptive statistics are changed. Thus, equations (18.2), (18.3), and (18.5), become

$$T_{i.} = \sum_{j=1}^{n_i} x_{ij} \tag{18.35}$$

$$T_{..} = \sum_{i=1}^{k}\sum_{j=1}^{n_i} x_{ij} \tag{18.36}$$

$$\bar{x}_{i.} = \frac{\sum_{j=1}^{n_i} x_{ij}}{n_i} \tag{18.37}$$

And, using equation (18.31), equation (18.6) becomes

$$\bar{x}_{..} = \frac{\sum_{i=1}^{k}\sum_{j=1}^{n_i} x_{ij}}{N} \tag{18.38}$$

EXAMPLE 18.10 For the data summarized in Table 18.2, take the first observation for variety 3, 18 in, and make it the first observation for variety 1. Now, the sample sizes are $n_1 = 6$, $n_2 = 5$, and $n_3 = 4$, with [equation (18.31)] $N = \sum_{i=1}^{3} n_i = 15$. Organize these data into a summary table like Tables 18.1 and 18.2.

Solution

The requested table, with totals and means calculated, is shown in Table 18.5.

Table 18.5

Wheat variety	Height (in)						Total	Mean
1	18	17	18	17	16	18	104 in	17.3 in
2	21	19	18	19	20		97 in	19.4 in
3	21	20	21	19			81 in	20.2 in
							282 in	18.8 in

18.20 GENERAL-PROCEDURE, ONE-WAY, FIXED-EFFECTS ANOVA: SUM OF SQUARES

For the general procedure, definitional formulas for the sum of squares, equations (18.8), (18.11), and (18.12), become

$$SST = \sum_{i=1}^{k}\sum_{j=1}^{n_i} (x_{ij} - \bar{x}_{..})^2 \tag{18.39}$$

$$SSA = \sum_{i=1}^{k} n_i(\bar{x}_{i.} - \bar{x}_{..})^2 \tag{18.40}$$

$$SSW = \sum_{i=1}^{k}\sum_{j=1}^{n_i} (x_{ij} - \bar{x}_{i.})^2 \tag{18.41}$$

The computational formulas for SST [equation (18.14)] and SSA [equation (18.15)] become

$$SST = \sum_{i=1}^{k}\sum_{j=1}^{n_i} x_{ij}^2 - \frac{T_{..}^2}{N} \tag{18.42}$$

$$SSA = \sum_{i=1}^{k} \frac{T_{i.}^2}{n_i} - \frac{T_{..}^2}{N} \tag{18.43}$$

And, as the sum-of-squares identity [equation (18.9)] remains valid, SSW can be calculated with equation (18.13): $SSW = SST - SSA$.

EXAMPLE 18.11 For the data summarized in Table 18.5, calculate SST, SSA, and SSW using the computational formulas.

Solution

$$SST = 5{,}336 \text{ in}^2 - (79{,}524 \text{ in}^2/15) = 34.40 \text{ in}^2$$
$$SSA = 5{,}324.72 \text{ in}^2 - (79{,}524 \text{ in}^2/15) = 23.12 \text{ in}^2$$
$$SSW = 34.40 \text{ in}^2 - 23.12 \text{ in}^2 = 11.28 \text{ in}^2$$

18.21 GENERAL-PROCEDURE, ONE-WAY, FIXED-EFFECTS ANOVA: DEGREES OF FREEDOM AND MEAN SQUARES

For the general case, degrees of freedom for SSA remains $k-1$ and thus equation (18.16) for MSA becomes

$$MSA = \frac{SSA}{k-1} = \frac{\sum_{i=1}^{k} n_i(\bar{x}_{i.} - \bar{x}_{..})^2}{k-1} \tag{18.44}$$

Degrees of freedom for SSW becomes $N-k$, and thus equation (18.17) for MSW becomes

$$MSW = \frac{SSW}{N-k} = \frac{\sum_{i=1}^{k}\sum_{j=1}^{n_i}(x_{ij} - \bar{x}_{i.})^2}{N-k} \tag{18.45}$$

Degrees of freedom for SST becomes $N-1$, and thus equation (18.18) becomes

$$MST = \frac{SST}{N-1} = \frac{\sum_{i=1}^{k}\sum_{j=1}^{n_i}(x_{ij} - \bar{x}_{..})^2}{N-1} \tag{18.46}$$

EXAMPLE 18.12 Using the values for SSA and SSW from Example 18.11, calculate MSA and MSW.

Solution

$$MSA = \frac{23.12 \text{ in}^2}{2} = 11.56 \text{ in}^2$$

$$MSW = \frac{11.28 \text{ in}^2}{12} = 0.94 \text{ in}^2$$

18.22 GENERAL-PROCEDURE, ONE-WAY, FIXED-EFFECTS ANOVA: THE F TEST

The test statistic used in the general procedure to test H_0: $\mu_1 = \mu_2 = \cdots = \mu_k$ is changed from equation (18.21) to

$$F = \frac{\dfrac{\sum_{i=1}^{k} n_i(\bar{X}_{i.} - \bar{X}..)^2}{k-1}}{\dfrac{\sum_{i=1}^{k}\sum_{j=1}^{n_i}(X_{ij} - \bar{X}_{i.})^2}{N-k}} \tag{18.47}$$

which can assume specific values

$$f = \frac{\dfrac{\sum_{i=1}^{k} n_i(\bar{x}_{i.} - \bar{x}..)^2}{k-1}}{\dfrac{\sum_{i=1}^{k}\sum_{j=1}^{n_i}(x_{ij} - \bar{x}_{i.})^2}{N-k}} = \frac{MSA}{MSW} \tag{18.48}$$

The critical-value decision rule [equation (18.23) with $\nu_1 = k - 1$ and $\nu_2 = N - k$] and P value formula [equation (18.24)] remain the same.

EXAMPLE 18.13 For the data in Table 18.5 and the results in Examples 18.11 and 18.12, do a right-tailed test of H_0: $\mu_1 = \mu_2 = \mu_3$, at $\alpha = 0.05$, using a critical-value decision rule.

Solution

(1) H_0: $\mu_1 = \mu_2 = \mu_3$, H_1: The three means are not all equal.

(2) $\alpha = 0.05$

(3) The right-tailed decision rule is the same as in Example 18.5(3): Reject H_0 if $f^* > (f_{0.05,2,12} = 3.89)$.

(4) The results of the ANOVA are shown in the ANOVA table in Table 18.6. From Table A.8, the P value is in the range $P < 0.005$.

(5) As $f^* > 3.89$, we reject H_0 and accept H_1. This result is confirmed by the fact that the P value is in the range $P < 0.005$. There is thus evidence at the 0.05 level of significance that not all three means are equal.

Table 18.6

Source of variation	Sum of squares	Degrees of freedom	Mean square	F
Among-samples	23.12	2	11.56	12.30
Within-samples	11.28	12	0.94	
Total	34.40	14		

18.23 GENERAL-PROCEDURE, ONE-WAY, FIXED-EFFECTS ANOVA: MULTIPLE COMPARISONS

Duncan's multiple-range test, used in Section 18.15 as an example of multiple comparison tests, requires equal sample sizes. There are, however, multiple comparison tests for the general case, for equal or unequal sample sizes, and we illustrate these with an extension of Duncan's test developed by *C. Y. Kramer*.

Again, the test compares the range of any subset p of the sample means $\bar{x}_1, \bar{x}_2, \ldots, \bar{x}_k$ with a least significant range. Now, however, this value, denoted by R'_p, is calculated with the formula

$$R'_p = \sqrt{MSW}\, r_p \tag{18.49}$$

where again r_p values (least significant studentized ranges), using $\nu = N - k$, are available from Table A.9, and MSW is the mean square within from the ANOVA. Also, to allow for the possibility of unequal sample sizes, it is necessary to correct the range between means to be compared with R'_p with the formula

$$(\bar{x}_{i.} - \bar{x}_{k.})\sqrt{\frac{2n_i n_k}{n_i + n_k}} \tag{18.50}$$

where $\bar{x}_i$ is the larger of the two means.

EXAMPLE 18.14 In Example 18.13, we rejected H_0: $\mu_1 = \mu_2 = \mu_3$, at $\alpha = 0.05$. For these data (see Table 18.5) and the same significance level, use Kramer's extension of Duncan's multiple-range test to determine differences between these means.

Solution

(1) The $k = 3$ sample means are arranged in linear order:

$\bar{x}_1$	$\bar{x}_2$	$\bar{x}_3$
17.3	19.4	20.2

(2) Next, using $MSW = 0.94$ from Example 18.12, and r_p values from Table A.9 for $\alpha = 0.05$ and $\nu = N - k = 12$, R'_p values are calculated using equation (18.49) and presented in a table:

p	2	3
r_p	3.082	3.225
R'_p	2.988	3.127

(3) The range is determined for the subgroup of $p = 3$ values that includes the largest and smallest sample means using equation (18.50).

$$(\bar{x}_3 - \bar{x}_1)\sqrt{\frac{2n_3 n_1}{n_3 + n_1}} = (20.2 - 17.3)\sqrt{\frac{48}{10}} = 6.354$$

Therefore, as $6.354 > R'_3 = 3.127$, we conclude that $\bar{x}_3$ and $\bar{x}_1$ are significantly different and thus $\mu_3 > \mu_1$.

(4) Because there is a significant difference in step (3), we must now test pairs within this range. First,

$$(\bar{x}_3 - \bar{x}_2)\sqrt{\frac{2n_3 n_2}{n_3 + n_2}} = (20.2 - 19.4)\sqrt{\frac{40}{9}} = 1.687$$

and as $1.687 < R'_2 = 2.988$, we conclude that $\bar{x}_3$ and $\bar{x}_2$ are not significantly different and thus $\mu_3 = \mu_2$.

Next,

$$(\bar{x}_2 - \bar{x}_1)\sqrt{\frac{2n_2n_1}{n_2+n_1}} = (19.4 - 17.3)\sqrt{\frac{60}{11}} = 4.905$$

and as $4.905 > R_2' = 2.988$, we conclude that $\bar{x}_2$ and $\bar{x}_1$ are significantly different and thus $\mu_2 > \mu_1$.

(5) From these results we can conclude that

$$\underline{\bar{x}_1} \quad \underline{\bar{x}_2 \quad \bar{x}_3}$$

and thus we can conclude that

$$\mu_1 < \mu_2 = \mu_3$$

18.24 GENERAL-PROCEDURE, ONE-WAY, FIXED-EFFECTS ANOVA: CALCULATING CONFIDENCE INTERVALS AND TESTING FOR HOMOGENEITY OF VARIANCE

In Section 18.16, equations (18.26), (18.27), and (18.28) are general formulas (for equal or unequal sample sizes) for calculating confidence intervals following multiple comparisons. Similarly, in Section 18.17, the equations presented are general formulas for testing for homogeneity of variance in the multisample case.

EXAMPLE 18.15 In Example 18.14, we concluded that $\mu_1 < \mu_2 = \mu_3$. For these data, calculate a 95% confidence interval for $\mu_2 - \mu_1$.

Solution

Using equation (18.28), the results shown in Tables 18.5 and 18.6, and a value from Table A.6

$$(\bar{x}_2 - \bar{x}_1) \pm t_{0.05/2,12}\sqrt{\frac{MSW}{n_2} + \frac{MSW}{n_1}}$$

$$(19.4 \text{ in} - 17.3 \text{ in}) \pm 2.179\sqrt{\frac{0.94 \text{ in}^2}{5} + \frac{0.94 \text{ in}^2}{6}}$$

$$2.1 \text{ in} \pm 1.28 \text{ in}$$

EXAMPLE 18.16 For the data in Table 18.5, test for homogeneity of variance at $\alpha = 0.05$ using Barlett's test.

Solution

Using equation (7.16) from Volume 1, the sample variances are $s_1^2 = 0.668$, $s_2^2 = 1.300$, $s_3^2 = 0.920$. Using equation (18.31) with $k = 3$,

$$N = \sum_{i=1}^{3} n_i = 6 + 5 + 4 = 15$$

Then, using equation (18.30),

$$s_p^2 = \frac{\sum_{i=1}^{3}(n_i - 1)s_i^2}{N - k} = \frac{11.30}{12} = 0.942$$

Next, using equation (18.33),

$$q = (N - k)\ \log s_p^2 - \sum_{i=1}^{3}(n_i - 1)\ \log s_i^2$$

$$= [12 \times (-0.0259)] - (-0.5290) = 0.2182$$

and using equation (18.34),

$$h = 1 + \frac{1}{6}\left(\sum_{i=1}^{3}\frac{1}{n_i - 1} - \frac{1}{15 - 3}\right) = 1.1167$$

Therefore, using equation (18.32),

$$b^* = 2.3026 \times \frac{0.2182}{1.1167} = 0.450$$

The test for homogeneity of variance can now be summarized as follows:

(1) H_0: $\sigma_1^2 = \sigma_2^2 = \sigma_3^2$, H_1: The three variances are not all equal.

(2) $\alpha = 0.05$

(3) Using the B statistic with a value from Table A.7 for $\alpha = 0.05$ and ($\nu = k - 1 = 3 - 1 = 2$), the critical-value decision rule is: Reject H_0 if $b^* > (\chi^2_{0.05,2} = 5.99)$.

(4) The value of the B statistic is $b^* = 0.450$, and from Table A.7 we can see that a comparable χ^{2*} value for the $\nu = 2$ distribution would be between $\chi^2_{0.900}$ and $\chi^2_{0.500}$ and thus the P value is in the range $0.5 < P < 0.9$.

(5) As $b^* < 5.99$, we accept H_0; there is homogeneity of variance. This is confirmed by the fact that $P > 0.05$.

18.25 VIOLATIONS OF ANOVA ASSUMPTIONS

The multisample techniques of one-way, fixed-effects ANOVA are called parametric techniques for the same reasons the one-sample (see Section 16.24) and two-sample (see Section 17.13) techniques are called parametric: they are used to estimate and test hypotheses about parameters, and many of the assumptions deal with parameters. The assumptions of the ANOVA (see Section 18.5) are therefore also called parametric assumptions.

The fundamental sampling assumptions of the ANOVA must be satisfied: independent random sampling of interval-level or ratio-level measurements. However, the ANOVA, like the t test (see Sections 16.25 and 17.14), is considered to be quite robust for the normal-distribution assumption, particularly for large sample sizes, and moderately robust for the homogeneity-of-variance assumption, particularly if the sample sizes are equal: $n_1 = n_2 = \cdots = n_k = n$.

Severe deviations from normality or homogeneity can seriously distort the ANOVA results. Therefore, as with one-sample and two-sample techniques (see Sections 16.25 and 17.14), the first step is to analyze the sample data for how well they satisfy these assumptions. In Section 16.25 we gave ways for evaluating the normal-distribution assumption, and in Sections 18.17 and 18.24 we showed how to test for homogeneity of variance in ANOVA. Again, however, as with the t test (see Section 17.14), the one-way, fixed-effects ANOVA is considered more robust to assumption violations then is the homogeneity test. For this reason, particularly if there are equal sample sizes, it is not recommended that homogeneity of variance be routinely tested for before attempting an ANOVA.

If it is determined that there are severe deviations from the assumptions, then the next step is to attempt a transformation of the data. The same transformations are suggested for ANOVA as were suggested for one-sample (see Section 16.25) and two-sample (see Section 17.14) techniques. If the transformation is successful, then ANOVA techniques can be used on the transformed data.

Again, as with one-sample and two-sample techniques, if no transformations can be found that satisfy the assumptions, then other aspects of the data can be analyzed with nonparametric procedures (see Chapter 20).

Solved Problems

EQUAL-SAMPLES, ONE-WAY, FIXED-EFFECTS ANOVA: H_0 AND H_1

18.1 An exercise physiologist develops the hypothesis that endurance athletes, such as long-distance runners, will perform best in races if they sleep at high altitude but train at a lower altitude. He tests this with 20 men who run 10 km races, all of whom have lived and trained at sea level. Five of the men are randomly assigned to each of four groups: (1) SH/TL (sleep in mountain town at 8,200 ft, train daily at 4,500 ft); (2) SH/TH (sleep and train at 8,200 ft); (3) SL/TH (sleep at 4,500 ft, train at 8,200 ft); (4) SL/TL (sleep and train at 4,500 ft). The training period lasts for 2 months in one summer, with all the men following the same training routine. Prior to the start of training, all the men do a 10 km race together at 4,500 ft, and each man's time for the race is recorded. After the two months of training, times are again taken in a 10 km race at 4,500 ft. The data to be analyzed are the differences (in seconds) for each man between their first and second race-times: second subtracted from first. Assuming that the populations of these differences are normally distributed with means μ_1, μ_2, μ_3, and μ_4, and that there is homogeneity of variance: $\sigma_1^2 = \sigma_2^2 = \sigma_3^2 = \sigma_4^2 = \sigma^2$, then if the physiologist wants to do a one-way, fixed-effects ANOVA on these data, what are H_0 and H_1?

Solution

$$H_0\colon \mu_1 = \mu_2 = \mu_3 = \mu_4$$

H_1: The four means are not all equal.

18.2 A manufacturer of battery-operated portable telephones is considering three comparable batteries (types 1, 2, and 3) for use with a new phone. You are asked to determine whether these batteries differ in *talk-time*, the life of the battery when in use. You take 10 randomly selected batteries of each type and time (to the nearest tenth of an hour) the talk-time for each battery in constant use in the new phone. Assuming that the populations of these times are normally distributed with means μ_1, μ_2, and μ_3, and that there is homogeneity of variance, $\sigma_1^2 = \sigma_2^2 = \sigma_3^2 = \sigma^2$, then if you want to do a one-way, fixed-effects ANOVA on these data, what are H_0 and H_1?

Solution

$$H_0\colon \mu_1 = \mu_2 = \mu_3$$

H_1: The three means are not all equal.

EQUAL-SAMPLES ANOVA: ORGANIZING THE DATA

18.3 These are the results of the training experiment in Problem 18.1, with the time difference for each man given to the nearest second: group 1 (11, 13, 10, 12, 11); group 2 (8, 9, 11, 10, 9); group 3 (7, 8, 10, 9, 7); group 4 (6, 7, 8, 6, 8). Organize these data into a summary table like Table 18.1.

Solution

The requested table, with totals and means calculated with equations (18.2), (18.3), (18.5), and (18.6), is shown in Table 18.7.

18.4 For the battery experiment in Problem 18.2, these are the mean talk-times for each group: $\bar{x}_{1.} = 1.34$ hr, $\bar{x}_{2.} = 1.26$ hr, $\bar{x}_{3.} = 1.06$ hr. From this information, determine: $T_{1.}, T_{2.}, T_{3.}, T_{..}$, and $\bar{x}_{..}$.

Table 18.7

Sleep/training group	Time difference (sec)					Total	Mean
1	11	13	10	12	11	57 sec	11.4 sec
2	8	9	11	10	9	47 sec	9.4 sec
3	7	8	10	9	7	41 sec	8.2 sec
4	6	7	8	6	8	35 sec	7.0 sec
						180 sec	9.0 sec

Solution

Using equations (18.2) and (18.5),

$$T_{1.} = n \times \bar{x}_{1.} = 10 \times 1.34 \text{ hr} = 13.4 \text{ hr}$$
$$T_{2.} = n \times \bar{x}_{2.} = 10 \times 1.26 \text{ hr} = 12.6 \text{ hr}$$
$$T_{3.} = n \times \bar{x}_{3.} = 10 \times 1.06 \text{ hr} = 10.6 \text{ hr}$$

Using equations (18.2) and (18.3)

$$T_{..} = T_{1.} + T_{2.} + T_{3.} = 13.4 \text{ hr} + 12.6 \text{ hr} + 10.6 \text{ hr} = 36.6 \text{ hr}$$

Using equation (18.6),

$$\bar{x}_{..} = \frac{T_{..}}{kn} = \frac{36.6 \text{ hr}}{10 \times 3} = 1.22 \text{ hr}$$

EQUAL-SAMPLES ANOVA: SUM OF SQUARES

18.5 For the training experiment, use the values in Table 18.7 and equations (18.13), (18.14), and (18.15) to calculate *SST*, *SSA*, and *SSW*.

Solution

$$SST = \sum_{i=1}^{4}\sum_{j=1}^{5} x_{ij}^2 - \frac{T_{..}^2}{kn} = 1{,}694 \text{ sec}^2 - (32{,}400 \text{ sec}^2/20) = 74.0 \text{ sec}^2$$

$$SSA = \frac{\sum_{i=1}^{4} T_{i.}^2}{n} - \frac{T_{..}^2}{kn} = (8{,}364 \text{ sec}^2/5) - (32{,}400 \text{ sec}^2/20) = 52.8 \text{ sec}^2$$

$$SSW = SST - SSA = 74.0 \text{ sec}^2 - 52.8 \text{ sec}^2 = 21.2 \text{ sec}^2$$

18.6 For the battery experiment, use the information in Problem 18.4 and this sum from the same data, $\sum_{i=1}^{3}\sum_{j=1}^{10} x_{ij}^2 = 45.62 \text{ hr}^2$, to calculate *SST*, *SSA*, and *SSW*, using equations (18.13), (18.14), and (18.15).

Solution

$$SST = \sum_{i=1}^{3}\sum_{j=1}^{10} x_{ij}^2 - \frac{T_{\cdot\cdot}^2}{kn} = 45.62\ \text{hr}^2 - (1{,}339.56\ \text{hr}^2/30) = 0.968\ \text{hr}^2$$

$$SSA = \frac{\sum_{i=1}^{3} T_{i\cdot}^2}{n} - \frac{T_{\cdot\cdot}^2}{kn} = (450.68\ \text{hr}^2/10) - (1{,}339.56\ \text{hr}^2/30) = 0.416\ \text{hr}^2$$

$$SSW = SST - SSA = 0.968\ \text{hr}^2 - 0.416\ \text{hr}^2 = 0.552\ \text{hr}^2$$

EQUAL-SAMPLES ANOVA: MEAN SQUARES

18.7 For the training experiment, use the values for SSA and SSW from Problem 18.5 to calculate MSA and MSW.

Solution

Using equation (18.16),

$$MSA = \frac{SSA}{k-1} = \frac{52.8\ \text{sec}^2}{4-1} = 17.60\ \text{sec}^2$$

Using equation (18.17),

$$MSW = \frac{SSW}{k(n-1)} = \frac{21.2\ \text{sec}^2}{4(5-1)} = 1.32\ \text{sec}^2$$

18.8 For the battery experiment, use the values for SSA and SSW from Problem 18.6 to calculate MSA and MSW.

Solution

Using equation (18.16),

$$MSA = \frac{SSA}{k-1} = \frac{0.416\ \text{hr}^2}{3-1} = 0.2080\ \text{hr}^2$$

Using equation (18.17),

$$MSW = \frac{SSW}{k(n-1)} = \frac{0.552\ \text{hr}^2}{3(10-1)} = 0.0204\ \text{hr}^2$$

EQUAL-SAMPLES ANOVA: THE F TEST

18.9 For the training experiment, use the information from Problems 18.1, 18.3, 18.5, and 18.7 to do a right-tailed test of H_0: $\mu_1 = \mu_2 = \mu_3 = \mu_4$, at $\alpha = 0.05$, using a critical-value decision rule.

Solution

(1) H_0: $\mu_1 = \mu_2 = \mu_3 = \mu_4$, H_1: The four means are not all equal.

(2) $\alpha = 0.05$.

(3) As we can assume independent sampling from normal distributions with homogeneity of variance, we can use the F statistic [equation (18.21)]. Thus, using Table A.8 for [$\nu_1 = k - 1 = 4 - 1 = 3$ and $\nu_2 = k(n-1) = 4(5-1) = 16$] the right-tailed decision rule is: Reject H_0 if $f^* > (f_{0.05,3,16} = 3.24)$.

(4) The results of the ANOVA are shown in the ANOVA table in Table 18.8. From Table A.8, we can say that the P value is in the range $P < 0.005$.

Table 18.8

Source of variation	Sum of squares	Degrees of freedom	Mean square	F
Among-samples	52.8	3	17.60	13.33
Within-samples	21.2	16	1.32	
Total	74.0	19		

(5) As $f^* > 3.24$, we reject H_0 and accept H_1. This result is confirmed by the fact that the P value is in the range $P < 0.005$. There is thus evidence at the 0.05 level of significance that the four means are not all equal.

18.10 For the battery experiment, use the information from Problems 18.2, 18.4, 18.6, and 18.8 to do a right-tailed test of H_0: $\mu_1 = \mu_2 = \mu_3$, at $\alpha = 0.05$, using a critical-value decision rule.

Solution

(1) H_0: $\mu_1 = \mu_2 = \mu_3$, H_1: The three means are not all equal.

(2) $\alpha = 0.05$

(3) As we can assume independent sampling from normal distributions with homogeneity of variance, we can use the F statistic [equation (18.21)]. Thus, using Table A.8 for [$\nu_1 = k - 1 = 3 - 1 = 2$ and $\nu_2 = k(n-1) = 3(10-1) = 27$], the right-tailed decision rule is: Reject H_0 if $f^* > (f_{0.05,2,27} = 3.35)$.

(4) The results of the ANOVA are shown in the ANOVA table in Table 18.9. From Table A.8, we can say that the P value is in the range $P < 0.005$.

Table 18.9

Source of variation	Sum of squares	Degrees of freedom	Mean square	F
Among-samples	0.416	2	0.2080	10.20
Within-samples	0.552	27	0.0204	
Total	0.968	29		

(5) As $f^* > 3.35$, we reject H_0 and accept H_1. This result is confirmed by the fact that the P value is in the range $P < 0.005$. There is thus evidence at the 0.05 level of significance that the three means are not all equal.

EQUAL-SAMPLES ANOVA: MULTIPLE COMPARISONS

18.11 In Problem 18.9 for the training experiment, we rejected H_0: $\mu_1 = \mu_2 = \mu_3 = \mu_4$ at $\alpha = 0.05$. For these data and the same significance level, use Duncan's multiple-range test (see Section 18.15) to determine differences between these means.

Solution

(1) First, the $k = 4$ sample means are arranged in a linear order from smallest to largest.

$\bar{x}_4$	$\bar{x}_3$	$\bar{x}_2$	$\bar{x}_1$
7.0	8.2	9.4	11.4

(2) Next, using $MSW = 1.32$ from Problem 18.7, and r_p values from Table A.9 for $\alpha = 0.05$ and $v = 16$, R_p values are calculated using equation (18.25) and presented in a table:

p	2	3	4
r_p	2.998	3.144	3.235
R_p	1.540	1.615	1.662

(3) The range is determined for the subgroup of $p = 4$ values that includes the largest and smallest sample means:

$$\bar{x}_1 - \bar{x}_4 = 11.4 - 7.0 = 4.4$$

Therefore, as $4.4 > R_4 = 1.662$, we conclude that $\bar{x}_1$ and $\bar{x}_4$ are significantly different and thus that $\mu_1 > \mu_4$.

(4) Because there is a significant difference in step (3), we must now test the difference between $\bar{x}_1$ and $\bar{x}_3$:

$$\bar{x}_1 - \bar{x}_3 = 11.4 - 8.2 = 3.2$$

Therefore, as $3.2 > R_3 = 1.615$, we conclude that $\bar{x}_1$ and $\bar{x}_3$ are significantly different and thus that $\mu_1 > \mu_3$.

(5) Because there is a significant difference in step (4), we must now test the difference between $\bar{x}_1$ and $\bar{x}_2$:

$$\bar{x}_1 - \bar{x}_2 = 11.4 - 9.4 = 2.0$$

Therefore, as $2.0 > R_2 = 1.540$, we conclude that $\bar{x}_1$ and $\bar{x}_2$ are significantly different and thus that $\mu_1 > \mu_2$.

(6) Next, we test the second largest against the smallest:

$$\bar{x}_2 - \bar{x}_4 = 9.4 - 7.0 = 2.4$$

Therefore, as $2.4 > R_3 = 1.615$, we conclude that $\bar{x}_2$ and $\bar{x}_4$ are significantly different and thus that $\mu_2 > \mu_4$.

(7) Because there is a significant difference in step (6), we must now test the difference between $\bar{x}_2$ and $\bar{x}_3$:

$$\bar{x}_2 - \bar{x}_3 = 9.4 - 8.2 = 1.2$$

Therefore, as $1.2 < R_2 = 1.540$, we conclude that $\bar{x}_2$ and $\bar{x}_3$ are not significantly different and thus that $\mu_2 = \mu_3$.

(8) Finally we test the difference between $\bar{x}_3$ and $\bar{x}_4$:

$$\bar{x}_3 - \bar{x}_4 = 8.2 - 7.0 = 1.2$$

Therefore, as $1.2 < R_2 = 1.540$, we conclude that $\bar{x}_3$ and $\bar{x}_4$ are not significantly different and thus that $\mu_3 = \mu_4$.

(9) From these results we conclude that

$$\bar{x}_4 \quad \bar{x}_3 \quad \bar{x}_2 \quad \bar{x}_1$$

and from this we can conclude unambiguously that $\mu_4 < \mu_2 < \mu_1$, but we can not, from this test, conclude how μ_3 is related to the other means.

18.12 In Problem 18.10 for the battery experiment, we rejected H_0: $\mu_1 = \mu_2 = \mu_3$ at $\alpha = 0.05$. For these data and the same significance level, use Duncan's multiple-range test (see Section 18.15) to determine differences between these means.

Solution

(1) First the $k = 3$ sample means are arranged in a linear order from smallest to largest:

$$\begin{array}{ccc} \bar{x}_3 & \bar{x}_2 & \bar{x}_1 \\ 1.06 & 1.26 & 1.34 \end{array}$$

(2) Next, we would like to calculate R_p values using $MSW = 0.0204$ from Problem 18.8, and r_p values from Table A.9 for $\alpha = 0.05$ and $v = 27$. However, as Table A.9 has only r_p values for $v = 24$ and $v = 30$, we must use the technique of linear interpolation (see Example 14.15) to get r_p values for $v = 27$. Thus, for $p = 2$, interpolating between $r_2 = 2.919$ for $v = 24$ and $r_2 = 2.888$ for $v = 30$, we get $r_2 = 2.904$ for $v = 27$. And, for $p = 3$, interpolating between $r_3 = 3.066$ for $v = 24$ and $r_3 = 3.035$ for $v = 30$, we get $r_3 = 3.050$ for $v = 27$. Using these values, R_p values are calculated with equation (18.25) and presented in a table:

p	2	3
r_p	2.904	3.050
R_p	0.131	0.138

(3) The range is determined for the subgroup $p = 3$ that includes the largest and smallest sample means:

$$\bar{x}_1 - \bar{x}_3 = 1.34 - 1.06 = 0.28$$

Therefore, as $0.28 > R_3 = 0.138$, we conclude that $\bar{x}_1$ and $\bar{x}_3$ are significantly different, and thus that $\mu_1 > \mu_3$.

(4) Because there is a significant difference in step (3), we must now test pairs within this range. First,

$$\bar{x}_1 - \bar{x}_2 = 1.34 - 1.26 = 0.08$$

Therefore, as $0.08 < R_2 = 0.131$, we conclude that $\bar{x}_1$ and $\bar{x}_2$ are not significantly different, and thus that $\mu_1 = \mu_2$. Next, we test

$$\bar{x}_2 - \bar{x}_3 = 1.26 - 1.06 = 0.20$$

and, as $0.20 > R_2 = 0.131$, we conclude that $\bar{x}_2$ and $\bar{x}_3$ are significantly different, and thus that $\mu_2 > \mu_3$.

(5) From these results we conclude that

$$\underline{\bar{x}_3} \qquad \underline{\bar{x}_2 \qquad \bar{x}_1}$$

and from this we can conclude that

$$\mu_3 < \mu_2 = \mu_1$$

EQUAL-SAMPLES ANOVA: CONFIDENCE INTERVALS

18.13 In Problem 18.11, we concluded unambiguously that $\mu_4 < \mu_2 < \mu_1$. From these data calculate a 95% confidence interval for μ_1.

Solution

Using equation (18.26),

$$\bar{x}_{i.} \pm t_{\alpha/2,\nu}\sqrt{\frac{MSW}{n_i}}$$

where from Table 18.7, $\bar{x}_{1.} = 11.4$ sec and $n_1 = 5$. From Table A.6, $t_{\alpha/2,\nu} = t_{0.05/2,16} = 2.120$. And, from Problem 18.7, $MSW = 1.32 \text{ sec}^2$. Therefore, the 95% confidence interval for μ_1 is

$$11.4 \text{ sec} \pm 2.120\sqrt{\frac{1.32 \text{ sec}^2}{5}}$$
$$11.4 \text{ sec} \pm 1.09 \text{ sec}$$

18.14 In Problem 18.12, we concluded that $\mu_3 < \mu_2 = \mu_1$. From these data calculate a 95% confidence interval for the overall mean μ_w for μ_1 and μ_2.

Solution

Using equation (18.27),

$$\bar{x}_w \pm t_{\alpha/2,\nu}\sqrt{\frac{MSW}{\sum n_i}}$$

where $\sum n_i = 2 \times 10 = 20$, and using equation (6.19) from Volume 1 and the values from Problem 18.4,

$$\bar{x}_w = \frac{\sum n_i \bar{x}_{i.}}{\sum n_i} = \frac{(10 \times 1.34 \text{ hr}) + (10 \times 1.26 \text{ hr})}{20} = \frac{26.0 \text{ hr}}{20} = 130 \text{ hr}$$

From Problem 18.8, we know that $MSW = 0.0204 \text{ hr}^2$ and from Table A.6 that $t_{\alpha/2,\nu} = t_{0.05/2,27} = 2.052$. Therefore, the 95% confidence interval for $\bar{x}_w$ is

$$1.30 \text{ hr} \pm 2.052\sqrt{\frac{0.0204 \text{ hr}^2}{20}}$$
$$1.30 \text{ hr} \pm 0.066 \text{ hr}$$

EQUAL-SAMPLES ANOVA: TESTING FOR HOMOGENEITY OF VARIANCE

18.15 For the data in Table 18.7, test for homogeneity of variance at $\alpha = 0.05$ using Bartlett's test.

Solution

Using equation (7.16) from Volume 1, the sample variances are $s_1^2 = 1.30$, $s_2^2 = 1.30$, $s_3^2 = 1.70$, $s_4^2 = 1.00$. Using equation (18.31) with $k = 4$,

$$N = \sum_{i=1}^{4} n_i = 4(5) = 20$$

Then, using equation (18.30),

$$s_p^2 = \frac{\sum_{i=1}^{4}(n_i - 1)s_i^2}{N - k} = \frac{21.20}{16} = 1.325$$

Next, using equation (18.33),

$$q = (N - k)\ \log s_p^2 - \sum_{i=1}^{4}(n_i - 1)\ \log s_i^2$$
$$= (16 \times 0.1222) - 1.8333 = 0.1219$$

And then, using equation (18.34),

$$h = 1 + \frac{1}{9}\left(\sum_{i=1}^{4} \frac{1}{n_i - 1} - \frac{1}{20-4}\right) = 1.1042$$

Therefore, using equation (18.32),

$$b^* = 2.3026 \times \frac{0.1219}{1.1042} = 0.254$$

The test for homogeneity of variance can now be summarized as follows:

(1) H_0: $\sigma_1^2 = \sigma_2^2 = \sigma_3^2 = \sigma_4^2$, H_1: The four variances are not all equal.

(2) $\alpha = 0.05$

(3) Using the B statistic with a value from Table A.7 for $\alpha = 0.05$ and ($\nu = k - 1 = 4 - 1 = 3$), the critical-value decision rule is: Reject H_0 if $b^* > (\chi^2_{0.05,3} = 7.81)$.

(4) The value of the B statistic is $b^* = 0.254$ and thus from Table A.7 we can see that a comparable χ^{2*} value for the $\nu = 3$ distribution would be between $\chi^2_{0.975}$ and $\chi^2_{0.950}$. Therefore, the P value is in the range $0.950 < P < 0.975$.

(5) As $b^* < 7.81$ we accept H_0; there is homogeneity of variance. This is confirmed by the fact that $P > 0.05$.

18.16 For the battery experiment in Problem 18.2, these are the sample variances: $s_1^2 = 0.01822$, $s_2^2 = 0.02267$, and $s_3^2 = 0.02044$. For these values, test for homogeneity of variance at $\alpha = 0.05$ using Bartlett's test.

Solution

Using equation (18.31) with $k = 3$,

$$N = \sum_{i=1}^{3} n_i = 3(10) = 30$$

Therefore, using equation (18.30),

$$s_p^2 = \frac{\sum_{i=1}^{3}(n_i - 1)s_i^2}{N - k} = \frac{0.55197}{27} = 0.02044$$

Next, using equation (18.33),

$$q = (N - k)\ \log s_p^2 - \sum_{i=1}^{3}(n_i - 1)\ \log s_i^2$$
$$= [27 \times (-1.6895)] - (-45.6617) = 0.04520$$

And then, using equation (18.34),

$$h = 1 + \frac{1}{6}\left(\sum_{i=1}^{3} \frac{1}{n_i - 1} - \frac{1}{20-3}\right) = 1.04575$$

Therefore, using equation (18.32),

$$b^* = 2.3026 \times \frac{0.04520}{1.04575} = 0.0995$$

The test for homogeneity of variance can now be summarized as follows:

(1) H_0: $\sigma_1^2 = \sigma_2^2 = \sigma_3^2$, H_1: The three variances are not all equal.

(2) $\alpha = 0.05$

(3) Using the B statistic with a value from Table A.7 for $\alpha = 0.05$ and ($\nu = k - 1 = 3 - 1 = 2$), the critical-

value decision rule is

$$\text{Reject } H_0 \text{ if } b^* > (\chi^2_{0.05,2} = 5.99)$$

(4) The value of the B statistic is $b^* = 0.0995$ and thus from Table A.7 we can see that a comparable χ^{2*} value for the $\nu = 2$ distribution would be between $\chi^2_{0.975}$ and $\chi^2_{0.950}$. Therefore, the P value is in the range $0.950 < P < 0.975$.

(5) As $b^* < 5.99$, we accept H_0; there is homogeneity of variance. This is confirmed by the fact that $P > 0.05$.

GENERAL-PROCEDURE, ONE-WAY, FIXED-EFFECTS ANOVA: H_0 AND H_1

18.17 You repeat the battery experiment in Problem 18.2, again taking constant-use talk-times for the new phone, for 10 batteries each of types 1, 2, and 3. This time, however, due to mechanical failures in the phones, some of the batteries do not complete the experiment: two of type 1 and one of type 3. These are the results of the experiment (to the nearest tenth of an hour) for the remaining 27 batteries: group 1 (1.5, 1.1, 1.3, 1.4, 1.5, 1.4, 1.2, 1.4); group 2 (1.4, 1.0, 1.2, 1.3, 1.2, 1.0, 1.3, 1.2, 1.4, 1.3); group 3 (1.0, 1.1, 1.3, 0.9, 1.2, 1.0, 1.1, 1.2, 1.0). Assuming, again, that the populations of these times are normally distributed with means μ_1, μ_2, and μ_3, and that there is homogeneity of variance, $\sigma_1^2 = \sigma_2^2 = \sigma_3^2 = \sigma^2$, then if you want to do a one-way, fixed-effects ANOVA on these data, what are H_0 and H_1?

Solution

H_0: $\mu_1 = \mu_2 = \mu_3$

H_1: The three means are not all equal.

GENERAL-PROCEDURE ANOVA: ORGANIZING THE DATA

18.18 For the results of the new battery experiment given in Problem 18.17, organize the data into a summary table like Table 18.1.

Solution

The requested table is given in Table 18.10, with totals and means calculated with equations (18.35), (18.36), (18.37), and (18.38).

GENERAL-PROCEDURE ANOVA: SUM OF SQUARES

18.19 For the data summarized in Table 18.10, calculate SST, SSA, and SSW using the computational formulas.

Table 18.10

Battery type	Time (hr)										Total	Mean
1	1.5	1.1	1.3	1.4	1.5	1.4	1.2	1.4			10.8 hr	1.35 hr
2	1.4	1.0	1.2	1.3	1.2	1.0	1.3	1.2	1.4	1.3	12.3 hr	1.23 hr
3	1.0	1.1	1.3	0.9	1.2	1.0	1.1	1.2	1.0		9.8 hr	1.09 hr
											32.9 hr	1.22 hr

Solution

Using equation (18.31),

$$N = \sum_{i=1}^{3} n_i = 8 + 10 + 9 = 27$$

Using equation (18.42),

$$SST = \sum_{i=1}^{3}\sum_{j=1}^{n_i} x_{ij}^2 - \frac{T_{..}^2}{N} = 40.83 \text{ hr}^2 - (1{,}082.41 \text{ hr}^2/27) = 0.741 \text{ hr}^2$$

Using equation (18.43),

$$SSA = \sum_{i=1}^{3} \frac{T_{i.}^2}{n_i} - \frac{T_{..}^2}{N} = 40.38 \text{ hr}^2 - (1{,}082.41 \text{ hr}^2/27) = 0.291 \text{ hr}^2$$

Using equation (18.9),

$$SSW = SST - SSA = 0.741 \text{ hr}^2 - 0.291 \text{ hr}^2 = 0.450 \text{ hr}^2$$

GENERAL-PROCEDURE ANOVA: MEAN SQUARES

18.20 Using the values for *SSA* and *SSW* from Problem 18.19, calculate *MSA* and *MSW*.

Solution

Using equation (18.44),

$$MSA = \frac{SSA}{k-1} = \frac{0.291 \text{ hr}^2}{3-1} = 0.146 \text{ hr}^2$$

Using equation (18.45),

$$MSW = \frac{SSW}{N-k} = \frac{0.450 \text{ hr}^2}{27-3} = 0.019 \text{ hr}^2$$

GENERAL-PROCEDURE: THE *F* TEST

18.21 For the data in Table 18.10 and the results in Problems 18.19 and 18.20, do a right-tailed test of H_0: $\mu_1 = \mu_2 = \mu_3$, at $\alpha = 0.05$, using a critical-value decision rule.

Solution

(1) H_0: $\mu_1 = \mu_2 = \mu_3$, H_1: The three means are not all equal.

(2) $\alpha = 0.05$

(3) Using Table A.8 for $\nu_1 = k - 1 = 2$ and $\nu_2 = N - k = 24$, the right-tailed decision rule is: Reject H_0 if $f^* > (f_{0.05,2,24} = 3.40)$.

(4) The results of the ANOVA are shown in the ANOVA table in Table 18.11. From Table A.8, the *P* value is in the range $P < 0.005$.

(5) As $f^* > 3.40$, we reject H_0 and accept H_1. This result is confirmed by the fact that the *P* value is in the range $P < 0.005$. There is thus evidence at the 0.05 level of significance that the three means are not all equal.

Table 18.11

Source of variation	Sum of squares	Degrees of freedom	Mean square	F
Among-samples	0.291	2	0.146	7.68
Within-samples	0.450	24	0.019	
Total	0.741	26		

GENERAL-PROCEDURE ANOVA: MULTIPLE COMPARISONS

18.22 In Problem 18.21 we rejected $H_0 : \mu_1 = \mu_2 = \mu_3$, at $\alpha = 0.05$. For these data (see Table 18.10) and the same significance level, use Kramer's extension of Duncan's multiple-range test to determine differences between these means.

Solution

(1) The $k = 3$ sample means are arranged in a linear order from smallest to largest:

$\bar{x}_3$	$\bar{x}_2$	$\bar{x}_1$
1.09	1.23	1.35

(2) Next, using $MSW = 0.019$ from Problem 18.20 and r_p values from Table A.9 for $\alpha = 0.05$ and $\nu = 24$, R'_p values are calculated using equation (18.49) and presented in a table:

p	2	3
r_p	2.919	3.066
R'_p	0.402	0.423

(3) The range is determined for the subgroup $p = 3$ values that includes the largest and smallest sample means using equaion (18.50):

$$(\bar{x}_1 - \bar{x}_3)\sqrt{\frac{2n_1n_3}{n_1 + n_3}} = (1.35 - 1.09)\sqrt{\frac{144}{17}} = 0.757$$

Therefore, as $0.757 > R'_3 = 0.423$, we conclude that $\bar{x}_1$ and $\bar{x}_3$ are significantly different and thus $\mu_1 > \mu_3$.

(4) Because there is a significant difference in step (3), we must now test pairs within this range. First,

$$(\bar{x}_1 - \bar{x}_2)\sqrt{\frac{2n_1n_2}{n_1 + n_2}} = (1.35 - 1.23)\sqrt{\frac{160}{18}} = 0.358$$

and as $0.358 < R'_2 = 0.402$, we conclude that $\bar{x}_1$ and $\bar{x}_2$ are not significantly different and thus $\mu_1 = \mu_2$. Next,

$$(\bar{x}_2 - \bar{x}_3)\sqrt{\frac{2n_2n_3}{n_2 + n_3}} = (1.23 - 1.09)\sqrt{\frac{180}{19}} = 0.431$$

and as $0.431 > R'_2 = 0.402$, we conclude that $\bar{x}_2$ and $\bar{x}_3$ are significantly different and thus that $\mu_2 > \mu_3$.

(5) From these results we can conclude that

$$\underline{\bar{x}_3} \quad \underline{\bar{x}_2 \quad \bar{x}_1}$$

and thus we can conclude that

$$\mu_3 < \mu_2 = \mu_1$$

GENERAL-PROCEDURE ANOVA: CALCULATING CONFIDENCE INTERVALS AND TESTING FOR HOMOGENEITY OF VARIANCE

18.23 In Problem 18.22, we concluded that $\mu_3 < \mu_2 = \mu_1$. For these data, calculate a 90% confidence interval for μ_3.

Solution

Using equation (18.26),

$$\bar{x}_{i\cdot} \pm t_{\alpha/2,\nu}\sqrt{\frac{MSW}{n_i}}$$

where from Table 18.10, $\bar{x}_3 = 1.09$ hr and $n_i = n_3 = 9$. From Table A.6, $t_{\alpha/2,\nu} = t_{0.10.2,24} = 1.711$. And, from Problem 18.20, $MSW = 0.019\text{ hr}^2$. Therefore, the 90% confidence interval for μ_3 is

$$1.09\text{ hr} \pm 1.711\sqrt{\frac{0.019\text{ hr}^2}{9}}$$

$$1.09\text{ hr} \pm 0.079\text{ hr}$$

18.24 For the data in Table 18.10, test for homogeneity of variance at $\alpha = 0.05$ using Bartlett's test.

Solution

Using equation (7.16) from Volume 1, the sample variances are $s_1^2 = 0.0200$, $s_2^2 = 0.0201$, and $s_3^2 = 0.0161$. Using equation (18.31) with $k = 3$,

$$N = \sum_{i=1}^{3} n_i = 8 + 10 + 9 = 27$$

Then, using equation (18.30),

$$s_p^2 = \frac{\sum_{i=1}^{3}(n_i - 1)s_i^2}{N - k} = \frac{0.4497}{24} = 0.0187$$

Next, using equation (18.33),

$$q = (N - k)\log s_p^2 - \sum_{i=1}^{3}(n_i - 1)\log s_i^2$$

$$= [24 \times (-1.7282)] - (-41.5094) = 0.0326$$

And, using equation (18.34),

$$h = 1 + \frac{1}{6}\left(\sum_{i=1}^{3}\frac{1}{n_i - 1} - \frac{1}{27 - 3}\right) = 1.0562$$

Therefore, using equation (18.32),

$$b^* = 2.3026 \times \frac{0.0326}{1.0562} = 0.0711$$

The test for homogeneity of variance can now be summarized as follows:

(1) H_0: $\sigma_1^2 = \sigma_2^2 = \sigma_3^2$, $\quad H_1$: The three variances are not all equal.

(2) $\alpha = 0.05$

(3) Using the B statistic with a value from Table A.7 for $\alpha = 0.05$ and ($\nu = k - 1 = 3 - 1 = 2$), the critical-value decision rule is: Reject H_0 if $b^* > (\chi^2_{0.05,2} = 5.99)$.

(4) The value of the B statistic is $b^* = 0.0711$, and from Table A.7 we can see that a comparable χ^{2*} value for the $\nu = 2$ distribution would lie between $\chi^2_{0.975}$ and $\chi^2_{0.950}$ and thus the P value is in the range $0.950 < P < 0.975$.

(5) As $b^* < 5.99$ we accept H_0; there is homogeneity of variance. This is confirmed by the fact that $P > 0.05$.

Supplementary Problems

EQUAL-SAMPLES, ONE-WAY, FIXED-EFFECTS ANOVA: H_0 AND H_1

18.25 You are a dietician testing five different diet/exercise programs, denoted by the numbers 1, 2, 3, 4, and 5. From 25 women who volunteer for your experiment, you randomly form five groups of 5 each, one for each program. You measure the weight of each woman (to the nearest pound) just before she begins the experiment and then after she has followed the program for 2 months. You calculate the difference between these weights for each woman: after subtracted from before. Assuming the populations of weight-differences are normally distributed with means μ_1, μ_2, μ_3, μ_4, and μ_5, and that there is homogeneity of variance, $\sigma_1^2 = \sigma_2^2 = \sigma_3^2 = \sigma_4^2 = \sigma_5^2 = \sigma^2$, then if you want to do a one-way, fixed-effects *ANOVA* on these data, what are H_0 and H_1?

Ans. H_0: $\mu_1 = \mu_2 = \mu_3 = \mu_4 = \mu_5$, H_1: The five means are not all equal.

EQUAL-SAMPLES ANOVA: ORGANIZING THE DATA

18.26 These are the results of the experiment in Problem 18.25, with the weight difference for each woman given to the nearest pound: group 1 (6, 7, 6, 8, 7); group 2 (8, 9, 10, 8, 9); group 3 (7, 9, 8, 6, 9); group 4 (14, 13, 12, 15, 14); group 5 (12, 13, 11, 11, 14). From these data, determine: $T_{1.}$, $T_{2.}$, $T_{3.}$, $T_{4.}$, $T_{5.}$, and $T_{..}$.

Ans. $T_{1.} = 34$ lb, $T_{2.} = 44$ lb, $T_{3.} = 39$ lb, $T_{4.} = 68$ lb, $T_{5.} = 61$ lb, $T_{..} = 246$ lb

18.27 From the results of the diet/exercise experiment in Problem 18.26, determine: $\bar{x}_{1.}$, $\bar{x}_{2.}$, $\bar{x}_{3.}$, $\bar{x}_{4.}$, $\bar{x}_{5.}$, and $\bar{x}_{..}$.

Ans. $\bar{x}_{1.} = 6.8$ lb, $\bar{x}_{2.} = 8.8$ lb, $\bar{x}_{3.} = 7.8$ lb, $\bar{x}_{4.} = 13.6$ lb, $\bar{x}_{5.} = 12.2$ lb, $\bar{x}_{..} = 9.8$ lb

EQUAL-SAMPLES ANOVA: SUM OF SQUARES

18.28 For the diet/exercise experiment, use the values from Problem 18.26 to determine *SST*, *SSA*, and *SSW*.

Ans. $SST = 195.4\ \text{lb}^2$, $SSA = 171.0\ \text{lb}^2$, $SSW = 24.4\ \text{lb}^2$

EQUAL-SAMPLES ANOVA: MEAN SQUARES

18.29 For the diet/exercise experiment, use the values of *SSA* and *SSW* from Problem 18.28 to determine *MSA* and *MSW*.

Ans. $MSA = 42.75\ \text{lb}^2$, $MSW = 1.22\ \text{lb}^2$

EQUAL-SAMPLES ANOVA: THE F TEST

18.30 For the diet/exercise experiment, using the values of *MSA* and *MSW* from Problem 18.29, do an F test, at $\alpha = 0.05$, of H_0: $\mu_1 = \mu_2 = \mu_3 = \mu_4 = \mu_5$. Give the f^* value. State whether you accept or reject H_0, and the approximate probability of getting this f^* value given that H_0 is true.

Ans. $f^* = 35.04$, reject H_0 because $f^* > 2.87$, $P < 0.005$

EQUAL-SAMPLES ANOVA: MULTIPLE COMPARISONS

18.31 In Problem 18.30 for the diet/exercise experiment, we rejected H_0: $\mu_1 = \mu_2 = \mu_3 = \mu_4 = \mu_5$ at $\alpha = 0.05$. For these data and the same significance level, use Duncan's multiple-range test to determine differences between these means. Give the R_p values, and show your conclusions for both the sample and population means.

Ans. $R_2 = 1.457$, $R_3 = 1.530$, $R_4 = 1.576$, $R_5 = 1.608$; $\bar{x}_1 \quad \bar{x}_3 \quad \bar{x}_2 \quad \bar{x}_5 \quad \bar{x}_4$; we can conclude unambiguously that $\mu_1 < \mu_2 < \mu_5 = \mu_4$, but we cannot, from this test, conclude how μ_3 is related to the other means.

EQUAL-SAMPLES ANOVA: CALCULATING CONFIDENCE INTERVALS AND TESTING FOR HOMOGENEITY OF VARIANCE

18.32 In Problems 18.31, we concluded unambiguously that $\mu_1 < \mu_2 < \mu_5 = \mu_4$. From these data calculate a 95% confidence interval for the overall mean μ_w for μ_4 and μ_5.

Ans. 12.9 lb $\pm$ 0.73 lb

18.33 From the information in Problems 18.26 and 18.27, test for homogeneity of variance at $\alpha = 0.05$ using Bartlett's test. Give the values for s_1^2, s_2^2, s_3^2, s_4^2, s_5^2, s_p^2, and b^*. State whether you accept or reject H_0: $\sigma_1^2 = \sigma_2^2 = \sigma_3^2 = \sigma_4^2 = \sigma_5^2$, and the approximate probability of getting this b^* value given that H_0 is true.

Ans. $s_1^2 = 0.70$, $s_2^2 = 0.70$, $s_3^2 = 1.70$, $s_4^2 = 1.30$, $s_5^2 = 1.70$, $s_p^2 = 1.22$, $b^* = 1.3962$, accept H_0 because $b^* < 9.49$, $0.5 < P < 0.9$

GENERAL-PROCEDURE, ONE-WAY, FIXED-EFFECTS ANOVA: H_0 AND H_1

18.34 Suppose that in the diet/exercise experiment in Problems 18.25 and 18.26, instead of all 25 women completing the experiment, two were not able to: a loser of 6 lb in group 1, and the loser of 15 lb in group 4. If normal distributions and homogeneity of variance can still be assumed, and you want to do a one-way, fixed-effects ANOVA on the data from the 23 women, then what are H_0 and H_1?

Ans. H_0: $\mu_1 = \mu_2 = \mu_3 = \mu_4 = \mu_5$, H_1: The five means are not all equal.

GENERAL-PROCEDURE ANOVA: ORGANIZING THE DATA

18.35 With the two women removed from the data in Problem 18.26, these are the new group weight-difference results: group 1 (7, 6, 8, 7); group 2 (8, 9, 10, 8, 9); group 3 (7, 9, 8, 6, 9); group 4 (14, 13, 12, 14); group 5 (12, 13, 11, 11, 14). From these data determine $T_{1.}$, $T_{2.}$, $T_{3.}$, $T_{4.}$, $T_{5.}$, and $T_{..}$.

Ans. $T_{1.} = 28$ lb, $T_{2.} = 44$ lb, $T_{3.} = 39$ lb, $T_{4.} = 53$ lb, $T_{5.} = 61$ lb, $T_{..} = 225$ lb

18.36 From the results of the diet/exercise experiment in Problem 18.35, determine $\bar{x}_{1.}$, $\bar{x}_{2.}$, $\bar{x}_{3.}$, $\bar{x}_{4.}$, $\bar{x}_{5.}$, and $\bar{x}_{..}$.

Ans. $\bar{x}_{1.} = 7.0$ lb, $\bar{x}_{2.} = 8.8$ lb, $\bar{x}_{3.} = 7.8$ lb, $\bar{x}_{4.} = 13.2$ lb, $\bar{x}_{5.} = 12.2$ lb, $\bar{x}_{..} = 9.8$ lb

GENERAL-PROCEDURE ANOVA: SUM OF SQUARES

18.37 For the diet/exercise experiment, use the values from Problem 18.35 to determine: SST, SSA, and SSW.

Ans. $SST = 153.9\ \text{lb}^2$, $SSA = 132.8\ \text{lb}^2$, $SSW = 21.1\ \text{lb}^2$

GENERAL-PROCEDURE ANOVA: MEAN SQUARES

18.38 For the diet/exercise experiment, use the values of SSA and SSW from Problem 18.37 to determine MSA and MSW.

Ans. $MSA = 33.20\ \text{lb}^2$, $MSW = 1.17\ \text{lb}^2$

GENERAL-PROCEDURE ANOVA: THE F TEST

18.39 For the diet/exercise experiment, using the values of *MSA* and *MSW* from Problem 18.38, do an F test, at $\alpha = 0.05$, of H_0: $\mu_1 = \mu_2 = \mu_3 = \mu_4 = \mu_5$. Give the f^* value. State whether you accept or reject H_0, and give the approximate probability of getting this f^* value given that H_0 is true.

Ans. $f^* = 28.38$, reject H_0 because $f^* > 2.93$, $P < 0.005$

GENERAL-PROCEDURE ANOVA: MULTIPLE COMPARISONS

18.40 In Problem 18.39 for the diet/exercise experiment, we rejected H_0: $\mu_1 = \mu_2 = \mu_3 = \mu_4 = \mu_5$ at $\alpha = 0.05$. For these data (see Problem 18.35) and the same significance level, use Kramer's extension of Duncan's multiple-range test to determine differences between these means. Give the R'_p values, and show your conclusions for the sample and population means.

Ans. $R'_2 = 3.214$, $R'_3 = 3.373$, $R'_4 = 3.472$, $R'_5 = 3.541$; $\bar{x}_1 \; \bar{x}_3 \; \bar{x}_2 \; \bar{x}_5 \; \bar{x}_4$; we can unambiguously conclude that $\mu_1 < \mu_2 < \mu_5 = \mu_4$, but we can not, from this test, conclude how μ_3 is related to the other means.

GENERAL-PROCEDURE ANOVA: CALCULATING CONFIDENCE INTERVALS AND TESTING FOR HOMOGENEITY OF VARIANCE

18.41 In Problem 18.40, we concluded unambiguously that $\mu_1 < \mu_2 < \mu_5 = \mu_4$. From these data, calculate a 95% confidence interval for $\mu_5 - \mu_2$.

Ans. 3.4 lb $\pm$ 1.44 lb

18.42 From the information in Problems 18.35 and 18.36, test for homogeneity of variance at $\alpha = 0.05$ using Bartlett's test. Give the values for s_1^2, s_2^2, s_3^2, s_4^2, s_5^2, s_p^2, and b^*. State whether you accept or reject H_0: $\sigma_1^2 = \sigma_2^2 = \sigma_3^2 = \sigma_4^2 = \sigma_5^2$, and the approximate probability of getting this b^* value given that H_0 is true.

Ans. $s_1^2 = 0.67$, $s_2^2 = 0.70$, $s_3^2 = 1.70$, $s_4^2 = 0.92$, $s_5^2 = 1.70$, $s_p^2 = 1.18$, $b^* = 1.4483$, accept H_0 because $b^* < 9.49$, $0.5 < P < 0.9$

CHAPTER 19

Regression and Correlation

19.1 ANALYZING THE RELATIONSHIP BETWEEN TWO VARIABLES

So far in this book, we have been concerned with *univariate data*, in which the sample observations are made on a single variable. We now consider *bivariate data*, in which the sample observations are made on two variables. Such a sample, for instance, may consist of observations on the temperature of the body and the consumption of oxygen in a population of beetles. A sample of n individual beetles would be taken, and both body temperature and oxygen consumption would be measured for each individual.

The first step in analyzing the relationship between two variables is to construct a *scatter diagram* (or a *scatter plot*) of the sample data. Such a diagram, for the body temperatures and oxygen consumptions of beetles, is shown in Fig. 19-1. A scatter diagram gives an initial impression of whether or not the data points form a pattern. If the points appear to lie along a straight line, as they do in Fig. 19-1, we can say that a *linear relationship* appears to exist between the two variables. If the points form a pattern, but do not lie along a straight line, then the two variables probably have a *nonlinear relationship*. This chapter deals only with linear relationships.

The relationship between two variables is analyzed statistically by either a *regression analysis* or a *correlation analysis*. In regression analysis, one of the variables is considered independent and the other is considered dependent (although the relationship does not have to be a cause-and-effect relationship; see Section 1.19 in Volume 1). The values of the independent variable are assumed not to have random variation; they are assigned by the investigator. The values of the dependent variable are assumed to have random variation; they are obtained through the process of sampling. Thus, if the study were repeated, the values of the independent variable would remain the same (as set by the investigator) but the values of the dependent variable would vary due to the process of sampling. The object of a regression analysis is to develop a mathematical equation that describes the relationship. This equation can then be used in the future to predict values of the dependent variable from values of the independent variable. An example of a regression analysis (seen in Fig. 19-1) is the relationship between oxygen consumption in beetles (the dependent variable) kept in the laboratory under different environmental temperatures (the independent variable). In correlation analysis, we study the strength of the relationship between two independent variables. Both variables are assumed to have random variation. An example of correlation analysis is oxygen consumption and body temperature in a population of beetles measured in the field, under different

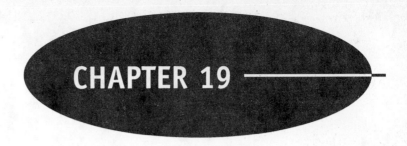

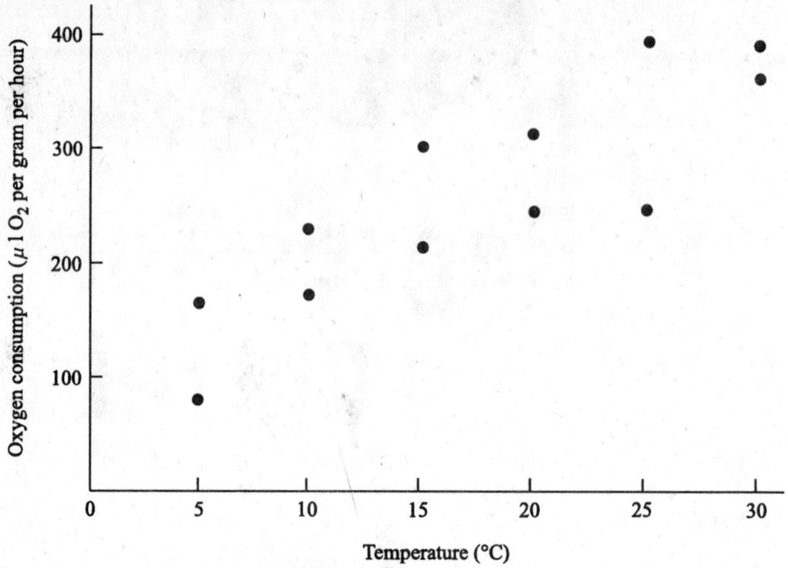

Fig. 19-1

environmental conditions. In this correlation analysis, the sample values of both variables are obtained through the process of sampling, and both would vary somewhat from one sample to another.

19.2 THE SIMPLE LINEAR REGRESSION MODEL

Simple linear regression analyzes the straight-line relationship between an independent variable and a dependent variable. The term "simple" distinguishes this two-variable analysis from a multiple-variable analysis (see Section 19.11). By convention, X denotes the independent variable and Y denotes the dependent variable. A perfect, straight-line relationship between X and Y is described by

$$Y = a + bX \tag{19.1}$$

where is a the y intercept and b is the slope of the line that describes the relation of Y to X. The constants a and b can be determined from any two points (x_1, y_1) and (x_2, y_2) on the line. The y intercept a is the value of Y when $X = 0$. The slope b measures the change in Y divided by a corresponding change in X:

$$b = \frac{y_2 - y_1}{x_2 - x_1} \tag{19.2}$$

When a value of the independent variable is known ($X = x_i$), equation (19.1) can be used to predict the corresponding value of the dependent random variable Y,

$$y_i = a + bx_i \tag{19.3}$$

where a and b are the parameters, often called the *regression coefficients*, of the relationship.

In the study of relations between real-world variables, Y cannot be exactly predicted from X because, for any particular value of x_i, there is random variation in the observed values of Y. The best we can do is to estimate Y from a random sample of y_i values for each x_i. The expected value of Y given x_i is then

$$E(Y|x_i) = \mu_{Y|x_i} = a + bx_i \tag{19.4}$$

where $Y|x_i$ denotes "the value of Y for a particular value of x."

In linear regression analysis, we use sample data to estimate the values of $\mu_{Y|x_i}$, a, and b. The estimator of the population mean $\mu_{Y|x_i}$ is denoted $\hat{\mu}_{Y|x_i}$ and the sample mean is denoted $\hat{\mu}^*_{Y|x_i}$. The estimator of a is denoted $\hat{a}$ and its point estimate (sample value) is denoted $\hat{a}^*$. The estimator of b is denoted $\hat{b}$ and its point estimate is denoted $\hat{b}^*$. Thus, the regression line developed from sample data is

$$\hat{\mu}^*_{Y|x_i} = \hat{a}^* + \hat{b}^* x_i \qquad (19.5)$$

The first step in estimating a and b is to choose n values of the independent variable $(x_1, x_2, \ldots, x_n)$ and then to take a sample of Y values for each of these x values. The next step is to prepare a scatter diagram of all the sample pairs (each value of x has two or more values of y). If there appears to be a linear relation between variable X and variable Y, then the next step is to develop an equation that describes the linear relationship.

19.3 THE LEAST-SQUARES REGRESSION LINE

A *least-squares regression line* (or *line of best fit*) is the line through the data points (x_i, y_i) that has the smallest possible sums of squares of deviations from the line. The method of finding this line, known as the *least-squares estimation*, is described below.

For a given value of X, the observed values of Y are unlikely to be the exact same value as predicted from equation (19.1). Such deviations from prediction are indicated with arrows in the scatter diagram shown in Fig. 19-2. The sum of squares (see Section 18.9) of these deviations in sample values of Y provide a measure of how well a line drawn through the data points "fits" the data.

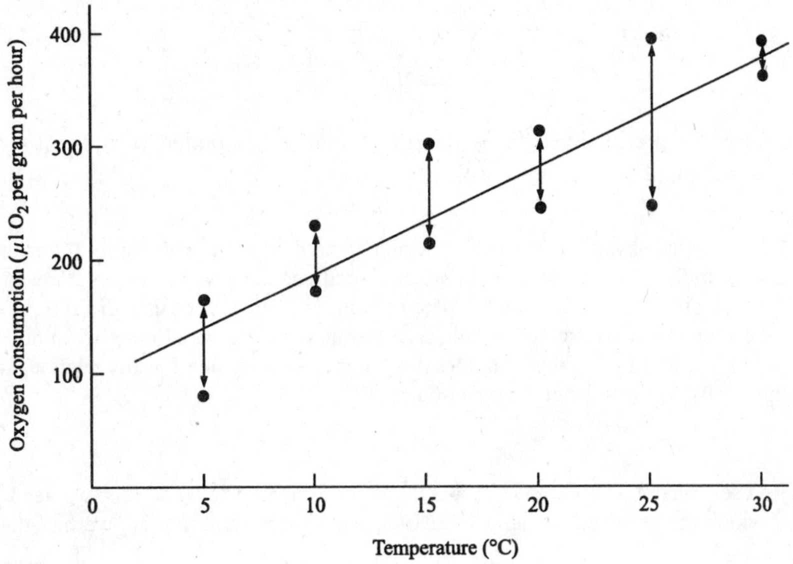

Fig. 19-2

We describe the least-squares regression line by our estimates of a and b, which are our point estimates $\hat{a}^*$ and $\hat{b}^*$. (The point estimates of a and b are also called *least-squares estimates* of a and b.) Without deriving the equations, we simply state that the point estimate of a is

$$\hat{a}^* = \bar{y} - \hat{b}^* \bar{x} \qquad (19.6)$$

and the point estimate of b is

$$\hat{b}^* = \frac{\sum (x_i - \bar{x})(y_i - \bar{y})}{\sum (x_i - \bar{x})^2} \qquad (19.7)$$

where $\bar{y}$ is the mean of the sample values of the random variable Y for each x, and $\bar{x}$ is the mean value of the variable X.

A regression line obtained in this way, from sample data, is valid only for the observed range of observations. The linear relation may not hold for all values of x, and so it should not be extrapolated beyond the range of values used in obtaining the regression line.

Calculation of the point estimates $\hat{a}^*$ and $\hat{b}^*$, as well as other equations in this chapter, is simplified by substituting these known equalities into definitional equations:

$$\sum(x_i - \bar{x})^2 = \sum x_i^2 - \frac{(\sum x_i)^2}{n} \tag{19.8}$$

$$\sum(y_i - \bar{y})^2 = \sum y_i^2 - \frac{(\sum y_i)^2}{n} \tag{19.9}$$

$$\sum(x_i - \bar{x})(y_i - \bar{y}) = \sum x_i y_i - \frac{(\sum x_i)(\sum y_i)}{n} \tag{19.10}$$

Thus, substituting equations (19.8) and (19.10) into equation (19.7), we get this computational version:

$$\hat{b}^* = \frac{\sum x_i y_i - \dfrac{\sum x_i \sum y_i}{n}}{\sum x_i^2 - \dfrac{(\sum x_i)^2}{n}} \tag{19.11}$$

where n is the number of paired values. The value of $\hat{\alpha}^*$ is then calculated with equation (19.6), using $\hat{b}^*$ and the mean values of x and y.

EXAMPLE 19.1 An exercise physiologist wants to be able to predict the cardiac output (liters of blood pumped by the heart each minute) from the level of exercise (kilograms lifted one meter per minute, abbreviated kg-m/min). He chooses four levels of exercise: 0, 300, 600, and 900 kg-m/min. His sample consists of 20 men, with 5 assigned at random to each of the four levels of exercise. Their cardiac output is measured after 15 minutes of exercise. The resulting data are shown in Table 19.1. What is the least-squares regression line for this relationship? For an exercise level of 700 kg-m/min, what is the expected cardiac output?

Solution

First, we use equation (19.11) to calculate the point estimate $\hat{b}^*$. To do this, we need $\sum x_i$, $\sum x_i^2$, $\sum y_i$, and $\sum x_i y_i$, which are provided in Table 19.2. Using these sums and $n = 20$, we find that

$$\hat{b}^* = \frac{128{,}790 - \dfrac{(9{,}000)(219.5)}{20}}{6{,}300{,}000 - \dfrac{(9{,}000)^2}{20}} = 0.01334 \text{ l/kg-m}$$

Next, we use equation (19.6) to calculate $\hat{a}^*$:

$$\hat{a}^* = \frac{219.5}{20} - (0.01334)\frac{9{,}000}{20} = 4.972 \text{ l/min}$$

(In reporting these values, the estimate of the Y intercept $\hat{a}^*$ is rounded off to one digit more than in the observed values of Y, and the estimate of the slope $\hat{b}^*$ is rounded off such that when multipled times the maximum value of x, it is one more digit than in the observed values of Y. Thus, we report $\hat{a}^*$ as 4.97 and $\hat{b}^*$ as 0.0133.)

The equation for the least-squares regession line is: $\hat{\mu}^*_{Y|x} = 4.97 + 0.0133x$. For a level of exercise equal to 700 kg-m/min, we expect a cardiac output of 14.28 l/min.

Table 19.1

Subject	Exercise level (kg-m per min)	Cardiac output (liters per min)
1	0	4.4
2	0	5.6
3	0	5.2
4	0	5.4
5	0	4.4
6	300	9.1
7	300	8.6
8	300	8.5
9	300	9.3
10	300	9.0
11	600	12.8
12	600	13.4
13	600	13.2
14	600	12.6
15	600	13.2
16	900	17.0
17	900	17.3
18	900	16.5
19	900	16.8
20	900	17.2

Table 19.2

	x_i	y_i	x_i^2	y_i^2	x_iy_i
	0	4.4	0	19.36	0
	0	5.6	0	31.36	0
	0	5.2	0	27.04	0
	0	5.4	0	29.16	0
	0	4.4	0	19.36	0
	300	9.1	90,000	82.81	2,730
	300	8.6	90,000	73.96	2,580
	300	8.5	90,000	72.25	2,550
	300	9.3	90,000	86.49	2,790
	300	9.0	90,000	81.00	2,700
	600	12.8	360,000	163.84	7,680
	600	13.4	360,000	179.56	8,040
	600	13.2	360,000	174.24	7,920
	600	12.6	360,000	158.76	7,560
	600	13.2	360,000	174.24	7,920
	900	17.0	810,000	289.00	15,300
	900	17.3	810,000	299.29	15,570
	900	16.5	810,000	272.25	14,850
	900	16.8	810,000	282.24	15,120
	900	17.2	810,000	295.84	15,480
$\sum$	9,000	219.5	6,300,000	2,812.05	128,790

19.4 THE ESTIMATOR OF THE VARIANCE $\sigma^2_{Y \cdot X}$

The variance of a least-squares regression line $\sigma^2_{Y \cdot X}$ is estimated by the amount of deviation of the variable Y around the population mean for all the values of x_i. For each value of the independent variable X, we assume that the sample values of the dependent variable Y form a normal distribution with a mean

$$\hat{\mu}_{Y|x} = \hat{a} + \hat{b}x \tag{19.12}$$

and that the variance of the distribution of Y values is the same for all values of x_i. The unbiased estimator of this variance is the mean square deviation of y_i values about the regression line,

$$s^2_{y \cdot x} = \frac{\sum(y_i - \hat{\mu}_{Y|x_i})^2}{n-2} \tag{19.13}$$

where the subscript $y \cdot x$ means that this estimator describes the variance of Y when we have the regression of y on x. The quantity $n - 2$ represents the sample size n minus two degrees of freedom, one for each of the two parameters (a and b) that are estimated.

The computational version of equation (19.13) is

$$s^2_{y \cdot x} = \frac{\sum y_i^2 - \hat{a}^* \sum y_i - \hat{b}^* \sum x_i y_i}{n-2} \tag{19.14}$$

and the standard deviation is

$$s_{y \cdot x} = \sqrt{s^2_{y \cdot x}} \tag{19.15}$$

This standard deviation, or *standard error of the estimate*, describes the deviation of the y_i values from the regression line. It represents the uncertainty in estimating Y from X.

EXAMPLE 19.2 For the experiment described in Example 19.1, what is the estimator of the variance and what is the standard error of the estimate?

Solution

Using equation (19.14) and inserting $n = 20$, $\hat{a}^* = 4.97$ liters per min, $\hat{b}^* = 0.0133$ l/kg-m, and sums from Table 19.2, we find the estimator of the variance is

$$s^2_{y \cdot x} = \frac{2{,}812.05 - (4.97)(219.5) - (0.0133)(128{,}790)}{20 - 2} = 0.4571 \text{ (l/min)}^2$$

Using equation (19.15), the standard error of the estimate is

$$s_{y \cdot x} = \sqrt{0.4571} = 0.6761, \quad \text{or } 0.68 \text{ l/min}$$

(The standard deviation, or standard error of the estimate, is rounded off to one digit more than the observed Y values.)

19.5 MEAN AND VARIANCE OF THE y INTERCEPT $\hat{a}$ AND THE SLOPE $\hat{b}$

We assume that, for each x_i, the y_i values are normally distributed (see Section 19.4). Because our estimators ($\hat{a}$ and $\hat{b}$) are linear functions of these Y_i values, we can assume that they also are normally distributed. Using this assumption of normality, the variances for the y intercept estimator $\hat{a}$ and the slope estimator $\hat{b}$ can be found.

Without deriving them, we simply state that for $\hat{a}$, the mean is $\mu_{\hat{a}} = a$ and the variance is

$$s^2_{\hat{a}} = s^2_{y \cdot x}\left(\frac{1}{n} + \frac{\bar{x}^2}{\sum(x_i - \bar{x})^2}\right) \tag{19.16}$$

where $s^2_{y \cdot x}$ is the best estimate of the population variance $\sigma^2_{Y \cdot X}$ for the random variable Y [see equations (19.13) and (19.14)]. Substituting the formula for calculating the mean and equation (19.8), we get a computational version of equation (19.16):

$$s^2_{\hat{a}} = s^2_{y \cdot x}\left[\frac{1}{n} + \frac{\left(\frac{\sum x}{n}\right)^2}{\sum x^2 - \frac{(\sum x)^2}{n}}\right] \tag{19.17}$$

Without deriving them, we state that for $\hat{b}$, the mean is $\mu_{\hat{b}} = b$ and the variance is

$$s^2_{\hat{b}} = \frac{s^2_{y \cdot x}}{\sum(x_i - \bar{x})^2} \tag{19.18}$$

where $s^2_{y \cdot x}$ is the best estimate of the population variance $\sigma^2_{Y \cdot X}$ for the random variable Y [see equations (19.13) and (19.14)]. The computational version of equation (19.18) is

$$s^2_{\hat{b}} = \frac{s^2_{y \cdot x}}{\sum x^2 - \frac{(\sum x)^2}{n}} \tag{19.19}$$

The standard deviations of these estimators are

$$s_{\hat{a}} = \sqrt{s^2_{\hat{a}}} \tag{19.20}$$

and

$$s_{\hat{b}} = \sqrt{s^2_{\hat{b}}} \tag{19.21}$$

EXAMPLE 19.3 For the experiment in Example 19.1, find the standard deviations of the point estimates of $\hat{a}$ and of $\hat{b}$.

Solution

We find the standard deviation of $\hat{a}^*$ by using equations (19.17) and (19.20), substituting the values of $s^2_{y \cdot x} = 0.4571$, $n = 20$, and sums from Table 19.2:

$$s_{\hat{a}^*} = \sqrt{s^2_{\hat{a}^*}} = \sqrt{0.4571\left(\frac{1}{20} + \frac{\left(\frac{9{,}000}{20}\right)^2}{6{,}300{,}000 - \frac{(9{,}000)^2}{20}}\right)} = \sqrt{0.063994} = 0.25297, \quad \text{or } 0.253 \text{ l/min}$$

We find the standard deviation of $\hat{b}^*$ by using equations (19.18) and (19.21), substituting the values of $s^2_{y \cdot x} = 0.4571$ and sums from Table 19.2:

$$s_{\hat{b}^*} = \sqrt{s^2_{\hat{b}^*}} = \sqrt{\frac{0.4571}{6{,}300{,}000 - \frac{(9{,}000)^2}{20}}} = \sqrt{0.0000002032} = 0.0004507, \quad \text{or } 0.00045 \text{ l/kg-m}$$

19.6 CONFIDENCE INTERVALS FOR THE *y* INTERCEPT *a* AND THE SLOPE *b*

Once we have established the least-squares regression line, we may want to know the range of values within which we are highly confident that the true parameters lie. From Section 19.5, we know that the estimator of the y intercept $\hat{a}$ and the estimator of the slope $\hat{b}$ can be assumed to be normally distributed with means a and b. Under this assumption of normality, we can use the t distribution to develop confidence intervals for a and b.

Without deriving the relationship, we simply state that the sampling distribution of the statistic

$$T = \frac{\hat{a} - a}{S_{\hat{a}}} \tag{19.22}$$

has a t distribution with $\nu = n - 2$ degrees of freedom. ($S_{\hat{a}}$ is the variable that can have values $s_{\hat{a}}$.) This statistic can assume specific values

$$t = \frac{\hat{a}^* - a}{s_{\hat{a}^*}}$$

For this t statistic we know that [see equation (14.15)]

$$P\left(-t_{\alpha/2,\nu} \le \frac{\hat{a} - a}{S_{\hat{a}}} \le t_{\alpha/2,\nu}\right) = 1 - \alpha$$

Rearranging the equation (see Section 14.8), we can say that

$$P(\hat{a} - t_{\alpha/2,\nu}S_{\hat{a}} < a < \hat{a} + t_{\alpha/2,\nu}S_{\hat{a}}) = 1 - \alpha \tag{19.23}$$

Thus, the $(1 - \alpha)100\%$ confidence limits for the y intercept are

$$[\hat{a}^* - t_{\alpha/2,\nu}s_{\hat{a}^*}, \hat{a}^* + t_{\alpha/2,\nu}s_{\hat{a}^*}]$$

A confidence interval for the slope b is developed in a similar manner. Without deriving the equation, we simply state that the sampling distribution of the statistic

$$T = \frac{\hat{b} - b}{S_{\hat{b}}} \tag{19.24}$$

has a t distribution with $\nu = n - 2$ degrees of freedom (where $S_{\hat{b}}$ is the variable that can have values $s_{\hat{b}}$). For this t statistic we know that [see equation (14.15)]

$$P\left(-t_{\alpha/2,\nu} \le \frac{\hat{b} - b}{S_{\hat{b}}} \le t_{\alpha/2,\nu}\right) = 1 - \alpha$$

or

$$P(\hat{b} - t_{\alpha/2,\nu}S_{\hat{b}} \le b \le \hat{b} + t_{\alpha/2,\nu}S_{\hat{b}}) = 1 - \alpha \tag{19.25}$$

The $(1 - \alpha)100\%$ confidence interval for the slope is then

$$[\hat{b}^* - t_{\alpha/2,\nu}s_{\hat{b}^*}, \hat{b}^* + t_{\alpha/2,\nu}s_{\hat{b}^*}]$$

To determine the confidence interval for a specific sample, we use the t distribution (Table A.6) to find the critical values for the particular degrees of freedom and level of significance.

EXAMPLE 19.4 For the experiment described in Example 19.1, find the 95% confidence interval for a and for b.

Solution

For a we use equation (19.23). From Example 19.1 we know that $\hat{a}^* = 4.97$ l/min, and from Example 19.3 we know that $s_{\hat{a}^*} = 0.253$ l/min. From Table A.6 for $\nu = n - 2 = 18$: $t_{0.05/2,18} = 2.101$. Thus the confidence interval for a is

$$4.97 \text{ l/min} \pm (2.101 \times 0.253 \text{ l/min})$$

$$4.97 \text{ l/min} \pm 0.532 \text{ l/min}$$

For b we use equation (19.25). From Example 19.1 we know that $\hat{b}^* = 0.0133$ l/kg-m, and from Example 19.3 we know that $s_{\hat{b}^*} = 0.00045$ l/kg-m. Using the same critical values and ν as above, the confidence interval for b is

$$0.0133 \text{ l/kg-m} \pm (2.101 \times 0.00045 \text{ l/kg-m})$$
$$0.0133 \text{ l/kg-m} \pm 0.00095 \text{ l/kg-m}$$

19.7 CONFIDENCE INTERVAL FOR THE VARIANCE $\sigma^2_{Y \cdot X}$

Given the sample pairs of x and y, the variance of the Y distribution is estimated by $s^2_{y \cdot x}$ as given by equations (19.13 and 19.14). This sample variance is the point estimate of the population variance $\sigma^2_{Y \cdot X}$.

Without deriving the equation, we simply state here that the sampling distribution of the statistic

$$X^2 = \frac{(n-2)S^2_{Y \cdot X}}{\sigma^2_{Y \cdot X}} \tag{19.26}$$

has a chi-square distribution with $\nu = n - 2$ degrees of freedom (where $S_{Y \cdot X}$ is the variable that can have values $s_{y \cdot x}$). Using this chi-square random variable, we know that [see equation (15.6)]

$$P\left[\chi^2_{1-\alpha/2,\nu} \leq \frac{(n-2)S^2_{Y \cdot X}}{\sigma^2_{Y \cdot X}} \leq \chi^2_{\alpha/2,\nu}\right] = 1 - \alpha$$

Rearranging terms (see Section 15.5), we find that

$$P\left[\frac{(n-2)S^2_{Y \cdot X}}{\chi^2_{\alpha/2,\nu}} \leq \sigma^2_{Y \cdot X} \leq \frac{(n-2)S^2_{Y \cdot X}}{\chi^2_{1-\alpha/2,\nu}}\right] = 1 - \alpha \tag{19.27}$$

This then is the confidence interval for $\sigma^2_{Y \cdot X}$:

$$\left[\frac{(n-2)s^2_{y \cdot x}}{\chi^2_{\alpha/2,\nu}}, \frac{(n-2)s^2_{y \cdot x}}{\chi^2_{1-\alpha/2,\nu}}\right]$$

To determine the confidence interval for a specific sample, we use the chi-square distribution (Table A.7) to find the critical values for the particular degrees of freedom ($\nu = n - 2$) and level of significance α.

A confidence interval for the population standard deviation $\sigma_{Y \cdot X}$ is found by taking the square roots of the confidence interval endpoints found for $\sigma^2_{Y \cdot X}$.

EXAMPLE 19.5 For the exercise study in Example 19.1, find the 95% confidence interval for the population variance $\sigma^2_{Y \cdot X}$ of the linear relationship between level of exercise and cardiac output.

Solution

We use equation (19.27) to develop a confidence interval for the variance. We know that $n = 20$, and from Example 19.2, we know that $s^2_{y \cdot x} = 0.4571 \text{ (l/min)}^2$. Using $\alpha/2 = 0.025$ and $1 - \alpha/2 = 0.975$, we find in Table A.7: $\chi^2_{0.025,18} = 31.35$, and $\chi^2_{0.975,18} = 8.23$. Using these values, we find that the confidence interval is

$$\left[\frac{(18 \times 0.4571)}{31.53}, \frac{(18 \times 0.4571)}{8.23}\right], \quad \text{or} \quad [0.261 \text{ (l/min)}^2, 1.000 \text{ (l/min)}^2]$$

19.8 PREDICTION INTERVALS FOR EXPECTED VALUES OF Y

The expected value of Y given X can be determined from the regression line

$$E(Y|x = x_0) = \mu_{Y|x_0} = a + bx_0 \tag{19.28}$$

where x_0 is the value of X for which the value of Y is predicted. The *prediction interval* is the range of values for which one can be $(1 - \alpha)100\%$ confident of the predicted value. It is established through use of the standard error of the mean (see Section 13.11) of the Y values, which is denoted by $s_{\hat{\mu}_{Y|x_0}}$:

$$s_{\hat{\mu}_{Y|x_0}} = s_{y \cdot x}\sqrt{1 + \frac{1}{n} + \frac{(x_0 - \bar{x})^2}{\sum(x_i - \bar{x})^2}} \tag{19.29}$$

where $s_{y \cdot x}$ is the standard deviation of the y_i values around the regression line [see equation (19.15)] and x_0 is the value of X that is being used to predict Y.

For small samples ($n < 30$), the prediction interval is obtained by using the t distribution

$$\hat{\mu}_{Y|x_0} \pm t_{\alpha/2,\nu} s_{\hat{\mu}_{Y|x_0}}$$

with degrees of freedom $\nu = n - 2$.

For large samples ($n \geq 30$), the prediction interval is obtained by using the Z distribution. Moreover, for large samples the equation for $s_{\hat{\mu}_{Y|x_0}}$ simplifies to

$$s_{\hat{\mu}_{Y|x_0}} = \frac{s_{y \cdot x}}{\sqrt{n}}$$

and the prediction interval becomes

$$\hat{\mu}_{Y|x_0} \pm z_{\alpha/2}\left(\frac{s_{y \cdot x}}{\sqrt{n}}\right)$$

EXAMPLE 19.6 You are an exercise physiologist and want to predict the cardiac output at a level of exercise equal to 750 kg-m per min. Use the line of least regression developed in Example 19.1 to make this prediction, and then find the 95% prediction interval.

Solution

From Example 19.1, we know that $\hat{\mu}^*_{Y|x} = 4.97 + 0.0133x$. Using this equation, the value of cardiac output (Y) when the level of exercise is 750 kg-m per min is predicted to be

$$\hat{\mu}_{Y|x=750} = 4.97 + 0.0133(750) = 14.945, \quad \text{or } 14.95 \text{ l/min}$$

As $n < 30$, we use the t distribution to find the prediction interval for this value. First, we use equation (19.29) to calculate the standard error of the mean of the Y values. Using $s_{y \cdot x} = 0.68$ l/min from Example 19.2, the computational version of $\sum(x - \bar{x})^2$ given by equation (19.8), and the sums provided in Table 19.2, we find

$$s_{\hat{\mu}_{Y|x_0}} = 0.68\sqrt{1 + \frac{1}{20} + \frac{\left(750 - \frac{9{,}000}{20}\right)^2}{6{,}300{,}000 - \frac{(9{,}000)^2}{20}}} = 0.7099, \quad \text{or } 0.71 \text{ l/min}$$

For $\hat{\mu}_{Y|x=750} = 14.95$ l/min, $s_{\hat{\mu}_{Y|x_0}} = 0.71$ l/min, and (from Table A.6) $t_{0.05/2,18} = 2.101$, we find the prediction interval

$$14.95 \text{ l/min} \pm (2.101 \times 0.71 \text{ l/min})$$

$$14.95 \text{ l/min} \pm 1.492 \text{ l/min}$$

19.9 TESTING HYPOTHESES ABOUT THE SLOPE b

In choosing to analyze the relationship between two variables by means of regression, we have assumed that one variable (Y) is dependent and the other variable (X) is independent. This assumption can be tested by seeing whether the slope of the regression line differs significantly from zero. If our assumption is wrong, and Y is independent of X, then the distribution of Y will not vary in a consistent way with the values of X. The mean Y, then, will be the same for each value of X and so the slope b will be equal to zero.

The regression line $\hat{\mu}_{Y|x} = \hat{a} + \hat{b}x$ allows us to obtain the expected (mean) value of Y for a given value of x. As long as b is not zero, the expected value of Y will be different for every value of x. On the other hand, if $b = 0$, then the expected value of Y is a for every value of x. We can test the null hypothesis H_0: $b = 0$ against one of the following alternatives: H_1: $b \neq 0$, H_1: $b > 0$, or H_1: $b < 0$.

We know that $\hat{b}$ is normally distributed with a mean of b (see Section 19.5). Therefore, we can use the t statistic [equation (19.24)] with $b = 0$. This statistic has a t distribution with $\nu = n - 2$ degrees of freedom when $b = 0$. The decision rules for the alternative hypotheses are

$$\text{For } H_1\text{: } b \neq 0, \text{ reject } H_0 \text{ if } t^* < -t_{\alpha/2,\nu} \text{ or if } t^* > t_{\alpha/2,\nu}$$

$$\text{For } H_1\text{: } b > 0, \text{ reject } H_0 \text{ if } t^* > t_{\alpha,\nu}$$

$$\text{For } H_1\text{: } b < 0, \text{ reject } H_0 \text{ if } t^* < -t_{\alpha,\nu}$$

EXAMPLE 19.7 In Example 19.1, we found that the slope of the least-squares regression line is $\hat{b}^* = 0.0133$ l/kg-m. In Example 19.3 we found that the standard deviation of $\hat{b}$ is equal to 0.00045 l/kg-m. Do a right-tailed test of H_0: $b = 0$, using $\alpha = 0.05$ and a critical-value decision rule.

Solution

(1) H_0: $b = 0$, $\quad H_1$: $b > 0$

(2) $\alpha = 0.05$

(3) Using equation (19.24), with $\alpha = 0.05$ and, from Table A.6, $t_{0.05,18} = 1.734$, the decision rule is: Reject H_0 if $t^* > 1.734$.

(4) The value of t is

$$t^* = \frac{0.0133 - 0}{0.00045} = 29.556$$

From Table A.6, we find that the approximate probability of getting this t^* is $P < 0.0005$.

(5) As $t^* > 1.734$, we reject H_0 and accept H_1. This result is confirmed by the fact that the probability of getting a t^* of 29.56 is less than 0.05. The cardiac output is dependent on the level of exercise.

19.10 COMPARING SIMPLE LINEAR REGRESSION EQUATIONS FROM TWO OR MORE SAMPLES

When linear regression equations are developed for two or more samples, statistical techniques are available for testing whether the equations are significantly different. Some of the techniques test for differences between the slopes and others test for differences between elevations (i.e., the y intercepts). When just two regression equations are being compared, the test statistic is based on the t distribution. When more than two equations are being compared, the test statistic is based on the F distribution. In either case, the object is to decide whether the samples come from the same or from different populations. The details of these tests are beyond the scope of this book.

19.11 MULTIPLE LINEAR REGRESSION

For many scientific studies, the variable of interest is influenced by more than one factor. Human height, for example, is influenced by both genes and nutrition. A linear relationship between a dependent variable and two or more independent variables can be analysed by means of *multiple linear regression*. As with simple linear regression, it is assumed that the dependent variable is a random variable, with sample values from a normal distribution with the same variance for each independent variable.

The multiple linear regression equation for a relationship between one dependent variable and two or more independent variables is a multinomial equation (see Section 1.11 in Volume 1). The simplest of these equations, for a dependent variable (Y) and the values of two independent variables (x and x'), is

$$\mu_{Y|x,x'} = a + bx + b'x'$$

A least-squares regression line is developed from the sample values. As with simple linear regression, the values of a, b, and b' are estimated by minimizing the sum of squares

$$\sum(y_i - \hat{a}^* - \hat{b}^* x_i - \hat{b}'^* x_i')^2$$

Equations have been developed that use sample values of Y to solve for these best estimates of the parameters of the equation. The computational procedures required for most multiple regression analyses are complex and so they are performed only by computer. Because of the complexity of the equations and the need for computer analysis, multiple regression analysis is not covered in this book.

19.12 SIMPLE LINEAR CORRELATION

Simple linear regression and simple linear correlation are two different ways of analyzing the relationship between variable X and variable Y in a sample of n pairs (x_i, y_i) of measurements. In simple linear regression [described in Sections 19.2 through 19.10)] the X variable is fixed (set by the experimenter) and the Y variable is a random variable. The goal of linear regression is to develop a linear equation so that the value of the X variable can be used to predict the average value of the Y variable. In simple linear correlation, by contrast, both X and Y are random variables, and the goal is to determine the strength of the linear relationship between them.

The relationship between two random variables can be seen on a scatter diagram (Fig. 19-3), where each point on the graph is a sample point consisting of a pair of measurements, one of the X variable and the other of the Y variable. The degree of linear association between the two variables is the degree to which the data points cluster around a straight line. A positive correlation [Fig. 19-3(*a*)] indicates a direct relationship between the two variables: as one variable increases, so does the other variable. A negative correlation [Fig. 19-3(*b*)] indicates an inverse relationship between the two variables: as one variable increases, the other decreases. A perfect linear relationship (either positive or negative) occurs when all the points lie on a straight line. No correlation may indicate no relationship [Fig. 19-3(*c*)] or a relationship that is not linear [Fig. 19-3(*d*)].

Simple linear correlation techniques, as described in the sections that follow, assume that the random variables X and Y have a *joint probability distribution* $f(x, y)$ (see Section 11.13) that is normally distributed, a characteristic known as a *bivariate normal distribution*. This assumption means that when X and Y are considered as pairs, the joint distribution takes on a smooth, symmetric, moundlike shape. (The exact shape depends on the degree of association.) Violations of the assumptions of normality are serious only when the distribution of X or Y is severely skewed.

19.13 DERIVATION OF THE CORRELATION COEFFICIENT r

In correlation analysis, we estimate the population parameter ρ, which is the degree of association between variables X and Y in the population. [ρ is the symbol for the lowercase letter *rho* (pronounced "row") of the Greek alphabet.] The most commonly used point estimate of ρ, denoted by the symbol r, is the *Pearson product-moment correlation coefficient* (or *simple linear correlation coefficient*, or *sample correlation coefficient*). It is named after the English scientist *Karl Pearson* (1857–1936) who developed it. To determine the equation for this statistic, we need to first understand covariation.

Covariation measures the simultaneous deviations of the two random variables from their means. It reflects the degree to which the two variables vary together. Suppose we are interested in the degree of association between the random variables X and Y, and obtain the sample points shown in Fig. 19-4(*a*) or (*b*). Each point (x_i, y_i) in the graph can be described in terms of its deviations from the sample mean $\bar{x}$ and

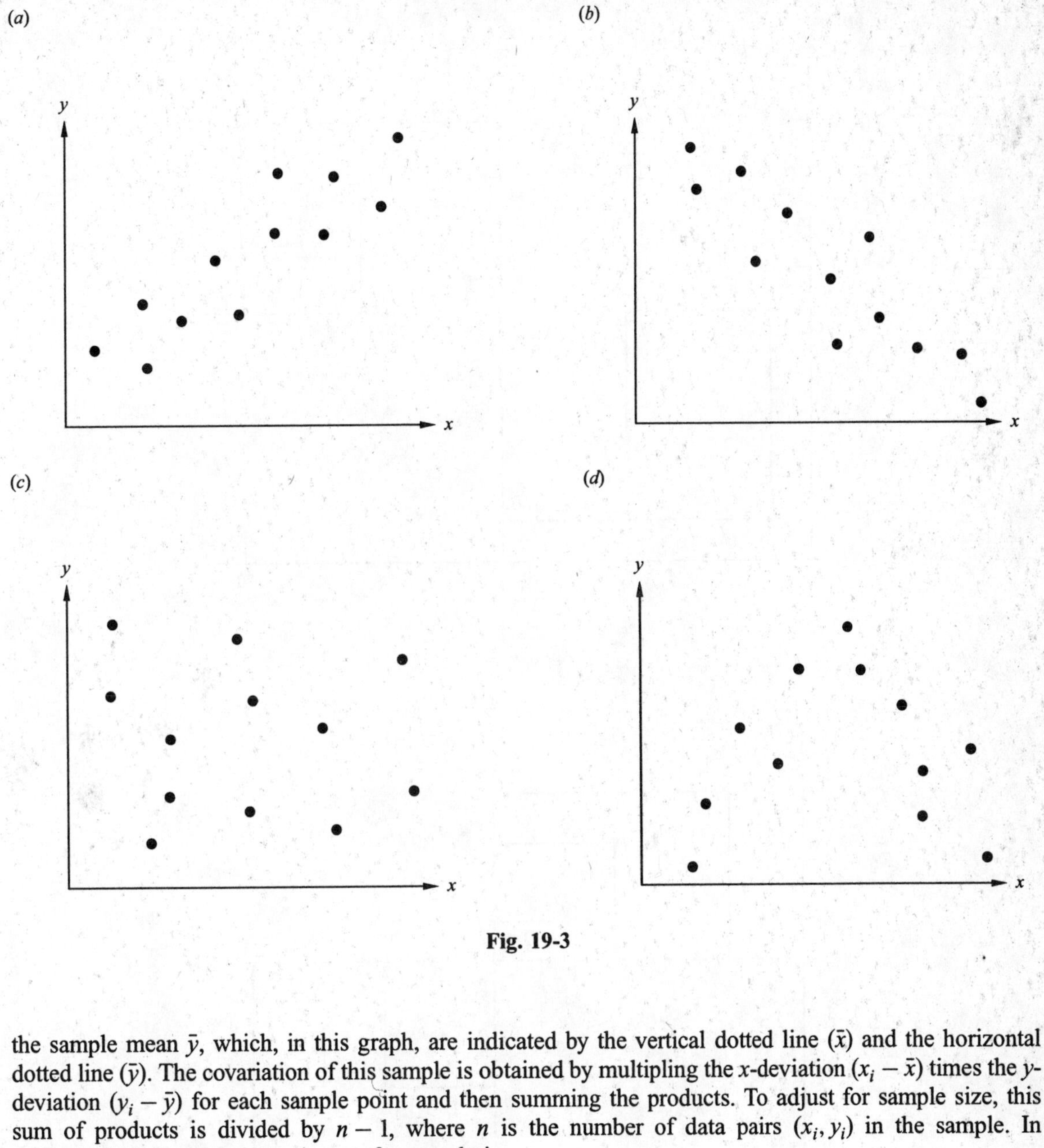

Fig. 19-3

the sample mean $\bar{y}$, which, in this graph, are indicated by the vertical dotted line ($\bar{x}$) and the horizontal dotted line ($\bar{y}$). The covariation of this sample is obtained by multipling the x-deviation $(x_i - \bar{x})$ times the y-deviation $(y_i - \bar{y})$ for each sample point and then summing the products. To adjust for sample size, this sum of products is divided by $n - 1$, where n is the number of data pairs (x_i, y_i) in the sample. In mathematical form, the covariance of a sample is

$$\text{cov}_{xy} = \frac{\sum_{i=1}^{n}(x_i - \bar{x})(y_i - \bar{y})}{n - 1} \tag{19.30}$$

The covariance cannot be used directly as a measure of correlation because its value depends on the units of measurement. This presents a problem when the two variables are measured in different units (for example, height in inches and weight in pounds). Moreover, the units of measurement determine the magnitude of the covariance. For example, if the heights and diameters of trees were measured in centimeters, their covariance would be larger than if they were measured in meters. For these reasons, the

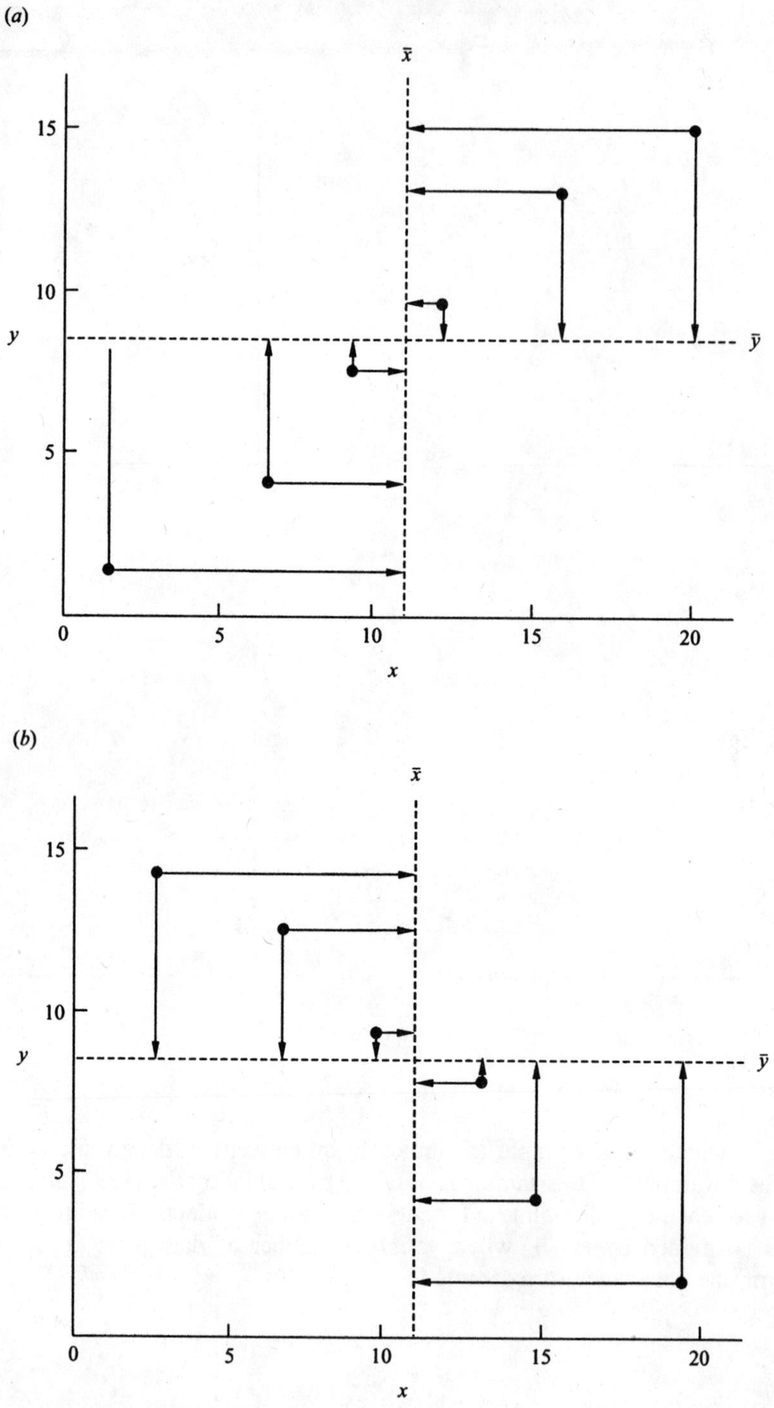

Fig. 19-4

covariance is standardized to make it dimensionless. The Pearson product-moment correlation is standardized by dividing the covariance by the product of the two standard deviations, s_x and s_y.

$$r = \frac{\dfrac{\sum_{i=1}^{n}(x_i - \bar{x})(y_i - \bar{y})}{n-1}}{\sqrt{\dfrac{\sum_{i=1}^{n}(x_i - \bar{x})^2}{n-1}}\sqrt{\dfrac{\sum_{i=1}^{n}(y_i - \bar{y})^2}{n-1}}}$$

or

$$r = \frac{\sum(x_i - \bar{x})(y_i - \bar{y})}{\sqrt{\sum(x_i - \bar{x})^2}\sqrt{\sum(y_i - \bar{y})^2}} \tag{19.31}$$

In this way, the units of measurement cancel out. Without units, r measures only the intensity of the association between the two variables.

The correlation coefficient, r, can assume values from -1 to $+1$. The sign of the correlation, positive or negative, depends entirely on the numerator, since the denominator consists of squared values and so is always positive. Considering the numerator, when the deviations of x and y both vary in the same way—i.e., as x gets farther above its mean, so also does the y with which it is paired [see Fig. 19-4(*a*)]—then the product $(x_i - \bar{x})$ $(y_i - \bar{y})$ is positive, since the product of two positive numbers is positive and the product of two negative numbers is also positive. If the deviations vary in the opposite way—i.e., as x gets farther above its mean, y gets farther below its mean [see Fig. 19-4(*b*)]—then the product $(x_i - \bar{x})$ $(y_i - \bar{y})$ is negative, since the product of a positive and a negative number is negative [see Fig. 19-4(*b*)]. If the deviations in x do not change in a linear pattern with the deviations in y, then there is a haphazard association of plus and minus deviations and the correlation coefficient r is near zero.

The maximum value of r is $+1$, which occurs when all the sample points lie on a straight line and the slope of the line is positive. It reflects the fact that the deviations of x_i from its mean $\bar{x}$ exactly match the deviations of y_i from its mean $\bar{y}$, in which case the term $(x_i - \bar{x})$ can be substituted for $(y_i - \bar{y})$ in equation (19.31):

$$r = \frac{\sum(x_i - \bar{x})(x_i - \bar{x})}{\sqrt{\sum(x_i - \bar{x})^2}\sqrt{\sum(x_i - \bar{x})^2}} = \frac{\sum(x_i - \bar{x})^2}{\sum(x_i - \bar{x})^2} = 1$$

This substitution makes the value of r equal to $+1$. The minimum value of r is -1, which occurs when all the sample points lie on a straight line and the slope of the line is negative. It reflects the fact that the deviations of x_i from its mean $\bar{x}$ are exactly opposite (the same magnitude, but of opposite sign) to the deviations of y_i from its mean $\bar{y}$, in which case the term $-(x_i - \bar{x})$ can be substituted for $(y_i - \bar{y})$ in equation (19.31). This substitution, similar to the one above, makes the value of r equal to -1.

The correlation coefficient given by equation (19.31) can be modified, by substituting equations (19.8), (19.9), and (19.10), to obtain this computational version:

$$r = \frac{\sum xy - \dfrac{\sum x \sum y}{n}}{\sqrt{(\sum x^2) - \dfrac{(\sum x)^2}{n}}\sqrt{(\sum y^2) - \dfrac{(\sum y)^2}{n}}} \tag{19.32}$$

EXAMPLE 19.8 In bumblebees, the temperature of the wing muscles is known to rise during flight. An insect physiologist wonders whether the temperature of the wing muscles is related in a linear fashion to the amount of work performed by the muscles. He uses the temperature of the thorax (where the wing muscles are located) as an indication of the temperature of the wing muscles, and weight of the abdomen as an indication of the amount of work the muscles do to achieve flight. He takes a random sample of 20 bees and measures, for each bee, the thoracic temperature (in °C) right after flight and the weight of the abdomen (in mg). The results are shown in Table 19.3. Estimate the linear correlation between these two variables.

Table 19.3

Bee	Weight of abdomen (mg)	Temperature of thorax (°C)
1	101.6	37.0
2	240.4	39.7
3	180.9	40.5
4	390.2	42.6
5	360.3	42.0
6	120.8	39.1
7	180.5	40.2
8	330.7	37.8
9	395.4	43.1
10	194.1	40.2
11	135.2	38.8
12	210.0	41.9
13	240.6	39.0
14	145.7	39.0
15	168.3	38.1
16	192.8	40.2
17	305.2	43.1
18	378.0	39.9
19	165.9	39.6
20	303.1	40.8

Solution

Because body temperature and weight of a population of bees can be assumed to have a bivariate normal distribution, we can estimate the population correlation coefficient ρ with the sample correlation coefficient r^*. To find this statistic, we need $\sum x$, $\sum x^2$, $\sum y$, $\sum y^2$, and $\sum xy$, which are provided in Table 19.4. Inserting these values into equation (19.32),

$$r^* = \frac{192{,}154.74 - \left[\frac{(4{,}739.7)(802.6)}{20}\right]}{\sqrt{(1{,}295{,}879.09) - P\frac{(4{,}739.7)^2}{20}}\sqrt{(32{,}264.56) - \frac{(802.6)^2}{20}}} = 0.626$$

This sample correlation coefficient, $r^* = 0.626$, suggests a direct relationship between thoracic temperature and abdominal weight.

Table 19.4

	x_i	y_i	x_i^2	y_i^2	$x_i y_i$
	101.6	37.0	10,322.56	1,369.00	3,759.20
	240.4	39.7	57,792.16	1,576.09	9,543.88
	180.9	40.5	32,724.81	1,640.25	7,326.45
	390.2	42.6	152,256.04	1,814.76	16,622.52
	360.3	42.0	129,816.09	1,764.00	15,132.60
	120.8	39.1	14,592.64	1,528.81	4,723.28
	180.5	40.2	32,580.25	1,616.04	7,256.10
	330.7	37.8	109,362.49	1,428.84	12,500.46
	395.4	43.1	156,341.16	1,857.61	17,041.74
	194.1	40.2	37,674.81	1,616.04	7,802.82
	135.2	38.8	18,279.04	1,505.44	5,245.76
	210.0	41.9	44,100.00	1,755.61	8,799.00
	240.6	39.0	57,888.36	1,521.00	9,383.40
	145.7	39.0	21,228.49	1,521.00	5,682.30
	168.3	38.1	28,324.89	1,451.61	6,412.23
	192.8	40.2	37,171.84	1,616.04	7,750.56
	305.2	43.1	93,147.04	1,857.61	13,154.12
	378.0	39.9	142,884.00	1,592.01	15,082.20
	165.9	39.6	27,522.81	1,568.16	6,569.64
	303.1	40.8	91,869.61	1,664.64	12,366.47
$\sum$	4,739.7	802.6	1,295,879.09	32,264.56	192,154.74

19.14 CONFIDENCE INTERVALS FOR THE POPULATION CORRELATION COEFFICIENT ρ

To determine a $(1 - \alpha)100\%$ confidence interval for the population parameter ρ, R. A. Fisher (see Section 17.17) developed a technique involving a new variable Z_r. First, sample correlation coefficients r are transformed into values of Z_r using this formula

$$z_r = 0.5 \log_e \left(\frac{1+r}{1-r} \right)$$

where $\log_e$ is the natural logarithm (see Problem 1.25 in Volume 1). Fortunately, there are tables available for this transformation, such as Table A.10 in the Appendix (*Transformation of r to z_r*). Using this table to convert, for example, $r = 0.634$ to z_r, the first two digits to the right of the decimal point, 0.63, are found in the left-hand column and the third digit, 0.004, is located in the row across the top of the table. The z_r value lies at the intersection of the column and row values: 0.7481. Table A.10 gives only positive values, but because the distributions of r and z_r are symmetric about zero, the negative values are the same as the positive values except for the negative sign.

With the transformation of r to z_r, the sampling distribution of r is transformed into a sampling distribution of z_r that has the standard error

$$\sigma_{z_r} = \sqrt{\frac{1}{n-3}} \tag{19.33}$$

where n is the number of sample pairs. Next, if the random variable Z_r can be assumed to be approximately normally distributed, then this statistic will have approximately a standard normal distribution

$$Z = \frac{Z_r - z_\rho}{\sigma_{z_r}} \tag{19.34}$$

where z_ρ is the z_r transformation value for ρ. Finally, substituting this statistic for Z in equation (14.4)

$$P(-z_{\alpha/2} \leq Z \leq z_{\alpha/2}) = 1 - \alpha$$

and doing the usual mathematical derivation (see Section 14.8), the approximate confidence limits for z_ρ are

$$\left(z_r - z_{\alpha/2}\sqrt{\frac{1}{n-3}},\ z_r + z_{\alpha/2}\sqrt{\frac{1}{n-3}}\right)$$

Once the confidence limits are found in terms of z_r, they are converted back into values of r by using Table A.10. As you will see when solving problems, the confidence limits for z_r are symmetrical but the confidence intervals for ρ (after conversion of z_r to r) are not symmetrical. Also, the breadth of the interval, which indicates the precision of the estimate, depends on the standard error σ_r, which in turn is affected by the sample size n. The larger the sample, the smaller the standard error and the more narrow the confidence limits.

EXAMPLE 19.9 Find the approximate 95% confidence interval for the population correlation coefficient using the sample correlation coefficient that you calculated in Example 19.8.

Solution

First we convert the correlation coefficient r into a z_r value. From Table A.10, for $r^* = 0.626$: $z_r = 0.7348$. The confidence interval is $[0.7348 - z_{\alpha/2}\sigma_{z_r},\ 0.7348 + z_{\alpha/2}\sigma_{z_r}]$. With $z_{0.05/2} = 1.96$, $n = 20$, and

$$\sigma_{z_r} = \sqrt{\frac{1}{n-3}} = \sqrt{\frac{1}{17}} = 0.2425$$

The approximate confidence limits are

$$[0.7348 - (1.96 \times 0.2425), 0.7348 + (1.96 \times 0.2425)]$$

$$(0.2595, 1.2101)$$

Returning to Table A.10, we convert these limits into r values. Thus, the 95% confidence interval for $r = 0.626$ is

$$(0.254, 0.837)$$

19.15 USING THE r DISTRIBUTION TO TEST HYPOTHESES ABOUT THE POPULATION CORRELATION COEFFICIENT ρ

Once a value of r has been calculated, it is important to know whether this value indicates a real linear association between the two variables, X and Y, or is caused by a haphazard association of values in the sample. If the two variables are not linearly associated, then the population correlation coefficient ρ is zero. Thus, we test the null hypothesis, H_0: $\rho = 0$ against one of these three alternatives, $H_1: \rho \neq 0$, H_1: $\rho > 0$, or H_1: $\rho < 0$. The logic of this test, as with other hypothesis tests, is to determine the probability of getting a point estimate $\hat{\theta}^*$ at least as different from the value hypothesized by the null θ_0 as the one calculated from the sample. For the correlation coefficient this statement is

$$P\,(\text{point estimate of } \rho \text{ at least as different from 0 as } r^* | H_0 \text{ is true})$$

Recall from Section 16.3 that a test statistic must: (1) allow comparison of the sample point estimate with the null's hypothesized value, and (2) be associated with a probability distribution that is known under the assumption that H_0 is true. The sample statistic r meets these two criteria. It allows comparison with the null's hypothesized value, $\rho = 0$, and has a known sampling distribution under the condition that $\rho = 0$. While the probability function for this distribution is too complex to describe here, the distribution of r is symmetric around a mean of zero, with and $r = -1$ and $r = +1$ as the two extreme values of the tails. The r distribution is a family of distributions, with a unique distribution for each degrees of freedom, $\nu = n - 2$ (where n is the number of pairs in the sample).

The critical values for rejecting the null hypothesis, using the sampling distribution of r under the null hypothesis of $\rho = 0$, are provided in tables for various levels of significance α and degrees of freedom ν. Table A.11 in the Appendix (*Critical Values of the Pearson Product-Moment Correlation Coefficient r*) is such a table. Only the right-tailed critical values are shown. Since the distribution of r is symmetric about $r = 0$, the left-tailed critical values are simply the negatives of the right-tailed critical values.

The critical value of r is reported as $r_{\alpha/2,\nu}$ (for a two-tailed hypothesis test) or as $r_{\alpha,\nu}$ (for a one-tailed test), where r is the tabulated value for a particular level of significance and degrees of freedom. The critical-value decision rules for rejecting the null hypothesis are:

For a two-tailed test (H_1: $\rho \neq 0$), reject the null hypothesis when $r^* > r_{\alpha/2,\nu}$ or when $r^* < -r_{\alpha/2,\nu}$.

For a right-tailed test (H_1: $\rho > 0$), reject the null hypothesis when $r^* > r_{\alpha,\nu}$.

For a left-tailed test (H_1: $\rho < 0$), reject the null hypothesis when $r^* < -r_{\alpha,\nu}$.

The approximate probability of getting a sample value r^* as different from the hypothesized population value $\rho = 0$, given that the null hypothesis is true, can be obtained directly from Table A.11. Simply find the sample value of r^* in the table for a given ν and note the range of probabilities within which it lies.

EXAMPLE 19.10 For the bumblebee study described in Example 19.8, we found that $r = 0.626$. Do a two-tailed test at $\alpha = 0.05$, using a critical-value decision rule, of H_0: There is no linear relationship between thoracic temperature and body weight. Use the r distribution shown in Table A.11.

Solution

(1) H_0: $\rho = 0$, H_1: $\rho \neq 0$

(2) $\alpha = 0.05$

(3) We use Table A.11 to find the critical r values for an r distribution with $\nu = n - 2 = 20 - 2$. For a two-tailed test, with $\nu = 18$ and $\alpha = 0.05$, we find that $r_{0.05/2,18} = 0.444$. Therefore, our decision rule is: Reject H_0 if $r^* < -0.444$ or if $r^* > 0.444$.

(4) From Table A.11, we find that the P value for $r^* = 0.626$ is <0.01.

(5) As $r^* > 0.444$, we reject H_0 and accept H_1. This result is confirmed by the fact that the probability of getting an $r^* = 0.626$ given that $\rho = 0$ is less than 0.05. There is a significant, linear relationship between thoracic temperature and abdominal weight.

19.16 USING THE t DISTRIBUTION TO TEST HYPOTHESES ABOUT ρ

In Section 19.15 we used the r distribution to test the null hypothesis $\rho = 0$. The t distribution can also be used for such a test, and is particularly useful for studies involving levels of significance not provided by tables of r values. To use the t distribution, the r value is transformed into a t value

$$t = \frac{r - (\rho = 0)}{\sqrt{\dfrac{1 - r^2}{n - 2}}} \tag{19.35}$$

where r is the sample correlation coefficient, ρ is the population correlation coefficient (hypothesized under the null to be equal to zero), and the denominator is s_r, the standard error of the correlation coefficient. This statistic has a t distribution with $n - 2$ degrees of freedom. The critical values are provided in Table A.6.

EXAMPLE 19.11 For the bumblebee study in Example 19.8, we found that $r^* = 0.626$. Do a two-tailed test at $\alpha = 0.05$, using a critical-value decision rule, of H_0: There is no linear relationship between thoracic temperature and abdominal weight. Use the t distribution to find the critical value.

Solution

(1) H_0: $\rho = 0$, H_1: $\rho \neq 0$

(2) $\alpha = 0.05$

(3) Using Table A.6, with $(\nu = n - 2 = 20 - 2 = 18)$ and $\alpha/2 = 0.05/2$ for a two-tailed test, the decision rule is: Reject H_0 if $t^* < -2.101$ or if $t^* > 2.101$.

(4) Using $r^* = 0.626$ and $n = 20$ in the t-statistic [equation (19.35)],

$$t^* = \frac{0.626 - 0}{\sqrt{\dfrac{1 - (0.626)^2}{20 - 2}}} = 3.4058$$

From Table A.6, we find that the approximate probability of getting a t value of 3.4058 in a two-tailed test with $\nu = 18$ is $0.001 < P < 0.01$.

(5) Because $t^* > 2.101$, we reject H_0 and accept H_1. This result is confirmed by the fact that the probability of getting a t value of 3.4058 (given that the null hypothesis is true) is less than 0.05. The correlation between thoracic temperature and abdominal weight is significantly different from zero.

19.17 USING THE Z DISTRIBUTION TO TEST THE HYPOTHESIS $\rho = c$

Neither the r distribution nor the t distribution can be used to test the null hypothesis that the population correlation coefficient is equal to some particular value other than zero (H_0: $\rho = c$, where $c \neq 0$). In such a test, the sample correlation coefficient r and the hypothesized population correlation coefficient ρ are transformed to z values, which can be done by using a mathematical formula or by using Table A.10 (see Section 19.14). These values, calculated from r and ρ, are denoted here as z_r and z_ρ, respectively. For values of r or ρ between 0 and 1, the corresponding values of z_r or z_ρ will lie between 0 and ∞; for values of r or ρ between -1 and 0, the corresponding values of z_r or z_ρ will lie between $-\infty$ and 0. We then calculate a value of the Z statistic with

$$z = \frac{z_r - z_\rho}{\sqrt{\dfrac{1}{n - 3}}} \tag{19.36}$$

where z_r is the transformed value of the sample r, z_ρ is the transformed value of the population ρ as hypothesized by the null, and the denominator is the standard error of the estimate. Critical values for the Z distribution are provided in Table A.5.

EXAMPLE 19.12 You repeat the bumblebee study described in Example 19.8, taking a sample of 15 bees from another location. You want to know whether the second sample comes from the same population as the first sample. This time your correlation coefficient is $r^* = 0.405$. Do a two-tailed test at $\alpha = 0.05$, using a critical-value decision rule, of H_0: The population correlation coefficient is $\rho = 0.626$.

Solution

(1) H_0: $\rho = 0.626$, H_1: $\rho \neq 0.626$

(2) $\alpha = 0.05$

(3) As you are testing whether the correlation coefficient is equal to a particular value ($\rho = 0.626$), you use the Z distribution (Table A.5) to find critical values for rejection. Thus, our decision rule is: Reject H_0 if $z^* < -1.96$ or if $z^* > 1.96$.

(4) Using Table A.10 to transform r and ρ values into z values, we find that $r = 0.405$ is equal to $z_r = 0.4296$ and that $\rho = 0.626$ is equal to $z_\rho = 0.7348$. Using equation (19.36) with $n = 15$, we find the sample value of z is

$$z^* = \frac{0.4296 - 0.7348}{\sqrt{1/12}} = -1.0572, \quad \text{or } -1.06$$

From Table A.5, we find that the area of the standard normal distribution that lies under the curve above the interval from 0 to $z = 1.06$ is 0.3554. Thus, the probability of getting this z value under the condition that the null hypothesis is true is

$$2[P(Z > 1.06)] = 2(0.5000 - 0.3554) = 2(0.1446) = 0.2892$$

(5) As $-1.96 < z^* < 1.96$, we accept H_0. This result is confirmed by the fact that the probability of getting an r value equal to 0.405 (under the condition that the population value is $\rho = 0.626$) is greater than 0.05. Thus, it is likely that the second sample of measurements comes from the same population, with regard to ρ, as the first sample.

19.18 INTERPRETING THE SAMPLE CORRELATION COEFFICIENT r

The sample correlation coefficient r is interpreted in terms of its squared value. The statistic r^2 is an estimate of the proportion of the total variation in X and Y that is explained by the linear relationship between the two variables. This proportion is usually converted to a percentage, $(100\%)r^2$, which is known as the *coefficient of determination*. A correlation coefficient of $r = 0.4$, for example, indicates that 16% of the variability in the sample can be explained by the linear relationship between X and Y. In a large sample, a small value of r may be statistically significant even though the percentage of the variation accounted for by the linear relationship is small.

Of all the statistical measures, the correlation coefficient is the one most often misinterpreted. A major problem arises with regard to cause and effect: a significant correlation coefficient, no matter how high, cannot be interpreted to mean that the relationship is a cause-and-effect relationship. Both variables may be dependent on a third variable that was not part of the analysis.

Another problem is that when a correlation coefficient r is not significantly different from zero, it cannot be interpreted to mean that the two variables are not associated. It means only that they do not have a linear association. The two variables may be associated in a nonlinear way.

Yet another misinterpretation of the correlation coefficient is to assume that the values of r themselves are on a linear scale, which they are not. The difference between $r = 0.400$ and $r = 0.500$, for example, is not of the same magnitude as the difference between $r = 0.500$ and $r = 0.600$. Similarly, when comparing two r values, say $r = 0.8$ and $r = 0.4$, we cannot conclude that $r = 0.8$ indicates a relationship that is twice as strong as $r = 0.4$. What we can say is that an r of 0.4 explains 16% of the variation and an r of 0.8 explains 64% of the variation in the sample.

Yet another source of potential error arises when the data are in the form of rates or averages. Rates and averages suppress the variation within a measurement sample, and are likely to inflate the correlation coefficient.

EXAMPLE 19.13 Describe the outcome of the bumblebee study (Example 19.8) in terms of the variance explained by the linear relationship between thoracic temperature and abdominal weight.

Solution

The coefficient of determination, r^2, estimates the amount of variation explained by the linear relationship between two variables. Here, $r^* = 0.626$, and $r^{*2} = 0.3919$. Thus, we can say that 39.2% of the variation in the values of thoracic temperature and abdominal weight can be explained by their linear relationship with each other.

19.19 MULTIPLE CORRELATION AND PARTIAL CORRELATION

Multiple correlation measures the strength of the relationship between more than two random variables. The goal is to estimate the proportion of the total variation in the sample that is accounted for by the variables being analyzed. The computational procedures for most multiple correlation analyses are so complex that they are performed only by computers.

The multiple correlation coefficient reflects the overall interrelationship of all the variables analyzed by the multiple correlation. The specific relationships between two of the variables cannot just be analyzed two at a time, because such correlations do not include the interactions of the other variables on the pair being analysed. A technique known as *partial correlation* is used for pairwise analysis of multiple variables. This technique considers the correlation between each pair of variables while holding constant the value of each of the other variables. Again, computer programs are the best way to analyze these relationships.

Solved Problems

THE LEAST-SQUARES REGRESSION LINE

19.1 A plant physiologist wants to be able to predict the growth of a species of rye grass from the concentration of phosphorus in the soil. She chooses four levels of phosphorus concentration: 2, 4, 8, and 16 parts per million (ppm), and grows four plants from seed in each of the concentrations. When the plants form flowers, she measures their dry weight in grams (g). The resulting data are shown in Table 19.5. What is the least-squares regression line for this relationship?

Table 19.5

Plant	Phosphorus (ppm)	Weight (g)
1	2	4.1
2	2	3.8
3	2	4.0
4	2	3.9
5	4	5.2
6	4	4.9
7	4	5.0
8	4	4.8
9	8	5.7
10	8	5.9
11	8	6.0
12	8	6.2
13	16	11.7
14	16	8.9
15	16	10.1
16	16	10.3

Solution

First, we use equation (19.11) to calculate a point estimate of the slope. The sums needed for this equation are provided in Table 19.6. Substituting these sums, as well as $n = 16$, into equation (19.11), we get

$$\hat{b}^* = \frac{957.6 - \dfrac{(120)(100.5)}{16}}{1{,}360 - \dfrac{(120)^2}{16}} = 0.443152, \quad \text{or } 0.44 \text{ g/ppm}$$

Table 19.6

	x_i	y_i	x_i^2	y_i^2	x_iy_i
	2	4.1	4	16.81	8.2
	2	3.8	4	14.44	7.6
	2	4.0	4	16.00	8.0
	2	3.9	4	15.21	7.8
	4	5.2	16	27.04	20.8
	4	4.9	16	24.01	19.6
	4	5.0	16	25.00	20.0
	4	4.8	16	23.04	19.2
	8	5.7	64	32.49	45.6
	8	5.9	64	34.81	47.2
	8	6.0	64	36.00	48.0
	8	6.2	64	38.44	49.6
	16	11.7	256	136.89	187.2
	16	8.9	256	79.21	142.4
	16	10.1	256	102.01	161.6
	16	10.3	256	106.09	164.8
$\sum$	120	100.5	1,360	727.49	957.6

Next, we use equation (19.6) to calculate a point estimate of the intercept:

$$\hat{a}^* = \frac{100.5}{16} - (0.443152)\frac{120}{16} = 2.96 \text{ g}$$

The equation for the least-squares regression line is

$$\hat{\mu}^*_{Y|x} = 2.96 + 0.44x$$

19.2 A population biologist wants to define the relationship between body size and population density in limpets. He grows limpets under five conditions of density: 300, 500, 700, 900, and 1,100 individuals per square meter. After 5 years, he randomly chooses and measures the maximum length (in mm) of four limpets from each density group. The resulting data are shown in Table 19.7. What is the least-squares regression line for this relationship? What size do you expect for limpets grown under these conditions but at a density of 600 individuals per square meter?

Table 19.7

Limpet	Density (number per m^2)	Length (mm)
1	300	66
2	300	65
3	300	63
4	300	64
5	500	63
6	500	61
7	500	60
8	500	58
9	700	55
10	700	56
11	700	57
12	700	58
13	900	51
14	900	54
15	900	53
16	900	53
17	1,100	46
18	1,100	48
19	1,100	50
20	1,100	47

Solution

To find the least-squares regression line, we need to calculate point estimates for the y intercept ($\hat{a}$) and the slope ($\hat{b}$). The sums needed for these calculations are provided in Table 19.8. Substituting these sums, as well as $n = 20$, into equation (19.11), we get

$$\hat{b}^* = \frac{756{,}000 - \dfrac{(14{,}000)(1{,}128)}{20}}{11{,}400{,}000 - \dfrac{(14{,}000)^2}{20}} = -0.021 \text{ mm/individual per m}^2$$

Using this value of $\hat{b}^*$ in equation (19.6), we get

$$\hat{a}^* = \frac{1{,}128}{20} - (-0.021)\frac{14{,}000}{20} = 71.1 \text{ mm}$$

The equation for the estimated least-squares regression line is

$$\hat{\mu}^*_{Y|x} = 71.1 - 0.021x$$

Using this equation to predict the size of limpets when grown for 5 years at a density of 600 individuals per square meter:

$$\hat{\mu}_{Y|x=600} = 71.1 - 0.021(600) = 58.5 \text{ mm}$$

Table 19.8

	x_i	y_i	x_i^2	y_i^2	$x_i y_i$
	300	66	90,000	4,356	19,800
	300	65	90,000	4,225	19,500
	300	63	90,000	3,969	18,900
	300	64	90,000	4,096	19,200
	500	63	250,000	3,969	31,500
	500	61	250,000	3,721	30,500
	500	60	250,000	3,600	30,000
	500	58	250,000	3,364	29,000
	700	55	490,000	3,025	38,500
	700	56	490,000	3,136	39,200
	700	57	490,000	3,249	39,900
	700	58	490,000	3,364	40,600
	900	51	810,000	2,601	45,900
	900	54	810,000	2,916	48,600
	900	53	810,000	2,809	47,700
	900	53	810,000	2,809	47,700
	1,100	46	1,210,000	2,116	50,600
	1,100	48	1,210,000	2,304	52,800
	1,100	50	1,210,000	2,500	55,000
	1,100	47	1,210,000	2,209	51,700
$\sum$	14,000	1,128	11,400,000	64,338	756,600

19.3 The manager of a pizza-delivery company wants to advertise how fast they can deliver an order to a customer. From her records, she selects 12 delivery distances, 2, 5, 8, and 15 miles, with three deliveries at each distance. She records, for each delivery, the time (in minutes) it takes to carry the pizzas from the company store to the customer. The resulting data are shown in Table 19.9. What is the least-squares regression line for this relationship? How long do you expect it to take for this company to deliver a pizza to an address that is exactly 8 miles from the store?

Table 19.9

Delivery	Distance (miles)	Time (min)
1	2	10.2
2	2	14.6
3	2	18.2
4	5	20.1
5	5	22.4
6	5	30.6
7	10	30.8
8	10	35.4
9	10	50.6
10	15	60.1
11	15	68.4
12	15	72.1

Solution

First we use equation (19.11) to calculate a point estimate for the slope. The sums needed for this calculation are provided in Table 19.10. Substituting these sums, as well as $n = 12$, into equation (19.11), we get

$$\hat{b}^* = \frac{4{,}628.5 - \frac{(96.0)(433.5)}{12}}{1{,}062.0 - \frac{(96.0)^2}{12}} = 3.9473, \quad \text{or } 3.95 \text{ min/mile}$$

Table 19.10

	x_i	y_i	x_i^2	y_i^2	$x_i y_i$
	2	10.2	4	104.04	20.4
	2	14.6	4	213.16	29.2
	2	18.2	4	331.24	36.4
	5	20.1	25	404.01	100.5
	5	22.4	25	501.76	112.0
	5	30.6	25	936.36	153.0
	10	30.8	100	948.64	308.0
	10	35.4	100	1,253.16	354.0
	10	50.6	100	2,560.36	506.0
	15	60.1	225	3,612.01	901.5
	15	68.4	225	4,678.56	1,026.0
	15	72.1	225	5,198.41	1,081.5
Σ	96	433.5	1,062	20,741.71	4,628.5

We then use this value of $\hat{b}^*$ in equation (19.6) to calculate a point estimate for the intercept:

$$\hat{a}^* = \frac{433.5}{12} - (3.9473)\frac{96.0}{12} = 4.55 \text{ min}$$

The equation for the estimated least-squares regression line is

$$\hat{\mu}^*_{Y|x} = 4.55 + 3.95x$$

Using this equation, we predict the time it will take to deliver a pizza 8 miles from the store to be

$$\mu_{Y|x=8} = 4.55 + (3.95)(8.0) = 36.15 \text{ min}$$

THE ESTIMATOR OF THE VARIANCE $\sigma^2_{Y \cdot X}$

19.4 For the plant-growth experiment described in Problem 19.1, what is the best estimate of the variance and what is the standard error of the estimate?

Solution

Substituting the values of $\hat{a}$, $\hat{b}$, and n from Problem 19.1 and sums from Table 19.6 in equation (19.14), we find the estimate of the variance is

$$s^2_{y \cdot x} = \frac{727.49 - (2.96)(100.5) - (0.44)(957.6)}{16 - 2} = 0.619 \text{ g}^2$$

and, using equation (19.15), the standard error of the estimate is

$$s_{y\cdot x} = \sqrt{0.619} = 0.7868, \quad \text{or } 0.79 \text{ g}$$

19.5 For the limpet-growth experiment described in Problem 19.2, what is the best estimate of the variance and what is the standard error of the estimate?

Solution

Substituting the values of $\hat{a}$, $\hat{b}$, and n from Problem 19.2 and using sums from Table 19.8 in equation (19.14) we find the estimate of the variance is

$$s^2_{y\cdot x} = \frac{64{,}338 - (71.1)(1{,}128) - (-0.021)(756{,}600)}{20 - 2} = 1.433 \text{ mm}^2$$

and, using equation (19.15), the standard error of the estimate is

$$s_{y\cdot x} = \sqrt{1.433} = 1.2 \text{ mm}$$

19.6 For the pizza-delivery experiment described in Problem 19.3, what is the best estimate of the variance and what is the standard error of the estimate?

Solution

Substituting the values of $\hat{a}$, $\hat{b}$, and n from Problem 19.3 and sums from Table 19.10 in equation (19.14), we find the estimate of the variance is

$$s^2_{y\cdot x} = \frac{20{,}741.71 - (4.55)(433.5) - (3.95)(4{,}628.5)}{12 - 2} = 48.671 \text{ min}^2$$

and, using equation (19.15), the standard error of the estimate is

$$s_{y\cdot x} = \sqrt{48.671} = 6.98 \text{ min}$$

VARIANCE OF $\hat{a}$ AND OF $\hat{b}$

19.7 For the experiment on rye grass described in Problem 19.1, find the standard deviations of the point estimates of $\hat{a}$ and $\hat{b}$.

Solution

We find the standard deviation of $\hat{a}^*$ by using equations (19.17) and (19.20), inserting the sample values of $s^2_{y\cdot x} = 0.619 \text{ g}^2$ from Problem 19.4, $n = 16$, and sums in Table 19.6:

$$s_{\hat{a}^*} = \sqrt{s^2_{\hat{a}^*}} = \sqrt{0.619\left[\frac{1}{16} + \frac{\left(\frac{120}{16}\right)^2}{1{,}360 - \frac{(120)^2}{16}}\right]} = 0.338 \text{ g}$$

We find the standard deviation of $\hat{b}^*$ by using equations (19.19) and (19.21), inserting the sample value of $s^2_{y\cdot x} = 0.619 \text{ g}^2$, $n = 16$, and sums provided in Table 19.6:

$$s_{\hat{b}^*} = \sqrt{s^2_{\hat{b}^*}} = \sqrt{\frac{0.619}{1{,}360 - \frac{(120)^2}{16}}} = 0.037 \text{ g/ppm}$$

19.8 For the experiment on limpets described in Problem 19.2, find the standard deviations of the point estimates of $\hat{a}$ and $\hat{b}$.

Solution

We find the standard deviation of $\hat{a}^*$ by using equations (19.17) and (19.20), inserting the sample value of $s_{y\cdot x}^2 = 1.433\ \text{mm}^2$ from Problem 19.5, $n = 20$, and sums provided in Table 19.8:

$$s_{\hat{a}^*} = \sqrt{s_{\hat{a}^*}^2} = \sqrt{1.433\left[\frac{1}{20} + \frac{\left(\frac{14{,}000}{20}\right)^2}{11{,}400{,}000 - \frac{(14{,}000)^2}{20}}\right]} = 0.714\ \text{mm}$$

We find the standard deviation of $\hat{b}^*$ by using equations (19.19) and (19.21), inserting the sample value of $s_{y\cdot x}^2 = 1.433\ \text{mm}^2$, $n = 20$, and sums provided in Table 19.8:

$$s_{\hat{b}^*} = \sqrt{s_{\hat{b}^*}^2} = \sqrt{\frac{1.433}{11{,}400{,}000 - \frac{(14{,}000)^2}{20}}} = 0.00095\ \text{mm/individual per m}^2$$

19.9 For the study of pizza delivery described in Problem 19.3, find the standard deviations of the point estimates of $\hat{a}$ and $\hat{b}$.

Solution

We find the standard deviation of $\hat{a}^*$ by using equations (19.17) and (19.20), inserting the sample value of $s_{y\cdot x}^2 = 48.671\ \text{min}^2$ from Problem 19.6, $n = 12$, and sums provided in Table 19.10:

$$s_{\hat{a}^*} = \sqrt{s_{\hat{a}^*}^2} = \sqrt{48.671\left[\frac{1}{12} + \frac{\left(\frac{96}{12}\right)^2}{1{,}062 - \frac{(96)^2}{12}}\right]} = 3.828\ \text{min}$$

We find the standard deviation of $\hat{b}^*$ by using equations (19.19) and (19.21), inserting the sample value of $s_{y\cdot x}^2 = 48.671$, $n = 12$, and sums provided in Table 19.10:

$$s_{\hat{b}^*} = \sqrt{s_{\hat{b}^*}^2} = \sqrt{\frac{48.671}{1{,}062 - \frac{(96)^2}{12}}} = 0.407\ \text{min/mile}$$

CONFIDENCE INTERVALS FOR a AND b

19.10 For the plant-growth experiment described in Problem 19.1, find the 95% confidence intervals for a and b.

Solution

We use equation (19.23) to develop a confidence interval for a. From Problem 19.1 we know that $n = 16$ and $\hat{a}^* = 2.96$ g. From Problem 19.7 we know that $s_{\hat{a}}^* = 0.338$ g. From Table A.6 we find that the critical value for $t_{\alpha/2,\nu} = t_{0.05/2,14} = 2.145$. Thus, the confidence interval for a is

$$2.96\ \text{g} \pm (2.145 \times 0.338\ \text{g})$$

$$2.96\ \text{g} \pm 0.725\ \text{g}$$

We use equation (19.25) to develop a confidence interval for b. From Problem 19.1 we know that $\hat{b}^* = 0.44$ g/ppm. From Problem 19.7 we know that $s_{\hat{b}^*} = 0.037$ g/ppm. Using the same critical value as above, we find the confidence interval for b is

$$0.44 \text{ g/ppm} \pm (2.145 \times 0.037 \text{ g/ppm})$$

$$0.44 \text{ g/ppm} \pm 0.079 \text{ g/ppm}$$

19.11 For the limpet-growth experiment described in Problem 19.2, find the 99% confidence intervals for a and b.

Solution

We use equation (19.23) to develop a confidence interval for a. From Problem 19.2 we know that $n = 20$ and $\hat{a}^* = 71.1$ mm. From Problem 19.8 we know that $s_{\hat{a}^*} = 0.714$ mm. From Table A.6 we find that the critical value for $t_{\alpha/2,v} = t_{0.01/2,18} = 2.878$. Thus, the confidence interval for a is

$$71.1 \text{ mm} \pm (2.878 \times 0.714 \text{ mm})$$

$$71.1 \text{ mm} \pm 2.05 \text{ mm}$$

We develop a confidence interval for b from equation (19.25). From Problem 19.2 we know that $\hat{b}^* = -0.021$ mm per individual per m^2. From Problem 19.8 we know that $s_{\hat{b}^*} = 0.00095$ mm per individual per m^2. Using the same critical value as above, we find the confidence interval for b is

$$-0.021 \text{ mm/individual per m}^2 \pm (2.878 \times 0.00095 \text{ mm/individual per m}^2)$$

$$-0.021 \text{ mm/individual per m}^2 \pm 0.0027 \text{ mm/individual per m}^2$$

19.12 For the pizza-delivery study described in Problem 19.3, find the 90% confidence intervals for a and b.

Solution

We use equation (19.23) to develop a confidence interval for a. From Problem 19.3 we know that $n = 12$ and $\hat{a}^* = 4.55$ min. From Problem 19.9 we know that $s_{\hat{a}}^* = 3.828$ min. From Table A.6, we find that the critical value for $t_{\alpha/2,v} = t_{0.10/2,10} = 1.812$. Thus, the confidence interval for a is

$$4.55 \text{ min} \pm (1.812 \times 3.828 \text{ min})$$

$$4.55 \text{ min} \pm 6.936 \text{ min}$$

We use equation (19.25) to develop a confidence interval for b. From Problem 19.3 we know that $\hat{b}^* = 3.95$ min/mile. From Problem 19.9 we know that $s_{\hat{b}^*} = 0.407$ min/mile. Using the same critical value as above, we find the confidence interval for b is

$$3.95 \text{ min/mile} \pm (1.812 \times 0.407 \text{ min/mile})$$

$$3.95 \text{ min/mile} \pm 0.737 \text{ min/mile}$$

CONFIDENCE INTERVAL FOR THE VARIANCE $\sigma^2_{Y \cdot X}$

19.13 For the rye-grass experiment described in Problem 19.1, find the 95% confidence interval for the population variance $\sigma^2_{Y \cdot X}$ of the linear relationship between plant growth and phosphorus concentration.

Solution

The confidence interval for the population variance is developed from equation (19.27), which requires specific values of n, $s^2_{y \cdot x}$, $\chi^2_{\alpha/2,v}$, and $\chi^2_{1-\alpha/2,v}$. We know from Problem 19.1 that $n = 16$ and from Problem 19.4 that $s^2_{y \cdot x} = 0.619$ g^2. From Table A.7, with $v = n - 2 = 14$, $\chi^2_{0.025,14} = 26.12$ and $\chi^2_{0.975,14} = 5.63$. Using these values, we get the confidence interval

$$\left[\frac{(14 \times 0.619\ \text{g}^2)}{26.12}, \frac{(14 \times 0.619\ \text{g}^2)}{5.63}\right]$$

$$(0.3318\ \text{g}^2, 1.5393\ \text{g}^2)$$

19.14 For the limpet experiment described in Problem 19.2, find the 99% confidence interval for the population variance $\sigma^2_{Y.X}$ of the linear relationship between the size of limpets and their population density.

Solution

The confidence interval for the population variance is developed from equation (19.27), which requires specific values of n, $s^2_{y\cdot x}$, $\chi^2_{\alpha/2,\nu}$, and $\chi^2_{1-\alpha/2,\nu}$. We know from Problem 19.2 that $n = 20$ and from Problem 19.5 that $s^2_{y\cdot x} = 1.433\ \text{mm}^2$. From Table A.7 with $\nu = n - 2 = 18$, $\chi^2_{0.005,18} = 37.16$, and $\chi^2_{0.995,18} = 6.26$. These values give the confidence interval

$$\left[\frac{(18 \times 1.433\ \text{mm}^2)}{37.16}, \frac{(18 \times 1.433\ \text{mm}^2)}{6.26}\right]$$

$$(0.6941\ \text{mm}^2, 4.1204\ \text{mm}^2)$$

19.15 For the study of pizza deliveries described in Problem 19.3, find the 90% confidence interval for the population variance $\sigma^2_{Y.X}$ of the linear relationship between delivery time and delivery distance.

Solution

The confidence interval for the population variance is developed from equation (19.27), which requires specific values of n, $s^2_{y\cdot x}$, $\chi^2_{\alpha/2,\nu}$, and $\chi^2_{1-\alpha/2,\nu}$. We know from Problem 19.3 that $n = 12$ and from Problem 19.6 that $s^2_{y\cdot x} = 48.671\ \text{min}^2$. From Table A.7 with $\nu = n - 2 = 10$, $\chi^2_{0.05,10} = 18.31$, and $\chi^2_{0.95,10} = 3.94$. These values give the confidence interval

$$\left[\frac{(10 \times 48.671\ \text{min}^2)}{18.31}, \frac{(10 \times 48.671\ \text{min}^2)}{3.94}\right]$$

$$(26.582\ \text{min}^2, 123.530\ \text{min}^2)$$

PREDICTION INTERVALS FOR EXPECTED VALUES OF Y

19.16 You plan to grow rye grass and want to predict the weight of a rye-grass plant grown at 5 ppm of phosphorus. Use the line of least-squares regression developed in Problem 19.1 to make this prediction and then find the 95% prediction interval.

Solution

We know from Problem 19.1 that $\hat{\mu}^*_{Y|x} = 2.96 + 0.44x$. Using this equation, the predicted weight of a plant when grown at 5 ppm of phosphorus is $\hat{\mu}_{Y|x=5} = 2.96 + (0.44 \times 5) = 5.16$ g. As n is equal to 16, which is less than 30, we use the t distribution to find the prediction interval. First, we use equation (19.29) to find the standard error of the mean of the Y values. We know from Problem 19.4 that $s_{y\cdot x} = 0.79$ g. Using $x_0 = 5$ ppm (the value of x at which Y is being predicted), equation (19.8), and sums provided in Table 19.6, we find that

$$s_{\hat{\mu}_{Y|x=5}} = 0.79\sqrt{1 + \frac{1}{16} + \frac{\left(5 - \dfrac{120}{16}\right)^2}{1{,}360 = \dfrac{(120)^2}{16}}} = 0.820\ \text{g}$$

Using the t distribution to find the critical values and substituting, $\hat{\mu}_{Y|x=5} = 5.16$ g, $s_{\mu_{Y|x}} = 0.820$ g, and, from Table A.6, $t_{0.05/2,14} = 2.145$, we get

$$5.16 \text{ g} \pm (2.145 \times 0.820 \text{ g})$$

$$5.16 \text{ g} \pm 1.759 \text{ g}$$

19.17 You find a patch of rocky shore where the limpet density is 850 per square meter, and want to predict the size of these limpets. Use the line of least-squares regression developed in Problem 19.2 to make this prediction and then find the 99% prediction interval.

Solution

We know from Problem 19.2 that $\hat{\mu}^{*}_{Y|x} = 71.1 - 0.021x$, and so the predicted length of a limpet that grew in a population density of 850 per meter^2 is $\hat{\mu}_{Y|x=850} = 71.1 - (0.021 \times 850) = 53.2$ mm. As n is equal to 20, which is less than 30, we use the t distribution to find the prediction interval. First, we use equation (19.29) to find the standard error of the mean of the Y values. We know from Problem 19.5 that $s_{y\cdot x} = 1.2$ mm and $x_0 = 850$ (the value of x at which Y is being predicted). Using equation (19.8) and sums in Table 19.8, we find that

$$s_{\hat{\mu}_{Y|x=850}} = 1.2\sqrt{1 + \frac{1}{20} + \frac{\left(850 - \dfrac{14{,}000}{20}\right)^2}{11{,}400{,}000 - \dfrac{(14{,}000)^2}{20}}} = 1.24 \text{ mm}$$

Using the t distribution to find the critical values and substituting the values of $\hat{\mu}_{Y|x=850} = 53.2$ mm, $s_{\mu_{Y|x=850}} = 1.24$ mm, and, from Table A.6, $t_{0.01/2,18} = 2.878$, we get

$$53.2 \text{ mm} \pm (2.878 \times 1.24 \text{ mm})$$

$$53.2 \text{ mm} \pm 3.57 \text{ mm}$$

19.18 You live 4.8 miles from the pizza-delivery store and want to predict how long it will take the company to deliver a pizza to you. Use the line of least-squares regression developed in Problem 19.3 to make this prediction and then find the 90% prediction interval.

Solution

We know from Problem 19.3 that $\hat{\mu}^{*}_{Y|x} = 4.55 + 3.95x$. The predicted time of pizza delivery to a house that is 4.8 miles from the store is $\hat{\mu}_{Y|x=4.8} = 4.55 + (3.95 \times 4.8) = 23.51$ min. As n is equal to 12, which is less than 30, we use the t distribution to find the prediction interval. First, we use equation (19.29) to find the standard error of the mean of the Y values. We know from Problem 19.6 that $s_{y\cdot x} = 6.98$ min. Here, $x_0 = 4.8$ miles (the value of x at which Y is being predicted). Using equation (19.8) and sums in Table 19.10, we find that

$$s_{\mu_{Y|x=4.8}} = 6.98\sqrt{1 + \frac{1}{12} + \frac{\left(4.8 - \dfrac{96}{12}\right)^2}{1{,}062.0 - \dfrac{(96)^2}{12}}} = 7.381 \text{ min}$$

Using the t distribution to find the critical values and substituting the values of $\hat{\mu}_{Y|x=4.8} = 23.51$ min, $s_{\mu_{Y|x=4.8}} = 7.381$ min, and, from Table A.6, $t_{0.10/2,10} = 1.812$, we get

$$23.51 \text{ min} \pm (1.812 \times 7.381 \text{ min})$$

$$23.51 \text{ min} \pm 13.374 \text{ min}$$

TESTING HYPOTHESES ABOUT THE SLOPE b

19.19 In Problem 19.1, we found the slope of the least-squares regression line is $\hat{b}^* = 0.44$ g per ppm. Then in Problem 19.7 we found that the standard deviation of $\hat{b}$ is 0.037 g/ppm. Do a right-tailed test of H_0: $b = 0$ using $\alpha = 0.01$ and a critical-value decision rule.

Solution

(1) H_0: $b = 0$, H_1: $b > 0$

(2) $\alpha = 0.01$

(3) We use the test statistic given by equation (19.24). From Table A.6 we find that, for a right-tailed test at $\alpha = 0.01$ and $\nu = n - 2 = 14$, the critical value is 2.624. The decision rule is: Reject H_0 if $t^* > 2.624$.

(4) Substituting $\hat{b}^* = 0.44$ g/ppm and $s_{\hat{b}^*} = 0.037$ g/ppm into the test statistic, we find that

$$t^* = \frac{0.44 - 0}{0.037} = 11.892$$

From Table A.6, for $\nu = 14$, we find that the approximate probability of getting this sample value is: $P < 0.0005$.

(5) As $t^* > 2.624$, we reject H_0 and accept H_1. This result is confirmed by the fact that the probability of getting a t^* of 11.892 (given that the null hypothesis is true) is less than 0.01. The slope of the relationship between plant weight and phosphorus concentration is greater than zero.

19.20 In Problem 19.2, we found the slope of the least-squares regression line is $\hat{b}^* = -0.021$ mm/individual per m^2. Then in Problem 19.8 we found that the standard deviation of $\hat{b}$ is 0.00095 mm/individual per m^2. Do a left-tailed test of H_0: $b = 0$ using $\alpha = 0.05$ and a critical-value decision rule.

Solution

(1) H_0: $b = 0$, H_1: $b < 0$

(2) $\alpha = 0.05$

(3) We use the test statistic given by equation (19.24). From Table A.6 we find that for a one-tailed test at $\alpha = 0.05$ and $\nu = n - 2 = 18$, the critical value is 1.734. The decision rule is: Reject H_0 if $t^* < -1.734$.

(4) Substituting $\hat{b}^* = -0.021$ mm per individual per m^2 and $s_{\hat{b}^*} = 0.00095$ mm per individual per m^2 into the test statistic, we find that

$$t^* = \frac{-0.021 - 0}{0.00095} = -22.105$$

From table A.6 for $\nu = 18$, we find that the approximate probability of getting this t^* is $P < 0.0005$.

(5) As $t^* < -1.734$, we reject H_0 and accept H_1. This result is confirmed by the fact that the probability of getting a t^* of -22.105 (given that $b = 0$) is less than 0.05. The slope of the relationship between limpet length and population density is less than zero.

19.21 In Problem 19.3, we found the slope of the least-squares regression line was $\hat{b}^* = 3.95$ min per mile. Then in Problem 19.9 we found that the standard deviation of $\hat{b}$ is 0.407 min per mile. Do a right-tailed test of H_0: $b = 0$ using $\alpha = 0.05$ and a critical-value decision rule.

Solution

(1) H_0: $b = 0$, H_1: $b > 0$

(2) $\alpha = 0.05$

(3) We use the test statistic given by equation (19.24). From Table A.6 we find that for a one-tailed test at $\alpha = 0.05$ and $\nu = n - 2 = 10$, the critical value is 1.812. The decision rule is: Reject H_0 if $t^* > 1.812$.

(4) Substituting $\hat{b}^* = 3.95$ min per mile and $s_{\hat{b}^*} = 0.407$ min per mile into the test statistic, we find that

$$t^* = \frac{3.95 - 0}{0.407} = 9.705$$

From Table A.6 for $\nu = 10$, we find that the approximate probability of getting this sample value is $P < 0.0005$.

(5) As $t^* > 1.812$, we reject H_0 and accept H_1. This result is confirmed by the fact that the probability of getting this sample value (given that $b = 0$) is less than 0.05. The slope of the relationship between delivery time and delivery distance is greater than zero.

CALCULATION OF THE SAMPLE CORRELATION COEFFICIENT r

19.22 A bird gets rid of excess heat by panting, and you want to know whether there is a linear relationship between body temperature and breathing rate. You take a random sample of 15 birds, under various conditions of environmental temperature, and measure, for each bird, the body temperature (°C) and the number of breaths per minute. Your results are shown in Table 19.11. Calculate the coefficient of correlation between these two variables.

Table 19.11

Bird	Body temperature (°C)	Breathing rate (breaths per min)
1	39.6	33
2	40.1	50
3	41.7	75
4	39.0	13
5	41.9	68
6	42.8	115
7	40.3	52
8	39.0	33
9	39.7	60
10	39.3	28
11	41.8	74
12	39.6	39
13	40.2	76
14	39.1	30
15	39.4	58

Solution

Because environmental temperature and number of breaths per minute can be assumed to have a bivariate normal distribution, we can estimate the population correlation coefficient ρ with the sample correlation coefficient r. To find this statistic, we need $\sum x$, $\sum x^2$, $\sum y$, $\sum y^2$, and $\sum xy$, which are provided in Table 19.12. Inserting these values into equation (19.32),

$$r^* = \frac{32{,}733.5 - \left[\frac{(603.5)(804)}{15}\right]}{\sqrt{(24{,}301.79) - \frac{(603.5)^2}{15}}\sqrt{(52{,}446) - \frac{(804)^2}{15}}} = 0.871$$

Table 19.12

	x_i	y_i	x_i^2	y_i^2	$x_i y_i$
	39.6	33	1,568.16	1,089	1,306.8
	40.1	50	1,608.01	2,500	2,005.0
	41.7	75	1,738.89	5,625	3,127.5
	39.0	13	1,521.00	169	507.0
	41.9	68	1,755.61	4,624	2,849.2
	42.8	115	1,831.84	13,225	4,922.0
	40.3	52	1,624.09	2,704	2,095.6
	39.0	33	1,521.00	1,089	1,287.0
	39.7	60	1,576.09	3,600	2,382.0
	39.3	28	1,544.49	784	1,100.4
	41.8	74	1,747.24	5,476	3,093.2
	39.6	39	1,568.16	1,521	1,544.4
	40.2	76	1,616.04	5,776	3,055.2
	39.1	30	1,528.81	900	1,173.0
	39.4	58	1,552.36	3,364	2,285.2
$\sum$	603.5	804	24,301.79	52,446	32,733.5

This correlation coefficient, $r^* = 0.871$, suggests a direct linear relationship between environmental temperature and breathing rate.

19.23 A biogeographer believes that an island gradually loses species after it becomes separated from the mainland. To find out whether there is a linear relationship between the amount of time that has elapsed since an island became separated from the mainland and the number of lizard species, she takes a random sample of 13 islands and finds out the age of each island and its number of lizard species. Her results are shown in Table 19.13. Calculate the coefficient of correlation between island age and number of lizard species.

Table 19.13

Island age (years)	Lizard diversity (number of species)
9,100	75
4,500	55
13,400	12
6,500	53
11,200	48
12,000	26
5,100	50
7,400	55
10,600	21
11,800	48
14,700	32
8,800	25
10,900	21

Solution

Because island age and number of species can be assumed to have a bivariate normal distribution, we can estimate the population correlation coefficient ρ with the sample corrrelation coefficient r. To find this statistic, we need $\sum x$, $\sum x^2$, $\sum y$, $\sum y^2$, and $\sum xy$, which are provided in Table 19.14. Inserting these values into equation (19.32)

$$r^* = \frac{4{,}655{,}200 - \left[\frac{(126{,}000)(521)}{13}\right]}{\sqrt{(1{,}339{,}020{,}000) - \frac{(126{,}000)^2}{13}}\sqrt{(24{,}943) - \frac{(521)^2}{13}}} = -0.570$$

Table 19.14

	x_i	y_i	x_i^2	y_i^2	$x_i y_i$
	9,100	75	82,810,000	5,625	682,500
	4,500	55	20,250,000	3,025	247,500
	13,400	12	179,560,000	144	160,800
	6,500	53	42,250,000	2,809	344,500
	11,200	48	125,440,000	2,304	537,600
	12,000	26	144,000,000	676	312,000
	5,100	50	26,010,000	2,500	255,000
	7,400	55	54,760,000	3,025	407,000
	10,600	21	112,360,000	441	222,600
	11,800	48	139,240,000	2,304	566,400
	14,700	32	216,090,000	1,024	470,400
	8,800	25	77,440,000	625	220,000
	10,900	21	118,810,000	441	228,900
$\sum$	126,000	521	1,339,020,000	24,943	4,655,200

This correlation coefficient, $r^* = -0.570$, suggests an inverse linear relationship between island age and number of lizard species.

19.24 The manager of a company wants to assure applicants for jobs that the salary at which an employee is hired is no indication of the salary after 10 years of employment. To be able to make this statement, he takes a random sample of 12 long-term employees and records their starting salary and their salary after 10 years of employment. The results are shown in Table 19.15. Calculate the coefficient of correlation between starting salary and salary 10 years later.

Solution

Because the two sets of salaries in this company can be assumed to have a bivariate normal distribution, we can estimate the population correlation coefficient ρ with the sample corrrelation coefficient r. To find this statistic, we need $\sum x$, $\sum x^2$, $\sum y$, $\sum y^2$, and $\sum xy$, which are provided in Table 19.16. Inserting these values

Table 19.15

Employee	Salary: starting	Salary: 10 years later
1	\$26,000	\$37,000
2	\$42,000	\$90,000
3	\$37,000	\$48,000
4	\$82,000	\$90,000
5	\$66,000	\$88,000
6	\$44,000	\$100,000
7	\$24,000	\$95,000
8	\$39,000	\$120,000
9	\$55,000	\$95,000
10	\$61,000	\$76,000
11	\$77,000	\$89,000
12	\$58,000	\$100,000

Table 19.16

	x_i	y_i	x_i^2	y_i^2	$x_i y_i$
	26,000	37,000	676,000,000	1,369,000,000	962,000,000
	42,000	90,000	1,764,000,000	8,100,000,000	3,780,000,000
	37,000	48,000	1,369,000,000	2,304,000,000	1,776,000,000
	82,000	90,000	6,724,000,000	8,100,000,000	7,380,000,000
	66,000	88,000	4,356,000,000	7,744,000,000	5,808,000,000
	44,000	100,000	1,936,000,000	10,000,000,000	4,400,000,000
	24,000	95,000	576,000,000	9,025,000,000	2,280,000,000
	39,000	120,000	1,521,000,000	14,400,000,000	4,680,000,000
	55,000	95,000	3,025,000,000	9,025,000,000	5,225,000,000
	61,000	76,000	3,721,000,000	5,776,000,000	4,636,000,000
	77,000	89,000	5,929,000,000	7,921,000,000	6,853,000,000
	58,000	100,000	3,364,000,000	10,000,000,000	5,800,000,000
$\sum$	611,000	1,028,000	34,961,000,000	93,764,000,000	53,580,000,000

into equation (19.32),

$$r^* = \frac{53{,}580{,}000{,}000 - \left[\dfrac{(611{,}000)(1{,}028{,}000)}{12}\right]}{\sqrt{(34{,}961{,}000{,}000) - \dfrac{(611{,}000)^2}{12}}\sqrt{(93{,}764{,}000{,}000) - \dfrac{(1{,}028{,}000)^2}{12}}} = 0.264$$

This correlation coefficient, $r^* = 0.264$, is low, which suggests there may be no linear relationship between the two sets of salaries.

CONFIDENCE INTERVALS FOR THE POPULATION CORRELATION COEFFICIENT ρ

19.25 For the relationship between body temperature and breathing rate described in Problem 19.22, find the 95% confidence interval for the population correlation coefficient.

Solution

First we convert the correlation coefficient r into a z_r value. From Table A.10, we find that for $r^* = 0.871$, $z_r = 1.3372$. The confidence limits (see Section 19.14), then, are

$$[1.3372 - z_{\alpha/2}\sigma_{z_r}, 1.3372 + z_{\alpha/2}\sigma_{z_r}]$$

For a 95% confidence interval, we know from Table A.5 that $z_{0.05/2} = z_{0.025} = 1.96$. Using $n = 15$ in equation (19.33) to calculate the standard error,

$$\sigma_{z_r} = \sqrt{\frac{1}{n-3}} = \sqrt{\frac{1}{12}} = 0.2887$$

The confidence limits are

$$[1.3372 - (1.96 \times 0.2887), 1.3372 + (1.96 \times 0.2887)]$$
$$(0.7713, 1.9031)$$

Returning to Table A.10, we convert these values into r values. Thus, the 95% confidence interval for $r^* = 0.871$ is (0.648, 0.956). We can say, with 95% confidence, that the population correlation coefficient ρ lies within the interval 0.648 to 0.956.

19.26 For the relationship between island age and lizard diversity described in Problem 19.23, find the 95% confidence interval for the population correlation coefficent.

Solution

First we convert the correlation coefficient r into a z_r value. From Table A.10, we find that for $r^* = -0.570$, $z_r = -0.6475$. The confidence limits (see Section 19.14) then are

$$[-0.6475 - z_{\alpha/2}\sigma_{z_r}, -0.6475 + z_{\alpha/2}\sigma_{z_r}]$$

For a 95% confidence interval, we know from Table A.5 that $z_{0.05/2} = 1.96$. Using $n = 13$ in equation (19.33) to calculate the standard error,

$$\sigma_{z_r} = \sqrt{\frac{1}{n-3}} = \sqrt{\frac{1}{10}} = 0.3162$$

The confidence limits are

$$[-0.6475 - (1.96 \times 0.3162), -0.6475 + (1.96 \times 0.3162)]$$
$$(-1.2673, -0.0277)$$

Returning to Table A.10, we convert these values into r values. Thus, the 95% confidence interval for $r^* = -0.570$ is $(-0.853, -0.028)$. We can say, with 95% confidence, that the population correlation coefficient ρ lies within the interval -0.853 to -0.028.

19.27 For the relationship between starting salary and salary 10 years later described in Problem 19.24, find the 95% confidence interval for the population correlation coefficient.

Solution

First we convert the correlation coefficient r into a z_r value. From Table A.10, we find that for $r^* = 0.264$, $z_r = 0.2704$. The confidence limits (see Section 19.14) then are

$$[0.2704 - z_{\alpha/2}\sigma_{z_r}, 0.2704 + z_{\alpha/2}\sigma_{z_r}]$$

For a 95% confidence interval, we know from Table A.5 that $z_{0.05/2} = 1.96$. Using $n = 12$ in equation (19.33) to calculate the standard error,

$$\sigma_{z_r} = \sqrt{\frac{1}{n-3}} = \sqrt{\frac{1}{9}} = 0.3333$$

The confidence limits are

$$[0.2704 - (1.96 \times 0.3333), 0.2704 + (1.96 \times 0.3333)]$$
$$(-0.3829, 0.9237)$$

Returning to Table A.10, we convert these values into r values. Thus, the 95% confidence interval for $r^* = 0.264$ is $(-0.365, 0.728)$. We can say, with 95% confidence, that the population correlation coefficient ρ lies within the interval -0.365 to 0.728.

USING THE r DISTRIBUTION TO TEST HYPOTHESES ABOUT THE CORRELATION COEFFICIENT ρ

19.28 Suppose that before you did the study described in Problem 19.22, you believed that the rate of breathing increases with body temperature. Do a right-tailed test of H_0: $\rho = 0$ for that study (in which $r^* = 0.871$) using $\alpha = 0.01$ and a critical-value decision rule.

Solution

(1) H_0: $\rho = 0$, H_1: $\rho > 0$

(2) $\alpha = 0.01$

(3) From Table A.11, for a right-tailed test, with $\nu = 13$ and $\alpha = 0.01$: $r_{0.01,13} = 0.592$. Therefore, our decision rule is: Reject H_0 if $r^* > 0.592$.

(4) From Table A.11, we find that the approximate probability of getting an r value of 0.871, with $\nu = 13$ in a one-tailed test, is less than 0.005.

(5) As $r^* > 0.592$, we reject H_0 and accept H_1. This result is confirmed by the fact that the probability of getting a sample value of $r^* = 0.871$ (given that $\rho = 0$) is less than 0.01. There is a significant, linear relationship between body temperature and breathing rate.

19.29 For the relationship between island age and lizard diversity (Problem 19.23), we found that $r^* = -0.570$. Do a two-tailed test of H_0: $\rho = 0$ using $\alpha = 0.05$ and a critical-value decision rule.

Solution

(1) H_0: $\rho = 0$, H_1: $\rho \neq 0$

(2) $\alpha = 0.05$

(3) From Table A.11, for a two-tailed test, with $\nu = 11$ and $\alpha = 0.05$: $r_{0.05/2,11} = 0.553$. Therefore, our decision rule is: Reject H_0 if $r^* < -0.553$ or if $r^* > 0.553$.

(4) From Table A.11, we find that the approximate probability of getting $r^* = 0.570$, with $\nu = 11$ in a two-tailed test, is in the range $0.02 < P < 0.05$. Because the r distribution is symmetric around zero, this is the same range of P values for $r^* = -0.570$.

(5) As $r^* < -0.553$, we reject H_0 and accept H_1. This result is confirmed by the fact that the probability of getting a sample value of $r^* = -0.570$ (given that $\rho = 0$) is less than 0.05. There is a significant, inverse linear relationship between island age and number of lizard species.

19.30 For the relationship between starting salary and salary 10 years later (see Problem 19.24), we found that $r^* = 0.264$. Do a two-tailed test of H_0: $\rho = 0$ using $\alpha = 0.05$ and a critical-value decision rule.

Solution

(1) H_0: $\rho = 0$, H_1: $\rho \neq 0$

(2) $\alpha = 0.05$

(3) From Table A.11, for a two-tailed test test, with $\nu = 10$ and $\alpha = 0.05$: $r_{0.05/2,10} = 0.576$, the decision rule is: Reject H_0 if $r^* < -0.576$ or if $r^* > 0.576$.

(4) From Table A.11, we find that the approximate probability for $r^* = 0.264$, in a two-tailed test with $\nu = 10$, is $P > 0.10$.

(5) As $-0.576 < r^* < 0.576$, we accept H_0. This result is confirmed by the fact that the probability of getting an $r^* = 0.264$ (when $\rho = 0$) is greater than 0.05. There is no significant, linear relationship between the two sets of salaries.

USING THE t DISTRIBUTION TO TEST HYPOTHESES ABOUT ρ

19.31 Repeat the test of the null hypothesis that there is no linear relationship between breathing rate and body temperature (see Problem 19.28), using the t transformation and the table of t values. Do this one-tailed test at $\alpha = 0.01$, using a critical-value decision rule.

Solution

(1) H_0: $\rho = 0$, H_1: $\rho > 0$

(2) $\alpha = 0.01$

(3) Using Table A.6, with ($\nu = n - 2 = 15 - 2 = 13$) and $\alpha = 0.01$ for a one-tailed test, the decision rule is: Reject H_0 if $t^* > 2.650$.

(4) We know from Problem 19.22 that $r^* = 0.871$. Using this value in equation (19.35),

$$t^* = \frac{0.871 - 0}{\sqrt{\dfrac{1 - (0.871)^2}{15 - 2}}} = 6.392$$

From Table A.6, we find that the approximate probability of getting this t^*, in a one-tailed test with $\nu = 13$, is $P < 0.0005$.

(5) Because $t^* > 2.650$, we reject H_0 and accept H_1. This result is confirmed by the fact that the approximate probability of getting a t^* value of 6.392 (given that the null hypothesis is true) is less than 0.01. There is a significant, positive correlation between body temperature and breathing rate.

19.32 Repeat the test of the null hypothesis that there is no linear relationship between island age and number of lizard species (Problem 19.29), using the t transformation and the table of t values. Do this two-tailed test at $\alpha = 0.05$, using a critical-value decision rule.

Solution

(1) H_0: $\rho = 0$, H_1: $\rho \neq 0$

(2) $\alpha = 0.05$

(3) Using Table A.6, with ($\nu = n - 2 = 13 - 2 = 11$) and $\alpha/2 = 0.05/2$ for a two-tailed test, we find the decision rule is: Reject H_0 if $t^* > 2.201$ or $t^* < -2.201$.

(4) We know from Problem 19.23 that $r^* = -0.570$. Using this value in equation (19.35), we find

$$t^* = \frac{-0.570 - 0}{\sqrt{\dfrac{1 - (-0.570)^2}{13 - 2}}} = -2.301$$

From Table A.6, we find that the approximate probability of getting a t^* value of -2.301 in a two-tailed test with $\nu = 11$ is in the range $0.02 < P < 0.05$.

(5) Because $t^* < -2.201$, we reject H_0 and accept H_1. This result is confirmed by the fact that the approximate probability of getting a t^* value of -2.301 (given that $\rho = 0$) is less than 0.05. There is a significant, inverse linear relationship between island age and number of lizard species.

19.33 Repeat the test of the null hypothesis that there is no linear relationship between starting salary and salary 10 years later (Problem 19.30), using the t transformation and the table of t values. Do this two-tailed test at $\alpha = 0.05$, using a critical-value decision rule.

Solution

(1) H_0: $\rho = 0$, H_1: $\rho \neq 0$

(2) $\alpha = 0.05$

(3) Using Table A.6, with $(\nu = n - 2 = 12 - 2 = 10)$ and $\alpha = 0.05$ for a two-tailed test, we find the decision rule is: Reject H_0 if $t^* > 2.228$ or if $t^* < -2.228$.

(4) We know from Problem 19.24 that $r^* = 0.264$. Using this value in equation (19.35), we find that

$$t^* = \frac{0.264 - 0}{\sqrt{\dfrac{1 - (0.264)^2}{12 - 2}}} = 0.866$$

From Table A.6, we find that the approximate probability of getting this t^*, in a two-tailed test when $\nu = 10$, is $P > 0.20$.

(5) Because $-2.228 < t^* < 2.228$, we accept H_0. This result is confirmed by the fact that the approximate probability of getting a t^* value of 0.866 (given that the null hypothesis is true) is greater than 0.05. There is no significant linear relationship between the two sets of salaries.

USING THE Z DISTRIBUTION TO TEST THE HYPOTHESIS $\rho = c$

19.34 You repeat the study of body temperature and breathing rate described in Problem 19.22, using a second sample of 15 birds from another species. This time, you get a correlation coefficient of $r^* = 0.600$. You want to know whether the relationship between body temperature and breathing rate in this second sample is the same as in the first sample. Do a two-tailed test at $\alpha = 0.05$, using a critical-value decision rule, of H_0: The population correlation coefficient is $\rho = 0.871$.

Solution

(1) H_0: $\rho = 0.871$, H_1: $\rho \neq 0.871$

(2) $\alpha = 0.05$

(3) As you are testing whether the correlation coefficient is equal to a particular value, you use the Z distribution (Table A.5) to find critical values for rejection. From this table, we find that $z_{0.05/2} = 1.96$. The decision rule is: Reject H_0 if $z^* < -1.96$ or if $z^* > 1.96$.

(4) Using Table A.10 to transform r and ρ values into z values, we find that $r = 0.600$ is equal to $z_r = 0.6931$ and that $\rho = 0.871$ is equal to $z_\rho = 1.3372$. Using these values and $n = 15$ in equation (19.36), we find that the sample value of z is

$$z^* = \frac{0.6931 - 1.3372}{\sqrt{1/12}} = -2.2312$$

From Table A.5, we find that the area of the standard normal distribution that lies under the curve above the interval from 0 to $z = 2.23$ is 0.4871. Thus, the probability of getting this z value under the condition that the null hypothesis is true is

$$2[P(Z > 2.23)] = 2(0.5000 - 0.4871) = 2(0.0129) = 0.0258$$

(5) As $z^* < -1.96$, we reject H_0 and accept H_1. This result is confirmed by the fact that the probability of getting an r value equal to 0.600 (under the condition that the population value is $\rho = 0.871$) is less than 0.05. Thus, it is unlikely that the second sample of measurements comes from the same population, with regards to ρ, as the first sample.

19.35 The study of island age and number of lizards (Problem 19.23) is repeated, this time with a sample of 20 islands. The correlation coefficient for this second study is $r^* = -0.410$. Do a one-tailed test at $\alpha = 0.05$, using a critical-value decision rule, of H_0: The population correlation coefficient is $\rho = -0.570$, against the alternative hypothesis that it is greater (i.e., less negative) than $\rho = -0.570$.

Solution

(1) H_0: $\rho = -0.570$, H_1: $\rho > -0.570$

(2) $\alpha = 0.05$

(3) As you are testing whether the correlation coefficient is equal to a particular value, you use the Z distribution (Table A.5) to find the critical value for rejection. From this table, we find that $z_{0.05} = 1.645$. The decision rule for this right-tailed test is: Reject H_0 if $z^* > 1.645$.

(4) Using Table A.10 to transform r and ρ values into z values, we find that $r = -0.410$ is equal to $z_r = -0.4356$ and that $\rho = -0.570$ is equal to $z_\rho = -0.6475$. Using these values, and $n = 20$, in equation (19.36), we find that the sample value of z is

$$z^* = \frac{-0.4356 - (-0.6475)}{\sqrt{1/17}} = 0.8737$$

From Table A.5, we find that the area of the standard normal distribution that lies under the curve above the interval from 0 to $z = 0.87$ is 0.3078. Thus, the probability of getting this z value under the condition that the null hypothesis is true is $P(Z > 0.87) = (0.5000 - 0.3078) = 0.1922$.

(5) As $z^* < 1.645$, we accept H_0. This result is confirmed by the fact that the probability of getting an r value equal to -0.410 (under the condition that the population value is $\rho = -0.570$) is greater than 0.05. It is likely that the second sample of measurements comes from the same population, with regard to ρ, as the first sample.

19.36 The study of starting salary and salary after 10 years (Problem 19.24) is repeated at another company, this time with a sample of 16 employees. The correlation coefficient for this second study is $r = 0.400$. Do a two-tailed test at $\alpha = 0.01$, using a critical-value decision rule, of H_0: The population correlation coefficient is $\rho = 0.264$.

Solution

(1) H_0: $\rho = 0.264$, H_1: $\rho \neq 0.264$

(2) $\alpha = 0.01$

(3) As you are testing whether the correlation coefficient is equal to a particular value, you use the Z distribution (Table A.5) to find the critical values for rejection. From this table, we find that $z_{0.01/2} = 2.575$. The decision rule is: Reject H_0 if $z^* > 2.575$ or if $z^* < -2.575$.

(4) Using Table A.10 to transform r and ρ values into z values, we find that $r = 0.400$ is equal to $z_r = 0.4236$ and that $\rho = 0.264$ is equal to $z_\rho = 0.2704$. Using these values, and $n = 16$, in equation (19.36), we find that the sample value of z is

$$z^* = \frac{0.4236 - 0.2704}{\sqrt{1/13}} = 0.5524$$

From Table A.5, we find that the area of the standard normal distribution that lies under the curve above the interval from 0 to $z = 0.55$ is 0.2088. Thus, the probability of getting this z value under the condition that the null hypothesis is true is

$$2[P(Z > 0.55)] = 2(0.5000 - 0.2088) = 2(0.2912) = 0.5824$$

(5) As $-2.575 < z^* < 2.575$, we accept H_0 at the 0.01 level of significance. This result is confirmed by the fact that the probability of getting an r value equal to 0.400 (under the condition that the population value is $\rho = 0.264$) is greater than 0.01. Thus, it is likely that the second sample of measurements comes from the same population, with regard to ρ, as the first sample.

INTERPRETATION OF THE CORRELATION COEFFICIENT r

19.37 Interpret the study described in Problem 19.22 in terms of how much of the total variation in body temperature and breathing rate is explained by the linear relationship between the two variables.

Solution

The coefficient of determination, r^2, estimates the amount of variance explained by the linear relationship between two variables. Here, $r^* = 0.871$ and $r^{*2} = 0.759$. Thus, we can say that 75.9% of the variation in the values of body temperature and breathing rate can be explained by their linear relationship with each other.

19.38 Interpret the study described in Problem 19.23 in terms of how much of the total variation in island age and number of lizard species is explained by the linear relationship between the two variables.

Solution

In this study, $r^* = -0.570$ and $r^{*2} = 0.325$. Thus, we can say that 32.5% of the variation in the values of island age and number of lizard species can be explained by their linear relationship with each other.

19.39 Interpret the study described in Problem 19.24 in terms of how much of the total variation in the two sets of salaries (starting and after 10 years) is explained by the linear relationship between the two variables.

Solution

In this study, $r^* = 0.264$ and $r^{*2} = 0.070$. Thus, we can say that 7.0% of the variation in the values of the salaries can be explained by their linear relationship with each other.

Supplementary Problems

THE LEAST-SQUARES REGRESSION LINE

19.40 A developmental biologist wants to be able to predict level of physical activity of duck embryos of various ages. She records the mean duration of periods of activity (in seconds) for each of four ages (in days), using three embryos for each age. The results are (days: duration): (5 days: 1, 3, 1 sec); (10 days: 18, 20, 22 sec); (15 days: 32, 36, 37 sec); (20 days: 44, 46, 48 sec). What is the least-squares regression line for these data? Using this line, what duration of activity can you predict for 13-day-old embryos?

Ans. $\hat{\mu}^*_{Y|x} = -11.33 + 2.96x, \quad \hat{\mu}_{Y|x=13} = 27.2$ sec

19.41 An oil-drilling company wants to establish the most economic system for exploratory drilling. They need to know the relationship between yield (in billions of dollars) and grid spacing (in miles). A preliminary study shows the following relationship (grid spacing: yield): (2 miles: 15.5, 17.0, 15.2); (4 miles: 11.0, 13.1, 9.8); (6 miles: 7.0, 8.5, 5.5); (8 miles: 2.3, 1.8, 1.7). What is the least-squares regression line for these data? What can the company predict for the amount of yield under a grid-spacing system of 5 miles?

Ans. $\hat{\mu}^*_{Y|x} = 20.583 - 2.31x, \quad \hat{\mu}_{Y|x=5} = \$9.033$ billion

19.42 A marketing analyst is studying hardware stores and wants to be able to predict the sales per month from the amount of money spent on advertising per month. She chooses three levels of spending ($200, $400, $600) and selects, at random, three stores for each of these levels. Her data set is as follows ($costs; $sales): ($200; $36,500), ($200; $35,400), ($200; $30,000), ($400; $41,200), ($400; $43,600), ($400; $46,000), ($600; $61,800), ($600; $52,500), ($600; $68,000). What is the least-squares regression line for these data? Using this line, how many dollars in sales per month can you predict for a hardware store that spends \$380 per month on advertising?

Ans. $\hat{\mu}^*_{Y|x} = 19{,}311 + 67.0x$, $\hat{\mu}_{Y|x=380} = \$44{,}771$

THE ESTIMATOR OF THE VARIANCE $\sigma^2_{Y \cdot X}$

19.43 For the experiment on duck embryos described in Problem 19.40, what is the best estimate of the variance of the estimate and of the standard error of the estimate?

Ans. $s^2_{y \cdot x} = 7.20\ \text{sec}^2$, $s_{y \cdot x} = 2.7$ sec

19.44 For the preliminary study of oil yields described in Problem 19.41, what is the best estimate of the variance of the estimate and of the standard error of the estimate?

Ans. $s^2_{y \cdot x} = \$^2 1.252$ billion, $s_{y \cdot x} = \$1.12$ billion

19.45 For the study of the relationship between advertising costs and sales described in Problem 19.42, what is the best estimate of the variance of the estimate and of the standard error of the estimate?

Ans. $s^2_{y \cdot x} = \$^2 26{,}553{,}571.4$, $s_{y \cdot x} = \$5{,}153.02$

THE VARIANCE OF $\hat{a}$ AND OF $\hat{b}$

19.46 For the experiment on duck embryos described in Problem 19.40, find the standard deviations of the point estimates of $\hat{a}$ and $\hat{b}$.

Ans. $s_{\hat{a}^*} = 1.90$ sec, $s_{\hat{b}^*} = 0.139$ sec/day

19.47 For the study of oil yields described in Problem 19.41, find the standard deviations of the point estimates of $\hat{a}$ and $\hat{b}$.

Ans. $s_{\hat{a}^*} = \$0.791$ billion, $s_{\hat{b}^*} = \$0.144$ billion/mile

19.48 For the study of advertising costs and sales described in Problem 19.42, find the standard deviations of the point estimates of $\hat{a}$ and $\hat{b}$.

Ans. $s_{\hat{a}^*} = \$4{,}544.5$, $s_{\hat{b}^*} = \$10.52$ in sales/dollar spent in advertising

CONFIDENCE INTERVALS FOR a AND b

19.49 For the duck-embryo experiment described in Problem 19.40, find the 95% confidence intervals for a and b.

Ans. a: (−15.56 sec, −7.10 sec), b: (2.650 sec/day, 3.270 sec/day)

19.50 For the oil-drilling experiment described in Problem 19.41, find the 90% confidence intervals for a and b.

Ans. a: (\$19.152 billion, \$22.016 billion), b: (−\$2.571 billion/mile, −\$2.049 billion/mile)

19.51 For the advertising study described in Problem 19.42, find the 99% confidence intervals for a and b.

Ans. a: (\$3,409.8, \$35,212.2), b: (\$30.19/dollar spent, \$103.81/dollar spent)

CONFIDENCE INTERVAL FOR THE VARIANCE $\sigma^2_{Y \cdot X}$

19.52 For the study of duck embryos described in Problem 19.40, what is the 95% confidence interval for the population variance $\sigma^2_{Y \cdot X}$ of the linear relation between duration of activity and age?

Ans. (3.516 sec², 22.154 sec²)

19.53 For the oil-drilling experiment described in Problem 19.41, what is the 90% confidence interval for the population variance $\sigma^2_{Y \cdot X}$ of the linear relation between yield and grid spacing?

Ans. ($\$^2 0.6838$ billion, $\$^2 3.1777$ billion)

19.54 For the marketing study described in Problem 19.42, what is the 99% confidence interval for the population variance $\sigma^2_{Y \cdot X}$ of the linear relation between advertising costs and sales?

Ans. ($\$^2 9,165,433.9$, $\$^2 187,942,365.8$)

PREDICTION INTERVALS FOR EXPECTED VALUES OF Y

19.55 You plan to do an experiment on duck embryos that are 14 days old and want to estimate the duration of activity at that age. Use the line of least-squares regression developed in Problem 19.40 to make this prediction. Then use $n = 12$ and $s_{y \cdot x} = 2.7$ sec to find the 99% prediction interval.

Ans. $\hat{\mu}_{Y|x=14} = 30.11$ sec, (21.180 sec, 39.040 sec)

19.56 An oil-drilling company wants to use a grid-spacing system of 3.0 miles, and wants to predict the yield (in dollars). Use the line of least-squares regression developed in Problem 19.41 to make this prediction. Then use $n = 12$ and $s_{y \cdot x} = \$1.12$ billion to find the 95% prediction interval.

Ans. $\hat{\mu}_{Y|x=3} = \$13.65$ billion, ($10.974 billion, $16.326 billion)

19.57 The owner of a hardware store wants to know how many dollars in sales per month that he can expect if he spends $150 per month in advertising. Use the line of least-squares regression developed in Problem 19.42 to make this prediction. Then use $n = 9$ and $s_{y \cdot x} = \$5,153.02$ to find the 90% prediction interval.

Ans. $\hat{\mu}_{Y|x=150} = \$29,361.0$, ($17,925.02, $40,796.98)

TESTING HYPOTHESES ABOUT THE SLOPE b

19.58 In Problem 19.40 we found the slope of the least-squares regression line to be 2.96 sec/day. Then in Problem 19.46 we found that the standard deviation of $\hat{b}$ is $s_{\hat{b}*} = \$0.139$ sec/day. Do a t test, at $\alpha = 0.01$, of H_0: $b = 0$, against the alternative hypothesis that $b > 0$. Give the value of the test statistic. State whether you accept or reject H_0 and give the approximate probability of getting this t^* given that H_0 is true.

Ans. $t^* = 21.295$, reject H_0 because $t^* > 2.764$, $P < 0.0005$

19.59 In Problem 19.41 we found the slope of the least-squares regression line to be -2.31 $billion/mile. Then in Problem 19.47 we found that the standard deviation of $\hat{b}$ is $s_{\hat{b}*} = \$0.144$ billion/mile. Do a t test, at $\alpha = 0.05$, of H_0: $b = 0$, against the alternative hypothesis that $b < 0$. Give the value of the test statistic. State whether you accept or reject H_0 and give the approximate probability of getting this t^* given that H_0 is true.

Ans. $t^* = -16.042$, reject H_0 because $t^* < -1.812$, $P < 0.0005$

19.60 In Problem 19.42 we found the slope of the least-squares regression line to be 67.0 dollars in sales per dollar in advertising. Then in Problem 19.48 we found that the standard deviation of $\hat{b}$ is $s_{\hat{b}*} = 10.52$ dollars in sales per dollar in advertising. Do a t test, at $\alpha = 0.05$, of H_0: $b = 0$, against the alternative hypothesis that $b > 0$. Give the value of the test statistic. State whether you accept or reject H_0 and give the approximate probability of getting this t^* given that H_0 is true.

Ans. $t^* = 6.369$, reject H_0 because $t^* > 1.895$, $P < 0.0005$

CALCULATION OF THE SAMPLE CORRELATION COEFFICIENT r

19.61 You are interested in knowing what governs the density of creosote bushes in the desert. One research hypothesis is that it is governed by precipitation. You locate, at random, six study sites and measure the amount of precipitation (in cm per year) and the density of creosote bushes (in numbers of plants per 100 m^2).

Listed by study site, your measurements are: (5.3 cm; 2 bushes), (15.8 cm; 3 bushes), (26.2 cm; 7 bushes), (29.9 cm; 5 bushes), (12.1 cm; 3 bushes), (18.0 cm; 4 bushes). What is the sample coefficient of correlation between these two variables?

Ans. $r^* = 0.865$

19.62 A designer of city parks plans to introduce goldfish into ponds and wants to know how much shade they will need. She decides to determine the linear relationship, if any, between water temperature and oxygen concentration, an important factor for goldfish survival. She chooses, at random, six ponds and measures both temperature (°C) and oxygen concentration (ml per liter of water). Her measurements, listed by ponds, are: (4.5°C; 9.2 ml), (9.3°C; 8.1 ml), (36.6°C; 5.8 ml), (24.0°C; 5.0 ml), (15.8°C; 7.2 ml), (30.1°C; 5.1 ml). What is the sample correlation coefficient for these two variables?

Ans. $r^* = -0.883$

19.63 An aerodynamics engineer supervises the design of model airplanes and wants to know the relationship between the weight of a plane and its flight velocity in still air. He samples, at random, six model planes and records the weight (in kg) and maximum flight velocity (in meters per second) for each plane. His results, listed by plane, are: (0.035 kg; 10.7 m/sec), (0.780 kg; 9.9 m/sec), (0.093 kg; 8.0 m/sec), (0.322 kg; 13.0 m/sec), (0.275 kg; 11.0 m/sec), (0.073 kg; 13.5 m/sec). What is the sample correlation coefficient for these two variables?

Ans. $r^* = -0.123$

CONFIDENCE INTERVALS FOR THE POPULATION CORRELATION COEFFICIENT ρ

19.64 For the relationship between precipitation and plant density described in Problem 19.61, what is the 95% confidence interval for the population correlation coefficient?

Ans. (0.179, 0.985)

19.65 For the relationship between temperature and oxygen concentration of ponds described in Problem 19.62, what is the 90% confidence interval for the population correlation coefficient?

Ans. $(-0.981, -0.413)$

19.66 For the relationship between weight and velocity of model planes described in Problem 19.63, what is the 95% confidence interval for the population correlation coefficient?

Ans. $(-0.850, 0.765)$

TESTING HYPOTHESES ABOUT THE CORRELATION COEFFICIENT ρ

19.67 For the relationship between precipitation and plant density described in Problem 19.61, we found that $r^* = 0.865$. Do a two-tailed test, at $\alpha = 0.05$, of H_0: There is no linear relationship between the two variables. Use the table of r values (Table A.11). State whether you accept or reject H_0 and give the approximate probability of getting this sample r.

Ans. Reject H_0 because $r^* > 0.811$, $0.02 < P < 0.05$

19.68 Repeat the test described in Problem 19.67, but this time use a t statistic.

Ans. $t^* = 3.448$, reject H_0 because $t^* > 2.776$, $0.02 < P < 0.05$

19.69 For the relationship between temperature and oxygen concentration of ponds described in Problem 19.62, we found that $r^* = -0.883$. Do a two-tailed test, at $\alpha = 0.05$, of H_0: There is no linear relationship between the two variables. Use the table of r values (Table A.11). State whether you accept or reject H_0 and give the approximate probability of getting this sample r value.

Ans. Reject H_0 because $r^* < -0.811$, $0.01 < P < 0.02$

19.70 Repeat the test described in Problem 19.69, but this time use a t statistic.

Ans. $t^* = -3.762$, reject H_0 because $t^* < -2.776, 0.01 < P < 0.02$

19.71 For the relationship between weight and velocity described in Problem 19.63, we found that $r^* = -0.123$. Do a two-tailed test, at $\alpha = 0.05$, of H_0 : There is no linear relationship between the two variables. Use the table of r values (Table A.11). State whether you accept or reject H_0 and give the approximate probability of getting this sample r value.

Ans. Accept H_0 because $-0.811 < r^* < 0.811, P > 0.10$

19.72 Repeat the test described in Probem 19.71, but this time use a t statistic.

Ans. $t^* = -0.248$, accept H_0 because $-2.776 < t^* < 2.776$, $P > 0.20$

USING THE Z DISTRIBUTION TO TEST THE HYPOTHESIS $\rho = c$

19.73 The study of the relationship between precipitation and plant density described in Problem 19.61 is repeated, this time with a sample of 10. The sample correlation coefficient r^* is 0.300. Do a two-tailed test, at $\alpha = 0.05$, of H_0: The population correlation coefficient is $\rho = 0.865$. Give the value of the test statistic. State whether you accept or reject H_0 and give the probability of getting this z^* given that H_0 is true.

Ans. $z^* = -2.655$, reject H_0 because $z^* < -1.96, P = 0.008$

19.74 The study of the relationship between the temperature and oxygen concentration in ponds described in Problem 19.62 is repeated, this time with a sample of 12. The sample correlation coefficient r^* is -0.640. Do a two-tailed test, at $\alpha = 0.05$, of H_0: The population correlation coefficient is $\rho = -0.883$. Give the value of the test statistic. State whether you accept or reject H_0 and give the probability of getting this z^* given that H_0 is true.

Ans. $z^* = 1.893$, accept H_0 because $-1.96 < z^* < 1.96$, $P = 0.06$

19.75 The study of the relationship between the weight and velocity of model planes described in Problem 19.63 is repeated, this time with a sample of 20. The sample correlation coefficient r^* is 0.248. Do a two-tailed test, at $\alpha = 0.05$, of H_0: The population correlation coefficient is $\rho = -0.123$. Give the value of the test statistic. State whether you accept or reject H_0 and give the probability of getting this z^* given that H_0 is true.

Ans. $z^* = 1.554$, accept H_0 because $-1.96 < z^* < 1.96$, $P = 0.12$

INTERPRETATION OF THE CORRELATION COEFFICIENT r

19.76 Interpret the results of the study described in Problem 19.61 in terms of how much of the variation in precipitation and plant density can be explained by the linear relationship between these two variables.

Ans. 74.8%

19.77 Interpret the results of the study described in Problem 19.62 in terms of how much of the variation in the temperature and oxygen concentration of ponds can be explained by the linear relationship between these two variables.

Ans. 78.0%

19.78 Interpret the results of the study described in Problem 19.63 in terms of how much of the variation in weight and velocity of model airplanes can be explained by the linear relationship between these two variables.

Ans. 1.5%

CHAPTER 20

Nonparametric Techniques

20.1 NONPARAMETRIC VS. PARAMETRIC TECHNIQUES

So far in this book, we have dealt only with parametric techniques, which test hypotheses about population parameters, such as μ and σ^2, and assume that the population being sampled has a particular distribution, such as a normal distribution. In this chapter, we consider *nonparametric techniques*, which test hypotheses about population distributions rather than about population parameters. Some nonparametric techniques are also *distribution-free techniques*, in that they do not require strict assumptions about the distribution of the population being sampled.

20.2 CHI-SQUARE TESTS

Chi-square tests are appropriate for nominal-level measurements (see Section 2.4 of Volume 1), in which the samples are counts of items arranged in categories. College students, for example, can be categorized according to whether they are freshmen, sophomores, juniors, or seniors. If a sample of college students is taken and the number of students in each of the four categories is recorded, then these data are nominal-level measurements that can be analyzed with a chi-square test.

Chi-square tests evaluate whether the observed frequencies in the various categories differ significantly from the frequencies that are expected under a specified set of assumptions. For such a test, we use the *chi-square test statistic*:

$$X^2 = \sum_{i=1}^{k} \frac{(O_i - E_i)^2}{E_i} \tag{20.1}$$

where O_i is the observed number of items in category i and E_i is the expected number of items in category i if the null hypothesis is true. The summation is over all k categories of the data. Note that the test statistic is based on the square of the differences, so that sample values are always positive.

When the observed frequencies are similar to the expected frequencies, then the sampling distribution of the test statistic is approximately a chi-square distribution, which is a family of distributions with the single parameter, degrees of freedom ν (see Section 15.2). For small degrees of freedom ($\nu < 10$), the X^2

distribution is skewed to the right, but as the degrees of freedom increase, the distribution approaches a normal distribution (see Fig. 15-1).

In the chi-square test, the degrees of freedom are set by the number of categories rather than by sample size. Sample size is important, however, in determining how closely the chi-square distribution approximates the sampling distribution of the test statistic: the larger the sample, the closer the approximation. Statistics books vary in their recommendation as to minimum sample size; the most common requirement is that all expected frequencies should be at least 5.

Chi-square tests have the following assumptions: (1) independent sampling (see Section 13.4), (2) mutually exclusive categories (i.e., each item fits one and only one category), and (3) an exhaustive list of categories (i.e., the k categories include all items in the sample). The tests are performed on frequencies; they are not appropriate for percentages or proportions.

The general procedure for a chi-square test is to obtain observed values from a random sample from the population, calculate expected values from the hypothesized distribution of the population, and then use the chi-square statistic [equation (20.1)] to calculate a chi-square value. The greater the differences between observed and expected frequencies, the higher the value of the chi-square statistic. This sample value is then compared with values in the X^2 distribution to determine the probability of obtaining, by chance, a χ^2 value as large as the sample value. Critical values of the chi-square distribution are provided in Table A.7. The null hypothesis is rejected when $\chi^{2*} > \chi^2_{\alpha,\nu}$, where χ^{2*} is the sample value, calculated with equation (20.1), and $\chi^2_{\alpha,\nu}$ is the critical value for the particular level of significance α and degrees of freedom ν.

In the following sections, we present chi-square procedures for testing three types of questions: *goodness-of-fit*, *independence of variables*, and *homogeneity of proportions*. The goodness-of-fit test deals with sample data in the form of two or more categories of a single variable, and the question is: Are the frequencies in the categories of the variable the same as the frequencies that we expect from some predetermined theoretical pattern? The independence of variables test deals with two variables, and the question is: Are the two variables independent of each other? The homogeneity of proportions deals with binomial proportions in more than two populations, and the question is: Are the proportions the same in all the populations?

20.3 CHI-SQUARE TEST FOR GOODNESS-OF-FIT

The *chi-square goodness-of-fit test* evaluates whether the distribution of frequencies within k categories of a single variable is the same as in a theoretical distribution. The term "goodness of fit" refers to how well the observed (sample) frequencies "fit" the expected (theoretical) frequencies. The test statistic is equation (20.1) with degrees of freedom $\nu = k - 1$, where k is the number of categories.

The hypotheses of the goodness-of-fit test are

$$H_0\colon \text{Distribution}_{\text{pop}} = \text{distribution}_{\text{theory}}$$
$$H_1\colon \text{Distribution}_{\text{pop}} \neq \text{distribution}_{\text{theory}}$$

The distribution of chi-square values obtained from samples is a discrete distribution, in that frequencies are whole numbers (i.e., 1, 4, 20), whereas the theoretical chi-square distribution is a continuous distribution. For this reason, the results from chi-square analyses are only approximations to the theoretical distribution. The approximation is good, however, except when there are only two categories of the variable ($\nu = k - 1 = 2 - 1 = 1$). For such two-category tests, most statistics books recommend the *Yates correction for continuity*:

$$X^2 = \sum_{i=1}^{k} \frac{(|O_i - E_i| - 0.5)^2}{E_i} \tag{20.2}$$

in which the absolute value of each deviation of the observed value minus the expected value is reduced by 0.5.

EXAMPLE 20.1 A specialists in college education wants know whether the undergraduates in small, private colleges form a uniform distribution, with equal numbers of students in each of the four classes: freshman, sophomore, junior, and senior. He samples, at random, 4500 undergraduates from such colleges and finds: 1,200 freshmen, 1,100 sophomores, 1,150 juniors, and 1,050 seniors. Do a chi-square goodness-of-fit test at $\alpha = 0.05$, using a critical-value decision rule, of H_0: The frequencies of students in the four classes form a uniform distribution.

Solution

(1) H_0: The frequencies of students in the four classes form a uniform distribution.
H_1: The frequencies of students in the four classes do not form a uniform distribution.

(2) $\alpha = 0.05$

(3) The critical value for this goodness-of-fit test is found in Table A.7. For $\alpha = 0.05$ and $\nu = 4 - 1 = 3$, we find that $\chi^2_{0.05,3} = 7.81$. The decision rule is: Reject H_0 if $\chi^{2*} > 7.81$.

(4) The test statistic is calculated with equation (20.1), for which we need the observed frequencies and the expected frequencies. The observed frequencies are: 1,200, 1,100, 1,150, and 1,050. The expected frequencies, if the distribution is uniform, are the same for all four categories: the total sample size divided by the number of categories: (1/4)(4,500) = 1,125. The sample value of the test statistic is

$$\chi^{2*} = \frac{(1{,}200 - 1{,}125)^2}{1{,}125} + \frac{(1{,}100 - 1{,}125)^2}{1{,}125} + \frac{(1{,}150 - 1{,}125)^2}{1{,}125} + \frac{(1{,}050 - 1{,}125)^2}{1{,}125} = 11.111$$

From Table A.7, we find that the approximate probability of getting this value for this distribution is: $0.010 < P < 0.025$.

(5) As $\chi^{2*} > 7.81$, we reject H_0 and accept H_1. This result is confirmed by the fact that the probability of getting a chi-square value of 11.11 (when the distribution is uniform) is less than 0.05. The distribution of students across the four undergraduate classes is not a uniform distribution.

20.4 CHI-SQUARE TEST FOR INDEPENDENCE: CONTINGENCY TABLE ANALYSIS

A *contingency table analysis* evaluates whether two variables, measured on a nominal level, are independent of one another or whether one variable is dependent (i.e., contingent) upon the other. The categories of one variable are arranged in columns and the categories of the other variable in rows. The intersection of a row and a column is called a cell, and the size of a contingency table is indicated as $r \times c$, where r denotes the number of rows and c denotes the number of columns. Consider a contingency table that evaluates whether the level of college education (four categories in rows: freshman, sophomore, junior, or senior) influences the grade (five categories in columns: A, B, C, D, or F) in a chemistry course. This particular table would be a 4×5 contingency table. The hypotheses tested by a contingency table are

H_0: The two variables are independent of one another.
H_1: The two variables are not independent of one another.

A contingency table presents observed and expected frequencies for the joint occurrence of categories within the two variables. The observed frequencies come from the data in the sample. The expected frequencies are obtained from the *marginal frequencies*, which are the row totals and the column totals. To find the expected frequencies, we calculate

$$E_{ij} = \frac{(\text{row}_i \text{ total})(\text{column}_j \text{ total})}{n} \tag{20.3}$$

where E_{ij} is the expected frequency for the cell in row i and column j, and n is the total sample size.

The observed and expected frequencies are typically presented within the same contingency table, in which each cell of the table has two values: observed frequency and expected frequency. The expected frequency is usually enclosed within a parenthesis.

Once the contingency table has been constructed, the observed and expected frequencies are compared using the chi-square test statistic [equation (20.1)] with a double subscript to indicate the particular categories of both variables:

$$X^2 = \sum \frac{(O_{ij} - E_{ij})^2}{E_{ij}} \tag{20.4}$$

where O_{ij} is the observed frequency and E_{ij} is the expected frequency for the cell in row i and column j. The summation is over all cells of the table. This test statistic has a sampling distribution that is approximately a chi-square distribution with degrees of freedom $v = (r - 1)(c - 1)$, where r is the number of rows and c is the number of columns in the contingency table. The sample value of χ^2, obtained with equation (20.4), is then compared with the critical value for $\chi^2_{\alpha,v}$ in a chi-square table (Table A.7). Since we are interested only in whether the sample value is larger than expected by chance, the null hypothesis is rejected when the sample value (χ^{2*}) exceeds the tabulated value ($\chi^2_{\alpha,v}$).

As with the goodness-of-fit test, the chi-square statistic tends to overestimate the association between the two variables when $v = 1$, which occurs in a 2×2 table. A more conservative estimate can be obtained through use of the Yates correction for continuity, in which the absolute value of the difference between O_i and E_i in each cell is reduced by 0.5 [see equation (20.2)].

EXAMPLE 20.2 A college professor wants to know whether level of college education influences the grade earned by students in his philosophy course. Last semester, 400 students completed his class: 150 freshmen, 100 sophomores, 100 juniors, and 50 seniors. At the end of the semester, 80 students earned an A, 148 earned a B, and 172 earned a C. The distribution of grades is shown in Table 20.1. Do a chi-square test, at $\alpha = 0.05$, using a critical-value decision rule, of H_0: The letter grades of the students are independent of the level of college education.

Table 20.1

	Freshmen	Sophomores	Juniors	Seniors	Total
A	25	12	25	18	80
B	47	31	50	20	148
C	78	57	25	12	172
Total	150	100	100	50	400

Solution

(1) H_0: The letter grades are independent of level of college education.
H_1: The letter grades are not independent of level of college education.

(2) $\alpha = 0.05$

(3) We use the chi-square distribution to find the critical value for this test. In Table A.7, with $\alpha = 0.05$ and degrees of freedom $v = (c - 1)(r - 1) = (4 - 1)(3 - 1) = 6$, we find that $\chi^2_{0.05,6} = 12.59$. The decision rule is: Reject H_0 if $\chi^{2*} > 12.59$.

(4) For this test, we use the test statistic for a contingency table [equation (20.4)], for which we need observed and expected frequencies for each cell of the contingency table. Observed frequencies are the sample values (see Table 20.1) and expected frequencies are calculated using equation (20.3). Thus, for example, the expected number of freshmen earning As if level of college education has no influence on grade is

$$\text{Expected number of freshmen earning As} = \frac{\text{(total number of freshmen)(total number of As)}}{\text{total number of students in sample}}$$

$$= \frac{(150)(80)}{400} = 30$$

The observed and expected frequencies are shown in Table 20.2. Each cell contains two numbers, the upper number is the observed frequency and the lower number, in parentheses, is the expected frequency if the two variables are independent. Using these values in equation (20.4),

$$\chi^{2*} = \frac{(25-30.0)^2}{30.0} + \frac{(12-20.0)^2}{20.0} + \frac{(25-20.0)^2}{20.0} + \frac{(18-10.0)^2}{10.0} + \frac{(47-55.5)^2}{55.5} + \frac{(31-37.0)^2}{37.0}$$
$$+ \frac{(50-37.0)^2}{37.0} + \frac{(20-18.5)^2}{18.5} + \frac{(78-64.5)^2}{64.5} + \frac{(57-43.0)^2}{43.0} + \frac{(25-43)^2}{43} + \frac{(12-21.5)^2}{21.5}$$
$$= 37.764$$

Table 20.2

	Freshmen	Sophomores	Juniors	Seniors
A	25	12	25	18
	(30.0)	(20.0)	(20.0)	(10.0)
B	47	31	50	20
	(55.5)	(37.0)	(37.0)	(18.5)
C	78	57	25	12
	(64.5)	(43.0)	(43.0)	(21.5)

From Table A.7, we find that the approximate probability of getting this chi-square value for this distribution is: $P < 0.005$.

(5) Because $\chi^{2*} > 12.59$, we reject H_0 and accept H_1. This result is confirmed by the fact that the probability of getting a chi-square value of 37.76 (given that the null hypothesis is true) is less than 0.05. The level of college education and the grade in the philosophy class are not independent of each other.

20.5 CHI-SQUARE TEST FOR HOMOGENEITY AMONG k BINOMIAL PROPORTIONS

The chi-square statistic for testing independence (see Section 20.4) can be used to test the hypothesis that the binomial proportions of k populations are the same (i.e., homogenous). [Recall from Sections 11.2 and 11.3 that a binomial trial has just two possible outcomes, success or failure, and a binomial proportion is the proportion of success outcomes (or failure outcomes) in a series of trials.] In Section 17.26, we tested for homogeneity (equality) of two population proportions, using this two-tailed pair of hypotheses:

$$H_0: p_1 = p_2$$
$$H_1: p_1 \neq p_2$$

The *chi-square test for homogeneity among k proportions* extends this two-sample test to include more than two populations. The hypotheses of this test are

$$H_0: p_1 = p_2 = p_3 = \cdots = p_k$$
$$H_1: \text{Not all } p \text{ are equal.}$$

If H_0 is rejected, then at least one of the populations is different, with regard to this proportion, from the others.

This test for homogeneity involves k independent samples from k populations. While the null hypothesis is about proportions, the sample data are left in the form of frequencies rather than converted to proportions. The first step is to arrange the frequencies in a table, with two rows (success and failure) and k columns. The test is then carried out in exactly the same manner as a contingency-table analysis. The expected cell frequencies are calculated, using equation (20.3), for the condition that the null hypothesis is true. These expected frequencies are then compared with the observed frequencies by means of the chi-square test statistic [equation (20.4)]. Finally, the sample chi-square value (χ^{2*}) is compared with the critical value in a table of the chi-square values (Table A.7) for the particular level of significance (α) and degrees of freedom [$v = (r-1)(c-1) = (2-1)(k-1) = k-1$]. The null hypothesis is rejected when the sample value is greater than the critical value.

EXAMPLE 20.3 A marine biologist is studying a species of tide-pool fish, and wants to know whether the proportion of males varies among the pools. She chooses, at random, four pools and counts the number of males and females in each pool. Her results are shown in Table 20.3. Do a chi-square test at $\alpha = 0.05$, using a critical-value decision rule, of H_0: The proportion of males is the same in all four pools.

Table 20.3

	Pool 1	Pool 2	Pool 3	Pool 4	Total
Males	59	68	47	56	230
Females	68	60	55	67	250
Total	127	128	102	123	480

Solution

(1) H_0: $p_1 = p_2 = p_3 = p_4$
H_1: p_1, p_2, p_3, and p_4 are not all equal.

(2) $\alpha = 0.05$

(3) From Table A.7, for $v = k - 1 = 3$: $\chi^2_{0.05,3} = 7.81$. The decision rule is: Reject H_0 if $\chi^{2*} > 7.81$.

(4) We use the test statistic described by equation (20.4) , for which we need both observed and expected frequencies. The observed frequencies are the sample values, shown in Table 20.3. The expected values are calculated with equation (20.3). Both sets of frequencies are shown in Table 20.4, where the expected values are shown in parentheses below the observed values. Inserting these values into equation (20.4)

$$\chi^{2*} = \frac{(59-60.854)^2}{60.854} + \frac{(68-61.333)^2}{61.333} + \frac{(47-48.875)^2}{48.875} + \frac{(56-58.938)^2}{58.938} + \frac{(68-66.146)^2}{66.146}$$
$$+ \frac{(60-66.667)^2}{66.667} + \frac{(55-53.125)^2}{53.125} + \frac{(67-64.062)^2}{64.062}$$
$$= 1.919$$

From Table A.7, we find the approximate probability of getting this value is $0.500 < P < 0.900$.

Table 20.4

	Pool 1	Pool 2	Pool 3	Pool 4
Males	59	68	47	56
	(60.854)	(61.333)	(48.875)	(58.938)
Females	68	60	55	67
	(66.146)	(66.667)	(53.125)	(64.062)

(5) Because $\chi^{2*} < 7.81$, we accept H_0. This result is confirmed by the fact that the probability of getting a chi-square value of 1.92 (given that the null hypothesis is true) is greater than 0.05. The proportion of males does not vary among the four tide pools.

20.6 RANK-ORDER TESTS

Rank-order tests require no strong assumptions about the distribution of the population being sampled. They are used only when parametric techniques are inappropriate, because they are less powerful and do not take advantage of all the information in the samples. Rank-order statistics are not, however, without assumptions. All the techniques described in the following sections have two assumptions. The first assumption is independent sampling (see Section 13.4). Some of the rank-order techniques assume independence of observations, while others assume independence of pairs of observations or of differences between observations. The second assumption is that the population being sampled has a continuous distribution, even when the sample is described by a discrete measure. With a continuous distribution, no two observations are equal, which means that there will be no ties among the ranks of the observations, or where differences between observations are tested, that there will be no differences with a value of zero. In real samples, however, tied ranks or zero differences do occur, and how these ties are handled is described for each technique.

The rank-order tests described in the following sections are used for ordinal-level measurements (see Section 2.5 in Volume 1), in which the observations can be ranked with respect to the degree to which they possess a certain characteristic. Ordinal-level measurements may be rank-order information about magnitudes (e.g., intensity of flavor); they may be sign information about the magnitude of direction (plus or minus) with regard to a standard; or they may be categorical information, involving verbal categories rather than magnitude.

All the techniques described in the following sections are based on ranks. Ranking of the observations can be done by visual inspection (for small samples) or by a hand-held calculator. Large data sets with many ties are typically ranked by computer programs.

20.7 ONE-SAMPLE TESTS: THE WILCOXON SIGNED-RANK TEST

One-sample, rank-order tests of central tendency determine whether the population median is equal to a hypothesized value (H_0: $\tilde{\mu} = \tilde{\mu}_0$). They are based on the definition of the median: if the median is as hypothesized, then half the sample values will be above and half will be below the hypothesized value. The test statistic then operates on the *difference scores*, which are obtained by subtracting the hypothesized median from the observed values.

There are two kinds of one-sample tests: sign tests and signed-rank tests. Sign tests assume only that the underlying distribution of the population of difference scores is continuous. They evaluate the number of positive difference scores (i.e., the observations are larger than the hypothesized median) as compared with the number of negative scores in the sample. Signed-rank tests assume that the underlying distribution of the population of difference scores is both continuous and symmetric about the median. They evaluate not only the signs of the difference scores, but their magnitude (expressed as ranks) as well. Here we describe the *Wilcoxon one-sample signed-rank test*, which is a nonparameteric alternative to the one-sample t test (see Section 16.19). The Wilcoxon signed-rank test has different procedures for small samples and large samples.

For small samples ($n < 30$), the Wilcoxon signed-rank procedure is to take a random sample and then subtract the null's hypothesized median from each observed value. The absolute values of these difference scores are assigned ranks from 1 to n, with the smallest difference assigned the rank of 1 and the largest assigned the rank of n. Where two difference scores are tied, the ranks are averaged (e.g., two difference scores both ranked 4th would each receive a rank of $4\frac{1}{2}$, which is the average of 4 and 5). Next, the sign (positive or negative) of the original difference score is restored to its corresponding rank. The positive ranks are summed to get W_+ and the negative ranks are summed to get W_-. If the null hypothesis is true, then each rank is just as likely to be assigned a positive sign as a negative sign, and the absolute value of W_+ will be approximately equal to the absolute value of W_-.

The test statistic has several versions. It may be the sum of the positive ranks (W_+), the sum of the negative ranks (W_-), the sum of all the signed ranks, or the smaller of the two sums. The test statistic W that we use here is the absolute value of either W_+ or W_-, whichever is smaller. If the null hypothesis is not true, then the smaller of the two values will be smaller than expected under conditions of the null's hypothesized value. The distribution of this test statistic W has been calculated and the critical values for various levels of significance α and sample size n are provided in Table A.12 of the Appendix (*Critical Values of the Wilcoxon W*). When the test statistic W is below the critical value, it is too small to have occurred by chance and the null hypothesis should be rejected.

EXAMPLE 20.4 A movie critic evaluates movies on a scale from 1 (worst) to 10 (best). After 20 years of experience, his median score is 6.3. He decides to retire and the manager of the newspaper hires a replacement. After one month of work, the replacement critic has seen 10 movies and has ranked them as follows: 3.8, 5.6, 1.8, 5.0, 2.4, 4.2, 7.3, 8.6, 9.1, and 5.2. The manager of the newspaper wants to know whether the ratings of the new critic are different from those of the previous critic. Do a two-tailed Wilcoxon signed-rank test at $\alpha = 0.05$, using a critical-value decision rule, of H_0: The median rank of the new critic is the same as of the previous critic.

Solution

(1) H_0: $\tilde{\mu} = 6.3$, H_1: $\tilde{\mu} \neq 6.3$

(2) $\alpha = 0.05$

(3) We use the W statistic and the critical value presented for a two-tailed test, with $\alpha = 0.05$ and $n = 10$. In Table A.12, we find the critical value for such a test is 8. Our decision rule is: Reject H_0 if $W < 8$.

(4) The value of W is calculated by subtracting the null's hypothesized median (6.3) from each observed value, ranking the absolute differences, and then restoring the $+$ or $-$ sign to each rank. These calculations are shown in Table 20.5. The sum of the positive signs, W_+, is 16 and the sum of the negative signs, W_-, is 39. The test statistic W is 16, the smaller of the two absolute values. From Table A.12, we find that the approximate probability of getting a value of 16 is $P > 0.10$.

Table 20.5

Observed minus $\tilde{\mu}_0$	Absolute difference	Rank	Signed rank
$3.8 - 6.3 = -2.5$	2.5	7	-7
$5.6 - 6.3 = -0.7$	0.7	1	-1
$1.8 - 6.3 = -4.5$	4.5	10	-10
$5.0 - 6.3 = -1.3$	1.3	4	-4
$2.4 - 6.3 = -3.9$	3.9	9	-9
$4.2 - 6.3 = -2.1$	2.1	5	-5
$7.3 - 6.3 = +1.0$	1.0	2	$+2$
$8.6 - 6.3 = +2.3$	2.3	6	$+6$
$9.1 - 6.3 = +2.8$	2.8	8	$+8$
$5.2 - 6.3 = -1.1$	1.1	3	-3
			$\lvert W_+ \rvert = 16$
			$\lvert W_- \rvert = 39$

(5) As $W > 8$, we accept H_0. This result is confirmed by the fact that the probability of getting a value of 16 (given that the null is true) is greater than 0.05. The ratings of the new movie critic are not significantly different from the ratings of the previous critic.

For large samples ($n \geq 30$), the distribution of the W statistic is approximately a normal distribution. The value of W is obtained in the same way as for the sample test described above. This W value (either $\lvert W_+ \rvert$ or $\lvert W_- \rvert$, whichever is smaller) is then inserted into the following formula for a Z transformation:

$$Z = \frac{W - \dfrac{n(n+1)}{4}}{\sqrt{\dfrac{n(n+1)(2n+1)}{24}}} \tag{20.5}$$

The Wilcoxon test evaluates whether the smaller of the two sums of ranks is smaller than expected under the null. Therefore, the decision rule is to reject H_0 when $z^* < -z_\alpha$ for a one-tailed test or $z^* < -z_{\alpha/2}$ for a two-tailed test. These critical values are obtained from Table A.7. The use of this table was described in Section 12.8.

EXAMPLE 20.5 A history teacher teaches a large lecture class of more than 200 students, and the median score of all the students over the past several years is 71.5 points. This year, he taught a smaller course of just 35 students and wants to know whether the median for this smaller class is higher than for the larger class. The absolute values of the sums of signed ranks for the scores of the 35 students are $|W_+| = 420$ and $|W_-| = 210$. Do a one-tailed Wilcoxon test at $\alpha = 0.05$, using a critical-value decision rule, of H_0: The median for the small class is the same as for the large class, and H_1: The median for the small class is higher than the median for the large class.

Solution

(1) H_0: $\tilde{\mu} = 71.5$, H_1: $\tilde{\mu} > 71.5$

(2) $\alpha = 0.05$

(3) As $n > 30$, we use the W statistic in the Z transformation to obtain z^*, the sample value of Z for these data. In Table A.5, we find that the critical value for a one-tailed test is $z_{0.05} = 1.645$. The decision rule is: Reject H_0 if $z^* < -1.645$.

(4) We know that W is 210, because it is the smaller absolute value of the two sums of ranks. We calculate z^* by inserting $W = 210$ and $n = 35$ into equation (20.5):

$$z^* = \frac{210 - \dfrac{35(35+1)}{4}}{\sqrt{\dfrac{35(35+1)[2(35)+1]}{24}}} = -1.7198, \quad \text{or } -1.72$$

To determine the P value, we use equation (16.5): $P = P[Z \leq (z^* = -a)|H_0 \text{ is true}]$. From Table A.5, we find that the area above the interval $0 \leq z \leq 1.72$ is 0.4573. Since the area to the right of zero is 0.5,

$$P = P(Z > 1.72) = 0.5 - 0.4573 = 0.0427$$

Because of the symmetry of the Z distribution, this result tells us that

$$P(Z < -1.72) = 0.5 - 0.4573 = 0.0427, \quad \text{or } 0.043$$

(5) As $z^* < -1.645$, we reject H_0 and accept H_1. This result is confirmed by the fact that the P value is less than 0.05. The students in the smaller course earned better scores than the students in the larger course.

20.8 TWO-SAMPLE TESTS: THE WILCOXON SIGNED-RANK TEST FOR DEPENDENT SAMPLES

Two-sample, rank-order tests for dependent samples evaluate differences between paired samples, in which the observations are taken in pairs (see Section 17.1). These tests are the same as the one-sample tests, except that the differences are between the medians of the two samples rather than between the sample median and the hypothesized median. The null hypothesis is that there is no difference between the medians of the two sampled populations. The *Wilcoxon paired-samples signed-rank test* evaluates both the sign and the magnitude (as ranks) of the difference scores. It is a substitute for the two-sample t test for paired samples (see Section 17.12) when the population distributions cannot be assumed to be normal or when the data are ordinal-level rather than interval-level or ratio-level measurements (see Sections 2.6 and 2.7 in Volume 1).

The procedure for the Wilcoxon test is as follows. A sample of n paired observations, all measured on the same scale, is taken and the difference between each pair of observations is calculated. The absolute values of these differences are then ranked from 1 (smallest) to n (largest). When two difference scores have the same value, they are both assigned the average rank. A plus sign is assigned to each rank for which the difference score is greater than zero; a negative sign is assigned to each rank for which the difference score is less than zero. Any difference score equal to zero (i.e., no difference between the matched pair) is deleted from the calculations and the test is carried out on the reduced sample size. Two sums are taken: one of the positive values (W_+) and the other of the negative values (W_-). The sum with the smaller absolute value becomes the test statistic W. Evaluation of this statistic depends on whether the sample is small or large.

For a small sample ($n < 30$), the test statistic W is evaluated by consulting Table A.12, which gives the critical values of W for various levels of significance α and sample size n. For large samples ($n \geq 30$), the value of W is transformed into a Z value and evaluated through use of Table A.5 (see the procedure described for large samples in Section 20.7).

EXAMPLE 20.6 A medical researcher wants to know whether a new exercise regimen has an effect on the pulse rate of women between 75 and 80 years old. She selects, at random, 12 such women and measures their pulse rate both before and after a 2-month period on the regimen. The pulse rates for these women (with the first number the "before" rate and the second number the "after" rate) are: (75, 71); (81, 83); (74, 70); (75, 60); (70, 75); (74, 67); (82, 85); (64, 65); (79, 69); (83, 71); (73, 65); (82, 76). Use a one-tailed Wilcoxon test at $\alpha = 0.05$, using a critical-value decision rule, of H_0: The median pulse rate is the same before and after the regime, and H_1: The median pulse rate is lower after the regimen.

Solution

(1) H_0: $\tilde{\mu}_1 = \tilde{\mu}_2$, H_1: $\tilde{\mu}_1 > \tilde{\mu}_2$

(2) $\alpha = 0.05$

(3) As $n < 30$, we use the small-sample test of the W statistic. From Table A.12, we find that for $n = 12$ in a one-tailed test, $W_{0.05} = 17$. The decision rule is: Reject H_0 if $W < 17$.

(4) The test statistic W is calculated by subtracting the "after" pulse rate from the "before" pulse rate for each paired sample (i.e., each woman). The absolute differences are ranked and then the original sign of the difference is restored to each rank. These calculations are shown in Table 20.6. The test statistic W is 12 because it is the smaller of the two absolute values. From Table A.12, we find that the approximate probability of getting $W = 12$ is $0.010 < P < 0.025$.

Table 20.6

Pulse (before minus after)	Absolute difference	Rank	Signed rank
$75 - 71 = +4$	4	4.5	+4.5
$81 - 83 = -2$	2	2.0	−2.0
$74 - 70 = +4$	4	4.5	+4.5
$75 - 60 = +15$	15	12.0	+12.0
$70 - 75 = -5$	5	6.0	−6.0
$74 - 67 = +7$	7	8.0	+8.0
$82 - 85 = -3$	3	3.0	−3.0
$64 - 65 = -1$	1	1.0	−1.0
$79 - 69 = +10$	10	10.0	+10.0
$83 - 71 = +12$	12	11.0	+11.0
$73 - 65 = +8$	8	9.0	+9.0
$82 - 76 = +6$	6	7.0	+7.0
			$\lvert W_+\rvert = 66.0$
			$\lvert W_-\rvert = 12.0$

(5) As $W < 17$, we reject H_0 and accept H_1. This result is confirmed by the fact that the probability of getting a W value of 12 (given that the null hypothesis is true) is less than 0.05. The median pulse rate after the exercise regimen is lower than before the exercise regimen.

20.9 TWO-SAMPLE TESTS: THE MANN-WHITNEY U TEST FOR INDEPENDENT SAMPLES

The *Mann-Whitney U test* (or the *Wilcoxon-Mann-Whitney test*) is a rank-order, nonparametric test for determining whether two independent samples come from the same population. It is a rank-sums test for ordinal-level measurements that assumes the two samples are independent and come from populations with continuous distributions. The null hypothesis is that the distributions of the two populations, from which the samples were taken, are the same; the alternative hypothesis is that they are not the same or that one is larger than the other (the bulk of one population is larger than the bulk of the other). The Mann-Whitney U test is a substitute for the two-sample t test for independent (i.e., nonpaired) samples (see Section 17.8) when the population distributions cannot be assumed to be normal or when the data are ordinal-level rather than interval-level or ratio-level measurements.

The first step in this test is to combine the scores (observations) from sample 1 (n_1) and sample 2 (n_2), and then to rank the combined list of scores from 1 for the smallest score to $n_1 + n_2$ for the largest score. Tied ranks are given the average of the ranks they would have if they were adjacent but not tied. If the distributions of the two populations are the same, then the ranks of the two samples will be randomly intermixed; if the distributions of the two populations are different, then the ranks of one sample will be higher than the ranks of the other sample. To determine which alternative is true, the ranks assigned to each sample are summed to get R_1 (the sum of ranks for sample 1) and R_2 (the sum of ranks for sample 2). These sums are then used to calculate U values for the two samples:

$$U_1 = n_1 n_2 + \frac{n_1(n_1 + 1)}{2} - R_1 \tag{20.6}$$

$$U_2 = n_1 n_2 + \frac{n_2(n_2 + 1)}{2} - R_2 \tag{20.7}$$

where n_1 is the size of sample 1, n_2 is the size of sample 2, R_1 is the sum of the ranks for sample 1, and R_2 is the sum of the ranks for sample 2. The smaller of these two values, U_1 or U_2, becomes the *Mann-Whitney test statistic U.*

For samples where ($n_1 \leq 20$ and $n_2 \leq 20$, the critical values for rejecting the null hypothesis are provided in Table A.13 of the Appendix (*Critical Values of the Mann-Whitney U*). (This table provides critical values for just two levels of significance for a one-tailed test and two levels for a two-tailed test; other tables can be consulted for additional levels of significance.) The critical value is at the intersection of the column indicated by n_1 (the smaller of the two samples) and the row indicated by n_2 (the larger of the two samples), for a particular level of significance α. (For equal samples, either can be n_1 or n_2.) If the null hypothesis is true, then U_1 will be approximately equal to U_2. If the null hypothesis is false, then the smaller of the two values (the test statistic U) will be smaller than expected under the null.

EXAMPLE 20.7 The dean of a college wants to know whether high-school language teachers and high-school science teachers receive the same salaries after 10 years of experience. He selects, at random, 10 language teachers and gets the following list of salaries: \$35,000, \$30,000, \$45,000, \$42,000, \$50,000, \$52,000, \$25,000, \$38,000, \$40,500, \$41,000. He selects, at random, 13 science teachers and gets the following list of salaries: \$35,500, \$40,000, \$48,000, \$53,000, \$58,000, \$57,000, \$54,000, \$49,000, \$49,500, \$51,000, \$51,500, \$57,500, \$52,500. Do a two-tailed Mann-Whitney U test at $\alpha = 0.05$, using a critical-value decision rule, of H_0: The distributions of the two sets of salaries are the same.

Solution

(1) H_0: The distribution of salaries for language teachers is the same as for science teachers.
H_1: The distribution of salaries for language teachers is not the same as for science teachers.

(2) $\alpha = 0.05$

(3) As $n_1 < 20$ and $n_2 < 20$, we use the small-sample version of the Mann-Whitney U test. From Table A.13 we find that with $n_1 = 10$, $n_2 = 13$, and $\alpha = 0.05$ in a two-tailed test, the decision rule is: Reject H_0 if $U < 33$.

(4) We obtain the test statistic U by using equations (20.6) and (20.7) to calculate U_1 and U_2. To find R_1 and R_2 for these equations, we combine the two samples and rank the combined list of values. The sums of ranks for each sample are R_1 and R_2, as shown in Table 20.7. U_1 then is calculated by inserting $n_1 = 10$, $n_2 = 13$, and $R_1 = 76$ into equation (20.6):

$$U_1 = (10)(13) + \frac{10(10+1)}{2} - 76 = 109$$

U_2 is calculated by inserting $n_1 = 10$, $n_2 = 13$, and $R_2 = 200$ into equation (20.7):

$$U_2 = (10)(13) + \frac{13(13+1)}{2} - 200 = 21$$

The test statistic U is 21, because it is the smaller of the two values.

Table 20.7

Salaries of English teachers	Rank	Salaries of science teachers	Rank
\$35,000	3	\$35,500	4
\$30,000	2	\$40,000	6
\$45,000	10	\$48,000	11
\$42,000	9	\$53,000	19
\$50,000	14	\$58,000	23
\$52,000	17	\$57,000	21
\$25,000	1	\$54,000	20
\$38,000	5	\$49,000	12
\$40,500	7	\$49,500	13
\$41,000	8	\$51,000	15
		\$51,500	16
		\$57,500	22
		\$52,500	18
$n_1 = 10$	$R_1 = 76$	$n_2 = 13$	$R_2 = 200$

(5) As $U < 33$, we reject H_0 and accept H_1. The salaries of language teachers and science teachers, after 10 years of experience, are different.

For larger samples ($n_1 > 20$ or $n_2 > 20$), the distribution of the test statistic U approaches a normal distribution, and so the U value can be transformed into a Z value,

$$Z = \frac{U - \dfrac{n_1 n_2}{2}}{\sqrt{\dfrac{(n_1)(n_2)(n_1 + n_2 + 1)}{12}}} \tag{20.8}$$

where U is the smaller of the two values, U_1 and U_2, n_1 is the size of sample 1, and n_2 is the size of sample 2.

Because the test statistic U is the smaller U of the two samples, the null hypothesis is rejected when the specific value of z is smaller than the critical value in the left tail of the Z distribution ($z^* < -z_\alpha$ for a one-tailed test or $z^* < -z_{\alpha/2}$ for a two-tailed test).

When there are many ties of ranks between the two samples (within-sample ties have no effect on the outcome), the Z statistic should include the correction factor

$$\sum T_i = \sum \frac{t_i^3 - t_i}{12} \tag{20.9}$$

where t is the number of scores tied for a given rank. If, for example, we have two scores of rank 6, three scores of rank 10, and four scores of rank 7, then we have t_i values of 2, 3, and 4. This correction factor is incorporated into the equation for the Z transformation

$$Z = \frac{U - \dfrac{n_1 n_2}{2}}{\sqrt{\left(\dfrac{n_1 n_2}{(n_1+n_2)^2 - (n_1+n_2)}\right)\left(\dfrac{(n_1+n_2)^3 - (n_1+n_2)}{12} - \sum T\right)}} \tag{20.10}$$

The correction factor raises the value of Z by a small amount, which may be important when the sample test statistic is near a critical value.

EXAMPLE 20.8 A town planner wants to know whether the houses in suburb 1 are more expensive than the houses in suburb 2. She samples 30 houses in suburb 1 and 40 houses in suburb 2, ranks the combined samples (no tied ranks), and gets the following R values: $R_1 = 1{,}241$, $R_2 = 1{,}244$. Do a one-tailed Mann-Whitney U test at $\alpha = 0.05$, using a critical-value decision rule, of H_0: Housing costs in suburb 1 are the same as housing costs in suburb 2, and H_1: Housing costs in suburb 1 are higher than in suburb 2.

Solution

(1) H_0: The distribution of housing costs in suburb 1 is the same as in suburb 2.
H_1: The distribution of housing costs in suburb 1 is higher than in suburb 2.

(2) $\alpha = 0.05$

(3) As $n_1 > 20$ and $n_2 > 20$, we use the large-sample version of the Mann-Whitney U test involving the Z transformation. From Table A.5, we find that for this one-tailed test, $z_{0.05} = 1.645$. The decision rule is: Reject H_0 if $z^* < -1.645$.

(4) We obtain the test statistic U by using equations (20.6) and (20.7) to calculate U_1 and U_2. Inserting $n_1 = 30$, $n_2 = 40$, $R_1 = 1{,}241$, and $R_2 = 1{,}244$, we get

$$U_1 = (30)(40) + \frac{30(30+1)}{2} - 1{,}241 = 424$$

and

$$U_2 = (30)(40) + \frac{40(40+1)}{2} - 1{,}244 = 776$$

The value of the test statistic U is 424, because it is the smaller of the two values. There are no ties in the ranks, so we do not apply the correction factor. Inserting $U = 424$, $n_1 = 30$, and $n_2 = 40$ into equation (20.8)

$$z^* = \frac{424 - \dfrac{(30)(40)}{2}}{\sqrt{\dfrac{(30)(40)(30+40+1)}{12}}} = -2.089$$

To determine the P value, we use equation (16.5): $P = P[Z \leq (z^* = -a) | H_0 \text{ is true}]$. From Table A.5, we find that the area above the interval $0 \leq z \leq 2.09 = 0.4817$. Because the area to the right of zero in the distribution is equal to 0.5,

$$P[Z \geq (z^* = a) | H_0 \text{ is true}] = 0.50 - 0.4817 = 0.0183$$

Because the Z distribution is symmetric around zero, it is also true that

$$P[Z \leq (z^* = -a) | H_0 \text{ is true}] = 0.0183$$

(5) As $z^* < -1.645$, we reject H_0 and accept H_1. This result is confirmed by the fact that the P value is less than 0.05. The costs of homes in suburb 1 are higher than in suburb 2.

20.10 MULTISAMPLE TESTS: THE KRUSKAL-WALLIS H TEST FOR k INDEPENDENT SAMPLES

The *Kruskal-Wallis H test* analyzes differences among k populations, where k is greater than 2. This rank-sums form of test is an extension of the two-sample Mann-Whitney U test. In the Kruskal-Wallis H test, as in the analysis of variance F test (see Section 18.12), the independent variable is called the *factor* and the categories of the factor are called *treatments*. Thus, in a study of how different levels of aerobic exercise affect pulse rate, the independent variable, or factor, is aerobic exercise and the treatments are different levels of aerobic exercise. The null hypothesis is that the k independent treatment-samples of sizes $n_1, n_2, \ldots, n_k$ come from the same population or that all sampled populations have the same distribution. The alternative hypothesis is that at least one treatment comes from a population that is different from the others. This rank-order test is a nonparametric substitute for the one-way analysis of variance F test when the population distributions cannot be assumed to be normal or when the data are ordinal-level rather than interval-level or ratio-level measurements.

The first step in the Kruskal-Wallis H test is to combine the observations from the k treatments and to rank the combined list from 1 for the smallest to N for the largest, where N is the total number of observations in all k treatments $\left(N = \sum_{i=1}^{k} n_i\right)$. Tied ranks are given the average of the ranks they would have if they were adjacent but not tied. The rank sum for each treatment, symbolized R_i, is then calculated.

The next step after getting the sums of ranks is to calculate a test statistic that measures the degree to which the sums of ranks differ from what is expected under the null hypothesis. As with the parametric analysis of variance (see Chapter 18), this test statistic is based on the sums of squares. Unlike the parametric analysis, which uses the actual values of observations, the Kruskal-Wallis test statistic H uses the sums of squares of the ranks. We will not derive the test statistic here, but simply state it as

$$H = \frac{12}{N(N+1)} \sum_{i=1}^{k} \left(\frac{R_i^2}{n_i}\right) - 3(N+1) \tag{20.11}$$

where N is the total number of observations, n_i is the number of observations in treatment i, and R_i^2 is the squared sum of the ranks for treatment i.

When more than 35 percent of the scores are tied, the test statistic H should include a correction factor

$$1 - \frac{\sum(t_i^3 - t_i)}{N^3 - N} \tag{20.12}$$

where t_i is the number of observations tied for a given rank i. Incorporating this correction factor into the test statistic H, we get

$$H = \frac{\dfrac{12}{N(N+1)} \sum_{i=1}^{k} \left(\dfrac{R_i^2}{n_i}\right) - 3(N+1)}{1 - \dfrac{\sum(t_i^3 - t_i)}{N^3 - N}} \tag{20.13}$$

The correction factor raises the value of H by a small amount, which may be important when H is near the critical value of a test.

The value of H indicates the distribution of ranks among the k treatments. The larger the value of H, the greater the differences in ranks. The null hypothesis is rejected when the value of H is larger than expected if the treatments came from the same population. Evaluation of the Kruskal-Wallis H depends on the number of treatments and the number of observations within each treatment. For small samples ($n \leq 5$) and just three treatments, the critical values of the H distribution are available in tables of exact probabilities. Table A.14 in the Appendix (*Critical Values of the Kruskal-Wallis H*) is such a table.

EXAMPLE 20.9 A real-estate developer wants to know whether size of town and size of house plots (in acres) are related. She samples four houses from each of three town sizes: small (less than 10,000 residents), medium (between 10,000 and 100,000 residents), and large (more than 100,000) residents). The house plot sizes (in acres) are: for the small town, 5.0, 0.8, 4.0, 4.5; for the medium-sized town, 1.0, 0.5, 3.0, 1.0; and for the large town, 0.25, 0.30, 0.50, 1.40. Do a Kruskal-Wallis H test at $\alpha = 0.05$, using a critical-value decision rule, of H_0: The distributions of house-plot sizes in the three town sizes are the same.

Solution

(1) H_0: The distributions of house-plot size in the three town sizes are the same.
H_1: The distributions of house-plot size in the three town sizes are not the same.

(2) $\alpha = 0.05$

(3) As $k = 3$ and the samples have less than five observations each, we use the small-sample version of the Kruskal-Wallis H test. From Table A.14, we find that with $n_1 = n_2 = n_3 = 4$, $H_{0.05} = 5.692$. The decision rule is: Reject H_0 if $H > 5.692$.

(4) We obtain the test statistic H by calculating R for each treatment. First, we combine the observations of the k treatments and rank the combined list, assigning a value of 1 to the smallest and a value of N to the largest, where $N = n_1 + n_2 + n_3 = 4 + 4 + 4 = 12$, the total number of observations in all treatments. Ties are given their average rank. R_i is then the sum of ranks for each treatment i. These calculations are shown in Table 20.8. As less than 35% of the observations are tied (2 of 12), we do not incorporate the correction for ties. Using equation (20.11) to compute the test statistic H:

$$H = \frac{12}{12(12+1)}\left(\frac{(38)^2}{4} + \frac{(25.5)^2}{4} + \frac{(14.5)^2}{4}\right) - 3(12+1) = 5.3173$$

From Table A.14, we find that the approximate probability of getting this sample value is $0.05 < P < 0.10$.

Table 20.8

Small town		Medium town		Large town	
Plot size (acres)	Rank	Plot size (acres)	Rank	Plot size (acres)	Rank
5.00	12.0	1.00	6.5	0.25	1.0
0.80	5.0	0.50	3.5	0.30	2.0
4.00	10.0	3.00	9.0	0.50	3.5
4.50	11.0	1.00	6.5	1.40	8.0
$n_1 = 4$	$R_1 = 38$	$n_2 = 4$	$R_2 = 25.5$	$n_3 = 4$	$R_3 = 14.5$

(5) As $H < 5.692$, we accept H_0. This result is confirmed by the fact that the approximate probability of getting a sample value of 5.3173 (given that the null is true) is greater than 0.05. The sizes of house plots in the three town sizes are not different.

For larger samples ($n > 5$) or more than three treatments, the sampling distribution of H is approximately a chi-square distribution with $k - 1$ degrees of freedom (where k is the number of treatments). The critical values for chi-square distributions are provided in Table A.7. As with the test for few treatments and few observations, this test determines when H is larger than expected (at a particular level of significance) under the conditions of the null hypothesis.

EXAMPLE 20.10 A college advisor wants to know whether class (freshman, sophomore, junior, and senior) has an effect on the number of hours a student spends in the library. He samples, at random, seven students from each class and records the number of hours that each student spends in the library during one week. The data are: for freshmen, 11.5, 15.0, 12.0, 6.0, 7.0, 9.0, 10.5 hours per week; for sophomores: 11.0, 19.0, 18.0, 14.0, 8.5, 6.5, 5.0 hours per week; for juniors, 12.5, 8.5, 4.0, 13.0, 19.5, 20.0, 10.0 hours per week; and for seniors, 16.0, 10.0, 7.5, 8.0, 17.0, 4.5, 21.0. Do a Kruskal-Wallis test at $\alpha = 0.05$, using a critical-value decision rule, of H_0: The distributions of times spent in the library are the same for all four classes of students.

Solution

(1) H_0: The distributions of times spent in the library are the same for the four classes of students.
H_1: The distributions of times spent in the library are not the same for the four classes of students.

(2) $\alpha = 0.05$

(3) As $k > 3$ and $n > 5$, we use the chi-square distribution to find the critical value. From Table A.7, we find that with $\nu = k - 1 = 4 - 1 = 3$ degrees of freedom, $\chi^2_{0.05,3} = 7.81$. The decision rule is: Reject H_0 if $H > 7.81$.

(4) We obtain the test statistic H by calculating R for each treatment. First, we combine the observations of the four treatments and rank the combined list, assigning a value of 1 to the smallest and a value of N to the largest, where $N = \sum_{i=1}^{k} n_i = 7 + 7 + 7 + 7 = 28$, the total number of observations. Ties are given the average rank. R_i is then the sum of ranks for each treatment i. These calculations are shown in Table 20.9. As there are only four ties (14.3% of the ranks), we do not need to apply the correction factor. Using equation (20.11) to compute the test statistic:

$$H = \frac{12}{28(28+1)}\left(\frac{89.0^2}{7} + \frac{101.5^2}{7} + \frac{113.0^2}{7} + \frac{102.5^2}{7}\right) - 3(28+1) = 0.6112$$

From Table A.7, we find that the approximate probability of getting a χ^2 of 0.6112 is $0.500 < P < 0.900$.

Table 20.9

Freshmen		Sophomores		Juniors		Seniors	
Hours	Rank	Hours	Rank	Hours	Rank	Hours	Rank
11.5	16.0	11.0	15.0	12.5	18.0	16.0	22.0
15.0	21.0	19.0	25.0	8.5	9.5	10.0	12.5
12.0	17.0	18.0	24.0	4.0	1.0	7.5	7.0
6.0	4.0	14.0	20.0	13.0	19.0	8.0	8.0
7.0	6.0	8.5	9.5	19.5	26.0	17.0	23.0
9.0	11.0	6.5	5.0	20.0	27.0	4.5	2.0
10.5	14.0	5.0	3.0	10.0	12.5	21.0	28.0
$n_1 = 7$	$R_1 = 89.0$	$n_2 = 7$	$R_2 = 101.5$	$n_3 = 7$	$R_3 = 113.0$	$n_4 = 7$	$R_4 = 102.5$

(5) As $H < 7.81$, we accept H_0. This result is confirmed by the fact that the probability of getting an H value of 0.6112 is greater than 0.05. The amount of time a student spends in the library is not related to the student's class in college.

20.11 THE SPEARMAN TEST OF RANK CORRELATION

The *Spearman test of rank correlation* is a nonparametric alternative to the Pearson product-moment correlation (see Section 19.13) when the measurements are ordinal-level rather than interval-level or ratio-level. It analyzes the relationship between variable X and variable Y in a sample of n pairs (x_i, y_i) of measurements. The individuals are ranked on each variable, and the degree of correspondence between the paired ranks is determined. Unlike the Pearson test, which evaluates the strength of the linear correlation, the Spearman test evaluates only whether the paired measurements have an *increasing monotonic relationship*, in which one variable increases as the other increases, or a *decreasing monotonic relationship*, in which one variable decreases as the other increases.

The null hypothesis of the Spearman test is that no relationship exists between the two variables. For alternative hypotheses, there are three possibilities: a relationship exists (a two-tailed test), an increasing monotonic relationship exists (a one-tailed test), or a decreasing relationship exists (a one-tailed test).

The first step is to assign ranks, from 1 to n, to the measurements on each variable. Thus, each individual has a rank on the X variable and on the Y variable. Tied ranks are assigned the mean of the ranks they would have received if they were adjacent but not tied. These paired ranks are then used to calculate the test statistic, known as the *Spearman rank coefficient* r_S (or the *Spearman rank order correlation coefficient*, or the *Spearman rho*). The coefficient is positive when the relationship is increasing monotonic (with $+1.00$ indicating a perfect correlation), negative when the relationship is decreasing monotonic (with -1.00 indicating a perfect correlation), and zero when there is no relationship. As with the Pearson coefficient, the square of the Spearman rank coefficient (r_S^2) is a measure of the proportion of the variation in X and Y that is explained by the relationship between the two variables. There are two ways to calculate this test statistic, depending on whether or not there are tied ranks.

Where there are ties among the ranks on the same variable, the Spearman coefficient is calculated by the equation for the Pearson product-moment corrrelation coefficient [equation (19.31)]:

$$r_S = \frac{\sum(x-\bar{x})(y-\bar{y})}{\sqrt{\sum(x-\bar{x})^2 \sum(y-\bar{y})^2}}$$

where for each individual (or item), x is the rank on one variable and y is the rank on the other variable. This is the computational version [equation (19.32)]:

$$r_S = \frac{\sum xy - \dfrac{\sum x \sum y}{n}}{\sqrt{\sum x^2 - \dfrac{(\sum x)^2}{n}}\sqrt{\sum y^2 - \dfrac{(\sum y)^2}{n}}}$$

Where there are no ties among the ranks in either variable, the above equation reduces to a simpler equation:

$$r_S = 1 - \frac{6\sum_{i=1}^{n} d_i^2}{n(n^2-1)} \tag{20.14}$$

where n is the number of paired ranks and d_i is the difference between the two ranks for each pair, obtained by ranking each individual on each variable separately, lowest to highest, and then computing the pairwise differences d between the ranks of x and y. Note that as the paired ranks become more similar, the values of d become smaller, the value of the fraction in the equation approaches zero, and r_S approaches $+1$. Conversely, as the paired ranks become less similar, the values of d become larger, and the fraction moves from a value of 1 (no correlation; $r_S = 0$) to a value of -2, and r_S approaches -1.

When the samples are small ($n < 30$), exact critical values for the sampling distribution of r_S are provided in Table A.15 (*Critical Values of the Spearman* r_S) in the Appendix. The value of n determines the row and the value of α determines the column in the table; the critical value is at the intersection of the row and column. While all the values in this table are positive, the critical values for negative correlations are the same except for sign.

EXAMPLE 20.11 The personnel manager of an insurance company wants to know whether performance in college is a good indicator of performance on the job. She chooses, at random, 12 employees and has their supervisor rank them, from 1 (best) to 12 (worst) on their job performance. She then compares these ranks with their grade points in college, as shown Table 20.10. [Note that for job performance, the highest rank (12) is the worst performance, whereas for grade-point average, the highest rank (12) is the best performance.] Do a one-tailed Spearman test of rank correlation at $\alpha = 0.05$, using a critical-value decision rule, of H_0: Job performance and grade point are not related, and H_1: Job performance and grade point have a decreasing monotonic relationship.

Table 20.10

Employee	Rank: job performance	Grade-point average	Rank: grade-point average	d_i	d_i^2
1	6	2.80	6	0	0
2	4	2.45	3	+1	1
3	2	3.55	11	−9	81
4	9	2.95	7	+2	4
5	12	2.50	4	+8	64
6	10	2.60	5	+5	25
7	5	3.15	9	−4	16
8	3	3.52	10	−7	49
9	1	3.75	12	−11	121
10	8	2.03	1	+7	49
11	7	3.00	8	−1	1
12	11	2.06	2	+9	81

Solution

(1) H_0: Job performance is not related to grade-point average.
H_1: Job performance and grade-point average have a decreasing monotonic relationship.

(2) $\alpha = 0.05$

(3) As the number of paired ranks is less than 30, we use Table A.15 to find the critical value. For $\alpha = 0.05$ and $n = 12$, we find that for this left-tailed test our decision rule is: Reject H_0 if $r_S < -0.503$.

(4) There are no tied ranks, so we use equation (20.14) to calculate the Spearman correlation coefficient. Our first step is to rank the college grade-point averages from 1 (lowest score) to 12 (highest score). The job performances are already ranked, from 1 (best) to 12 (worst). We then subtract the paired ranks for each individual to get values of d_i, and square each difference to get values of d_i^2 for all pairs of ranks from $i = 1$ to $i = 12$. These calculations are shown in Table 20.10. We find that

$$\sum_{i=1}^{12} d_i^2 = 492$$

Inserting into equation (20.14) the value of 492 for $\sum_{i=1}^{n} d_i^2$ and the value of 12 for n,

$$r_S = 1 - \frac{6(492)}{12(12^2 - 1)} = -0.7203$$

From Table A.15, we find that the approximate probability of getting this sample value is: $0.005 < P < 0.010$.

(5) As $r_S < -0.503$, we reject H_0 and accept H_1. This result is confirmed by the fact that the probability of getting a correlation coefficient of $r_S = -0.7203$ (given that the null is true) is less than 0.05. There is a negative correlation between college grade-point average and rank of job performance: the higher the

grade-point average, the better the job performance. The amount of the total variation in these two variables that can be accounted for by their correlation is 51.9%.

When the samples are large ($n \geq 30$), the sampling distribution of r_S is approximately a normal distribution with a standard deviation of $\frac{1}{\sqrt{n-1}}$. Thus, the value of r_S can be transformed into a value of Z:

$$z = \frac{r_S - 0}{\frac{1}{\sqrt{n-1}}} = r_S\sqrt{n-1} \tag{20.15}$$

This Z statistic is approximately distributed as the standard normal distribution, with critical values provided in Table A.5. Two-tailed or one-tailed tests can be done by using critical values with the appropriate $\alpha/2$ or α, respectively.

EXAMPLE 20.12 A college algebra teacher wants to know whether there is a negative relationship between number of times a student is absent from class and performance in the class. At the end of the semester, he ranks each of his 35 students on two variables, assigning a rank of 1 to the student with the most absences and a rank of 1 to the student with the highest class rank. Do a one-tailed Spearman rank correlation test at $\alpha = 0.01$, using a critical-value decision rule, of H_0: There is no relationship between class performance and number of absences, and H_1: Class performance has a decreasing monotonic relationship with number of absences.

Solution

(1) H_0: Class performance and number of absences are not related.
H_1: Class performance and number of absences have a decreasing monotonic relationship.

(2) $\alpha = 0.01$

(3) With more than 30 paired ranks, we use a Z transformation of r_S and the Z distribution to find the critical value. From Table A.5, we find that $z_{0.01} = 2.33$. For this left-tailed test, the decision rule is: Reject H_0 if $z^* < -2.33$.

(4) The teacher ranked the number of absences (variable X) from 1 (most) to 35 (least) and class performance (variable Y) from 1 (best) to 35 (worst). There are tied ranks, so we use the Pearson product-moment correlation coefficient [equation (19.31)] to calculate the Spearman correlation coefficient. Calculations of the required sums are shown in Table 20.11. Inserting these sums into equation (19.32), we get

$$r_S = \frac{10{,}229.5 - \frac{(630)(630)}{35}}{\sqrt{14{,}897 - \frac{630^2}{35}}\sqrt{14{,}910 - \frac{630^2}{35}}} = -0.3116$$

Using equation (20.15) to transform r_S to z^*,

$$z^* = -0.3116\sqrt{35-1} = -1.8169$$

We use equation (16.5), $P = P[Z \leq (z^* = -a)|H_0 \text{ is true}]$, to find the probability of getting this sample value. From Table A.5, we find that the area under the curve between $z = 0$ and $z = 1.82$ is 0.4656. Thus

$$P[Z \geq (z^* = a)|H_0 \text{ is true}] = 0.5000 - 0.4656 = 0.0344$$

As the Z distribution is symmetric about zero, this means that the probability of getting a sample value of $z^* = -1.82$ is also equal to 0.0334.

(5) As $z^* > -2.33$, we accept H_0 at the 0.01 level of significance. This result is confirmed by the fact that the probability of getting this sample value (given that the null hypothesis is true) is greater than 0.01. The ranks of class performance are not related to the ranks of class absences. Moreover, we can say that only 9.7% (-0.3116^2) of the variation in class rank is explained by the rank in number of absences.

Table 20.11

	Absences		Performance		
Student	x_i	x_i^2	y_i	y_i^2	$(x_i)(y_i)$
1	10.5	110.25	25.0	625	262.5
2	17.5	306.25	11.0	121	192.5
3	28.0	784.00	17.0	289	476.0
4	24.0	576.00	18.0	324	432.0
5	9.0	81.00	33.0	1,089	297.0
6	33.5	1,122.25	35.0	1,225	1,172.5
7	2.0	4.00	1.0	1	2.0
8	19.0	361.00	5.0	25	95.0
9	17.5	306.25	22.0	484	385.0
10	1.0	1.00	34.0	1,156	34.0
11	35.0	1,225.00	3.0	9	105.0
12	7.5	56.25	27.0	729	202.5
13	25.0	625.00	12.0	144	300.0
14	10.5	100.25	4.0	16	42.0
15	33.5	1,122.25	10.0	100	335.0
16	3.0	9.00	26.0	676	78.0
17	22.0	484.00	19.0	361	418.0
18	27.0	729.00	13.0	169	351.0
19	7.5	56.25	6.0	36	45.0
20	29.0	841.00	29.0	841	841.0
21	15.5	240.25	28.0	784	434.0
22	20.0	400.00	16.0	256	320.0
23	4.5	20.25	32.0	1,024	144.0
24	12.0	144.00	24.0	576	288.0
25	31.0	961.00	2.0	4	62.0
26	13.0	169.00	23.0	529	299.0
27	32.0	1,024.00	9.0	81	288.0
28	6.0	36.00	30.0	900	180.0
29	30.0	900.00	21.0	441	630.0
30	21.0	441.00	15.0	225	315.0
31	14.0	196.00	7.0	49	98.0
32	4.5	20.25	31.0	961	139.5
33	26.0	676.00	20.0	400	520.0
34	15.5	240.25	8.0	64	124.0
35	23.0	529.00	14.0	196	322.0
$\sum$	630.0	14,897.00	630.0	14,910	10,229.5

Solved Problems

CHI-SQUARE TEST FOR GOODNESS-OF-FIT

20.1 A geneticist wants to know whether flower color in a species of aster is inherited in a simple Mendelian fashion without dominance. If so, then when he crosses two pink-flowered plants, the offspring will occur in a ratio of 1white to 2 pink to 1 red. He does the cross and examines 100 offspring, finding that 21 are white, 61 are pink, and 18 are red. Do a chi-square test at $\alpha = 0.05$, using a critical-value decision rule, of H_0: The distribution of flower colors is a 1 : 2 : 1 ratio.

Solution

(1) H_0: The population distribution is a 1 : 2 : 1 ratio.
H_1: The population distribution is not a 1 : 2 : 1 ratio.

(2) $\alpha = 0.05$

(3) The critical value for this one-tailed test is found in Table A.7. For $\alpha = 0.05$ and degrees of freedom $\nu = k - 1 = 2$, we find that $\chi^2_{0.05,2} = 5.99$. The decision rule is: Reject H_0 if $\chi^{2*} > 5.99$.

(4) We use equation (20.1) to calculate the test statistic. The observed values are: 21, 61, and 18. The expected values for a 1 : 2 : 1 ratio in a sample of 100 are $\frac{1}{4}(100)$, $\frac{1}{2}(100)$, $\frac{1}{4}(100) = 25, 50, 25$. Thus,

$$\chi^{2*} = \frac{(21-25)^2}{25} + \frac{(61-50)^2}{50} + \frac{(18-25)^2}{25} = 5.020$$

From Table A.7, we find that the approximate probability of getting this value is $0.050 < P < 0.100$.

(5) As $\chi^{2*} < 5.99$, we accept H_0. This result is confirmed by the fact that the probability of getting a χ^2 value of 5.02 (given that the null hypothesis is true) is greater than 0.05. The offspring of this cross exhibit a 1 : 2 : 1 ratio.

20.2 A fish geneticist wants to know whether inheritance of lip shape (curved is dominant over straight) and the inheritance of scale shape (flat is dominant over ridged) are controlled by two different gene loci on different chromosomes. If so, then offspring of two heterozygous fish (each with two versions of the gene for lip shape and two versions of the gene for scale shape) will occur in a 9 : 3 : 3 : 1 ratio. She does the cross and examines 160 offspring, finding that 72 have curved lips and flat scales, 38 have curved lips and ridged scales, 32 have straight lips and flat scales, and 18 have straight lips and ridged scales. Do a chi-square test at $\alpha = 0.05$, using a critical-value decision rule, of H_0: The distribution of traits is a 9 : 3 : 3 : 1 ratio.

Solution

(1) H_0: The population distribution is a 9 : 3 : 3 : 1 ratio.
H_1: The population distribution is not a 9 : 3 : 3 : 1 ratio.

(2) $\alpha = 0.05$

(3) The critical value for this chi-square test is found in Table A.7. For $\alpha = 0.05$ and degrees of freedom $\nu = k - 1 = 3$, we find that $\chi^2_{0.05,3} = 7.81$. The decision rule is: Reject H_0 if $\chi^{2*} > 7.81$.

(4) We use equation (20.1) to calculate the test statistic. The observed values are: 72, 38, 32, 18. With a sample size of 160, the expected values are 9/16(160), 3/16(160), 3/16(160), 1/16(160) = 90, 30, 30, 10. Thus,

$$\chi^{2*} = \frac{(72-90)^2}{90} + \frac{(38-30)^2}{30} + \frac{(32-30)^2}{30} + \frac{(18-10)^2}{10} = 12.267$$

From Table A.7, we find that the approximate probability of getting this sample value is $0.005 < P < 0.010$.

(5) As $\chi^{2*} > 7.81$, we reject H_0 and accept H_1. This result is confirmed by the fact that the probability of getting a chi-square value of 12.27 (given that the null hypothesis is true) is less than 0.05. The offspring of this test do not exhibit a 9 : 3 : 3 : 1 ratio.

20.3 A history professor teaches a large lecture class on Monday through Friday, and wants to know whether class attendance is the same for every day of the week. He counts the number of students attending class each day of the week and finds: 283 attended on Monday, 332 on Tuesday, 360 on Wednesday, 307 on Thursday, and 243 on Friday. Do a chi-square test at $\alpha = 0.05$, using a critical-value decision rule, of H_0: The distribution of attendances is a uniform distribution (i.e., the same for each of the five days).

Solution

(1) H_0: The population distribution is a uniform distribution.
H_1: The population distribution is not a uniform distribution.

(2) $\alpha = 0.05$

(3) The critical value for this chi-square test is found in Table A.7. For $\alpha = 0.05$ and degrees of freedom $\nu = k - 1 = 4$, we find that $\chi^2_{0.05,4} = 9.49$. The decision rule is: Reject H_0 if $\chi^{2*} > 9.49$.

(4) We use equation (20.1) to calculate the test statistic. The observed values are: 283, 332, 360, 307, and 243. The expected value (for a uniform distribution) is the average attendance:

$$E_i = \frac{283 + 332 + 360 + 307 + 243}{5} = 305$$

Thus,

$$\chi^{2*} = \frac{(283 - 305)^2}{305} + \frac{(332 - 305)^2}{305} + \frac{(360 - 305)^2}{305} + \frac{(307 - 305)^2}{305} + \frac{(243 - 305)^2}{305} = 26.511$$

From Table A.7, we find that the approximate probability of getting this sample value is $P < 0.005$.

(5) As $\chi^{2*} > 9.49$, we reject H_0 and accept H_1. This result is confirmed by the fact that the probability of getting a χ^2 value of 26.511 (given that the null hypothesis is true) is less than 0.05. The distribution of attendances over the five days is not a uniform distribution.

CHI-SQUARE TEST FOR INDEPENDENCE : CONTINGENCY TABLE ANALYSIS

20.4 The manager of a chain of restaurants wants to know whether customer satisfaction is related to the salary of a waitperson. She takes a random sample of 100 customers, asking the name of the waitperson and whether the service was excellent, good, or poor. She then categorizes the salaries of the waitpersons as low, medium, or high. Her results are shown, as frequencies not within parentheses, in Table 20.12. Do a chi-square test at $\alpha = 0.05$, using a critical-value decision rule, of H_0: The quality of service is independent of the waitperson's salary.

Solution

(1) H_0: The quality of service is independent of salary of waitperson.
H_1: The quality of service is not independent of salary of waitperson.

(2) $\alpha = 0.05$

(3) We use the chi-square distribution, with degrees of freedom $\nu = (c - 1)(r - 1)$, where c (number of columns) = 3 and r (number of rows) = 3, to find the critical value. In Table A.7, for $\alpha = 0.05$ and $\nu = 4$, we find that $\chi^2_{0.05,4} = 9.49$. The decision rule is: Reject H_0 if $\chi^{2*} > 9.49$.

(4) The test statistic is equation (20.4). The expected frequencies, computed with equation (20.3), are shown in parentheses in Table 20.12. Inserting the observed and expected frequencies into equation (20.4),

Table 20.12

	Low salary	Medium salary	High salary	Total
Excellent service	9	10	7	26
	(8.32)	(7.02)	(10.66)	
Good service	11	9	31	51
	(16.32)	(13.77)	(20.91)	
Poor service	12	8	3	23
	(7.36)	(6.21)	(9.43)	
Total	32	27	41	100

we get

$$\begin{aligned}\chi^{2*} &= \frac{(9-8.32)^2}{8.32} + \frac{(10-7.02)^2}{7.02} + \frac{(7-10.66)^2}{10.66} + \frac{(11-16.32)^2}{16.32} + \frac{(9-13.77)^2}{13.77} \\ &\quad + \frac{(31-20.91)^2}{20.91} + \frac{(12-7.36)^2}{7.36} + \frac{(8-6.21)^2}{6.21} + \frac{(3-9.43)^2}{9.43} \\ &= 18.658\end{aligned}$$

From Table A.7, we find that the approximate probability of getting this sample value is $P < 0.005$.

(5) Because $\chi^{2*} > 9.49$, we reject H_0 and accept H_1. This result is confirmed by the fact that the probability of getting a chi-square value of 18.66 (given that the null is true) is less than 0.05. Customer satisfaction is not independent of salary of waitperson.

20.5 A car manufacturer wants to know whether the buyer's age influences the color of car purchased. For 500 buyers, selected at random, he records age of the buyer and color of the car purchased (blue, red, white, or black). He places the ages in three categories: young (under 30), middle (30 to 50), and old (over 50). His results are shown, as numbers not within parentheses, in Table 20.13. Do a chi-square test at $\alpha = 0.05$, using a critical-value decision rule, of H_0: The color of the car purchased is independent of the age of the buyer.

Table 20.13

	Blue	Red	White	Black	Total
Young	73	32	74	21	200
	(72.0)	(24.0)	(76.0)	(28.0)	
Middle-aged	59	16	65	20	160
	(57.6)	(19.2)	(60.8)	(22.4)	
Old	48	12	51	29	140
	(50.4)	(16.8)	(53.2)	(19.6)	
Total	180	60	190	70	500

Solution

(1) H_0: The color of the car purchased is independent of age of the buyer.
H_1: The color of the car purchased is not independent of age of the buyer.

(2) $\alpha = 0.05$

(3) We use the chi-square distribution, with degrees of freedom $v = (c - 1)(r - 1) = (4 - 1)(3 - 1) = 6$, to find the critical value. In Table A.7, we find that $\chi^2_{0.05,6} = 12.59$. The decision rule is: Reject H_0 if $\chi^{2*} > 12.59$.

(4) The test statistic is equation (20.4). The expected frequencies, computed with equation (20.3), are shown in parentheses in Table 20.13. Using the observed and expected frequencies in equation (20.4),

$$\begin{aligned}\chi^{2*} &= \frac{(73-72.0)^2}{72.0} + \frac{(32-24.0)^2}{24.0} + \frac{(74-76.0)^2}{76.0} + \frac{(21-28.0)^2}{28.0} + \frac{(59-57.6)^2}{57.6} \\ &+ \frac{(16-19.2)^2}{19.2} + \frac{(65-60.8)^2}{60.8} + \frac{(20-22.4)^2}{22.4} + \frac{(48-50.4)^2}{50.4} + \frac{(12-16.8)^2}{16.8} \\ &+ \frac{(51-53.2)^2}{53.2} + \frac{(29-19.6)^2}{19.6} \\ &= 11.683\end{aligned}$$

From Table A.7, we find that the approximate probability of getting this χ^{2*} is $0.050 < P < 0.100$.

(5) Because $\chi^{2*} < 12.59$, we accept H_0. This result is confirmed the the fact that the probability of getting a chi-square value of 11.68 (given that the null is true) is greater than 0.05. Age of the buyer and color of the car purchased are independent variables.

20.6 The manager of an insurance company wants to know whether the frequency of car accidents is related to the distance that a person travels to work. She accumulates information for the past 10 years on 200 customers, categorizing the frequency of car accidents in a 10-year period as: less than 5, between 5 and 10, and more than 10. She categorizes the one-way distance travelled to work as: less than 10 miles, between 10 and 20 miles, and more than 20 miles. Her results are shown, as numbers not within parentheses, in Table 20.14. Do a chi-square test at $\alpha = 0.01$, using a critical-value decision rule, of H_0: The frequency of accidents is independent of the distance travelled to work.

Table 20.14

	<5 accidents	5–10 accidents	>10 accidents	Total
<10 miles	42	31	30	103
	(47.895)	(31.415)	(23.690)	
10–20 miles	32	23	5	60
	(27.900)	(18.300)	(13.800)	
>20 miles	19	7	11	37
	(17.205)	(11.285)	(8.510)	
Total	93	61	46	200

Solution

(1) H_0: The frequency of car accidents is independent of distance travelled to work.
H_1: The frequency of car accidents is not independent of distance travelled to work.

(2) $\alpha = 0.01$

(3) We use the chi-square distribution, with degrees of freedom $v = (c - 1)(r - 1) = (3 - 1)(3 - 1) = 4$, to find the critical value. In Table A.7, we find that $\chi^2_{0.01,4} = 13.28$. The decision rule is: Reject H_0 if $\chi^{2*} > 13.28$.

(4) The test statistic is equation (20.4). The expected frequencies, computed with equation (20.3), are shown in parentheses in Table 20.14. Using the observed and expected frequencies in the test statistic,

$$\begin{aligned}\chi^{2*} &= \frac{(42-47.895)^2}{47.895}+\frac{(31-31.415)^2}{31.415}+\frac{(30-23.690)^2}{23.690}+\frac{(32-27.900)^2}{27.900}+\frac{23-18.300)^2}{18.300}\\ &+\frac{(5-13.800)^2}{13.800}+\frac{(19-17.205)^2}{17.205}+\frac{(7-11.285)^2}{11.285}+\frac{(11-8.51)^2}{8.51}\\ &= 12.376\end{aligned}$$

From Table A.7, we find that the approximate probability of getting this sample value is $0.010 < P < 0.025$.

(5) Because $\chi^{2*} < 13.28$, we accept H_0 at the 0.01 level of significance. This result is confirmed by the fact that the probability of getting a chi-square value of 12.38 (given that the null is true) is greater than 0.01. Number of accidents and distance travelled to work are independent variables.

CHI-SQUARE TEST FOR HOMOGENEITY AMONG k BINOMIAL PROPORTIONS

20.7 The promoter of a 10,000-meter race wants to know whether the proportion of females in his race has increased since the race began 4 years ago. He checks his records and finds that the number of female runners in the first year was 98 out of 210 runners; in the second year, 100 out of 190 runners; in the third year, 133 out of 220 runners; and in the fourth year, 169 out of 280 runners. Do a chi-square test at $\alpha = 0.05$, using a critical-value decision rule, of H_0: The proportion of female runners has not changed in the past four years.

Solution

(1) H_0: $p_1 = p_2 = p_3 = p_4$
H_1: p_1, p_2, p_3, and p_4 are not all equal.

(2) $\alpha = 0.05$

(3) We use the chi-square distribution, with degrees of freedom $\nu = k - 1 = 4 - 1 = 3$, to find the critical value. From Table A.7, we find that $\chi^2_{0.05,3} = 7.81$. The decision rule is: Reject H_0 if $\chi^{2*} > 7.81$.

(4) The test statistic is equation (20.4). The expected frequencies are calculated using marginal frequencies [equation (20.3)]. Thus, for example, the number of women expected in the first race is

$$E_1 = \frac{\text{(number of runners in the 1st race)(total number of women runners in all 4 years)}}{\text{total number of runners in all 4 years}}$$

$$E_1 = \frac{(210)(500)}{900} = 116.667$$

The observed and expected frequencies are shown in Table 20.15. Using these values in the test statistic, we find

$$\begin{aligned}\chi^{2*} &= \frac{(98-116.667)^2}{116.667}+\frac{(100-105.556)^2}{105.556}+\frac{(133-122.222)^2}{122.222}+\frac{(169-155.556)^2}{155.556}\\ &+\frac{(112-93.333)^2}{93.333}+\frac{(90-84.444)^2}{84.444}+\frac{(87-97.778)^2}{97.778}+\frac{(111-124.444)^2}{124.444}\\ &= 12.131\end{aligned}$$

From Table A.7, we find that the approximate probability of getting this sample value is $0.005 < P < 0.010$.

(5) As $\chi^{2*} > 7.81$, we reject H_0 and accept H_1. This result is confirmed by the fact that the probability of getting a chi-square value of 12.13 (given that the null hypothesis is true) is less than 0.05. The proportion of female runners has changed over the past 4 years.

Table 20.15

	First race	Second race	Third race	Fourth race	Total
Females	98	100	133	169	500
	(116.667)	(105.556)	(122.222)	(155.556)	
Males	112	90	87	111	400
	(93.333)	(84.444)	(97.778)	(124.444)	
Total	210	190	220	280	900

20.8 A distributor of baseball caps wants to know whether his potential market at baseball games changes as the season progresses. He samples 100 people each month as they enter the ball field during the months of May, June, July, August, and September, and records whether or not they are wearing a cap. He finds that the number of people wearing caps, listed in order of the sequence of months, is: 59, 61, 65, 68, and 47. Do a chi-square test at $\alpha = 0.01$, using a critical-value decision rule, of H_0: The proportion of people wearing caps does not change with month of the season.

Solution

(1) H_0: $p_1 = p_2 = p_3 = p_4 = p_5$
H_1: p_1, p_2, p_3, p_4, and p_5 are not all equal.

(2) $\alpha = 0.01$

(3) We use the chi-square distribution, with degrees of freedom $\nu = k - 1 = 5 - 1 = 4$, to find the critical value. From Table A.7, we find that $\chi^2_{0.01,4} = 13.28$. The decision rule is: Reject H_0 if $\chi^{2*} > 13.28$.

(4) The test statistic is equation (20.4). The expected frequencies are calculated using marginal frequencies [equation (20.3)]. The observed and expected frequencies are shown in Table 20.16. Inserting these values into the test statistic, we find

$$\begin{aligned}\chi^{2*} &= \frac{(59-60)^2}{60} + \frac{(61-60)^2}{60} + \frac{(65-60)^2}{60} + \frac{(68-60)^2}{60} + \frac{(47-60)^2}{60} \\ &\quad + \frac{(41-40)^2}{40} + \frac{(39-40)^2}{40} + \frac{(35-40)^2}{40} + \frac{(32-40)^2}{40} + \frac{(53-40)^2}{40} \\ &= 10.833\end{aligned}$$

From Table A.7, we find that the approximate probability of getting this sample value is: $0.025 < P < 0.050$.

Table 20.16

	May	June	July	Aug.	Sept.	Total
Wearing caps	59	61	65	68	47	300
	(60)	(60)	(60)	(60)	(60)	
Not wearing caps	41	39	35	32	53	200
	(40)	(40)	(40)	(40)	(40)	
Total	100	100	100	100	100	500

(5) As $\chi^{2*} < 13.28$, we accept the null hypothesis at the 0.01 level of significance. This result is confirmed by the fact that the probability of getting a chi-square value of 10.833 (given that the null hypothesis is true) is greater than 0.01. The proportion of people wearing caps did not change over the 5-month period.

20.9 The administrators of a college are developing a plan to reduce the amount of alcohol consumed by freshmen. To find out the pattern of drinking throughout the school year, they take six random samples, of 100 freshmen each, at various times during the year. Each sampled student is asked how many alcoholic drinks they have had during the previous week, and the responses are divided into two categories: more than 10 drinks, and 10 drinks or fewer. They find that the number of students (out of 100) who have had more than 10 drinks during the previous week are: 40 in September, 31 in October, 36 in November, 35 in February, 18 in May, and 20 in April. Do a chi-square test at $\alpha = 0.01$, using a critical-value decision rule, of H_0: The proportion of freshmen who had more than 10 drinks in the past week is the same in all six samples.

Solution

(1) H_0: $p_1 = p_2 = p_3 = p_4 = p_5 = p_6$
H_1: p_1, p_2, p_3, p_4, p_5, and p_6 are not all equal.

(2) $\alpha = 0.01$

(3) We use the chi-square distribution, with degrees of freedom $\nu = k - 1 = 6 - 1 = 5$, to find the critical value. From Table A.7, we find that $\chi^2_{0.01,5} = 15.09$. The decision rule is: Reject H_0 if $\chi^{2*} > 15.09$.

(4) The test statistic is equation (20.4). The expected frequencies are calculated using marginal frequencies [equation (20.3)]. Both observed and expected frequencies are shown in Table 20.17. Inserting these values in the test statistic, we find

$$\chi^{2*} = \frac{(40-30)^2}{30} + \frac{(31-30)^2}{30} + \frac{(36-30)^2}{30} + \frac{(35-30)^2}{30} + \frac{(18-30)^2}{30} + \frac{(20-30)^2}{30}$$
$$+ \frac{(60-70)^2}{70} + \frac{(69-70)^2}{70} + \frac{(64-70)^2}{70} + \frac{(65-70)^2}{70} + \frac{(82-70)^2}{70} + \frac{(80-70)^2}{70}$$
$$= 19.333$$

From Table A.7, we find that the approximate probability of getting this sample value is $P < 0.005$.

Table 20.17

	Sept.	Oct.	Nov.	Feb.	Mar.	Apr.	Total
More than 10 drinks	40	31	36	35	18	20	180
	(30)	(30)	(30)	(30)	(30)	(30)	
10 drinks or fewer	60	69	64	65	82	80	420
	(70)	(70)	(70)	(70)	(70)	(70)	
Total	100	100	100	100	100	100	600

(5) As $\chi^{2*} > 15.09$, we reject H_0 and accept H_1. This result is confirmed by the fact that the probability of getting a chi-square value of 19.33 (given that the null hypothesis is true) is less than 0.01. The proportion of freshmen who had more than 10 drinks during the previous week is not the same in all six samples.

ONE-SAMPLE TESTS: THE WILCOXON SIGNED-RANK TEST

20.10 A team of 12 geologists sampled rock outcrops of a geological formation and found a median number of 34 species per 1,000 fossil specimens. A new outcrop has been discovered and the team wants to know whether the number of species per 1,000 specimens is the same as in the previous outcrops. Each geologist collects specimens from the new outcrop and calculates the median number of species per 1,000 specimens. These medians, one per geologist, are: 39, 21, 33, 64, 40,

43, 37, 42, 54, 36, 47, 38. Do a two-tailed Wilcoxon test at $\alpha = 0.05$, using a critical-value decision rule, of H_0: $\tilde{\mu} = \tilde{\mu}_0$ and H_1: $\tilde{\mu} \neq \tilde{\mu}_0$.

Solution

(1) H_0: $\tilde{\mu} = 34$, H_1: $\tilde{\mu} \neq 34$

(2) $\alpha = 0.05$

(3) As $n < 30$, we use the small-sample test of the W statistic. From Table A.12, we find that for $n = 12$ in a two-tailed test, $W_{0.05} = 14$. The decision rule is: Reject H_0 if $W < 14$.

(4) The specific value of W is calculated by subtracting the null's hypothesized median (34) from each observed median, ranking the absolute differences, and then restoring the + or − sign to each rank. The positive ranks are summed to get W_+ and the negative ranks are summed to get W_-. These calculations are shown in Table 20.18. The absolute value of the smaller W, which is 10.5 in this case, is the test statistic. From Table A.12, we find that the approximate probability of getting this test statistic is $0.02 < P < 0.05$.

Table 20.18

Observed minus $\tilde{\mu}_0$	Absolute difference	Rank	Signed rank
$39 - 34 = +5$	5	5.0	+5.0
$21 - 34 = -13$	13	9.5	−9.5
$33 - 34 = -1$	1	1.0	−1.0
$64 - 34 = +30$	30	12.0	+12.0
$40 - 34 = +6$	6	6.0	+6.0
$43 - 34 = +9$	9	8.0	+8.0
$37 - 34 = +3$	3	3.0	+3.0
$42 - 34 = +8$	8	7.0	+7.0
$54 - 34 = +20$	20	11.0	+11.0
$36 - 34 = +2$	2	2.0	+2.0
$47 - 34 = +13$	13	9.5	+9.5
$38 - 34 = +4$	4	4.0	+4.0
			$\lvert W_+ \rvert = 67.5$
			$\lvert W_- \rvert = 10.5$

(5) As $W < 14$, we reject H_0 and accept H_1. This result is confirmed by the fact that the probability of getting a W value of 10.5 (given that the null is true) is less than 0.05. The median number of species per 1,000 specimens in the new rock outcrop is not the same as in the previous outcrop.

20.11 The geologists in Problem 20.10 decide to take more samples from the new outcrop in order to determine, from a larger sample, whether there are more species per 1,000 specimens in the new outcrop as compared with the previous one, which had a median of 34 species. Fifty samples are taken. The sum of the positive ranks is 830 and the sum of the negative ranks is −445. Do a one-tailed Wilcoxon test at $\alpha = 0.05$, using a critical-value decision rule, of H_0: $\tilde{\mu} = \tilde{\mu}_0$ and H_1: $\tilde{\mu} > \tilde{\mu}_0$.

Solution

(1) H_0: $\tilde{\mu} = 34$, H_1: $\tilde{\mu} > 34$

(2) $\alpha = 0.05$

(3) As $n > 30$, we use the W statistic in the Z transformation, and so the critical value comes from the Z distribution. From Table A.5, for a one-tailed test we find that $z_{0.05} = 1.645$. The decision rule is: Reject H_0 if $z^* < -1.645$.

(4) Using $W = 445$ (the smaller absolute value of the two sums) and $n = 50$ in equation (20.5),

$$z^* = \frac{445 - \frac{50(50+1)}{4}}{\sqrt{\frac{50(50+1)[2(50)+1]}{24}}} = -1.858, \quad \text{or } -1.86$$

To determine the P value, we use equation (16.5): $P = P[Z \leq (z^* = -a)|H_0 \text{ is true}]$. From Table A.5, we find that the area above the interval $0 \leq z \leq 1.86$ is 0.4686. Since the area to the right of zero is 0.5,

$$P = P(Z \geq 1.86|H_0 \text{ is true}) = 0.5 - 0.4686 = 0.0314$$

Because the distribution of Z is symmetric about zero, this means that

$$P = P(Z \leq -1.86|H_0 \text{ is true}) = 0.5 - 0.4686 = 0.0314, \quad \text{or } 0.031$$

(5) As $z^* < -1.645$, we reject H_0 and accept H_1. This result is confirmed by the fact that the P value is less than 0.05. The median number of species per 1,000 specimens in the new outcrop is higher than in the previous outcrop.

20.12 The median property tax rate per \$1,000 value for state A is \$21.42. A family is considering moving to state B and wants to know whether the tax rate there is higher. They randomly sample 12 counties in state B and find the following rates: \$31.70, \$31.80, \$28.70, \$31.12, \$25.00, \$13.90, \$20.01, \$33.12, \$15.00, \$34.84, \$25.32, \$18.01. Do a one-tailed Wilcoxon test at $\alpha = 0.05$, using a critical-value decision rule, of H_0: $\tilde{\mu} = \tilde{\mu}_0$ and H_1: $\tilde{\mu} > \tilde{\mu}_0$.

Solution

(1) H_0: $\tilde{\mu} = \$21.42$, $\quad H_1$: $\tilde{\mu} > \$21.42$

(2) $\alpha = 0.05$

Table 20.19

Observed minus $\tilde{\mu}_0$	Absolute difference	Rank	Signed rank
\$31.70−\$21.42= +\$10.28	10.28	9	+9
\$31.80−\$21.42= +\$10.38	10.38	10	+10
\$28.70−\$21.42= +\$7.28	7.28	6	+6
\$31.12−\$21.42= +\$9.70	9.70	8	+8
\$25.00−\$21.42= +\$3.58	3.58	3	+3
\$13.90−\$21.42= −\$7.52	7.52	7	−7
\$20.01−\$21.42= −\$1.41	1.41	1	−1
\$33.12−\$21.42= +\$11.70	11.70	11	+11
\$15.00−\$21.42= −\$6.42	6.42	5	−5
\$34.84−\$21.42= +\$13.42	13.42	12	+12
\$25.32−\$21.42= +\$3.90	3.90	4	+4
\$18.01−\$21.42= −\$3.41	3.41	2	−2
			$\lvert W_+\rvert = 63$
			$\lvert W_-\rvert = 15$

(3) As $n < 30$, we use the W statistic. From Table A.12, we find that for $n = 12$ in a one-tailed test, $W_{0.05} = 17$. The decision rule is: Reject H_0 if $W < 17$.

(4) The specific value of W is calculated by subtracting the null's hypothesized median ($21.42) from each observed median, ranking the differences, and then restoring the + or − sign to each rank. The sum of the positive values is W_+; the sum of the negative values is W_-. These calculations are shown in Table 20.19. The statistic W is 15, the smaller absolute value of these two sums. From Table A.12, we find that the approximate probability of getting this test statistic is $0.025 < P < 0.050$.

(5) As $W < 17$, we reject H_0 and accept H_1. This result is confirmed by the fact that the probability of getting a W of 15 (given that the null is true) is less than 0.05. The tax rates in state B are higher than the tax rates in state A.

20.13 A medical researcher wants to know whether air conditioning raises the amount of calories that a person consumes. She knows that, for a large city in a warm environment, the median number of kilocalories consumed per woman is 2,500 kcal per day. She selected 40 women, at random, to live in the cooler temperatures of air-conditioned apartments for 10 days. Then, on day 11, their food consumption was monitored. The differences between the observed value and the median value of 2,500 were calculated and ranked. The absolute value of W_+ was found to be 520 and the absolute value of W_- was found to be 300. Do a one-tailed Wilcoxon test at $\alpha = 0.05$, using a critical-value decision rule, of H_0: $\tilde{\mu} = \tilde{\mu}_0$ and H_1: $\tilde{\mu} > \tilde{\mu}_0$.

Solution

(1) H_0: $\tilde{\mu} = 2,500$, $\quad H_1$: $\tilde{\mu} > 2,500$

(2) $\alpha = 0.05$

(3) As $n > 30$, we use the W statistic in the Z transformation. From Table A.5, we find that for $\alpha = 0.05$ in a one-tailed test, $z_{0.05} = 1.645$. The decision rule is: Reject H_0 if $z^* < -1.645$.

(4) We know that $W = 300$, because it is the smaller of the two absolute values. The sample value of Z is calculated by substituting this value of W and $n = 40$ in equation (20.5):

$$z^* = \frac{300 - \dfrac{40(40+1)}{4}}{\sqrt{\dfrac{40(40+1)[2(40)+1]}{24}}} = -1.479, \quad \text{or } -1.48$$

To determine the P value, we use equation (16.5): $P = P[Z \leq (z^* = -a)|H_0 \text{ is true}]$. From Table A.5, we find that the area above the interval $0 \leq z \leq 1.48$ is 0.4306. Since the area to the right of zero is 0.5,

$$P = P(Z \geq 1.48|H_0 \text{ is true}) = 0.5 - 0.4306 = 0.0694$$

Because the distribution of Z is symmetric about zero, we know that

$$P = P(Z \leq -1.48|H_0 \text{ is true}) = 0.5 - 0.4306 = 0.0694, \quad \text{or } 0.069$$

(5) As $z^* > -1.645$, we accept H_0. This result is confirmed by the fact that the P value is greater than 0.05. An air-conditioned environment does not raise the caloric consumption of women.

TWO-SAMPLE TESTS: THE WILCOXON SIGNED-RANK TEST FOR DEPENDENT SAMPLES

20.14 The exercise experiment described in Example 20.6 is repeated with a sample of 35 women between the ages of 75 and 80. Now the sum of the positive ranks is 402 and the sum of the negative ranks is −228. Do a Wilcoxon test at $\alpha = 0.01$, using a critical value decision rule, of H_0: The median pulse rate is the same after the exercise regimen as before the exercise regimen, and H_1: The median pulse rate is lower after the exercise regimen ($\tilde{\mu}_2$) than before the exercise regimen ($\tilde{\mu}_1$).

Solution

(1) H_0: $\tilde{\mu}_1 = \tilde{\mu}_2$, H_1: $\tilde{\mu}_1 > \tilde{\mu}_2$

(2) $\alpha = 0.01$

(3) As $n > 30$, we use the W statistic in the Z transformation and the Z distribution to find the critical value. From Table A.5, we find that for a one-tailed test, $z_{0.01} = 2.33$. The decision rule is: Reject H_0 if $z^* < -2.33$.

(4) We know that W is 228, because it is the smaller absolute value of the two sums of ranks. We calculate z^* by inserting $W = 228$ and $n = 35$ into equation (20.5):

$$z^* = \frac{228 - \dfrac{35(35+1)}{4}}{\sqrt{\dfrac{35(35+1)[2(35)+1]}{24}}} = -1.425$$

To determine the P value, we use equation (16.5): $P = P[Z \leq (z^* = -a)|H_0 \text{ is true}]$. From Table A.5, we find that the area above the interval $0 \leq z \leq 1.43$ is 0.4236. Since the area to the right of zero is 0.5, which is symmetric with the area to the left of zero,

$$P = P(Z \leq -1.43|H_0 \text{ is true}) = 0.50 - 0.4236 = 0.0764$$

(5) As $z^* > -2.33$, we accept H_0 at the 0.01 level of significance. This result is confirmed by the fact that the probability of getting a sample value of -1.425 is greater than 0.01. The pulse rates of the subjects were not lower after the exercise regimen than before the regimen.

20.15 A dairy farmer wants to know whether a new hormone will increase the milk production of his cows. He is reluctant to expose his entire herd to the hormone before he has evidence that the hormone works, and so he takes a random sample of just 10 cows and records, for each cow, milk production during the week before and during the week after hormone treatment. Milk production, in gallons per week with the "before" value listed first and the "after" value listed second, is as follows: (30, 34); (25, 35); (22, 27); (25, 24); (23, 25); (34, 26); (33, 24); (30, 24); (24, 27); (32, 21). Do a one-tailed Wilcoxon test at $\alpha = 0.05$, using a critical-value decision rule, of H_0: Milk production is the same after the hormone treatment ($\tilde{\mu}_2$) as before ($\tilde{\mu}_1$), and H_1: Milk production is higher after the hormone treatment.

Solution

(1) H_0: $\tilde{\mu}_1 = \tilde{\mu}_2$, H_1: $\tilde{\mu}_1 < \tilde{\mu}_2$

(2) $\alpha = 0.05$

(3) As $n < 30$, we use the small-sample test of the W statistic. Using Table A.12, we find that for $n = 10$ in a one-tailed test, $W_{0.05} = 11$. The decision rule is: Reject H_0 if $W < 11$.

(4) The test statistic W is calculated by subtracting the "after" production from the "before" production for each cow, ranking the absolute differences, and then restoring the + or − sign to each rank. The positive ranks are summed to get W_+ and the negative ranks are summed to get W_-. These calculations are shown in Table 20.20. The test statistic W is 23, because it is the smaller of the two absolute values. From Table A.12, we find that the approximate probability of getting this sample value is $P > 0.05$.

(5) As $W > 11$, we accept H_0. This result is confirmed by the fact that the probability of getting a W of 23 (given that the null is true) is greater than 0.05. The amount of milk produced by the cows is the same before and after hormone treatment.

Table 20.20

Milk: before minus after	Absolute difference	Rank	Signed rank
$30 - 34 = -4$	4	4	-4
$25 - 35 = -10$	10	9	-9
$22 - 27 = -5$	5	5	-5
$25 - 24 = +1$	1	1	$+1$
$23 - 25 = -2$	2	2	-2
$34 - 26 = +8$	8	7	$+7$
$33 - 24 = +9$	9	8	$+8$
$30 - 24 = +6$	6	6	$+6$
$24 - 27 = -3$	3	3	-3
$32 - 21 = +11$	11	10	$+10$
			$\lvert W_+ \rvert = 32$
			$\lvert W_- \rvert = 23$

20.16 A shoe manufacturer wants to know whether his new-style boots last longer than the boots he presently sells. He takes a random sample of 13 hikers and has each hiker wear the new-style boot on one foot (which foot is chosen at random) and the present boot on the other foot, and then records how many miles it takes for each boot to reach a certain level of deterioration. He gets the following results, in miles, for the 13 hikers, with the present boot (boot 1) listed first and the new-styled boot (boot 2) listed second: (460, 530); (420, 525); (520, 500); (515, 505); (490, 520); (490, 450); (500, 495); (550, 575); (480, 474); (530, 515); (518, 490); (515, 480); (475, 493). Do a Wilcoxon test at $\alpha = 0.05$, using a critical-value decision rule, of H_0: The median time to deterioration is the same in the two kinds of boots, and H_1: The median time to deterioration is longer in the new-styled boot.

Solution

(1) $H_0\colon \tilde{\mu}_1 = \tilde{\mu}_2, \qquad H_1\colon \tilde{\mu}_1 < \tilde{\mu}_2$

(2) $\alpha = 0.05$

(3) As $n < 30$, we use the small-sample test of the W statistic. From Table A.12, we find that with $n = 13$ in a one-tailed test, $W_{0.05} = 21$. The decision rule is: Reject H_0 if $W < 21$.

(4) The test statistic W is calculated by subtracting the miles-to-deterioration of the new-style boot from the miles-to-deterioration of the present boot for each paired sample. The absolute differences are ranked and then the original sign of the difference is restored to each rank. The positive ranks are summed to get W_+ and the negative ranks are summed to get W_-. These calculations are shown in Table 20.21. The test statistic W is equal to 45, because it is the smaller of the two absolute values. From Table A.12, we find that the probability of getting this sample value is $P > 0.05$.

(5) As $W > 21$, we accept H_0. This result is confirmed by the fact that the probability of getting a W of 45 (given that the null is true) is greater than 0.05. The new-style hiking boot does not last longer than the previous one.

20.17 The shoe manufacturer in Problem 20.16 repeats the experiment on his new-style boot and present boot, this time with a sample of 50 hikers. He subtracts the miles-to-deterioration of the new style boot (boot 2)from the present boot (boot 1), ranks the difference scores, and gets the following sum of signed ranks: $W_+ = 850$ and $W_- = -425$. Do a Wilcoxon test at $\alpha = 0.05$, using a critical-value decision rule, of H_0: The median time to deterioration is the same in the two kinds of boots, and H_1: The median time to deterioration is longer in the new-styled boot.

Table 20.21

Miles: boot 1 minus boot 2	Absolute difference	Rank	Signed rank
$460 - 530 = -70$	70	12	-12
$420 - 525 = -105$	105	13	-13
$520 - 500 = +20$	20	6	$+6$
$515 - 505 = +10$	10	3	$+3$
$490 - 520 = -30$	30	9	-9
$490 - 450 = +40$	40	11	$+11$
$500 - 495 = +5$	5	1	$+1$
$550 - 575 = -25$	25	7	-7
$480 - 474 = +6$	6	2	$+2$
$530 - 515 = +15$	15	4	$+4$
$518 - 490 = +28$	28	8	$+8$
$515 - 480 = +35$	35	10	$+10$
$475 - 493 = -18$	18	5	-5
			$\lvert W_+ \rvert = 45$
			$\lvert W_- \rvert = 46$

Solution

(1) H_0: $\tilde{\mu}_1 = \tilde{\mu}_2$, $\quad H_1$: $\tilde{\mu}_1 < \tilde{\mu}_2$

(2) $\alpha = 0.05$

(3) As $n > 30$, we use the W statistic in the Z transformation and obtain the critical value from the Z distribution. From Table A.5, we find that for a one-tailed test, $z_{0.05} = 1.645$. The decision rule is: Reject H_0 if $z^* < -1.645$.

(4) We know that W is 425, because it is the smaller absolute value of the two sums of ranks. We calculate z^* by inserting $W = 425$ and $n = 50$ into equation (20.5):

$$z^* = \frac{425 - \dfrac{50(50+1)}{4}}{\sqrt{\dfrac{50(50+1)[2(50)+1]}{24}}} = -2.051, \quad \text{or } -2.05$$

To determine the P value, we use equation (16.5): $P = P[Z \leq (z^* = -a) | H_0 \text{ is true}]$. From Table A.5, we find that the area above the interval $0 \leq z \leq 2.05$ is 0.4798. Since the area to the right of zero is 0.5,

$$P = P(Z > 2.05) = 0.5 - 0.4798 = 0.0202$$

Because of the symmetry of the Z distribution, we know that

$$P = P(Z > 2.05) = 0.5 - 0.4798 = 0.0202$$

(5) As $z^* < -1.645$, we reject H_0 and accept H_1. This decision is confirmed by the fact that the probability of getting a z value of -2.05 (given that the null is true) is less than 0.05. The new-style hiking boots lasts longer (in miles to deterioration) than the present boots.

TWO-SAMPLE TESTS: THE MANN-WHITNEY U TEST FOR INDEPENDENT SAMPLES

20.18 An exercise physiologist wants to know the effect of two brands of sport drink on the performance of elite runners in 10-kilometer races. She chooses, at random, 8 women to drink brand A and 8 women to drink brand B. The 16 women run a race and the results (in minutes) are, for brand A:

33.30, 30.10, 38.62, 38.94, 42.63, 41.96, 46.30, 43.25; for brand B: 31.62, 46.33, 31.82, 40.21, 45.72, 39.80, 45.60, 41.25. Do a two-tailed Mann-Whitney U test at $\alpha = 0.05$, using a critical-value decision rule, of H_0: The distributions of the two populations of running times are the same.

Solution

(1) H_0: The distribution of race times for women using brand A is the same as for women using brand B. H_1: The distribution of race times for women using brand A is not the same as for women using brand B.

(2) $\alpha = 0.05$

(3) As $n_1 < 20$ and $n_2 < 20$, we use the small-sample version of the Mann-Whitney U test. From Table A.13, we find that with $n_1 = 8$ and $n_2 = 8$ in a two-tailed test, $U_{0.05} = 13$. The decision rule is: Reject H_0 if $U < 13$.

(4) We obtain the test statistic U by using equations (20.6) and (20.7) to calculate U_1 and U_2. For this equation, we know that $n_1 = 8$ and $n_2 = 8$. To find R_1 and R_2, we combine the two samples and rank the combined list of values. The sums of ranks for each sample are R_1 and R_2. These calculations are shown in Table 20.22. U_1 is found by inserting $n_1 = 8$, $n_2 = 8$, and $R_1 = 64$ into equation (20.6):

$$U_1 = (8)(8) + \frac{(8)(8+1)}{2} - 64 = 36$$

U_2 is found by inserting $n_1 = 8$, $n_2 = 8$, and $R_2 = 72$ into equation (20.7):

$$U_2 = (8)(8) + \frac{(8)(8+1)}{2} - 72 = 28$$

The test statistic U is 28, because it is the smaller of the two values.

(5) As $U > 13$, we accept H_0. The race times of women using brand A are not different from those using brand B.

Table 20.22

Times: brand A	Ranks of times	Times: brand B	Ranks of times
33.30	4	31.62	2
30.10	1	46.33	16
38.62	5	31.82	3
38.94	6	40.21	8
42.63	11	45.72	14
41.96	10	39.80	7
46.30	15	45.60	13
43.25	12	41.25	9
$n_1 = 8$	$R_1 = 64$	$n_2 = 8$	$R_2 = 72$

20.19 The exercise physiologist described in Problem 20.18 repeats her study with a larger sample. Now, $n_1 = 30$ and $n_2 = 30$. She finds that $R_1 = 830$ and $R_2 = 1{,}000$, with no tied ranks. Do a two-tailed Mann-Whitney U test at $\alpha = 0.05$, using a critical-value decision rule, of H_0: The race times for women using brand A is the same as the race times for women using brand B.

Solution

(1) H_0: The distribution of race times for women using brand A is the same as for women using brand B. H_1: The distribution of race times for women using brand A is not the same as for women using brand B.

(2) $\alpha = 0.05$

(3) As $n_1 > 20$ and $n_2 > 20$, we use the large-sample version of the Mann-Whitney U test involving the Z transformation. From Table A.5, we find that for a two-tailed test, $z_{0.05} = 1.96$. Our decision rule is: Reject H_0 if $z^* < -1.96$.

(4) We obtain the test statistic U by using equations (20.6) and (20.7) to calculate U_1 and U_2. Inserting $n_1 = 30$, $n_2 = 30$, and $R_1 = 830$, we get

$$U_1 = (30)(30) + \frac{(30)(30+1)}{2} - 830 = 535$$

Inserting $n_1 = 30$, $n_2 = 30$, and $R_2 = 1{,}000$, we get

$$U_2 = (30)(30) + \frac{(30)(30+1)}{2} - 1{,}000 = 365$$

The test statistic U is 365, because it is the smaller of the two values. There are no ties in the ranks, so we do not apply the correction factor. Inserting $U = 365$, $n_1 = 30$, and $n_2 = 30$ into equation (20.8):

$$z^* = \frac{365 - \dfrac{(30)(30)}{2}}{\sqrt{\dfrac{(30)(30)(30+30+1)}{12}}} = -1.2567$$

To determine the P value, we use equation (16.4): $P = 2[P(Z \geq \langle z^* = a \rangle | H_0 \text{ is true})]$. From Table A.5 we find that the area above the interval $0 \leq z \leq 1.26$ is 0.3962. Because the area to the right of zero in the distribution is equal to 0.5,

$$P = 2[P(Z \geq 1.26 | H_0 \text{ is true})] = 2(0.5 - 0.3962) = 0.2076$$

(5) As $z^* > -1.96$, we accept H_0. This result is confirmed by the fact that the probability of getting $z^* = -1.257$ (given that the null hypothesis is true) is greater than 0.05. The effects of brand A are not different from the effects of brand B on the running times of women.

20.20 Consider the same experiment as described in Problem 20.19, but this time with the following ties in ranks: two scores of 8, three scores of 10, and five scores of 11. Determine the effect of these ties on your decision to accept H_0.

Solution

To find out the effect of ties, we need to calculate z^* using equation (20.10) and then compare this result with the one above, where we used equation (20.8). First, using equation (20.9), we calculate $\sum T_i$:

$$\sum T_i = \sum \frac{t_i^3 - t_i}{12} = \frac{2^3 - 2}{12} + \frac{3^3 - 3}{12} + \frac{5^3 - 5}{12} = 12.5$$

Incorporating $\sum T_i = 12.5$ into equation (20.10):

$$z^* = \frac{365 - \dfrac{(30)(30)}{2}}{\sqrt{\left(\dfrac{(30)(30)}{(30+30)^2 - (30+30)}\right)\left(\dfrac{(30+30)^3 - (30+30)}{12} - 12.5\right)}} = -1.2571$$

Incorporating ties lowers the value of z^* from -1.2567 to -1.2571. With the ties, z^* is still less negative than the critical value, -1.96, and the probability P of getting this value is $P = 0.208$, the same as the calculation without ties.

We conclude that incorporating these ties into our calculations has a small effect on z^*, but not enough to alter our decision to accept H_0. The probability of getting this sample value (if the null hypothesis is true) remains the same, at least to three decimal points.

MULTISAMPLE TESTS: THE KRUSKAL-WALLIS H TEST FOR k INDEPENDENT SAMPLES

20.21 A conservationist wants to know whether mule deer use one type of habitat more than others. He counts the number of deer found per hectare in four areas of pine forest, four areas of spruce-fir forest, and three areas of aspen forest. His results are: for the pine forest, 12, 11, 8, 6 deer; for the spruce-fir forest, 8, 10, 4, 5 deer; for the aspen forest, 13, 7, 9 deer. Do a Kruskal-Wallis test at $\alpha = 0.05$, using a critical-value decision rule, of H_0: The densities of deer are the same among all three forest types.

Solution

(1) H_0: The densities of deer are the same among the three forest types.
H_1: The densities of deer are different among the three forest types.

(2) $\alpha = 0.05$

(3) As $k = 3$ and the n values are all less than 6, we use the small-sample version of the Kruskal-Wallis H test. From Table A.14, we find that with $n_1 = 4$, $n_2 = 4$, and $n_3 = 3$, $H_{0.05} = 5.598$. The decision rule is: Reject H_0 if $H > 5.598$.

(4) We obtain the test statistic H by calculating R for each treatment. First, we combine the observations of the three treatments and rank the combined list, assigning a value of 1 to the smallest and a value of 11 (the total number of observations) to the largest observation. Ties are given the average rank. R_i is then the sum of ranks for each treatment i. The calculations are shown in Table 20.23. As less than 35% of the observations are tied (2 of 11), we do not apply the correction factor. Using equation (20.11) to compute the test statistic:

$$H = \frac{12}{11(11+1)}\left(\frac{(27.5)^2}{4} + \frac{(16.5)^2}{4} + \frac{(22.0)^2}{3}\right) - 3(11+1) = 2.0417$$

From Table A.14, we find that the approximate probability of getting this H value is $P > 0.10$.

Table 20.23

Pine forest		Spruce-fir forest		Aspen forest	
Number of deer	Rank	Number of deer	Rank	Number of deer	Rank
12	10.0	8	5.5	13	11.0
11	9.0	10	8.0	7	4.0
8	5.5	4	1.0	9	7.0
6	3.0	5	2.0		
$n_1 = 4$	$R_1 = 27.5$	$n_2 = 4$	$R_2 = 16.5$	$n_3 = 3$	$R_3 = 22.0$

(5) As $H < 5.598$, we accept H_0. This result is confirmed by the fact that the probability of getting a sample H value of 2.0417 (given that the null hypothesis is true) is greater than 0.05. The numbers of deer per hectare are not different among the three forest types.

20.22 A geologist wants to know whether the amount of potash differs among five outcrops of a rock formation. He takes eight samples from each outcrop and measures the amount of potash in parts per million. The results are: outcrop A, 2.70, 7.50, 5.00, 2.25, 2.80, 6.00, 4.35, 3.00; outcrop B, 4.10, 7.40, 6.65, 5.70, 5.30, 7.20, 6.30, 6.95; outcrop C, 3.50, 3.20, 3.10, 4.20, 3.15, 4.30, 4.45, 5.25; outcrop D, 6.85, 4.00, 4.25, 4.40, 6.55, 3.25, 2.20, 1.80; outcrop E, 6.25, 6.05, 4.10, 4.05, 6.90, 6.45, 6.70, 5.30. Do a Kruskal-Wallis test at $\alpha = 0.01$, using a critical-value decision rule, of H_0: The potash contents in the outcrops are the same.

Solution

(1) H_0: The potash contents of the five outcrops are the same.
H_1: The potash contents of the five outcrops are not the same.

(2) $\alpha = 0.01$

(3) As $k > 3$ and $n_i > 5$ for all samples, we use the chi-square distribution to obtain the critical value. From Table A.7, we find for $\nu = 5 - 1 = 4$, that $\chi^2_{0.01,4} = 13.28$. The decision rule is: Reject H_0 if $H > 13.28$.

(4) We obtain the test statistic H by calculating R for each treatment. First, we combine the observations of the five treatments and rank the combined list, assigning a value of 1 to the smallest and a value of 40 (the total number of observations) to the largest. Ties are given the average rank. R_i is then the sum of ranks for each treatment i. These calculations are shown in Table 20.24. As there are only four ties (10% of the ranks), we do not apply the correction factor. Using equation (20.11) to compute the test statistic H,

$$H = \frac{12}{40(41)}\left(\frac{(126)^2}{8} + \frac{(242)^2}{8} + \frac{(113)^2}{8} + \frac{(129)^2}{8} + \frac{(210)^2}{8}\right) - 3(40+1) = 12.3201$$

From Table A.7, we find that the approximate probability of getting this H value is $0.010 < P < 0.025$.

Table 20.24

Potash content (in parts per million)									
Outcrop A		Outcrop B		Outcrop C		Outcrop D		Outcrop E	
Content	Rank	Content	Rank	Content	Rank	Content	Rank	Content	Rank
2.70	4.0	4.10	14.5	3.50	11.0	6.85	35.0	6.25	29.0
7.50	40.0	7.40	39.0	3.20	9.0	4.00	12.0	6.05	28.0
5.00	22.0	6.65	33.0	3.10	7.0	4.25	17.0	4.10	14.5
2.25	3.0	5.70	26.0	4.20	16.0	4.40	20.0	4.05	13.0
2.80	5.0	5.30	24.5	3.15	8.0	6.55	32.0	6.90	36.0
6.00	27.0	7.20	38.0	4.30	18.0	3.25	10.0	6.45	31.0
4.35	19.0	6.30	30.0	4.45	21.0	2.20	2.0	6.70	34.0
3.00	6.0	6.95	37.0	5.25	23.0	1.80	1.0	5.30	24.5
$n_1 = 8$	$R_1 = 126$	$n_1 = 8$	$R_2 = 242$	$n_3 = 8$	$R_3 = 113$	$n_4 = 8$	$R_4 = 129$	$n_5 = 8$	$R_5 = 210$

(5) As $H < 13.28$, we accept H_0 at the 0.01 level of significance. This result is confirmed by the fact that the probability getting an H of 12.3201 (given that the null is true) is greater than 0.010. The potash contents of the five outcrops are not different.

20.23 Suppose, in the study described in Problem 20.22, that the geologist had rounded off the values for potash content so that there were more ties, specifically two ties at 3.2, three ties at 4.1, two ties at 4.3, two ties at 4.4, three ties at 5.3, two ties at 6.3, and two ties at 6.7. Using the same values of R_i calculated in Problem 20.22, apply the correction for ties and then repeat the statistical test, at $\alpha = 0.01$, of H_0: The potash contents of the outcrops are the same.

Solution

(1) H_0: The potash contents of the five outcrops are the same.
H_1: The potash contents of the five outcrops are not the same.

(2) $\alpha = 0.01$

(3) As $k > 3$ and $n_i > 5$ for all samples, we use the large-sample version of the Kruskal-Wallis H test, using the chi-square distribution. From Table A.7, we find for $\nu = 5 - 1 = 4$ and $\alpha = 0.01$, that $\chi^2_{0.01,4} = 13.28$. The decision rule is: Reject H_0 if $H > 13.28$.

(4) We obtain the test statistic H by calculating R for each treatment. From Problem 20.22, we know that $R_1 = 126$, $R_2 = 242$, $R_3 = 113$, $R_4 = 129$, $R_5 = 210$, and that $n_1 = n_2 = n_3 = n_4 = n_5 = 8$. As there are 16 ties (40% of the ranks), we should calculate H with the correction factor, as described by equations (20.12) and (20.13):

$$H = \frac{\dfrac{12}{40(41)}\left(\dfrac{(126)^2}{8} + \dfrac{(242)^2}{8} + \dfrac{(113)^2}{8} + \dfrac{(129)^2}{8} + \dfrac{(210)^2}{8}\right) - 3(40+1)}{1 - \dfrac{(2^3-2)+(3^3-3)+(2^3-2)+(2^3-2)+(3^3-3)+(2^3-2)+(2^3-2)}{(40)^3 - 40}} = 12.3352$$

From Table A.7, we find that the approximate probability of getting this H value is $0.01 < P < 0.025$.

(5) The correction factor raised the value of H from 12.3201 to 12.3352, but not enough to reach the critical value of 13.28. The approximate probability of getting this H value (given that the null is true) is the same as without the correction factor. Thus, we again accept the null hypothesis at the 0.01 level of significance. The potash contents of the five outcrops are not different.

THE SPEARMAN TEST OF RANK CORRRELATION

20.24 The chemistry department of a college has received research money for three undergraduate students. Ten students apply for the research, and two professors are assigned the task of ranking the students based on their research proposals. The students are listed (from A to J) and each professor ranks them from 1 (best) to 10 (worst). From the list (arranged in order from A to J), Professor A ranks the students as: 2, 5, 7, 1, 3, 8, 9, 6, 10, 4. From the same list, Professor B ranks them as: 1, 3, 8, 2, 5, 7, 10, 4, 9, 6. Do a Pearson test of rank correlation at $\alpha = 0.05$, using a critical-value decision rule, of H_0: The ranks of the two professors are not related, and H_1: The ranks of the two professors have an increasing monotonic relationship.

Solution

(1) H_0: The two populations of ranks have no relationship.
H_1: The two populations of ranks have an increasing monotonic relationship.

(2) $\alpha = 0.05$

(3) As the number of paired ranks is less than 30, we use Table A.15 to find the critical value. For a one-tailed test with $\alpha = 0.05$ and $n = 10$, we find that the critical value is 0.564. The decision for this right-tailed test is: Reject H_0 if $r_S > 0.564$.

(4) There are no tied ranks, so we use equation (20.14) to calculate the correlation coefficient. To do this, we obtain the difference in ranks for the paired observations and then square this difference to get a d_i^2 for each pair. These calculations are shown in Table 20.25. The sum of these squares (22) is then inserted, along with $n = 10$, into equation (20.14):

$$r_S = 1 - \frac{6(22)}{10(10^2 - 1)} = 0.8667$$

From Table A.15, we find that the approximate probability of getting this corrrelation coefficient is: $0.001 < P < 0.0025$.

(5) As $r_S > 0.564$, we reject H_0 and accept H_1. This result is confirmed by the fact that the probability of getting an r_S of 0.8667 is less than 0.05. The two ranking systems are similar, with an increasing positive monotonic relationship.

20.25 The research awards described in Problem 20.24 are so successful that 32 students apply the next time they are offered. Again, the two professors rank the applicants (no ties) from an anonymous list of students. From a table of ranks and differences between ranks, the sums of squares of rank

Table 20.25

Student	Rank by Professor A	Rank by Professor B	d_i	d_i^2
A	2	1	+1	1
B	5	3	+2	4
C	7	8	−1	1
D	1	2	−1	1
E	3	5	−2	4
F	8	7	+1	1
G	9	10	−1	1
H	6	4	+2	4
I	10	9	+1	1
J	4	6	−2	4
				$\sum = 22$

differences is calculated to be 3,010. Do a Spearman test of rank correlation, at $\alpha = 0.01$, using a critical-value decision rule, of H_0: The rankings of the professors are not related, and H_1: The rankings of the professors have an increasing monotonic relationship.

Solution

(1) H_0: The two populations of ranks have no relationship.
H_1: The two populations of ranks have an increasing monotonic relationship.

(2) $\alpha = 0.01$

(3) As the number of paired ranks is more than 30, we do a Z transformation and use the Z distribution to find the critical value. From Table A.5, we find that for a one-tailed test, $z_{0.01} = 2.33$. The decision rule for this right-tailed test is: Reject H_0 if $z^* > 2.33$.

(4) There are no tied ranks, so we use equation (20.14) to calculate the correlation coefficient. Knowing that $\sum_{i=1}^{32} d_i^2 = 3{,}010$ and $n = 32$, we insert these values into the equation:

$$r_S = 1 - \frac{6(3{,}010)}{32(32^2 - 1)} = 0.4483$$

Using equation (20.15) to transform r_S into z:

$$z^* = 0.4483\sqrt{32 - 1} = 2.4960, \quad \text{or } 2.50$$

From Table A.5, we find that the probability of getting this sample value is $P = 0.5 - 0.4938 = 0.0062$.

(5) As $z^* > 2.33$, we reject H_0 at the 0.01 level of significance. This result is confirmed by the fact that the probability of getting this sample correlation coefficient is less than 0.01. The two sets of ranks have an increasing monotonic relationship.

20.26 The athletic director of a university wants to know whether there is a relationship between end-of-season rank of a college basketball team and the average height of its starting-five players. His league has eight teams and the average height of their starting-five players, listed in order of end-of-season team rank the previous year, are: 6 ft 5.5 in; 6 ft. 5.0 in; 6 ft 6.5 in; 6 ft 3.8 in; 6 ft 7.2 in; 6 ft 4.4 in; 6 ft 6.2 in; 6 ft 6.1 in. Do a Spearman test of rank correlation at $\alpha = 0.05$, using a critical-value decision rule, of H_0: The rank of the team is not related to the rank of average team height, and H_1: The rank of the team has an increasing monotonic relationship to the rank of average team height.

Solution

(1) H_0: The team ranks and average heights have no relationship.
H_1: The team ranks and average heights have an increasing monotonic relationship.

(2) $\alpha = 0.05$

(3) With fewer than 30 paired ranks, we use Table A.15 to find the critical value. For $\alpha = 0.05$ and $n = 8$, we find that the decision rule for a right-tailed test is: Reject H_0 if $r_S > 0.643$.

(4) There are no tied ranks, so we use equation (20.14) to calculate the correlation coefficient. The first step in the calculation of r_S is to rank the observations. The end-of-season team ranks are provided, so we need only rank the average team heights. We then find d_i and d_i^2 for each team, as shown in Table 20.26. Using equation (20.14) with the sum of squared differences equal to 98 and $n = 8$,

$$r_S = 1 - \frac{6(98)}{8(8^2 - 1)} = -0.1667$$

From Table A.15, we find that the approximate probability of getting this sample correlation coefficient is: $P > 0.25$.

Table 20.26

Team rank	Average height	Rank of height	d_i	d_i^2
1	6 ft 5.5 in	5	−4	16
2	6 ft 5.0 in	6	−4	16
3	6 ft 6.5 in	2	+1	1
4	6 ft 3.8 in	8	−4	16
5	6 ft 7.2 in	1	+4	16
6	6 ft 4.4 in	7	−1	1
7	6 ft 6.2 in	3	+4	16
8	6 ft 6.1 in	4	+4	16
				$\sum = 98$

(5) As $r_S < 0.643$, we accept H_0 at the 0.05 level of significance. This result is confirmed by the fact that the probability of getting $r_S = -0.1667$ (given that the null hypothesis is true) is greater than 0.05. The end-of-season ranks in his basketball division are not related to the average height of the starting-five players.

Supplementary Problems

CHI-SQUARE TEST FOR GOODNESS-OF-FIT

20.27 A die is tossed 60 times. (Each one of the six faces has a different number of dots: 1, 2, 3, 4, 5, or 6). As each face has an equal probability (1/6) of landing upward, the expected frequency of a particular face is $(\frac{1}{6})(60) = 10$. The observed frequencies, listed from one dot to six dots, are: 7, 7, 11, 12, 13, 10. Do a chi-square test, at $\alpha = 0.05$, of H_0: The observed frequencies have a uniform distribution. Give the value of the test statistic. State whether you accept or reject H_0 and give the approximate probability of getting this χ^{2*} given that H_0 is true.

Ans. $\chi^{2*} = 3.20$, accept the null hypothesis because $\chi^{2*} < \chi^2_{0.05,5} = 11.07$, $0.500 < P < 0.900$

20.28 A drug store sells five kinds of toothbrushes and the manager wants to know whether all five sell in equal frequencies. He takes a random sample of 500 toothbrush sales and records the brand. The expected frequencies, if all five sell in equal frequencies, are 100 of each brand. The observed frequencies are: 81, 135, 97, 90, 97. Do a chi-square test, at $\alpha = 0.05$, of H_0: The observed frequences have a uniform distribution. Give the value of the test statistic. State whether you accept or reject H_0 and give the approximate probability of getting this χ^{2*} given that H_0 is true.

Ans. $\chi^{2*} = 17.04$, reject the null hypothesis because $\chi^{2*} > \chi^2_{0.05,4} = 9.49$, $P < 0.005$

20.29 A geneticist wants to know whether inheritance of a trait is in the form of a simple Mendelian inheritance without dominance. If so, the genotypes of the offspring from matings between two heterozygotes (each with two versions of the gene) will occur in a ratio of 1 : 2 : 1. He does the experiment and finds, among 200 offspring, a ratio of 35 : 95 : 70. Do a chi-square test, at $\alpha = 0.01$, of H_0: The observed frequencies are in a 1 : 2 : 1 ratio. Give the value of the test statistic. State whether you accept or reject H_0 and give the approximate probability of getting this χ^{2*} given that H_0 is true.

Ans. $\chi^{2*} = 12.75$, reject the null hypothesis because $\chi^{2*} > \chi^2_{0.01,2} = 9.21$, $P < 0.005$

CHI-SQUARE TEST FOR INDEPENDENCE: CONTINGENCY TABLE ANALYSIS

20.30 A college recruiter wants to know whether the college that a student attends (in-state or out-of-state) depends on parental status (a single parent or married parents). He randomly chooses, from a large city, 60 students and finds 25 students are from families with a single parent and 35 are from families with married parents. Of the single-parent students, 15 went to college within the state and 10 went to college out of the state. Of the married-parent students, 27 went to college within the state and 8 went to college out-of-state. Do a chi-square test, at $\alpha = 0.05$ with the correction factor, of H_0: Whether a student goes to a college within the state or out-of-state is not related to whether they come from a single-parent household or a married-parent household. Give the value of the test statistic. State whether you accept or reject H_0 and give the approximate probability of getting this χ^{2*} given that H_0 is true.

Ans. $\chi^{2*} = 1.306$, accept H_0 because $\chi^{2*} < \chi^2_{0.05,1} = 3.84$, $0.100 < P < 0.500$

20.31 A high-school administrator wants to know whether urban and rural parents differ with regard to the number of hours they want their children to attend school. She takes two random samples of parents, 200 from urban areas and 300 from rural areas, asking each parent whether they favor, oppose, or have no opinion on longer school days. Of the urban parents, she finds that 123 favor, 36 oppose, and 41 have no opinion. Of the rural parents, she finds that 145 favor, 85 oppose, and 70 have no opinion. Do a chi-square test, at $\alpha = 0.01$, of H_0: Opinion about lengthening the school day is not related to whether the parents live in an urban area or in a rural area. Give the value of the test statistic. State whether you accept or reject H_0 and give the approximate probability of getting this χ^{2*} given that H_0 is true.

Ans. $\chi^{2*} = 9.610$, reject H_0 because $\chi^{2*} > \chi^2_{0.01,2} = 9.21$, $0.005 < P < 0.010$

20.32 A county is considering building a new highway between its two major cities, and a newspaper reporter wants to know whether the position of citizens with regard to this project depends on their political affiliation. He interviews 1,000 citizens, selected at random, and finds that: (1) among the 420 Democrats in the sample, 211 are in favor, 144 are opposed, and 65 have no opinion; (2) among the 440 Republicans in the sample, 248 are in favor, 141 oppose, and 51 have no opinion; and (3) among the 140 citizens with no political affiliation, 76 are in favor, 40 are opposed, and 24 have no opinion. Do a chi-square test, at $\alpha = 0.05$, of H_0: Opinion with regard to building the new highway is independent of political affiliation. Give the value of the test statistic. State whether you accept or reject H_0 and give the approximate probability of getting this χ^{2*} given that H_0 is true.

Ans. $\chi^{2*} = 6.096$, accept H_0 because $\chi^{2*} < \chi^2_{0.05,4} = 9.49$, $0.100 < P < 0.500$

CHI-SQUARE TEST FOR HOMOGENEITY AMONG k BINOMIAL PROPORTIONS

20.33 The owner of a stationery store buys pencils of four brands (A, B, C, and D), and wants to know whether the proportion of unacceptable pencils varies among the brands. She takes a poll of 1,000 customers, 250 for each of the four kinds of pencils, and finds the number of customers who say the pencils are unacceptable is: 70 for brand A, 40 for brand B, 30 for brand C, and 60 for brand D. Do a chi-square test, at $\alpha = 0.01$, of H_0: The proportion of unacceptable pencils is the same for all four brands of pencils. Give the value of the test statistic. State whether you accept or reject H_0 and give the approximate probability of getting this χ^{2*} given that H_0 is true.

Ans. $\chi^{2*} = 25.00$, reject H_0 because $\chi^{2*} > \chi^2_{0.01,3} = 11.34$, $P < 0.005$

20.34 A sociologist wants to know whether the proportion of teen-age boys who belong to the Boy Scouts changes with age. He samples boys of five ages (13 through 17), 100 boys each, and finds that the numbers of boys belonging to a scout troop in the samples are: 26 for age 13, 29 for age 14, 32 for age 15, 31 for age 16, and 30 for age 17. Do a chi-square test, at $\alpha = 0.05$, of H_0: The proportion of boys that belong to a scout troop is the same for all five age groups. Give the value of the test statistic. State whether you accept or reject H_0 and give the approximate probability of getting this χ^{2*} given that H_0 is true.

Ans. $\chi^{2*} = 1.017$, accept H_0 because $\chi^{2*} < \chi^2_{0.05,4} = 9.49$, $0.900 < P < 0.950$

20.35 A high-school administrator wants to help high-school students pass their drivers' tests. She samples four driving schools, 30 customers each, and finds out how many customers passed the driver's test on their first try. She finds that the numbers who pass are: school A, 18; school B, 26; school C, 17; school D, 19. Do a chi-square test, at $\alpha = 0.05$, of H_0: The proportion of students who pass the driver's test the first time is the same for all four driving schools. Give the value of the test statistic. State whether you accept or reject H_0 and give the approximate probability of getting this χ^{2*} given that H_0 is true.

Ans. $\chi^{2*} = 7.500$, accept H_0 because $\chi^{2*} < \chi^2_{0.05,3} = 7.81$, $0.050 < P < 0.100$

ONE-SAMPLE TESTS: THE WILCOXON SIGNED-RANK TEST

20.36 A large population of lizards is known to have a median length of 54 mm from snout to vent. You want to know whether the body length is the same in a much smaller island population, which was formed by colonists from the larger population. You take a random sample of 25 lizards from this smaller population and find that $W_+ = 98$ and $W_- = -227$. Do a two-tailed Wilcoxon test, at $\alpha = 0.05$, of H_0: $\tilde{\mu} = \tilde{\mu}_0$ and H_1: $\tilde{\mu} \neq \tilde{\mu}_0$. Give the value of the test statistic. State whether you accept or reject H_0 and give the approximate probability of getting this W given that H_0 is true.

Ans. $W = 98$, accept H_0 because $W > 90$, $0.05 < P < 0.10$

20.37 The manager of a chain of shoe stores plans to open a new store and is told by the local government that the median income per household in the town is \$36,000. The manager thinks this estimate is too high. He takes a random sample of eight households and gets the following incomes: \$20,000, \$37,000, \$36,500, \$36,400, \$21,000, \$32,600, \$30,000, \$37,000. Do a one-tailed Wilcoxon test, at $\alpha = 0.05$, of H_0: $\tilde{\mu} = \tilde{\mu}_0$ and H_1: $\tilde{\mu} < \tilde{\mu}_0$. Give the value of the test statistic. State whether you accept or reject H_0 and give the approximate probability of getting this W given that H_0 is true.

Ans. $W = 10$, accept H_0 because $W > 6$, $P > 0.05$

20.38 The median IQ of high-school students is 100. A teacher wonders whether the median of her class is also 100. She checks the IQ scores of 12 of her students, chosen at random, and finds the following scores: 110, 98, 120, 130, 110, 97, 95, 125, 135, 128, 94, 96. Do a two-tailed Wilcoxon test, at $\alpha = 0.05$, of H_0: $\tilde{\mu} = \tilde{\mu}_0$ and H_1: $\tilde{\mu} \neq \tilde{\mu}_0$. Give the value of the test statistic. State whether you accept or reject H_0 and give the approximate probability of getting this W given that H_0 is true.

Ans. $W = 15$, accept H_0 because $W > 14$, $0.05 < P < 0.10$.

TWO-SAMPLE TESTS: THE WILCOXON SIGNED-RANK TEST FOR DEPENDENT SAMPLES

20.39 A secretarial school offers a speed-typing course and checks, each year, to see whether the course actually increases the number of words typed per minute. The manager takes a random sample of 15 students and measures their rate of typing, in words per minute, before (sample 1) and after (sample 2) the class. The scores of these students, with the "before" rate listed first, are: (100, 120); (105, 100); (90, 96); (120, 118); (110, 128); (95, 94); (98, 121); (97, 135); (86, 93); (95, 87); (99, 111); (115, 140); (115, 112); (120, 130); (120, 109). Do a small-sample Wilcoxon test, at $\alpha = 0.05$, of H_0: $\tilde{\mu}_1 = \tilde{\mu}_2$ and H_1: $\tilde{\mu}_1 < \tilde{\mu}_2$. Give the value of the test statistic. State whether you accept or reject H_0 and give the approximate probability of getting this W given that H_0 is true.

Ans. $W = 26$, reject H_0 because $W < 30$, $0.025 < P < 0.050$

20.40 The manager of the secretarial school wants to make a stronger argument for its speed-typing course in its advertisements. She takes a larger sample of 50 students, measures their typing speed, in words per minute, before (sample 1) and after (sample 2) the course. She calculates the differences, in words per minute, ranks the difference scores, and restores the signs of the difference scores to their corresponding ranks. She finds that $W_+ = 365$ and $W_- = -910$. Do a large-sample Wilcoxon test, at $\alpha = 0.01$, of H_0: $\tilde{\mu}_1 = \tilde{\mu}_2$ and H_1: $\tilde{\mu}_1 < \tilde{\mu}_2$. Give the value of the test statistic. State whether you accept or reject H_0 and give the approximate probability of getting this z^* given that H_0 is true.

Ans. $z^* = -2.631$, reject H_0 because $z^* < -z_{0.01} = -2.33$, $P \approx 0.004$

20.41 A garage manager receives two kinds of tires to sell, brand A and brand B. He wants to know whether the two brands are equally good, in terms of miles-to-deterioration. He chooses eight cars at random and puts one brand on the left-front side and the other on the right-front side of each car (the side for each brand is selected at random). He then records the number of miles-to-deterioration, and gets these results (brand A is listed first): (41,000, 40,000); (38,000, 40,000); (38,500, 40,000); (43,000, 40,000); (42,500, 41,400); (41,500, 42,300); (40,100, 40,200); (39,600, 41,300). Do a two-tailed Wilcoxon test, at $\alpha = 0.05$, of H_0: $\tilde{\mu}_1 = \tilde{\mu}_2$ and H_1: $\tilde{\mu}_1 \neq \tilde{\mu}_2$. Give the value of the test statistic. State whether you accept or reject H_0 and give the approximate probability of getting this W given that H_0 is true.

Ans. $W = 15$, accept H_0 because $W > 4$, $P > 0.10$

TWO-SAMPLE TESTS: THE MANN-WHITNEY U TEST FOR INDEPENDENT SAMPLES

20.42 A psychologist has developed two new methods of teaching arithmetic to fourth-grade students. To find out whether method A is better than method B, he chooses, at random, 6 fourth-graders for learning under method A (sample A) and 8 fourth-graders for learning under method B (sample B). After 16 weeks of classes, he gives both groups the same test, and records the time it takes to correctly solve a set of problems. Times (in minutes) for sample A are: 50, 45, 30, 42, 36, 33. Times for sample B are: 52, 51, 47, 35, 40, 38, 53, 34. Do a one-tailed Mann-Whitney test, at $\alpha = 0.05$, of H_0: The distribution of scores in population A is not different from the distribution of scores in population B, and H_1: The distribution of scores in population A is smaller than the distribution of scores in population B. Give the value of the test statistic and state whether you accept or reject H_0.

Ans. $U = 15$, accept H_0 because $U > 10$

20.43 The psychologist described in Problem 20.42 repeats the experiment with larger samples: 40 students for each method. He finds that $R_1 = 1{,}250$ and $R_2 = 1{,}990$, with no ties between groups. Do a one-tailed Mann-Whitney U test, at $\alpha = 0.01$, of H_0: The distribution of scores in population A is the same as in population B, and H_1: The distribution of scores in population A is lower than in population B. Give the value of the test statistic. State whether or not you accept H_0 and the probability of getting this z^* given that H_0 is true.

Ans. $z^* = -3.560$, reject H_0 because $z^* < -2.33$, $P = 0.0002$

20.44 Repeat the statistical test described above, but incorporating these tied ranks: three ties at rank 2, five ties at rank 5, and eight ties at rank 10. Give the value of the test statistic. State whether or not you accept H_0 and the approximate probability of getting this z^* if H_0 is true.

Ans. $z^* = -3.563$, reject H_0 because $z^* < -2.33$, $P = 0.0002$

MULTISAMPLE TESTS: THE KRUSKAL-WALLIS H TEST FOR k INDEPENDENT SAMPLES

20.45 A mathematics teacher is experimenting with three different methods of teaching geometry to eighth-grade students. He chooses, at random, four students for each method and, after two semesters of classes, evaluates them on the basis of their score on a comprehensive examination. His results are: method A, 60, 55, 78, 66; method B, 61, 74, 60, 63; method C, 72, 77, 82, 80. Do a Kruskal-Wallis H test, at $\alpha = 0.05$, of H_0: The distributions of scores for the three methods are the same. Give the value of the test statistic and state whether you accept or reject H_0.

Ans. $H = 4.875$, accept H_0 because $H < H_{0.05} = 5.692$

20.46 The mathematics teacher described in Problem 20.45 repeats his study, choosing 10 students at random for each of the three methods. His results are: method A, 50, 60, 64, 67, 63, 75, 81, 55, 51, 53; method B, 58, 43, 49, 65, 74, 68, 71, 70, 57, 66; method C, 70, 78, 80, 76, 86, 74, 72, 73, 83, 84. Do a Kruskal-Wallis H test, at $\alpha = 0.01$, of H_0: The distributions of scores for the three methods are the same. Give the value of the test statistic. State whether you accept or reject H_0 and give the approximate probability of getting this sample value given that H_0 is true.

Ans. $H = 13.659$, reject H_0 because $H > \chi^2_{0.01,2} = 9.21$, $P < 0.005$

20.47 A golf instructor wants to know whether there is a relationship between age of golfer and amount of money won in a tournament. He chooses, at random, four golfers from each of three age classes and gets these results: under 25 years of age, \$7,535, \$10,000, \$13,000, \$12,000; from 26 to 30 years of age, \$25,000, \$18,500, \$13,500, \$20,000; over 30 years of age, \$21,900, \$30,000, \$33,000, \$28,000. Do a Kruskal-Wallis H test, at $\alpha = 0.05$, of H_0: The distributions of winnings for the three age groups are the same. Give the value of the test statistic and state whether you accept or reject H_0.

Ans. $H = 9.269$, reject H_0 because $H > H_{0.05} = 5.692$

20.48 The golf instructor in Problem 20.47 repeats his study with larger samples. He chooses, at random, seven golfers from each of the three age classes and gets these results: under 25 years of age, \$28,000, \$12,000, \$15,000, \$15,500, \$12,500, \$14,000, \$14,500; from 26 to 30 years of age, \$30,000, \$34,000, \$16,000, \$18,000, \$21,000, \$16,500, \$17,000; over 30 years of age, \$20,000, \$25,000, \$28,000, \$35,000, \$29,500, \$42,500, \$41,000. Do a Kruskal-Wallis H test, $\alpha = 0.01$, of H_0: The distributions of winnings for the three age groups are the same. Give the value of the test statistic. State whether you accept or reject H_0 and give the approximate probability of getting this χ^{2*} value given that H_0 is true.

Ans. $H = 11.668$, reject H_0 because $H > \chi^2_{0.01,2} = 9.21$, $P < 0.005$

THE SPEARMAN TEST OF RANK CORRELATION

20.49 A panel of critics has ranked 10 college towns on two criteria: quality of life (rank 1 has the best quality) and crime rate (rank 1 has the most crime). There are no ties within the ranks of either variable. Subtracting the rank for crime rate from the rank for quality of life, we get: $-7, -7, -3, 1, 0, -2, 0, 4, 8, 8$. Do a two-tailed Spearman test of rank correlation, at $\alpha = 0.05$, of H_0: The rank for quality of life is not related to the rank for crime rate. Give the value of the test statistic and state whether you accept or reject H_0.

Ans. $r_S = -0.552$, accept H_0 because $r_S > -0.648$

20.50 A rock-climbing instructor thinks that more climbing accidents occur on easy climbs, due to more amateur climbers, than on hard climbs. He has kept records on the number of accidents that have occurred over a 5-year period on 12 rock climbs, which are ranked from 1 (least difficult) through 12 in terms of difficulty. The number of accidents, listed in order of climbing difficulty, are: 2 (least difficult), 3, 5, 3, 4, 3, 3, 4, 4, 2, 1, 1 (most difficult). Note the large proportion of ties within the rankings. Do a one-tailed Spearman test of rank correlation, at $\alpha = 0.05$, of H_0: There is no relation between number of accidents and difficulty of climb, and H_1: There is a decreasing, monotonic relation between number of accidents and difficulty of climb. Give the value of the test statistic and state whether you accept or reject H_0.

Ans. $r_S = -0.4371$, accept H_0 because $r_S > -0.503$

20.51 A travel agent wants to know whether there is a correlation between vacation cost and distance traveled. She interviews 40 vacationers and ranks their distance traveled, from 1 through 40, without ties. She finds out the weekly cost of each vacation (without ties). Subtracting the ranks of distances from the ranks of costs, she gets these differences: −10, −29, −6, −8, −8, +5, −10, +6, −9, +6, −4, −4, +6, −20, −4, +6, −8, +10, −18, −6, −6, −18, −5, −5, +1, +3, −6, +23, +26, −8, +9, −3, +27, +5, +21, +6, +17, +17, +7, +4. Do a one-tailed Spearman test of rank correlation, at $\alpha = 0.01$, of H_0: There is no relation between vacation cost and distance traveled, and H_1: There is an increasing monotonic relationship between vacation cost and distance traveled. Give the value of the test statistic. State whether you accept or reject H_0 and give the approximate probability of getting this z^* given that H_0 is true.

Ans. $r_S = 0.4263$, $z^* = 2.66$, reject H_0 because $z^* > 2.33$, $P < 0.004$

Appendix

Table A.3 Cumulative Binomial Probabilities

This table gives cumulative probabilities calculated using

$$F(a) = \sum_{x \le a} \left[f(x) = \binom{n}{x} p^x q^{n-x} \right]$$

for $n = 2, 3, \ldots, 10$ and $p = 0.01, 0.05, \ldots, 0.50$. To find $F(a)$ for $p > 0.50$, enter the table at the appropriate n, find the intersection of row $n - (x + 1)$ and column $1 - p$ and then subtract this intersection-value from 1.

		p											
n	*a*	0.01	0.05	0.10	0.15	0.20	0.25	0.30	1/3	0.35	0.40	0.45	0.50
2	0	0.9801	0.9025	0.8100	0.7225	0.6400	0.5625	0.4900	0.4444	0.4225	0.3600	0.3025	0.2500
	1	0.9999	0.9975	0.9900	0.9775	0.9600	0.9375	0.9100	0.8889	0.8775	0.8400	0.7975	0.7500
	2	1.0000	1.0000	1.0000	1.0000	1.0000	1.0000	1.0000	1.0000	1.0000	1.0000	1.0000	1.0000
3	0	0.9703	0.8574	0.7290	0.6141	0.5120	0.4219	0.3430	0.2963	0.2746	0.2160	0.1664	0.1250
	1	0.9997	0.9927	0.9720	0.9393	0.8960	0.8437	0.7840	0.7407	0.7183	0.6480	0.5748	0.5000
	2	1.0000	0.9999	0.9990	0.9966	0.9920	0.9844	0.9730	0.9630	0.9571	0.9360	0.9089	0.8750
	3	1.0000	1.0000	1.0000	1.0000	1.0000	1.0000	1.0000	1.0000	1.0000	1.0000	1.0000	1.0000
4	0	0.9606	0.8145	0.6561	0.5220	0.4096	0.3164	0.2401	0.1975	0.1785	0.1296	0.0915	0.0625
	1	0.9994	0.9860	0.9477	0.8905	0.8192	0.7383	0.6517	0.5926	0.5630	0.4752	0.3910	0.3125
	2	1.0000	0.9995	0.9963	0.9880	0.9728	0.9492	0.9163	0.8889	0.8735	0.8208	0.7585	0.6875
	3	1.0000	1.0000	0.9999	0.9995	0.9984	0.9961	0.9919	0.9877	0.9850	0.9744	0.9590	0.9375
	4	1.0000	1.0000	1.0000	1.0000	1.0000	1.0000	1.0000	1.0000	1.0000	1.0000	1.0000	1.0000
5	0	0.9510	0.7738	0.5905	0.4437	0.3277	0.2373	0.1681	0.1317	0.1160	0.0778	0.0503	0.0312
	1	0.9990	0.9774	0.9185	0.8352	0.7373	0.6328	0.5282	0.4609	0.4284	0.3370	0.2562	0.1875
	2	1.0000	0.9988	0.9914	0.9734	0.9421	0.8965	0.8369	0.7901	0.7648	0.6826	0.5931	0.5000
	3	1.0000	1.0000	0.9995	0.9978	0.9933	0.9844	0.9692	0.9547	0.9460	0.9130	0.8688	0.8125
	4	1.0000	1.0000	1.0000	0.9999	0.9997	0.9990	0.9976	0.9959	0.9947	0.9898	0.9815	0.9687
	5	1.0000	1.0000	1.0000	1.0000	1.0000	1.0000	1.0000	1.0000	1.0000	1.0000	1.0000	1.0000
6	0	0.9415	0.7351	0.5314	0.3771	0.2621	0.1780	0.1176	0.0878	0.0754	0.0467	0.0277	0.0156
	1	0.9985	0.9672	0.8857	0.7765	0.6554	0.5339	0.4202	0.3512	0.3191	0.2333	0.1636	0.1094
	2	1.0000	0.9978	0.9841	0.9527	0.9011	0.8306	0.7443	0.6804	0.6471	0.5443	0.4415	0.3437
	3	1.0000	0.9999	0.9987	0.9941	0.9830	0.9624	0.9295	0.8999	0.8826	0.8208	0.7447	0.6562
	4	1.0000	1.0000	0.9999	0.9996	0.9984	0.9954	0.9891	0.9822	0.9777	0.9590	0.9308	0.8906
	5	1.0000	1.0000	1.0000	1.0000	0.9999	0.9998	0.9993	0.9986	0.9982	0.9959	0.9917	0.9844
	6	1.0000	1.0000	1.0000	1.0000	1.0000	1.0000	1.0000	1.0000	1.0000	1.0000	1.0000	1.0000
7	0	0.9321	0.6983	0.4783	0.3206	0.2097	0.1335	0.0824	0.0585	0.0490	0.0280	0.0152	0.0078
	1	0.9980	0.9556	0.8503	0.7166	0.5767	0.4449	0.3294	0.2634	0.2338	0.1586	0.1024	0.0625
	2	1.0000	0.9962	0.9743	0.9262	0.8520	0.7564	0.6471	0.5706	0.5323	0.4199	0.3164	0.2266
	3	1.0000	0.9998	0.9973	0.9879	0.9667	0.9294	0.8740	0.8267	0.8002	0.7102	0.6083	0.5000
	4	1.0000	1.0000	0.9998	0.9988	0.9953	0.9871	0.9712	0.9547	0.9444	0.9037	0.8471	0.7734
	5	1.0000	1.0000	1.0000	0.9999	0.9996	0.9987	0.9962	0.9931	0.9910	0.9812	0.9643	0.9375
	6	1.0000	1.0000	1.0000	1.0000	1.0000	0.9999	0.9998	0.9995	0.9994	0.9984	0.9963	0.9922
	7	1.0000	1.0000	1.0000	1.0000	1.0000	1.0000	1.0000	1.0000	1.0000	1.0000	1.0000	1.0000

Table A.3 (*continued*)

		p											
n	*a*	0.01	0.05	0.10	0.15	0.20	0.25	0.30	1/3	0.35	0.40	0.45	0.50
8	0	0.9227	0.6634	0.4305	0.2725	0.1678	0.1001	0.0576	0.0390	0.0319	0.0168	0.0084	0.0039
	1	0.9973	0.9428	0.8131	0.6572	0.5033	0.3671	0.2553	0.1951	0.1691	0.1064	0.0632	0.0352
	2	0.9999	0.9942	0.9619	0.8948	0.7969	0.6785	0.5518	0.4682	0.4278	0.3154	0.2201	0.1445
	3	1.0000	0.9996	0.9950	0.9786	0.9437	0.8862	0.8059	0.7414	0.7064	0.5941	0.4770	0.3633
	4	1.0000	1.0000	0.9996	0.9971	0.9896	0.9727	0.9420	0.9121	0.8939	0.8263	0.7396	0.6367
	5	1.0000	1.0000	1.0000	0.9998	0.9988	0.9958	0.9887	0.9803	0.9747	0.9502	0.9115	0.8555
	6	1.0000	1.0000	1.0000	1.0000	0.9999	0.9996	0.9987	0.9974	0.9964	0.9915	0.9819	0.9648
	7	1.0000	1.0000	1.0000	1.0000	1.0000	1.0000	0.9999	0.9998	0.9998	0.9993	0.9983	0.9961
	8	1.0000	1.0000	1.0000	1.0000	1.0000	1.0000	1.0000	1.0000	1.0000	1.0000	1.0000	1.0000
9	0	0.9135	0.6302	0.3874	0.2316	0.1342	0.0751	0.0404	0.0260	0.0207	0.0101	0.0046	0.0020
	1	0.9966	0.9288	0.7748	0.5995	0.4362	0.3003	0.1960	0.1431	0.1211	0.0705	0.0385	0.0195
	2	0.9999	0.9916	0.9470	0.8591	0.7382	0.6007	0.4628	0.3772	0.3373	0.2318	0.1495	0.0898
	3	1.0000	0.9994	0.9917	0.9661	0.9144	0.8343	0.7297	0.6503	0.6089	0.4826	0.3614	0.2539
	4	1.0000	1.0000	0.9991	0.9944	0.9804	0.9511	0.9012	0.8552	0.8283	0.7334	0.6214	0.5000
	5	1.0000	1.0000	0.9999	0.9994	0.9969	0.9900	0.9747	0.9576	0.9464	0.9006	0.8342	0.7461
	6	1.0000	1.0000	1.0000	1.0000	0.9997	0.9987	0.9957	0.9917	0.9888	0.9750	0.9502	0.9102
	7	1.0000	1.0000	1.0000	1.0000	1.0000	0.9999	0.9996	0.9990	0.9986	0.9962	0.9909	0.9805
	8	1.0000	1.0000	1.0000	1.0000	1.0000	1.0000	1.0000	0.9999	0.9999	0.9997	0.9992	0.9980
	9	1.0000	1.0000	1.0000	1.0000	1.0000	1.0000	1.0000	1.0000	1.0000	1.0000	1.0000	1.0000
10	0	0.9044	0.5987	0.3487	0.1969	0.1074	0.0563	0.0282	0.0173	0.0135	0.0060	0.0025	0.0010
	1	0.9957	0.9139	0.7361	0.5443	0.3758	0.2440	0.1493	0.1040	0.0860	0.0464	0.0233	0.0107
	2	0.9999	0.9855	0.9298	0.8202	0.6778	0.5256	0.3828	0.2991	0.2616	0.1673	0.0996	0.0547
	3	1.0000	0.9990	0.9872	0.9500	0.8791	0.7759	0.6496	0.5593	0.5138	0.3823	0.2660	0.1719
	4	1.0000	0.9999	0.9984	0.9901	0.9672	0.9219	0.8497	0.7869	0.7515	0.6331	0.5044	0.3770
	5	1.0000	1.0000	0.9999	0.9986	0.9936	0.9803	0.9527	0.9234	0.9051	0.8338	0.7384	0.6230
	6	1.0000	1.0000	1.0000	0.9999	0.9991	0.9965	0.9894	0.9803	0.9740	0.9452	0.8980	0.8281
	7	1.0000	1.0000	1.0000	1.0000	0.9999	0.9996	0.9984	0.9966	0.9952	0.9877	0.9726	0.9453
	8	1.0000	1.0000	1.0000	1.0000	1.0000	1.0000	0.9999	0.9996	0.9995	0.9983	0.9955	0.9893
	9	1.0000	1.0000	1.0000	1.0000	1.0000	1.0000	1.0000	1.0000	1.0000	0.9999	0.9997	0.9990
	10	1.0000	1.0000	1.0000	1.0000	1.0000	1.0000	1.0000	1.0000	1.0000	1.0000	1.0000	1.0000

Source: Wilfrid J. Dixon and Frank J. Massey, *Introduction to Statistical Analysis* (4th ed.), McGraw-Hill, New York, 1983. Reproduced with permission of The McGraw-Hill Companies.

Table A.4 Cumulative Poisson Probabilities

This table gives cumulative Poisson probabilities calculated using

$$F(a) = \sum_{x \leq a} \left[f(x) = \frac{\mu^x e^{-\mu}}{x!} \right]$$

for $\mu = 0.001, \ldots, 1.00$, and $\mu = 1.1, \ldots, 8.0$.

	μ														
a	0.001	0.01	0.05	0.10	0.15	0.20	0.25	0.30	0.40	0.50	0.60	0.70	0.80	0.90	1.00
0	0.999	0.990	0.951	0.905	0.861	0.819	0.779	0.741	0.670	0.607	0.549	0.497	0.449	0.407	0.368
1	1.000	1.000	0.991	0.995	0.990	0.982	0.974	0.963	0.938	0.910	0.878	0.844	0.809	0.772	0.736
2			1.000	1.000	0.999	0.999	0.998	0.996	0.992	0.986	0.977	0.966	0.953	0.937	0.920
3					1.000	1.000	1.000	1.000	0.999	0.998	0.997	0.994	0.991	0.987	0.981
4									1.000	1.000	1.000	0.999	0.999	0.998	0.996
5												1.000	1.000	1.000	0.999
6															1.000

	μ														
a	1.1	1.5	2.0	2.5	3.0	3.5	4.0	4.5	5.0	5.5	6.0	6.5	7.0	7.5	8.0
0	0.333	0.223	0.135	0.082	0.050	0.030	0.018	0.011	0.007	0.004	0.002	0.002	0.001	0.001	0.000
1	0.699	0.558	0.406	0.287	0.199	0.136	0.092	0.061	0.040	0.027	0.017	0.011	0.007	0.005	0.003
2	0.900	0.809	0.677	0.544	0.423	0.321	0.238	0.174	0.125	0.088	0.062	0.042	0.030	0.020	0.014
3	0.974	0.934	0.857	0.758	0.647	0.537	0.433	0.342	0.265	0.202	0.151	0.112	0.082	0.059	0.042
4	0.995	0.981	0.947	0.891	0.815	0.725	0.629	0.532	0.440	0.358	0.285	0.224	0.173	0.132	0.100
5	0.999	0.996	0.983	0.958	0.916	0.858	0.785	0.703	0.616	0.529	0.446	0.369	0.301	0.241	0.191
6	1.000	0.999	0.995	0.986	0.966	0.935	0.889	0.831	0.762	0.686	0.606	0.527	0.450	0.378	0.313
7		1.000	0.999	0.996	0.988	0.973	0.949	0.913	0.867	0.809	0.744	0.673	0.599	0.525	0.453
8			1.000	0.999	0.996	0.990	0.979	0.960	0.932	0.894	0.847	0.792	0.729	0.662	0.593
9				1.000	0.999	0.997	0.992	0.983	0.968	0.946	0.916	0.877	0.830	0.776	0.717
10					1.000	0.999	0.997	0.993	0.986	0.975	0.957	0.933	0.901	0.862	0.816
11						1.000	0.999	0.998	0.995	0.989	0.980	0.966	0.947	0.921	0.888
12							1.000	0.999	0.998	0.996	0.991	0.984	0.973	0.957	0.936
13								1.000	0.999	0.998	0.996	0.993	0.987	0.978	0.966
14									1.000	0.999	0.999	0.997	0.994	0.990	0.983
15										1.000	0.999	0.999	0.998	0.995	0.992
16											1.000	1.000	0.999	0.998	0.996
17													1.000	0.999	0.998
18														1.000	0.999
19															1.000

Source: Wilfrid J. Dixon and Frank J. Massey, *Introduction to Statistical Analysis* (4th ed.), McGraw-Hill, New York, 1983. Reproduced with permission of The McGraw-Hill Companies.

Table A.5 Areas of the Standard Normal Distribution

This table gives areas of the standard normal distribution that lie under the curve above the interval from 0 to z (the shaded area in the figure), where z represents specific positive values of the standard normal variable Z.

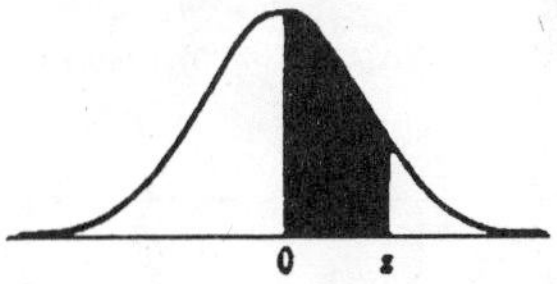

z	0.00	0.01	0.02	0.03	0.04	0.05	0.06	0.07	0.08	0.09
0.0	0.0000	0.0040	0.0080	0.0120	0.0160	0.0199	0.0239	0.0279	0.0319	0.0359
0.1	0.0398	0.0438	0.0478	0.0517	0.0557	0.0596	0.0636	0.0675	0.0714	0.0754
0.2	0.0793	0.0832	0.0871	0.0910	0.0948	0.0987	0.1026	0.1064	0.1103	0.1141
0.3	0.1179	0.1217	0.1255	0.1293	0.1331	0.1368	0.1406	0.1443	0.1480	0.1517
0.4	0.1554	0.1591	0.1628	0.1664	0.1700	0.1736	0.1772	0.1808	0.1844	0.1879
0.5	0.1915	0.1950	0.1985	0.2019	0.2054	0.2088	0.2123	0.2157	0.2190	0.2224
0.6	0.2258	0.2291	0.2324	0.2357	0.2389	0.2422	0.2454	0.2486	0.2518	0.2549
0.7	0.2580	0.2612	0.2642	0.2673	0.2704	0.2734	0.2764	0.2794	0.2823	0.2852
0.8	0.2881	0.2910	0.2939	0.2967	0.2996	0.3023	0.3051	0.3078	0.3106	0.3133
0.9	0.3159	0.3186	0.3212	0.3238	0.3264	0.3289	0.3315	0.3340	0.3365	0.3389
1.0	0.3413	0.3438	0.3461	0.3485	0.3508	0.3531	0.3554	0.3577	0.3599	0.3621
1.1	0.3643	0.3665	0.3686	0.3708	0.3729	0.3749	0.3770	0.3790	0.3810	0.3830
1.2	0.3849	0.3869	0.3888	0.3907	0.3925	0.3944	0.3962	0.3980	0.3997	0.4015
1.3	0.4032	0.4049	0.4066	0.4082	0.4099	0.4115	0.4131	0.4147	0.4162	0.4177
1.4	0.4192	0.4207	0.4222	0.4236	0.4251	0.4265	0.4279	0.4292	0.4306	0.4319
1.5	0.4332	0.4345	0.4357	0.4370	0.4382	0.4394	0.4406	0.4418	0.4429	0.4441
1.6	0.4452	0.4463	0.4474	0.4484	0.4495	0.4505	0.4515	0.4525	0.4535	0.4545
1.7	0.4554	0.4564	0.4573	0.4582	0.4591	0.4599	0.4608	0.4616	0.4625	0.4633
1.8	0.4641	0.4649	0.4656	0.4664	0.4671	0.4678	0.4686	0.4693	0.4699	0.4706
1.9	0.4713	0.4719	0.4726	0.4732	0.4738	0.4744	0.4750	0.4756	0.4761	0.4767
2.0	0.4772	0.4778	0.4783	0.4788	0.4793	0.4798	0.4803	0.4808	0.4812	0.4817
2.1	0.4821	0.4826	0.4830	0.4834	0.4838	0.4842	0.4846	0.4850	0.4854	0.4857
2.2	0.4861	0.4864	0.4868	0.4871	0.4875	0.4878	0.4881	0.4884	0.4887	0.4890
2.3	0.4893	0.4896	0.4898	0.4901	0.4904	0.4906	0.4909	0.4911	0.4913	0.4916
2.4	0.4918	0.4920	0.4922	0.4925	0.4927	0.4929	0.4931	0.4932	0.4934	0.4936
2.5	0.4938	0.4940	0.4941	0.4943	0.4945	0.4946	0.4948	0.4949	0.4951	0.4952
2.6	0.4953	0.4955	0.4956	0.4957	0.4959	0.4960	0.4961	0.4962	0.4963	0.4964
2.7	0.4965	0.4966	0.4967	0.4968	0.4969	0.4970	0.4971	0.4972	0.4973	0.4974
2.8	0.4974	0.4975	0.4976	0.4977	0.4977	0.4978	0.4979	0.4979	0.4980	0.4981
2.9	0.4981	0.4982	0.4982	0.4983	0.4984	0.4984	0.4985	0.4985	0.4986	0.4986
3.0	0.4987	0.4987	0.4987	0.4988	0.4988	0.4989	0.4989	0.4989	0.4990	0.4990
3.1	0.4990	0.4991	0.4991	0.4991	0.4992	0.4992	0.4992	0.4992	0.4993	0.4993
3.2	0.4993	0.4993	0.4994	0.4994	0.4994	0.4994	0.4994	0.4995	0.4995	0.4995
3.3	0.4995	0.4995	0.4995	0.4996	0.4996	0.4996	0.4996	0.4996	0.4996	0.4997
3.4	0.4997	0.4997	0.4997	0.4997	0.4997	0.4997	0.4997	0.4997	0.4997	0.4998
3.5	0.4998	0.4998	0.4998	0.4998	0.4998	0.4998	0.4998	0.4998	0.4998	0.4998
3.6	0.4998	0.4998	0.4999	0.4999	0.4999	0.4999	0.4999	0.4999	0.4999	0.4999
3.7	0.4999	0.4999	0.4999	0.4999	0.4999	0.4999	0.4999	0.4999	0.4999	0.4999
3.8	0.4999	0.4999	0.4999	0.4999	0.4999	0.4999	0.4999	0.4999	0.4999	0.4999
3.9	0.5000	0.5000	0.5000	0.5000	0.5000	0.5000	0.5000	0.5000	0.5000	0.5000

Source: Murray R. Spiegel, *Schaum's Outline of Theory and Problems of Statistics* (2nd ed.), McGraw-Hill, New York, 1988. Reproduced with permission of The McGraw-Hill Companies.

Table A.6 Critical Values of the *t* Distribution

This table gives positive critical $t_{\alpha/2,\nu}$ and $t_{\alpha,\nu}$ values for selected t distributions ($\nu = 1, \ldots, 30, 40, 60, 120, \infty$). Use of the table is explained in Section 14.20.

	$t_{\alpha/2}$					
	$t_{0.20/2}$	$t_{0.10/2}$	$t_{0.05/2}$	$t_{0.02/2}$	$t_{0.01/2}$	$t_{0.001/2}$
	t_{α}					
ν	$t_{0.10}$	$t_{0.05}$	$t_{0.025}$	$t_{0.01}$	$t_{0.005}$	$t_{0.0005}$
1	3.078	6.314	12.706	31.821	63.657	636.619
2	1.886	2.920	4.303	6.965	9.925	31.598
3	1.638	2.353	3.182	4.541	5.841	12.941
4	1.533	2.132	2.776	3.747	4.604	8.610
5	1.476	2.015	2.571	3.365	4.032	6.859
6	1.440	1.943	2.447	3.143	3.707	5.959
7	1.415	1.895	2.365	2.998	3.499	5.405
8	1.397	1.860	2.306	2.896	3.355	5.041
9	1.383	1.833	2.262	2.821	3.250	4.781
10	1.372	1.812	2.228	2.764	3.169	4.587
11	1.363	1.796	2.201	2.718	3.106	4.437
12	1.356	1.782	2.179	2.681	3.055	4.318
13	1.350	1.771	2.160	2.650	3.012	4.221
14	1.345	1.761	2.145	2.624	2.977	4.140
15	1.341	1.753	2.131	2.602	2.947	4.073
16	1.337	1.746	2.120	2.583	2.921	4.015
17	1.333	1.740	2.110	2.567	2.898	3.965
18	1.330	1.734	2.101	2.552	2.878	3.922
19	1.328	1.729	2.093	2.539	2.861	3.883
20	1.325	1.725	2.086	2.528	2.845	3.850
21	1.323	1.721	2.080	2.518	2.831	3.819
22	1.321	1.717	2.074	2.508	2.819	3.792
23	1.319	1.714	2.069	2.500	2.807	3.767
24	1.318	1.711	2.064	2.492	2.797	3.745
25	1.316	1.708	2.060	2.485	2.787	3.725
26	1.315	1.706	2.056	2.479	2.779	3.707
27	1.314	1.703	2.052	2.473	2.771	3.690
28	1.313	1.701	2.048	2.467	2.763	3.674
29	1.311	1.699	2.045	2.462	2.756	3.659
30	1.310	1.697	2.042	2.457	2.750	3.646
40	1.303	1.684	2.021	2.423	2.704	3.551
60	1.296	1.671	2.000	2.390	2.660	3.460
120	1.289	1.658	1.980	2.358	2.617	3.373
∞	1.282	1.645	1.960	2.326	2.576	3.291

Source: Table III of Ronald A. Fisher and Frank Yates, *Statistical Tables for Biological, Agricultural and Medical Research* (6th ed.), Longman Group Ltd., London, 1974. (Previously published by Oliver & Boyd Ltd., Edinburgh.) Reprinted by permission of Pearson Education Limited.

Table A.7 Critical Values of the Chi-square Distribution

This table gives critical $\chi^2_{\alpha,\nu}$ values for selected chi-square distributions ($\nu = 1, \ldots, 30, 40, 50, 60, 70, 80, 90, 100$). Use of the table is explained in Section 15.4.

	χ^2_α										
ν	$\chi^2_{0.995}$	$\chi^2_{0.990}$	$\chi^2_{0.975}$	$\chi^2_{0.950}$	$\chi^2_{0.900}$	$\chi^2_{0.500}$	$\chi^2_{0.100}$	$\chi^2_{0.050}$	$\chi^2_{0.025}$	$\chi^2_{0.010}$	$\chi^2_{0.005}$
1	0.00004	0.00016	0.00098	0.00393	0.0158	0.455	2.71	3.84	5.02	6.63	7.88
2	0.0100	0.0201	0.0506	0.103	0.211	1.386	4.61	5.99	7.38	9.21	10.60
3	0.072	0.115	0.216	0.352	0.584	2.366	6.25	7.81	9.35	11.34	12.84
4	0.207	0.297	0.484	0.711	1.064	3.357	7.78	9.49	11.14	13.28	14.86
5	0.412	0.554	0.831	1.145	1.61	4.251	9.24	11.07	12.83	15.09	16.75
6	0.676	0.872	1.24	1.64	2.20	5.35	10.64	12.59	14.45	16.81	18.55
7	0.989	1.24	1.69	2.17	2.83	6.35	12.02	14.07	16.01	18.48	20.28
8	1.34	1.65	2.18	2.73	3.49	7.34	13.36	15.51	17.53	20.09	21.96
9	1.73	2.09	2.70	3.33	4.17	8.34	14.68	16.92	19.02	21.67	23.59
10	2.16	2.56	3.25	3.94	4.87	9.34	15.99	18.31	20.48	23.21	25.19
11	2.60	3.05	3.82	4.57	5.58	10.34	17.28	19.68	21.92	24.73	26.76
12	3.07	3.57	4.40	5.23	6.30	11.34	18.55	21.03	23.34	26.22	28.30
13	3.57	4.11	5.01	5.89	7.04	12.34	19.81	22.36	24.74	27.69	29.82
14	4.07	4.66	5.63	6.57	7.79	13.34	21.06	23.68	26.12	29.14	31.32
15	4.60	5.23	6.26	7.26	8.55	14.34	22.31	25.00	27.49	30.58	32.80
16	5.14	5.81	6.91	7.96	9.31	15.34	23.54	26.30	28.85	32.00	34.27
17	5.70	6.41	7.56	8.67	10.09	16.34	24.77	27.59	30.19	33.41	35.72
18	6.26	7.01	8.23	9.39	10.86	17.34	25.99	28.87	31.53	34.81	37.16
19	6.84	7.63	8.91	10.12	11.65	18.34	27.20	30.14	32.85	36.19	38.58
20	7.43	8.26	9.59	10.85	12.44	19.34	28.41	31.41	34.17	37.57	40.00
21	8.03	8.90	10.28	11.59	13.24	20.34	29.62	32.67	35.48	38.93	41.40
22	8.64	9.54	10.98	12.34	14.04	21.34	30.81	33.92	36.78	40.29	42.80
23	9.26	10.20	11.69	13.09	14.85	22.34	32.01	35.17	38.08	41.64	44.18
24	9.89	10.86	12.40	13.85	15.66	23.34	33.20	36.42	39.36	42.98	45.56
25	10.52	11.52	13.12	14.61	16.47	24.34	34.38	37.65	40.65	44.31	46.93
26	11.16	12.20	13.84	15.38	17.29	25.34	35.56	38.89	41.92	45.64	48.29
27	11.81	12.83	14.57	16.15	18.11	26.34	36.74	40.11	43.19	46.96	49.64
28	12.46	13.56	15.31	16.93	18.94	27.34	37.92	41.34	44.46	48.28	50.99
29	13.12	14.26	16.05	17.71	19.77	28.34	39.09	42.56	45.72	49.59	52.34
30	13.79	14.95	16.79	18.49	20.60	29.34	40.26	43.77	46.98	50.89	53.67
40	20.71	22.16	24.43	26.51	29.05	39.34	51.81	55.76	59.34	63.69	66.77
50	27.99	29.71	32.36	34.76	37.69	49.33	63.17	67.50	71.42	76.15	79.49
60	35.53	37.43	40.48	43.19	46.46	59.33	74.40	79.08	83.30	88.38	91.95
70	43.28	45.44	48.76	51.74	55.33	69.33	85.53	90.53	95.02	100.4	104.2
80	51.17	53.54	51.17	60.39	64.28	79.33	98.58	101.9	106.6	112.3	116.3
90	59.20	61.75	65.65	69.13	73.29	89.33	107.6	113.1	118.1	124.1	128.3
100	67.33	70.06	74.22	77.93	82.36	99.33	118.5	124.3	129.6	135.8	140.2

Source: Table IV of Ronald A. Fisher and Frank Yates, *Statistical Tables for Biological, Agricultural and Medical Research* (6th ed.), Longman Group Ltd., London, 1974. (Previously published by Oliver & Boyd Ltd., Edinburgh.) Reprinted by permission of Pearson Education Limited.

Table A.8 Critical Values of the *F* Distribution

This table gives critical f_{α,ν_1,ν_2} values for selected *F* distributions. Use of the table is explained in Section 17.19

ν_2	α	ν_1 = 1	2	3	4	5	6	7	8	9
1	0.100	39.86	49.50	53.59	55.83	57.24	58.20	58.91	59.44	59.86
	0.050	161.4	199.5	215.7	224.6	230.2	234.0	236.8	238.9	240.5
	0.025	647.8	799.5	864.2	899.6	921.8	937.1	948.2	956.7	963.3
	0.010	4052.0	4999.5	5403.0	5625.0	5764.0	5859.0	5928.0	5982.0	6022.0
	0.005	16211	20000	21615	22500	23056	23437	23715	23925	24091
2	0.100	8.53	9.00	9.16	9.24	9.29	9.33	9.35	9.37	9.38
	0.050	18.51	19.00	19.16	19.25	19.30	19.33	19.35	19.37	19.38
	0.025	38.51	39.00	39.17	39.25	39.30	39.33	39.36	39.37	39.39
	0.010	98.50	99.00	99.17	99.25	99.30	99.33	99.36	99.37	99.39
	0.005	198.5	199.0	199.2	199.2	199.3	199.3	199.4	199.4	199.4
3	0.100	5.54	5.46	5.39	5.34	5.31	5.28	5.27	5.25	5.24
	0.050	10.13	9.55	9.28	9.12	9.01	8.94	8.89	8.85	8.81
	0.025	17.44	16.04	15.44	15.10	14.88	14.73	14.62	14.54	14.47
	0.010	34.12	30.82	29.46	28.71	28.24	27.91	27.67	27.49	27.35
	0.005	55.55	49.80	47.47	46.19	45.39	44.84	44.43	44.13	43.88
4	0.100	4.54	4.32	4.19	4.11	4.05	4.01	3.98	3.95	3.94
	0.050	7.71	6.94	6.59	6.39	6.26	6.16	6.09	6.04	6.00
	0.025	12.22	10.65	9.98	9.60	9.36	9.20	9.07	8.98	8.90
	0.010	21.20	18.00	16.69	15.98	15.52	15.21	14.98	14.80	14.66
	0.005	31.33	26.28	24.26	23.15	22.46	21.97	21.62	21.35	21.14
5	0.100	4.06	3.78	3.62	3.52	3.45	3.40	3.37	3.34	3.32
	0.050	6.61	5.79	5.41	5.19	5.05	4.95	4.88	4.82	4.77
	0.025	10.01	8.43	7.76	7.39	7.15	6.98	6.85	6.76	6.68
	0.010	16.26	13.27	12.06	11.39	10.97	10.67	10.46	10.29	10.16
	0.005	22.78	18.31	16.53	15.56	14.94	14.51	14.20	13.96	13.77
6	0.100	3.78	3.46	3.29	3.18	3.11	3.05	3.01	2.98	2.96
	0.050	5.99	5.14	4.76	4.53	4.39	4.28	4.21	4.15	4.10
	0.025	8.81	7.26	6.60	6.23	5.99	5.82	5.70	5.60	5.52
	0.010	13.75	10.92	9.78	9.15	8.75	8.47	8.26	8.10	7.98
	0.005	18.63	14.54	12.92	12.03	11.46	11.07	10.79	10.57	10.39
7	0.100	3.59	3.26	3.07	2.96	2.88	2.83	2.78	2.75	2.72
	0.050	5.59	4.74	4.35	4.12	3.97	3.87	3.79	3.73	3.68
	0.025	8.07	6.54	5.89	5.52	5.29	5.12	4.99	4.90	4.82
	0.010	12.25	9.55	8.45	7.85	7.46	7.19	6.99	6.84	6.72
	0.005	16.24	12.40	10.88	10.05	9.52	9.16	8.89	8.68	8.51
8	0.100	3.46	3.11	2.92	2.81	2.73	2.67	2.62	2.59	2.56
	0.050	5.32	4.46	4.07	3.84	3.69	3.58	3.50	3.44	3.39
	0.025	7.57	6.06	5.42	5.05	4.82	4.65	4.53	4.43	4.36
	0.010	11.26	8.65	7.59	7.01	6.63	6.37	6.18	6.03	5.91
	0.005	14.69	11.04	9.60	8.81	8.30	7.95	7.69	7.50	7.34
9	0.100	3.36	3.01	2.81	2.69	2.61	2.55	2.51	2.47	2.44
	0.050	5.12	4.26	3.86	3.63	3.48	3.37	3.29	3.23	3.18
	0.025	7.21	5.71	5.08	4.72	4.48	4.32	4.20	4.10	4.03
	0.010	10.56	8.02	6.99	6.42	6.06	5.80	5.61	5.47	5.35
	0.005	13.61	10.11	8.72	7.96	7.47	7.13	6.88	6.69	6.54
10	0.100	3.29	2.92	2.73	2.61	2.52	2.46	2.41	2.38	2.35
	0.050	4.96	4.10	3.71	3.48	3.33	3.22	3.14	3.07	3.02
	0.025	6.94	5.46	4.83	4.47	4.24	4.07	3.95	3.85	3.78
	0.010	10.04	7.56	6.55	5.99	5.64	5.39	5.20	5.06	4.94
	0.005	12.83	9.43	8.08	7.34	6.87	6.54	6.30	6.12	5.97
11	0.100	3.23	2.86	2.66	2.54	2.45	2.39	2.34	2.30	2.27
	0.050	4.84	3.98	3.59	3.36	3.20	3.09	3.01	2.95	2.90
	0.025	6.72	5.26	4.63	4.28	4.04	3.88	3.76	3.66	3.59
	0.010	9.65	7.21	6.22	5.67	5.32	5.07	4.89	4.74	4.63
	0.005	12.23	8.91	7.60	6.88	6.42	6.10	5.86	5.68	5.54
12	0.100	3.18	2.81	2.61	2.48	2.39	2.33	2.28	2.24	2.21
	0.050	4.75	3.89	3.49	3.26	3.11	3.00	2.91	2.85	2.80
	0.025	6.55	5.10	4.47	4.12	3.89	3.73	3.61	3.51	3.44
	0.010	9.33	6.93	5.95	5.41	5.06	4.82	4.64	4.50	4.39
	0.005	11.75	8.51	7.23	6.52	6.07	5.76	5.52	5.35	5.20
13	0.100	3.14	2.76	2.56	2.43	2.35	2.28	2.23	2.20	2.16
	0.050	4.67	3.81	3.41	3.18	3.03	2.92	2.83	2.77	2.71
	0.025	6.41	4.97	4.35	4.00	3.77	3.60	3.48	3.39	3.31
	0.010	9.07	6.70	5.74	5.21	4.86	4.62	4.44	4.30	4.19
	0.005	11.37	8.19	6.93	6.23	5.79	5.48	5.25	5.08	4.94
14	0.100	3.10	2.73	2.52	2.39	2.31	2.24	2.19	2.15	2.12
	0.050	4.60	3.74	3.34	3.11	2.96	2.85	2.76	2.70	2.65
	0.025	6.30	4.86	4.24	3.89	3.66	3.50	3.38	3.29	3.21
	0.010	8.86	6.51	5.56	5.04	4.69	4.46	4.28	4.14	4.03
	0.005	11.06	7.92	6.68	6.00	5.56	5.26	5.03	4.86	4.72

Table A.8 (*continued*)

ν_2	α	ν_1									
		10	12	15	20	24	30	40	60	120	∞
1	0.100	60.19	60.71	61.22	61.74	62.00	62.26	62.53	62.79	63.06	63.33
	0.050	241.9	243.9	245.9	248.0	249.1	250.1	251.1	252.2	253.3	254.3
	0.025	968.6	976.7	984.9	993.1	997.2	1001	1006	1010	1014	1018
	0.010	6056	6106	6157	6209	6235	6261	6287	6313	6339	6366
	0.005	24224	24426	24630	24836	24940	25044	25148	25253	25359	25465
2	0.100	9.39	9.41	9.42	9.44	9.45	9.46	9.47	9.47	9.48	9.49
	0.050	19.40	19.41	19.43	19.45	19.45	19.46	19.47	19.48	19.49	19.50
	0.025	39.40	39.41	39.43	39.45	39.46	39.46	39.47	39.48	39.49	39.50
	0.010	99.40	99.42	99.43	99.45	99.46	99.47	99.47	99.48	99.49	99.50
	0.005	199.4	199.4	199.4	199.4	199.5	199.5	199.5	199.5	199.5	199.5
3	0.100	5.23	5.22	5.20	5.18	5.18	5.17	5.16	5.15	5.14	5.13
	0.050	8.79	8.74	8.70	8.66	8.64	8.62	8.59	8.57	8.55	8.53
	0.025	14.42	14.34	14.25	14.17	14.12	14.08	14.04	13.99	13.95	13.90
	0.010	27.23	27.05	26.87	26.69	26.60	26.50	26.41	26.32	26.22	26.13
	0.005	43.69	43.39	43.08	42.78	42.62	42.47	42.31	42.15	41.99	41.83
4	0.100	3.92	3.90	3.87	3.84	3.83	3.82	3.80	3.79	3.78	3.76
	0.050	5.96	5.91	5.86	5.80	5.77	5.75	5.72	5.69	5.66	5.63
	0.025	8.84	8.75	8.66	8.56	8.51	8.46	8.41	8.36	8.31	8.26
	0.010	14.55	14.37	14.20	14.02	13.93	13.84	13.75	13.65	13.56	13.46
	0.005	20.97	20.70	20.44	20.17	20.03	19.89	19.75	19.61	19.47	19.32
5	0.100	3.30	3.27	3.24	3.21	3.19	3.17	3.16	3.14	3.12	3.10
	0.050	4.74	4.68	4.62	4.56	4.53	4.50	4.46	4.43	4.40	4.36
	0.025	6.62	6.52	6.43	6.33	6.28	6.23	6.18	6.12	6.07	6.02
	0.010	10.05	9.89	9.72	9.55	9.47	9.38	9.29	9.20	9.11	9.02
	0.005	13.62	13.38	13.15	12.90	12.78	12.66	12.53	12.40	12.27	12.14
6	0.100	2.94	2.90	2.87	2.84	2.82	2.80	2.78	2.76	2.74	2.72
	0.050	4.06	4.00	3.94	3.87	3.84	3.81	3.77	3.74	3.70	3.67
	0.025	5.46	5.37	5.27	5.17	5.12	5.07	5.01	4.96	4.90	4.85
	0.010	7.87	7.72	7.56	7.40	7.31	7.23	7.14	7.06	6.97	6.88
	0.005	10.25	10.03	9.81	9.59	9.47	9.36	9.24	9.12	9.00	8.88
7	0.100	2.70	2.67	2.63	2.59	2.58	2.56	2.54	2.51	2.49	2.47
	0.050	3.64	3.57	3.51	3.44	3.41	3.38	3.34	3.30	3.27	3.23
	0.025	4.76	4.67	4.57	4.47	4.42	4.36	4.31	4.25	4.20	4.14
	0.010	6.62	6.47	6.31	6.16	6.07	5.99	5.91	5.82	5.74	5.65
	0.005	8.38	8.18	7.97	7.75	7.65	7.53	7.42	7.31	7.19	7.08
8	0.100	2.54	2.50	2.46	2.42	2.40	2.38	2.36	2.34	2.32	2.29
	0.050	3.35	3.28	3.22	3.15	3.12	3.08	3.04	3.01	2.97	2.93
	0.025	4.30	4.20	4.10	4.00	3.95	3.89	3.84	3.78	3.73	3.67
	0.010	5.81	5.67	5.52	5.36	5.28	5.20	5.12	5.03	4.95	4.86
	0.005	7.21	7.01	6.81	6.61	6.50	6.40	6.29	6.18	6.06	5.95
9	0.100	2.42	2.38	2.34	2.30	2.28	2.25	2.23	2.21	2.18	2.16
	0.050	3.14	3.07	3.01	2.94	2.90	2.86	2.83	2.79	2.75	2.71
	0.025	3.96	3.87	3.77	3.67	3.61	3.56	3.51	3.45	3.39	3.33
	0.010	5.26	5.11	4.96	4.81	4.73	4.65	4.57	4.48	4.40	4.31
	0.005	6.42	6.23	6.03	5.83	5.73	5.62	5.52	5.41	5.30	5.19
10	0.100	2.32	2.28	2.24	2.20	2.18	2.16	2.13	2.11	2.08	2.06
	0.050	2.98	2.91	2.85	2.77	2.74	2.70	2.66	2.62	2.58	2.54
	0.025	3.72	3.62	3.52	3.42	3.37	3.31	3.26	3.20	3.14	3.08
	0.010	4.85	4.71	4.56	4.41	4.33	4.25	4.17	4.08	4.00	3.91
	0.005	5.85	5.66	5.47	5.27	5.17	5.07	4.97	4.86	4.75	4.64
11	0.100	2.25	2.21	2.17	2.12	2.10	2.08	2.05	2.03	2.00	1.97
	0.050	2.85	2.79	2.72	2.65	2.61	2.57	2.53	2.49	2.45	2.40
	0.025	3.53	3.43	3.33	3.23	3.17	3.12	3.06	3.00	2.94	2.88
	0.010	4.54	4.40	4.25	4.10	4.02	3.94	3.86	3.78	3.69	3.60
	0.005	5.42	5.24	5.05	4.86	4.76	4.65	4.55	4.44	4.34	4.23
12	0.100	2.19	2.15	2.10	2.06	2.04	2.01	1.99	1.96	1.93	1.90
	0.050	2.75	2.69	2.62	2.54	2.51	2.47	2.43	2.38	2.34	2.30
	0.025	3.37	3.28	3.18	3.07	3.02	2.96	2.91	2.85	2.79	2.72
	0.010	4.30	4.16	4.01	3.86	3.78	3.70	3.62	3.54	3.45	3.36
	0.005	5.09	4.91	4.72	4.53	4.43	4.33	4.23	4.12	4.01	3.90
13	0.100	2.14	2.10	2.05	2.01	1.98	1.96	1.93	1.90	1.88	1.85
	0.050	2.67	2.60	2.53	2.46	2.42	2.38	2.34	2.30	2.25	2.21
	0.025	3.25	3.15	3.05	2.95	2.89	2.84	2.78	2.72	2.66	2.60
	0.010	4.10	3.96	3.82	3.66	3.59	3.51	3.43	3.34	3.25	3.17
	0.005	4.82	4.64	4.46	4.27	4.17	4.07	3.97	3.87	3.76	3.65
14	0.100	2.10	2.05	2.01	1.96	1.94	1.91	1.89	1.86	1.83	1.80
	0.050	2.60	2.53	2.46	2.39	2.35	2.31	2.27	2.22	2.18	2.13
	0.025	3.15	3.05	2.95	2.84	2.79	2.73	2.67	2.61	2.55	2.49
	0.010	3.94	3.80	3.66	3.51	3.43	3.35	3.27	3.18	3.09	3.00
	0.005	4.60	4.43	4.25	4.06	3.96	3.86	3.76	3.66	3.55	3.44

Table A.8 *(continued)*

ν_2	α	ν_1								
		1	2	3	4	5	6	7	8	9
15	0.100	3.07	2.70	2.49	2.36	2.27	2.21	2.16	2.12	2.09
	0.050	4.54	3.68	3.29	3.06	2.90	2.79	2.71	2.64	2.59
	0.025	6.20	4.77	4.15	3.80	3.58	3.41	3.29	3.20	3.12
	0.010	8.68	6.36	5.42	4.89	4.56	4.32	4.14	4.00	3.89
	0.005	10.80	7.70	6.48	5.80	5.37	5.07	4.85	4.67	4.54
16	0.100	3.05	2.67	2.46	2.33	2.24	2.18	2.13	2.09	2.06
	0.050	4.49	3.63	3.24	3.01	2.85	2.74	2.66	2.59	2.54
	0.025	6.12	4.69	4.08	3.73	3.50	3.34	3.22	3.12	3.05
	0.010	8.53	6.23	5.29	4.77	4.44	4.20	4.03	3.89	3.78
	0.005	10.58	7.51	6.30	5.64	5.21	4.91	4.69	4.52	4.38
17	0.100	3.03	2.64	2.44	2.31	2.22	2.15	2.10	2.06	2.03
	0.050	4.45	3.59	3.20	2.96	2.81	2.70	2.61	2.55	2.49
	0.025	6.04	4.62	4.01	3.66	3.44	3.28	3.16	3.06	2.98
	0.010	8.40	6.11	5.18	4.67	4.34	4.10	3.93	3.79	3.68
	0.005	10.38	7.35	6.16	5.50	5.07	4.78	4.56	4.39	4.25
18	0.100	3.01	2.62	2.42	2.29	2.20	2.13	2.08	2.04	2.00
	0.050	4.41	3.55	3.16	2.93	2.77	2.66	2.58	2.51	2.46
	0.025	5.98	4.56	3.95	3.61	3.38	3.22	3.10	3.01	2.93
	0.010	8.29	6.01	5.09	4.58	4.25	4.01	3.84	3.71	3.60
	0.005	10.22	7.21	6.03	5.37	4.96	4.66	4.44	4.28	4.14
19	0.100	2.99	2.61	2.40	2.27	2.18	2.11	2.06	2.02	1.96
	0.050	4.38	3.52	3.13	2.90	2.74	2.63	2.54	2.48	2.42
	0.025	5.92	4.51	3.90	3.56	3.33	3.17	3.05	2.96	2.88
	0.010	8.18	5.93	5.01	4.50	4.17	3.94	3.77	3.63	3.52
	0.005	10.07	7.09	5.92	5.27	4.85	4.56	4.34	4.18	4.04
20	0.100	2.97	2.59	2.38	2.25	2.16	2.09	2.04	2.00	1.96
	0.050	4.35	3.49	3.10	2.87	2.71	2.60	2.51	2.45	2.39
	0.025	5.87	4.46	3.86	3.51	3.29	3.13	3.01	2.91	2.84
	0.010	8.10	5.85	4.94	4.43	4.10	3.87	3.70	3.56	3.46
	0.005	9.94	6.99	5.82	5.17	4.76	4.47	4.26	4.09	3.96
21	0.100	2.96	2.57	2.36	2.23	2.14	2.08	2.02	1.98	1.95
	0.050	4.32	3.47	3.07	2.84	2.68	2.57	2.49	2.42	2.37
	0.025	5.83	4.42	3.82	3.48	3.25	3.09	2.97	2.87	2.80
	0.010	8.02	5.78	4.87	4.37	4.04	3.81	3.64	3.51	3.40
	0.005	9.83	6.89	5.73	5.09	4.68	4.39	4.18	4.01	3.88
22	0.100	2.95	2.56	2.35	2.22	2.13	2.06	2.01	1.97	1.93
	0.050	4.30	3.44	3.05	2.82	2.66	2.55	2.46	2.40	2.34
	0.025	5.79	4.38	3.78	3.44	3.22	3.05	2.93	2.84	2.76
	0.010	7.95	5.72	4.82	4.31	3.99	3.76	3.59	3.45	3.35
	0.005	9.73	6.81	5.65	5.02	4.61	4.32	4.11	3.94	3.81
23	0.100	2.94	2.55	2.34	2.21	2.11	2.05	1.99	1.95	1.92
	0.050	4.28	3.42	3.03	2.80	2.64	2.53	2.44	2.37	2.32
	0.025	5.75	4.35	3.75	3.41	3.18	3.02	2.90	2.81	2.73
	0.010	7.88	5.66	4.76	4.26	3.94	3.71	3.54	3.41	3.30
	0.005	9.63	6.73	5.58	4.95	4.54	4.26	4.05	3.88	3.75
24	0.100	2.93	2.54	2.33	2.19	2.10	2.04	1.98	1.94	1.91
	0.050	4.26	3.40	3.01	2.78	2.62	2.51	2.42	2.36	2.30
	0.025	5.72	4.32	3.72	3.38	3.15	2.99	2.87	2.78	2.70
	0.010	7.82	5.61	4.72	4.22	3.90	3.67	3.50	3.36	3.26
	0.005	9.55	6.66	5.52	4.89	4.49	4.20	3.99	3.83	3.69
25	0.100	2.92	2.53	2.32	2.18	2.09	2.02	1.97	1.93	1.89
	0.050	4.24	3.39	2.99	2.76	2.60	2.49	2.40	2.34	2.28
	0.025	5.69	4.29	3.69	3.35	3.13	2.97	2.85	2.75	2.68
	0.010	7.77	5.57	4.68	4.18	3.85	3.63	3.46	3.32	3.22
	0.005	9.48	6.60	5.46	4.84	4.43	4.15	3.94	3.78	3.64
26	0.100	2.91	2.52	2.31	2.17	2.08	2.01	1.96	1.92	1.88
	0.050	4.23	3.37	2.98	2.74	2.59	2.47	2.39	2.32	2.27
	0.025	5.66	4.27	3.67	3.33	3.10	2.94	2.82	2.73	2.65
	0.010	7.72	5.53	4.64	4.14	3.82	3.59	3.42	3.29	3.18
	0.005	9.41	6.54	5.41	4.79	4.38	4.10	3.89	3.73	3.60
27	0.100	2.90	2.51	2.30	2.17	2.07	2.00	1.95	1.91	1.87
	0.050	4.21	3.35	2.96	2.73	2.57	2.46	2.37	2.31	2.25
	0.025	5.63	4.24	3.65	3.31	3.08	2.92	2.80	2.71	2.63
	0.010	7.68	5.49	4.60	4.11	3.78	3.56	3.39	3.26	3.15
	0.005	9.34	6.49	5.36	4.74	4.34	4.06	3.85	3.69	3.56
28	0.100	2.89	2.50	2.29	2.16	2.06	2.00	1.94	1.90	1.87
	0.050	4.20	3.34	2.95	2.71	2.56	2.45	2.36	2.29	2.24
	0.025	5.61	4.22	3.63	3.29	3.06	2.90	2.78	2.69	2.61
	0.010	7.64	5.45	4.57	4.07	3.75	3.53	3.36	3.23	3.12
	0.005	9.28	6.44	5.32	4.70	4.30	4.02	3.81	3.65	3.52

Table A.8 *(continued)*

ν_2	α	ν_1									
		10	12	15	20	24	30	40	60	120	∞
	0.100	2.06	2.02	1.97	1.92	1.90	1.87	1.85	1.82	1.79	1.76
	0.050	2.54	2.48	2.40	2.33	2.29	2.25	2.20	2.16	2.11	2.07
15	0.025	3.06	2.96	2.86	2.76	2.70	2.64	2.59	2.52	2.46	2.40
	0.010	3.80	3.67	3.52	3.37	3.29	3.21	3.13	3.05	2.96	2.87
	0.005	4.42	4.25	4.07	3.88	3.79	3.69	3.58	3.48	3.37	3.26
	0.100	2.03	1.99	1.94	1.89	1.87	1.84	1.81	1.78	1.75	1.72
	0.050	2.49	2.42	2.35	2.28	2.24	2.19	2.15	2.11	2.06	2.01
16	0.025	2.99	2.89	2.79	2.68	2.63	2.57	2.51	2.45	2.38	2.32
	0.010	3.69	3.55	3.41	3.26	3.18	3.10	3.02	2.93	2.84	2.75
	0.005	4.27	4.10	3.92	3.73	3.64	3.54	3.44	3.33	3.22	3.11
	0.100	2.00	1.96	1.91	1.86	1.84	1.81	1.78	1.75	1.72	1.69
	0.050	2.45	2.38	2.31	2.23	2.19	2.15	2.10	2.06	2.01	1.96
17	0.025	2.92	2.82	2.72	2.62	2.56	2.50	2.44	2.38	2.32	2.25
	0.010	3.59	3.46	3.31	3.16	3.08	3.00	2.92	2.83	2.75	2.65
	0.005	4.14	3.97	3.79	3.61	3.51	3.41	3.31	3.21	3.10	2.98
	0.100	1.98	1.93	1.89	1.84	1.81	1.78	1.75	1.72	1.69	1.66
	0.050	2.41	2.34	2.27	2.19	2.15	2.11	2.06	2.02	1.97	1.92
18	0.025	2.87	2.77	2.67	2.56	2.50	2.44	2.38	2.32	2.26	2.19
	0.010	3.51	3.37	3.23	3.08	3.00	2.92	2.84	2.75	2.66	2.57
	0.005	4.03	3.86	3.68	3.50	3.40	3.30	3.20	3.10	2.99	2.87
	0.100	1.96	1.91	1.86	1.81	1.79	1.76	1.73	1.70	1.67	1.63
	0.050	2.38	2.31	2.23	2.16	2.11	2.07	2.03	1.98	1.93	1.88
19	0.025	2.82	2.72	2.62	2.51	2.45	2.39	2.33	2.27	2.20	2.13
	0.010	3.43	3.30	3.15	3.00	2.92	2.84	2.76	2.67	2.58	2.49
	0.005	3.93	3.76	3.59	3.40	3.31	3.21	3.11	3.00	2.89	2.78
	0.100	1.94	1.89	1.84	1.79	1.77	1.74	1.71	1.68	1.64	1.61
	0.050	2.35	2.28	2.20	2.12	2.08	2.04	1.99	1.95	1.90	1.84
20	0.025	2.77	2.68	2.57	2.46	2.41	2.35	2.29	2.22	2.16	2.09
	0.010	3.37	3.23	3.09	2.94	2.86	2.78	2.69	2.61	2.52	2.42
	0.005	3.85	3.68	3.50	3.32	3.22	3.12	3.02	2.92	2.81	2.69
	0.100	1.92	1.87	1.83	1.78	1.75	1.72	1.69	1.66	1.62	1.59
	0.050	2.32	2.25	2.18	2.10	2.05	2.01	1.96	1.92	1.87	1.81
21	0.025	2.73	2.64	2.53	2.42	2.37	2.31	2.25	2.18	2.11	2.04
	0.010	3.31	3.17	3.03	2.88	2.80	2.72	2.64	2.55	2.46	2.36
	0.005	3.77	3.60	3.43	3.24	3.15	3.05	2.95	2.84	2.73	2.61
	0.100	1.90	1.86	1.81	1.76	1.73	1.70	1.67	1.64	1.60	1.57
	0.050	2.30	2.23	2.15	2.07	2.03	1.98	1.94	1.89	1.84	1.78
22	0.025	2.70	2.60	2.50	2.39	2.33	2.27	2.21	2.14	2.08	2.00
	0.010	3.26	3.12	2.98	2.83	2.75	2.67	2.58	2.50	2.40	2.31
	0.005	3.70	3.54	3.36	3.18	3.08	2.98	2.88	2.77	2.66	2.55
	0.100	1.89	1.84	1.80	1.74	1.72	1.69	1.66	1.62	1.59	1.55
	0.050	2.27	2.20	2.13	2.05	2.01	1.96	1.91	1.86	1.81	1.76
23	0.025	2.67	2.57	2.47	2.36	2.30	2.24	2.18	2.11	2.04	1.97
	0.010	3.21	3.07	2.93	2.78	2.70	2.62	2.54	2.45	2.35	2.26
	0.005	3.64	3.47	3.30	3.12	3.02	2.92	2.82	2.71	2.60	2.48
	0.100	1.88	1.83	1.78	1.73	1.70	1.67	1.64	1.61	1.57	1.53
	0.050	2.25	2.18	2.11	2.03	1.98	1.94	1.89	1.84	1.79	1.73
24	0.025	2.64	2.54	2.44	2.33	2.27	2.21	2.15	2.08	2.01	1.94
	0.010	3.17	3.03	2.89	2.74	2.66	2.58	2.49	2.40	2.31	2.21
	0.005	3.59	3.42	3.25	3.06	2.97	2.87	2.77	2.66	2.55	2.43
	0.100	1.87	1.82	1.77	1.72	1.69	1.66	1.63	1.59	1.56	1.52
	0.050	2.24	2.16	2.09	2.01	1.96	1.92	1.87	1.82	1.77	1.71
25	0.025	2.61	2.51	2.41	2.30	2.24	2.18	2.12	2.05	1.98	1.91
	0.010	3.13	2.99	2.85	2.70	2.62	2.54	2.45	2.36	2.27	2.17
	0.005	3.54	3.37	3.20	3.01	2.92	2.82	2.72	2.61	2.50	2.38
	0.100	1.86	1.81	1.76	1.71	1.68	1.65	1.61	1.58	1.54	1.50
	0.050	2.22	2.15	2.07	1.99	1.95	1.90	1.85	1.80	1.75	1.69
26	0.025	2.59	2.49	2.39	2.28	2.22	2.16	2.09	2.03	1.95	1.88
	0.010	3.09	2.96	2.81	2.66	2.58	2.50	2.42	2.33	2.23	2.13
	0.005	3.49	3.33	3.15	2.97	2.87	2.77	2.67	2.56	2.45	2.33
	0.100	1.85	1.80	1.75	1.70	1.67	1.64	1.60	1.57	1.53	1.49
	0.050	2.20	2.13	2.06	1.97	1.93	1.88	1.84	1.79	1.73	1.67
27	0.025	2.57	2.47	2.36	2.25	2.19	2.13	2.07	2.00	1.93	1.85
	0.010	3.06	2.93	2.78	2.63	2.55	2.47	2.38	2.29	2.20	2.10
	0.005	3.45	3.28	3.11	2.93	2.83	2.73	2.63	2.52	2.41	2.29
	0.100	1.84	1.79	1.74	1.69	1.66	1.63	1.59	1.56	1.52	1.48
	0.050	2.19	2.12	2.04	1.96	1.91	1.87	1.82	1.77	1.71	1.65
28	0.025	2.55	2.45	2.34	2.23	2.17	2.11	2.05	1.98	1.91	1.83
	0.010	3.03	2.90	2.75	2.60	2.52	2.44	2.35	2.26	2.17	2.06
	0.005	3.41	3.25	3.07	2.89	2.79	2.69	2.59	2.48	2.37	2.25

Table A.8 (*continued*)

ν_2	α	ν_1 = 1	2	3	4	5	6	7	8	9
	0.100	2.89	2.50	2.28	2.15	2.06	1.99	1.93	1.89	1.86
	0.050	4.18	3.33	2.93	2.70	2.55	2.43	2.35	2.28	2.22
29	0.025	5.59	4.20	3.61	3.27	3.04	2.88	2.76	2.67	2.59
	0.010	7.60	5.42	4.54	4.04	3.73	3.50	3.33	3.20	3.09
	0.005	9.23	6.40	5.28	4.66	4.26	3.98	3.77	3.61	3.48
	0.100	2.88	2.49	2.28	2.14	2.05	1.98	1.93	1.88	1.85
	0.050	4.17	3.32	2.92	2.69	2.53	2.42	2.33	2.27	2.21
30	0.025	5.57	4.18	3.59	3.25	3.03	2.87	2.75	2.65	2.57
	0.010	7.56	5.39	4.51	4.02	3.70	3.47	3.30	3.17	3.07
	0.005	9.18	6.35	5.24	4.62	4.23	3.95	3.74	3.58	3.45
	0.100	2.84	2.44	2.23	2.09	2.00	1.93	1.87	1.83	1.79
	0.050	4.08	3.23	2.84	2.61	2.45	2.34	2.25	2.18	2.12
40	0.025	5.42	4.05	3.46	3.13	2.90	2.74	2.62	2.53	2.45
	0.010	7.31	5.18	4.31	3.83	3.51	3.29	3.12	2.99	2.89
	0.005	8.83	6.07	4.98	4.37	3.99	3.71	3.51	3.35	3.22
	0.100	2.79	2.39	2.18	2.04	1.95	1.87	1.82	1.77	1.74
	0.050	4.00	3.15	2.76	2.53	2.37	2.25	2.17	2.10	2.04
60	0.025	5.29	3.93	3.34	3.01	2.79	2.63	2.51	2.41	2.33
	0.010	7.08	4.98	4.13	3.65	3.34	3.12	2.95	2.82	2.72
	0.005	8.49	5.79	4.73	4.14	3.76	3.49	3.29	3.13	3.01
	0.100	2.75	2.35	2.13	1.99	1.90	1.82	1.77	1.72	1.68
	0.050	3.92	3.07	2.68	2.45	2.29	2.17	2.09	2.02	1.96
120	0.025	5.15	3.80	3.23	2.89	2.67	2.52	2.39	2.30	2.22
	0.010	6.85	4.79	3.95	3.48	3.17	2.96	2.79	2.66	2.56
	0.005	8.18	5.54	4.50	3.92	3.55	3.28	3.09	2.93	2.81
	0.100	2.71	2.30	2.08	1.94	1.85	1.77	1.72	1.67	1.63
	0.050	3.84	3.00	2.60	2.37	2.21	2.10	2.01	1.94	1.88
∞	0.025	5.02	3.69	3.12	2.79	2.57	2.41	2.29	2.19	2.11
	0.010	6.63	4.61	3.78	3.32	3.02	2.80	2.64	2.51	2.41
	0.005	7.88	5.30	4.28	3.72	3.35	3.09	2.90	2.74	2.62

Table A.8 *(continued)*

ν_2	α	ν_1 = 10	12	15	20	24	30	40	60	120	∞
29	0.100	1.83	1.78	1.73	1.68	1.65	1.62	1.58	1.55	1.51	1.47
	0.050	2.18	2.10	2.03	1.94	1.90	1.85	1.81	1.75	1.70	1.64
	0.025	2.53	2.43	2.32	2.21	2.15	2.09	2.03	1.96	1.89	1.81
	0.010	3.00	2.87	2.73	2.57	2.49	2.41	2.33	2.23	2.14	2.03
	0.005	3.38	3.21	3.04	2.86	2.76	2.66	2.56	2.45	2.33	2.21
30	0.100	1.82	1.77	1.72	1.67	1.64	1.61	1.57	1.54	1.50	1.46
	0.050	2.16	2.09	2.01	1.93	1.89	1.84	1.79	1.74	1.68	1.62
	0.025	2.51	2.41	2.31	2.20	2.14	2.07	2.01	1.94	1.87	1.79
	0.010	2.98	2.84	2.70	2.55	2.47	2.39	2.30	2.21	2.11	2.01
	0.005	3.34	3.18	3.01	2.82	2.73	2.63	2.52	2.42	2.30	2.18
40	0.100	1.76	1.71	1.66	1.61	1.57	1.54	1.51	1.47	1.42	1.38
	0.050	2.08	2.00	1.92	1.84	1.79	1.74	1.69	1.64	1.58	1.51
	0.025	2.39	2.29	2.18	2.07	2.01	1.94	1.88	1.80	1.72	1.64
	0.010	2.80	2.66	2.52	2.37	2.29	2.20	2.11	2.02	1.92	1.80
	0.005	3.12	2.95	2.78	2.60	2.50	2.40	2.30	2.18	2.06	1.93
60	0.100	1.71	1.66	1.60	1.54	1.51	1.48	1.44	1.40	1.35	1.29
	0.050	1.99	1.92	1.84	1.75	1.70	1.65	1.59	1.53	1.47	1.39
	0.025	2.27	2.17	2.06	1.94	1.88	1.82	1.74	1.67	1.58	1.48
	0.010	2.63	2.50	2.35	2.20	2.12	2.03	1.94	1.84	1.73	1.60
	0.005	2.90	2.74	2.57	2.39	2.29	2.19	2.08	1.96	1.83	1.69
120	0.100	1.65	1.60	1.55	1.48	1.45	1.41	1.37	1.32	1.26	1.19
	0.050	1.91	1.83	1.75	1.66	1.61	1.55	1.50	1.43	1.35	1.25
	0.025	2.16	2.05	1.94	1.82	1.76	1.69	1.61	1.53	1.43	1.31
	0.010	2.47	2.34	2.19	2.03	1.95	1.86	1.76	1.66	1.53	1.38
	0.005	2.71	2.54	2.37	2.19	2.09	1.98	1.87	1.75	1.61	1.43
∞	0.100	1.60	1.55	1.49	1.42	1.38	1.34	1.30	1.24	1.17	1.00
	0.050	1.83	1.75	1.67	1.57	1.52	1.46	1.39	1.32	1.22	1.00
	0.025	2.05	1.94	1.83	1.71	1.64	1.57	1.48	1.39	1.27	1.00
	0.010	2.32	2.18	2.04	1.88	1.79	1.70	1.59	1.47	1.32	1.00
	0.005	2.52	2.36	2.19	2.00	1.90	1.79	1.67	1.53	1.36	1.00

Source: M. Merrington and C. M. Thompson, "Tables of percentage points of the inverted beta (*F*) distribution," *Biometrika*, vol. 33 (1943), and from Table 18 of E.S. Pearson and H.O. Hartley, *Biometrika Tables for Statisticians*, vol. 1, Cambridge University Press, Cambridge, 1954. Reproduced by permission of *Biometrika* Trustees.

Table A.9 Least Significant Studentized Ranges r_p

	$\alpha = 0.05$						$\alpha = 0.01$				
	p						p				
v	2	3	4	5	6	v	2	3	4	5	6
1	17.97	17.97	17.97	17.97	17.97	1	90.03	90.03	90.03	90.03	90.03
2	6.085	6.085	6.085	6.085	6.085	2	14.04	14.04	14.04	14.04	14.04
3	4.501	4.516	4.516	4.516	4.516	3	8.261	8.321	8.321	8.321	8.321
4	3.927	4.013	4.033	4.033	4.033	4	6.512	6.677	6.740	6.756	6.756
5	3.635	3.749	3.797	3.814	3.814	5	5.702	5.893	5.898	6.040	6.065
6	3.461	3.587	3.649	3.680	3.694	6	5.243	5.439	5.549	5.614	5.655
7	3.344	3.477	3.548	3.588	3.611	7	4.949	5.145	5.260	5.334	5.383
8	3.261	3.399	3.475	3.521	3.549	8	4.746	4.939	5.057	5.135	5.189
9	3.199	3.339	3.420	3.470	3.502	9	4.596	4.787	4.906	4.986	5.043
10	3.151	3.293	3.376	3.430	3.465	10	4.482	4.671	4.790	4.871	4.931
11	3.113	3.256	3.342	3.397	3.435	11	4.392	4.579	4.697	4.780	4.841
12	3.082	3.225	3.313	3.370	3.410	12	4.320	4.504	4.622	4.706	4.767
13	3.055	3.200	3.289	3.348	3.389	13	4.260	4.442	4.560	4.644	4.706
14	3.033	3.178	3.268	3.329	3.372	14	4.210	4.391	4.508	4.591	4.654
15	3.014	3.160	3.250	3.312	3.356	15	4.168	4.347	4.463	4.547	4.610
16	2.998	3.144	3.235	3.298	3.343	16	4.131	4.309	4.425	4.509	4.572
17	2.984	3.130	3.222	3.285	3.331	17	4.099	4.275	4.391	4.475	4.539
18	2.971	3.118	3.210	3.274	3.321	18	4.071	4.246	4.362	4.445	4.509
19	2.960	3.107	3.199	3.264	3.311	19	4.046	4.220	4.335	4.419	4.483
20	2.950	3.097	3.190	3.255	3.303	20	4.024	4.197	4.312	4.395	4.459
24	2.919	3.066	3.160	3.226	3.276	24	3.956	4.126	4.239	4.322	4.386
30	2.888	3.035	3.131	3.199	3.250	30	3.889	4.056	4.168	4.250	4.314
40	2.858	3.006	3.102	3.171	3.224	40	3.825	3.988	4.098	4.180	4.244
60	2.829	2.976	3.073	3.143	3.198	60	3.762	3.922	4.031	4.111	4.174
120	2.800	2.947	3.045	3.116	3.172	120	3.702	3.858	3.965	4.044	4.107
∞	2.772	2.918	3.017	3.089	3.146	∞	3.643	3.796	3.900	3.978	4.040

Source: H.L. Harter, "Critical values for Duncan's new multiple range test," *Biometrics*, vol. 16 (1960). Reproduced with permission from the International Biometric Society.

Table A.10 Transformation of r to z_r

This table gives values of z_r for values of the Pearson product-moment correlation coefficient r. Use of this table is explained in Section 19.14.

r	0.000	0.001	0.002	0.003	0.004	0.005	0.006	0.007	0.008	0.009
0.000	0.0000	0.0010	0.0020	0.0030	0.0040	0.0050	0.0060	0.0070	0.0080	0.0090
0.010	0.0100	0.0110	0.0120	0.0130	0.0140	0.0150	0.0160	0.0170	0.0180	0.0190
0.020	0.0200	0.0210	0.0220	0.0230	0.0240	0.0250	0.0260	0.0270	0.0280	0.0290
0.030	0.0300	0.0310	0.0320	0.0330	0.0340	0.0350	0.0360	0.0370	0.0380	0.0390
0.040	0.0400	0.0410	0.0420	0.0430	0.0440	0.0450	0.0460	0.0470	0.0480	0.0490
0.050	0.0501	0.0511	0.0521	0.0531	0.0541	0.0551	0.0561	0.0571	0.0581	0.0591
0.060	0.0601	0.0611	0.0621	0.0631	0.0641	0.0651	0.0661	0.0671	0.0681	0.0691
0.070	0.0701	0.0711	0.0721	0.0731	0.0741	0.0751	0.0761	0.0771	0.0782	0.0792
0.080	0.0802	0.0812	0.0822	0.0832	0.0842	0.0852	0.0862	0.0872	0.0882	0.0892
0.090	0.0902	0.0912	0.0922	0.0933	0.0943	0.0953	0.0963	0.0973	0.0983	0.0993
0.100	0.1003	0.1013	0.1024	0.1034	0.1044	0.1054	0.1064	0.1074	0.1084	0.1094
0.110	0.1105	0.1115	0.1125	0.1135	0.1145	0.1155	0.1165	0.1175	0.1185	0.1195
0.120	0.1206	0.1216	0.1226	0.1236	0.1246	0.1257	0.1267	0.1277	0.1287	0.1297
0.130	0.1308	0.1318	0.1328	0.1338	0.1348	0.1358	0.1368	0.1379	0.1389	0.1399
0.140	0.1409	0.1419	0.1430	0.1440	0.1450	0.1460	0.1470	0.1481	0.1491	0.1501
0.150	0.1511	0.1522	0.1532	0.1542	0.1552	0.1563	0.1573	0.1583	0.1593	0.1604
0.160	0.1614	0.1624	0.1634	0.1644	0.1655	0.1665	0.1676	0.1686	0.1696	0.1706
0.170	0.1717	0.1727	0.1737	0.1748	0.1758	0.1768	0.1779	0.1789	0.1799	0.1810
0.180	0.1820	0.1830	0.1841	0.1851	0.1861	0.1872	0.1882	0.1892	0.1903	0.1913
0.190	0.1923	0.1934	0.1944	0.1954	0.1965	0.1975	0.1986	0.1996	0.2007	0.2017
0.200	0.2027	0.2038	0.2048	0.2059	0.2069	0.2079	0.2090	0.2100	0.2111	0.2121
0.210	0.2132	0.2142	0.2153	0.2163	0.2174	0.2184	0.2194	0.2205	0.2215	0.2226
0.220	0.2237	0.2247	0.2258	0.2268	0.2279	0.2289	0.2300	0.2310	0.2321	0.2331
0.230	0.2342	0.2353	0.2363	0.2374	0.2384	0.2395	0.2405	0.2416	0.2427	0.2437
0.240	0.2448	0.2458	0.2469	0.2480	0.2490	0.2501	0.2511	0.2522	0.2533	0.2543
0.250	0.2554	0.2565	0.2575	0.2586	0.2597	0.2608	0.2618	0.2629	0.2640	0.2650
0.260	0.2661	0.2672	0.2682	0.2693	0.2704	0.2715	0.2726	0.2736	0.2747	0.2758
0.270	0.2769	0.2779	0.2790	0.2801	0.2812	0.2823	0.2833	0.2844	0.2855	0.2866
0.280	0.2877	0.2888	0.2898	0.2909	0.2920	0.2931	0.2942	0.2953	0.2964	0.2975
0.290	0.2986	0.2997	0.3008	0.3019	0.3029	0.3040	0.3051	0.3062	0.3073	0.3084
0.300	0.3095	0.3106	0.3117	0.3128	0.3139	0.3150	0.3161	0.3172	0.3183	0.3195
0.310	0.3206	0.3217	0.3228	0.3239	0.3250	0.3261	0.3272	0.3283	0.3294	0.3305
0.320	0.3317	0.3328	0.3339	0.3350	0.3361	0.3372	0.3384	0.3395	0.3406	0.3417
0.330	0.3428	0.3439	0.3451	0.3462	0.3473	0.3484	0.3496	0.3507	0.3518	0.3530
0.340	0.3541	0.3552	0.3564	0.3575	0.3586	0.3597	0.3609	0.3620	0.3632	0.3643
0.350	0.3654	0.3666	0.3677	0.3689	0.3700	0.3712	0.3723	0.3734	0.3746	0.3757
0.360	0.3769	0.3780	0.3792	0.3803	0.3815	0.3826	0.3838	0.3850	0.3861	0.3873
0.370	0.3884	0.3896	0.3907	0.3919	0.3931	0.3942	0.3954	0.3966	0.3977	0.3989
0.380	0.4001	0.4012	0.4024	0.4036	0.4047	0.4059	0.4071	0.4083	0.4094	0.4106
0.390	0.4118	0.4130	0.4142	0.4153	0.4165	0.4177	0.4189	0.4201	0.4213	0.4225
0.400	0.4236	0.4248	0.4260	0.4272	0.4284	0.4296	0.4308	0.4320	0.4332	0.4344
0.410	0.4356	0.4368	0.4380	0.4392	0.4404	0.4416	0.4429	0.4441	0.4453	0.4465
0.420	0.4477	0.4489	0.4501	0.4513	0.4526	0.4538	0.4550	0.4562	0.4574	0.4587
0.430	0.4599	0.4611	0.4623	0.4636	0.4648	0.4660	0.4673	0.4685	0.4697	0.4710
0.440	0.4722	0.4735	0.4747	0.4760	0.4772	0.4784	0.4797	0.4809	0.4822	0.4835
0.450	0.4847	0.4860	0.4872	0.4885	0.4897	0.4910	0.4923	0.4935	0.4948	0.4961
0.460	0.4973	0.4986	0.4999	0.5011	0.5024	0.5037	0.5049	0.5062	0.5075	0.5088
0.470	0.5101	0.5114	0.5126	0.5139	0.5152	0.5165	0.5178	0.5191	0.5204	0.5217
0.480	0.5230	0.5243	0.5256	0.5279	0.5282	0.5295	0.5308	0.5321	0.5334	0.5347
0.490	0.5361	0.5374	0.5387	0.5400	0.5413	0.5427	0.5440	0.5453	0.5466	0.5480

Table A.10 (*continued*)

r	0.000	0.001	0.002	0.003	0.004	0.005	0.006	0.007	0.008	0.009
0.500	0.5493	0.5506	0.5520	0.5533	0.5547	0.5560	0.5573	0.5587	0.5600	0.5614
0.510	0.5627	0.5641	0.5654	0.5668	0.5681	0.5695	0.5709	0.5722	0.5736	0.5750
0.520	0.5763	0.5777	0.5791	0.5805	0.5818	0.5832	0.5846	0.5860	0.5874	0.5888
0.530	0.5901	0.5915	0.5929	0.5943	0.5957	0.5971	0.5985	0.5999	0.6013	0.6027
0.540	0.6042	0.6056	0.6070	0.6084	0.6098	0.6112	0.6127	0.6141	0.6155	0.6170
0.550	0.6184	0.6198	0.6213	0.6227	0.6241	0.6256	0.6270	0.6285	0.6299	0.6314
0.560	0.6328	0.6343	0.6358	0.6372	0.6387	0.6401	0.6416	0.6431	0.6446	0.6460
0.570	0.6475	0.6490	0.6505	0.6520	0.6535	0.6550	0.6565	0.6579	0.6594	0.6610
0.580	0.6625	0.6640	0.6655	0.6670	0.6685	0.6700	0.6715	0.6731	0.6746	0.6761
0.590	0.6777	0.6792	0.6807	0.6823	0.6838	0.6854	0.6869	0.6885	0.6900	0.6916
0.600	0.6931	0.6947	0.6963	0.6978	0.6994	0.7010	0.7026	0.7042	0.7057	0.7073
0.610	0.7089	0.7105	0.7121	0.7137	0.7153	0.7169	0.7185	0.7201	0.7218	0.7234
0.620	0.7250	0.7266	0.7283	0.7299	0.7315	0.7332	0.7348	0.7364	0.7381	0.7398
0.630	0.7414	0.7431	0.7447	0.7464	0.7481	0.7497	0.7514	0.7531	0.7548	0.7565
0.640	0.7582	0.7599	0.7616	0.7633	0.7650	0.7667	0.7684	0.7701	0.7718	0.7736
0.650	0.7753	0.7770	0.7788	0.7805	0.7823	0.7840	0.7858	0.7875	0.7893	0.7910
0.660	0.7928	0.7946	0.7964	0.7981	0.7999	0.8017	0.8035	0.8053	0.8071	0.8089
0.670	0.8107	0.8126	0.8144	0.8162	0.8180	0.8199	0.8217	0.8236	0.8254	0.8273
0.680	0.8291	0.8310	0.8328	0.8347	0.8366	0.8385	0.8404	0.8423	0.8442	0.8461
0.690	0.8480	0.8499	0.8518	0.8537	0.8556	0.8576	0.8595	0.8614	0.8634	0.8653
0.700	0.8673	0.8693	0.8712	0.8732	0.8752	0.8772	0.8792	0.8812	0.8832	0.8852
0.710	0.8872	0.8892	0.8912	0.8933	0.8953	0.8973	0.8994	0.9014	0.9035	0.9056
0.720	0.9076	0.9097	0.9118	0.9139	0.9160	0.9181	0.9202	0.9223	0.9245	0.9266
0.730	0.9287	0.9309	0.9330	0.9352	0.9373	0.9395	0.9417	0.9439	0.9461	0.9483
0.740	0.9505	0.9527	0.9549	0.9571	0.9594	0.9616	0.9639	0.9661	0.9684	0.9707
0.750	0.9730	0.9752	0.9775	0.9799	0.9822	0.9845	0.9868	0.9892	0.9915	0.9939
0.760	0.9962	0.9986	1.0010	1.0034	1.0058	1.0082	1.0106	1.0130	1.0154	1.0179
0.770	1.0203	1.0228	1.0253	1.0277	1.0302	1.0327	1.0352	1.0378	1.0403	1.0428
0.780	1.0454	1.0479	1.0505	1.0531	1.0557	1.0583	1.0609	1.0635	1.0661	1.0688
0.790	1.0714	1.0741	1.0768	1.0795	1.0822	1.0849	1.0876	1.0903	1.0931	1.0958
0.800	1.0986	1.1014	1.1041	1.1070	1.1098	1.1127	1.1155	1.1184	1.1212	1.1241
0.810	1.1270	1.1299	1.1329	1.1358	1.1388	1.1417	1.1447	1.1477	1.1507	1.1538
0.820	1.1568	1.1599	1.1630	1.1660	1.1692	1.1723	1.1754	1.1786	1.1817	1.1849
0.830	1.1870	1.1913	1.1946	1.1979	1.2011	1.2044	1.2077	1.2111	1.2144	1.2178
0.840	1.2212	1.2246	1.2280	1.2315	1.2349	1.2384	1.2419	1.2454	1.2490	1.2526
0.850	1.2561	1.2598	1.2634	1.2670	1.2708	1.2744	1.2782	1.2819	1.2857	1.2895
0.860	1.2934	1.2972	1.3011	1.3050	1.3089	1.3129	1.3168	1.3209	1.3249	1.3290
0.870	1.3331	1.3372	1.3414	1.3456	1.3498	1.3540	1.3583	1.3626	1.3670	1.3714
0.880	1.3758	1.3802	1.3847	1.3892	1.3938	1.3984	1.4030	1.4077	1.4124	1.4171
0.890	1.4219	1.4268	1.4316	1.4366	1.4415	1.4465	1.4516	1.4566	1.4618	1.4670
0.900	1.4722	1.4775	1.4828	1.4883	1.4937	1.4992	1.5047	1.5103	1.5160	1.5217
0.910	1.5275	1.5334	1.5393	1.5453	1.5513	1.5574	1.5636	1.5698	1.5762	1.5825
0.920	1.5890	1.5956	1.6022	1.6089	1.6157	1.6226	1.6296	1.6366	1.6438	1.6510
0.930	1.6584	1.6659	1.6734	1.6811	1.6888	1.6967	1.7047	1.7129	1.7211	1.7295
0.940	1.7380	1.7467	1.7555	1.7646	1.7736	1.7828	1.7923	1.8019	1.8117	1.8216
0.950	1.8318	1.8421	1.8527	1.8635	1.8745	1.8857	1.8972	1.9090	1.9210	1.9333
0.960	1.9459	1.9588	1.9721	1.9857	1.9996	2.0140	2.0287	2.0439	2.0595	2.0756
0.970	2.0923	2.1095	2.1273	2.1457	2.1649	2.1847	2.2054	2.2269	2.2494	2.2729
0.980	2.2976	2.3223	2.3507	2.3796	2.4101	2.4426	2.4774	2.5147	2.5550	2.5988
0.990	2.6467	2.6996	2.7587	2.8257	2.9031	2.9945	3.1063	3.2504	3.4534	3.8002

r	z_r
0.9999	4.95172
0.99999	6.10303

Source: Albert E. Waugh, *Statistical Tables and Problems*, McGraw-Hill, New York, 1952, as adapted in Herbert M. Blalock Jr., *Social Statistics*, McGraw-Hill, New York, 1979. Reproduced with permission of The McGraw-Hill Companies.

Table A.11 Critical Values of the Pearson Product-Moment Correlation Coefficient *r*

This table gives critical values for selected *r* distributions and levels of signficance α. Use of this table is explained in Section 19.15.

	Levels of significance for a one-tailed test					Levels of significance for a one-tailed test			
	0.05	0.025	0.01	0.005		0.05	0.025	0.01	0.05
	Levels of significance for a two-tailed test					Levels of significance for a two-tailed test			
v	0.10	0.05	0.02	0.01	*v*	0.10	0.05	0.02	0.01
1	0.988	0.997	0.9995	0.9999	24	0.330	0.388	0.453	0.496
2	0.900	0.950	0.980	0.990	26	0.317	0.374	0.437	0.479
3	0.805	0.878	0.934	0.959	28	0.306	0.361	0.423	0.463
4	0.729	0.811	0.882	0.917	30	0.296	0.349	0.409	0.449
5	0.669	0.755	0.833	0.875	35	0.275	0.325	0.381	0.418
6	0.622	0.707	0.789	0.834	40	0.257	0.304	0.358	0.393
7	0.582	0.666	0.750	0.798	45	0.243	0.288	0.338	0.372
8	0.549	0.632	0.716	0.765	50	0.231	0.273	0.322	0.354
9	0.521	0.602	0.685	0.735	55	0.220	0.261	0.307	0.339
10	0.497	0.576	0.658	0.708	60	0.211	0.250	0.295	0.325
11	0.476	0.553	0.634	0.684	70	0.195	0.232	0.274	0.302
12	0.458	0.532	0.612	0.661	80	0.183	0.217	0.256	0.283
13	0.441	0.514	0.592	0.641	90	0.173	0.205	0.242	0.267
14	0.426	0.497	0.574	0.623	100	0.164	0.195	0.230	0.254
15	0.412	0.482	0.558	0.606	120	0.150	0.178	0.210	0.232
16	0.400	0.468	0.542	0.590	150	0.134	0.159	0.189	0.208
17	0.389	0.456	0.529	0.575	200	0.116	0.138	0.164	0.181
18	0.378	0.444	0.516	0.561	300	0.095	0.113	0.134	0.148
19	0.369	0.433	0.503	0.549	400	0.082	0.098	0.116	0.128
20	0.360	0.423	0.492	0.537	500	0.073	0.088	0.104	0.115
22	0.344	0.404	0.472	0.515	1000	0.052	0.062	0.073	0.081

Source: Table VI of Ronald A. Fisher and Frank Yates, *Statistical Tables for Biological, Agricultural and Medical Research* (6th ed.), Longman Group Ltd., London, 1974. (Previously published by Oliver & Boyd Ltd., Edinburgh.) Reprinted by permission of Pearson Education Limited. As adapted by E.W. Minium and R.B. Clarke, *Elements of Statistical Reasoning*, John Wiley & Sons, Inc., 1982. Reprinted by permission of John Wiley & Sons, Inc.

Table A.12 Critical Values of the Wilcoxon W

This table gives critical values of the test statistic W for $n \leq 50$ and selected values of α. Use of this table is explained in Section 20.7.

One-tailed	Two-tailed	$n = 5$	$n = 6$	$n = 7$	$n = 8$	$n = 9$	$n = 10$
$\alpha = 0.05$	$\alpha = 0.10$	1	2	4	6	8	11
$\alpha = 0.025$	$\alpha = 0.05$		1	2	4	6	8
$\alpha = 0.01$	$\alpha = 0.02$			0	2	3	5
$\alpha = 0.005$	$\alpha = 0.01$				0	2	3
One-tailed	**Two-tailed**	$n = 11$	$n = 12$	$n = 13$	$n = 14$	$n = 15$	$n = 16$
$\alpha = 0.05$	$\alpha = 0.10$	14	17	21	26	30	36
$\alpha = 0.025$	$\alpha = 0.05$	11	14	17	21	25	30
$\alpha = 0.01$	$\alpha = 0.02$	7	10	13	16	20	24
$\alpha = 0.005$	$\alpha = 0.01$	5	7	10	13	16	19
One-tailed	**Two-tailed**	$n = 17$	$n = 18$	$n = 19$	$n = 20$	$n = 21$	$n = 22$
$\alpha = 0.05$	$\alpha = 0.10$	41	47	54	60	68	75
$\alpha = 0.025$	$\alpha = 0.05$	35	40	46	52	59	66
$\alpha = 0.01$	$\alpha = 0.02$	28	33	38	43	49	56
$\alpha = 0.005$	$\alpha = 0.01$	23	28	32	37	43	49
One-tailed	**Two-tailed**	$n = 23$	$n = 24$	$n = 25$	$n = 26$	$n = 27$	$n = 28$
$\alpha = 0.05$	$\alpha = 0.10$	83	92	101	110	120	130
$\alpha = 0.025$	$\alpha = 0.05$	73	81	90	98	107	117
$\alpha = 0.01$	$\alpha = 0.02$	62	69	77	85	93	102
$\alpha = 0.005$	$\alpha = 0.01$	55	61	68	76	84	92
One-tailed	**Two-tailed**	$n = 29$	$n = 30$	$n = 31$	$n = 32$	$n = 33$	$n = 34$
$\alpha = 0.05$	$\alpha = 0.10$	141	152	163	175	188	201
$\alpha = 0.025$	$\alpha = 0.05$	127	137	148	159	171	183
$\alpha = 0.01$	$\alpha = 0.02$	111	120	130	141	151	162
$\alpha = 0.005$	$\alpha = 0.01$	100	109	118	128	138	149
One-tailed	**Two-tailed**	$n = 35$	$n = 36$	$n = 37$	$n = 38$	$n = 39$	
$\alpha = 0.05$	$\alpha = 0.10$	214	228	242	256	271	
$\alpha = 0.025$	$\alpha = 0.05$	195	208	222	235	250	
$\alpha = 0.01$	$\alpha = 0.02$	174	186	198	211	224	
$\alpha = 0.005$	$\alpha = 0.01$	160	171	183	195	208	
One-tailed	**Two-tailed**	$n = 40$	$n = 41$	$n = 42$	$n = 43$	$n = 44$	$n = 45$
$\alpha = 0.05$	$\alpha = 0.10$	287	303	319	336	353	371
$\alpha = 0.025$	$\alpha = 0.05$	264	279	295	311	327	344
$\alpha = 0.01$	$\alpha = 0.02$	238	252	267	281	297	313
$\alpha = 0.005$	$\alpha = 0.01$	221	234	248	262	277	292
One-tailed	**Two-tailed**	$n = 46$	$n = 47$	$n = 48$	$n = 49$	$n = 50$	
$\alpha = 0.05$	$\alpha = 0.10$	389	408	427	446	466	
$\alpha = 0.025$	$\alpha = 0.05$	361	379	397	415	434	
$\alpha = 0.01$	$\alpha = 0.02$	329	345	362	380	398	
$\alpha = 0.005$	$\alpha = 0.01$	307	323	339	356	373	

Source: W.H. Beyer (ed.), *CRC Handbook of Tables for Probability and Statistics* (2nd ed.), CRC Press, Inc., Boca Raton, Florida, 1968. Reprinted by permission of CRC Press, Inc.

Table A.13 Critical Values of the Mann-Whitney U

This table gives critical values for small samples ($n_1 \leq 20$ and $n_2 \leq 20$) and for selected levels of significance α. The values are for a one-tailed test at $\alpha = 0.05$ (roman type) and $\alpha = 0.025$ (boldface type) and for a two-tailed test at $\alpha = 0.10$ (roman type) and $\alpha = 0.05$ (boldface type). Dashes in the body of the table indicate no decision is possible at the given α. Use of the table is explained in Section 20.9.

n_2 \ n_1	1	2	3	4	5	6	7	8	9	10	11	12	13	14	15	16	17	18	19	20
1	–	–	–	–	–	–	–	–	–	–	–	–	–	–	–	–	–	–	0	0
																			–	**–**
2	–	–	–	–	0	0	0	1	1	1	1	2	2	2	3	3	3	4	4	4
					–	**–**	**–**	**0**	**0**	**0**	**0**	**1**	**1**	**1**	**1**	**1**	**2**	**2**	**2**	**2**
3	–	–	0	0	1	2	2	3	3	4	5	5	6	7	7	8	9	9	10	11
	–	**–**	**–**	**–**	**0**	**1**	**1**	**2**	**2**	**3**	**3**	**4**	**4**	**5**	**5**	**6**	**6**	**7**	**7**	**8**
4	–	–	0	1	2	3	4	5	6	7	8	9	10	11	12	14	15	16	17	18
	–	**–**	**–**	**0**	**1**	**2**	**3**	**4**	**4**	**5**	**6**	**7**	**8**	**9**	**10**	**11**	**11**	**12**	**13**	**13**
5	–	0	1	2	4	5	6	8	9	11	12	13	15	16	18	19	20	22	23	25
	–	**–**	**0**	**1**	**2**	**3**	**5**	**6**	**7**	**8**	**9**	**11**	**12**	**13**	**14**	**15**	**17**	**18**	**19**	**20**
6	–	0	2	3	5	7	8	10	12	14	16	17	19	21	23	25	26	28	30	32
	–	**–**	**1**	**2**	**3**	**5**	**6**	**8**	**10**	**11**	**13**	**14**	**16**	**17**	**19**	**21**	**22**	**24**	**25**	**27**
7	–	0	2	4	6	8	11	13	15	17	19	21	24	26	28	30	33	35	37	39
	–	**–**	**1**	**3**	**5**	**6**	**8**	**10**	**12**	**14**	**16**	**18**	**20**	**22**	**24**	**26**	**28**	**30**	**32**	**34**
8	–	1	3	5	8	10	13	15	18	20	23	26	28	31	33	36	39	41	44	47
	–	**0**	**2**	**4**	**6**	**8**	**10**	**13**	**15**	**17**	**19**	**22**	**24**	**26**	**29**	**31**	**34**	**36**	**38**	**41**
9	–	1	3	6	9	12	15	18	21	24	27	30	33	36	39	42	45	48	51	54
	–	**0**	**2**	**4**	**7**	**10**	**12**	**15**	**17**	**20**	**23**	**26**	**28**	**31**	**34**	**37**	**39**	**42**	**45**	**48**
10	–	1	4	7	11	14	17	20	24	27	31	34	37	41	44	48	51	55	58	62
	–	**0**	**3**	**5**	**8**	**11**	**14**	**17**	**20**	**23**	**26**	**29**	**33**	**36**	**39**	**42**	**45**	**48**	**52**	**55**
11	–	1	5	8	12	16	19	23	27	31	34	38	42	46	50	54	57	61	65	69
	–	**0**	**3**	**6**	**9**	**13**	**16**	**19**	**23**	**26**	**30**	**33**	**37**	**40**	**44**	**47**	**51**	**55**	**58**	**62**
12	–	2	5	9	13	17	21	26	30	34	38	42	47	51	55	60	64	68	72	77
	–	**1**	**4**	**7**	**11**	**14**	**18**	**22**	**26**	**29**	**33**	**37**	**41**	**45**	**49**	**53**	**57**	**61**	**65**	**69**
13	–	2	6	10	15	19	24	28	33	37	42	47	51	56	61	65	70	75	80	84
	–	**1**	**4**	**8**	**12**	**16**	**20**	**24**	**28**	**33**	**37**	**41**	**45**	**50**	**54**	**59**	**63**	**67**	**72**	**76**
14	–	2	7	11	16	21	26	31	36	41	46	51	56	61	66	71	77	82	87	92
	–	**1**	**5**	**9**	**13**	**17**	**22**	**26**	**31**	**36**	**40**	**45**	**50**	**55**	**59**	**64**	**67**	**74**	**78**	**83**
15	–	3	7	12	18	23	28	33	39	44	50	55	61	66	72	77	83	88	94	100
	–	**1**	**5**	**10**	**14**	**19**	**24**	**29**	**34**	**39**	**44**	**49**	**54**	**59**	**64**	**70**	**75**	**80**	**85**	**90**
16	–	3	8	14	19	25	30	36	42	48	54	60	65	71	77	83	89	95	101	107
	–	**1**	**6**	**11**	**15**	**21**	**26**	**31**	**37**	**42**	**47**	**53**	**59**	**64**	**70**	**75**	**81**	**86**	**92**	**98**
17	–	3	9	15	20	26	33	39	45	51	57	64	70	77	83	89	96	102	109	115
	–	**2**	**6**	**11**	**17**	**22**	**28**	**34**	**39**	**45**	**51**	**57**	**63**	**67**	**75**	**81**	**87**	**93**	**99**	**105**
18	–	4	9	16	22	28	35	41	48	55	61	68	75	82	88	95	102	109	116	123
	–	**2**	**7**	**12**	**18**	**24**	**30**	**36**	**42**	**48**	**55**	**61**	**67**	**74**	**80**	**86**	**93**	**99**	**106**	**112**
19	0	4	10	17	23	30	37	44	51	58	65	72	80	87	94	101	109	116	123	130
	–	**2**	**7**	**13**	**19**	**25**	**32**	**38**	**45**	**52**	**58**	**65**	**72**	**78**	**85**	**92**	**99**	**106**	**113**	**119**
20	0	4	11	18	25	32	39	47	54	62	69	77	84	92	100	107	115	123	130	138
	–	**2**	**8**	**13**	**20**	**27**	**34**	**41**	**48**	**55**	**62**	**69**	**76**	**83**	**90**	**98**	**105**	**112**	**119**	**127**

Source: This table is reprinted from Table D.10 in Roger E. Kirk, *Elementary Statistics* (2nd ed.), Brooks/Cole Publishing Company, 1984, with the kind permission of Roger E. Kirk.

Table A.14 Critical Values of the Kruskal-Wallis H

This table gives values of H for small samples ($n \leq 5$) in three treatments and for selected values of α. Use of this table is explained in Section 20.10.

n_1	n_2	n_3	$\alpha = 0.10$	0.05	0.01	n_1	n_2	n_3	$\alpha = 0.10$	0.05	0.01
3	2	1	4.286			5	2	1	4.200	5.000	
3	2	2	4.500	4.714		5	2	2	4.373	5.160	6.533
3	3	1	4.571	5.143		5	3	1	4.018	4.960	
3	3	2	4.556	5.361		5	3	2	4.651	5.251	6.909
3	3	3	4.622	5.600	7.200	5	3	3	4.533	5.648	7.079
4	2	1	4.500			5	4	1	3.987	4.986	6.954
4	2	2	4.458	5.333		5	4	2	4.541	5.273	7.204
4	3	1	4.056	5.208		5	4	3	4.549	5.656	7.445
4	3	2	4.511	5.444	6.444	5	4	4	4.619	5.657	7.760
4	3	3	4.709	5.727	6.746	5	5	1	4.109	5.127	7.309
4	4	1	4.167	4.967	6.667	5	5	2	4.623	5.338	7.338
4	4	2	4.554	5.455	7.036	5	5	3	5.545	5.705	7.578
4	4	3	4.546	5.598	7.144	5	5	4	4.523	5.666	7.823
4	4	4	4.654	5.692	7.654	5	5	5	4.560	5.780	8.000

Source: W.H. Kruskal and W.A. Wallis, "Use of ranks in one-criterion variance analysis," *The Journal of the American Statistical Association*, vol. 47 (1952). Reprinted with permission from *The Journal of the American Statistical Association*.

Table A.15 Critical Values of the Spearman r_S

This table gives critical values of r_S for small samples ($n \leq 30$). Use of this table is explained in section 20.11.

	Levels of significance for a one-tailed test								
	0.25	0.10	0.05	0.025	0.01	0.005	0.0025	0.001	0.0005
	Levels of significance for a two-tailed test								
n	0.50	0.20	0.10	0.05	0.02	0.01	0.005	0.02	0.001
5	0.500	0.800	0.900	1.000	1.000				
6	0.371	0.657	0.829	0.886	0.943	1.000	1.000		
7	0.321	0.571	0.714	0.786	0.893	0.929	0.964	1.000	1.000
8	0.310	0.524	0.643	0.738	0.833	0.881	0.905	0.952	0.976
9	0.267	0.483	0.600	0.700	0.783	0.833	0.867	0.917	0.933
10	0.248	0.455	0.564	0.6648	0.745	0.794	0.830	0.879	0.903
11	0.236	0.427	0.536	0.618	0.709	0.755	0.800	0.845	0.873
12	0.224	0.406	0.503	0.587	0.671	0.727	0.776	0.825	0.860
13	0.209	0.385	0.484	0.560	0.648	0.703	0.747	0.802	0.835
14	0.200	0.367	0.464	0.538	0.622	0.675	0.723	0.776	0.811
15	0.189	0.354	0.443	0.521	0.604	0.654	0.700	0.754	0.786
16	0.182	0.341	0.429	0.503	0.582	0.635	0.679	0.732	0.765
17	0.176	0.328	0.414	0.485	0.566	0.615	0.662	0.713	0.748
18	0.170	0.317	0.401	0.472	0.550	0.600	0.643	0.695	0.728
19	0.165	0.309	0.391	0.460	0.535	0.584	0.628	0.677	0.712
20	0.161	0.299	0.380	0.447	0.520	0.570	0.612	0.662	0.696
21	0.156	0.292	0.370	0.435	0.508	0.556	0.599	0.648	0.681
22	0.152	0.284	0.361	0.425	0.496	0.544	0.586	0.634	0.667
23	0.148	0.278	0.353	0.415	0.486	0.532	0.573	0.622	0.654
24	0.144	0.271	0.344	0.406	0.476	0.521	0.562	0.610	0.642
25	0.142	0.265	0.337	0.398	0.466	0.511	0.551	0.598	0.630
26	0.138	0.259	0.331	0.390	0.457	0.501	0.541	0.587	0.619
27	0.136	0.255	0.324	0.382	0.448	0.491	0.531	0.577	0.608
28	0.133	0.250	0.317	0.375	0.440	0.483	0.522	0.567	0.598
29	0.130	0.245	0.312	0.368	0.433	0.475	0.513	0.558	0.589
30	0.128	0.240	0.306	0.362	0.425	0.467	0.504	0.549	0.580

Source: J.H. Zar, "Significance testing of the Spearman rank correlation coefficient," *The Journal of the American Statistical Association*, vol. 67 (1972). Reprinted with permission from *The Journal of the American Statistical Association*.

INDEX